CRIME AND NO PUNISHMENT

Crime and No Punishment

WEALTH, POWER, AND VIOLENCE
IN AMERICA

MARIE GOTTSCHALK

PRINCETON UNIVERSITY PRESS

PRINCETON & OXFORD

Published by Princeton University Press
41 William Street, Princeton, New Jersey 08540
99 Banbury Road, Oxford OX2 6JX

press.princeton.edu

GPSR Authorized Representative: Easy Access System Europe - Mustamäe tee 50, 10621 Tallinn, Estonia, gpsr.requests@easproject.com

All Rights Reserved

ISBN 9780691275253
ISBN (e-book) 9780691275260

Library of Congress Control Number: 2024049976

British Library Cataloging-in-Publication Data is available

Editorial: David McBride and Alena Chekanov
Production Editorial: Natalie Baan
Jacket Design: Heather Hansen
Production: Erin Suydam
Publicity: James Schneider

This book has been composed in Arno

10 9 8 7 6 5 4 3 2 1

MIX
Paper | Supporting
responsible forestry
FSC® C008955
FSC
www.fsc.org

To Tara, in loving honor of your triumphs and struggles

To Atul, for everything

As nightfall does not come all at once, neither does oppression. In both instances, there is twilight when everything remains seemingly unchanged. And it is in such twilight that we all must be most aware of change in the air—however slight—lest we become unwitting victims of the darkness.

JUSTICE WILLIAM O. DOUGLAS, 1976

CONTENTS

ABBREVIATIONS

ACA	Affordable Care Act
ACLU	American Civil Liberties Union
ADA	Americans with Disabilities Act
ADHD	Attention deficit hyperactivity disorder
AFL-CIO	American Federation of Labor–Congress of Industrial Organizations
AID	Agency for International Development
AIG	American International Group
AP	Associated Press
BG	*Boston Globe*
BJS	Bureau of Justice Statistics
BOP	Bureau of Prisons
BR	*Boston Review*
CARA	Comprehensive Addiction and Recovery Act
CBO	Congressional Budget Office
CDC	Centers for Disease Control and Prevention
CDO	Collateralized debt obligation
CDS	Credit default swap
CFMA	Commodity Futures Modernization Act
CFPB	Consumer Financial Protection Bureau
CFTC	Commodity Futures Trading Commission
CIA	Central Intelligence Agency
CLN	*Criminal Legal News*
COINTELPRO	Counter Intelligence Program (FBI)
COP	Congressional Oversight Panel
CR	*Crime Report*
CRS	Congressional Research Service
CSM	*Christian Science Monitor*

CSPOA	Constitutional Sheriffs and Peace Officers Association
CVA	Concerned Veterans for America
DEA	Drug Enforcement Administration
DHS	Department of Homeland Security
DOA	Department of Agriculture
DOD	Department of Defense
DOJ	Department of Justice
DPA	Deferred prosecution agreement
FAA	Federal Aviation Administration
FBI	Federal Bureau of Investigation
FCIC	Financial Crisis Inquiry Commission
FDA	Food and Drug Administration
FDIC	Federal Deposit Insurance Corporation
FERA	Fraud Enforcement and Recovery Act
FHLBB	Federal Home Loan Bank Board
FIRREA	Financial Institutions Reform, Recovery, and Enforcement Act of 1989
FOIA	Freedom of Information Act
FOP	Fraternal Order of Police
FRBNY	Federal Reserve Bank of New York
FSOC	Financial Stability Oversight Council
FTC	Federal Trade Commission
GAO	Government Accountability Office
GPO	Government Publishing Office (formerly Government Printing Office)
HAMP	Home Affordable Modification Program
HHS	Department of Health and Human Services
HM	*Harper's Magazine*
HOEPA	Home Ownership and Equity Protection Act
ICE	Immigration and Customs Enforcement
IED	Improvised explosive device
IPO	Initial public offering
IRS	Internal Revenue Service
IUPA	International Union of Police Associations
JWCCC	*Journal of White Collar and Corporate Crime*
LAT	*Los Angeles Times*
LEAA	Law Enforcement Assistance Administration
LFO	Legal financial obligation

MAT	Medication-assisted treatment
MERS	Mortgage Electronic Registration System
NAACP	National Association for the Advancement of Colored People
NACCD	National Advisory Commission on Civil Disorders (Kerner Commission)
NAFTA	North American Free Trade Agreement
NAS	National Academy of Sciences
NATO	North Atlantic Treaty Organization
NCVS	National Crime Victimization Survey
NCFIRRE	National Commission on Financial Institution Reform, Recovery, and Enforcement
NEJM	*New England Journal of Medicine*
NIBRS	National Incident-Based Reporting System
NIDA	National Institute on Drug Abuse
NPA	Nonprosecution agreement
NR	*New Republic*
NSA	National Security Agency
NY	*New Yorker*
NYM	*New York Magazine*
NYP	*New York Post*
NYPD	New York Police Department
NYRB	*New York Review of Books*
NYT	*New York Times*
OCC	Office of the Comptroller of the Currency
OECD	Organisation for Economic Co-operation and Development
OMB	Office of Management and Budget
ONDCP	Office of National Drug Control Policy
OPS	Office of Public Safety
OTC	Over-the-counter
OTS	Office of Thrift Supervision
PAC	Political action committee
PI	*Philadelphia Inquirer*
PLN	*Prison Legal News*
PRC	Pew Research Center
PTSD	Post-traumatic stress disorder
R&D	Research and development
S&L	Savings and loan
SAR	Suspicious activity report

SEADOC   Senior Officers Civil Disturbance Orientation Course
SEC   Securities and Exchange Commission
SIGTARP   Special inspector general for the Troubled Asset Relief Program
SIV   Structured investment vehicle
SPV   Special purpose vehicle
STEM   Science, technology, engineering, and math
SWAT   Special weapons and tactics
TAP   *The American Prospect*
TARP   Troubled Asset Relief Program
TRAC   Transactional Records Access Clearinghouse
UCR   Uniform Crime Reporting (FBI)
USSC   US Sentencing Commission
VA   Department of Veterans Affairs
VHA   Veterans Health Administration
WHO   World Health Organization
WP   *Washington Post*
WSJ   *Wall Street Journal*
YLJ   *Yale Law Journal*

FOR NEARLY two decades, I have been teaching courses on mass incarceration, the carceral state, and race at the University of Pennsylvania. Like most scholars of crime and the criminal legal system, I mostly ignored white-collar and corporate crime in my teaching and research. Several years ago, I began gesturing in my courses toward the corporate crime waves that occurred over the last five decades while the US was locking up record numbers of people convicted of drug offenses, street crimes, and immigration violations.

But my gestures fell short of reckoning with the intimate relationship between the carceral state, crime in the streets, crime in the suites, the US empire, and other state violence that has made America exceptionally lethal, unstable, violent, and punitive (for some people). This book is my reckoning. It takes an expansive view of violence that encompasses not only the conventional focus on homicides, assaults, and other so-called street crimes but also corporate violence, structural violence, and state violence perpetrated by local police, the US military, and other government entities.

I hope this book resonates with students and members of the public anguished over mass incarceration and the carceral state. I hope it illuminates how developments in the US political economy and US military are vital to understanding the surge of violence and punishment in the United States, including why US police forces are so lethal; why America cages so many of its people; why the white power movement has become so virulent; and why Donald Trump ended up in the White House twice.

Like students across the country, mine have flocked to introductory courses in economics, which have become the gatekeepers for lucrative jobs in finance and consulting. But the Great Recession is a ghost in most of these courses. The deepest economic downturn since the Great Depression a century ago left barely a trace on the syllabi of introductory courses in economics—or for that matter, political science. As John Kenneth Galbraith warned in his presidential address to the American Economic Association in 1972, in "eliding power," the discipline of economics "destroys its relation with the real world," preventing citizens and students from seeing how they are or will be governed. Much of political science has run the same risk as it has sought to model itself after economics and, increasingly, computer science.[1]

In this book, I have tried to make the causes of the financial crisis, the rise in corporate crime that goes unprosecuted and unpunished, and the political ramifications of so much corporate, state, and structural violence in America comprehensible to students and the public. No advanced training in economics, math, law, or political science is necessary.

Escalating economic inequalities, the 2007–9 financial and foreclosure crises, and blowback from the forever wars set off a political earthquake that Donald Trump shrewdly exploited. But Trump is almost incidental in my account. Trump's exceptionalism—his swagger, cronyism, contempt for democracy, unabashedly racist appeals, misogyny, alleged sexual assaults, and embrace of political violence—obscures how this political earthquake had been in the making for decades.

Trump may be a simple man, but the tens of millions of people who voted for him are not. Writing off everyone who voted for him as "deplorable" obscures how, for decades, the political, economic, and criminal legal systems, along with the US military, have been churning out an increasing number of people who are disposable in the United States. My efforts to explain why many of these people felt they had nowhere else to go but to embrace Trump should not be interpreted as justifications or excuses for the abhorrent activities and attitudes of some of his supporters.

This is a big picture book. My goal is to make visible some vital connections that have been hiding in plain sight at the margins of academic and public discussions; to reframe how we think about crime, violence, punishment, power, wealth, and inequality; and to foster greater ambition in how we understand the problems and seek solutions.

This book is admittedly incomplete. It should have a whole chapter on gun violence. On tax policy. On the climate emergency. But it doesn't. Readers will undoubtedly discover other omissions. I hope this book sets an agenda for others to follow and inspires them to keep asking the big questions.

I have been gratified over the years that my teaching and research on the carceral state have inspired many of my students to volunteer in jails and prisons, to teach about crime and punishment, and to become public defenders, civil rights lawyers, and health-care professionals serving the underserved. These are all vital pursuits. But they will not on their own dismantle the carceral state or radically reduce violence in America. I hope this book will inspire more people to take the fight against mass incarceration, the carceral state, and violence in America to other related and critical arenas, including tax policy, military and foreign policy, and the battle against global warming.

This is a deeply personal book. In writing it, I returned to concerns from the most formative period in my intellectual development when, as an undergraduate, my mentor and thesis adviser was Walter LaFeber, the preeminent revisionist historian of the American empire. I also returned to my earlier research interests that centered on the US political economy, the welfare state, the power of business, and the dysfunctional US health-care system. This book also reflects themes from the course on the American presidency that I have been teaching at Penn since Bill Clinton's second term.

The adage that books don't have to be brilliant, but they must get finished, is especially true at this fraught political moment. As I was writing this book the past few years, I felt at times like I was writing an obituary for the United States and the world I once knew. As I got closer to the end, I felt like I was frantically trying to finish a timed test, and the time was running out. I feared I wouldn't be able to finish before that world, for all its faults, dissolved into something worse and unrecognizable.

The harms and violence I analyze in this book have touched some of the people closest to me. I often feel powerless to help them despite my best efforts. Writing this book has given me some solace. Illuminating the larger forces that they and I are up against makes me more forgiving of them and perhaps of myself.

I harvest hope and strength from seeing problems as they are—however enormous and interconnected they may be—because this is the real world we live in. It is paralyzing and ultimately self-defeating to pretend otherwise. "We should remember that sorrow does produce flowers of its own," Shirley Hazzard once wrote. "It is a misunderstanding always to look for joy."

And so, I end here on a hopeful note. As James Baldwin once said, "I can't be a pessimist because I am alive."

June 30, 2025

PART I

Introduction

1

Social Murder

WEALTH, POWER, AND VIOLENCE
IN AMERICA

I asked a man in prison once how he happened to be there and he said he had
stolen a pair of shoes. I told him if he had stolen a railroad he would be a
United States Senator.

—MOTHER JONES, 1925[1]

THE UNITED States is an exceptionally militarized, lethal, and violent country. The growing concentration of economic, political, and military power is draining America of vital resources to sustain healthy and peaceful communities. It is pushing more people to the margins, where a police officer, a prison cell, a tent, a military recruiter, or a deadly dose of fentanyl-laced heroin is waiting for them.

Rates of homicide, gun violence, suicide, drug overdoses, incarceration, traffic deaths, poverty, and police use of force are exceptionally high in the United States compared to those of other Western countries. In a historic reversal, US life expectancy has fallen below that of much poorer countries as a growing number of people in this country are at risk of losing their homes, health, livelihoods, and savings. Tens of millions of US gun owners are locked and loaded, ready to take the law into their own hands or to turn their guns on themselves. And escalating political violence has put the electoral system and democracy in America in mortal danger.

The United States is increasingly unable or unwilling to stem violence in its many forms. Powerful economic and political interests are rendering less powerful groups and individuals in the United States more susceptible to premature

3

death and other harms. Friedrich Engels called this social murder. Social murder is harder to defend against than everyday homicides "because no man sees the murderer, because the death of the victim seems a natural one, since the offence is more one of omission than of commission. But murder it remains."[2]

US corporations commit social murder with impunity on an even grander scale than they once did. Pharmaceutical executives have been responsible for enormous harms, including the deadly opioid epidemic, and have escaped serious legal or other consequences. So have the titans of Wall Street who unleashed the 2007–9 financial and foreclosures crises. And so have the oil and gas company executives who knew for decades that the burning of fossil fuels would have catastrophic results but stayed silent as they continued doing business as usual.

Since the country's founding, the US criminal legal system has been more forgiving and less punitive toward the well-to-do and well-connected.[3] Over the centuries, this punishment gap has waxed and waned. As the US incarceration rate skyrocketed to record levels starting in the 1970s, this gap widened considerably.

Executives in the C-suites escaped accountability as they amassed more economic and political power. Meanwhile, the country doubled down on pursuing people accused of street crimes, drug offenses, and immigration violations. Today the United States incarcerates more of its people than nearly every other country, even as it decriminalizes or turns a blind eye to elite-level corporate crime. Public and scholarly attention remains fixated on street crime—although corporate malfeasance directly and indirectly harms far more people in the United States.

Penal and social policies have long been two sides of the same coin in governing social marginality.[4] But penal policy has become the policy of first resort to address the massive economic and social dislocations of the last half century in the United States. America is vexed by pervasive state violence thanks to its unprecedented prison boom and the militarization of its police forces.

The country's deep investment in its overseas empire—including the massive military budget and the unassailable assumption that the United States is the indispensable nation destined to police the world—has compounded the problem of violence in America. The global war on terror launched after 9/11 shattered numerous countries and communities around the world. Back home in the United States, it eroded the will and capacity to stem violence in its many forms. For all the talk of political polarization in the United States, the bloated US military budget sails through Congress most years with just a handful of dissenters, if that. Meanwhile, a growing number of people in the United States, including veterans, are denied adequate food, shelter, and health care, let alone opportunities to lead dignified and meaningful lives.

When discussing violence in America, we need to widen the analytic lens to include structural violence.[5] As legal scholar Paul Butler explains, structural violence encompasses deaths and other harms that are the result of "a process or ongoing social condition embedded in our everyday lives" that robs people of their potential. Structural violence stands in contrast to the more familiar and narrow understanding of violence as a single event, such as a homicide, robbery, or back-alley beating by a police officer.[6]

Political, economic, corporate, legal, military, social, and other structures that we take for granted are meting out extraordinary levels of structural violence—or social murder—that is less visible but often more deadly. Unprecedented drops in US life expectancy due to rising rates of suicide, drug overdoses, alcoholism, obesity, and chronic illnesses like diabetes and hypertension are not just the product of individual choices, individual pathologies, or individual circumstances.[7] They stem from social, economic, and political developments that foster structural violence and poverty. As sociologist Matthew Desmond states, "poverty is an injury, a taking." Millions of people in the United States "do not end up poor by a mistake of history or personal conduct. Poverty persists because some wish and will it to."[8]

A central argument of this book is that corporate impunity, the financialization of the economy, militarized policing, the burgeoning carceral state, and the forever wars in Afghanistan, Iraq, and elsewhere have fostered state, structural, and economic violence in America. They have also been impediments to stemming interpersonal violence or so-called street crimes. The growing concentration of military, economic, and political power has siphoned off vital resources, preying on the most vulnerable communities and individuals and normalizing violence and death. It has impeded the United States from mitigating the root causes of violent and other street crimes and has contributed to falling rates of life expectancy. These developments have furthered the consolidation of what geographer and prison abolitionist Ruth Wilson Gilmore calls the "anti-state state" in which guaranteeing social well-being and preventing premature deaths are no longer considered the government's raison d'être.[9]

The US failure to protect its people from all these harms has increased the brittleness of democracy in America. Punishment serves a vital role in reinforcing the moral bounds of society by demarcating what actions are considered wrong and who is blameworthy, as French sociologist Émile Durkheim once noted.[10] The repeated failure to hold corporations, their executives, and their political patrons accountable has fostered political instability and undermined the legitimacy of US political and economic institutions. So has the related rise in state and structural violence. Taken together, these developments raise the prospect of a bleak, undemocratic future as violence begets more violence, and America morphs into a failed state.[11]

State Violence: The Changing Carceral State

A country's incarceration rate is an important barometer of state violence and control. As underlying economic and political conditions have shifted over the past fifty years, so have patterns of incarceration and other penal sanctions. But discussions of the carceral state and criminal justice reform in the United States still tend to focus on urban areas and African American people, particularly the hyperincarceration of Black men. The ways in which interlocking systems of punishment, disadvantage, and violence have been diffusing to other groups and communities in the United States have not been central issues in most scholarly analyses and public discussions.[12] But since the race to incarcerate began more than five decades ago, there have been important demographic and geographic shifts in who is ending up in prison and jail, as detailed in chapter 2.

Between the mid-1970s and the turn of the twenty-first century, the United States became the world's leading warden as its incarceration rate increased more than fourfold, and hundreds of new prisons, jails, and immigrant detention facilities were built.[13] Thanks to a political stampede coming from many directions, the country ratcheted up penalties for crimes ranging from homicide to burglary to immigration and drug offenses as public officials turned to "governing through crime."[14] The prison boom and punitive turn in the United States did not wane even as rates of violent street crime began falling in the mid-1990s and plunged to historic lows over the next two decades. The massive increase in US incarceration rates was responsible for at most only a small portion of this historic drop in street crime.[15] Other factors were more consequential, including a shrinking proportion of young people, new policing strategies, shifts in the market for illegal drugs, and investments in public housing and public services.[16]

Deindustrialization and other changes in urban economies and polities in the 1950s and 1960s helped fuel mass incarceration and get-tough policies targeted at African American people in urban areas.[17] More recently, the economic hollowing out of rural and Rust Belt communities in the United States that are not riding the crest of urban gentrification and the high-tech boom has rendered those left behind more vulnerable to state and structural violence today, including incarceration and premature death.[18] Over the last twenty-five years, Black-white disparities in incarceration have certainly not closed in the United States, but they have narrowed.[19] In dozens of states (both blue and red), incarceration rates are slowing or declining in urban areas while rising in rural and suburban communities.[20] Furthermore, as the US incarceration rate decreased slightly over the past few years, the rate for women remained at a historic high; and immigrant detention and convictions for sex offenses (some of them quite minor) became major drivers of the carceral state. With Donald Trump's return to the White House, immigration policy is turbocharging state violence and the carceral state.

State Violence: The Police

Police use of excessive force is another major barometer of state violence. Police officers in the United States are accustomed to deploying extraordinary levels of violence and coercion shielded from outside scrutiny and control. The resources available to US police departments and law enforcement agencies have increased dramatically without a commensurate increase in their accountability to the communities they are supposed to serve, as detailed in chapter 3.

Categorizing police killings of civilians as acts of state violence shifts the emphasis from the actions and biases of individual officers to the larger institutional, structural, racial, and historical forces that are at the root of excessive use of force in the United States. Doing so "calls attention to the systemic forces" that permit individual officers "to act with impunity," explains historian Keeanga-Yamahtta Taylor.[21]

Black people in the United States are more than twice as likely as white people to be killed by the police.[22] But compared to the rates of police violence in Western Europe and Canada, white people in the United States are also victims of police violence at exceptional rates. Police use of excessive force in the United States is widely assumed to be primarily a problem for urban areas. But homicides by police have been declining in the largest cities while continuing to rise in rural and suburban communities.[23]

The lethalness of US police forces has proximate and deeper historical causes. The tendency to focus on the culpability of individual officers, most notably the impact of their implicit and explicit racial and other biases, occludes the institutional factors that are far more consequential in explaining levels of police violence. These institutional factors, as chronicled in chapter 3, include differences in training, weaponry, and standards for the use of force; the clout of police unions; and a string of court decisions that largely immunize US police officers from criminal charges and civil lawsuits.

As for the deeper historical factors, many critics of US policing single out the country's history of slavery, white supremacy, Jim Crow, and the "new Jim Crow" to explain why police in the United States are so violent and deadly. But additional historical factors are also culprits. As discussed in chapters 4 and 5, America's exceptionally violent history of suppressing workers, organized labor, and political unrest left a bloody imprint on the development of US police forces. So did the emergence of the United States as a global empire in the twentieth century. More recently, the tightening ties between law enforcement, the US military, and the white power movement have fueled the lethalness of US police forces.

State Violence: The Warfare State

When it comes to wealth, power, and violence in America, developments at home and abroad are "mutually constitutive."[24] Rising US militarization has generated violence not only overseas but also back in the United States.[25] Blowback on the homefront from the global empire and war on terror has been a problem hiding in plain sight, just like mass incarceration once was.

Like the carceral state, the warfare state has metastasized into the political, social, and economic fabric of the United States. It has been compromising and enfeebling democratic institutions and heaping more disadvantages onto already disadvantaged groups, as detailed in chapter 5.[26] The warfare state has fueled political marginalization and alienation as people in small towns and rural communities are more likely to serve in the military and be wounded or killed in action. It also has fostered the militarization of local police departments and the surges of the white power movement and political violence. Furthermore, the warfare state has plundered the country of vital political and material resources to stem crime in the streets, crime in the suites, and premature deaths.

Today, the United States operates more than 750 military bases in at least eighty countries—though no one, not even the Pentagon, knows exactly how many.[27] (China has nine or so.)[28] The United States has active and reserve troops stationed in nearly every country, and US drones conduct bombing raids and missile attacks in numerous countries. United States special forces, which reportedly number seventy-four thousand, have been deployed in over 150 countries, where they carry out missions shrouded in secrecy.[29] The official tab for US expenditures on the military and defense was over $900 million in 2023—or more than what the next nine countries spent in total. Actual US spending on the military and defense may be nearly twice the official figures.[30]

The ways in which militarization is imperiling US democratic institutions and contributing to the increase in all kinds of violence in the United States have not been central to recent public and academic discussions about violence and the enfeebled state of democracy in America. Indeed, as President Donald Trump surrounded himself in 2017 with a cordon of generals in top civilian positions that was unprecedented in modern US history, the political establishment and mainstream media approvingly referred to the president's civilian generals as "the adults in the room."[31] A major multiyear project funded by the Social Science Research Council on the "anxieties of democracy," which involved dozens of leading scholars, did not include a single essay on the US military or the forever wars.[32]

Military conquest and occupation have been central features of American state building since the first colonies were established.[33] Yet while military conquest was a key feature of American political development, military adventures were regarded as intermittent rather than integral to the American state and society for much of US history. Over the course of the twentieth century, there was a basic shift. The quest for perpetual global military supremacy congealed as a central feature of the American state and American identity by the late 1940s.[34]

In the aftermath of the Second World War, the United States forged what historian and former military officer Andrew Bacevich calls the "Washington rules," which were premised on constructing an unrivaled global empire.[35] The US defeat in Vietnam in 1975, the end of the Cold War in 1989, and the dissolution of the Soviet Union in 1991 provided important openings to jettison the Washington rules. But those opportunities were quickly forfeited. After 9/11, the global war on terror and forever wars became a codicil to the Washington rules, "accepted policy, hardly more controversial than the practice of stationing US troops abroad."[36] During the 2016 presidential campaign, Donald Trump appeared to set the Washington rules on fire as he excoriated the US invasion of Iraq and the forever wars.[37] The US wars in Afghanistan, Iraq, and elsewhere were an accelerant for Trump's narrative of betrayal that propelled him into the White House that year.

Corporate Violence and Corporate Crime:
The Culture of Little or No Control

The aftershocks of the 2007–9 financial and foreclosure crises were also accelerants for Trump's narrative of betrayal. The wreckage from these twin crises and the failure to pursue and punish the main culprits created a huge political opening that Trump brashly stepped into. Trump seized this political moment, but he did not create it. Indeed, it had been decades in the making, as shown in chapters 6 to 9.

Over the last fifteen years or so, mass incarceration in the United States has become a central concern in criminology and in public discussions of crime and punishment.[38] But scholars, policymakers, and the public have generally ignored the concurrent de facto decriminalization of crime in the suites and how it has transformed the criminal legal system, fostered violence in its many forms, and put US democracy at risk.[39]

In identifying the causes of mass incarceration, sociologist David Garland argued years ago that societal angst stemming from deep changes in the US economy and society in the decades immediately following World War II ushered in a "culture of control."[40] The widespread perception of the government's impotency to mitigate the economic upheavals of the 1970s, notably the twin shocks of stagflation and the oil crisis, fueled the culture of control. The government's failure to tame these economic demons cast doubt on its efficacy, legitimacy, and raison d'être. As public officials struggled to curb inflation and restore economic growth, they lashed out. They promoted harsher measures to punish crime in the streets for their symbolic and expressive value, according to Garland.

While the culture of control was taking hold in the United States, another radical transformation was under way that has received far less attention. A culture of no control—or little control—over elite-level corporate crime was taking root away from the political limelight. As it doubled down on pursuing and punishing people accused of street and drug crimes and immigration offenses, the United States retreated from regulating corporations and prosecuting and punishing their executives despite a tsunami of elite-level criminal activities by leading banks, accounting firms, and major corporations. Keeping the public focus on immigration offenses, drug crimes, homicides, robberies, and other street crimes was a winning strategy to rivet political attention and public resources on battling crime in the streets, not crime in the suites.[41]

In hailing the so-called great crime drop that began in the 1990s, criminologists, public figures, and the media focused on trends in street crimes. They did not take into account the huge corporate crime waves that were buffeting the country.[42] As President Bill Clinton was about to leave office, the dot-com bubble burst under the weight of fraudulent initial public offerings (IPOs). In the early aughts, the energy giant Enron and several other large corporations went under in a sea of fraudulent reports about their earnings and debt. Epic fraud in the subprime mortgage market hurled the country and the world toward the Great Recession, which began in 2007. Since then, white-collar and corporate prosecutions have plummeted to record lows. Meanwhile financial crimes, including eye-popping cases of money laundering, accounting fraud, and market manipulation, have escalated.[43] So have cases of mass-market consumer fraud and internet-related crimes.[44]

Victims and Costs of Corporate Violence and Crime

Crime in the suites victimizes more people and causes more harm than crime in the streets. Yet the US media don't acknowledge much of it; criminologists mostly ignore it; and the country's leading clearinghouses for crime statistics don't really track it. And the word *corruption* is seldom used to refer to the criminal activities of US corporations, their executives, and their political patrons.[45]

The harms from corporate malfeasance "are often the result of criminal recklessness" but are seldom prosecuted.[46] Those harms are huge.[47] How huge is hard to say because the data the government collects on white-collar and corporate crime are sketchy compared to what it compiles on street crime.[48] An estimated 125,000 people in the United States die each year from traumatic injuries on the job and from occupational diseases, such as black lung and asbestosis—or more than five times the number of people who were murdered in 2021.[49] The "silent violence of pollution, contaminated food, hazardous consumer products, and hospital malpractice" kills tens of thousands of people yearly and injures many more.[50]

Wage theft by employers—another crime that is seldom prosecuted—robs low-wage workers of an estimated $50 billion each year. This sum is equivalent to about three and a half times the total yearly losses due to all robberies, burglaries, larcenies, and motor vehicle thefts in the United States.[51] Estimates of health-care fraud range from $240 billion to $750 billion annually.[52] But who really knows how much. The subprime mortgage scandal was the catalyst for the Great Recession, during which US households lost an estimated $19–22 trillion in wealth, including real estate, stocks, and retirement savings.[53] The crisis rocked financial and political systems around the world because the global economy was (and is) deeply entangled with Wall Street and the US real estate market.[54] Fraudulent foreclosures during the subprime mortgage scandal robbed millions of people in the United States of their homes. The foreclosure crisis spurred the biggest mass movement of people in the United States since the Great Depression. It also fueled today's housing crisis.[55]

Corporate crime in just one industry can result in more deaths, injuries, and property losses annually than all kinds of street crime combined.[56] One of the most notorious examples is the pharmaceutical industry, which has a long and well-documented history of shamelessly marketing dangerous drugs and committing bribery and fraud on an epic scale.[57] Pharmaceutical companies also routinely engage in shockingly unethical behavior, including unscrupulous off-label marketing, price gouging, and exploiting loopholes in the patent system to reap billions of dollars by delaying the release of safer and more efficacious versions of their drugs.[58]

Widespread criminal and unethical behavior in the pharmaceutical industry sparked the opioid crisis, which has killed hundreds of thousands of people in the United States since the turn of the twenty-first century. Fatal drug overdoses increased more than fivefold between 2000 and 2022 and contributed to unprecedented declines in the country's life expectancy rate.[59] Drug overdoses are now the leading cause of accidental death in the United States, surpassing motor vehicle accidents, and the top cause of death by far for people under age fifty.[60] The Joint Economic Committee of the US Congress estimated that the toll of the opioid crisis was $1.5 trillion in 2020 alone—or 7 percent of the GDP.[61]

In the latest war on drugs, the harshest words and most punitive policies have been aimed at people who use opioids, not at the pharmaceutical companies, medical providers, government regulators, and policymakers who triggered and perpetuated the opioid crisis, as detailed in chapters 10 and 11. The individuals and companies that opened the floodgates for tens of billions of high-dosage opioid pills to flow through the United States have largely escaped punishment and accountability.

The Limits of Neoliberalism as an Explanation

Political and institutional factors mediated the construction of the culture of little or no control of corporate malfeasance and corporate violence in the United States. Its emergence was not preordained but rather contingent, fluid, and multilayered. The drive to radically reorient the criminal legal system toward a hands-off approach to elite-level corporate crime while mercilessly cracking down on people accused of street and drug crimes and immigration violations was not seamless. Just as the construction of the carceral state was not linear, neither was the decriminalization of crime in the suites and the construction of the shield of corporate impunity.[62]

The shift toward corporate decriminalization over the last five decades occurred by fits and starts as regulators, law enforcement, policymakers, and legislators alternately lightened up and toughened up on white-collar and corporate crime. But the overall trend was toward more leniency. The waves of deregulation and a growing bipartisan enthusiasm for neoliberalism since the 1970s are important factors. But they cannot on their own explain this trend toward easing up on corporate criminality.

Neoliberalism is a useful shorthand way to sum up a cluster of political and economic beliefs and policies, including deifying the market and disdaining government intervention. Neoliberalism is rooted in the premise that free markets produce the most efficient and just outcomes, so governments should just get out of the way. As Bill Clinton pronounced in his 1996 State of the Union address, "The era of big government is over." The hallmarks of neoliberalism include deregulation, fealty to so-called free trade, retrenchment of the welfare state, low taxes (at least for corporations and wealthy people), and the privatization of everything from schools to sewer systems.

Neoliberalism also reifies the individual over the society. As British Prime Minister Margaret Thatcher famously once said, "there's no such thing as society."[63] People are seen primarily as market actors—on the job, in their communities, on dating apps, and even in their families—always striving to secure a competitive advantage by building up their human capital and, increasingly, their individual brand, even when money is not the main issue. Neoliberalism is not just a package of economic beliefs and policies. By crowding out a vocabulary of politics and replacing it with a lexicon of economics in which the allegedly neutral "free" market rules, neoliberalism renders the operation of power much less visible.[64] As Alan Greenspan, the former chairman of the Federal Reserve, brashly declared in 2007: "National security aside, it hardly makes any difference who will be the next president. The world is governed by market forces."[65]

Fraught with contradictions, neoliberalism's political power has long rested on political and ideological sleights of hand that keep those contradictions out of the public eye and public debates. Foremost among them is the myth that the state has retreated under the neoliberal order. The government did not retreat but rather repositioned itself. It pulled back or was forced back in areas such as providing health and social services, public education, public transportation, and workplace protections. Meanwhile, the government's power and capacity to police and punish people in the United States for street crimes, drug offenses, and immigration violations grew vastly thanks to the unprecedented expansion of the carceral state. So did its capacity to police the globe.

Neoliberalism's reputed disdain for government goes only so far. For example, Charles Koch, one of the richest people in the United States, is a die-hard crusader against taxes and the social safety net. He is also a longtime champion of the so-called free market. But he became a billionaire many times over thanks to how his Koch Industries expanded primarily "into businesses that are uncompetitive, dominated by monopolistic firms, and deeply intertwined with government subsidies and regulation."[66] Fracking, the hazardous method of extracting fossil fuels deeply embedded in shale, became profitable only through government-sponsored research and generous government subsidies, which Koch and other producers of natural gas and oil have profited from and ardently defended.[67] Similarly, pharmaceutical companies have fought to eviscerate numerous government regulations that protect patients and consumers. Meanwhile they have doggedly defended patent laws and government regulations that permit them to maintain lucrative monopolies on drugs, many of which were developed with generous government support.

To understand the quiescence toward corporate malfeasance, a fine-grained understanding of the political, historical, institutional, and ideological terrain that neoliberalism traverses is necessary. Treating neoliberalism as an all-powerful, all-encompassing, ahistorical force obscures the varied and at times interlocking economic, political, ideological, cultural, racial, and other factors that shape this terrain and fuel the many strands of violence in America.[68]

Sociologist Barrington Moore railed against ideological and cultural explanations that neglected how political conflicts, institutional developments, and shifting elite interests transmit certain values and ideologies from one generation to the next. "To maintain and transmit a value system," Moore explained, "human beings are punched, bullied, sent to jail, thrown into concentration camps, cajoled, bribed, made into heroes, encouraged to read newspapers, stood up against a wall and shot, and sometimes even taught sociology."[69] In that spirit, we need to understand how the ideology of neoliberalism is maintained and transmitted—or forced to pull back—as the political, economic, social, racial, institutional, and international context shifts.

Financialization and the Politics of Entitlement

The financialization of the US economy, polity, and society over the last half century is a major contour of this context, as detailed in chapters 6 to 9. One expert on the US political economy likens financialization to a "Copernican revolution" in which business and society now orbit around a financial sector that has grown to an unprecedented size.[70] The financial sector encompasses firms and individuals that make their money primarily through financial services, including banks, hedge funds, pension funds, insurance companies, and private equity firms.[71] The ideologies and activities of the financial industry now permeate not just the economy but also the polity, society, and even the educational system and family life.

Since the mid-1980s, the financial sector has been generating only 4 to 5 percent of all jobs in the United States. But this sector typically accounts for almost a third of yearly corporate profits—up from between 10 and 15 percent in the 1950s and 1960s.[72] The financial sector has been consuming disproportionate slices not only of corporate profits and the country's wealth but also of its educational elite.[73]

Financialization facilitated an astounding upward redistribution of wealth and political power. In 1980, the richest 1 percent of people in the United States were receiving 9 percent of overall income—a division that had remained relatively constant since World War II. By 2007, the share of the top 1 percent had skyrocketed to 23 percent.[74] Wealth has become even more concentrated than income. As of 2022, the top 1 percent held about 35 percent of the total personal wealth in the United States, up from a modern low of 22 percent in 1978. During roughly that same period, wealth held by the 0.1 percent more than doubled to nearly 20 percent (see figure 1.1). In 1982, the combined worth of the 400 richest people in the United States was $225 billion in today's dollars.[75] Four decades later, the United States had some 735 billionaires, who together were worth $4.7 trillion.[76]

On the political spectrum, these multibillionaires tend to lean toward the right, the hard right, and the antidemocratic, neofascist right.[77] As billionaire financier Warren Buffett quipped in 2006, "There's class warfare, all right, but it's my class, the rich class, that's making war, and we're winning."[78] Economic elites and organized groups representing their interests largely determine US government policy. Average citizens and interest groups have little to no influence if they do not have the backing of a billionaire or at least a decamillionaire.[79] More money than ever is corrupting the political system thanks to the

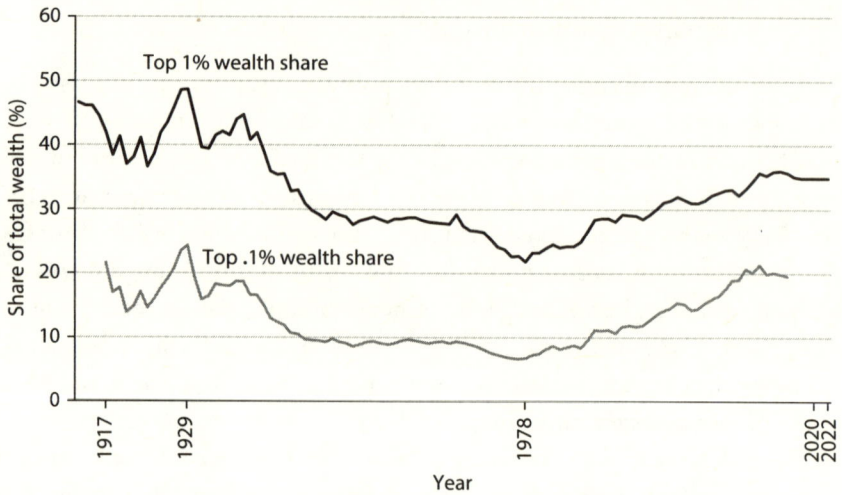

FIGURE 1.1. US Wealth Inequality, 1913–2022. *Sources*: World Inequality Database, "Wealth Inequality, USA, 1963–2023," n.d., https://wid.world /country/usa/ (accessed February 23, 2025); and Emmanuel Saez and Gabriel Zucman, "The Rise of Income and Wealth Inequality in America: Evidence from Distributional Macroeconomic Accounts," *Journal of Economic Perspectives* 34, no. 4 (Fall 2020): 10, fig. 1; original data courtesy of the authors.

huge personal fortunes that financialization and militarization facilitated. The US Supreme Court's *Citizens United* decision in 2010 and *McCutcheon* ruling in 2014 compounded these problems as they swept away vestiges of restrictions on corporate campaign donations and other political activities.[80]

Thanks to the unprecedented political and economic clout of the financial and high-tech sectors—including the revolving door between Wall Street, leading corporate law firms, and the top rungs of government—financiers and high-tech executives have amassed overwhelming authority and resources to define the economic and political narrative, dictate the political and policy solutions, and escape major penalties or other consequences for their criminal activities. Call it the politics of entitlement.

As financialization accelerated, leading financial institutions and their executives also had greater personal and institutional incentives to take the economy on a rough ride to the edge of the cliff. And if they misjudged where the edge was, chances had increased that the government would rescue them in the name of rescuing the economy because these financial institutions had become too big to fail and too big to jail.

The Courts, Corporate Crime, and Violence in America

Since the 1970s, the courts have been instrumental in the buildup of the carceral state as they sanctioned all sorts of exceptionally punitive laws and practices that have made it easier for the criminal legal system to apprehend, convict,
and severely punish people accused of street and drug crimes and immigration
offenses. Meanwhile, the courts have been galvanizing the culture of little or
no control over corporations and their executives, which has fueled structural
violence and social murder. The judicial turn toward business accelerated
under Chief Justice John Roberts, who has helmed the most business-friendly
US Supreme Court in almost a century. The Second Circuit Court in New
York City, the most consequential federal appeals court for securities law, also
enabled this shift.[81]

The judiciary has stripped prosecutors of key weapons to investigate and
prosecute corporate malfeasance while expanding the legal protections for corporations and their executives.[82] The US Supreme Court has doggedly strip-
mined the administrative state of its regulatory powers, including striking down
the decades-old *Chevron* ruling in.[83] In a series of decisions, the US Supreme
Court has been immunizing public officials from charges of corruption for accepting bribes, kickbacks, and "gratuities." In his dissent in the 2010 *Citizens
United* decision, Justice John Paul Stevens denounced the court's tighter embrace of a "crabbed view of corruption" over the prior quarter century.[84]

A growing cadre of judges on the US Supreme Court and elsewhere pro-
claim their fealty to the "original" meaning of the US Constitution. But they
blithely ignore how corruption was a central issue at the constitutional and
ratifying conventions and how the framers took an expansive view of what
constitutes official corruption.[85] In her stinging dissent to the landmark
2024 *Snyder v. United States* decision, which greatly circumscribes federal
safeguards against public corruption, Justice Ketanji Brown Jackson denounced the majority's "absurd and atextual reading of the law." She warned
that legally sanctioning gratuities to reward greedy public officials for past
actions "makes government—at every level—less responsive, less efficient,
and less trustworthy."[86]

Corporations and their executives became more adept at maneuvering
themselves beyond the reach not only of the criminal courts but also of the
civil courts thanks to a slew of corporate-friendly legal decisions. People victimized by corporations were increasingly shut out from receiving monetary
compensation and other redress through civil lawsuits. They were denied their

day in court thanks to the proliferation of binding mandatory arbitration clauses that favor businesses and employers; nondisclosure agreements that keep corporate malfeasance shrouded; and higher hurdles to file and prevail in class-action lawsuits.[87]

The courts and lawmakers have contributed to escalating violence in America in additional ways. The US Supreme Court's radical reinterpretation of the Second Amendment's so-called right to bear arms helped put an estimated 400 million guns in private hands in the United States (including at least twenty million military-style assault rifles).[88] This death march has propelled the country's exceptional rates of homicide, shootings, and suicide.[89] Every year for the past quarter century, the number of gun suicides has outpaced the number of gun homicides.[90] Black people in the United States are much more likely to be murdered, while non-Hispanic white people, especially men, are far more likely to die of suicide. Indeed the suicide rate for non-Hispanic white people is close to the homicide rate for Black people.[91] In California and some other states, gun homicide rates in rural and semirural towns and counties far surpass the rates in major cities. Kern County, a rural area north of Los Angeles, is California's deadliest county, with people shot to death at a rate nearly twice that of the state's largest city.[92]

The Great Recession, the Financial Crisis, and the Criminal Legal System

Scholars have ably excavated the underlying causes, as well as some of the far-reaching consequences, of the financialization of the US economy and the 2007–9 financial and foreclosure crises.[93] They also have shown how the Republican and Democratic parties were deeply culpable in the financialization of the US economy and in the ascent of the uber-rich's politics of entitlement.[94] But the seismic impact that financialization has had on the criminal legal system has garnered less attention.

Experts on the carceral state have identified some important aspects of the direct impact of financialization on the criminal legal system. They have shown, for example, how financiers and their political allies shrewdly repurposed financial instruments, such as lease revenue bonds, to obscure the real costs of the jail and prison boom; how the push for privatization of prisons, jails, immigrant detention facilities, parole, and probation also helped to keep the real costs of the carceral state out of the public eye; how new financial gimmicks, such as social impact bonds, were not likely to reduce the incarceration rate even as they lined the pockets of Goldman Sachs and other financiers that promoted them; and how the neoliberal and deregulatory impulses that fueled financialization also fueled enthusiasm for emphasizing reentry, justice reinvestment, and reducing recidivism as the cures for mass incarceration, even though centering the reform agenda on these three R's would likely bolster, not dismantle, the carceral state.[95]

But the impact of financialization on the criminal legal system and the carceral state is much more extensive than this. With the political and economic ascent of the financial sector, the criminal legal system has radically retreated from policing, prosecuting, and punishing elite-level corporate criminal misconduct. Furthermore, financialization, the corporate crime waves, and the de facto decriminalization of crime in the suites have robbed individuals, communities, and the country of critical financial and other resources to vanquish the root causes of violent street crime. They also have left more people vulnerable to structural violence and propelled a political legitimacy crisis.

The Democratic and Republican parties have both been culprits in institutionalizing and normalizing the decriminalization of crime in the suites since the 1970s. Despite loud warnings early on, criminality and unethical behavior festered for years in the mortgage market and infected the wider financial sector. When the White House, Congress, and the Federal Reserve finally acted under President George W. Bush and then President Barack Obama, they ladled trillions of taxpayer dollars on the financial institutions that were the prime culprits. The government bailed out the leading banks and other financial institutions and did not demand much in return, not even meaningful restraints on executive compensation. Banks, financial firms, and their top executives faced no serious criminal penalties. The fines levied against them were minuscule compared to the quarterly profits they raked in.

After promising hope and change in the 2008 election, Barack Obama and his administration forfeited a major political opening to set the country on a new track. The political will to sanction the culprits, heal the harms, and prevent such violence in the future by restructuring the financial sector quickly dissipated, as detailed in chapters 8 and 9. In his memoirs, Obama contends that meting out criminal sanctions to the financiers who triggered the financial and foreclosure crises would have done "violence to the social order."[96] Instead, his administration pursued modest regulatory reforms that left in place many of the pathogens that triggered the financial and foreclosure crises.

As Wall Street rapidly rebounded from the Great Recession, much of the country remained mired in debt, unemployment, underemployment, and foreclosures. Standards of living deteriorated for many people, and income inequality, poverty, and homelessness increased. The shrinking tax base and the attacks on deficit spending from the right and center (including President Obama's jabs in his 2011 State of the Union address) further imperiled the social safety net, which was already threadbare.[97] Public services to mitigate this pain withered as tax revenues plummeted thanks to regressive tax policies and rising unemployment and foreclosure rates.

By the end of the Obama administration, a new regime to deal with elite-level corporate crime by top executives and their companies had congealed into a "corporate shield" that protected them from charges of "colossal fraud."[98] The consolidation of this corporate shield had enormous economic and political implications. It cast widespread doubt not only on the legitimacy and fairness of the criminal legal system but also on the legitimacy and fairness of the economic and political systems. The uber-wealthy's politics of entitlement shielded top executives and their corporations from serious legal consequences and protected their growing stockpiles of assets, bonuses, and profits.

Crime in the Streets and "Thick Public Safety"

This maldistribution of economic and political power robbed the government and ultimately the wider society of the vital resources needed to foster safe, thriving, and healthy communities with low levels of despair, violence, and premature deaths. The giant fiscal and political investment in the country's global empire compounded these problems.

Violent street crime is not exceptionally high in the United States compared to affluent democracies. The one big exception—and it is a big one—is homicide and gun-related deaths and injuries.[99] Since the mid-1990s, rates of violent crime have plummeted in the United States, but they remain remarkably high. Between 1990 and 2019, the homicide victimization rate for African American people fell by nearly 40 percent.[100] Nonetheless, about 217,000 Black males were homicide victims between 1990 and 2019—a figure that exceeds the total number of US military casualties during the decade-long American war in Southeast Asia by about 400 percent.[101] And for every Black male killed by gun violence, another twenty-four incurred nonfatal injuries from shootings.[102] Black women are also victims of exceptionally high rates of violence, including homicide and sexual assault.[103]

As US rates of street crime fell from their peak in the mid-1990s, violent street crime became more unequally distributed in this country.[104] Celebrating the great crime drop while ignoring these facts is like heralding the record highs of the US stock market or gains in US per capita income without considering trends in income distribution or poverty rates.[105] Violent street crime is highly stratified by race, class, and neighborhood.[106] In one striking example, when Barack Obama became president in 2009, the homicide rate in Chicago's Washington Park, whose population is overwhelmingly poor and 98 percent African American, was more than twenty-five times higher than the rate in neighboring affluent Hyde Park, home to the Obama family.[107]

With the rise in the number of people living in residentially segregated neighborhoods, and of Black people living in concentrated poverty, the deleterious effects of growing up and residing in poor, segregated, urban neighborhoods are now well documented.[108] But it is extremely hard—perhaps impossible—to disentangle the race effects from the class effects in urban violence because there are virtually no urban white neighborhoods as poor as the poorest Black neighborhoods to make comparisons.[109]

That said, the findings of decades of research on what explains trends in violent street crime *over the long term*, especially homicide rates, are remarkably robust. Certain structural factors, including higher rates of poverty, income inequality, and gun ownership, predict higher rates of homicide. So do other structural factors that are often related to income inequality, including residential segregation, pervasive economic discrimination, and the lack of thriving neighborhood and community groups.[110] One additional factor in the US case appears to be the growing demand for opioids in certain communities since the late 1990s.[111]

Differences in policing resources and policing strategies also likely explain some of the variations in rates of violent street crime (at least over the short term) between similarly situated communities. But experts on crime and policing do not agree on just how much to credit the police for sustained drops in rates of homicide and other violent crimes.[112] Small-bore solutions to stem violent street crime, notably the various "community violence intervention" programs, have attracted more scholarly and public attention recently. But these programs have had checkered success in fostering sustained—rather than just short-term—declines in violence in high-crime neighborhoods.[113]

Experts on crime generally agree that swift and certain apprehension and punishment deter street crime while ratcheting up penalties does not.[114] But frightening people living in high-crime neighborhoods—many of whom are already alienated from law enforcement and the wider society—into obeying the law by wielding credible threats that they will be arrested and punished if they don't obey is at best a second-rate solution.[115] The better fix is to prevent crime by improving the social and economic conditions and the life chances of people who reside in marginalized and disadvantaged communities.[116] But that would entail more money and resources. Lots more.

We need to foster what sociologist Bruce Western calls the "restorative power of thick public safety," which keeps the peace by nurturing thriving communities and neighborhoods rather than by relying on intrusive and militarized police forces.[117] But since the days of President Lyndon B. Johnson's Great Society and war on poverty in the 1960s, conservatives on the right have hammered away at the social and economic supports that foster thick public safety and reduce homicides and other violent crimes. They succeeded in mainstreaming the view that public assistance and other public investments increase rather than reduce street crime, despite overwhelming evidence to the contrary.[118] The extraordinary 8-to-1 Black-white disparity in US homicide victims overshadows the fact that the United States is a remarkably lethal country for other demographic groups.[119] On the eve of the pandemic, non-Hispanic white people in the United States were two to five times more likely to be murdered than people living in Western Europe.[120]

Crime prevention policies in Western Europe have followed different trajectories from those in the United States. In much of Western Europe, they have been "bound up with concerns about social exclusion and urban renewal in disadvantaged communities."[121] Police forces in Canada and Western Europe tend to be better trained, more highly educated, less militaristic, and more subject to civilian control. Canada and Western Europe also have more expansive social welfare and economic programs that curtail crime by ameliorating poverty and inequality and by providing high-quality day care, good schools, universal health care, public housing, and other vital social and economic supports.[122] That model is now under great strain thanks to the rise in the number of migrants to Canada and Europe and other political and economic shifts.

Racism, Racial Disparities, and Violence

In any account of violence in America, race-related factors are key. The historical evidence is overwhelming that racial animus and the quest to preserve white supremacy have been central factors in American political development, including the disproportionate violence meted out to African American people, Indigenous people, and other historically marginalized groups. But racism does not on its own explain how state, corporate, economic, structural, and interpersonal violence is perpetuated; why such violence fluctuates; why some groups are harmed more than others; or how to staunch the violence. Racism, just like neoliberalism, capitalism, and other isms, is not a historical actor itself but rather part of complex historical processes. The form and impact of these isms depend on the interplay of economic, institutional, political, and social factors over time and the choices individuals and groups make in a given moment and context. In the case of policing, for example, there is not a straight line from the antebellum slave patrols to the cops in armed personnel carriers patrolling the streets of Ferguson, Missouri, in summer 2014 after a police officer killed Michael Brown, a Black teenager.

Furthermore, as the racial order invents new ways and resurrects old ones to target African American people, it has generated punitive, often violent, policies and practices that diffuse to other people in the United States and abroad. At the dawn of the Jim Crow era more than a century ago, the massive disenfranchisement of African American people through poll taxes, literacy tests, and violence overshadowed the vast and simultaneous disenfranchisement of poor white people in the South that stunted the Populist movement during the Gilded Age. Likewise, the hyperincarceration of Black men today and the disproportionate number of African American people killed by the police have overshadowed the lethal consequences of state and other violence for other groups of people in the United States.

Researchers have devised sophisticated statistical models to measure the Black-white disparities in life expectancy and other realms, including education, employment, health care, income, incarceration, and wealth. The tendency to focus on racial disparities has overshadowed disparities related to class, ethnicity, geography, gender, sexuality, and so forth. Furthermore, the degree to which certain inequalities "that appear statistically as 'racial' disparities" may in fact be embedded in other political, social, and economic relations has not received sufficient scholarly or public attention.[123] Measuring racial and other disparities in incarceration rates, war casualties, police killings of civilians, suicides, overdoses, and other premature deaths does not tell us much about the underlying factors that generate so much violence in America.[124] To borrow from political scientist Cedric Johnson, rising violence on these many fronts is not "a uniquely black predicament."[125]

The forces of financialization, globalization, and rapid technological change that have transformed the US economy are not exceptional to the United

States.[126] But they have had exceptionally toxic consequences here. The United States is in the midst of a "reversal in fortunes" in life expectancy.[127] A global leader in life expectancy for much of the twentieth century, the United States is now a laggard.[128] An unprecedented twenty-year chasm has opened up between US counties with the longest and shortest life expectancies.[129] The mortality rate is still higher for African American people than for white people, but that gap is narrowing quickly thanks to rising mortality rates for white men and women, especially less-educated white people, who have experienced a catastrophic drop in life expectancy.[130]

Canada, Japan, and Western Europe have not experienced the epic drops in life expectancy that have gripped the United States.[131] On the eve of the pandemic in 2019, nearly one-quarter of all US deaths would not have occurred that year if US mortality rates had matched the average rate of wealthy democracies.[132] Those "missing Americans" totaled nearly 623,000 premature deaths in 2019.[133]

Wrong on Crime and Violence

In the early 2000s, leading conservatives in the United States appeared to make a major shift on the issues of crime, punishment, and mass incarceration. With pressures mounting to reduce the country's prison and jail population, name-brand conservatives—including billionaire Charles Koch, former Speaker of the House Newt Gingrich, and tax slayer Grover Norquist—aligned with Right on Crime, a national initiative led by the Texas Public Policy Foundation, one of the country's leading hard-right organizations. Supporters of Right on Crime, established in 2007, pressed the case for criminal justice reform, including lowering the incarceration rate, in the name of reducing the burden that the criminal legal system placed on government budgets.[134] Their shift fostered a burst of optimism across the political spectrum that the United States might be reaching the beginning of the end of mass incarceration.[135]

The optimism fostered by Right on Crime and its coalition partners on the left, on the right, and in between turned out to be unwarranted. Since Right on Crime was established, the US incarceration rate has barely dipped. Meanwhile, the "prison beyond the prison," including parole, probation, community sanctions, drug courts, immigrant detention, and other forms of penal control, has continued to expand. Justice reinvestment initiatives have failed to channel major savings from the penal system to the communities and people most harmed by mass incarceration. The actual savings have been relatively small, and they have often ended up in the pockets of law enforcement.[136]

But Right on Crime did yield enormous political payoffs for the far right and its corporate and wealthy patrons. It allowed them to don the cloak of bipartisanship and political reasonableness as they supported small-bore solutions—most notably the federal First Step Act, signed into law by President Donald Trump in December 2018—that would not significantly reduce the incarceration rate.[137] Meanwhile, they continued to promote their radical agenda, including the decades-long push to starve the government by forcing Congress and the states to divest from the very items proven to reduce violent street crime, stem premature deaths, and improve the quality of life in the country's most disadvantaged communities and elsewhere, including good schools, good health care, living-wage jobs, and a robust social safety net.[138] In one of its biggest political achievements, Right on Crime succeeded in rebranding Texas as a model of criminal justice reform. "Be more like Texas" became a rallying cry for public figures across the political spectrum, including President Obama, even though the Lone Star State has one of the country's highest incarceration rates, some of the most brutal and inhumane lockups, and one of the most threadbare social safety nets.[139]

Furthermore, as leading conservatives were endorsing modest reforms such as the First Step Act, they also pressed for concessions on the issue of corporate crime. They aligned with major business groups and top corporate executives, including Charles and David Koch, in pushing for legislation to create a higher standard of criminal intent that critics nicknamed "The White Collar Immunity Act."[140] Federal prosecutors, consumer and environmental advocates, and other critics charged that such measures, if enacted, would gut many protections by making it even harder to hold top executives and their firms accountable to the criminal legal system.

Democracy in America

When asked why he robbed banks, legendary thief Willie Sutton reportedly answered: "Because that's where the money is."[141] The police, prisons, and rest of the US criminal legal system consume a greater proportion of public budgets than they once did. But the total amount is still trivial compared to other public spending and to the tax breaks lavished on corporations and the wealthiest Americans.[142] The real money is the nearly $1 trillion in military expenditures each year, and the trillions of dollars lost to tax subsidies, tax cuts, tax loopholes, and tax dodges that have engorged wealthy corporations and individuals at great cost to the rest of society, as discussed in chapter 12.

In the wake of the killing of George Floyd in May 2020, the police were not defunded, despite escalating calls to do so. In fact, many law enforcement budgets increased.[143] But even if advocates of defunding the police had succeeded in trimming or even gutting police budgets, this would have provided only a trickle of the money and other resources needed to significantly reduce street crime and curtail premature deaths by addressing their root causes. As Cynthia Lum, an expert on policing and a former police officer, observes, "The idea that these communities need resources to be shuffled from one group to another to help them is frankly a privileged perspective. These communities need more resources across all services."[144]

In the wake of 9/11, the Great Recession, and the pandemic, curtailing interpersonal, state, corporate, and structural violence is a more formidable task. Compared to the days of the savings and loan banking scandal of the 1980s, the wealthiest financial institutions, high-tech corporations, and individuals now possess vastly superior weapons to loot and destabilize the broader economy. Far from disarming them, the government's response to the financial and foreclosure crises of 2007–9 emboldened them. Policymakers rendered the financial world "far more criminogenic" and yet further beyond the reach of regulators and law enforcement.[145] The unprecedented political and economic dominance that the financial industry achieved in the wake of these crises amounted to a "quiet coup," according to Simon Johnson, former chief economist at the International Monetary Fund.[146]

The United States remains acutely vulnerable to another major economic upheaval brought on by the financial industry, the 0.1 percent, and their accomplices in the government for many of the same reasons that caused the Great Recession and then some. The stakes are even higher now because the country is facing a political crisis in which the very future of democracy is at stake here and in many other countries. As George Mason, a delegate from Virginia, warned at the outset of the constitutional convention nearly 250 years ago, "If we do not provide against corruption, our government will soon be at an end."[147]

The perilous state of democracy in America has become a central concern of numerous scholars and public commentators.[148] Some contend that the United States has become an "anocracy"—neither a democracy nor an autocracy, but rather something in between. Others suggest the country may be on its way to becoming a "zombie democracy," an authoritarian state, or a new variant of totalitarianism.[149] A decade ago, former President Jimmy Carter declared that the United States had become an oligarchy and was no longer a democracy.[150] In his farewell address to the nation in January 2025, President Joe Biden warned that "an oligarchy is taking shape in America of extreme wealth, power, and influence that literally threatens our entire democracy, our basic rights and freedoms, and a fair shot for everyone to get ahead."[151]

The collapse of public confidence in all kinds of government institutions, including Congress, the presidency, and the US Supreme Court, has drawn much media and scholarly attention. Less noticed is that the public's confidence in capitalism and corporations has also declined, even among Republican voters.[152] By the mid-1980s, public opinion research had "punctured the notion that the criminal immunity enjoyed by white-collar offenders was the will of the people—that it was somehow democracy taking its course."[153] Surveys since then reveal that the public remains deeply troubled by crime in the suites and favors bringing criminal charges and levying penalties against executives and corporations.[154]

On the eve of the financial crisis, surveys found that the public continued to view numerous white-collar crimes to be as serious as street crimes; wanted more resources devoted to controlling crime in the suites; and favored getting tougher with corporate executives who violate the law. Furthermore, members of the public agreed by overwhelming margins that executives of large corporations were grossly overpaid, dishonest, and unethical. In a 2006 Gallup poll, big business and health maintenance organizations (HMOs) tied for dead last in a national poll gauging how much confidence the public had in sixteen major US institutions, including Congress (which ranked just above them, at number 14).[155]

The downward slide of so many poor and working-class people in the United States—many of whom are white, many of whom are not—and the precarious state of other people struggling to keep their toehold on a middle-class life have been misunderstood, ignored, dismissed, or mischaracterized. This is why the Democratic and Republican establishment and the mainstream media could not fathom that Senator Bernie Sanders (I-VT) and Donald Trump were anything more than entertaining political sideshows when they first ran for president in 2016. Until they weren't.

Many people in the United States continued to struggle years after the Great Recession had been declared officially over. But the power brokers in the Democratic Party under Obama's leadership resumed business as usual and marginalized Bernie Sanders, Senator Elizabeth Warren (D-MA), and others calling to break up the banks and reverse the radical upward redistribution of wealth and political power. No wonder that people were ready to heed Donald Trump's siren call to "drain the swamp," wherever that might lead.[156]

Trump's racial, ethnic, and other taunts in the 2016 election reinforced the view that unreconstructed white supremacists, militias, and misogynists centered in rural America and the white working class were the cement that held his base together. In short, the "basket of deplorables" that Hillary Clinton reviled in her remarks to a well-heeled New York City audience during the 2016 campaign.[157] But while Donald Trump may be a simple man, his base of supporters is not.[158] In his three quests for the presidency, Trump tapped into and cultivated a vein of racial resentment and rage. But his electoral success is not comprehensible without a deeper understanding of how the forever wars, the de facto decriminalization of crime in the suites, the opioid crisis, and the grossly unequal economic recovery from the Great Recession have contributed to all kinds of violence in America and reshaped American politics.

As he railed against the forever wars, conjured up his "mutant populism," and attacked the corporate and government swamp, Trump also vowed to double down on people who were charged with street crimes, drug offenses, and immigration violations.[159] Meanwhile, the white power movement, which had been decades in the making, was ready to seize the moment and play its part in normalizing political violence as it forged closer ties to Donald Trump, the Republican Party, the police, and the US military.[160]

Trump stoked and braided together many strands of resentment and rage—against women, against people of color, against immigrants but also against the widely perceived sellout of the government to corporations, as captured by his frequent refrain to "drain the swamp."[161] His final commercial to close the deal in the 2016 election was riveting. It featured cameos of a rainbow of everyday working-class Americans interspersed with clips of the world's economic and political elite, including Hillary and Bill Clinton, Lloyd Blankfein of Goldman Sachs, and billionaire investor and philanthropist George Soros. Much of the ad looked like something that the Bernie Sanders campaign could have produced, except that the voiceover was unmistakably Trump's as he warned: "It's a global power structure that is responsible for the economic decisions that have robbed our working class, stripped our economy of its wealth and put that money into the pockets of a handful of large corporations and political entities."[162]

Slaying the anti-state state, reducing violence in its many manifestations in the United States and overseas, and revitalizing democracy in America will depend on building broad coalitions that incorporate many of the disposable people that the US empire and its political and economic system are churning out. Many of the people that Hillary Clinton reviled as deplorable are living precarious lives.

The most successful periods of political mobilization to foster economic and political equality in the United States—Reconstruction, the New Deal, the civil rights era—rested on expansive political and social movements. These movements did not single-mindedly focus on racial disparities but sought to forge broader political agendas centered on racial, social, and economic justice that drew in a wide range of groups.[163] Likewise, throughout US history, major movements against war and militarism have been broad and multifaceted ones that rested on complex, often imperfect, coalitions. Successfully rolling back the various tentacles of violence in America today will depend on fostering alliances that stretch from the hollers of Appalachia to the streets of North Philadelphia to the victims of the US empire overseas.

PART II

State Violence at Home and Abroad

2

Breaking Bad in America

STATE VIOLENCE AND THE
CHANGING CARCERAL STATE

The contempt with which American leaders treat American blacks is very obvious; what is not so obvious is that they treat the bulk of the American people with the very same contempt. But it will be sub-zero weather in a very distant August when the American people find the guts to recognize this fact. They will recognize it only when they have exhausted every conceivable means of avoiding it.

—JAMES BALDWIN, 1972[1]

THE REACH of the carceral state is a major barometer of state and structural violence. As the geography of poverty and marginality has been shifting in the United States, so have the geography and demographics of punishment. Scholarly and public attention on the hyperincarceration of African American men has overshadowed how and why the cruel, dehumanizing, unjust, and violent policies and institutions of the carceral state are ensnaring other groups of people, including women, immigrants, and people living in small towns and rural areas.[2]

Nonmetropolitan counties, especially those with higher rates of poverty and other social disadvantages, more conservative politics, and relatively larger Black populations, are now more likely than urban areas to send their residents—including both people of color and white people—to prison.[3] These findings are consistent with long-standing research findings that concentrated disadvantage and the related impulse to control people perceived as threatening to the social order are key drivers of punitive practices and policies.[4]

Social theorists have long contended that people who are poor, unemployed, or underemployed are disproportionally seen as threats to the social
order and thus subjected to more punitive measures. During periods of unsettling economic transformations and growing economic inequalities, the so-
called dangerous classes appear even more threatening and more in need of
punitive measures to control them—all the more so if they are politically mobilized.[5] Judges, prosecutors, legislators, the media, and the public are more
supportive of punitive measures during hard economic times out of the often
unfounded fear that street crime inevitably rises as the economy stumbles. A
related factor is the more generalized fear that the growing number of dispos-
sessed people poses a threat not only to public safety but also to the wider
social, political, and economic order and therefore must be dealt with severely.[6] Tough-on-crime policies premised on harsh punishment and extensive surveillance are also a way for public officials to restore their legitimacy
and raison d'être in the face of public anxiety and dismay about their failure to
revive a sputtering economy.[7]

In its comprehensive 2014 report on the causes and consequences of mass
incarceration, the National Academy of Sciences (NAS) concluded that several social, institutional, political, and economic factors came together in the
1960s and 1970s to create the perfect storm that launched the prison boom.
The NAS report identified long-term structural changes in urban economies
as a key catalyst of mass incarceration. As working-class and middle-class
families migrated to the suburbs, they left behind isolated communities mired
in severe and concentrated poverty in US cities. African American people
disproportionally resided in these communities and faced diminished life
chances due to the disappearance of living-wage jobs for low-skilled workers,
rising residential segregation, and declining public investment in cities. The
wrenching political and economic restructuring spurred by the collapse of
the Fordist model of production was a central factor in the spike in violence
in urban areas and the origins of the prison boom.[8] As unemployment rates
soared, the illegal economy—especially the drug trade—became the em-
ployer of first and last resort.

Certain urban neighborhoods and groups—especially young African
Americans and other people of color—were subjected to higher rates of policing not only because of growing concerns about crime but also because of
rising fears about social disorder and political unrest.[9] Some US politicians
and policymakers fanned these fears, triggering a bipartisan bidding war for
more punishment and more prisons that did not subside, even as crime rates

plummeted in the 1990s. The commitment to mass incarceration remained steadfast, even though this costly public experiment had a negligible effect on reducing crime and a devastating effect on the residents of poor urban neighborhoods where people of color disproportionately resided.

On the heels of the deindustrialization of US cities, rural America has been undergoing a wrenching restructuring of its own since the 1980s. Factories and industries in urban areas that fled to greenfield sites and right-to-work states in the 1960s and 1970s have since packed up and moved to Mexico, China, and other low-wage, low-regulation countries, thanks to the North American Free Trade Agreement (NAFTA), China's entry into the World Trade Organization (WTO) in 2001, and other trade policies. Factory farms run by large corporations replaced family farms. Well-paying, unionized jobs in rural areas, notably in coal mines, meat processing plants, and paper mills, disappeared. With the public disinvestment in rural health care and other public services, the rural social safety net became more threadbare. As the high-tech sector and "knowledge economy" regenerated major US cities over the last couple of decades, the economic and political gulf between large metro areas, on the one hand, and small cities and rural America, on the other, surged.[10]

Albuquerque, New Mexico, is one of these small cities. No wonder, then, that the critically acclaimed television series *Breaking Bad* was set there. Walter White, the main lead in the series, was an underpaid, white chemistry teacher with terminal cancer and shoddy health insurance who regenerates his life by other means. To pay for his cancer treatment and keep his family from becoming destitute after he dies, White embarks on a second career as a meth drug kingpin.

This chapter first chronicles major racial and geographic shifts in who has ended up in prison or jail since the race to incarcerate began five decades ago. It then examines trends in the punishment of women, immigrants, and people convicted of sex offenses, three groups that should be more central to analyses of state violence and the carceral state. Next it explores how changing fronts in the wars (yes, wars!) on drugs, including the war on methamphetamines in rural areas, have altered the carceral state.

The chapter concludes by discussing the impact of "culture of poverty" arguments and the Great Recession on state and structural violence in America. Culture of poverty arguments have long served to stigmatize African American people and legitimize investing more in prisons and law enforcement rather than in housing, education, jobs, health care, and other public assistance to alleviate their economic and political marginalization. Periodi-

cally, claims of a culture of poverty have also served to justify public quiescence toward alleviating the structural and state violence that rural residents
and poor and working-class white people experience, including, most recently,
the reverberations from the wrenching Great Recession and the 2007–9 financial and foreclosure crises.

Geographic and Racial Shifts of the Carceral State

More than three decades ago, geographer Charles Aiken pioneered the concept
of the rural ghetto to draw attention to the racial, economic, and other disadvantages concentrated in rural areas.[11] Large-scale studies of rural distress took
hold about fifteen years later as sociologists mapped concentrations of Black
poverty and residential segregation in rural America. But their work did not
alter broader discussions of poverty, marginality, and disadvantage, which continued to focus on urban areas, not the suburbs or rural communities, even as
the carceral state was transforming the geography of punishment.[12]

National and state data on incarceration rates mask important geographic
and other shifts in who is being sent to prison or jail and why. They can cast
the so-called era of criminal justice reform era in "too rosy a light," warned a
2018 report from the Vera Institute.[13] In dozens of states, incarceration rates
have been slowing or declining in urban areas while rising in rural and suburban communities.[14] Annual prison admissions for big cities have been plummeting, driving statewide drops in incarceration rates in California, Texas,
New York State, and elsewhere.

Incarceration rates for jails in rural and smaller metro areas have continued
to rise despite falling rates of street crime (see figure 2.1).[15] In the mid-aughts,
residents of rural, suburban, and urban areas had about an equal chance of
being sent to prison. A decade later, people in small counties were about
50 percent more likely to end up in prison than people in larger urban areas.[16]
Dearborn County—a small, rural, nearly all-white county in Indiana where
violent crime is rare—sent more people to prison per capita in 2014 than almost any other county in the United States.[17]

Going to prison or jail has become a common experience in the United
States. One out of every two adults reports that they have an immediate family
member who has spent at least one night in prison or jail, including 63 percent
of African American adults, 48 percent of Latino adults, and 42 percent of
white adults surveyed. These reported rates of family incarceration are nearly
identical for Democrats and Republicans and for Black and white people with-

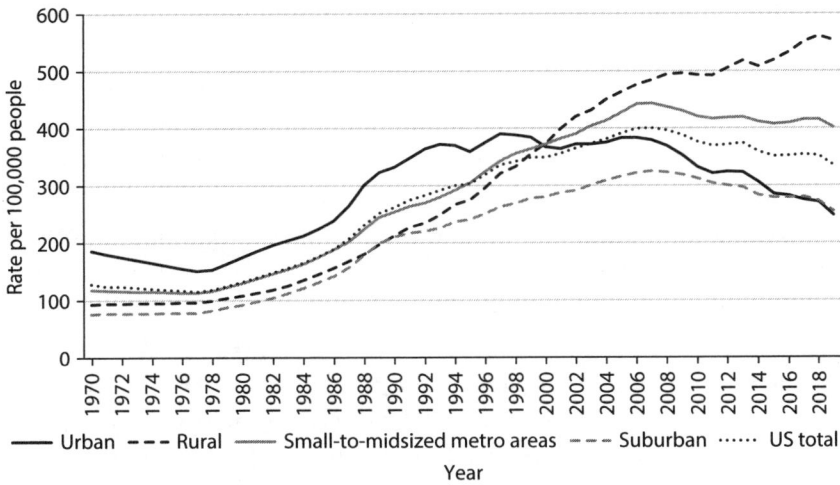

FIGURE 2.1. Incarceration Rates for US Jails by Geography, 1970–2019.
Source: Vera Institute of Justice, "Incarceration Trends: Jail Incarceration by Geography," June 11, 2024, https://trends.vera.org.

out high school degrees.[18] As for longer time served, one in ten white adults reports that a close family member was incarcerated for a year or more in prison or jail. This finding looks unremarkable only when compared to the nearly one in three African American adults and one in six Latino adults who reported so.[19]

The cumulative risks of imprisonment have risen faster for Latino men and white males than for African American men, and at faster rates for low-income white men than for low-income Black males and low-income Latino men.[20] Over one-quarter of white males who dropped out of high school have served time in prison by the age of thirty-four. Once again, that extraordinary figure looks unremarkable only when compared to the 68 percent figure for African American men who did not complete high school.[21] These numbers understate the likelihood of serving time because they do not include time spent in jails, which house about a third of all people who are incarcerated in the United States.

The racial disparities in incarceration rates have certainly not closed in the United States, but they have narrowed considerably since the turn of the twenty-first century.[22] After reaching a high of about 7:1 in 2000, the Black-white ratio in incarceration fell to about 4:1 in 2019 on the eve of the pandemic.[23] This is slightly lower than the 5:1 ratio that prevailed for much of the twentieth century before the US incarceration rate began its steep upward climb in the 1970s.[24]

I have chosen to use prepandemic figures here to analyze trends in incarceration because it is still too early to tell what lasting impact Covid-19 and the related spike in violent street crimes will have on prison and jail populations. What we do know for sure is that the virus was exceptionally deadly for incarcerated people, killing them at a rate at least six times greater than the Covid-19 death rate for the general population.[25]

After peaking in 2008, incarceration rates for African American people had fallen by 30 percent by late 2019. Rates for Latino people had declined by 26 percent and for non-Hispanic white people by less than 5 percent. Decreases in the number of incarcerated African American people have driven most of the recent modest drop in the total number of people incarcerated in US prisons and jails. The number of Black people held in state and federal prisons fell by nearly 23 percent—or approximately 203,000 people—between 2008 and 2019. The drop for non-Hispanic white people was approximately 76,000—or about 9 percent. It was 3 percent for Hispanic people.[26]

As for the jail population specifically, after escalating sharply in the early 2000s, the number of people incarcerated in local jails held steady at about three-quarters of a million people between 2010 and 2019. But this masks a huge divergence in who is going to jail. After a significant spike in the early 2000s, the Black jail population fell back to where it was in 2000—about one-quarter of a million people. The total number of Latino people in US jails was about 107,000 people in 2019, an increase of about 12 percent since 2000. The number of non-Hispanic whites in local jails climbed steadily between 2000 and the eve of the pandemic, hitting 363,000 people in 2019—an increase of 39 percent.[27]

By 2013, the incarceration rate for African American people held in local jails had fallen back to about where it was three decades earlier. This national drop masked important regional differences in the pace of decline. For much of this period, the rate for African American people continued to climb in small and medium-sized metro areas and in rural communities, where it more than doubled between 1990 and 2013. In the West and Northeast, the incarceration rate for African American people held in local jails peaked in the mid-1990s. In the South and Midwest, it continued to grow for another decade before starting to decrease. As for white people, by 2013, jails in rural and small and medium-sized metro areas were holding more white people than the total number of white people held by urban and suburban jails.[28]

The United States would still have an incarceration crisis even if it were locking up African American people at "only" the rate at which white people in the United States are currently incarcerated—or if it were not locking up any African American people at all. The US incarceration rate for white people of about 450 per 100,000 residents in 2019 appears relatively low compared to the rates for African American people (about 2,000 per 100,000 residents) and Latino people (about 900 per 100,000 residents) but is extraordinarily high compared with the rates in affluent democracies (see figure 2.2).[29] On the eve of the pandemic, the incarceration rate for white people in the United States was three to eleven times the rate that the countries of Western Europe and Japan were locking up their residents (see figure 2.2). Ten US states were incarcerating their white residents at a pace that would put them at the top or in second place in global incarceration rankings if they were independent countries.[30]

Southern states generally have the country's highest imprisonment rates for both Black and white people but below-average Black-white racial disparities in imprisonment.[31] In this respect, Southern states are, relatively speaking, more equal opportunity incarcerators. White people residing in the South tend to be poorer than white people elsewhere, while Black people living in the South "have a disadvantage equal to or less than that of U.S. blacks generally," which helps explain these patterns.[32] New Jersey and Texas are good examples. New Jersey has one of the highest Black-white disparities in imprisonment (12.5:1). But the Garden State has below-average imprisonment rates for African American people and one of the lowest imprisonment rates overall among the fifty states.[33] As for the Lone Star State, it has some of the lowest racial and ethnic disparities in imprisonment but some of the highest imprisonment rates for white, Black, and Latino people.[34]

Gender, Race, and the Carceral State

With just 4 percent of the world's female population, the United States accounts for 30 percent of all the incarcerated women worldwide.[35] Leaving aside Thailand, El Salvador, and the United States itself, the top forty-seven jurisdictions in the world with the highest rates of incarcerating women are individual American states.[36] Oklahoma's incarceration rate for women is 281 per 100,000—which is the highest of any state and over fifty-five times the rate for women in Denmark, which has one of the lowest rates among affluent democracies.[37]

Rates of incarceration in prisons and jails have risen much faster for women than for men and have declined more slowly for women.[38] Between 1978 and

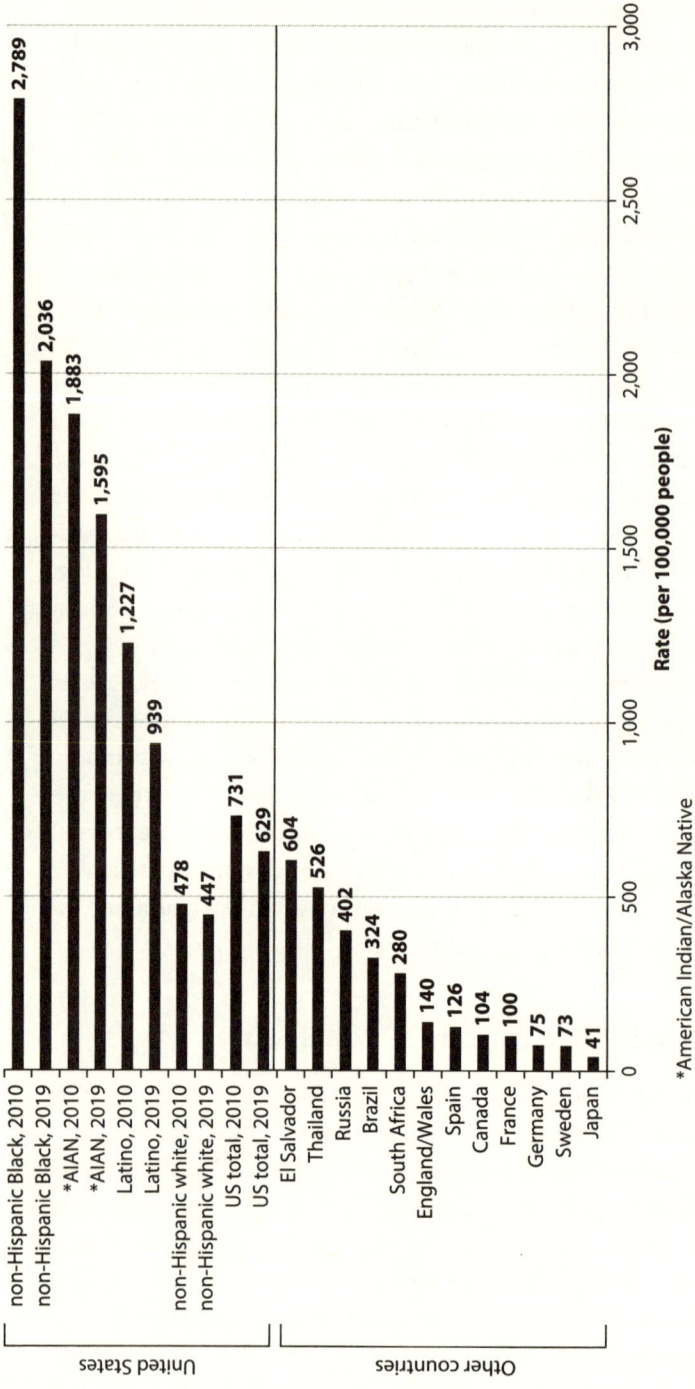

Rate (per 100,000 people)

*American Indian/Alaska Native

Chart data (Rate per 100,000 people):

United States:
- non-Hispanic Black, 2010: 2,789
- non-Hispanic Black, 2019: 2,036
- *AIAN, 2010: 1,883
- *AIAN, 2019: 1,595
- Latino, 2010: 1,227
- Latino, 2019: 939
- non-Hispanic white, 2010: 478
- non-Hispanic white, 2019: 447
- US total, 2010: 731
- US total, 2019: 629

Other countries:
- El Salvador: 604
- Thailand: 526
- Russia: 402
- Brazil: 324
- South Africa: 280
- England/Wales: 140
- Spain: 126
- Canada: 104
- France: 100
- Germany: 75
- Sweden: 73
- Japan: 41

FIGURE 2.2. Incarceration Rates of Select Countries and US Demographic Groups in 2010 and 2019. *Sources:* National figures are the most recent prepandemic figures prior to February 2020 available from Roy Walmsley, "World Population List," 12th ed. and 13th ed., n.d., Institute for Criminal Policy Research and Birkbeck University of London, https://www.prisonstudies.org/sites/default/files /resources/downloads/wppl_12.pdf, and https://www.prisonstudies.org/sites/default/files/resources/downloads/world_prison _population_list_13th_edition.pdf (accessed September 9, 2024). US demographic figures were calculated from Zhen Zeng and Todd D. Minton, "Jail Inmates in 2019," DOJ BJS, March 2021, https://bjs.ojp.gov/content/pub/pdf/ji19.pdf, 4, table 2; and E. Ann Carson, "Prisoners in 2020," DOJ BJS, December 2021, https://bjs.ojp.gov/content/pub/pdf/p20st.pdf, 14, table 6.

its peak around 2007, the state imprisonment rate for women increased nearly sevenfold.[39] Women made up 7 percent of people locked up in state and federal prisons in 2019, up from 3 percent in 1970. In 2019, women constituted 15 percent of people confined in local jails, or about double the proportion held in the mid-1980s.[40] The number of women locked up in city and county jails rose by nearly one-quarter between 2009 and 2018, an increase that offset more than 40 percent of the simultaneous drop in the men's jail population.[41]

The number of women held in state prisons for violent, property, and public order offenses has increased substantially, which has offset some of the drop in women serving time for drug offenses. With the scaling back of the penalties for crack cocaine and some other illegal drugs, the slowing of the war on drugs in major urban areas, and the decriminalization of marijuana in many jurisdictions, the state imprisonment rate for Black women has plummeted. After having risen nearly nonstop since the 1970s, it fell by more than half between 2000 and 2019 (see figures 2.3 and 2.4).

The overall decline in women serving time for drug offenses in the United States between 2000 and 2019 was the result of the *600 percent* drop in African American women sent to state prison for drug crimes. That drop masked a 65 percent increase in the number of white women held in state prisons for drug crimes.[42] The rising rates of contact with the criminal legal system for low-income white women are likely a consequence not only of shifts in the war on drugs and opioid use but also of a sharp deterioration in their health and social conditions.[43] These include rising rates of health-care uninsurance, chronic illnesses, poverty, and unemployment, all of which have likely contributed to an exceptional five-year drop in life expectancy at birth between 1990 and 2008 for white females who dropped out of high school. The life expectancy rate during this period also fell for white males who dropped out but not for Black or Latino people who did not complete high school. As of 2008, the life expectancy rate at birth for white and Black females who dropped out of high school was identical, and the rate for white and Black males who dropped out was nearly identical.[44]

Imprisonment rates for Black and white women in state prisons have converged sharply (see figure 2.4). As the state imprisonment rate for non-Latino Black females plummeted between 2000 and 2019, it increased by nearly two-thirds for non-Latino white females.[45] On the eve of the pandemic, the imprisonment rate for white females was considerably higher than the rate for Black females in 1980 just as the race to incarcerate women was taking off (see figures 2.3 and 2.4).[46]

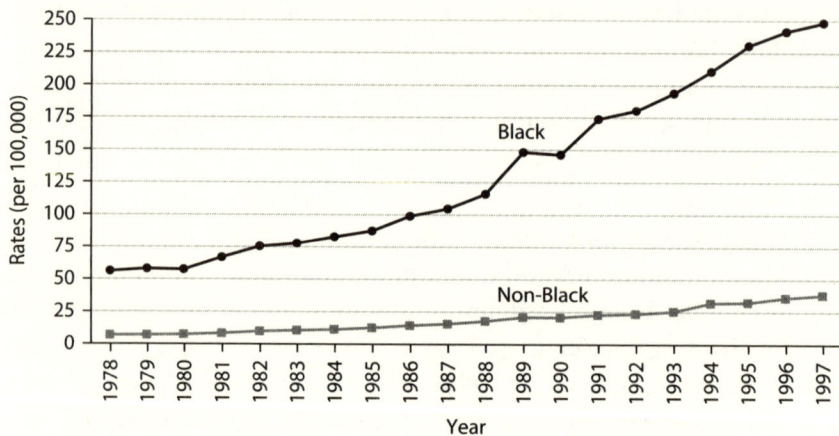

FIGURE 2.3. Black and Non-Black Female State Imprisonment Rates in the United States, 1978–97. *Source*: Courtesy of Karen Heimer, Sarah E. Malone, and Stacy De Coster, "Trends in Women's Incarceration Rates in US Prisons and Jails," *Annual Review of Criminology* 6 (2023): 90, fig. 3. Prior to 2000, the US Bureau of Justice Statistics generally used only two racial categories— Black and white—to classify incarcerated people.

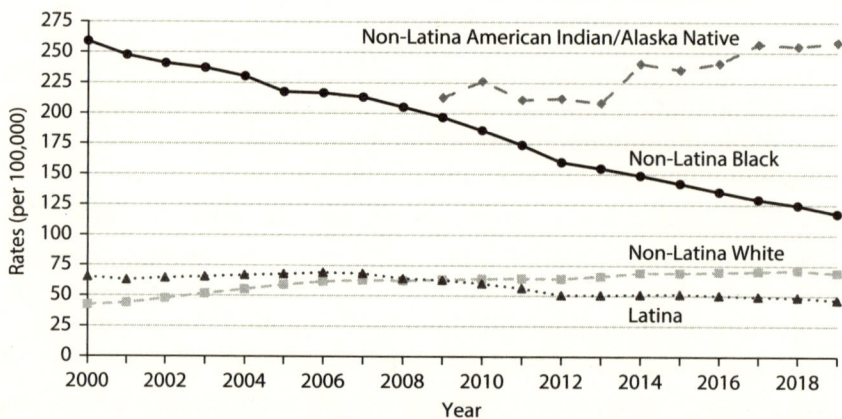

FIGURE 2.4. Female State Imprisonment Rates in US by Race and Ethnicity, 2000–2019. *Source*: Courtesy of Karen Heimer, Sarah E. Malone, and Stacy De Coster, "Trends in Women's Incarceration Rates in US Prisons and Jails," *Annual Review of Criminology* 6 (2023): 91, fig. 4.

As a result of these trends, the Black-white imprisonment gap for women plummeted from 6:1 in 2000 to about 1.7:1 in 2019, which is a historic low.[47] By 2016, Black women made up about a quarter of all women in state prisons, down from about half in 1995. Meanwhile, white women constituted 61 percent, up from 41 percent in the mid-1990s.[48] After reaching a peak around 2006, the state imprisonment rate for Latino women began declining and fell below the rate for non-Latino white women around 2010 (see figure 2.4).[49] The combined state imprisonment rate for American Indian/Alaskan Native women exceeds all other demographic groups for women. It is close to the peak incarceration rate for Black women before their imprisonment rates began declining around the turn of the twenty-first century (see figure 2.4). These national trends obscure enormous state-level variations in the pace of the convergence of imprisonment rates for Black and white women.[50]

Immigrants and the Carceral State

Since the early aughts, immigration policy has become a major engine of the carceral state, with jails, prisons, and detention centers holding a growing number of documented and undocumented immigrants and migrants, especially people from South and Central America.[51] The US Department of Homeland Security (DHS), which oversees Immigration and Customs Enforcement (ICE), refers more cases to the Justice Department for prosecution than do all other major law enforcement agencies combined.[52] For many years now, criminal prosecutions for immigration-related offenses have constituted the largest proportion of all federal criminal prosecutions, far exceeding prosecutions for drug and white-collar crimes.[53] Furthermore, federal spending on immigration enforcement has greatly exceeded funding for all the principal federal law enforcement agencies combined.[54] If Donald Trump carries out his 2024 campaign pledges to deport millions of undocumented and other immigrants, federal law enforcement and other resources earmarked for immigration policies will skyrocket much further. The final version of Trump 2.0's Big Beautiful Bill, which Congress enacted in July 2025, included an additional $170 billion to further militarize the border, expand ICE, and add over 100,000 immigrant detention beds.[55]

Important legislative and institutional changes dating back to the 1990s facilitated the criminalization and localization of immigration policy. Over the last three decades or so, a whole new apparatus to apprehend, detain, and

punish immigrants was constructed. It was built by importing many of the
theories, objectives, and methods of law enforcement into immigration enforcement, as well as some of the inflammatory law-and-order and racial rhetoric that fostered the punitive turn in the criminal legal system.[56] Nearly one-
third of all people serving time in federal prisons as of late 2024 were Latino,
as were nearly half of all defendants sentenced in federal courts in 2022.[57] The
crackdown on immigration offenses and the related influx of Latino people
and other immigrants into federal penitentiaries and other penal facilities fed
the misperception that immigrants commit a disproportionate amount of serious or violent crimes. This, in turn, fueled pressure for tougher immigration
policies, including accelerating the militarization of the southwesten border of
the United States.[58]

Long before Donald Trump first took office in 2017, the immigration enforcement system had morphed into a vast and ever-growing web of Border
Patrol agents, police, prosecutors, courts, jails, prisons, and detention centers.
It has a well-documented history of human rights violations and procedural
shortcuts that run roughshod over due process and other protections for immigrants.[59] Most ICE detention facilities are modeled after jails and prisons,
even though many of the people they are holding have not been accused of a
crime. Immigration and Customs Enforcement also runs an extensive network
of secret detention jails. As a top ICE official once boasted, "If you don't have
enough evidence to charge someone criminally but you think he's illegal, we
can make him disappear."[60]

Arrests for minor violations became a pretext to funnel noncitizens into
deportation proceedings, where they are not entitled to defense counsel and
other legal protections accorded to people who have been charged with
crimes. Under the Obama administration, the United States began deporting
record numbers of immigrants, most of whom posed no risk to public safety
and many of whom had extensive family and other ties to the United States.[61]
United States law defines deportation as a so-called administrative measure,
not a type of punishment. But deportation is one of the most extreme forms
of punishment, for it often precipitates the loss of home, family, and property
for people who are members of US society.

Some of the people who were deported had committed serious crimes.
But most of them were exiled for having committed traffic violations or
other minor criminal offenses, such as petty larceny, or for entering the
country without proper authorization. People deported to "home" countries that they had not lived in for years, decades, or even lifetimes often

faced discriminatory, inhumane, and, in some cases, life-threatening situations.[62]

During Donald Trump's first term, deportations fell considerably below the record modern-day highs of the Obama years. They fell even further under Joe Biden before spiking to a ten-year high during his final year in office.[63] The intense militarization of the border has raised the costs and risks of crossing into the United States. Immigrants must increasingly rely on expensive "coyotes" to help smuggle them into the country. Forced to attempt crossings in more desolate and physically dangerous desert and mountain areas, they now face a much higher risk of perishing. In a perverse outcome for those who want to slash the number of unauthorized people residing permanently in the United States, more migrants began settling down in this country because crossing back and forth—once a common pattern—became so expensive and risky.[64]

The intense focus on apprehending people for petty immigration violations has come at the cost of diverting resources from more serious threats to public safety, including elite-level corporate criminal activities, as well as the sophisticated drug, human trafficking, and firearms smuggling enterprises responsible for much of the border violence. Requiring assistant US attorneys along the border to focus most of their time and energy on low-level immigration prosecutions has come at the expense of developing the skills necessary to successfully investigate and prosecute more serious crimes, including corporate malfeasance. All these problems with immigration policy escalated upon Donald Trump's return to the White House.

The Carceral State and Sex Crimes

Racial disparities in the many wars on drugs have been a central focus of research on mass incarceration and a catalyst for political mobilization against the carceral state. People convicted of sex offenses have received comparatively little scholarly attention or public sympathy. Since the early 1990s, sex crimes have been major targets of political energy and public fears in the United States.[65] The category of sex offenses is expansive. It can include everything from public urination to making obscene phone calls, to consensual sex between a sixteen-year-old and an eighteen-year-old, to possession of child pornography, to rape.

The war against people charged with sex offenses does not fit into the "new Jim Crow" framework for understanding the origins and tenacity of the carceral state. People of color have not been disproportionately targeted for police crackdowns on sex offenses since the 1970s, unlike in the case of the many wars on drugs over the last five decades.[66] Furthermore, in the war on sex crimes, legislators and policymakers have been less likely to invoke the racialized language that they have deployed to justify locking up so many people of color for drug and other offenses.[67] Major sex crimes laws often do valorize white victims—especially young white women and girls, who are memorialized in measures such as Megan's Law. These laws have disproportionately swept up white men. About 17 percent of white men serving time in state prisons as of 2019 had been convicted of serious sexual offenses. The comparable figure for Black men is about 8 percent.[68] People convicted of child pornography offenses at the state and federal levels are overwhelmingly older white men.[69]

Key features of the war on sex offenses include the demonization of people charged with sex crimes; the ratcheting up of penalties, including castration; and the federalization of what had once been largely a matter for local or state law enforcement.[70] People found guilty of sex offenses are ensnared in a web of restrictions long after they have served their sentences. These restrictions far exceed the onerous "civil death" measures (such as denial of the right to vote, to serve on a jury, or to reside in public housing) that hound people convicted of drug and other crimes. People convicted of sex offenses are subject to not only civil death but also an Alice-in-Wonderland maze of civil commitment laws and community notification, registration, and residency restrictions that amount to a kind of "ritual exile."[71] This punitive maze of laws and restrictions is exceptional. Other Western countries do not impose such punitive sentences on people convicted of sex crimes or keep them ensnared long after they have served their time.[72]

The Carceral State and the Wars (Yes, Wars) on Drugs

Likewise, US drug policy has been and remains exceptionally punitive. The term *war on drugs* became widely used after President Richard Nixon officially declared that drug abuse was "public enemy number one" in 1971. At the time, Nixon called for waging "a new, all-out offensive" against illegal drugs.[73] But war on drugs is a misnomer, for it implies a single war against a constant enemy. In fact, for more than a century now, the United States has waged a series of *wars* on drugs in which the main targets have varied: Chinese immigrants and opium at the turn of the twentieth century; Mexican migrants and marijuana in the 1930s; African American people and cocaine, heroin, crack, and marijuana from the 1940s onward; and white people and methamphetamines and opioids the past few decades.[74] Moral panics that further stigmatized already liminal groups in the United States fueled these wars and propelled punitive laws and policies to attack what drug warriors charged was a mortal threat to the United States.

The wars on drugs waged by Nixon and many of his successors in the White House were highly racialized. They disproportionately targeted African American people despite surveys showing that they were no more likely to use or sell illegal drugs than white people were.[75] Police and prosecution tactics—including racial profiling, intense surveillance of poor, inner-city neighborhoods, and the widespread use of buy-and-bust and stop-and-frisk tactics in these communities—fostered racial disparities in arrests and sentences for drug offenses. The social scientific evidence largely supported the *Wire*-esque world portrayed on the award-winning HBO television series in which young African American men in distressed Baltimore neighborhoods were the main targets of an urban war on drugs that had few heroes.[76]

Deploying racially coded and not so racially coded language, public officials and commentators blamed people who would not "just say no" to illegal substances for rising rates of crime, violence, poverty, homelessness, unemployment, single-parent families, and premature births in cities. (First Lady Nancy Reagan immortalized the phrase "just say no" during Ronald Reagan's war against drugs in the 1980s.) In these accounts, larger structural forces, such as deindustrialization, white flight, redlining, residential segregation, eroding tax bases, and public disinvestment in cities, were invisible and thus blameless. This helped to legitimize an urban agenda premised on deregulating the private sector, privatizing the public sector, and just saying no to adequately funding public schools, public housing, the social safety net, public transportation, and health care. This urban agenda also recoiled from creating more public-sector jobs and supporting a strong labor movement—two proven means to reduce economic inequality for African American people and other disadvantaged groups.[77]

With the introduction of crack, which pharmacologically is nearly identical to powder cocaine but much cheaper, so-called crackheads became the most prominent target in the wars on drugs beginning in the mid-1980s. These crackheads took the rap for high rates of violence, unemployment, concentrated poverty, and homelessness in US cities. A moral panic ensued as politicians, with the help of an acquiescent media, promulgated exaggerated and racialized accounts of crack as a "devil's drug" that was "instantly and inevitably addictive" and that inculcated extremely violent and antisocial behavior in users.[78] Sensationalist media accounts and early scientific research stoked fears of a new generation of severely disabled "crack babies" in need of costly medical care for the rest of their lives. These apocalyptic claims were eventually proven to be unfounded.[79]

Large swaths of urban areas were in crisis in the 1980s and 1990s thanks to deeper structural forces and not just because of the introduction of crack. But politicians, police, and some residents of these neighborhoods heaped much of the blame on crack and so-called crackheads for rising rates of violence, crime, and social decay in urban areas, much as they had blamed heroin and people addicted to heroin in the 1960s and 1970s.[80] This justified greater investment in law enforcement, especially militarized policing, and cracking down on poor urban neighborhoods and their residents, especially young Black men. These crackdowns helped quash nodules of political mobilization against police violence and the deeper structural problems in US cities that were hitting low-income people and people of color the hardest.[81]

As President Ronald Reagan's war on drugs took off in the mid-1980s, racial disparities in incarceration grew.[82] The gross racial disparities in how drug cases were punished (epitomized by the 100-to-1 disparity in cocaine sentences) and the courts' persistent indifference or hostility to claims of racial bias in the criminal legal system solidified the view among many critics of US penal policy that racism and the wars on drugs were the main propellants of mass incarceration.[83]

The impact of these wars on drugs on the size of the prison population was significant but overstated.[84] The era of mass incarceration that began in the 1970s comprised distinct periods driven by different engines.[85] From the early 1970s to the mid-1980s, the main engine was a general rise in committing more people to prison, with few discernible patterns by type of crime or type of offender.[86] During the 1985–92 period commitments to prison for drug crimes far outpaced the rate of growth in commitments for other offenses.[87] Beginning in the early 1990s, the main engine was longer sentences and time served for a wider range of offenses thanks to a more punitive political climate that fostered penal innovations like "three strikes and you're out," truth-in-sentencing laws, and an explosion in life sentences and life in prison without the possibility of parole (LWOP).[88]

Since the mid-1990s, powerful criminal legal reform movements centered in urban areas—from Drop the Rock in New York State in the 1990s, to Black Lives

Matter, to the wave of progressive prosecutors in large cities—have had some success in slowing or rolling back the wars on drugs and reducing sanctions for some other offenses in urban areas. Individuals convicted of drug crimes constituted about 14 percent of all people held in state prisons in 2019, down from nearly one-quarter in 1991.[89] As discussed earlier, racial disparities in drug enforcement have narrowed as arrests of Black people for drug offenses plummeted. The growing number of white people arrested for possession of methamphetamine between 2009 and 2019 offset reductions in marijuana arrests of African Americans and helped propel the decline in racial disparities in drug arrests and prison sentences.[90] Between 2000 and 2019, the Black-white ratio for imprisonment for drug offenses reversed, shifting from 2.5:1 to 1:1.3.[91]

Drug offenses are no longer a primary driver of new prison admissions nationwide. Nonetheless, the political and public policy reverberations of the wars on drugs launched beginning in the 1970s, which coincided with the escalation of the incarceration rate, continue to be seismic. Among other things, these wars on drugs bequeathed a starkly racialized framework through which to view the carceral state. This helped obfuscate, among other things, the wider toll of state violence in the United States, including the impact of the wars on drugs and carceral state on white people and rural America.

The Wars on Drugs in Rural America

As the debate over mass incarceration riveted on how the urban wars on drugs disproportionately targeted African Americans, wars on methamphetamines, opioids, and the people who use them were unfolding out of the national spotlight in rural America and some of the whitest states.[92] As policymakers sought to find scapegoats to blame for mounting economic and other distress in rural areas, the drug of choice they reached for first was meth.

Since it was first launched in the late 1980s, the war on methamphetamines has waxed and waned. Just about the time that the war on crack was cresting in urban areas in the early 2000s, the war on meth surged once again in rural areas. Some of the weapons deployed by law enforcement, politicians, and other public figures in the war on meth were remarkably like those used in the war on crack even though the geographic terrain and the groups they targeted were different. In the early aughts, the Drug Enforcement Administration (DEA) and public officials began warning that "crystal meth could become the new crack."[93] This fueled a moral panic in rural areas, even though meth use was not escalating.

In his ethnographic study of a small rural community in West Virginia, anthropologist William Garriott documents how the culture of control and what Jonathan Simon called "governing through crime" transformed rural communities.[94] Local police and prosecutors deployed new federal resources specifically designed to target methamphetamine use and production. Schools, employers, and law enforcement in rural areas intensified their efforts to detect drugs and surveil their students, employees, and residents. Just as crack users were the designated scapegoats for urban decay, meth users served as scapegoats for social and economic distress in rural areas and the Rust Belt, obscuring the deeper structural causes. The moral panic over methamphetamine depicted a causal link between meth and rising rates of crime and violence that was unfounded.

The war against meth was racialized in its own way. As Oklahoma Governor Frank Keating explained in 1999, "It's a white trash drug—methamphetamines largely are consumed by the lower socio-economic element of white people, and I think we need to shame it. Just like crack cocaine was a black trash drug and is a black trash drug."[95] Movies, television shows, the media, antimeth campaigns, and public officials deployed caricatures of "white trash" in their war against meth users. Antimeth campaigns included mugshots of people alleged to be meth addicts arrayed next to their "before" photos, in which they did not have body sores, rotting teeth, and swollen faces; graphic images of white women prostituting themselves to get their meth fix; disturbing pictures of "meth zombies"; and frequent references to "white man's crack" and "redneck coke."[96]

The government and wealthy individuals, including William I. Koch, the lesser-known brother of billionaires Charles and David Koch, generously funded antimeth campaigns.[97] These campaigns blanketed radio, television, and billboards in rural areas with images and messages that characterized the meth problem as an epidemic that was "uniquely white and rural."[98] The alleged meth epidemic was widely portrayed as a threat to the soul of the country—the idealized Norman Rockwell rural heartland. This threat was explicitly equated with the post-9/11 terrorism threat from overseas, so much so that the Combat Methamphetamine Epidemic Act was included as part of the 2006 reauthorization of the USA Patriot Act.[99] In his signing statement for the measure, President George W. Bush lauded the reauthorization legislation for providing "law enforcement new tools to combat threats to our citizens, from international terrorists to local drug dealers."[100] In rural areas, meth and so-called meth heads were the scapegoats, which obscured how deindustrialization, factory farms, and declining investment in public institutions and services were upending rural communities and propelling them to latch on to prison construction as a last resort in economic development.

The Prison Boom in Rural America

Over the last four decades or so, the United States has constructed nearly twelve hundred new prisons, more than tripling the number of facilities.[101] These new fortresses of mass incarceration were disproportionately located in rural areas. In a marked historical shift, rural communities competed to become prison towns as the United States embarked on a massive public works project in which prison construction became the de facto economic development strategy for many distressed rural communities.

With a few notable exceptions, the rural prison boom has received relatively little analytical attention.[102] Most analyses of the rural prison boom have centered on the narrow question of whether the promised economic rewards of new prison construction ever actually materialized. The scholarly consensus was that the rural prison boom, contrary to the claims of its boosters, actually impeded economic growth, contributing to higher rates of unemployment and poverty in prison towns.[103]

In his case study of a prison town in Arkansas, sociologist John Eason challenges some of these claims. He presents a nuanced analysis of the impact of the prison boom on the political economy of rural communities. Prisons were once uniformly stigmatized, even in rural areas, he argues. That changed beginning in the 1970s. For poor, marginalized, highly stigmatized rural communities, a new prison was no longer a LULU—a locally undesirable land use, others being incinerators and dumps. Communities that were highly stigmatized by high rates of crime, violence, poverty, deindustrialization, and fraught racial relations sought to reframe new prison construction as a "savior." A new prison was "the best of the last options" for towns that had hit rock bottom and had nowhere to go but up. Eason shows how prison construction slowed economic decline and served as a "stabilizing force for rural communities headed toward the precipice of economic and social despair."[104]

Eason challenges the widespread view that pure and simple racism propelled rural communities that were overwhelmingly white to premise their economic development strategy on building prisons to house people of color from urban areas. Contrary to the conventional wisdom, many of the new prisons were built in rural areas in the South that had sizable numbers of poor

Black and Latino residents. Eason documents how local Black leaders supported prison construction and were co-opted into a growth coalition fostered by local white elites. The siting of a prison provided a bridge for major players in the community—both Black and white—to find common ground in "an otherwise racially contentious political climate."[105] Eason contends that shuttering these penal facilities would likely leave giant economic holes in prison towns. It would increase their economic precarity, much as the passage of NAFTA and the closing of local factories once did, unless major resources are allocated to smooth the transition.[106]

The Culture of Poverty, Once Again

For decades, cultural explanations rooted in various incarnations of the culture of poverty thesis were key in diverting public attention and resources away from the structural reasons for rising rates of unemployment, homelessness, crime, violence, and economic despair in US cities.[107] More recently, cultural explanations of what's the matter with rural America and poor and working-class people have diverted attention and resources from what's really the problem for them.

Sociologist Robert Crutchfield likens culture of poverty arguments to "zombies and vampires." Despite the overwhelming evidence marshalled against them, they live on, stalking debates over criminal justice and social policy for decades. They fostered highly racialized understandings of crime that portray African American people as "carriers of pro-crime norms and values" and were used to justify the get-tough measures that fueled mass incarceration.[108] But this does not fully capture the strange career of culture of poverty arguments, which have been wielded to demonize African American people but also periodically to demonize other groups, including immigrants and poor and working-class white people.

Discussions of the culture of poverty often identify the mid-1960s as ground zero for the popularization and legitimization of claims that cultural pathologies passed down from one generation to the next best explain concentrations of poverty, crime, and violence. Daniel Moynihan's 1965 report on the Black family is generally considered a seminal, if not founding, text for such claims.[109] This report portrayed Black families as damaged, pathological, and beholden to criminal subcultures. It was central to fostering an ideological and political environment conducive to the punitive turn directed at people of color and to a highly racialized understanding of the crime problem. Black parents, especially mothers, were blamed for transmitting pathological cultural values and behaviors that doom their children, including disdain for education and hard work, an unwillingness to defer gratification, and high rates of out-of-wedlock births, domestic violence, and substance abuse.[110]

The Moynihan report was not the founding text for the culture of poverty thesis, however. It was the third chapter. Anthropologist Oscar Lewis had written the founding text six years earlier when he introduced the term *culture of poverty* in his study of five impoverished Mexican families.[111] Lewis argued that oppositional subcultures emerged from social and economic conditions that marginalized certain groups. He singled out these structural factors—not pathological parents—as the incubators of cultural behaviors that appeared to lie outside the mainstream but could be considered rational adaptations to the environment in which Mexico's urban poor lived. In his account, structural forces, such as discrimination and an inequitable economic system, created conditions that kept poor people on a poverty treadmill. For example, the children of poor parents were more likely to attend failing schools, thus diminishing their motivation to succeed. Even if they succeeded, their job prospects upon graduation were dim, so why bother.[112] Lewis's thesis "was easily co-opted into arguments that poor people were to blame for their own poverty and deserved to be disciplined and shamed into changing their behaviors."[113]

The second chapter of the strange career of the culture of poverty thesis imported Lewis's findings into the US context. Michael Harrington's *The Other America*, a searing account of poverty in urban and rural enclaves across the United States, was pivotal in popularizing Lewis's key ideas.[114] In this 1962 bestseller, which helped launch President Lyndon B. Johnson's war on poverty, Harrington attempted to show how poor people in the United States are also locked into structural forces largely beyond their control that perpetuate behaviors that appear self-defeating. Harrington "did not hesitate to present the seedier side of the Other America, including domestic violence, sexual promiscuity, and substance abuse."[115] His self-consciously Dickensian portrayal of the lives of poor white people as "nasty, brutish, and short" bolstered long-standing stereotypes of white trash and a hillbilly culture of moonshine, inbreeding, illegitimate children, and vengeful violence.[116] But along with Lewis, Harrington challenged popular claims that the growing economy would eliminate poverty and thus obviate the need for government interventions to address the economy's structural problems.

The nuances of Lewis's and Harrington's work quickly got lost in debates about crime and poverty.[117] A view of poverty coalesced in the early 1960s in which cultural conditions overshadowed structural inequalities. With increased attention to the poverty problem came a reinvention of what poverty constituted. Poverty no longer denoted "an economic condition: a lack of wealth, a lack of money" but rather "a social, psychological, and ethnic condition."[118]

Although Harrington crisscrossed the United States to examine poverty in both rural and urban America, *The Other America*'s accounts of poor white people in Appalachia garnered disproportionate attention. For a time, the main face of poverty was white. Senator John F. Kennedy (D-MA) appeared taken aback by the grinding poverty he witnessed in 1960 while stumping in West Virginia's Democratic primary. He pledged to end poverty in the United States if he became president. Lyndon B. Johnson, his successor, frequently invoked his own hardscrabble upbringing in the poor Texas hill country as a core part of his political identity. A 1964 photo of LBJ crouched down on a dilapidated front porch in Kentucky talking with Tom Fletcher, an unemployed white man and father of eight, about the lack of jobs became an iconic image of the war on poverty.[119]

Lewis's and Harrington's work set the stage for the more familiar third chapter of the culture of poverty. As mentioned earlier, with the release of the Moynihan report on the Black family, the culture of poverty debate pivoted to the purported cultural deficiencies or pathologies of African American people. Moynihan's account rendered structural factors—residential and school segregation, persistent job discrimination, flawed law enforcement strategies, deindustrialization of the cities, and government policies that favored the burgeoning suburbs over the inner cities—invisible, blameless, or of secondary importance. So did many popular and academic discussions of the causes of poverty and crime. Critics of LBJ's Great Society and other public assistance crucified government programs for allegedly fostering cultural deficiencies and thus keeping people poor.[120]

Decades later on the campaign trail and then in the White House, Barack Obama channeled Moynihan. Shortly after he secured the Democratic presidential nomination in June 2008, Obama gave a Father's Day speech at a predominantly Black church in Chicago that was aimed at a wider national audience, especially white Americans. Taking a page from the culture of poverty playbook, Obama downplayed the structural factors that perpetuate poverty and other disadvantages—foremost among them, mass incarceration, which has taken so many African American fathers (and mothers) away from their children—as he castigated Black fathers for being AWOL.[121]

Around that time, conservatives to the right of Obama were opening a new chapter in the strange career of the culture of poverty. Although African American people retained top billing in their analyses, poor and working-class whites were once again a central part of the story. *Coming Apart,* the 2013 bestseller by conservative lightning rod Charles Murray, charged that large numbers of poor and working-class white people have succumbed to many of the cultural pathologies that he and others had previously associated with African American people.[122] Three years later, *Hillbilly Elegy,* JD Vance's coming-of-age memoir about growing up destitute in a small town in Ohio and spending summers with family in Appalachia, became a bestseller. The future Republican senator from Ohio and vice president recounted how "the white working class has followed the black underclass and Native Americans" down the road of "family disintegration, addiction and other pathologies," in the words of one enthusiastic reviewer of the book.[123]

Vance repackaged and updated a familiar story as he blamed the reputed cultural pathologies of poor and working-class white people for their plight. He does acknowledge that certain structural factors are also to blame for hollowing out their lives and communities, and that some government interventions are warranted to alleviate their plight. But in the end, he circles back to culture as the main culprit. He concludes with a quote from Moynihan: "The central conservative truth is that it is culture, not politics, that determines the success of a society."[124]

The Great Recession and the Changing Carceral State

Major economic and technological transformations are extremely stressful for societies and countries. The United States has been less equipped to ameliorate the strains of these transformations because of its economic and political institutions.[125] The Great Recession, which was the largest economic downturn since the Great Depression in the 1930s, exacerbated these strains across the country.

The Great Recession ushered in a "lost decade" of public investment for many states. Despite a decade of national economic growth in the decade after the Great Recession, states were still reeling from the effects of losing out on at least $283 billion because of the drop in tax revenues, which stayed below 2008 levels until 2013. After adjusting for inflation, nearly half of all states were spending less in 2018 than a decade earlier. Overall, state funding was drastically down in key areas, including education, health care, infrastructure, and aid to local governments.[126]

Disadvantage and distress deepened more in rural and suburban areas than in cities in the wake of the Great Recession.[127] During the 1980s and 1990s, rates of deep poverty were comparable in rural and urban areas (around 5 percent) but then diverged significantly.[128] Poverty rates hit at least thirty-year highs in rural, suburban, and urban areas during the Great Recession and financial crisis, but metropolitan areas rebounded more quickly.[129] On the eve of the pandemic, one out of every four rural counties was classified as having high rates of poverty compared to one out of every ten urban counties.[130] The urban-rural divide in extreme poverty was even grimmer. In 2018, all the counties meeting the criteria for extreme poverty (40 percent or more of the population living below the poverty line) were in rural areas.[131]

The Great Recession fomented conditions conducive to a doubling down on the culture of control in the United States.[132] Deteriorating economic conditions do not necessarily propel crime rates upward—but members of the public (and politicians) often believe they do. Despite major decreases in the street crime rate, more people reported that crime was a serious and growing problem after the Great Recession.[133]

For several reasons, historically disadvantaged groups in major urban areas were better positioned than marginalized people in rural communities and small cities to resist a reassertion of the culture of control in the wake of the Great Recession. One important factor was the growing strength since the 1990s of urban-based criminal justice reform movements that have pushed for reducing criminal penalties, expanding alternatives to incarceration, and ending the wars on drugs. Another key factor is how the economic recovery was geographically exceptional. As major urban areas rebounded, many rural communities and small cities remained mired in economic distress. Unlike earlier recoveries, the gains in real estate values, new jobs, new businesses, investment, GDP, and labor force participation were overwhelmingly concentrated in large urban centers.

With social safety nets that are even more threadbare than those in urban areas, rural communities lack vital services and programs to keep people out of prison and jail and to assist in their reentry after serving time. These include substance abuse and mental health programs and housing and employment assistance.[134] Furthermore, charitable giving and private philanthropy disproportionately flow toward urban, not rural, communities.[135] In addition, many rural areas have acute shortages of trained professionals, including prosecutors, judges, and public defenders. Rural communities struggle to provide even basic legal services, such as timely bail hearings and constitutionally mandated legal aid for indigent defendants. Rural areas often do not have the resources to establish diversion programs and pursue other alternatives to incarceration that have been credited with reducing incarceration rates in major urban areas. Rural communities are also more likely to be civic deserts that lack opportunities and institutions "for civic and political learning and engagement," including youth programs, cultural and arts groups, and religious congregations.[136]

The American carceral state is dynamic, not static. Its extraordinary impact on African American people has overshadowed its extensive impact on other groups. People living in rural and Rust Belt America are more vulnerable to state violence than they once were as evidenced by, among other things, the changing geography and demographics of the carceral state. Furthermore, while the race to incarcerate African American people had some distinct engines, we can draw some parallels with the race to incarcerate other groups in the United States. The next two chapters focus on two other exceptional features of state violence in America—the excessive use of force by police officers and domestic blowback from the country's global empire.

3

Tougher Than the Rest

STATE VIOLENCE AND US POLICE FORCES

HOW YOU TRAIN WILL AFFECT HOW YOU PERFORM IN COMBAT.
—POSTER FOR ROOKIE US POLICE OFFICERS

POLICE IN the United States deploy extraordinary levels of violence and co-ercion shielded from outside scrutiny and control. From shootings to choke-holds, US police officers use force in ways that are prohibited or more tightly restricted in other Western countries. What sets the United States apart is not just the fifty or one hundred "grossly unjustified" police killings of civilians each year but also the hundreds of "routine" killings.[1] These "routine" fatali-ties are not blatant violations of US law or department policies. But they do violate international law and standards and would be prosecuted elsewhere as murder.[2]

The disparities in police use of lethal force between the United States and elsewhere are seismic. Police kill people in the United States at five times the rate they do in Australia, more than twenty-five times the rate in Germany, and at least twice the rate in Canada.[3] The United States is the only Western country in which police killings are a daily event. In less than a month, police officers in the United States typically kill more people than police in England and Wales kill in a quarter century.[4] In a global ranking of rates of police kill-ings, the top thirty countries were all from the Global South, except for the United States.[5]

The proliferation of smartphones, security cameras, body-worn cameras for police officers, and dashboard cameras for patrol cars has made it more difficult to hide abuses by law enforcement—as least in densely populated urban areas. Over the past decade or so, shocking videos of police brutality and killings of Black men have sparked massive protests and the greatest legitimacy crisis for US law enforcement since the 1960s. But this public outroar has not resulted in major reductions in police homicides of civilians or a meaningful rise in successful prosecutions of law enforcement for excessive use of force and other misconduct. Officers do not face significant consequences for their misbehavior, be it killing civilians or cursing them out (the most frequent complaint lodged against the police in many cities).[6]

The racial disparities in officer-involved deaths and the proliferation of videos of police officers killing Black men have bolstered claims that racism is the main engine of the use of deadly force. Racial biases and discriminatory behavior on the part of individual police officers and their departments are certainly factors. But the immediate and underlying causes of officer-involved fatalities are complex. Some of the causes are race related but not necessarily in ways readily reducible to racial bias and discrimination on the part of individual police officers and their departments. Other causes are not related to race or are only tangentially so. Efforts to mitigate racial and ethnic biases and discrimination on the part of individual police officers—even if they were 100 percent successful—would not necessarily result in a dramatic reduction in police shootings.

Despite burgeoning research on police use of force, results are mixed or inconclusive with respect to the relationship between officer-involved deaths and racially biased or discriminatory policing.[7] Racial factors are consequential but not in ways that are well understood or easily summed up. Furthermore, there is a dearth of data on the victims of police violence and the circumstances of their deaths. In discussions of police use of excessive force, public attention has riveted on the culpability of individual officers rather than on systemic failures—on a few "bad apples" rather than on the bad barrels, as one expert on police misconduct explained.[8] Solutions fixated on weeding out a handful of "bad apples" obfuscate the more fundamental problem—that the "*institution* of policing has been ungovernable."[9]

The roots of excessive state violence by the police extend far beyond how individual police departments and the wider criminal legal system operate. Exceptionally high levels of household gun ownership, socioeconomic disadvantage, and gun violence set an important context for high levels of state and structural violence that feed off each other, as discussed in this chapter. In short, the "crisis in policing is the culmination of a thousand other failures."[10]

This chapter first examines the government's failure to collect vital information on the extent and circumstances of police use of force. It then surveys the demographics and geography of police killings in the United States and the greatest risk factors for police violence. Next, it scrutinizes the militarization of US police departments; the standards (or lack of standards) for police use of lethal and other force; how the doctrine of "qualified immunity" shields officers from civil lawsuits; the limited success of consent decrees in mitigating police brutality and other abuses; and how police unions impede investigating and disciplining officers for misconduct, including egregious behavior.

The Victims of Police Use of Excessive Force

Police use of lethal force in the United States is widely thought to be primarily a problem for urban areas, especially for African American men living in cities. But police use of excessive force is a major problem for Black women and other historically disadvantaged groups and for people living in nonmetropolitan areas.[11] Police killings have been declining in the largest cities and rising in rural and suburban communities, which accounted for about three-quarters of such fatalities in 2020.[12] This fact is not widely known for several reasons. Research on police homicides overwhelmingly focuses on large cities, even though most of these fatalities occur in communities with fewer than one hundred thousand people.[13] Furthermore, major cities tend to have more political networks, organizational resources, and media outlets, so police killings in urban areas are more likely to attract public attention.[14] Indigenous people are the most at risk of being killed by the police. But their deaths, which typically occur in rural, underpopulated areas without witnesses to record the deadly encounters on smartphones, do not garner wider public attention.[15]

African American people are more than twice as likely to be killed by a police officer than are white people.[16] Latino people are slightly more likely than white people to be killed by the police.[17] That said, white people in the United States are victims of police violence at alarming rates compared to the rates of police violence in Canada and Western Europe. A white person in the United States is twenty-six times more likely to be shot to death by the police than a white person in Germany.[18]

More white people are killed by US police officers each year than people from any other racial or ethnic group.[19] Eight of the ten states with the highest rates of fatal police shootings are in the West, where Black people constitute barely 3 percent of state populations on average. As for the other leading states, one is West Virginia, which is one of the whitest and least diverse states. The other is Louisiana, one of the most racially and ethnically diverse states.[20] White people make up the majority of people in rural areas in nearly every state, and also constitute two-thirds of the people killed by the police in rural communities, according to a *New York Times* investigation. That said, the rate at which police kill Black rural residents is disproportionately high in several states, with Louisiana leading the list. The city, state, and regional differences in the rate of officer-involved deaths are vast. Residents of New Mexico—a leader in fatal police shootings—are more than eleven times more at risk of being shot to death by the police than residents of New York State, which has the lowest rate of fatal police shootings. Between 2015 and 2017, police shot more people to death in New Mexico (sixty-two) than in New York State (fifty-two), which has nine times as many residents.[21]

Dead and Disappeared

Until the 2014 death of Michael Brown—an unarmed African American teenager suspected of shoplifting who was shot by a police officer in Ferguson, Missouri—police killings attracted only sparse and sporadic scholarly and public attention.[22] Public authorities do not collect reliable figures on how many people are killed or injured by law enforcement each year, the circumstances of their deaths and injuries, or the demographics and other characteristics of the victims and the police officers involved.[23] Following Brown's death, James Comey, director of the Federal Bureau of Investigation (FBI), confessed that the lack of accurate government data on officer-involved deaths was "embarrassing" and "ridiculous."[24]

The failure to collect comprehensive data on police killings is not an innocent oversight. It is part of the "fetish of secrecy" that shrouds policing in the United States, observes legal scholar Barry Friedman. For example, government officials usually insist that court orders to access cell phone records from telecom companies remain secret. The FBI and police departments across the country "have engaged in a massive conspiracy to cover up the use of Stingray cell phone tracking technology, which scoops up the data on countless Americans with no cause." Even basic information "about law enforcement, essential to sound oversight," is not collected or is "regularly kept from public view." These include the circumstances surrounding the use of stop and frisk, paramilitary special weapons and tactical (SWAT) teams, the indemnification of officers held liable for misconduct, and the list goes on.[25] Furthermore, the obstacles to accessing police misconduct records are huge for prosecutors and defense attorneys and nearly insurmountable for the media and members of the public.[26]

Since the 1930s, the FBI has collected detailed data on the number of law enforcement officers who are killed or die accidentally in the line of duty, as well as the circumstances of their deaths. But it has yet to establish a reliable, comprehensive, and valid database on officer killings of civilians and excessive use of force. The Violent Crime Control and Law Enforcement Act of 1994 required the Justice Department to collect and publish statistics on police use of excessive force. But this mandate has not been adequately funded or enforced. The FBI's reports on police use of force are ridden with inaccuracies and vexed by omissions.[27] Official databases severely undercount officer-involved deaths. They also are not subject to audits, including independent confirmation of police assertions that the victim was armed, and that the death was "justifiable."[28]

Many US law enforcement agencies, including some of the largest police departments, do not regularly file reports to the FBI on civilians killed by their officers. Some states have gone decades without filing any. The New York Police Department (NYPD) has had lapses of several years.[29] By contrast, many European countries carefully tabulate each person killed by the police. Germany and Finland even require that every shot fired by the police be entered into a national database.[30] (In 2013, police in Finland fired a total of six bullets—far fewer than police in the United States routinely fire in a single incident.)[31]

In 2015, the FBI vowed to collect better use-of-force data, including more comprehensive information on officer-involved fatalities, serious injuries, and firearm discharges. But so far, the FBI has made little of this information public—not even the total number of incidents—because too few departments have participated in this voluntary program.[32] A number of states explicitly forbid the release of key information on officer-involved killings or give their departments wide leeway on what to release.[33] Legislation to require all law enforcement agencies, including local and state police departments, to submit comprehensive data to the Department of Justice (DOJ) on the use of deadly force or else forfeit some of their federal funding has repeatedly stalled in Congress.[34]

Over the past decade, media and other organizations have established several open-source databases that pool information on police killings from news reports, social media postings, police reports, and elsewhere.[35] The database Fatal Encounters reportedly provides the most comprehensive portrait of officer-involved deaths, including police homicides, citizens killed during vehicle chases, medical emergencies during an encounter with the police, and suicides when police are on the scene.[36] Independent databases calculated that police officers in the United States killed nearly fourteen hundred people in 2024. This figure, which is more than twice the annual figures compiled by the FBI from voluntary reports submitted by local police departments, is likely an undercount.[37]

The Centers for Disease Control and Prevention (CDC) tallies officer-involved deaths, but its figures are undercounts. If a death certificate does not list words like "police" and "law enforcement," the fatality is not counted as a death involving "legal intervention." A 2017 recommendation by leading pathologists to add a checkbox to standard US death certificates to identify fatalities involving law enforcement (as is the case of deaths associated with use of tobacco or pregnancy) has not gained traction.[38]

Nonfatal Police Violence and Abuse

While killings by the police have become a major issue in recent years, other types of police violence and abuse have received comparatively little national attention. Sexual assault and sexual misconduct are among the most frequently reported forms of police misconduct, second only to excessive use of force.[39] Low-income women, LGBTQ people, Black women, and members of other historically disadvantaged groups are most likely to be victims of sexual assault and sexual misconduct by law enforcement.[40] Police officers across the country conduct "roadside digital anal and vaginal exams on the thinnest of pretexts."[41] Furthermore, school officials and police nationwide persist in strip-searching students, from preschoolers to high schoolers, "in violation of the Constitution because courts cannot bring themselves to impose a penalty upon them for doing so."[42]

Police use of deadly or lethal force "is physical force *capable* of [sic] or *likely* to kill" but "does not always kill."[43] When police discharge their weapons, usually no one is killed. In 2022 alone, an estimated seventy-four thousand people in the United States were treated in hospital emergency rooms for nonfatal injuries inflicted by law enforcement, including broken bones, bruises, dog bites, and internal injuries.[44] Figures on people injured by the police are undoubtedly gross undercounts. Many of the country's law enforcement agencies do not tally or make public the number of people needing medical attention after a violent encounter with the police.[45] They do not even require officers to take an injured person to the emergency room before booking them in jail.[46]

Use of so-called nonlethal restraints by the police, including electronic stun guns, chokeholds, attack dogs, and sedatives, can be deadly.[47] Electronic devices, notably Tasers, have been promoted as safe alternatives, but many police officers and prison guards have not been properly trained in their use.[48] Dozens of people die each year after receiving paralyzing shocks from these devices, and many more are seriously injured. The precise number is unknown because no government agency tracks these fatalities and injuries.[49] The Associated Press identified dozens of instances in which people died after they were given sedatives without their consent during encounters with the police. In some cases, police officers urged paramedics to administer the drugs, including the powerful sedative ketamine, even though law enforcement is unqualified to make this recommendation.[50]

Police killings of pet dogs is another controversial use of force issue that has received little public attention. The DOJ estimates that police kill twenty-five dogs every day, but the Puppycide Database Project claims the real number is closer to five hundred dogs each day. Federal courts have ruled that barking or moving is sufficient cause for police to open fire on a dog. In 20 percent of these shootings, a child was nearby or in the line of fire.[51]

Warrior Cops

With their battle dress uniforms, military-grade equipment and weapons, SWAT teams, and military-style training, police in the United States are taught to behave as "warrior cops," not guardians of the public.[52] Training in firearms and survival in an "intensely hostile world" that is "quite literally, gunning for them" is the focus of US police academies.[53] New recruits spend almost twenty times as many hours learning how to use their guns and other weapons as they do in learning how to de-escalate conflicts.[54] United States police academies "relentlessly show terrifying videos that can lead to only one conclusion: that *failure* to shoot can be fatal."[55] By contrast, in Western Europe there is "a relentless emphasis . . . on alternatives to pulling a trigger."[56] As one top German police official explained: "We try to make all police officers recognize that you are not a good guy if you are shooting. You are a good guy if you are not shooting."[57]

Training to become a police officer in Germany, Norway, and some other European countries typically lasts at least three years—compared to just nineteen weeks on average in the United States (and often as little as eleven weeks). Many states have higher standards to become a licensed barber or manicurist than to become a police officer.[58] The instructors in European police academies include experts in sociology, criminology, law, and psychology, not just law enforcement, in contrast to most US police academies. These countries also tend to have higher educational and other requirements for people seeking to become police officers. While many police departments in the United States go begging for recruits, getting accepted at a police academy in some European countries can be as tough as getting admitted to the most selective colleges and universities in the United States.[59]

Decentralization and intense local control are major roadblocks to imposing national standards for training and the use of force. The United States has a hyperlocalized law enforcement system with its more than eighteen thousand independent state and local police agencies. These range from police departments with just a single cop to the NYPD, which employs some fifty thousand people, including about thirty-four thousand uniformed officers. The most common type of law enforcement agency is a small-town police department with ten or fewer officers.[60] Even if smaller police departments wanted to raise their standards for recruitment, training, and monitoring their officers, they do not necessarily have the resources to do so.

Most US police departments have at least one SWAT team or other paramilitary unit.[61] Trained by current and former Navy SEALs and Army Rangers, SWAT teams and other paramilitary units conduct an estimated eighty thousand deployments each year.[62] The precise figures are unknown because most police agencies are not required to publicly report on the activities of their paramilitary units.[63] Most SWAT missions do not involve emergency situations, such as hostage taking, but rather more mundane police work, such as raiding homegrown cannabis operations or serving warrants.[64]

Paramilitary units, including SWAT teams, deliver tens of thousands of no-knock warrants each year in terrorizing operations usually conducted before dawn by heavily armed officers cloaked in black. These teams rapidly enter homes, often using specialized battering rams, explosives, and flashbang grenades to disorient residents.[65] The 2020 death of Breonna Taylor, a twenty-six-year-old African American woman killed during a SWAT attack in Louisville, Kentucky, spurred some cities and states to restrict or ban no-knock warrants. But these reforms do not appear to have significantly altered how these paramilitary units operate.[66] Research suggests that SWAT teams do not reduce violent crime or make police officers safer but do harm the reputation of the police.[67]

For decades, the Defense Department's so-called 1033 program has funneled surplus military equipment, including drones, grenade launchers, and mine-resistant vehicles, to local police departments and even some school districts.[68] Police departments that are more militarized, as measured by the amounts of surplus military equipment they receive, have higher rates of police killings.[69] Between 1990 and 2014, a Department of Defense (DOD) unit, whose unofficial motto is "from warfighter to crimefighter," distributed $5 billion in surplus equipment under this program.[70] The 1033 program, which had never exceeded $34 million annually since it was formally established in 1997, surged under the Obama administration, increasing twenty-four-fold between 2008 and 2014.[71] The DOD transferred $787 million in weaponry and military gear to local police in 2014, the year that Michael Brown was killed.[72]

Images of police patrolling the streets of Ferguson, Missouri, in August 2014 with combat gear, military-grade assault rifles, and armored vehicles sparked a public outcry over the militarization of the police. After his administration issued a searing report in late 2014 on transfers of military equipment to civilian police forces, Obama placed modest, mostly toothless restrictions on the 1033 program.[73] The first Trump administration lifted these restrictions, and the Biden administration reinstated some of them.[74] Congress, including the Congressional Black Caucus, has been reluctant to seriously reduce or disband the program.[75] Hours after his return to the White House for a second term, President Donald Trump signed an executive order rolling back the Biden administration's restrictions on military equipment transfers to police.

Even more consequential than the 1033 program is the Department of Homeland Security's "terrorism grants," which as of 2014 had distributed $34 billion to police departments for the purchase of military equipment, as well as sophisticated technology to surveil the public.[76] Permissive civil asset forfeiture laws and policies have also facilitated the buildup of police arsenals. These measures permit police to confiscate cash and property from people they suspect of criminal activity, often without first securing warrants, indictments, or convictions. Police departments have used these slush funds to go on spending sprees to purchase everything from military-grade equipment to lavish parties.[77]

Standards for the Use of Force

When it comes to the use of force by law enforcement, the United States is shockingly permissive. All 50 states, the District of Columbia, and all federal law enforcement agencies fail to meet international law and standards for police use of lethal force that are set out in key treaties, including the International Covenant on Civil and Political Rights.[78] As a signatory to those international agreements, the United States is legally obligated to comply with them, but it doesn't. According to international law and standards, police officers are permitted to use lethal force only if they are facing a threat of imminent death or severe injury and if no other means are available. Furthermore, the amount of force must not exceed the minimum necessary and must be proportionate to what they are trying to achieve.[79] Police also are obligated to provide medical assistance as soon as possible for people who are injured.

American case law, standards for the use of force, and other factors make it nearly impossible to hold police officers criminally accountable for injuring or killing civilians. They also make it difficult to hold officers accountable in the civil courts. As of 2015, nine states and Washington, DC, did not even have any laws spelling out the circumstances under which use of lethal force by police is sanctioned; and laws in thirteen other states did not even comply with the bare minimum standards for the use of lethal force established by the US courts and constitutional law.[80] Until recently, the deployment of police dogs to apprehend someone "was completely ungoverned by sound policies."[81] Many departments trained their K-9 units to bite suspects regardless of whether the person is actively resisting arrest or attempting to escape.[82]

Barely 1 percent of officers who fatally shot civilians between 2005 and 2020 were charged with manslaughter or homicide. Of these, less than one-third were convicted, usually for a lesser offense that resulted in probation or a short jail or prison sentence.[83] As one expert on police use of force explained, "To charge an officer in a fatal shooting, it takes something so egregious, so over the top, that it cannot be explained in any rational way."[84] In the great majority of cases in which an officer was charged, the person killed was unarmed. But it usually took more than that for prosecutors to press charges.[85] Most of the cases in which officers were criminally charged involved at least one other factor that made them exceptional: a victim shot in the back, video evidence of the incident, incriminating testimony from other police officers, or allegations of a cover-up.

The hurdles to successfully prosecuting officers who use excessive force are enormous. Victims often do not know the names of the officers who abused them.[86] District attorneys are reluctant to file criminal charges against police officers for many reasons. Prosecutors by temperament tend to side with the police. Moreover, unlike in most other countries, nearly all district attorneys in the United States are elected officials. Prosecutors and other politicians are wary of powerful and well-funded police unions and other groups that can imperil their political fortunes. Furthermore, by the time crimes committed by police officers become known or acknowledged, the relevant statute of limitations has expired in more than three-quarters of these cases, according to an analysis by legal scholar Angelica Hendricks.[87]

State and local police are usually the ones who are responsible for investigating civilian deaths involving their own officers, which raises troubling conflict-of-interest issues. Since the murder of George Floyd, pressure to mandate independent investigations of civilian deaths involving police officers or guards in prisons and jails has intensified.[88] The attorneys general in a number of states have become more active in investigating local police departments and lodging civil suits against them.[89] But state agencies do not necessarily conduct more evenhanded investigations of local police or local jails. A *New York Times* analysis of deaths in local custody in Texas, for example, revealed that investigations conducted by the statewide Texas Rangers "fell short of basic standards" and were vexed by biases in favor of the police and guards.[90] A special unit of the New York State attorney general's office established in 2015 to investigate and prosecute officer-involved deaths has a dismal record.[91] So did Chicago's now-defunct Independent Police Review Authority.[92]

Even when a prosecutor is motivated to press criminal charges, the legal hurdles are nearly insurmountable. Police officers seldom testify against their colleagues, and perjury is common among officers.[93] Judges and juries tend to side with the police. Furthermore, decades of case law laid down by the Supreme Court and lower courts protect the police from being found guilty in cases of officer-involved deaths.

As late as the early 1970s, police departments had no meaningful guidelines for use of deadly force by their officers.[94] Until the mid-1980s, use of deadly force against a fleeing suspect was considered constitutional, even if the person posed no imminent threat. The 1985 *Tennessee v. Garner* decision appeared to narrow the circumstances in which deadly force is permitted. The US Supreme Court rejected a Tennessee law that permitted police to use force indiscriminately on suspects fleeing arrest—in this case, Edward Garner, an unarmed teenager suspected of burglary who was shot and killed by a Memphis police officer as he climbed a fence.[95] However, the court gave wide berth for police officers to use deadly force if they have probable cause to believe a suspect poses a threat to police or others by brandishing a weapon or if the suspect "has committed a crime involving the infliction or threatened infliction of serious physical harm"—even if there is no evidence the suspect would inflict such harm in the future.[96]

In the 1989 *Graham v. Connor* decision, the Supreme Court determined that use of force must adhere to a standard of "reasonableness"—that is, what a "reasonable officer on the scene," often forced to make "split-second decisions," would do. But the courts have failed to implement the reasonableness standard in a consistent or meaningful way. The prevailing approach has resulted in "an incoherent hodgepodge of pro-police excessive force decisions" that undermine public confidence in the ability of the criminal legal system and police departments to rein in police violence.[97]

A review of excessive force decisions since *Graham* reveals that many courts shortsightedly focus "on only one aspect of policing—its dangerousness." They do not consider the training, experience, and standards of professional conduct that should make police officers "better able than civilians to deal with that danger without using excessive force."[98] The judiciary's stance reflects the common perception that policing is exceptionally dangerous, and thus officers need wide leeway to perform their jobs. Police unions and their advocates have aggressively cultivated these sentiments. But law enforcement is not even among the top ten most deadly occupations in the United States.[99] Taxi, limo, and Uber drivers are twice as likely as police officers to be the victim of an on-the-job homicide.[100]

Being a police officer is a far less dangerous job than it once was. The death rate for police officers killed in the line of duty fell by about 75 percent between 1976 and 2012, thanks to Kevlar bullet-proof vests and other innovations in policing.[101] One hundred or so police officers die in the line of duty each year, typically a little more than half of them from shootings and other assaults and most of the rest from accidents.[102] The on-the-job risk of death for a police officer is below the total homicide risk for an average male. In 1976, it was twice the risk.[103] The death rate for police killed on the job has plummeted since the late 1970s. But the rate of police use of lethal force has remained fairly constant, falling just 9 percent over this forty-year period.[104]

Although being a cop in the United States is less dangerous compared to years ago and to many other occupations, it is still a risky job in comparison to being a police officer in many other countries. Police in the United States are thirty-five times more likely to be killed in the line of duty compared to police in Germany, according to one estimate. In some years, not a single police officer is killed in Germany, the most populous country in Europe.[105] Policing in the United States is risky in less direct ways. United States police officers have higher rates of suicide, PTSD, depression, and other mental health problems than the general population does. They also have lower life expectancy.[106]

The courts have determined that judges and jurors do not necessarily have to consider a police officer's "training, experience, and adherence to department policies and procedures" in determining whether an officer acted reasonably in a use-of-force case.[107] For example, the courts have ruled that the police are acting reasonably even when they engage in activities that are prohibited by their departments—such as using a chokehold on a suspect.[108] The courts have even determined that firing multiple shots at someone who appears to be surrendering with hands up in the air as they walk toward a police officer can still be considered a "reasonable" use of force. The Justice Department referred to this case law in explaining why it had determined that Ferguson police officer Darren Wilson was acting lawfully when he fatally shot Michael Brown.[109]

The Supreme Court has all but abandoned the "reasonableness" standard with respect to car chases, which the Justice Department once characterized as "the most dangerous of all ordinary police activities."[110] Thanks to a 2007 decision, officers are permitted to open fire on a fleeing vehicle or force it off the road merely on the fear that the driver might cause an accident.[111] That 8–1 ruling overturned a lower court decision that "the chase itself cannot create the danger that justifies shooting [the] suspect."[112] A *USA Today* analysis found that 11,500 people were killed in high-speed police chases between 1979 and 2013. Nearly half of them were bystanders or passengers in the fleeing vehicles. Tens of thousands more have been injured in dangerous chases as officers pursued drivers, usually for minor traffic violations or misdemeanors.[113]

In the face of the Supreme Court's permissive standards for car chases and the lethal use of force, some police departments have imposed stricter standards. Some major cities now forbid officers from engaging in high-speed chases of drivers suspected of breaking traffic laws or committing other low-level offenses.[114] The NYPD's patrol guide states that police officers should not fire at fleeing vehicles unless deadly force is being used against them or someone else present "by means other than a moving vehicle."[115] Officers of the NYPD are also not permitted to shoot a fleeing suspect "who presents no threat of imminent death or serious injury to themselves or another person present."[116]

Although imminence is certainly a stricter standard than the one laid down in *Garner*, it still is subject to wide interpretation. Most police in the United States are not held to a "necessary standard," which prohibits the use of deadly force if less lethal options are available and feasible. Furthermore, only a handful of states legally require police to give a warning whenever possible before deploying lethal force.[117]

In 1995, the DOJ adopted a "necessary standard" for the use of force, but it was a discretionary policy and applied only to federal law enforcement agencies, not local police forces. In May 2022, the department adopted a new policy that permits federal officers to "use force only when no reasonably effective, safe, and feasible alternative appears to exist."[118] The Biden administration also ordered federal agencies to comply with DOJ standards for use of force. While an improvement, these revised standards are woefully inadequate compared to European standards.[119]

Most European countries adhere to the standards set out in the European Convention on Human Rights, which permit use of lethal force only when it is "absolutely necessary." In several European countries, the typical police officer does not even carry a firearm.[120] "Killings excused under America's 'reasonable belief' standards often violate Europe's 'absolute necessity' standards," according to one expert on the use of force.[121] These would include the many police killings in the United States in which the victim was armed.

Some European countries have established stricter regulations that go beyond the convention's legal framework. When feasible, police in Finland and Norway are supposed to receive permission from a supervisor before deploying lethal force. Police in Spain are required to incrementally escalate, first with verbal warnings, then warning shots, and then shots fired at nonvital parts of the body before delivering deadly force.[122] By contrast, police supervisors in Vallejo, California, praised their officers for their proficiency in using "zipper drills"—that is, firing many shots into a suspect, beginning in their lower body and "zipping" toward their head while firing nonstop.[123]

People reportedly brandishing firearms account for a little over half of all the individuals shot to death by the police in the United States. Police kill hundreds of people every year who are holding less lethal weapons or no weapons at all. A substantial portion of these people—over 16 percent by one calculation—were holding knives.[124] In 2020 alone, US police killed at least 180 people who were allegedly holding a sharp object.[125] Opening fire on someone with a knife is standard operating procedure in the United States (but not in European countries). For decades, rookie police officers in the United States have been taught the "21-foot rule"—a controversial and unproven claim that police are at great risk of death or serious injury if they let anyone with a sharp object get closer than that distance.[126] In fact, police in the United States are almost never killed or seriously injured by people holding knives or other sharp objects.[127] Neither are police in other countries.[128]

Most European countries ban or strictly restrict the use of chokeholds, a standard tactic used by many US police departments. Chokeholds drew little public attention until mobile phones graphically captured Eric Garner in 2014 gasping for breath and pleading "I can't breathe" as a NYPD officer put him in a chokehold and suffocated him to death.[129] Minneapolis police officer Derek Chauvin killed George Floyd in May 2020 by pressing his knee against the forty-six-year-old Black man's neck for nearly nine minutes. At the time, the Minneapolis Police Department permitted the use of dangerous neck restraints if officers feared for their lives. A year after Floyd was killed, Chauvin was convicted of manslaughter and murder in a rare instance in which fellow officers breached the blue wall of silence. They testified that Chauvin had not adhered to department policies and training. Chauvin was found guilty in part because he could not claim that he was making a split-second decision in self-defense when he suffocated Floyd.

After the uproar over Floyd's death, pressure mounted on lawmakers at all levels of government to impose greater restraints on police use of force, including banning chokeholds outright or putting more restrictions on them.[130] But bans are no guarantee that officers will not use chokeholds or that they will be criminally prosecuted if they violate department policies. In the case of Eric Garner, the medical examiner ruled that his death was a homicide. But a grand jury refused to indict NYPD officer Daniel Pantaleo, who used a prohibited chokehold when he apprehended the forty-three-year-old African American man suspected of selling single cigarettes. After dithering for five years, the DOJ declined in 2019 to bring charges against Pantaleo under federal civil rights laws.[131] In the six years after Garner's death, New York City's Civilian Complaint Review Board, which investigates police misconduct, substantiated forty instances of NYPD officers using prohibited chokeholds. Not even one of the officers was fired. The most common sanction: loss of vacation days. Some officers were not sanctioned at all.[132]

The Shield of Qualified Immunity

Like the criminal legal system, the civil courts are extremely deferential to the police (and prison guards). The obstacles to suing police officers, prison guards, and government officials for serious misconduct and civil rights violations, including excessive use of force, are daunting and have been growing. Thanks to a 1961 decision in *Monroe v. Pape*, Section 1983 of the US Code was transformed into "by far the most important vehicle" for pressing such claims.[133]

Section 1983 is derived from the Civil Rights Act of 1871, which the administration of President Ulysses S. Grant wielded to vanquish the Ku Klux Klan during Reconstruction. In *Monroe*, the Supreme Court determined that section 1983 applied not only to private actors like the Ku Klux Klan who violated civil rights but also to government officials who exceeded their authority in unauthorized behavior. At issue in *Monroe* was a violent, threatening, warrantless police invasion of a home with six children.[134]

Civil suits brought under section 1983 put pressure on police departments to be more legally accountable, resulting in a drop in the use of force and other changes in police behavior.[135] But over the last half century, the courts have waged a "procedural assault" on section 1983. Their most powerful ammunition is the expansive judicial interpretation of the once esoteric doctrine of "qualified immunity." In a 2018 dissent, Supreme Court Justice Sonia Sotomayor charged that qualified immunity had become "an absolute shield for law enforcement officers."[136]

The courts have determined that police officers and other government officials are immune from liability claims unless the constitutional right in question was "clearly established" law in a prior case with nearly identical circumstances in the same jurisdiction.[137] Nearly identical cases adjudicated in other federal jurisdictions may not be used as precedents in later cases. Trivial differences in earlier cases are cause to deny victims of police brutality and other misconduct their day in court to seek compensation or other redress. As one specialist on qualified immunity explains, "Courts have granted officers qualified immunity even when they have engaged in egregious behavior—not because what the officers did was acceptable, but because there wasn't a prior case in which that precise conduct had been held unconstitutional."[138]

For example, the Sixth Circuit Court ruled in 2018 that two Nashville policemen were not liable for injuries and civil rights violations after they sicced a police dog on an unarmed burglary suspect who had just surrendered with his hands up in the air. A prior case in that jurisdiction had established that a police officer had violated the Fourth Amendment rights of a nonthreatening suspect by deploying a police dog on the man, who was lying on the ground and had already surrendered. But that precedent did not apply in the more recent case because the surrendering suspect was sitting on the ground—not lying down—with his hands raised.[139] In another case, federal judges sided with a deputy sheriff who shot at a family dog without any provocation, missing the animal but striking a ten-year-old child, because of the "unique facts of this case."[140]

In 2009, the Supreme Court determined that lower courts are allowed to grant qualified immunity on the grounds that the law was not clearly established without first even deciding whether officers had violated any constitutional rights. This has created a catch-22. Since the courts tend to rule in favor of the police in qualified immunity cases, many police misconduct cases are thrown out of court without providing any clear judicial guidance for future cases about what types of constitutional violations meet the court's "clearly established law" standard.[141] Furthermore, "if courts grant qualified immunity without at least deciding the merits question, then the same defendant could continue committing exactly the same misconduct indefinitely—and never be held accountable."[142]

If a district court denies a defendant's motion to dismiss on grounds of qualified immunity, the police officer may immediately appeal the decision even before the case goes to trial. In most other types of cases, a trial court's decision may not be appealed until the verdict has been rendered. The legal costs of these protracted pretrial appeals in qualified immunity cases often induce plaintiffs to settle the case under less favorable terms rather than go to trial.[143] George Floyd's family reached a $27 million settlement with the city of Minneapolis before a lawsuit was ever filed.[144] Had Floyd's death not attracted such national notoriety, the city's lawyers might well have chosen to engage in a lengthy legal case as they pressed claims that qualified immunity shielded Minneapolis from liability.

Some jurisdictions have sought to deny qualified immunity to officers in wrongful-death lawsuits if their actions violate department policies or training. This can have a perverse effect. It encourages departments to refrain from spelling out their use-of-force policies and from adopting standards that are higher than the low bar set by the Supreme Court because doing so would make their officers more vulnerable to losing the shield of qualified immunity. Lexipol, a Texas-based company that works with thousands of law enforcement agencies, including many police departments, specializes in writing policies and training manuals that are vague and permissive so as to elude civil lawsuits.[145] "They want to make it impossible, or nearly impossible, for anybody to point to the policy and say it was violated," explains an expert on police misconduct.[146] Some of the policies that Lexipol promotes are even at odds with recommendations from major police organizations.[147]

The courts have shielded law enforcement from civil liability and public accountability in other ways. In 1983, the US Supreme Court handed down a landmark decision involving chokeholds and the use of force that expanded the legal shield for police in civil cases, even in instances of unconstitutional use of force. In *City of Los Angeles v. Lyons*, the US Supreme Court refused to uphold injunctive relief for Adolph Lyons, an unarmed twenty-four-year-old Black man pulled over in 1976 for a broken taillight and then subjected to a chokehold by a Los Angeles Police Department (LAPD) officer. His legal team presented evidence that between 1975 and when the Supreme Court heard Lyons's case in 1982, the LAPD killed sixteen people, including twelve African American people, using chokeholds. The Supreme Court upheld the lower court's decision that Lyons was entitled to compensation for his injuries, pain, and suffering. But the Supreme Court also ruled that Lyons did not have standing to seek a court order restricting chokeholds because he was not likely to be subjected to a chokehold again.[148]

In a series of 5–4 decisions in the 1980s and 1990s, the Rehnquist Court constructed an expansive concept of state immunity. As a result, suing individual officers—not state or municipal governments or agencies—is often the only avenue open to seek damages in Section 1983 cases.[149] Furthermore, the courts have ruled that supervisors of frontline officers—including police commissioners—are generally not liable for their employees' misconduct or for failing to provide proper training and supervision.[150] They also have rejiggered how plaintiffs' attorney fees are calculated and awarded, making it harder for victims of police violence to secure adequate legal representation to successfully pursue their claims.[151]

A growing number of judges, scholars, and advocates spanning the ideological spectrum are belatedly recognizing "that qualified immunity doctrine is legally unsound, unnecessary to shield government officials from the costs and burdens of litigation, and destructive of police accountability efforts."[152] As protests convulsed the country after George Floyd was killed in May 2020, qualified immunity emerged as a leading issue in debates over police reform.

Costly Settlements

Even when plaintiffs successfully navigate the shoals of qualified immunity, settlements in civil lawsuits do not necessarily deter police misconduct. Federal lawsuits under section 1983 are most successful in recovering significant monetary damages in use of force cases involving death or bodily injury. Suits pertaining to police violations of the Fourth Amendment's protections from unreasonable searches and seizures, for example, are less likely to result in high monetary awards because the harms are deemed far less significant.[153]

Governments—not individual officers—typically pay nearly all the costs of civil settlements.[154] Police officers personally shelled out only 0.02 percent of the money that plaintiffs were awarded, according to one study.[155] Almost all police union contracts include provisions that indemnify their members in legal actions. Bad cops seldom pay punitive damages "even when officers were disciplined, terminated, or prosecuted for their conduct."[156] Furthermore, cities usually pay for these settlements out of general operating revenues—not police budgets—so these payments seldom directly impact police operations. Some advocates for police reform have been pushing to require police officers to carry individual liability insurance—much as doctors are obligated to have medical malpractice insurance. They also have called on local governments to be more open about which officers have had judgments against them; the full costs of these settlements, including servicing the debt; and who ends up shouldering these costs.[157]

Police killings of civilians are a relatively small portion of police misconduct costs. Very few fatal shootings result in any monetary settlement or a public accounting. Of the estimated 160 lethal police shootings in Los Angeles between 2000 and 2009, only thirteen (or about 8 percent) resulted in some payment. Most of the amounts were relatively trivial given the loss of life—typically less than $250,000. In over 90 percent of these cases, the cost of damages paid out to victims' families was not made public.[158]

The tab for cities in police misconduct cases, most of which do not involve lethal shootings, is huge but submerged. Those costs "are cloaked, if they are mentioned at all, in the opaque legalese of bond offerings and tax bills."[159] Like most civil liability cases, lawsuits leveled against the police—if they are not thrown out of court altogether because of qualified immunity and other claims—are usually settled short of full litigation. These private settlements are often kept secret, making it difficult to track the number of settlements against the police and their dollar amounts. A 2015 *Wall Street Journal* study found that the country's ten largest police departments paid more than $1 billion over the previous five years to settle cases that included beatings, shootings, and wrongful imprisonment.[160] Between 2010 and 2019, the city of Chicago doled out more than $930 million, including interest, to settle cases of wrongdoing by its officers—a total equal to about two-thirds of the police department's annual budget.[161] A single multimillion-dollar settlement can force smaller cities into bankruptcy. Insurance companies have been spurring some changes in police use of excessive force by threatening to cancel liability coverage for departments.[162]

Large and small municipalities often must float what critics deride as "police brutality bonds" to cover the settlements. Once the expense of servicing the debt is added in, the actual cost of a settlement can more than double.[163] The residents of impoverished urban neighborhoods, who are more at risk of being victimized by police killings and brutality, are thus victimized twice more. Thanks to the regressive tax systems that prevail in many cities, they end up shouldering a disproportionate share of the financial burden of compensating the victims of police violence.[164] Furthermore, to pay for these police settlements and for costly liability insurance, cities have less to spend on essential services that people in poor neighborhoods depend on, such as lead poisoning screenings, after school programs, and mental health clinics.[165] Cities end up slashing the very services and programs "that reduce violence and crime, and thereby reduce the perceived need for aggressive policing" that spurs excessive use of force.[166]

Consent Decrees

Until recently, civil rights organizations and their allies did not prioritize eliminating or circumscribing qualified immunity through legislation, even though civil lawsuits have been key in expanding rights in other realms, notably in curbing employment discrimination.[167] They preferred that government— rather than private—actors take the lead in pressing civil rights claims in law enforcement cases and in monitoring police departments.

A provision in the 1994 crime bill permits the Justice Department, but not individuals, to seek injunctive relief in cases involving police departments with a proven history of misconduct.[168] The DOJ is permitted to investigate, sue, enter into consent decrees, and appoint independent monitors to compel police departments to change their behavior. Consent decrees are court-supervised settlements to resolve illegal actions or systematic misconduct uncovered during federal investigations of state or local law enforcement groups. These settlements can be costly to implement—$300 million in the case of the LAPD—and their success may be short-lived.[169] After the decrees are lifted, some research suggests, the police start to relapse.[170]

The DOJ has yet to do a comprehensive quantitative analysis of the impact of consent decrees on police behavior.[171] Independent analyses of these negotiated settlements suggest they have had mixed success.[172] In some departments, the decrees have spurred reductions in lethal and abusive behavior, but in others they have not.[173] Consent decrees have had more success at compelling police departments to track, investigate, and respond to citizen complaints of misconduct and abusive behavior. In a number of cases, public satisfaction with the police rose, including among Black residents, even when pedestrian and vehicle stops increased during the decree.[174]

The DOJ pursues few civil rights investigations of police departments each year—typically just two or three.[175] Since the DOJ handles so few civil rights investigations, "the scope of its enforcement activity is minuscule" and "should not be considered an adequate substitute for or alternative to private enforcement under Section 1983."[176] When the DOJ does step in, it is usually after an egregious case of police use of force that has become a national issue. Notable examples include the 2014 killing of Michael Brown, the 2015 death of Freddie Gray (a twenty-five-year-old African American man who succumbed to spinal injuries he received while being transported in a Baltimore police van), and the death of Laquan McDonald (a Black teenager who died after being shot sixteen times by a Chicago police officer in October 2014).[177]

The DOJ investigation of the Ferguson police grimly documented how the city and its officers had for years systematically engaged in abusive behavior and violated the civil rights of the residents of this predominantly Black city. The report concluded that Ferguson needed to double down on creating a "robust system of true community policing."[178] But the concept of community policing is not well defined. Calls for more community policing have often been a cover for expanding the power of the police at the expense of empowering citizens.[179] In response to the report and the lack of funding to implement its other recommendations, Ferguson city officials and the consent decree's federal monitor prioritized increasing expenditures for the city's police force and its school resource officers (a euphemism for school-based cops).[180]

The national uproar over Chicago's shoddy investigation of and attempts to cover up the circumstances of McDonald's death prompted the DOJ to get involved. In January 2017, the outgoing Obama administration issued a scathing report charging that the Chicago Police Department engaged in a pattern of excessive use of force that was unconstitutional. It faulted the department for the lack of any "meaningful, systematic accountability for officers who use force in violation of the law or CPD policy."[181]

The Obama administration stepped up DOJ investigations of police departments, entered into more consent decrees, and in late 2014 established a national task force on policing. But in general, the administration's response to the excessive use of force and other abuses by law enforcement was muted or misdirected.[182] It did not spend much political capital on pursuing more far-reaching reforms, including advocating for the courts and legislators to abolish or restrict qualified immunity. Furthermore, the Obama administration sided with the police in every Supreme Court case that sought "to hold police officers accountable to constitutional constraints in their encounters with citizens."[183]

During President Donald Trump's first term, the Justice Department was overtly hostile to federal investigations of police departments, contending that state or local authorities, not federal ones, should be responsible for monitoring the police.[184] In late 2019, Attorney General William Barr warned critics of US policing that if they did not show more "support and respect" for the police, "they may find themselves without the police protection they need."[185] After the police killing of George Floyd in May 2020, Trump threatened to deploy the military against protesters outraged at his death. Wielding an incendiary phrase dating back to police suppression of popular unrest in the 1960s, Trump warned them, "When the looting starts, the shooting starts."[186] At a June Rose Garden ceremony that was filled with police union officials but no victims of police violence, Trump unveiled a tepid proposal to improve police training and track misconduct.[187]

During Joe Biden's first year in office, congressional negotiations to enact the George Floyd Justice in Policing Act collapsed as lawmakers disagreed over proposed restrictions on qualified immunity and police use of deadly force and on the creation of a national database to track police misconduct. Weeks later, President Biden signed three bills supportive of law enforcement, including measures to add one thousand new police officers, expand mental health services for law enforcement, and increase death and disability payments for officers.[188] By fall 2022, states had enacted nearly three hundred police-related measures in the aftermath of Floyd's death. Many of these measures fell far short of what reformers had hoped for and were subsequently rolled back as the push for police reform stalled.[189] But a handful of states and local governments did enact measures to bar or limit qualified immunity.[190]

The DOJ under Biden enforced fifteen court-ordered oversight agreements from previous administrations. Merrick Garland, Biden's attorney general, also loosened the rules to make it easier for the government to enter into consent decrees. During his tenure, the DOJ conducted a dozen civil rights investigations of polices forces, documenting extensive and "shocking examples of brutality, racial profiling, illegal arrests and impunity for officers who had committed misconduct." These investigations resulted in a couple of oversight agreements finalized in the waning months of the Biden administration. But days before the five-year anniversary of the murder of George Floyd, the second Trump administration announced plans to abandon oversight agreements and investigations of nearly two dozen police departments.[191]

Officer Misconduct and Police Unions

Collective bargaining agreements are another powerful shield to protect police officers from criminal charges, civil lawsuits, and public accountability. "It is a given," according to one expert on policing, that many police chiefs "do not really run their departments," thanks to the clout of police unions and police associations and to case law fashioned by the Supreme Court, all of which makes it almost impossible to hold police officers accountable.[192]

The history of the relationship between the labor movement and fights for racial, social, and economic justice is fraught. Segments of organized labor fought to exclude African Americans and other historically disadvantaged groups from their ranks, treating them as second-class members and siding with politicians and groups seeking to bolster Jim Crow. But left-leaning labor organizers and unions were at the forefront of fights against police brutality and other injustices in the early twentieth century.[193] For that, they paid a high price as organized labor purged its ranks of card-carrying and alleged members of the Communist Party in the 1940s and 1950s and contributed to the political decapitation of the left during the heyday of McCarthyism.[194]

In response to rising criticisms of the police and mounting efforts to rein them in, droves of police officers began in the 1960s to organize themselves into unions and police associations, which were de facto unions. Law enforcement ended up becoming one of the most heavily unionized sectors of the workforce, with unions and police associations today representing over seven hundred thousand officers—or more than 80 percent of all officers.[195] Police sought unionization to enhance their power not only to negotiate bread-and-butter issues like wages and benefits but also to defend their prerogatives in policy matters, such as the discipline and deployment of officers. Police unions ended up "unparalleled in their ability to successfully advocate for policy proposals that conflict with traditional democratic values of accountability and transparency," according to one expert on police misconduct.[196] Police unions, working closely with public officials, prison guards' unions, and associations of sheriffs and district attorneys, were also major drivers of the punitive policies and politics that built the carceral state and remain major obstacles to dismantling it.[197]

With the spread of police unionization in the 1960s, police became openly involved in politics and emerged "as a self-conscious, organized, and militant constituency bidding for far-reaching political power in their own right."[198] Police unions backed policies and supported politicians antithetical to the interests of the wider labor movement, as well as other movements for social justice, including the civil rights movement. Police organized "in relative isolation from the rest of the labor movement," forming police-only unions and associations, or defecting from unions that represent public-sector workers, notably the American Federation of State, County, and Municipal Employees (AFSCME).[199] As one expert on policing put it, police "organize as police, not as workers."[200]

As the clout of political machines receded over the course of the twentieth century, police departments ended up further insulated from political and civilian control. With the spread of civil service procedures and unionization, public officials lost authority to hire, fire, promote, and discipline officers. Mayors and other public figures would lament police use of excessive force, corruption, and discrimination. They would claim they had no real clout to ameliorate these problems since police chiefs had the ultimate authority over their officers. As for reform-minded police chiefs, they had to contend with civil service protections, pressures to maintain the loyalty of their officers, and a wave of unionization that further insulated police from civilian oversight and control.[201]

Police unions began bestowing political endorsements and running their own candidates. Police cast off their traditional role of enforcing established policies and sought greater clout to shape policies, including the rights of defendants, the budget for law enforcement, and calls for greater public accountability.[202] In doing so, they radically challenged the authority of police chiefs, the courts, and civilian leaders. In one infamous example, to protest proposed budget cuts that included police layoffs, New York City's Patrolmen's Benevolent Association "ordered a rampage through the city's black and Puerto Rican communities" that lasted several nights in 1975.[203] In another notorious incident, thousands of off-duty NYPD cops rioted in 1992, successfully derailing efforts to establish a civilian review board and imperiling the reelection of David Dinkins, the city's first African American mayor.

Police and their political benefactors have stridently resisted creating independent civilian review boards with real teeth to monitor departments and discipline police officers. Police contracts routinely restrict the interrogation of officers after a police shooting or allegation of misconduct; forbid civilian oversight; mandate the destruction of disciplinary records; ban anonymous civilian complaints; put severe time and other limits on internal investigations; and indemnify officers from civil lawsuits.[204] Unionized police departments tend to receive more use-of-force complaints compared to nonunionized ones and to have higher rates of police killings.[205] In the words of Charles McClelland, Houston's former police chief, police management and municipal authorities have allowed police unions to "go too far."[206]

Collective bargaining agreements give police unions considerable clout to select arbitrators in the appeals process, often leaving chiefs of police, other city officials, and civilian oversight bodies wielding only symbolic power to discipline officers.[207] Between 2012 and 2020, citizens in Minneapolis filed more than twenty-six hundred misconduct complaints, but only a dozen of these resulted in penalties for an officer. The most severe sanction was a forty-hour suspension.[208] In the rare instance when an officer is fired for abuse or other misconduct, they usually can readily find new positions in other departments because the federal government and most states do not maintain clearinghouses to track police misconduct. Weeks after Trump returned to office, the DOJ shut down a national database used to track misconduct by federal law enforcement officers, which the president had supported during his first term.[209]

Police brutality and misconduct have become wedge issues for organized labor. While union membership has been anemic in most sectors, it has been surging in law enforcement. When Republican Governor Scott Walker of Wisconsin led a successful drive in 2011 to eliminate collective bargaining for most of the state's public employees, he shrewdly won the support of the police and firefighters by carving out exceptions for their unions. Pressure has been mounting for the labor movement to distance itself from police unions and associations. In the summer of 2015, the United Auto Workers local that represents over thirteen thousand teaching assistants and other student workers on the University of California campuses became the first local to demand that the American Federation of Labor–Congress of Industrial Organizations (AFL-CIO), the country's leading labor organization, expel the International Union of Police Associations (IUPA), the federation's only all-police union.[210]

The AFL-CIO has remained firmly behind police unions, even in the wake of political uproars over police use of excessive force. Shortly after Michael Brown was killed in 2014, AFL-CIO President Richard Trumka called for demilitarization of the police, ending mass incarceration, and a reckoning with the labor movement's checkered record on racial matters. But he also made a sympathetic nod to the police, saying, "Think about what it means to be a police officer in this country where violence is so often the norm."[211]

The recommendations of the AFL-CIO's Task Force on Racial Justice, established in June 2020 after the murder of George Floyd, were tepid. The task force framed the problem as one of a few bad apples, not a deeply flawed system in need of radical change. Its central recommendation was a program designed to facilitate better self-policing by police officers.[212] The task force did not side with the growing chorus demanding meaningful independent oversight and sanctions of police departments and their officers.[213]

Some states and jurisdictions have moved to curtail the power of police unions. Among other things, they have sought to restrict the power of police unions to negotiate over disciplinary and oversight measures; to limit the ability of arbitrators to overturn disciplinary actions; to repeal measures that seal the disciplinary records of police officers; and to require police officers to report or prevent misconduct.[214]

The uproar over US policing has not deterred police groups from pushing to expand their autonomy through "Blue Lives Matter" bills that would cast police as an independent protected class, criminalize actions such as insulting an officer, and treat attacks on officers as hate crimes.[215] Since the mid-1970s, more than twenty states have adopted some version of the Law Enforcement Officers' Bill of Rights, which grants special legal protections to police officers under investigation for misconduct. Lawmakers in some states have pushed to repeal such measures, while others have moved to enact or strengthen them.[216]

Police unions and associations have donated troves of cash at the local, state, and federal levels to defeat reform-minded prosecutors and other candidates and to crush legislation that would rein in their clout.[217] With the political ascent of Donald Trump, police unions and associations have moved even closer to the Republican Party. The National Association of Police Organizations (NAPO) endorsed the Obama-Biden ticket in 2008 and 2012, thanks to Biden's long history of championing law enforcement.[218] But NAPO abandoned the Democratic ticket during Donald Trump's three runs for the White House.[219] The Fraternal Order of Police, the largest police association, representing 350,000 members, has not endorsed a Democrat for president since Bill Clinton in 1996. The IUPA broke with the AFL-CIO to endorse Trump in 2020 and 2024.[220]

The political activities of the police extend far beyond campaign contributions and electoral endorsements. The "policing machine," as described by sociologist Tony Cheng, has a remarkable ability to co-opt community organizations and create an illusion of public input as it steers public sentiment away from meaningful institutional reforms of the police.[221] Civil rights lawyer Alec Karakatsanis has charted the vast system of "copaganda." He documents how police, prosecutors, prison administrators, and other members of the "punishment bureaucracy" induce a complicit media to narrow the understanding of threats to public safety to crimes committed by the poorest and most vulnerable members of society while letting the most powerful off the hook; to "manufacture crises and panics about this narrow category of threats"; and to promote increased spending on police, prisons, and the like "while downplaying the connection between safety and the material, structural conditions of people's lives."[222]

Racial Bias, Racial Discrimination, and Police Killings of Civilians

Systemic and structural factors, some of them related to race, some of them not, contribute to such high levels of police violence.[223] As political scientist Cedric Johnson argues, focusing on racism as the main problem of the police and antiracism as the main solution "truncates the policing problem as one of endemic antiblackness." Doing so, among other things, cuts off potential allies, including victims of police abuse who are not Black.[224]

The research findings are mixed regarding whether police forces that are racially diverse engender community trust, lawful policing, and fewer police killings.[225] The DOJ's *Ferguson Report* cited research findings that African American officers are less prejudiced than white ones are. But it also noted that Black police officers are just as likely to fire their weapons, to arrest people, to have public complaints lodged against them, and, in some cases, to harbor prejudices against Black citizens.[226] The effectiveness of implicit bias training in curbing police bias, let alone police brutality and excessive use of force, remains unproven.[227] Some research suggests that, under certain conditions, training in implicit bias reinforces racial stereotypes rather than countering them.[228]

The implicit or explicit biases of individual officers appear to be less consequential in determining rates and patterns of excessive use of force than are other characteristics related to individual officers, the rules and policies of their departments, the communities they police, and the victims of deadly force. Officers with higher levels of education (especially four-year degrees) are less likely to use force and are more likely to deploy lower levels of force when they do.[229] Police with prior instances of misconduct and civilian complaints are more prone to using excessive force.[230] So are police officers who have just come from an emotionally demanding situation—such as a suicide or a domestic abuse incident involving a child.[231]

Police officers with military experience are more likely to use force, discharge their guns, and kill people.[232] An estimated 19 to 28 percent of US police officers have current or prior military service, compared to around 7 percent of the general population.[233] Today and historically, US police officers have been disproportionately drawn from the military.[234] This is partly thanks to special government programs and preferential hiring requirements that channel veterans into law enforcement.[235] For example, in 2012 as the unemployment rate for veterans hovered at 12 percent, the Justice Department allocated $100 million to facilitate employment of post-9/11 veterans in law enforcement.[236]

As for systemic and structural factors, states that score higher on racism indexes (which include socioeconomic indicators) and neighborhoods, cities, and states with higher levels of racial segregation tend to have greater racial disparities in the deadly use of force and more police killings of Black and Latino men.[237] Communities with higher rates of socioeconomic disadvantages have higher rates of police killings.[238] So do jurisdictions and communities with higher rates of violence—"but only up to a point."[239] The US homicide rate is three to six times the homicide rate of affluent democracies. But the magnitude of lethal police violence in the United States compared to peer countries is much greater than the differentials between homicide rates in the United States and these other countries. This suggests that higher rates of overall violence do not on their own explain why police in the United States are so exceptionally lethal.[240]

Another key structural factor is gun ownership. The United States has the highest rate of firearm possession in the world by far. Yemen is way behind in second place.[241] Numerous studies have concluded that people who possess a weapon, especially a firearm, are at the greatest risk of being shot by the police.[242] Results are mixed on whether the police are more or less likely to shoot armed or unarmed African American people than armed or unarmed white people, especially once other characteristics of the community and the victim (including rate of arrests for weapons charges and violent crimes) are factored in.[243]

After controlling for levels of violent crime, states with higher levels of gun ownership—both legal and illegal—have significantly higher rates of civilians shot and killed by the police, especially armed civilians.[244] Higher levels of gun ownership in the United States are associated with not only state-by-state variations in killings *by* police but also state-by-state variations in killings *of* police. Officers in states with high rates of gun ownership are three times more likely to be killed than those in states with low rates of gun ownership.[245] This may help explain why the Western mountain states have some of the highest rates of police use of deadly force.[246]

Three decades ago, police organizations were supportive of modest gun control measures, such as banning military-style assault weapons and requiring licenses to carry concealed weapons. For a variety of racial and political reasons, the police are now more closely allied with pro-gun-rights groups, including the National Rifle Association (NRA), even though wider private ownership and circulation of guns in the United States put officers at greater risk of harm.[247]

The evidence is conclusive that certain institutional differences between police departments, especially regarding training and rules for the use of deadly force, are highly consequential in explaining variations over time and place in police killings. Between the late 1960s and early aughts, the national rate of officer-involved killings plummeted, largely because of a precipitous decline in police killings of African American people.[248] As a result, the Black-white ratio in these fatalities also fell. After rising sharply in the 1960s to hit a peak of 10 to 1 in 1969, the Black-white disparity in police killings plunged. Over the past two decades, it has held reasonably steady at just over 2 to 1.[249] The imposition of certain standards for the use of lethal force and more stringent training and other requirements for police officers drove this decline. Policy differences in these key areas help explain why certain police departments are far more deadly than others today.[250]

Take the case of Philadelphia. A dozen years ago, it had one of the deadliest police forces of any major US city, second only to Phoenix. In response to a federal review that Philadelphia Police Commissioner Charles Ramsey requested in 2013, the DOJ issued a scathing report two years later. The federal investigation attributed Philadelphia's high number of fatal police shootings (in many years, more deaths than in New York City, which has over five times as many residents) to poor training, confusing and inconsistent standards for the use of force, and a lack of transparency.[251] In the aftermath of changes instituted under Ramsey, police killings fell significantly. Between 2015 and 2023, they averaged about four per year in Philadelphia, down from an average of about eleven per year in the five years prior to the DOJ report.[252] This is a major achievement. But it needs to be considered in an international context. In 2019, police in the United Kingdom, which has nearly seventy times the population of Philadelphia, killed three people.[253]

The Police and People with Mental Health Problems

One of the biggest risk factors for police use of excessive force is mental illness. People with mental health problems are sixteen times more likely to be killed by the police than other people approached or stopped by the authorities.[254] At least one in four people killed by police—and perhaps as many as one in two—was grappling with a mental health issue at the time of their death.[255] The lower levels of mental health services in rural communities and the West coupled with the wider availability of firearms likely help explain why police killings are more common in Western states.[256]

With the radical cutbacks in the social safety net, including psychiatric beds, community mental health centers, and public housing, the role of the police and the criminal legal system in managing people with mental health disorders has expanded massively over the last five decades. Deinstitutionalization beginning in the 1970s emptied mental health hospitals, but the promised robust system of community mental health treatment centers never materialized to take their place. Deinstitutionalization unfolded at a time when other critical support services for people with mental health illnesses—affordable housing, health care, jobs programs, and disability payments—were under attack and being dismantled or scaled back. This perfect storm contributed to an increase in contact between people with mental health problems and law enforcement.[257]

This contact also increased as more departments embraced "broken windows" policing. This controversial approach to policing, in which officers increase arrests and sanctions for low-level offenses such as public urination, panhandling, or jumping subway turnstiles, was premised on the theory that taking a harder line on these quality-of-life offenses would reduce more serious crimes. This claim revolutionized policing in many departments even though it did not withstand rigorous evaluation.[258]

Relatives and members of the community often feel they have no option other than to call 911 when someone is experiencing serious mental health distress. But police officers are ill equipped to be the first responders to these crises or even to everyday mental health problems. Even police officers with more training in mental health and de-escalation cannot make meaningful clinical assessments of someone in the field.[259] Furthermore, most communities lack adequate mental health services for police to refer someone to, especially individuals in crisis. County jails have become the primary facility to house people with mental illnesses in most states. The

Los Angeles County jail is now the largest mental health facility in the country.[260]

Shouting commands and brandishing weapons—routine behavior for US police officers—can spur "a mentally ill person to flee or become more aggressive."[261] People having delusions or a psychotic episode may be less able to hear, understand, or comply with commands from officers, which likely helps explain why they are more likely to resist the police.[262] Police are no more likely to use force against people with mental health problems but are significantly more likely to escalate the levels of force deployed against them, including pepper spray, batons, Tasers, and guns.[263] Even after controlling for other factors, such as criminal history and substance abuse, the police are more likely to shoot people with mental health problems who are resisting arrest than other people who are resisting arrest.[264]

Some US jurisdictions have created specialized teams of police officers to deal with mental health crises. Sometimes these teams include mental health workers. But unlike in Canada and elsewhere, US mental health workers are typically not in the driver's seat, with the police standing by to assist only "if absolutely necessary."[265] Some US cities are experimenting with mental health crisis teams composed entirely of civilians and no police officers.[266]

Most mental-health-related calls to police do not involve crisis situations. More typically they involve people with chronic mental health and other health problems who need services (including anything from a shower and change of clothes to housing and substance abuse treatment) and the conflicts and other difficulties created because of the lack of these services.[267] Some US municipalities have established specialized units of police officers to oversee outreach for such assistance. But deploying armed police officers for such tasks is expensive compared to using civilian workers trained in mental health, public health, and social services. Furthermore, civilian outreach workers are better suited than police officers are to build trust and long-term relationships with people who have complex mental, physical, and social problems. The "implied threat of coercive response that police pose drives" these individuals "further into isolation, not into proper care."[268]

Systemic Wrongdoing

Police violence and the militarization of the police are widespread problems in the United States. The lack of comprehensive and reliable databases on police brutality and deadly use of force has crippled research in this area. What we do know is that, when it comes to violence inflicted by the police, the United States is in a class all its own compared to wealthy democracies and to many countries in the Global South. Focusing on how individual police officers fail people in need obscures how the system fails people in need and also individual officers. To reduce police violence, some experts contend that law enforcement needs to learn from the experiences of the airline industry and hospital sector, which do not stop at identifying an individual culprit. When a plane goes down or a deadly infection breaks out in a neonatal unit, mandatory investigations are conducted to consider what systemic flaws may have contributed to the tragedy.[269]

Systemic reviews are not mandatory in many police departments. They are conducted on an idiosyncratic, ad hoc basis, usually in the case of a high-profile killing of a civilian. The hundreds of other "routine" police killings each year receive little public or official scrutiny. Systemic reviews are no substitute for disciplining and prosecuting police officers when they break the law. But they do have "the effect of spreading the blame so that individual officers are *not* the only ones held responsible" and forced to bear the consequences of killing someone.[270]

The focus on racial disparities in police killings contributes to a narrow understanding of the proximate and structural factors that have fostered such lethal and ungovernable police forces. The proximate factors include the dearth of data and research on police violence; how US police officers are trained and equipped to be "warrior cops"; permissive standards for the use of force; the political clout of police unions and associations; and the shield of qualified immunity.

Changes in administrative policy can reduce excessive use of force—but only up to a point.[271] It is not enough to improve training and impose stricter use-of-force policies. Or to identify the Derek Chauvins in law enforcement and then fire them before they kill someone. Or to aggressively prosecute police officers who kill without compelling cause. More far-reaching reforms are necessary. Chauvin's knee was the immediate cause of Floyd's death. A key underlying cause was the overemphasis in Minneapolis and police departments across the country on apprehending people for minor offenses—in George Floyd's case, an arrest on suspicion of using a counterfeit $20 bill—at the cost of focusing on crime prevention, community engagement, and problem solving.[272]

Furthermore, changes in administrative policy will not fix the failing social safety net and other structural factors that contribute to exceptional rates of police killings and other types of violence. We know that jurisdictions and neighborhoods with higher levels of socioeconomic disadvantage, violent street crime, and racial segregation tend to have higher rates of police use of deadly force. So do states with higher levels of gun ownership and lower levels of social services. And people in rural communities tend to be at greater risk than residents of large urban areas.

Misunderstandings about the proximate reasons why US police forces are so deadly and violent have yielded shortsighted solutions to reduce this state violence, including Band-aids centered on diversifying police departments and increased training in implicit and explicit racial biases, as detailed in this chapter. So have misunderstandings about or neglect of deeper institutional and historical factors that have fostered the exceptional lethalness and danger-ousness of US law enforcement, as discussed in the next chapter.

The historical legacies of slavery, white supremacy, Jim Crow, and the "new Jim Crow" help explain why US police are so deadly and why they dispropor-tionately kill African American people. But additional historical developments that have received less attention are also culprits. These include the country's long and bloody history of suppressing insurgencies and rebellions at home and abroad as it rapidly industrialized and sought to build and defend a global empire, which is discussed in the next chapter. Ironically, a country born out of a suspicion of state power and standing armies ended up creating multiple layers of public and private police forces and a massive military that operate with enormous autonomy from the political authorities and the public. The United States must reckon with how this past reverberates in the present if it is to move forward to a more peaceful future without such exceptional levels of all kinds of violence.

4

Deadly and Professional

THE ORIGINS AND DEVELOPMENT
OF US POLICE FORCES

There is no way that we can fix policing without fixing America. The institution of policing is really America itself, this country that is still struggling to deal with race and class and inequity. You can't divorce the police from that. And so the flaws the country has, the police will display in a more virulent way because they have guns and are in people's faces.

—RAS BARAKA, MAYOR OF NEWARK, NEW JERSEY[1]

OVER THE last decade or so, the United States has been undergoing a controversial public reckoning with how its history of white supremacy shaped law enforcement and other institutions. In the case of the police, attention has centered on how slave patrols and fugitive slave laws fortified a brutal, violent, racialized, quasi-private system of social control, and how a succession of institutions established after the Civil War that harkened back to slavery—including the "Black Codes," convict leasing, Jim Crow, and the "new Jim Crow"—were the main forebearers of today's police forces.[2] But other historical developments that have drawn less public attention were also critical in forging US police forces that today routinely deploy excessive and lethal force with little legal or public accountability.[3]

Several historical developments spanning the period from the end of the Civil War to the aftermath of 9/11 have left their mark on policing in the United States. They have contributed to the lethalness and unaccountability of US police forces and fueled other types of violence in the United States. This chapter examines several of them, including how private interests and public authorities responded to the social and economic upheavals of the late nineteenth and early twentieth centuries as the country rapidly urbanized and industrialized; the emergence of the United States as a global and imperial power following the Spanish-American War in 1898; the impact of the Cold War on US police forces; how the United States sought to crush left-leaning insurgencies in Vietnam and other countries in the 1960s and 1970s while contending with a spike in political rebellions and violent street crime back home; and the consolidation of a new model of hypermilitarized policing in the aftermath of 9/11.

Localism and Decentralization

Three defining features of US police forces that help shield them from outside scrutiny and control—entrenched localism, decentralization, and claims of professionalism—have deep historical roots. The localism and decentralization of US police date back to the establishment of the first municipal police forces nearly two centuries ago. Beginning in the 1830s, massive disorders, including gang warfare, racial and ethnic riots, and Election Day mob violence, routinely gripped Northern cities.[4] These urban upheavals were catalysts to establish public police forces, first in major cities and then elsewhere in the United States.

Urban reformers in America who wanted to model their new police forces on the highly centralized, nationalized, and elitist London Metropolitan Police established in 1829 were not successful because the political context was radically different. Founded before the emergence of widespread suffrage in the United Kingdom, London's new police force was expected to be a neutral arm of the national government and insulated from local control and parochial interests. By contrast, the debates over policing in the United States unfolded at a time when universal suffrage for white men had become the norm. With the election of Andrew Jackson as president in 1828 and the dawning of the Age of the Common Man, electoral politics hinged on intense partisan competition between political parties with strong local ties. Established in a highly partisan atmosphere in a country with a long history of local governance, self-rule, and suspicion of centralized government, the new municipal police forces in the United States tended to be highly parochial and decentralized.[5]

As a consequence, police in the United States had much closer ties to the communities they patrolled than English police did. They were responsible for a wider range of functions—everything from maintaining weather records to providing temporary housing to running soup kitchens. United States police departments also mirrored and reinforced local partisan, ethnic, and racial cleavages. Ward leaders in major cities used the police force to provide employment and upward mobility for their supporters and to consolidate their political bases. Operating with little outside supervision and training in a highly decentralized system, the cop on the beat in the United States had more discretion on the job, which facilitated corruption and brutality.[6]

The rapid industrialization and urbanization in the late nineteenth and early twentieth centuries brought additional upheavals and strains—so much so that some business and political leaders feared the United States might be on the brink of revolution and social collapse.[7] Major industrialists and other business leaders had widespread doubts that the urban police forces, with their strong local and partisan ties, could be counted on to suppress the upsurge of socialists, anarchists and, especially, workers seeking to form unions. They began to invest heavily in private police forces, including the notorious Pinkerton National Detective Agency, to infiltrate unions, mobilize strikebreakers, provide guards, and intimidate workers.

The US government also turned to private police forces. The Department of Justice (DOJ), established in 1871, lacked sufficient resources to investigate and prosecute violations of federal law, so it contracted with the Pinkertons for assistance. The Pinkertons' involvement in violently suppressing the 1892 Homestead strike with the help of the National Guard sparked a series of congressional investigations about using private police agencies to preserve public order and break strikes and unions. Critics, including leaders of the surging Populist movement, charged that the Pinkertons represented a throwback to the lawlessness of the Middle Ages, when the absence of effective public authorities spurred the establishment of private feudal armies. In 1893, Congress enacted the Anti-Pinkerton Act, which restricted the federal government in hiring mercenaries and private security agencies such as the Pinkertons.[8] Although private police forces came under fire, they were not vanquished. At the start of the twentieth century, the Pinkertons were still the largest private police force in the world.

As the Pinkertons came under harsh public scrutiny in the late nineteenth century, government reformers associated with the Progressive movement remained uneasy about public police forces. They were aghast at the patronage and partisanship endemic to municipal police forces. Political machines controlled the hiring, promotion, transfer, and discipline of officers. Whenever city hall changed hands, the police department usually changed hands as well.[9]

The Progressives were alarmed at burgeoning municipal corruption as cities moved to concentrate brothels, bars, and gambling establishments in certain neighborhoods. The formation of red-light districts created lucrative opportunities for the police. Officers hauled in bribes, kickbacks, and protection money, some of which they funneled to local political machines.[10]

Urban elites and industrialists did not want to pay the taxes necessary for regular public police forces and to grant them a larger role beyond harassing impoverished city residents.[11] But as general strikes and other worker unrest started to overwhelm private security forces, industrialists and other elites began "to see the virtues of a permanent, well-trained, paramilitary force speaking the neutral language of law and order."[12]

Progressives started calling for more "professional" police insulated from local politics and corruption.[13] The solution that emerged was to add more layers of public police forces; "professionalize" local police through military-style training, techniques, and organization; and retain the largely unregulated private police forces and guards that corporations relied on to suppress workers and otherwise protect their political and economic interests. Furthermore, as moral crusades against liquor, sex work, illegal drugs, and other alleged vices swept the country during the Progressive era, cities relocated their red-light districts to Black neighborhoods. Over the course of the twentieth century, "white moral outrage" over police corruption periodically flared up.[14] White so-called reformers demanded police crackdowns that criminalized residents of these neighborhoods and that targeted sex work, interracial relationships, queer relationships, gay and lesbian bars, and allegations of promiscuity.[15] All of this diverted public attention from police corruption.

Individual states also began creating statewide police forces to supplement the local police. The hope was that the state police, staffed by officers recruited from across the state, would be reliable allies in quelling labor disputes because they had fewer ties to local police and communities. States also invested heavily in National Guard units housed in imposing armories built in cities across the country, figuring that they would be less reticent than local police to fire on striking workers and to contain the "dangerous classes."[16]

Police played a divisive role in the early history of organized labor, breaking strikes and warring on labor unions and their supporters in the nineteenth and early twentieth centuries.[17] In 1897, the nascent American Federation of Labor (AFL) rejected a petition from a group of Cleveland police officers seeking a union charter. The federation declared, "It is not within the province of the trade union movement to especially organize policemen, no more than to organize militiamen, as both policemen and militiamen are often controlled by forces inimical to the labor movement."[18]

During this period, legislators and the courts relied on the police to enforce court injunctions and other measures designed to curtail labor unions by criminalizing strikes, boycotts, and picketing.[19] Police ruthlessly beat and fired on workers demonstrating against unemployment and poor working conditions and seeking to form unions. They also raided newspapers sympathetic to workers and radical causes and set up special "red squads" in the 1910s and 1920s to blackmail, spy on, and crush rival politicians, unionists, anarchists, opponents of World War I, socialists, communists, civil rights activists, and other political dissenters.[20] Veterans who had served in the US war in the Philippines were key figures in the establishment of these red squads.

Policing, Professionalism, and the US War in the Philippines

Claims of so-called professionalism have served as powerful shields to preserve the autonomy of police in the United States. When lawmakers and members of the public have periodically pushed for more control over law enforcement, promises to double down on professionalization have held them at bay. What constitutes professionalism for US policing is rooted in a military model derived from the country's extensive experience suppressing working people and other so-called dangerous classes at home and establishing and maintaining an empire overseas. The United States has a long history of conflating professionalization with militarization rather than with alternatives, such as nonviolent de-escalation.

From the early twentieth century onward, reform-minded police chiefs shrewdly embraced the banner of professionalism, which helped to disarm their critics. In doing so, they garnered more resources for their departments while also carving out wide autonomy to police themselves with little control and oversight from state and federal authorities. But what did professionalism actually mean in practice?

These early debates about professionalism and police reform unfolded while the United States was emerging as a global and imperial power and as the country was fiercely divided over its future role in the world. The initial embrace of professionalism was shaped and bolstered by the experience of the US Army in suppressing rebellions and independence movements overseas in the Philippines and elsewhere beginning around the turn of the twentieth

century. Initially, the US move to acquire overseas territories was highly controversial with lawmakers and the public. But the anti-imperialists ultimately
lost out to the expansionists, setting the country on a new path of empire
building overseas with a fortified army and navy.

Veterans of these overseas military campaigns were well positioned to lever-
age their military experience and credentials to play pivotal roles in the unfolding debates about police reform back home, as well as in the mission to bolster
Jim Crow. The US conquest of the Philippines also shaped US drug policy
back home. The United States inherited a legal opium regime in the Philippines at a time of growing concern that permissive state and municipal laws
were failing to contain narcotics addiction in the United States. Federal lawmakers responded with passage of the Harrison Act in 1914, which ramped up
Washington's role in drug control.[21]

In February 1899, a deeply divided US Senate narrowly approved the Treaty
of Paris to settle the Spanish-American War. Spain ceded the Philippines,
Puerto Rico, and Guam to the United States and relinquished all claims of
sovereignty over Cuba. A massive anti-imperialism movement emerged to
ensure that the US victory in the Spanish-American War "did not transform
the United States into a colonial power." Major public figures spoke out against
annexing these islands. By mid-1899, the nascent Anti-Imperialist League had
hundreds of thousands of members; and new groups, such as the Colored
National Anti-Imperialist League, were sprouting up in several cities, creating
a massive antiwar movement.[22]

As the anti-imperialists had predicted, US annexation stoked a rebellion in
the Philippines, and the United States became involved in a full-scale war to
crush the archipelago's independence movement. For a time, government censorship kept the lid on what the "disciplined" US soldiers were doing. As
censorship broke down, an uproar ensued with reports that US soldiers were
abusing Filipinos, including administering the "water cure," a form of torture
dating back to the Spanish Inquisition when it was used to punish heretics. Filipinos had learned the "water cure," in which water was forced down someone's
throat to simulate drowning, from Spanish soldiers and then passed it on to the
US military in 1899. The US military and supporters of the war in the Philippines dismissed reports of US soldiers administering the "water cure" and
committing other abuses as the actions of a few bad apples.[23] (The "water cure"
became infamous once again a century later when the United States deployed
"waterboarding" in its global war on terror.)

The fate of the Philippines was a leading issue in the 1900 presidential election, in which Democrat William Jennings Bryan faced off once again against Republican William McKinley, who had won the 1896 election. The anti-imperialist movement demanded that the United States withdraw its troops and grant the Philippines independence. But leading expansionists, most notably Theodore Roosevelt, McKinley's running mate, insisted that the US military ramp up its efforts to suppress the independence movement.

Even though the Democratic platform stridently opposed expansionism in the strongest language of any major party platform up to then or since, Bryan's candidacy divided the anti-imperialists.[24] Some of them detested and feared Bryan's economic policies.[25] Steel magnate Andrew Carnegie, an outspoken anti-imperialist, could not bring himself to vote for Bryan, who had warned four years earlier when he ran on the Democratic-Populist ticket not to "crucify mankind on a cross of gold." Carnegie declared that while McKinley "stands for war and violence abroad," the Democratic presidential candidate "stands for those scourges at home."[26]

The anti-imperialist movement and Bryan's candidacy were enfeebled by not only economic antagonisms but also racial ones. The Anti-Imperialist League was a direct descendant of the abolitionist movement. One of its leading figures, Moorfield Storey, would later become the first president of the National Association for the Advancement of Colored People (NAACP). At the time, Ida B. Wells, Booker T. Washington, and other prominent African Americans drew parallels between foreign wars abroad and oppression at home in the first major mobilization of African American people on a foreign policy issue. Mark Twain, the country's most famous writer, became the country's best known and most vitriolic opponent of colonization, denouncing the subjugation, racism, and exploitation on which it was built. He sarcastically suggested that the flag for the Philippines should be a modeled on "our usual flag, with the white stripes painted black and the stars replaced by a skull and cross-bones."[27]

Other leading foes of imperialism declared their opposition in starkly racist terms. Samuel Gompers, head of the AFL, said he feared that annexing overseas lands would open "the flood-gates of immigration" to "hordes of Chinese and the semi-savage races" and would imperil the embryonic labor movement.[28] Senator Benjamin Tillman (D-SC), a champion of Jim Crow, denounced annexing islands populated by "tens of millions of the colored race, one-half or more of whom are barbarians of the lowest type."[29]

The 1900 election was a referendum on empire, and the imperialists re-soundingly won as McKinley's supporters successfully exploited the racial and economic divisions that enfeebled the anti-imperialist camp. Backed by an unprecedented campaign war chest of corporate contributions, McKinley was resoundingly reelected. After the election, McKinley unleashed the US Army to carry out a scorched-earth campaign in the Philippines. General Arthur MacArthur, commander of the US forces in the Philippines, obliged. He issued new orders to kill captured insurgents, burn towns and villages, cut off the food supplies, and herd villagers into fortified towns or camps where they could be closely monitored.[30] Reports of torture and other atrocities committed by the US Army in the Philippines provoked an initial public outcry. But it was quelled by sympathetic media accounts and an investigation by the US Senate that resulted in a whitewashed report in 1902 that largely absolved the American forces.[31]

Reports of atrocities persisted, however. Five years after the Senate report, W.E.B. Du Bois wrote a letter to Moorfield Storey of the NAACP inquiring whether a photograph in an Anti-Imperialist League pamphlet could be enlarged. Du Bois told Storey that the image of US soldiers casually standing over a trench filled with the corpses of Filipinos killed in the infamous Bud Dajo Massacre of 1906 was "the most illuminating thing I have ever seen." He declared that the photograph should be displayed in classrooms "to impress upon the students what wars and especially Wars of Conquest really mean."[32] Major General Leonard Wood, commander of the US troops that massacred as many as one thousand Filipinos, including women and children who had taken refuge in the volcanic crater at Bud Dajo, apparently witnessed the photographer taking the picture. He "asked to see the negative which, strangely enough, (!) he dropped and let break while handing it back to the photographer," according to the secretary of the Anti-Imperialist League. Unbeknownst to Wood, the photographer had another negative of the scene.[33]

The United States did not rely on brute force alone to conquer the Philippines. The archipelago was a natural laboratory for pioneering the establishment of an expansive surveillance state with the help of state-of-the art technology, a network of contacts and informers, a local police force of Filipino people under the control of the US Army, and the creation of new institutions to centralize the collection and use of intelligence information.[34] The aim was not only to suppress the independence movement but also to manipulate public opinion and empower local elites who supported US civilian and military leaders. Captain Ralph Van Deman, who served in the Philippines and directed its Division of Military Information, which gathered massive amounts of counterintelligence on Filipino citizens, was later nicknamed the father of US military intelligence. He had a formative role in the establishment of stand-alone intelligence organizations during and after World War I. These organizations were the progenitors of the full-blown centralized national security state that President Harry Truman and the US Congress brought into being with the National Security Act of 1947, which established the National Security Council (NSC) and the Central Intelligence Agency (CIA).[35]

Despite numerous reports of atrocities and other abuses, the expansionists vanquished the anti-imperialist movement, thanks to the splintering of the Anti-Imperialist League on racial and economic shoals in the 1900 election; the US Army's scorched-earth campaign; the capture of the guerilla movement's leader in the Philippines; a string of military victories for US forces that buoyed the patriotic, rally 'round the flag appeals of military and civilian leaders (foremost among them the indomitable Theodore Roosevelt, who became president after McKinley was assassinated in 1901); and the outsized political influence of a cluster of business leaders who sought to exploit new overseas markets in the Philippines and elsewhere.[36]

Another blow for the anti-imperialists was a series of US Supreme Court decisions in 1901 that sanctioned imposing essentially martial rule indefinitely on overseas territories annexed by the United States. In what became known as the Insular Cases, the court ruled that people living in the Philippines, Guam, Puerto Rico, and Cuba did not enjoy the protections of the US Constitution, including due process, free speech, a free press, and the right to vote. The court carved out what one justice called "'practically two national governments,' one bound by the Bill of Rights, the other not," in a decision that echoed the 1896 *Plessy v. Ferguson* decision, which upheld racial segregation.[37]

United States expansionism also won out because it was a powerful salve to heal the political wounds of the Civil War and redeem the South. The US war in the Philippines created a pact between the North and the South that fueled US expansionism abroad and white supremacy at home.[38] Dispatching Southern troops to pacify Indigenous people on the frontier shortly after the Civil War and sending troops abroad to pacify the Philippines and other overseas territories allowed the South to rehabilitate the Confederacy's image.[39] Expansionism allowed the South to redeem the military values and symbols idealized in Southern political culture, as well as the "Lost Cause" itself.[40] During military campaigns stretching from the Spanish-American War to the

Korean War half a century later, federal troops widely brandished the Confederate flag, carrying it into battle and sewing it on their uniforms.[41]

Expansionists argued for denying people in the Philippines and other overseas territories ruled by the US military the right to vote, let alone self-determination and independence, on the grounds that they were not ready for full citizenship—and might never be. Their claims, which echoed antebellum arguments in defense of US slavery and the views of John Stuart Mill and other British liberals in defense of the British empire, were repurposed to fortify Jim Crow.[42] At the time, Southern states were busy rewriting their constitutions and imposing new voting and other restrictions that disenfranchised millions of African American people, as well as millions of poor white people, with the demise of Reconstruction.

Professionalism and the War Back Home

By the time President Theodore Roosevelt prematurely declared victory on July 4, 1902, hundreds of thousands of people in the Philippines had perished of war-related causes. Thousands more would die over the next decade as the US Army finally subdued the archipelago's outlying islands.[43] The US war in the Philippines is the country's second longest after the twenty-year war in Afghanistan that ended in August 2021 with the rout of US-backed forces.

American soldiers returning home from military campaigns in the Philippines and elsewhere were well positioned to play leading roles in bolstering Jim Crow, answering the call to reform and professionalize US police forces, and curbing dissent. Veterans were central players in obliterating the last vestiges of Reconstruction, including spearheading the coup and massacre in November 1898 that ousted the elected multiracial coalition governing Wilmington, North Carolina. They also were at the forefront of the revival of the Ku Klux Klan in the 1910s and 1920s; in meting out vigilante "frontier justice" to African Americans, Mexican Americans, and other groups; and in the establishment of the brutal and militarized US Border Patrol as part of the 1924 Immigration Act, which sharply curtailed immigration to the United States.[44]

Leading proselytizers of police professionalization in the early twentieth century had served with the US Army in the Philippines, and many police departments were led by police chiefs who were veterans.[45] These police commanders singled out their military service overseas as formative in how they thought about policing back home. August Vollmer, "considered the grandfather of US police professionalization," enlisted in the US Army in 1898 and got his "first taste of law enforcement in the Philippines."[46] Decades later he told a Los Angeles Police Department (LAPD) audience, "For years, ever since the Spanish-American War days, I've studied military tactics and used them to good effect in rounding up crooks." He continued, "After all we're conducting a war, a war against the enemies of society and we must never forget that."[47]

Vollmer and other so-called reformers repatriated elements of the overseas counterinsurgency campaigns back to the United States, where they became important building blocks to professionalize local police forces. They advocated for collecting extensive records on local populations, including fingerprints, to aid in apprehending criminal suspects and keeping tabs on the community; establishing highly centralized, hierarchical command structures to oversee police units dispersed around a city so as to disrupt the relationship between local political bosses and the police officers who patrolled their wards; and investing in rigorous training for new recruits and experienced officers, especially in the use of firearms.[48]

In the decades after the US war in the Philippines, torture became a standard operating procedure in many police departments in the United States. In 1931, the country's first national commission on law enforcement documented the widespread use of the "third degree" to obtain information, extract confessions, and mete out punishment. The National Commission on Law Observance and Enforcement (better known as the Wickersham Commission, after its chair, George Wickersham) concluded that US police officers routinely used many of the tactics deployed by US armed forces in the war in the Philippines, including stress positions, beatings, psychological torture, and the infamous "water cure."[49] But the Wickersham Report had little impact on policy. Growing concerns about the Depression and the coming of war in Europe overshadowed its findings.

Vollmer, who became president of the International Association of Chiefs of Police (IACP) in 1926, initially advocated a dual role for professional police—serving as soldiers in waging war against criminals and as quasi social workers in addressing the needs of the local community. This approach harkened back to the experience of the United States in the Philippines, where the US Army deployed the stick of its scorched-earth campaign alongside the promise of social uplift to quell the rebellion and independence movement. But Vollmer's many disciples and ultimately Vollmer himself sided with professionalization—not social uplift—based on a military model insulated from civilian and political oversight and control. These reformers emphasized how discipline was key to professionalism and to carving out wide autonomy for the police to operate free of public scrutiny and accountability. Promises to maintain a chain of command, discipline wayward officers, and provide ongoing training for police officers helped to disarm critics calling for greater civilian and political oversight of the police.[50]

Veterans played pivotal roles in running local police departments and establishing new statewide police forces. In 1905, Pennsylvania created the country's first state police force. It was modeled directly on the US colonial government's Philippine Constabulary, a paramilitary police force. Other state police got their start as highway patrols to deal with the rise of automobiles or as the private paramilitaries of industrialists.[51] Sergeant Jesse Garwood, who served in the Philippines, helped found the Pennsylvania Constabulary, which was nicknamed the "American Cossack" by organized labor. Garwood was renowned for the brutal tactics he deployed in the Philippines, including offering bounties for severed ears and even requiring a potential ally to first bring him the severed head of an alleged criminal.[52] Most of the constabulary's officers were former or current members of the armed forces, including veterans of the Philippine Constabulary.[53] The Pennsylvania Constabulary and some other state police forces became well known for violently suppressing labor actions involving workers who were immigrants.[54]

An Empire of Police Officers

The United States occupied the Philippines for nearly five decades, finally granting it independence in 1946. With nationalist movements sweeping the globe in the aftermath of World War II, direct military rule became less politically tenable. The United States sought alternative means to maintain its informal empire while it was mobilizing to wage what became the Cold War against the Soviet Union. America ended up creating an empire of police officers around the world, which had important boomerang effects on local police forces back home, enhancing their political autonomy while supercharging them with military gear and training, all in the name of professionalization.

Assistance to the military and local police in other countries emerged as a major plank of US foreign policy following World War II.[55] The goal was to mold and co-opt local police in other countries to serve as allies in managing global decolonization and the strains of economic modernization. Local police would become the first line of defense in quelling brewing challenges to political and economic elites overseas who were close US allies.

Back in the United States, rising political unrest and violence were also sources of growing concern as Black veterans of World War II returning home to the South were attacked and killed; as hundreds of disturbances convulsed US cities, including the 1943 rebellion in Detroit that left thirty-four people dead, most of them African American people killed by white police officers; and as workers walked off their jobs in an unprecedented strike wave. The uproar over police brutality and police inaction in the face of organized and wide-scale white violence against African American people and other groups forced President Harry Truman and other so-called race liberals to act. They were the first to raise calls for "law and order" as they advocated for better-trained and better-equipped police forces to protect Black people, Mexican American people, and others from violence meted out by the defenders of Jim Crow and their allies in law enforcement.[56]

In signing the executive order creating the President's Committee on Civil Rights in December 1946, President Truman pointedly referred to the many lynchings and other violent attacks on Black people that were being carried out with the tacit or explicit support of local authorities, including the police.[57] While Truman and other race liberals were concerned about the plight of Black people, they also were troubled by how this violence threatened a central plank of US foreign policy: promoting the United States as a beacon of freedom, democracy, and human rights in waging what would become the decades-long Cold War against the Soviet Union and China.[58]

Truman and other race liberals sought a greatly expanded role for the federal government in the administration of criminal justice and law enforcement at the local and state levels and in the prosecution and punishment of civil rights crimes.[59] They introduced a flurry of bills in the 1940s and 1950s to provide federal assistance to equip, train, and professionalize local and state police forces so that they would be better able to protect Black people and their allies from violence perpetrated by white people defending the color line. They also introduced dozens of bills to federalize many crimes, including antilynching legislation, most of which did not pass.

Southern Democrats opposed to desegregation and civil rights sought to counter race liberals by formulating their own association between civil rights, criminality, and race. They cast their opposition to major civil rights legislation in criminological terms, arguing that segregation upholds law and order, while integration fosters crime. Southern Democrats shrewdly used civil rights bills as vehicles to stiffen and broaden criminal penalties.[60] They also began pushing for enhanced police forces and law enforcement, but for reasons different from those of the race liberals associated with Truman. They sought an expanded criminal legal system to stem what they charged was the increased lawlessness on the part of Black people and their supporters seeking to bring down the Jim Crow regime. But local police departments and opponents of the civil rights movement were also wary of the federalization of crime control. They craved more federal dollars and other federal resources, but they also feared that Washington would tread on local autonomy and states' rights—euphemisms for the Jim Crow regime.[61]

The stalemate over the police was finally broken in June 1968 when President Lyndon B. Johnson signed into law the Omnibus Crime Control and Safe Streets Act. This measure marked an unprecedented expansion of the federal government's role in law enforcement and crime control while preserving wide latitude for the local police. In waging his war on poverty, Johnson had explicitly called for addressing the root causes of crime by investing more in education, health care, welfare, affordable housing, and job programs, not just law enforcement. But this approach was decisively defeated in the final version of the Safe Streets Act. The centerpiece of the act was the establishment of the Law Enforcement Assistance Administration (LEAA), which over the next two decades channeled large and unprecedented amounts of money and other resources to local law enforcement in the name of professionalizing and upgrading the police.[62] Claims by liberal Democrats and Johnson himself that the president had been forced into signing the Safe Streets Act by Republican presidential nominee Richard Nixon and other Republicans campaigning in 1968 on promises to restore law and order obscure how much liberals were responsible for the punitive turn.[63]

Experts on this punitive turn tend to focus on domestic racial, economic, and political factors to explain why the root-causes approach to addressing crime and reducing inequalities lost out to investing in more police and prisons.[64] But foreign policy considerations were a key factor as well. The major shift in US foreign policy over the previous twenty-five years toward suppressing incipient insurgencies abroad by training, professionalizing, and co-opting overseas police forces had helped to prepare the political, ideological, and institutional ground for passage of the Safe Streets Act, with its overweening emphasis on police and law enforcement.

In the years immediately after World War II, assistance to police forces overseas "was always considered at best an adjunct to military assistance."[65] That began to change toward the end of the Eisenhower administration as Democrats in Congress, prodded by Senator John F. Kennedy (D-MA), began to formulate a new blueprint for US foreign policy. With political protests against the United States erupting from Latin America to East Asia during the Eisenhower years, concerns rose that the strategy of building up military forces in other countries might be counterproductive because it aligned the United States with authoritarian regimes. Furthermore, a focus on interstate wars did not address the problem of how to quash domestic political challenges to ruling elites overseas who were close allies of the United States.

The Kennedy administration broke with its predecessor by popularizing the term *counterinsurgency* and making it—not nuclear deterrence—the top priority of its national security policy.[66] His administration identified assistance to foreign police forces, coupled with economic aid for modernization and building up covert US special forces, as the cornerstones of US efforts to preemptively combat counterinsurgencies and communist threats. By these means, US policymakers sought to manage the dismantling of colonial empires while ensuring that rising nationalism and calls for a more equitable postcolonial world did not thwart the Pax Americana of world domination that they envisioned.[67]

After much bureaucratic wrangling, the Kennedy administration succeeded in creating the Office of Public Safety (OPS) in 1962. It was located within the Agency for International Development (AID), the country's leading civilian agency for dispersing overseas economic development assistance. The OPS became the nerve center of US efforts to create an empire of well-trained, professional police officers in other countries to wage war on not only crime but also political subversion. It conflated these two missions because, after all, "Keystone Kops could not catch communists."[68]

Initially promoted as an alternative to direct US military assistance and intervention to combat insurgencies, OPS morphed into a complement to US military interventions, as demonstrated most acutely in the US war in Vietnam. Over the years, OPS assisted police forces in dozens of countries and trained over a million police officers from around the world at academies and local precincts in the United States, as well as in overseas programs. Police assistance was seen as an inexpensive, flexible form of indirect rule to quash incipient insurgencies and political unrest. Champions of overseas police assistance also viewed recruiting, training, and equipping people drawn from the local society to be police officers as a way to deftly sidestep charges of racism and foreign occupation and "spread color-blind Americanism abroad."[69] Similarly, calls to professionalize, upgrade, and diversify polices forces back in the United States were aimed at curtailing the threat that Jim Crow violence posed to winning the Cold War.

The Johnson Administration and the Police State

This model of professionalized policing became a critical component of US national security policy overseas without much fanfare. It also soon became the centerpiece of efforts to stem political unrest and insurgencies back at home. As street crime and political rebellions escalated in the United States during the 1960s, police reformers and researchers who specialized in the science of policing sought to domesticate the lessons promulgated by OPS, as historians Stuart Schrader and Micol Seigel document in riveting detail.[70] They sought ways to tamp down what many leading political and public figures viewed as dangerous counterinsurgencies and communist threats back in the United States.

"Training, technologies, and tactics" deployed to suppress counterinsurgencies, left-leaning political movements, and communism overseas became a part of everyday policing in the United States.[71] As "domestic and international conflicts intensified," Americans across the political spectrum "increasingly used metaphors from or references to the war in Vietnam to organize their understandings of domestic conditions." Conservatives characterized inner cities as jungles that needed to be pacified by warrior cops while the Black Panthers and other insurgent groups portrayed inner cities as colonized war zones in need of liberation.[72] William H. Parker—chief of the LAPD during the 1965 Watts uprising in which police officers killed thirty-one people—bluntly remarked that battling protesters was "very much like fighting the Viet Cong."[73]

The enormous social and political unrest of the 1960s took shape amid a crime shock as the national homicide rate doubled between the mid-1960s and early 1970s and as violent street crime became more geographically concentrated in poor, predominantly Black urban areas.[74] The lack of a consensus on what was driving the alarming increase in violent crime opened up a chasm of political space to redefine the "law-and-order problem" and its solutions. Opponents of civil rights worked "vociferously to conflate crime and disobedience, with its obvious extensions to civil rights."[75]

The mid-1960s escalation of political unrest and the national crime rate coincided with the launch of Lyndon Johnson's Great Society. Critics charged that greater investment in social and other programs did not reduce crime and indeed was contributing to personal pathologies that were reportedly the real roots of crime.[76] They alleged that welfare and other public assistance programs were creating a culture of dependency that fostered delinquent parents and children. Pointing to how rising crime rates coincided with the welfare state expansion of the Great Society, leading conservatives sought to cast doubt on claims from some liberals about the structural causes of crime and poverty. This helped foster so-called laissez-faire racism in which African American people were blamed for Black-white disparities in income, wealth, poverty, and other measures of inequality, including incarceration rates. This bolstered public resistance to policies that sought to ameliorate racism and the structural factors responsible for these disparities.[77]

The escalation in the crime rate took place amid the beginning stages of a vast economic restructuring as the manufacturing base of major urban areas was hollowed out, fueling high rates of unemployment and concentrated poverty. The high rates of violent crimes in these areas prompted some politicians to stoke public fears of a marauding underclass.[78] As popular faith in the government's ability to ensure public safety and manage the economy dwindled, so did confidence in elite expertise to guide government policies, giving wide berth to politicians to define the crime problem and its solutions.[79] All this provided a fertile environment for public fears of crime to escalate and for politicians to exploit those fears even after crime rates began to ebb.

In July 1967, Johnson established the National Advisory Commission on Civil Disorders, headed by Illinois Governor Otto Kerner, to investigate the causes of dozens of rebellions in cities across the United States. In its report released in early 1968, the Kerner Commission, as it became widely known, recommended a huge injection of federal spending and resources to alleviate the racial and economic inequalities that were fueling the unrest and public alarm about a crime wave. Although transforming the police was a second-tier recommendation of the Kerner Report, it became the centerpiece of the Omnibus Crime Control and Safe Streets Act of 1968.[80]

In its final report, the Kerner Commission included near verbatim several paragraphs of testimony from Byron Engle, who was largely unknown to the public but was one of the most influential voices in law enforcement circles at home and abroad.[81] Engle headed OPS from its creation in 1962 until his retirement in 1973, a year before the agency was forced to shut down. In his testimony, Engle extolled the US experience of combatting insurgencies overseas by professionalizing the police, expanding the use of so-called nonlethal weapons in riot control, and conflating battling crime with battling political unrest.

The Safe Streets Act accorded the federal government a new and much larger role in the criminal legal system with the creation of LEAA.[82] This agency was modeled after OPS with the help of Engle and others who had close ties to the program. Under the guise of professionalization, OPS had been fostering the decentralization, militarization, and autonomy of police forces around the world. The OPS served as a model for how to get buy-in from local police forces by directly channeling enormous new resources to them for training and equipment without diminishing their local autonomy. The agency was a source for ideas, resources, and personnel to transform policing in the United States as former OPS personnel took positions advising or working directly for local US police departments.[83]

Aiming to neutralize conservative critics at the time, Johnson Democrats reformulated the law-and-order problem. Liberal Democrats viewed modernizing, professionalizing, and federalizing the criminal justice system as a solution to the problem of state and interpersonal violence directed at African American people and other groups. They also contended that an expanded, professionalized law enforcement apparatus would render the criminal legal system fairer and more legitimate in the eyes of African American people, rendering them less likely to commit crimes.[84]

As the Safe Streets Act moved through Congress, Southern Democrats and their Republican allies outmaneuvered race liberals time and again. They enshrined funding formulas that gave state governments—not cities—enormous leeway to distribute the money as they saw fit through block grant funding from the federal government. In the face of massive urban unrest that was increasingly criminalized and racialized in public debates, many states opted to accord riot control and militarization of the police priority over crime prevention and rehabilitation, two of the stated goals of the Safe Streets Act.[85]

The ups and downs of LEAA's budget over the years and its eventual demise in 1982 belie the agency's significance. The LEAA legitimized a major role for the federal government in crime policy. It also created incentives for state and local governments to inflate their crime statistics so as to tap into more of the federal largesse. The LEAA legitimized and institutionalized the idea that greater law enforcement capacity modeled on the military was needed to combat crime and political unrest, two problems that were increasingly conflated in public debates.

Modeled on key features of OPS, the Safe Streets Act facilitated a kind of "devolutionary state-building."[86] Defending Jim Crow and its vestiges rested on protecting local power structures, including the police. While public officials and the police toned down or jettisoned the rhetoric of white supremacy as they amplified their crime-fighting mission, LEAA supercharged them with new resources to bolster the racial hierarchy over which they presided. During the Nixon administration, LEAA administrators began channeling block grants directly to state and local police departments, bypassing state officials. They established a pattern in the war on crime in which the federal government not only provided enormous new resources to state and local police but also gave them wide latitude to determine "the scope of law enforcement, with few constraints" from state or local political authorities.[87] Under Nixon, LEAA also developed a "long-range master plan" to increase the country's prison capacity, which would facilitate the country's embrace of mass incarceration beginning in the 1970s.[88]

The LEAA fostered a conservative, zero-sum view of victims' rights premised on the idea that the best way to help survivors of crime was to severely punish the people who victimized them. The agency advocated shoveling more resources to police, prosecutors, and prisons, all in the name of helping victims.[89] In funding select victims' groups and law enforcement organizations, LEAA promoted this punitive vision of victims' rights despite the lack of evidence that this was what victims wanted. The agency's vision of victims' rights was at odds with how Western European countries were addressing the needs of victims by building up the welfare state's capacity to provide them with housing, health care, economic assistance, and other supports to aid their recovery.

The LEAA was a hothouse for implementing the New Federalism of the Nixon administration, which sought to empower its supporters at the local level by providing federal funding with few strings attached. This disempowered other local groups seeking more civilian control of the police since the locus of the political action was in Washington, DC, where they were relatively powerless compared to federal administrators and lawmakers. The use of block grants leached into other areas of policymaking and contributed to the evisceration of federal social welfare programs intended to alleviate poverty and inequality and address the root causes of crime. In this way, the war on crime, fomented by Republican and Democratic lawmakers and law enforcement officials, helped lay the groundwork "for decades of devolutionary dismantling of federal social programs."[90]

The Demise and Reincarnation of OPS

Congress finally shut down OPS in 1974. The agency had come under withering attacks at home and abroad for supporting unsavory regimes and practices, including death squads, assassinations, torture, disappearances, and corruption.[91] Its critics included a motley coalition of Black radicals, antiwar activists, the New Left, and anti-imperialists, who drew direct connections between abusive, militarized policing in the United States and the abuses of the US empire abroad. A US Senate investigation of OPS unearthed numerous research theses—a graduation requirement for students enrolled in its International Police Academy—that condoned torture.[92] As Jack O'Dell, an adviser to Martin Luther King Jr. and critic of OPS, observed, in 1967: "Policemanship as a style of government is no longer confined to the Southern-way-of-life but is now becoming institutionalized on a national level." Channeling a comment Frederick Douglass once made on the passage of the Fugitive Slave Act, O'Dell went on say, "And the line between foreign and domestic policy is fading out as well, as militarism and the military presence become 'coextensive with the Star Spangled Banner.'"[93]

Although OPS was finally forced to close up shop in 1974, its aftershocks continued to shape US law enforcement. The LEAA broadened its mission to include activities that OPS had once performed.[94] Former OPS employees and contractors sought positions working with US police departments and other parts of the criminal legal system, including prison administration.[95] Others landed at federal agencies, including LEAA and the Drug Enforcement Administration (DEA), established in 1973 as part of President Nixon's war on drugs.[96] Some former employees of OPS played central roles in the burgeoning private security industry, launching or advising firms that contracted with corporations and foreign governments to provide everything from bodyguards to training for paramilitary units.[97] When President Ronald Reagan declared his own war on drugs in the 1980s, US training of overseas police officers resumed, morphing into a major endeavor that involved multiple federal agencies as well as private contractors. The DEA and a program run out of the State Department "became in many respects the successors to OPS" as the US budget for drug control overseas increased several-fold in just a few years.[98]

By the late 1960s, the views of Southern Democrats, Republicans, and some Northern liberals had converged with respect to key aspects of the law-and-order question. For Republicans and Southern Democrats, the expansion of civil rights had fostered crime by "disrupting the harmonious segregation of the races and validating black civil disobedience."[99] For race liberals, the incomplete civil rights agenda was the main cauldron of crime. Both explanations, in their own way, conflated political unrest and crime and cast African American people as the main subjects of the crime question.[100]

This formulation was compatible with OPS's model of policing, which conflated militarization with professionalization; merged the missions of battling insurgencies and battling crime; maintained wide autonomy for the police; and sought to diffuse charges of racism and colonialism by recruiting police officers from the ranks of the communities they patrolled. The combination of these domestic and international factors helps explain why the root-causes approach to reducing crime decidedly lost out in the 1968 crime bill in favor of a vast expansion of law enforcement that fortified local police departments without subjecting them to more political oversight.

Military-Grade Police Departments

Professionalizing the police entailed a revolution not only in tactics and training but also in the use of military weapons and technology, thanks to the Kerner Commission, LEAA, and OPS.[101] In the 1960s, surplus military equipment began flowing to local police departments. Legislation in the 1980s and 1990s formalized and facilitated these weapons transfers.[102] With the influx of federal funds from LEAA and other sources, police departments went on spending sprees for military hardware. Defense contractors targeted local police departments and other domestic law enforcement agencies as the market in military-grade equipment exploded. With the defeat of US forces in Vietnam and the anticipated contraction of the armed forces, defense contractors focused even more intently on cultivating the domestic law enforcement market for military-grade weapons and other equipment.[103] They exploited fears of crime and urban unrest as they promoted items like "the Curdler," a sonic weapon deployed by the US military in Vietnam.[104]

The Kerner Commission noted how the triggering event for political unrest in dozens of US cities was often the routine arrest of Black people by white officers for minor offenses.[105] It also condemned how the police, National Guard, and US Army wielded indiscriminate force to quell urban disturbances, resulting in wide-scale civilian injuries and deaths.[106] The commission denounced "moves to equip police departments with mass destruction weapons, such as automatic rifles, machine guns and tanks." It declared that weapons that "are designed to destroy, not to control, have no place in densely populated urban communities."[107] As a solution to this wanton state violence, the Kerner Commission recommended not only more resources to upgrade and professionalize the police but also enhanced training in riot control and the use of so-called nonlethal weapons.[108] But in the end, the political and legislative response to the Kerner Report hastened the further militarization of policing in the United States.

Nonlethal weapons have an ignominious history stemming from how the Kennedy and Johnson administrations deployed chemical weapons to crush overseas insurgencies, most notably in the US war in Vietnam. After the Kennedy administration's pivot toward counterinsurgency, national security experts and the US military began clamoring for the greater use of chemical weapons, notably CS, a talcum-like powder that incapacitates people by simulating suffocation, severely burning their eyes, and blistering their skin.[109] In 1965, the media began reporting that the US Army was deploying poisonous gases in Vietnam. This was in apparent violation of the ban on chemical weapons in the Geneva Protocol of 1925, which the United States had never signed, but claimed to adhere to.[110]

To stem the controversy, US national security officials and the military popularized the then-obscure term *nonlethal weapon*. Used by US forces in Vietnam to "flush out" people in hiding and kill them, CS was rebranded as "tear gas."[111] United States officials claimed that CS was not being used as a weapon of war but as a "riot-control agent." They falsely claimed that police departments in the United States and around the world were already using CS to control riots. In making this claim, they conflated the use of CS with that of CN, a less potent chemical weapon. In 1965, President Johnson reassured a leading journalist off the record: "Every police chief in the United States has them."[112]

Rebranding CS as mere "tear gas" helped to tamp down controversies over its use, paving the way for deploying massive quantities of this substance delivered by ever more sophisticated and lethal means during the US war in Vietnam.[113] The routine use of CS by US forces and their allies in Vietnam quickly had boomerang effects back in the United States. The Kerner Commission's endorsement of "nonlethal weapons" in riot control cleared the way for the US Army, National Guard, and local police to begin routinely deploying CS on demonstrators in the United States. As in Vietnam, police and other law enforcement agencies also started using CS in situations other than riot control, notably in waging war against Black radical organizations and in apprehending suspects in the war on crime. Back in the United States, some police chiefs and their supporters initially feared that nonlethal weapons would effectively disarm cops. But these so-called nonlethal weapons did not end up replacing "pistols, rifles, and shotguns; rather they supplemented them."[114]

In theory, counterinsurgency policing emphasized de-escalation, demilitarization, and use of minimal force, but in practice it was often just the opposite. The special weapons and tactics (SWAT) teams that LAPD Chief Daryl Gates helped to develop and popularize in the 1960s deployed overwhelming firepower, including CS, armored vehicles, highly trained snipers, and officers outfitted in body armor and brandishing semiautomatic rifles. These paramilitary units emerged in US police departments in the 1960s and 1970s and then exploded across the country in the 1980s and 1990s.[115] They also became popular overseas, thanks to OPS, which served as a relay team to export policing innovations developed in the United States and to import policing practices from overseas.[116] Local police in the United States started deploying SWAT teams not only for emergency situations, like rescuing hostages, but also for routine police activities, most notably serving warrants.

Police Departments and Military Veterans

The US war in Vietnam facilitated the militarization of US police forces in additional ways. As veterans returned home from fighting in Southeast Asia, concerns grew that the enfeebled economy would be unable to absorb them. Veterans of the war surged into law enforcement, prodded to become police officers by government programs and the sputtering US economy. In a major turnabout, the US Army, which had generally been excluded from direct involvement in civilian policing in the United States, became a leader in recruiting and training domestic law enforcement.

As he waged the war in Vietnam, President Johnson promoted military service as a way to steer youths—especially Black youths from disadvantaged backgrounds—away from crime. Johnson also championed programs that channeled veterans into law enforcement, hoping to diversify police departments and quell the political unrest breaking out in cities across the country. In the 1960s and 1970s, the US Department of Defense instituted programs that permitted early discharge for active military personnel to take up jobs as civilian police officers and that encouraged police forces to recruit on military bases and among veterans.[117]

Police chiefs and their political supporters have a long history of seeking to burnish their legitimacy and maintain control with periodic attempts to diversify their ranks with nonwhite officers. These efforts have been uneven but have tended to surge after major wars, including the Spanish-American War, World War II, and the US war in Vietnam. Since African American people enlisted in the military at higher rates than white people did after the all-volunteer army was established in 1973, they provided a disproportionate share of the pool of veterans for law enforcement.[118] During the 1960s and 1970s, mayors and other public officials rushed to channel Black veterans into policing. They sought to diffuse racial tensions and criticisms over deploying white police forces to quash protests and rebellions by African American people in urban areas. But some officials also feared that Black veterans would use their military training to become "militant black ghetto organizers."[119]

With the anticipated contraction of the armed forces after the US defeat in Vietnam, concerns grew that the military could no longer serve as a safety valve to employ young men and transform them into responsible, law-abiding citizens. President Gerald Ford, whose role in ramping up the war on crime has long been underestimated, openly worried that the contraction of the armed forces was fueling unemployment among young men.[120] The unprecedented demographic bulge of young adults as the baby boomers were coming of age intensified these worries. Just as deindustrialization fueled pressures for ramping up punitive policies to contain the so-called dangerous classes, so did the demobilization and contraction of the armed forces.[121]

A bifurcated view of veterans emerged. The "good" veterans would be channeled into employment in police departments, prisons, and private security firms. As for the "bad" ones, politicians and the media stoked public alarm over crime and drugs by promoting what turned out to be a myth about an alleged epidemic of drug-addicted, crime-prone veterans.[122] This view of veterans was tinged with racism. "The specter of the violent, crazed, or drugged black veteran was widespread, even if the image of white vets was scarcely better," explains historian Michael Sherry. Law enforcement and the criminal legal system were growing sectors "that vets, at least high-functioning ones, were well placed to enter," according to Sherry. By large numbers, members of the cohort of nearly eight million Vietnam-era veterans disproportionately took up positions in policing and in "protective services," including guards in the public and private sectors. But veterans also ended up swelling the ranks of people serving time in prison.[123]

The military was a major vehicle not only to recruit police officers but also to train them. Thanks to an influx of money from the Justice Department, the US Army established the Senior Officers Civil Disturbance Orientation Course (SEADOC) at Fort Gordon, Georgia, in the late 1960s. At SEADOC, midlevel police officers, members of the National Guard, US soldiers, and reservists learned how to work together in a mock urban setting called "Riotsville" to quell riots, protests, and demonstrations. When Ronald Reagan was governor of California, the Golden State established its own version of SEADOC with the help of LEAA funding. The California facility ended up training tens of thousands of officers from around the country and overseas.[124]

The LEAA was the spark for an explosion in government, private, and foundation support to fund US police training and education, including police academies and the proliferation of criminology and criminal justice programs at colleges and universities. These programs promised to create more well-rounded, humane, professional police officers who were less likely to use force and more open to fresh ideas and reforms. But they did not deliver on what they promised.[125] The programs tightly circumscribed what courses police officers and officers-to-be were permitted to take. Many of the instructors had law enforcement and military backgrounds, including former OPS employees who took up teaching positions after the agency was disbanded. A 1978 Police Foundation report charged that criminal justice programs tended to be "intellectually shallow, conceptually narrow, and provided by a faculty that is far from scholar[ly]."[126] Highly dependent on government funding, including state-funded research, criminology and criminal justice programs were less critical of the criminal legal system, including policing.[127]

Torture and the Red Squads

The United States was a signatory to a spate of international agreements to ban torture and inhumane treatment that were enacted in the 1940s after the vast abuses of the Nazi regime became more widely known. But as the United States marched into the Cold War, US officials sought to develop "clean" torture techniques that would "inflict immense physical, psychological, or emotional pain" while leaving few or no physical marks.[128] In 1946, President Truman approved Project Paperclip, which would bring more than one thousand German scientists, many of whom had been committed Nazis, to the United States. Their expertise would be critical to US advances in rocketry and chemical and biological warfare but also in developing techniques for "clean" torture.[129]

The CIA was at the forefront of pioneering such techniques, including administering psychedelic drugs to unsuspecting members of the public, incarcerated people, and even its own employees. Dozens of public and private institutions, including leading universities and medical centers, received vast sums of government money to carry out experiments using drugs, alcohol, sleep and sensory deprivation, and other means to induce mental and physical distress. Under Project MKUltra, the CIA funded an extensive program to study the effects of induced physical and mental stresses on the brain and people's behavior.[130]

The US war in Vietnam provided another opportunity to experiment with torture. In 1965, the same year the United States agreed to abide by the Geneva Conventions in Vietnam, including the ban on the torture or abuse of people who are captured, it launched the Phoenix Program. Vietnamese people suspected of being members of or sympathizers with the Viet Cong were systematically taken to dozens of interrogation centers, where CIA personnel and their South Vietnamese allies subjected them to physical and mental torture to obtain information. Some of these captured people were murdered to induce others to break their silence.[131]

As Vietnam veterans took positions with local police departments after returning home from Southeast Asia, some of them repatriated the torture techniques they had learned overseas. Jon Burge, who served tours of duty in Korea and Vietnam before joining the Chicago Police Department in 1970, was one of the most notorious examples. Over the course of many years, Burge and his unit of rogue cops subjected more than one hundred African American people—we'll likely never know the total number—to what they called the "Vietnam special" or "Vietnamese treatment." This torture treatment included electric shocks, sexual assaults, beatings, sleep deprivation, suffocation, and mock executions.[132] After Burge and his fellow officers were accused of systematic torture, Chicago's Fraternal Order of Police (FOP) spearheaded a decades-long campaign to defend them. The FOP even attempted to honor Burge with a float in the city's South Side Irish Parade after he was fired from the force.[133]

During the 1960s and early 1970s, red squads proliferated in police departments nationwide as authorities sought to crush the antiwar, civil rights, Black power, feminist, and other movements. These squads worked closely with the US Army, CIA, and Federal Bureau of Investigation (FBI), which tutored them in the ABC's of clandestine activities, including surveillance, eavesdropping, secretive searches, and the manufacture and use of explosives.[134] Local police collaborated closely with the FBI's Counter Intelligence Program (COINTELPRO), established in the mid-1950s, and the CIA's Operation CHAOS, the domestic intelligence program established in 1967 to conduct covert and illegal activities, including blackmail, forgery, infiltration, false reports to the media, illegal imprisonment, and even assassinations.[135]

In 1974, the *New York Times* published excerpts from the "Family Jewels," which were internal CIA reports documenting a massive, illegal intelligence operation during the Nixon administration that targeted antiwar protesters and other dissidents in violation of the CIA's charter. The reports, which had been commissioned by CIA Director James Schlesinger, also revealed dozens of other illegal activities by CIA operatives inside the United States since the 1950s.[136] Media exposés of the gross abuses of the red squads and their close connections to the FBI, CIA, and US military prompted major congressional investigations in the mid-1970s that revealed the extensive involvement of local police in illegal activities.[137] These revelations, a string of lawsuits, and growing political pressure forced many cities to dissolve their red squads and destroy files about their activities.[138]

But the rollback of the red squads was short-lived. Local police successfully pushed for greater powers and to lift the modest limits that had been imposed on their activities in the 1970s. County and state police established their own special intelligence units. At the federal level, the FBI began fostering joint task forces comprising local, state, and federal law enforcement officers to wage numerous wars against drugs, sex crimes, terrorism, immigrants, and other designated scourges. These task forces allowed local police officers to skirt public scrutiny and accountability. Since local police officers were "ostensibly acting as federal agents, their activities" were "not subject to the supervision of local authorities," and the information they gathered remained secret.[139] Joint task forces also allowed the FBI to dodge allegations of intrusive federal involvement in local law enforcement.[140]

Hypermilitarized Policing and Crushing Dissent

The United States has a long and disquieting history of labeling political dissenters, including people challenging the "color line," as terrorists and exaggerating the threat they pose to justify ramping up law enforcement and the national security state. After 9/11, a new model of policing to crush dissent congealed. It rested on confronting protesters with overwhelming force, including massive numbers of heavily armed, military-style police officers, and infiltrating and destabilizing their networks and organizations.[141] Law enforcement pioneered and perfected these tactics during the high-profile crackdowns on the 1999 Seattle protests against the World Trade Organization, the 2003 demonstrations during the Free Trade of Americas meetings, the political unrest during the 2004 Republican National Convention, and then again during the 2011 Occupy Wall Street movement. The New York Police Department's abusive tactics at the 2004 Republican convention ended up costing the city $18 million in 2014 to settle the claims of about eighteen hundred people in what the New York Civil Liberties Union described as the "largest protest settlement in history."[142] Crushing demonstrations with overwhelming and hypermilitarized police forces and criminalizing protesters help explain why Occupy Wall Street and other movements could not sustain their momentum.[143]

In the wake of 9/11, the FBI, CIA, and other arms of the national security state exploited fears of foreign terrorists and "Islamic terrorism" to jettison many of the remaining restraints imposed on them during the 1970s in response to public outrage over abuses by COINTELPRO. The FBI morphed from a law enforcement agency into a domestic intelligence agency.[144] In 2014, without much fanfare, the FBI even removed "law enforcement" from its mission statement.[145]

With enactment of the Patriot Act in October 2001, the authority of law enforcement to investigate and prosecute so-called domestic terrorism skyrocketed, as did abuses of that authority. For over two decades now, Muslims and people of Middle Eastern, South Asian, and African heritage living in the United States have been subject to sting operations, infiltration of their places of worship and organizations, and overly broad prosecution, all in the name of fighting the global war on terror. The US government has wantonly labeled more than one million people in the United States (who are disproportionately drawn from Muslim and immigrant communities) as security threats and placed them on its watchlist, which has been denounced as a "due process nightmare."[146] Federal agents wield the threat of placement on the watchlist to coerce people into becoming informants.[147] For many years, the vast Suspicious Activity Reporting Initiative, run out of the Justice Department, has promoted the collection and dissemination of information about individuals labeled as "suspicious" despite the absence of evidence of possible criminal activity.[148]

The separation that the 1878 Posse Comitatus Act established between the military and domestic law enforcement is rapidly eroding in the United States.[149] Local police routinely participate in joint operations with the military, including antidrug and antiterrorism activities.[150] The national network of fusion centers, established after 9/11, permits federal agencies, local police, and the private sector to gather and share reams of intelligence information collected on citizens and residents of the United States, including surveillance and infiltration of lawful groups, public gatherings, and demonstrations.[151]

This model of crushing dissent and protests with militarized policing diffused across the United States and around the world.[152] It eroded the legitimacy of the police and citizens' trust in them. Even the Obama administration's special commission on policing, established after the uproar over the 2014 police killing of Michael Brown in Ferguson, conceded this point.[153]

These problems predate the Trump and Biden administrations but worsened under them. Threats to invoke the centuries-old (and dangerously vague) Insurrection Act to enlist the military in crushing domestic protests and carrying out mass deportations of undocumented immigrants have been part of the repertoire of Donald Trump and his allies for years.[154] In response to the wave of protests over the climate emergency, excessive use of police force, and now the war in Gaza, states and municipalities have enacted dozens of new laws that restrict the right of free and peaceful assembly and that ramp up criminal penalties and fines for acts of civil disobedience. These include stiffer penalties for trespassing, blocking traffic, damaging public property, vandalizing statues, demonstrating near oil or gas pipelines, and participating in "riots," which are capaciously defined to include acts of nonviolent protest and that sometimes involve as few as three people. States have sought to broaden the definition of "domestic terrorism" to include demonstrations, boycotts, and other forms of protest and political expression; to criminalize "economic terrorism"; to permit municipalities to charge protest organizers upfront "security deposits" to cover the costs of cleanup, law enforcement, and other expenses; and to enact measures that shield drivers who injure or kill protesters with their cars from liability and prosecution. The push in Congress to ramp up federal penalties for acts of civil disobedience and dissent has also intensified.[155]

As protests over the war in Gaza broke out in 2023 and 2024, university and college administrators and campus police forces emerged as a leading edge in legitimizing hypermilitarized policing to quell dissent. In October 2024, the University of Pennsylvania even called out a SWAT team to carry out a terrorizing predawn search of an off-campus apartment and deliver a warrant to a student allegedly accused of a minor act of vandalism.[156] University and college administrators across the country have called on campus and local police to enforce new Orwellian standards for free expression that they rammed through as a new big chill descended on many campuses.

To sum up, developments at home and abroad have been mutually constitutive in molding US police forces. The burgeoning US empire and national security state were vital sources for the establishment of militarized police forces that have eluded civilian and political control and fostered exceptional state violence. As the size, resources, and power of the federal government expanded in the realm of law enforcement over the course of the twentieth

century, local police paradoxically became even more powerful and autono-
mous. They amassed greater capacity to coerce and control with little outside
accountability, shielded behind their badge of so-called professionalism, their
powerful unions and associations, and the extremely decentralized system of
law enforcement in the United States. Time and again, the police and their
champions sought refuge in professionalism defined in militaristic terms to
stave off their critics, as shown in this chapter. Blowback at home from the
quest to police the world has contributed to violence in America in additional
ways, as detailed in the next chapter.

5

Enemies Here, There, and Everywhere

FOREVER AT WAR AT HOME AND ABROAD

A long habit of not thinking a thing *wrong*, gives it a superficial appearance of being *right*.

—THOMAS PAINE[1]

AMERICA'S DEEP and long-standing commitment to maintaining a global empire has fostered violence not only overseas but also back home in this country. Blowback from the US response to its defeat in Vietnam, the end of the Cold War, and the 9/11 attacks has contributed to state, structural, inter-personal, and political violence in America and put US democracy at risk. The US political and military debacle in Southeast Asia left its mark on the US military, local law enforcement, and the political landscape in numerous ways. The fall of Saigon in 1975 was a brief setback for the empire but not for milita-rized policing back home. Vietnam veterans flowed into local police depart-ments, hastening their militarization. So did the surplus military equipment that ended up with local police officers. The US defeat was also instrumental in fostering a narrative of betrayal that incubated the contemporary white power movement.

After the US defeat in Vietnam, the future scope and mission of the US military appeared uncertain. The armed forces and the country grappled with the implications of the resounding defeat in Vietnam, the deep vein of antiwar sentiment that the war had pricked, the abolition of the draft, the dawn of the all-volunteer military, and a lumbering economy gripped by unprecedented stagflation. The defeat provided an opportunity to jettison the "Washington rules" forged after World War II.[2] But that opportunity was forfeited. The core tenets of the Washington rules remained largely intact: maintaining a global military that greatly exceeds what is required for self-defense; projecting US power in hundreds of bases around the world; and countering existing or anticipated threats with military interventionism throughout the world.[3] The end of the Cold War in 1989 and the dissolution of the Soviet Union in 1991 were other lost opportunities to abandon the Washington rules.

After 9/11, President George W. Bush launched two major wars—against Afghanistan in October 2001 and against Iraq eighteen months later—that resulted in decades of warfare, occupation, and finally defeat for the United States. Fighting dragged on in Iraq and Afghanistan. Iraqis and others radicalized by the US invasion and occupation of Iraq founded ISIS, which spread to at least a dozen countries in Africa and the Middle East. Casualties skyrocketed for civilians in other countries. United States troops found themselves enmeshed in conflicts in which the lines between enemy and ally were blurred. No light was visible at the end of a tunnel that looked more like a replay of the quagmire in Vietnam than a replay of the US military's Operation Desert Storm, which expelled Iraq from Kuwait in 1991.

Military and civilian leaders in the United States responded by digging in "for the Long War, a conflict defined not by purpose, adversary, or location but by duration, which was indeterminate."[4] Under his watch, President Barack Obama escalated the global war on terror, though he hesitated to use that term, by expanding special forces operations and targeted assassinations, including of US citizens overseas.[5] Obama also initiated and institutionalized a vast air war in which intelligence and military operators manning computers at bases back in the United States launched bombing raids and other attacks with unmanned drones that terrorized wide swaths of people in numerous countries.[6]

Blowback, a term the Central Intelligence Agency (CIA) coined decades ago, connotes the unintended negative consequences of US policies overseas for the United States and other countries. Political scientist Chalmers Johnson popularized the term *blowback* with his series of books excoriating how the US empire jeopardized its economy, polity, and national security.[7] Discussions of blowback in the aftermath of 9/11 mostly centered on whether the manner in which the United States waged the global war on terror—the invasions of Afghanistan and Iraq, the US-led war in Libya, the expansive and terrorizing drone war, the torture of "enemy combatants" detained at Guantánamo Bay and "black sites" in other countries, and the denunciations of "Islamic terrorism"—undermined the country's long-term foreign policy and other national security interests, and in particular, whether the global war on terror rendered the United States more vulnerable to terrorist attacks at home and abroad. But blowback from the war on terror had other negative consequences.

The relatively low number of US combat deaths in Iraq, Afghanistan, and elsewhere in the post-9/11 wars helped obscure how the forever wars have contributed to violence in America and put US democracy in jeopardy. Rural and Rust Belt communities disproportionately shouldered the human costs of the war on terror and the forever wars thanks to the establishment of the all-volunteer armed forces after the abolition of the draft in 1973, as detailed in this chapter. These were many of the same communities reeling from the economic hollowing out spurred by the 1994 North American Free Trade Agreement (NAFTA), China's admission to the World Trade Organization in 2001, the 2007–9 financial and foreclosure crises, and the accelerated flight of capital to urban and coastal financial and high-tech centers. Residents of these communities were more likely to don a military uniform, die or be injured in combat, and succumb to the opioid epidemic. As medical and other needs of veterans and active-duty personnel escalated, lawmakers and other public officials were slashing and privatizing their health care and other benefits, eroding what had been one of the most robust pieces of the US welfare state.

Waging the global war on terror cost the United States more than $8 trillion as of 2021, according to the Costs of War Project.[8] People in rural and Rust Belt communities had ringside seats not only to the economic hollowing out of the heartland, but also to the massive waste, corruption, and destruction of the forever wars. They and their families excoriated the military for sending US soldiers into battle without vital basic gear, including body armor and vehicles equipped to withstand roadside bombs and other low-tech improvised explosive devices (IEDs). It was no secret to soldiers in the field that the United States, which spent more on the wars in Iraq and Afghanistan than it spent on the Marshall Plan to rebuild Europe after World War II, had little to show for its trillions of dollars. Meanwhile, back at home, rural hospitals and clinics in the United States were closing, roads and bridges were crumbling, education budgets were shrinking, and living-wage jobs were vanishing, with even teachers forced to moonlight to make ends meet.

The preoccupation after 9/11 with rounding up tens of thousands of Muslim people in the United States and constructing a massive dragnet to combat "Islamic terrorism" diverted attention and resources from combatting the growing threat of the contemporary white power movement and its militias.[9]

Blowback from the global war on terror fostered a new wave of recruits to the white power movement and private militias, which were bolstering their ties to US military personnel, local police departments, and sheriffs.

The human, political, and fiscal costs of the forever wars launched after 9/11 plundered the United States of vital resources. They robbed the country of the will and the means to stem the deaths of despair, the alarming erosion in the quality of life for so many people, and the surge in various forms of violence in rural America and across the country. And the countries that the United States shattered in the forever wars remained mostly shattered.

Brown University's Watson Institute conservatively estimates that over nine hundred thousand people have been killed because of direct violence related to the post-9/11 wars, including three hundred thousand people in Iraq and 176,000 people in Afghanistan.[10] An additional 3.6 million deaths—likely more—are indirectly attributable to the forever wars. These include deaths from fatal diseases and malnutrition caused by damage to the food, water, and health-care systems, infrastructure, environment, and economies in Iraq, Afghanistan, Libya, Pakistan, Syria, Somalia, and Yemen.[11] A staggering thirty-eight million people have been displaced by the US post-9/11 wars, a greater flow of refugees for any war or disaster since 1900 except for World War II.[12] The mass migration of refugees to Europe as a consequence of the forever wars has empowered right-wing parties and politicians fanning the flames of nativism and political extremism.

The White Power Movement

Since its emergence in the 1970s and its consolidation in the 1980s and 1990s, the white power movement has repositioned itself to wage war on its enemies in the United States and to engineer a regime change in which democracy itself may be cast out. The movement has been on a long march that has taken it from the margins to the centers of power in the United States. Along the way it has aligned with private militias, embraced organized violence as a political strategy, and cultivated closer ties with local police, active-service military personnel, sheriffs, and other public officials. The movement also incubated a radical reinterpretation of the Second Amendment to create a locked and loaded nation with no significant limits on carrying weapons—be they handguns or military-style assault weapons.[13] More recently, the white power movement, which once shunned electoral politics, has sought to be a player and disrupter in campaigns and elections. It has undergone a major shift toward mixing politics with armed militancy, including backing candidates for local, state, and national elected offices who are covertly and openly aligned with the movement.[14]

The emergence of the white power movement as a major force in American politics and society is another instance of the mutually constitutive relationship between state violence abroad and the spread of state and other violence at home. The contemporary white power movement is a "broad and diverse social movement" that brought together Klansmen, skinheads, radical tax resisters, neo-Nazis, militiamen, white separatists, and Christian identity groups beginning in the late 1970s, explains historian Kathleen Belew. With its aim of fomenting "a wholesale revolution through race war," the movement is "distinct in many ways from earlier mobilizations of racist and vigilante violence."[15]

The US debacle in Southeast Asia galvanized groups across the political spectrum, radicalizing and militarizing the extreme left and the extreme right in the United States. But the "militarization of the left never matched that of the paramilitary right," partly because of "the right's cultural embrace of weapons" and its ties to the US armed forces and law enforcement.[16] The far left also withered in the 1970s thanks to ideological and tactical disputes and the war of infiltration, intimidation, and violence carried out by the red squads, Federal Bureau of Investigation (FBI), CIA, and US military.[17] The far left ended up splintered and enfeebled while groups on the far right congealed into a powerful and militarized white power movement that today rivals the second coming of the Ku Klux Klan in the 1920s.[18] And like the Klan at that time, the movement has cultivated close and unsettling ties with local police, sheriffs, the military, and government officials.

A small but influential group of Vietnam veterans played a vital role in mobilizing previously disparate and often antagonistic groups on the far right to declare war on the government and embark on a joint mission to overthrow it. These veterans and their supporters fostered a narrative of betrayal that served as the cauldron for the consolidation and expansion of the white power movement. They charged that the corrupt US government "sent American boys to Vietnam and then denied them permission to win by limiting their use of force against a beastly, subhuman enemy. Many met gruesome injury and death, and all faced hardship, insects, abandonment, rot, and disease," explains Belew.[19] The Watergate scandal and the government's failure to stem the wave of factory closures and farm foreclosures in the 1970s and 1980s were additional fuel for an explosion in mistrust of government that the leaders of the white power movement stoked. So was growing apprehension about the influx of immigrants and about the expansion of rights for African American people, women, and other historically disadvantaged groups.

Paramilitarism and a cohesive social network forged by strategic marital and other personal ties helped unite the disparate groups on the right.[20] So did several key events involving violence in which members of white extremist groups were acquitted of criminal charges.[21] The movement's deft use of leaderless cells and its pioneering use of computers, the internet, and later social media to recruit and mobilize new members also facilitated its growth and consolidation.[22] Furthermore, as World War II and the battle against Nazi Germany became more distant memories, the earlier reluctance of some Klansmen and other ultraright groups to join forces with neo-Nazis dissipated. And with the fall of the Berlin Wall in 1989 and the breakup of the Soviet Union, political space opened up to pivot from an obsession with battling communism's evil empire to a fixation on battling the alleged evils of their own government.[23]

In the 1980s, the white power movement made a major strategic shift from a focus on carrying out acts of vigilante violence to declaring war on the state—especially the federal government—in its quest to establish a white homeland. As the movement embraced paramilitarism, it stepped up its efforts to recruit veterans, active-duty military personnel, law enforcement officers, and people serving time in prison, especially penal facilities with high levels of racial violence. It also stockpiled weapons stolen from US military bases. In the face of rising white nationalism in the ranks and the disappearance of large amounts of matériel, the Defense Department generally looked the other way.[24]

Overkill by law enforcement in rural communities also propelled the white power movement. Public criticism of special weapons and tactics (SWAT) operations and other heavy-handed measures has tended to center on how militarized policing has targeted urban areas and Black people in particular, seeding alienation, rage, and a deep distrust of the government, especially the police.[25] (The most notorious example of police overkill in an urban area during the 1980s was the Philadelphia Police Department's deadly 1985 siege and bombing of MOVE, an Afrocentric, antitechnology group. The attack, carried out jointly with federal authorities, killed eleven people and destroyed dozens of homes.)[26] But rural communities have also been the victims of deadly government sieges carried out by heavily armed local, state, and federal authorities. These sieges fueled rage, mistrust, and alienation and were a boon for the white power movement.

The 1992 confrontation in Ruby Ridge, Idaho, and the 1993 assault against the Branch Davidians in Waco, Texas, spurred the surge of private militias and deepened the white power movement's commitment to the violent overthrow of the government.[27] In the Ruby Ridge siege, hundreds of heavily armed local police and federal agents descended on a remote mountaintop cabin to apprehend Randy Weaver, a white separatist accused of selling two illegally modified weapons. His wife, Vicki Weaver, became a martyr to the movement after an FBI sniper shot her to death as she stood holding her ten-month-old daughter at the doorway of their cabin.[28]

Months later, federal authorities began a seven-week siege of the Branch Davidians, a millennialist religious community in Waco, Texas. The siege ended on April 19, 1993, with the deaths of some eighty people, including dozens of children, as hundreds of federal agents and state and local police manning tanks, armored personnel carriers, and military helicopters stormed the compound, firing hundreds of canisters of CS gas and igniting a deadly inferno. Ruby Ridge and Waco, occurring just as the Cold War appeared to be winding down, facilitated the white power movement's pivot from battling communism to battling a federal government accused of attempting to create an all-powerful New World Order. As one of the leaders of the movement proclaimed in 1992, "Communism now represents a threat to no one in the United States, while federal tyranny represents a threat to *everyone.*"[29]

Sociologist Amy Cooter cautions against viewing white power groups and the proliferating private militias as part of a single movement. She suggests that their relationship is more like a Venn diagram in which they have overlapping but also distinct characteristics, priorities, and resources. "Unlike white power organizations, most militia groups' aims were not racially oriented," she contends.[30] What the militias and white power groups do share is deep antipathy toward a government that they perceive as overweening and abusive. They are also united in their interpretation of the Second Amendment as a constitutional right to "practically unlimited personal gun ownership."[31]

Growing fears about gun control galvanized the white power movement and the formation of militias in the 1990s. In the late 1960s, sales and possession of firearms began to skyrocket. Widely publicized images at the time of members of the Black Panthers armed with guns and rifles as they rode around in the back of pickup trucks and called for an armed defense likely spurred the upward spiral in gun purchases by Black and white people.[32] A desire to force the Black Panthers to surrender their guns by rescinding open-carry laws spurred calls for more gun control. But opposition to gun control quickly emerged as a central mobilizing issue for the white power movement and the militias it was spawning.

Former advisers of the federal Office of Public Safety (OPS) parlayed their expertise in firearms and their enthusiasm for weapons into the push to liberalize US gun laws.[33] Byron Engle, the longtime leader of OPS, was instrumental in a mid-1970s coup at the National Rifle Association that shifted the country's largest organization for gun owners "toward the far more extreme and fundamentalist gun-rights positions it has maintained over the past few decades."[34] The militias and supporters of the white power movement viewed passage of the 1993 Brady Handgun Violence Prevention Act, which imposed modest regulations on handguns, and a provision in the 1994 crime bill that levied some restrictions on military-style assault rifles, with alarm.[35] (The crime bill's restrictions on AR-15-style rifles turned out to be a pyrrhic victory for gun-control advocates. The so-called ban on these weapons made them even more desirable. As sales of other firearms flagged, the market for AR-15s would soar.)[36] Opposition to gun control legislation is at the top of the creed of ten orders that members of the Oath Keepers, a militia group founded in 2009, have vowed to follow.[37]

On April 19, 1995, two years to the day after the government raid on the Branch Davidians, a bomb went off in the federal office building in Oklahoma City, killing 168 people. Despite some evidence that the men charged in the bombing may have had ties to the white power movement and its militias, the attack became popularly understood as "an example of 'lone wolf' terrorism."[38] Around this time, the FBI institutionalized a policy of focusing on individual actors and not considering their violent crimes in relation to a wider white power movement. This strategy helped erase the white power movement and the militias it was spawning from public awareness in the years ahead.[39]

The "American Century" and Staying the Course

As the burgeoning white power movement was reckoning with the US defeat in Vietnam, so was the US military and foreign policy establishment. Soon after the fall of Saigon in 1975, the US military leadership and much of the Washington establishment forged a consensus that the country's defeat in Vietnam was a one-off event. They attributed the loss to "specific misjudgments and miscalculations, not deep-seated systemic flaws in the American way of life, in the American tradition of statecraft," or in the Washington rules.[40] The United States doubled down on battling the Soviet Union and its allies, despite growing evidence from the CIA and elsewhere that the "evil empire" that President Ronald Reagan and others railed against was increasingly a paper tiger enfeebled by mounting political and economic strains.[41]

During his final two years in office, President Jimmy Carter pivoted toward more militaristic policies, including the start of what became billions of dollars of military support funneled through the CIA over the next decade to support the mujahideen fighting the Soviet Union in Afghanistan. Leaders of the mujahideen would emerge years later as key figures in the Taliban, which the United States would fail to overthrow after 9/11 despite two decades of waging war against them.[42] Carter's actions paved the way for the biggest peacetime military buildup in the country's history under his successor, Ronald Reagan.[43] That said, Reagan's military policies did not go unchallenged. They faced vigorous opposition in Congress and ignited a major peace movement.[44] In June 1982, in one of the largest political rallies in US history, an estimated one million people gathered in New York City's Central Park to demand an end to the nuclear arms race.

The fall of the Berlin Wall in 1989 and the 1991 breakup of the Soviet Union provided other potential turning points to fundamentally rethink US foreign and military policy. But the Washington establishment demurred. Instead, it viewed the demise of the Soviet Union as an opportunity to fully realize publisher Henry Luce's mid-twentieth-century vision of the "American Century."[45] In this view, the United States would be the sole superpower, policing the peace and protecting US interests with a military presence spanning the globe. In cases where military conflicts did break out, the United States would wield its unrivaled military might to assure that they were settled quickly, surgically, and with minimum loss of life, as least for US forces and American citizens.

With the end of the Cold War, Colin Powell, the chairman of the Joint Chiefs of Staff, joked in 1991, "I'm running out of demons, I'm running out of villains."[46] But the following year he found his demons and villains, and they were everywhere. In 1992, Powell endorsed a strategy to use military action unilaterally and preemptively to ensure US supremacy and "dete[r] competitors from even aspiring to a larger regional or global role."[47]

Under President George H. W. Bush, Powell and the Joint Chiefs of Staff preempted any serious discussion of a "peace dividend" by capitalizing on the prestige they garnered with Operation Desert Storm in 1991. They portrayed liberating Kuwait from Iraq as the "paradigmatic 'good war'"—fast, decisive, with minimum loss of life for US forces.[48] They invoked Operation Desert Storm to bolster claims that in the post–Cold War world the United

States was well positioned to be the one and only superpower pursuing unrivaled military might.

In the decade leading up to the 9/11 attacks in 2001, debates over US military posture were intense, but they oscillated within a narrow range defined by military insiders led by Powell and military outsiders led by Donald Rumsfeld, Dick Cheney, and Paul Wolfowitz. Both camps had serious disagreements over which strategic posture, force structure, and weapons systems were most likely to secure and maintain the United States as the unrivaled superpower. But they were united in their commitment dating back to the 1970s to restore the credibility of US armed forces battered by the ghosts of the US war in Vietnam and to pursue "a thoroughly militarized conception of statecraft."[49]

This was a thoroughly bipartisan vision. Facing a war hero president who topped out at over 90 percent in the public opinion polls after Operation Desert Storm, Democratic presidential candidate Bill Clinton—draft dodger, foe of the US war in Vietnam—refashioned himself as a "new Democrat." He promised to "not only maintain but even enhance U.S. military strength" and to pursue an activist, interventionist foreign policy.[50] Once in the White House, Clinton made good on his word. He authorized major air wars against several countries and dispatched tens of thousands of US troops to fight in Bosnia.[51] His "military initiatives were remarkable both for their frequency and the absence of any institutional checks, either legislative or judicial."[52] Clinton also burnished his "new Democrat" credentials by brashly embracing the death penalty people; backing the most draconian crime bill in US history; dissing organized labor (most notably by championing NAFTA); picking high-profile spats with leading African American people; killing off Aid to Families with Dependent Children (AFDC, a pillar of the New Deal's social welfare programs for poor families); and championing measures to deregulate the financial sector that set the stage for the 2007–9 financial crisis and Great Recession.[53]

With the end of the Cold War, Clinton and other top Democrats did not make even a halfhearted effort to pursue a "peace dividend" premised on significant reductions in military spending and pursuit of collective security and burden sharing rather than the singular military dominance of the United States. Clinton vowed toward the end of his administration to reverse the purported decline in defense spending that began in 1985 even though "from the perspective of the entire Cold War, the military budgets of the 1990s were surprisingly high."[54] Furthermore, under Clinton the United States emerged as the world's leading arms-trading nation, despite his campaign platform in 1992 to reduce US arms sales abroad.[55]

The All-Volunteer Force and the Military Welfare State

The US debacle in Vietnam and the end of the Cold War did not put the Washington rules or the gigantic military budget to fund them in jeopardy. But they did set in motion a radical shift in who served in the armed forces and who died or was wounded in action. In the face of strong support from President Richard Nixon and vociferous objections from the military, Congress abolished the draft in 1973.

During World War II, the burden of military service was widely shared.[56] At the time, the military heavily relied on conscription to fill its ranks, thanks to the Selective Training and Service Act, the nation's first peacetime draft, which Democratic President Franklin D. Roosevelt signed into law in 1940 before the United States officially entered World War II. Poor people were disproportionately rejected for military service during World War II because of illiteracy and failure to meet fitness and mental health standards.[57] While there was not a major socioeconomic gap in who served in the military at the time, there was a significant rural-urban divide. Men living in rural communities were less likely to be drafted during World War II because of a provision in the Selective Service Act, inserted at the behest of powerful agricultural interests, that permitted wide exemptions for farmers and agricultural workers.[58]

As the army's personnel needs shrank following World War II, policymakers and draft boards had more leeway to expand the number of student deferments and occupational exemptions.[59] In the early 1940s, volunteers constituted only one-third of the military. During the US war in Vietnam, the proportion of volunteers nearly doubled to 60 percent.[60] As the US military became more dependent on volunteers, not conscription, to fill its ranks after World War II, a casualty gap opened up, beginning with the US war in Korea and growing wider with each major war. Residents from poorer, less-educated communities were more likely to enlist and to be assigned combat positions than people living in better-off towns and cities.[61]

Poorer communities with fewer educational opportunities began paying a "disproportionate share of the human costs of war," including combat deaths and injuries.[62] So did people residing in the South and in rural communities.[63] Poor white communities "suffered casualty rates even higher than those suffered by communities with larger black populations and identical socioeconomic conditions" during the US wars in Korea and Vietnam.[64]

With the end of the draft in 1973, the military became entirely dependent on volunteers. *All-volunteer* force is really a misnomer. *All-recruited* force is more accurate.[65] The Defense Department is keenly sensitive to how it periodically must recalibrate its recruitment strategies, especially for the US Army, because of demographic, economic, political, social, and cultural shifts.[66]

To lure and retain recruits after the draft ended, the military developed an extensive welfare state that included housing, education, medical, childcare, and other benefits.[67] With the advent of the all-volunteer force, the Pentagon was forced to engage in a delicate political and public relations dance to simultaneously construct, defend, deny, and obscure its relatively generous social safety net for military personnel as the push to slash health care, pensions, and other benefits for civilians was becoming a stampede. With the launch of the global war on terror after 9/11, choreographing that dance became even more challenging.

Soon after the establishment of the all-volunteer force, the military's burgeoning welfare state came under attack. Critics faulted the US Army in particular for attracting a new caliber of recruits who were enlisting because they lacked the skills and wherewithal to succeed in civilian life and who were becoming wards of the state, dependent on the military's costly government handouts.[68] These criticisms echoed widespread attacks on the social safety net for civilians as critics deployed thinly veiled racialized appeals to allege that social welfare programs were fostering a so-called culture of poverty.[69] The image of the army, with its expanding package of benefits, became "dangerously blurred" with denigrated civilian social welfare programs and the "dysfunctional poor."[70] Critics in Congress and elsewhere also charged that the military's growing package of benefits, which likely accounted for nearly half of the Defense Department's budget in some years, was depleting its fighting capabilities and siphoning off money from other essential items, such as weapons procurement.[71]

The spike in African American people serving in the US Army soon after the creation of the all-volunteer force raised additional concerns. The proportion of the US Army comprising Black people peaked at over 30 percent in the mid-1980s.[72] Military officials worried at the time that the "quality" of recruits was declining and feared that the armed forces, especially the army, might reach a "tipping point" in which "white men would no longer be willing to join what they saw as the low-status 'all-black Army.'"[73] Critics also charged that efforts to recruit more women were contributing to the "feminization" of the army and fueling a culture of dependency and passivity.[74] In response to these concerns, recruiters began shifting their sights during the Nixon and Ford administrations "from the relatively easy territory of urban ghettos, where employment opportunities were few, to the more difficult terrain of middle-class white suburbs and small towns" in search of "better recruits."[75]

In the 1980s and early 1990s, the Pentagon successfully repelled mounting pressures to slash benefits for military personnel. Concerned about falling short of their recruitment goals and a possible drive for unionization of the armed forces, military leaders and their supporters fought back and triumphed in expanding the military welfare state.[76] This was a remarkable victory, coming at a time when employment-based benefits for nonmilitary workers in the public and private sectors were under attack, as was the public safety net.

To combat unionization pressures, the army also ought to rebrand military service as a calling and an act of self-sacrifice, not just another job.[77] But in much of its marketing, the army deemphasized notions of citizenship, stressing instead individual opportunities for personal transformation, acquiring marketable skills, and going on exciting adventures overseas.[78] A key part of the army's strategy was to rebrand itself as an escalator for middle-class, high-achieving young men (and some women) who sought to "be all you can be," according to its ubiquitous marketing mantra from the 1980s and 1990s.[79]

A new GI bill that expanded education and other benefits for soldiers that became law in the 1980s was an important piece of this rebranding. Reagan championed the measure while leading the charge to slash federal higher education loan and grant programs for civilians and to gut core pieces of the public social safety net, including Medicaid, Social Security, and AFDC. Reagan argued that the publicly funded social safety net should be reserved for people who volunteered to serve their country.[80]

A grassroots movement of army wives was instrumental in efforts to defend and expand the military welfare state. Inspired by second-wave feminism, these women emphasized the unpaid labor they performed that was vital to keep the military going. Initially sympathetic to their concerns, army leaders soon became uneasy about the growing influence of these women. To stem their clout, the army began fashioning its family programs around the Christian right's model of family life at a time when the power and number of white conservative evangelicals in the armed forces were accelerating. The leaders of the religious right advocated for a more robust military welfare state by promoting the army as "an enclave of virtue" and portraying other US institutions and nonmilitary families as degenerate.[81]

The rebranding of the army did not deliver the upper- and professional middle-class recruits that had been hoped for. Recruits continued to hail disproportionately from working-class and lower-middle-class backgrounds. But the rebranding, with its emphasis on educational benefits, succeeded in transforming the image of the army from a dumping ground for misfits in search of government handouts to a magnet for high-achieving, patriotic go-getters.[82]

The All-Recruited Armed Forces

Throughout US history, socioeconomic factors have been critically important in determining rates of enlistment.[83] Like the carceral state, the warfare state has become an important feature of the political economy of rural America. The penal industry and state departments of corrections trawled the countryside and used misleading or false feasibility studies to promote building new prisons and jails as the key to the economic revival of rural communities. Likewise, military recruiters targeted rural communities in distress to meet their quotas.[84] The military's new recruitment strategies, coupled with wider changes in the political and economic context, did spur a geographic and racial realignment in the army. Beginning in the mid-1980s, the proportion of enlistees from the South and West accelerated, thanks to the Sunbelt's booming population, the military's new recruitment strategies, and the region's greater "propensity to serve," in the words of the Defense Department.[85] As the number of recruits from rural areas and small towns rose—so much that the US Navy was nicknamed the "prairie navy"—the proportion of African American recruits declined.[86]

With pressures to privatize all kinds of government programs and public services growing in the 1980s and early 1990s, the military was initially successful in repelling efforts to cede pieces of the military welfare state to the private sector. But as pressures intensified to reduce the defense budget, military leaders eventually did an about-face and became champions of privatization and subcontracting out services and programs.[87] They extolled the alleged greater efficiency and savings due to the reputedly lower-cost "free" market. (The true costs of the military's contracts with the private sector were often obscured by accounting gimmicks, much as the costs of the prison buildup and the privatization of penal services and facilities had been obscured or misrepresented.)[88] As the army began ceding portions of the military welfare state to private or semiprivate interests, health, housing, education, and other benefits for military personnel and their families started to erode. Military officials began promoting the army as an institution in which the best soldiers and their families did not look to the army to take care of them but rather to teach them how to take care of themselves.[89]

In 1979, the army failed to meet its recruiting goals for the first time since the start of the all-volunteer force.[90] In the early 1980s, the army met its goals once again, largely thanks to the deep economic recession and the lure of the military welfare state's package of benefits.[91] But in 1999, two years before the 9/11 attacks, all the armed services fell short of their recruiting goals for the first time.[92] The growing momentum for privatization and related cutbacks in military benefits, services, and programs in the 1990s had tarnished the attractiveness of military service. Furthermore, the rebounding economy was drawing away potential recruits, as was the opening of more opportunities for Black people in the private sector.

Unequal Sacrifices and Paying for the Post-9/11 US Military

The 9/11 attacks "provided the political cover" for huge increases in military spending to achieve "unprecedented military superiority."[93] While the Pentagon went on a buying spree for advanced weaponry, it neglected the needs of soldiers on the front lines, including providing them with basic protective gear such as safe, high-quality helmets and earplugs to minimize injuries from bomb blasts. Lethal gaps emerged between the needs of US troops who fought the forever wars and the defense industry that profited from the permanent state of war.

The US fighting force in Afghanistan and Iraq was radically different from the one that fought in World War II, Korea, and Vietnam. The US wars in Afghanistan and Iraq were the first major wars since the end of World War II that had to rely on an all-volunteer force. As a result, there was an unprecedented geographic and socioeconomic gap in who was killed or injured in combat during the forever wars. In short, "Iraq and Afghanistan have been working class wars."[94] Furthermore, during the US wars in Iraq and Afghanistan, the Defense Department contracted out to private firms many services previously performed by the military directly—everything from disposing of hazardous waste to food preparation to providing security to staffing and maintaining high-tech weaponry—which resulted in huge unaccountable costs and outright corruption.[95]

In the aftermath of the 9/11 attacks, it was a major political project for the George W. Bush administration to engineer a gigantic, intrusive, and expensive expansion of the national security state and to put the country on a perpetual war footing without breaking its commitment to slashing taxes and shrinking the government. The expansion of the warfare state entailed keeping its full costs obscured and beyond the reach of public scrutiny and accountability, just as in the case of the costly prison buildup. In an age dominated by antitax and antigovernment fever, lawmakers and prison administrators had relied on accounting gimmicks and other measures to conceal the full costs of the prison boom.[96] The unprecedented reliance on emergency supplemental budget requests purportedly to fund the wars in Iraq and Afghanistan served a similar function for military spending after 9/11. Supplemental requests became a backdoor way to greatly increase total spending on the military. Before 9/11, these requests constituted only a small percentage of all military spending. By 2007, they equaled 28 percent of all military expenditures.[97]

Supplemental budget appropriations for the military are not subject to the scrutiny of the normal budget process or to congressional restrictions to contain the budget deficit.[98] These so-called emergency appropriations ended up funding huge increases in weapons procurement for big-ticket items that had little to do with winning the wars in Iraq or Afghanistan but were a boon to defense contractors.[99] All branches of the armed services sought to exploit 9/11 to retain and increase funding for controversial legacy weapons systems, such as the F-22 ($412 million per aircraft) and the F-35 (the F-22's bargain-basement cousin at $135 million per aircraft), that were extraordinarily expensive to purchase, operate, and maintain. These weapons systems were like the "good china that stays in the dining room buffet rather than run the risk of being chipped," quipped one astute analyst.[100] The armed forces also used these supplemental requests to secure money for the lighter, faster, high-tech forces of the future that Donald Rumsfeld, secretary of Defense in the Ford and George W. Bush administrations, proselytized about. As the Pentagon invested heavily in new digitalized, high-tech systems beloved by Rumsfeld, it also tenaciously defended the expensive legacy weapons programs of the Cold War.[101]

The Bush administration and its supporters deployed additional mechanisms besides supplemental budget requests to minimize or obscure the record-setting increases in military spending. Champions of the largest military buildup since World War II characterized it as "only" 4 percent of the economy—compared to an annual average of nearly 8 percent between 1950 and 1990 at the height of the Cold War. With their "Four Percent for Freedom" campaign, they succeeded in making this figure the accepted benchmark for leaders of both political parties. Thus, spending on national security "would not have to be justified by facts on the ground" or "by demonstrated need, but rather by its relatively light burden on the economy."[102] In a similar fashion, advocates of the prison boom were masters at reframing the spikes in spending on corrections as fiscally insignificant.[103]

By 2007 or so, annual spending in inflation-adjusted dollars exceeded the peak in spending on the military during the Cold War, including the US wars in Korea and Vietnam and the Reagan military buildup.[104] The Bush administration's final budget request for fiscal year 2009 marked the "eleventh straight year of real increases in the defense budget."[105] Once supplemental outlays for the war were included, military spending was at its highest level since World War II.[106] Even as public support for the war in Iraq plummeted along with support for President Bush, few legislators of either party voted against the defense appropriations bills.[107] A national security expert who worked for the Bush and Obama administrations confessed that during these years the United States developed a "phenomenal killing machine."[108]

The defense sector's drain on brainpower also accelerated. Since World War II, the STEM (science, technology, engineering, and math) fields have gravitated away from bettering the human condition and toward advancing defense and corporate interests.[109] As federal and state funding for higher education plummeted, universities took on a growing share of research for the Defense Department and defense industry.[110] Lockheed Martin, the manufacturer of Black Hawks, F-35 fighter jets, and Hellfire missiles, is the government's largest contractor. In 2020, federal funding for Lockheed Martin surpassed the budget of the US Department of Education for the first time. At least a dozen universities participate in Lockheed Martin Day, part of a push by defense contractors to draw more STEM students into the defense industry. Lockheed has established extensive recruiting programs and research partnerships at historically Black colleges and universities, including Howard University, which has a storied history of opposition to military recruiting.[111]

Privatization and Mercenaries

Advocates of increased military spending used privatization to obscure the real costs of the warfare state and the forever wars, just as champions of the war on crime deployed privatization to conceal the real costs of the prison boom.[112] Dating as far back as at least the Civil War, mercenary troops have been integral to US military operations. But with the launch of the global war on terror and forever wars, mercenary forces assumed a gigantic role, at times dwarfing the footprint of regular US military personnel.

Privatization permitted the US military presence in Iraq, Afghanistan, and elsewhere to appear much smaller than it was. Contractors carried out numerous tasks in the war on terror, including interrogating, abusing, and torturing so-called enemy combatants held at Iraq's Abu Ghraib prison and

Guantánamo Bay in Cuba, providing security for US officials, and performing support services, including food preparation, transportation, and communications. Contractors who carried out combat and security functions for the United States overseas tended to be white male US veterans in their forties, while citizens from low-income countries predominated in contracted-out menial jobs.[113]

Employees working for private military contractors performed jobs in Iraq and elsewhere that in another era would have been done by US military personnel. In 2007, the number of contracted personnel in Iraq (about 180,000) exceeded the total number of US troops (approximately 160,000).[114] To this day, we cannot be sure of how many US military personnel are still stationed in Iraq, Syria, and elsewhere because official US figures do not include the shadow army of private contractors and often exclude special forces operations, many of which are run out of the CIA, not the Pentagon.[115] By some accounts, as of 2019, there were 50 percent more contractors than troops serving under the US Central Command region that encompasses the Middle East and Central and South Asia.[116]

Contracting out "inflated the already exorbitant costs" of the US wars in Iraq and Afghanistan.[117] During the two-decades-long US war in Afghanistan, the US government spent $145 billion on reconstruction and aid and an additional $845 billion on fighting the war. (This spending dwarfed Afghanistan's GDP, which ranged from $4 billion to $20 billion.) A 2008 study estimated that 40 percent of the money earmarked for Afghanistan actually found its way back to the United States and other donor countries in the form of corporate profits and salaries for consultants.[118] Between 2000 and 2006, Vice President Dick Cheney's old firm Halliburton—whose "very name became a shorthand for waste, fraud, and abuse in Iraq"—rocketed from twenty-eighth to sixth largest contractor with the US government thanks to its war-related contracts.[119]

With the escalation in weapons procurement and privatization of military personnel and services, the number of no-bid contracts skyrocketed. Meanwhile, the number of federal employees responsible for overseeing contracts did not increase. Private contractors were even enlisted to oversee other private contractors.[120] The Government Accountability Office (GAO) reported that the "largely unsupervised and unrestricted boom in weapons research and production" had produced vast cost overruns, widespread violations of contracting rules, and poorly managed programs.[121] These developments paralleled how the surge in privatization of prisons, jails, and penal services was matched by a drop in state and federal monitoring of the penal industry.[122]

American troops in Iraq and Afghanistan had frontline seats to how the Pentagon and State Department were shoveling billions of dollars to private contractors such as Blackwater and Halliburton while US troops were forced to scavenge for protective gear and struggled to keep their equipment in working order.[123] The Pentagon and its champions exploited the frontline shortages in Iraq to press claims that the US war in Iraq was underfunded, even as large portions of the emergency supplemental requests were siphoned off to fund weapons systems that had little bearing on winning the war in Iraq. United States soldiers found themselves unequipped to battle the growing insurgencies in Afghanistan and Iraq, whose main weapons were IEDs buried on highways and hidden in vehicles, not Soviet-era MIG jets.

The media reported how US soldiers had to resort to fashioning do-it-yourself body armor and retrofitting Humvees to withstand roadside bombs, and how parents stateside were purchasing basic equipment for their children serving overseas, including socks, boots, leg holsters, and night-vision goggles.[124] In December 2004, Iraqi-bound US National Guard troops stationed in Kuwait confronted Rumsfeld in a town meeting. They complained to the Defense secretary that US soldiers had to resort to "hillbilly armor"—rusty scrap metal and bulletproof glass scrounged from local landfills and bolted on their trucks—for protection against roadside bombs. To this Rumsfeld dismissively responded: "You go to war with the army you have, not the army you might want or wish to have at a later time."[125]

Hooah! The All-Volunteer Force and the Forever Wars

The global war on terror put additional and unprecedented strains on the all-volunteer force.[126] With the US invasions of Afghanistan in 2001 and Iraq in 2003, the military had to contend with meeting its enlistment goals during an extended war for the first time since the draft was abolished. The Department of Defense found itself spending hundreds of millions of dollars each year and deploying seventy-five hundred military recruiters with the goal of enlisting about eighty thousand new recruits annually into the US Army.[127]

Military recruiters massively retooled their recruitment and marketing strategies to meet the needs of the forever wars. They stepped up efforts to target white youths, especially males, from working-class and lower-class backgrounds who resided in declining, deindustrialized rural areas and small towns in what some critics called the "poverty draft."[128] As military recruiters embedded themselves in these communities, they fostered militarized and highly surveilled environments in local schools.[129] A provision in the No Child Left Behind Act of 2001 requires all public high schools receiving federal funds to provide military recruiters with personal contact information for students unless their parents have opted out.[130] (Project 2025, the Heritage Foundation's controversial blueprint for Trump's second term, called for mandating that all these students take the military entrance examination.)[131]

In some rural communities and small towns, recruiters became fixtures in local high schools, dispensing advice and privy to information and confidences from students, teachers, and parents that were useful in refining their enlistment pitches. Recruiters even served as substitute teachers, free of charge, in some school districts.[132] These developments had troubling parallels with the proliferation of school resource officers—a euphemism for school-based cops—that turned urban public schools into heavily surveilled and policed environments that critics charge fostered a school-to-prison pipeline.

Facing a recruitment crisis as the forever wars dragged on, as well as escalating calls to slash and privatize the military welfare state, the army sought once again to rebrand itself. The army began to reemphasize its "warrior ethos," and that military service was an obligation, not just a personal choice.[133] It no longer promoted itself as a provider of social goods, such as diversity and inclusion or humanitarian relief after natural disasters. Nor did it continue to laud itself as an escalator to the middle class for ambitious young people. The army adopted a new creed in 2003: "I am a Warrior and a member of a team." All soldiers now vowed: "I stand ready to deploy, engage, and destroy, the enemies of the United States of America in close combat."[134] The growing use of the exclamation "Hooah!" throughout the army signified the new emphasis on the warrior ethos.[135]

During the first few years of the wars in Afghanistan and Iraq, the army met its enlistment goals. But in 2005, it missed them by the highest margin since 1979. Furthermore, enlistment improprieties were at unprecedented levels as recruiters bent or broke the rules to meet their quotas.[136] The army soon began meeting its numerical goals once again, but the "quality" of recruits fell as it lowered admission standards. It issued more waivers for applicants with criminal records and accepted more people who performed poorly on the military's standardized entrance examination. The US military also accepted more recruits with extremist views, notably neo-Nazis and white supremacists. In 2006, Representative Charles Rangel (D-NY) introduced legislation to reinstate the draft, but it made no headway in Congress or with President Bush.

To meet its targets, the army increased bonuses for enlistment and reenlistment and began deploying troops for multiple tours of duty in war zones. The Defense Department relied heavily on its unpopular "stop-loss" program, which allows the Pentagon to unilaterally extend a service member's enlistment contract, a practice that critics likened to a "backdoor draft." These frequent deployments took a toll on the physical and mental health of military personnel. They also took a toll on their families, as troops were subjected to longer and more frequent deployments in combat conditions with shorter breaks in between at home.[137] The military established new programs to assist families in weathering the forever wars. But these programs "proved less successful," in part because they sought to "make families more resilient without alleviating the underlying source of stress."[138]

During the forever wars, the military relied heavily on the National Guard and Army Reserve units, which carry about eight hundred thousand people on their rolls.[139] After General Creighton Abrams became chief of staff of the US Army in 1972 during the US war in Vietnam, he sought to make the army "operationally dependent on the reserves" so that the United States could not fight a major war without calling them up.[140] If the president and other civilian leaders wanted to take the country into another war, Abrams reasoned, they would have to take the "politically sensitive and economically costly step of calling up" its "weekend warriors."[141]

With the forever wars in Afghanistan and Iraq, these "weekend warriors," many of whom never anticipated military careers, were pulled away from their families, jobs, and communities to serve one, two, or even three tours of duty overseas.[142] Calling up the Reserves and National Guard had a disproportionate impact on rural communities and small towns and in the South and West, which tend to have more "weekend warriors." By 2004, members of the National Guard were dying at a higher rate than regular active-duty soldiers, "partly because they were often given the dangerous task of guarding convoys."[143]

In the early years of the global war on terror, the racial and ethnic realignment of the military accelerated. New enlistments by Black Americans, which had dipped with the Gulf War in 1991, plummeted after 9/11.[144] Between 2001 and 2006, the share of African American people among active-duty recruits declined by 35 percent as a wide gap opened up between the views of Black and white Americans on military service and the war in Iraq.[145] Black Americans were much more likely to oppose the US war in Iraq and to question serving in the military and dying in combat for a cause they did not believe in.[146] But the number of Latino people serving in the US military skyrocketed thanks to aggressive recruitment tactics that targeted immigrants and to new policies to expedite citizenship for noncitizens who joined the armed forces.[147] By 2008, Latino people made up about 15 percent of all new military recruits—a figure that matched the rate for Black people and was a threefold increase since the establishment of the all-volunteer force in 1973.[148]

The financial crisis that struck in 2007 ended up being a godsend for military recruiters. Thanks to the Great Recession, the drop in African American recruits bottomed out and their numbers in the military began to turn upward.[149] As a top military official acknowledged at the time, "We do benefit when things look less positive in civil society."[150] Military recruiters were once again able to meet their numerical goals and attract higher-quality recruits even though casualties for US forces and the civilian population in Afghanistan were spiking to record levels with the troop surge President Obama ordered in 2009.[151]

Mind the Casualty Gap

During the forever wars, an unprecedented and politically explosive casualty gap opened up that surpassed the gaps during the US wars in Korea and Vietnam.[152] As the military became more dependent on recruits from the South, rural areas, the Reserves, and the National Guard to fight the forever wars, poorer, less educated communities with fewer economic opportunities disproportionately bore the burden of soldiers killed and wounded in combat.[153] Southern and interior Western states led the country by far in the proportion of their residents serving in post-9/11 military operations overseas.[154] All else being equal, residents of rural communities in the United States shouldered a greater share of the human costs of the global war on terror compared to residents of US cities, in a reversal from World War II and the US wars in Korea and Vietnam.[155]

Many residents of rural communities and small towns personally knew someone, or of someone, who had died in combat in Iraq—a friend, family member, acquaintance, coworker, or neighbor.[156] Senator John Kerry (D-MA) sparked a firestorm in 2006 when, during the height of the US war in Iraq, he tacitly acknowledged the casualty gap. Kerry told students at a community college: "You know, education—if you make the most of it, you study hard, and you do your homework, and you make an effort to be smart, you can do well. If you don't, you get stuck in Iraq."[157] Kerry's acknowledgment of the casualty gap was exceptional. Public officials and scholars "routinely overlook" the inequalities that undergird military service, and a large portion of the public "mistakenly believes there is shared sacrifice."[158]

Timely and accurate casualty figures are often a casualty of war. Fearful of jeopardizing public support for military actions, governments go to great lengths to suppress this information. The United States is no exception.[159] With the launch of the forever wars after 9/11, presidents, military officials, and other policymakers became even more circumspect and less transparent about the number of US troops killed or injured in overseas operations. They also obfuscated or outright lied about fatalities caused by US forces, including civilians killed in Iraq, Afghanistan, and elsewhere by the country's drone arsenal.[160] President Bush imposed a media blackout on coverage of the flag-draped coffins of deceased military personnel arriving at US bases in Ramstein, Germany, and in Dover, Delaware. President Obama lifted the ban, but his administration was not much more forthcoming about releasing information on the number of nonfatal combat casualties and rates of mental health problems, including suicide and post-traumatic stress disorder (PTSD), for troops returning from tours of duty in Iraq and Afghanistan.

Researchers at Brown University's Costs of War Project reported that seven thousand US troops and an additional eight thousand people working on contract with the US government had been killed as of 2019 in the global war on terror in the Middle East.[161] Although the number of US soldiers killed in combat in Iraq and Afghanistan was relatively low compared to other major wars, a high proportion of US troops experienced hostile fire and were friends or colleagues of soldiers who were killed or injured.[162] Furthermore, the number of US soldiers who were wounded in Iraq and Afghanistan was huge. But nonfatal casualties do not have "the same resonance with voters as fatal casualties."[163]

Thanks to medical and technical advances, US soldiers who sustained serious injuries in Iraq and Afghanistan were much more likely to survive (90 percent of them) compared to soldiers wounded during the American war in Vietnam (only 40 percent).[164] As of December 2013, more than 58,500 military personnel had been wounded in Afghanistan and Iraq, many of them severely, including major brain injuries.[165] The high incidence of brain injuries was partly due to the Defense Department's failure to distribute state-of-the art helmet pads as standard gear to members of the infantry.[166]

Elite troops, such as special forces, did receive the more expensive helmet pads. The army deemed that these soldiers were "quite frankly, smarter" than the average soldier, and that they took better care of their equipment.[167] The elite troops were thought to be worth the extra expense (about twenty dollars per helmet), even though treating soldiers with brain injuries and PTSD was already costing the Veterans Health Administration (VHA) hundreds of millions of dollars in the early years of the US wars in Iraq and Afghanistan.[168] The US Army continued to insist on supplying many nonelite soldiers with faulty helmets from "a favored contractor that enhance the effects of blasts."[169] These troops had to resort to purchasing the more protective helmet pads at their own expense or turning to a nonprofit group for assistance in modifying their helmets. Many veterans who served in Afghanistan and Iraq also experienced hearing loss and tinnitus due to faulty earplugs.[170]

The forever wars took a huge mental toll on the troops. Tens of thousands of soldiers were diagnosed with PTSD.[171] Military suicides, which were once rare, began rising among active-duty service personnel and post-9/11 veterans. Soon they significantly outpaced the rate for civilians.[172] The only other time that had occurred was during the US war in Vietnam. The rise in military suicides was attributed to many factors, including the increase in traumatic brain injuries and multiple injuries due to the proliferation of IEDs; the length of the forever wars; the multiple tours of duty; advances in medical care that made it possible to redeploy troops who had sustained severe injuries; and sexual violence and other sexual trauma in the ranks.[173] Even as deaths in combat declined considerably after 2007, suicide rates continued to climb almost unabated. Between 2001 and 2018, more than four times as many active-duty personnel and veterans of the post-9/11 wars died by suicide (30,177) than were killed in combat operations in the global war on terror.[174]

The Military Welfare State Under Attack

The military had no model for "fighting a prolonged, violent insurgency with a small volunteer force" and lacked "the resources necessary to ensure troops' mental health."[175] The Bush administration proposed few increases in the budget for the Department of Veterans Affairs (VA) despite the increased stresses of the US wars in Iraq and Afghanistan. For a time, the VA was not even spending all the money it had been allocated for mental health.[176] As the wars ground on, some senior military leaders became more outspoken about the toll that the forever wars were taking on the mental health of US troops. They advocated extraordinary and controversial measures to prevent suicides and address other mental health needs.[177]

People who served in Iraq and Afghanistan have a greater need for health services than veterans who served in the US war in Vietnam and other prior wars. This is because of "more frequent and longer deployments, higher levels of exposure to combat, higher rates of survival from injuries, higher incidence of serious disability, and more complex medical treatments."[178]

Total government expenditures for health care and other benefits for post-9/11 military personnel are expected to total a staggering $2.5 trillion by 2050—and even more if the rapid privatization of veterans' health care and the push to shift more health-care costs onto veterans is slowed down or reversed.[179] As it is, fewer than half of all regular-service veterans receive health benefits through the VA, which has complicated formulas for determining who qualifies and the amount of coverage they are entitled to. People who serve in National Guard or Reserve units typically do not qualify for health-care benefits after they are deactivated.[180]

Even prior to the global war on terror, policymakers in Washington seldom acknowledged the severity of veterans' physical and mental health problems.[181] For decades, Vietnam veterans struggled to get the US military to provide treatment and disability benefits for cancer and other illnesses caused by its widespread use of the defoliant Agent Orange in the jungles of Southeast Asia. The Pentagon also long denied allegations of a "Gulf War syndrome," despite widespread complaints of a cluster of acute and chronic symptoms, including memory loss, fatigue, and respiratory problems, among US troops who served in the 1990–91 Gulf War. Researchers have attributed the syndrome to several factors, including exposure to pesticides, anti-nerve-gas drugs, and munitions with depleted uranium, which the US military used widely for the first time during that war. The syndrome reportedly afflicted nearly one-third of the seven hundred thousand military personnel who served in Operation Desert Storm.[182]

During the post-9/11 wars in Iraq and Afghanistan, an estimated 3.5 million troops were exposed to dangerous burn pits run by the private contractor KBR, a former subsidiary of Vice President Dick Cheney's Halliburton Company. The Pentagon responded to health and disability claims stemming from exposure to the burn pits—dubbed the "Agent Orange" of the wars in Iraq and Afghanistan—with "bureaucratic skepticism and outright hostility." Military officials even accused service members of lying about their ailments.[183] These pits incinerated everything from human remains to pesticides to polyvinyl chloride pipes and other hazardous materials at hundreds of bases in Iraq and Afghanistan. Thousands of cases of cancer, including leukemia, and debilitating respiratory problems have been attributed to the open-air burn pits, which violated Environmental Protection Agency (EPA) standards and the Pentagon's own regulations. In 2016, Joe Biden suggested publicly for the first time that these toxic pits may have caused the brain cancer that killed his son Beau, who had served in Iraq.[184] In August 2022, President Biden signed legislation expanding federal assistance for veterans sickened by exposure to burn pits.

After 9/11, the military uplifted its "warrior ethos" in its recruitment campaigns and called for more "self-sufficient" troops. At the same time, however, it was vastly expanding the health-care benefits for retired military personnel, their families, and members of the Reserves and National Guard who were not on active duty.[185] But as the Defense Department's outlays for health care skyrocketed (from about 6 percent of its base budget in 2000 to nearly 10 percent in 2012), so did concerns about how the expanding military welfare state was coming at the cost of other budget items, notably weapons procurement.[186] Pressure escalated to shift more costs directly onto active-duty military personnel and retirees and to replace TRICARE, the military's main health program for active-duty personnel, with commercial insurance. So did pressure to cut expenses by outsourcing more military tasks to private contractors, who tended to skimp on providing benefits, including workers' compensation and other benefits that their employees are entitled to regardless of their nationality.[187] Companies often refused to purchase insurance for their contracted workers or to assist them in filing claims as required by the law. Furthermore, insurers routinely denied or delayed claims for disability and death payments.[188]

While the military was doubling down on the theme of self-reliance, a coalition of military officials, business interests, and conservative and far-right groups was pushing for a radical privatization of the military welfare state that would gut comprehensive pension, medical, and other benefits for the armed forces. Their attacks on the military welfare state mirrored their unrelenting efforts to slash public services and the social safety net for civilians by privatizing Social Security, replacing guarantees of medical care with vouchers, abolishing comprehensive pensions, and defunding public schools.[189]

This push to privatize and cut military benefits did not ease up, even as hundreds of thousands of people who served in Iraq and Afghanistan were returning home with grave mental and physical disabilities and as complaints escalated that they were not receiving adequate care and treatment. A 2007 *Washington Post* exposé documenting the shocking conditions for wounded US soldiers returning from the Middle East who were treated at Washington, DC's Walter Reed Hospital sparked outrage. Walter Reed was reputed to be the country's premier medical facility for military personnel. But care had deteriorated after this facility had been partially privatized.[190]

The American Legion (one of the country's largest and oldest veterans' groups) and younger veterans' organizations, including Iraq Veterans Against the War and Veterans for Peace, opposed wide-scale privatization. They pushed to rivet public attention on the formidable medical and mental health needs of veterans of the post-9/11 wars.[191] To counter this opposition, billionaires Charles and David Koch bankrolled a new organization in 2011, the Concerned Veterans for America (CVA), which promoted itself as a grassroots group. But CVA was Astroturf. Within a short period of time, it emerged as "one of the most muscular arms" of the Koch brothers' elite-led conservative advocacy network.[192] Other veterans' groups disparaged CVA as a political lobbying firm that represented the interests of its wealthy supporters, not those of the average veteran.[193]

As the physical and mental toll that the forever wars were taking on the troops escalated, the ideological battle over the military welfare state did not abate. Koch-funded groups and their lobbyists, as well as other conservative and far-right organizations, intensified their "long, brutal, and largely one-sided" war against benefits for veterans and active-duty personnel.[194] They sought not only to hasten the radical privatization of military benefits and services, but also to discredit the accomplishments of the Department of Veterans Affairs in social welfare provision, including health care and a pioneering program to end homelessness among veterans.

After Donald Trump won the 2016 election, CVA's influence soared. Former CVA leaders and other Koch insiders secured key appointments in the first Trump administration and mainstreamed what were once fringe ideas on veterans' affairs.[195] Pete Hegseth served as executive director of CVA beginning in 2011. Five years later, Hegseth was ousted from the veterans' organization amid allegations of sexual and other misconduct. He went on to become a star pundit at Fox News and then Defense secretary in Trump's second term.[196] Koch-funded groups and their supporters aimed to cast the VHA as a "failed experiment in socialized medicine," even though this federal agency had long outperformed the private-health-care sector on key metrics, including quality, cost, efficiency, and reduction in racial disparities in health outcomes.[197] The Koch brothers also targeted the VHA because it is heavily unionized.

The VHA provides care for a diverse patient population of about nine million people and has an outsized role in delivering health care to underserved rural areas. Until recently, it was the only US government health-care program that negotiated major discounts with the pharmaceutical companies.[198] Critics of the VHA contrived scandals and misrepresented data to tarnish the agency's reputation as a model of public provision of health care. Their most notorious claim (which was widely publicized in the media and later proven to be false by the VA's Office of Inspector General) was that veterans were facing life-threatening waits for care.[199] By undermining the VHA, the Koch brothers and other critics hoped to slow the momentum for "Medicare for All" championed by Senator Bernie Sanders (I-VT) and others pushing for a public system of universal health care.

The VA and VHA scrambled to maintain services as they were being plundered by privatization and budget cuts. More costs were directly shifted onto veterans, which enraged them. Passage of the Veterans Choice Act in 2014 "funneled millions of veterans into unaccountable and often substandard private care" and "enriched massive health care contractors."[200] The endgame was to transform the VHA from a direct provider of comprehensive care to veterans into something akin to a privatized health insurance program.[201] Privatization impacted members of the armed services and veterans in other ways. Thanks to a regulatory loophole in the GI bill enacted in the 1980s, military personnel and veterans became attractive prey for the for-profit college industry's high-pressure and fraudulent recruitment tactics.[202]

During his first term, President Trump promoted himself as a champion of military veterans and boasted that the VA budget reached historic highs under his watch. Left unsaid was that a growing proportion of that money was being siphoned off to private-sector providers. David Shulkin, Trump's first VA secretary, pushed back against the administration's aggressive drive to privatize the VHA and was removed from office. As the first Trump administration accelerated the contracting out of veterans' health services to private-sector providers and insurers, it pursued a multipronged public relations strategy that brazenly denied it was doing so.[203]

The VA Mission Act of 2018, enacted with the support of the Trump administration and eventually a coalition of veterans' groups, diverted billions of dollars from VHA facilities to private-sector providers.[204] The legislation, which included few mechanisms to hold the private sector accountable for the quality and cost of care it delivered, resulted in wide-scale fraudulent billing.[205] During Trump's first term, the VHA's acute staffing problems reached crisis levels as his appointees undermined recruitment and retention efforts.[206] As a result, the VHA's reputation for delivering high-quality care at lower costs was further besmirched, which played into the efforts by the Koch-funded

CVA and its allies to destroy the agency's reputation as a model for comprehensive, high-quality care delivered by the public sector. The push for privatization and outsourcing barreled forward under the Biden administration. Veterans Health Administration workers, their patients, and veterans' groups continued to be alarmed at the ongoing deterioration in the quality of care and the skyrocketing costs.[207]

The Political Consequences of the Casualty Gap

The casualty gap, the US defeats in Iraq and Afghanistan, and the privatization and retrenchment of the military welfare state had enormous political consequences. Wars that end in clear victories or that require mass mobilizations—such as the Civil War and the two world wars—tend to result in sustained increases in civic and political participation, in contrast with wars that end in stalemate or defeat, notably the US wars in Korea and Vietnam.[208] The costly and controversial US war in Vietnam initially spurred greater political engagement by fostering the massive antiwar movement to end the conflict. But the long-term political consequences of the US defeat in Vietnam included declining public confidence in the government's competence and declining public trust in the government. Communities that suffered the highest casualty rates during the US wars in Korea and Vietnam experienced the greatest drops in levels of trust in government, political engagement, and political participation, including voting.[209] The US wars in Iraq and Afghanistan, which fell far short of victory, have had some comparable political consequences.[210]

The casualty gap of the forever wars has long been an invisible issue at the national level. But for many years, it has been acutely felt and experienced in certain localities, even as much of the country mistakenly believed there has been shared sacrifice in waging the war on terror.[211] In the 2004 presidential campaign, criticism of the war in Iraq was still muted. Senator John Kerry, a Vietnam vet, ran against the mismanagement of the US war in Iraq, not the war itself. The Democratic nominee for president memorably took the stage at the party's convention with a salute and a vow that he was reporting for duty. But by 2006, with public support for the wars in Afghanistan and Iraq withering, Democrats ran on a modest antiwar platform that helped them win back the House and Senate in the midterm elections, returning them to power for the first time since the 1994 Republican takeover of Congress. Support for the Republican Party in the 2006 midterm elections was lower in communities that had shouldered more combat deaths.[212]

As the Iraq war slogged on, some of the most outspoken critics of the war were lawmakers from rural areas.[213] Members of Congress from districts and states with large contingents of veterans were more likely to condemn the war (after controlling for other factors, like ideology and partisanship).[214] In late 2006, Representative Nancy Pelosi (D-CA), the incoming Speaker of the House, vowed that ending the war in Iraq was her "highest priority."[215] But then she and other leading Democrats largely stepped aside as President Bush doubled down on the US commitment to the war in Iraq with a surge of another twenty thousand troops in early 2007.[216]

In the 2008 presidential campaign, the economy, not Iraq, was the preeminent issue thanks to the Great Recession and the financial crisis.[217] All the major Republican and Democratic candidates for president except Senator John Edwards (D-NC) were gung-ho on increasing defense spending even beyond what Bush had requested in the final year of his presidency. Although the economy was the main national issue in the 2008 election, the US casualty gap in the wars in Iraq and Afghanistan resonated with rural voters. Politicians from rural areas singled out the disproportionately higher rates of military casualties and service as evidence that rural residents were more patriotic.[218] Sarah Palin, the 2008 Republican vice-presidential candidate, made this a key theme as she barnstormed the country extolling how "the best of America" is found in the small towns that have been "fighting our wars for us."[219]

In the 2008 contest, Senator Barack Obama (D-IL), who had opposed the US invasion of Iraq years earlier when he was serving in the Illinois legislature, shrewdly positioned himself as against the wrong war but not antiwar. This was an important distinction that many of his supporters failed to recognize. Obama castigated the Bush administration for failing to get the job done in Afghanistan—the good war—because troops and resources had been diverted to the bad war in Iraq. Even though Obama campaigned against Bush's national security policies, he ended up embracing the Washington rules. He retained Robert Gates, Bush's Defense secretary, and appointed Hillary Clinton, one of the most hawkish Democrats, to be his secretary of State. Upon taking office, Obama declared Bush's surge in Iraq a success (despite ample public and private evidence to the contrary) and pivoted toward Afghanistan.[220]

On the advice of Gates and other military officials, Obama backed a surge that ended up increasing the number of US troops in Afghanistan from about sixty thousand to more than one hundred thousand during his first year in office.[221] As a result, casualties for US troops and Afghan civilians soared. The troop increase and then the unprecedented public campaign by General

David Petraeus (commander of US forces in Iraq) and other military officials in 2010–11 to pressure Obama to not begin withdrawing US forces from Afghanistan raised questions about whether the president controlled the generals or the generals controlled the president.[222] In his memoir, Obama reported that Vice President Biden had warned him to be wary of generals who "are trying to box in a new president."[223]

Years later, internal government documents dubbed the Afghanistan Papers revealed that US military and civilian leaders had lied to the public and had known for years that the United States was on a doomed mission in Afghanistan.[224] Obama supported the surge in Afghanistan and maintaining troops there despite widespread doubts among military officials and members of his administration that the US war in Afghanistan was winnable or worth the costs. Douglas Lute, the three-star army general who was the "war czar" for Afghanistan and Iraq for much of the Bush and Obama administrations, privately confessed in 2015 to investigators compiling the Afghanistan Papers: "What are we trying to do here? We didn't have the foggiest notion of what we were undertaking."[225]

Obama expanded the war on terror far beyond Bush's focus on Afghanistan and Iraq. He widened it to at least eight other countries as special forces operations and a vast arsenal of predator drones became integral, not incidental, to fighting the global war on terror.[226] In 2011, Obama essentially declared war on Libya, authorizing a massive bombing campaign and other interventions to topple the regime of Muammar Gaddafi. His war in Libya succeeded in overthrowing Libya's longtime leader at the cost of shattering the country in what Obama later confessed was the biggest mistake of his presidency.[227] Deploying secrecy, obfuscation, and outright deception, the Obama administration went to great lengths to conceal the staggering number of civilians killed by US forces in Libya and elsewhere as part of the American-led global war on terror. Official government reports on US air and drone strikes regularly failed to accurately note civilian casualties. Meaningful investigations of these deaths were rare. Sanctions for misconduct in choosing targets and related activities were even rarer.[228]

The White Power Movement Since 9/11

As the US global war on terror upended numerous other countries, it had enormous blowback at home. The Obama administration consolidated, expanded, and legitimized the government's massive surveillance program of

US citizens. Despite the blockbuster revelations by National Security Agency (NSA) contractor Edward Snowden in 2013 about this program, this dragnet continued to operate with no major judicial or congressional oversight.[229]

The war on terror and the 2007–9 financial crisis were boons for the white power movement. The Department of Homeland Security (DHS) reported in 2009 that the economic crisis and political climate were fueling a resurgence of "rightwing extremism," and that veterans were a primary target for recruitment.[230] The DHS warned that veterans returning from fighting in Iraq and Afghanistan who had difficulty reintegrating could "lead to the potential emergence of terrorist groups or lone wolf extremists capable of carrying out violent attacks."[231] Around this time, the FBI warned that members of white supremacist groups and their sympathizers were infiltrating law enforcement and the military and even compromising investigations of these groups.[232] The FBI reported that people with military backgrounds were assuming leadership positions in white power groups, helping to "reinvigorate" the movement in the post-9/11 era.[233]

The Republican Party attacked the DHS report, stoking a political firestorm. Faced with intense pressure from veterans' groups, the DHS withdrew the report and scaled back its monitoring of the white power movement. That action contributed to, among other things, serious undercounts of violent incidents committed by white supremacist groups.[234] Federal agents and other law enforcement groups prioritized instead policing the activities of Muslim groups and individuals, animal rights groups, environmental groups, student groups, peace activists, and civil rights groups. In the process, they trampled on the constitutionally protected rights of these groups and individuals, all in the name of combatting "domestic terrorism."[235] The FBI treated suspicions about potential minor, local crimes that are not federal offenses, such as vandalism and acts of nonviolent civil disobedience, as cause to launch domestic terrorism investigations of these groups, according to a scathing 2010 report by the Justice Department's inspector general.[236]

The federal government, the Pentagon, local governments, and police departments failed to prioritize tackling violence and other criminal activities committed by white power extremists and their militias.[237] They were also slow to acknowledge and address the growing presence of white power supporters and sympathizers in law enforcement and the military. As heavily armed far-right groups held well-publicized demonstrations designed to draw counterprotestors and mete out violence against them in the name of self-defense, local police increasingly stood back, looked the other way, or actively aided white nationalist groups.[238] During the 2020 wave of protests against the police killing of George Floyd, police officers openly fraternized and coordinated with armed vigilantes and militia members, ignored their curfew violations and other offenses, and even offered them bottled water and other support.[239] This was part of a troubling shift in law enforcement dating back more than a decade.

White power groups and private militias have recruited an expansive national network of members disproportionately drawn from local police, sheriffs, the US Border Patrol, and former and active-duty military personnel. Veterans and active-duty personnel constitute at least one-quarter of the rosters of some militias.[240] Thousands of members of the Oath Keepers, a paramilitary group that was at the forefront of the January 6 siege of the US Capitol, and of the American Patriots Three Percent, another antigovernment militia, have direct ties to the military and law enforcement.[241]

The country's three-thousand-plus sheriffs have become prize recruits for the white power movement.[242] Founded in 2011 by Richard Mack, a onetime sheriff in Arizona and former board member of the Oath Keepers, the Constitutional Sheriffs and Peace Officers Association (CSPOA) has been holding so-called training sessions for law enforcement.[243] The association's central tenet is that local sheriffs have the right and authority to not enforce laws or other measures that they deem unconstitutional—everything from gun restrictions to mask mandates. Hundreds of current and former sheriffs reportedly belong to CSPOA.[244] In 2021, John Eastman, one of the masterminds behind the attempt to overturn the 2020 election, launched the Sheriffs Fellowship program at the Claremont Institute, his base of operations. This fellowship program seeks to develop a "countervailing network of uncorrupted law enforcement officials" to combat "the perversion of the justice system" as evidenced by the response to the George Floyd protests, the Covid-19 lockdowns, and the "electoral disaster of 2020," according to its mission statement.[245] During his first term, Donald Trump held more meetings at the White House with sheriffs than any other president had in US history.[246]

Tallying how many white extremist and militia groups are operating in the United States and the size of their memberships is difficult. The number of white nationalist organizations in the United States reportedly escalated from thirty in 2008 to a peak of over three hundred in 2011 before falling to about two hundred as of 2022, according to some experts.[247] The Southern Poverty Law Center counted forty militia movement groups in the United States as of 2022.[248] Total membership figures for militia groups range widely from fifteen thousand to one hundred thousand.[249] After the January 6 attack on Congress, a number of white extremist groups and militias disbanded or went underground. But they prominently resurfaced as Trump won a second term and issued a sweeping grant of clemency to all of the nearly sixteen hundred people charged in connection with the 2021 insurrection, including two hundred people who pleaded guilty to assaulting police officers. On the first full day of his second term, Trump indicated there could be a place in American politics for the Proud Boys and Oath Keepers, two extremist groups whose leaders were found guilty of seditious conspiracy against the United States and were serving long sentences in federal prison when Trump commuted their sentences.[250]

Law enforcement agencies have significant authority and resources to combat the white power movement. But many of them have failed to do so. For example, dozens of states have laws that prohibit groups from organizing as private military units without the authorization of state governments. They also have statutes that specifically criminalize certain paramilitary activities, such as "parading" or "drilling" in public with firearms or teaching people how to use explosives to incite civil disorder.[251] But these statutes are generally not enforced, partly because they "are less clear-cut in their application than may seem to be true at first glance."[252] Some state lawmakers have sought to circumvent prohibitions on private militias by pushing legislation that would "effectively deputize private gun owners as members of volunteer state militias."[253]

Few law enforcement agencies specifically forbid their officers from affiliating with the white power movement.[254] If officers are subject to discipline related to their white power associations and sympathies, it is typically for violating general prohibitions against conduct that hurts the department or violates antidiscrimination or social media regulations. Police commanders and other public officials often mistakenly claim they cannot do more to root out extremism in the ranks because the First Amendment protects police officers' rights to free speech and free association. But the courts permit placing certain curbs on the First Amendment rights of law enforcement and other public employees.[255] Prosecutors also possess powerful tools to expose extremism in the ranks of law enforcement, but they have been loath to wield them.[256]

According to a Defense Department directive updated in 2012, military personnel "must not actively advocate supremacist, extremist, or criminal gang doctrine, ideology, or causes." They also "must reject active participation" in groups that promote such causes.[257] But what constitutes "active participation" appears open to debate, and it is not obvious that past activities are a bar to future enlistment. Furthermore, individual unit commanders, who have the responsibility to identify and discharge extremists, do not necessarily have the time, training, or inclination to do so.[258]

In 2017, the FBI and DHS conceded that the "white supremacist extremist movement" poses a persistent threat of lethal violence and has killed far more people since 2000 than any other "domestic extremist movement."[259] The proportion of militia attacks and plots aimed at the US military or local police jumped to 40 percent in 2017, a nearly threefold increase since the 1990s, according to one academic database.[260] But during President Trump's first term, the DHS further scaled back resources to track the white power movement, including disbanding a group of analysts focused on domestic terrorism in the Office of Intelligence and Analysis.[261] An uproar ensued in 2017 when leaked documents revealed that the FBI's Counterterrorism Division called for investigating "Black identity extremists"—a provocative name for a group that does not actually exist—as a "domestic terrorism" threat.[262] The FBI had pulled out its playbook from the 1960s and 1970s, implementing a new program called IRON FIST, which deployed undercover agents and other resources to counter the alleged threat of domestic terrorism posed by Black Lives Matter and its supporters.[263]

In a 2020 report to Congress, the Pentagon acknowledged that members of the military were "highly prized recruits" for the white power movement.[264] The report noted that leaders of white extremist groups have been joining the armed services and encouraging their followers to enlist to obtain weapons and get specialized training.[265] About one-third of active-duty personnel have witnessed signs of white supremacy in the ranks, according to surveys by *Military Times*.[266] Nearly half of active-duty personnel consider white supremacy to be a greater threat to the United States than North Korea and almost as threatening as foreign terrorism.[267] The armed forces continue to stonewall about releasing information about the number of weapons that have gone AWOL.[268]

Leaders of white extremist groups and militias have reviled the FBI and some federal, state, and local prosecutors for their roles in investigating Donald Trump and his associates. Their denunciations escalated in the aftermath of the January 6 attack as the Justice Department probed the assault and prosecuted the participants. An estimated one in ten people charged with crimes related to the insurrection had military ties, and one-quarter of participants with a military background were associated with far-right extremist groups like the

Oath Keepers and the Proud Boys.[269] Leaders of the attack on the Capitol deployed combat tactics and formations that were "instantly recognizable to any US soldier or Marine who served in Iraq and Afghanistan."[270]

Taking office in the wake of the January 6 insurrection, Secretary of Defense Lloyd Austin III ordered the military to take a two-month pause in training and other activities to address the problem of extremism in the ranks. He also announced new screening measures designed to weed out people with extremist ties from enlisting in the military. Just as Austin was issuing his executive order, a prominent white nationalist was finishing up boot camp after having enlisted in the US Air Force.[271] This is but one in a string of embarrassing and disturbing examples of how individuals with deep ties to the white power movement have been operating in plain sight in the military and other branches of the government, sometimes in high-level positions.[272] A 2022 report from the Defense Department's inspector general concluded that the Pentagon has been unable to implement policies to address extremism in the ranks because it does not understand the extent of the problem and what activities were prohibited.[273] This echoed the findings of a 2005 Defense Department report that concluded "the military has a 'don't ask, don't tell' policy pertaining to extremism."[274]

The selection of Pete Hegseth as Defense secretary in the second Trump administration suggested that the Pentagon may be more tolerant of open displays of white supremacy in the ranks going forward. One of the many controversies swirling around Hegseth after he was nominated was the large "Deus Vult" tattoo inked on his arm. The tattoo first drew attention when Hegseth was a member of the National Guard around the time of the January 6 uprising. The Latin phrase, which means "God Wills It," was a rallying cry during the Crusades a thousand years ago and is now a popular slogan among white power groups.[275]

After the January 6 siege of the Capitol, calls escalated to wage a "domestic war on terrorism" and to address the growing ties between the military, law enforcement, and the white power movement. Top Democrats endorsed legislation modeled on the Patriot Act, which sailed through Congress just weeks after the 9/11 attacks and has since been widely characterized by critics on the right and left as a grievous assault on civil rights and civil liberties. Some members of Congress, mostly Democrats, called for measures that would expand the criminal charges that could be brought under the vague, overly expansive definition of "domestic terrorism" and that would stiffen punishments for violations.[276] These proposals drew sharp criticisms from civil rights groups.[277]

During his confirmation hearings to become Biden's attorney general, Merrick Garland testified that combatting domestic terrorism would be his top priority.[278] In June 2021, President Biden became the first president in US history to unveil a national strategy to address "domestic terrorism."[279] That strategy was modeled in disquieting ways on the global war on terror. It called for further expanding the capacity of law enforcement and the national security apparatus to surveil and monitor at the cost of further eroding civil rights and civil liberties.[280] By further empowering the military, law enforcement, and domestic and foreign intelligence agencies, it risked legitimizing the white power movement's claims about an increasingly repressive state.

The fight over US immigration policy, especially along the southwestern border, has further emboldened the white power movement and the militias. It has also contributed to the militarization of law enforcement. Texas is the epicenter of these efforts. Republican Governor Greg Abbott has bolstered private militias by enlisting them in policing the border with Mexico. Furthermore, under Operation Lone Star launched in 2021, Texas essentially created its own independent military force, complete with Black Hawk helicopters, C-130 cargo planes, and ten thousand National Guard troops and law enforcement officers, to carry out its own version of immigration enforcement in defiance of the Biden administration. As of late 2024, Texas had spent $11 billion on this initiative, which has been linked to shocking human rights abuses.[281] In December 2023, Abbott signed SB4, a controversial bill that accords the state of Texas power to usurp the federal government's control of immigration enforcement. The legislation, which critics charge is unconstitutional, has since been winding its way through the courts. The Texas statute makes unauthorized migration—already a federal offense—into a state crime and permits local police to arrest migrants.[282]

Donald Trump and the Forever Wars

In the 2016 election, the forever wars burst through as a central issue in American politics thanks to Donald Trump. On the Democratic side, the party doubled down on the Washington rules. The Democratic convention featured so many generals and other military figures that some observers noted that the proceedings could be mistaken for a Republican convention of yore.[283] On the Republican side, however, the Washington rules were beginning to show some unprecedented cracks.

During the campaign, Trump relentlessly criticized the forever wars. He denounced the US invasion of Iraq (though he lied about having opposed the war from its start) and called for a US withdrawal from Afghanistan. His calls to bring the troops home resonated in areas of the country that disproportionately shouldered the burden of the forever wars. They also tapped into the vein of anti-imperialism and skepticism of overseas military adventures that courses through some segments of the white power movement. For some members of the white power movement, the US wars overseas were a distraction and drain on resources needed to wage the war against its enemies on the home front.[284]

Trump, who reportedly dodged military service in Vietnam after being diagnosed with bone spurs by a podiatrist friendly with his father, mocked Gold Star families who had lost loved ones in combat. He also ridiculed Senator John McCain (R-AZ), the 2008 Republican presidential candidate and a decorated veteran who had been a POW for more than five years in the "Hanoi Hilton." The Democrats and some leading Republicans lobbed a fusillade of criticisms at Trump for lashing out at McCain and Khizr and Ghazala Khan, the Gold Star parents who lost a son in Iraq and were featured at the Democratic convention.[285] Despite these attacks on the military, veterans stood by Trump, choosing him over Hillary Clinton by a two-to-one margin.[286] Trump won a greater proportion of voters who were veterans than McCain had won eight years earlier.[287] A targeted get-out-the-vote effort by GOPVETS, an organization aligned with the Republican Party, helped boost vet voter turnout by about 3 million voters compared to 2012.[288]

During Trump's first term, his stance on the military and forever wars was complicated. For all his bellicose rhetoric and gestures, Trump was the first president in decades who did not launch a new war. That said, he loosened the Obama-era rules for airstrikes in Afghanistan, leading to a spike in civilian casualties there. Trump also expanded the already gigantic Special Operations Command at a "frantic" pace, according to its former commander.[289] He backed a hike in defense spending, much of it directed at the procurement of advanced weaponry.[290] Trump contended that the US military was "totally depleted" and poorly positioned to wage major wars against "great power" enemies such as China and Russia because it was too enmeshed in battling the unwinnable wars in Iraq, Afghanistan, and elsewhere.[291]

In the 2020 election, veterans stuck by Trump once again despite his administration's rampant cronyism, scandals, and cutbacks in key programs for veterans and military personnel.[292] Veterans did not widely defect from Trump even as he continued to denigrate US troops killed or wounded in action as "losers" and "suckers."[293] After a slight dip in 2020, Trump's support among veterans soared in 2024, even though Project 2025, the Heritage Foundation's blueprint for his second term, called for deep cuts in veterans' benefits, including health-care and disability benefits. With Trump 2.0, the chaotic cost-cutting, layoffs, and edicts of the so-called Department of Government Efficiency (DOGE) have hit the VA hard. Despite a congressional mandate in the 2022 PACT Act to expand certain care for veterans, plans were underway to close VA hospitals, slash staff, cut services, and even hobble or abandon clinical trials, including for treatment of cancer and opioid use disorder.[294]

Deeply Wounded

The forever wars launched after 9/11 deeply wounded the political system and US democracy while leaving defense contractors and the Pentagon, but not US troops and veterans, unscathed. Rural communities and states in the South and interior West disproportionately shouldered the direct human costs of the post-9/11 wars. Their residents were more likely to be killed or wounded in combat and to return home with PTSD and other serious mental health disorders. The opioid epidemic also took a disproportionate toll on veterans.[295]

Many veterans, active-duty personnel, and members of the National Guard and Reserves were treated with cruel indifference. They were sent into combat without basic equipment and forced to endure multiple tours of duty. As they grappled with serious physical and mental health problems, they also had to grapple with privatization, budget cuts, and cost shifting that were hollowing out health care and other services for them. And the situation was even worse for people who served the United States as mercenaries hired by private firms under contract with the US government.

The public soured on the forever wars, but not on the US military. Even after the Afghanistan Papers revealed that US military leaders had lied to the public and had known for years that the United States was on a doomed mission in Afghanistan, the public's view of the military remained mostly untarnished.[296] Meanwhile, public opinion of other US institutions, both governmental and nongovernmental, sank even lower.[297]

In 2016, Donald Trump tapped into public discontent with the Washington rules and the forever wars as he waged what appeared to be a long-shot bid for the White House. His campaign fueled the white power movement, which emerged as an important part of his base. Public discontent with burgeoning corporate malfeasance also helped clear Trump's path to the White House, as discussed in the coming chapters. Decades of decriminalization of crime in the suites, the fallout from the financial and foreclosure crises, and the opioid epidemic created the perfect storm for his political ascent.

PART III

Corporate and Economic Violence

6

The Banksters Hiding
in Plain Sight

THE CORPORATE CRIME WAVES
FROM CARTER TO CLINTON

Better, so the image runs, to take one dime from each of ten million people at
the point of a corporation than $100,000 from each of ten banks at the point
of a gun.

—C. WRIGHT MILLS, *THE POWER ELITE*[1]

DURING THE 1920s and 1930s, the federal government and many states expanded their criminal legal systems as they waged Prohibition's war on alcohol and then sought to contain an alleged wave of violent street crime.[2] Shortly after taking office in 1933, President Franklin D. Roosevelt exploited sensational crimes, including high-profile kidnappings and murders (but not racialized lynchings), to push for an unprecedented expansion of the federal government's role in crime control.[3] But he also was forced to broaden the public understanding of crime to include corporate crime. The seismic wave of corporate crime that crashed the economy and sparked the misery of the Great Depression spurred a major public and political backlash against business and corporations. It resulted in an outpouring of landmark measures to regulate banks and corporations, stem economic inequality, and identify, contain, and punish corporate malfeasance.[4]

The US Senate's riveting Pecora hearings during the waning days of President Herbert Hoover's administration and the start of Roosevelt's presidency turned a scorching public spotlight on the banking sector's malfeasance and

163

its complicity in igniting the Great Depression. As he put the House of Morgan and other bankers on trial, Ferdinand Pecora, chief counsel of the Senate Banking Committee, helped popularize during the age of bootlegger and gangster Al Capone a term not heard today—the "bankster." These hearings compelled Roosevelt to support stricter controls of banks and corporations than he might have otherwise.[5]

By contrast, eight decades later, the financial sector, its top executives, and its political patrons emerged remarkably unscathed from the financial crisis that sparked the Great Recession, which was the largest economic collapse since the Depression. No top executive was prosecuted, let alone sent to prison, despite widespread evidence of criminal activities. With the assistance of record bailouts, the top financial institutions (including Goldman Sachs, JPMorgan Chase, Citigroup, and Morgan Stanley) that were instrumental in crashing the economy emerged from the Great Recession with even more wealth and political power and even greater immunity from prosecution and regulation.

This chapter first examines the long-standing dearth of scholarly and public attention to the issue of crime in the suites, including the lack of comprehensive databases to track corporate criminality and its victims. It then surveys how the escalating financialization of the US economy enhanced the privileged political position of the financial sector. More specifically, financialization spurred a radical transformation in how the criminal legal system deals with elite-level financial and other corporate crimes.

Financialization contributed to a shift toward a de facto decriminalization of corporate crime. This shift was not linear. It was decades in the making, with advances and modest and short-lived retreats. Fallout from the brazen criminality of the savings and loan (S&L) scandal during the Reagan years, as discussed in this chapter, spurred the George H. W. Bush administration to reimpose some important guardrails on the financial sector and beef up the regulatory and judicial apparatus to pursue corporate crime.

Bill Clinton, Bush's successor, hastened the financialization of the US economy and the decriminalization of corporate malfeasance, as detailed in this chapter. His administration set the stage for a series of corporate crime waves that inflicted great harm but went largely unpunished. These included the financial and foreclosure crises and the wreckage of the Great Recession, which are analyzed in chapters 7 to 9. The Clinton administration's soft touch toward corporate malfeasance starkly contrasted with its punitive and unforgiving stance toward street and drug crimes, which helped fuel the prison boom and a record increase in the US incarceration rate during the 1990s.

Corporate Crime and Violence: Out of Sight, Out of Mind

When sociologist Edwin Sutherland coined the term *white-collar crime* in 1939, he chastised criminologists and the criminal legal system for not taking crimes committed by people of high status and respectability in the course of their jobs more seriously.[6] In the decades since, popular use of the term *white-collar crime*, rather than *corporate crime* or *corruption*, has perpetuated a narrow focus on individuals, typically low-level employees or other people who commit offenses such as fraud and embezzlement.[7] This narrow focus has occluded the systemic nature of corporate crime engineered by elite-level executives aided and abetted by high-powered corporate law firms and their political patrons. It also has obscured the extensive harms that their criminal activities have perpetrated.

That was hardly Sutherland's intention when he developed the term *white-collar crime* decades ago. His conception of white-collar crime was an expansive one. It encompassed the criminal activities of high-status individuals who exploited the public's trust and their positions of power and respectability for personal gain. It also included the organized criminal activities of corporations that the criminal legal system adjudicated, as well as unethical and harmful business practices that were channeled into the civil courts or administrative bodies.[8] Sutherland observed that "white-collar criminals are segregated administratively from other criminals, and largely as a consequence of this are not regarded as real criminals by themselves, the general public, or the criminologists."[9]

Sutherland's pathbreaking *White Collar Crime*, published in 1949, spurred a handful of up-and-coming criminologists to focus on crime in the suites.[10] But this spurt of interest soon subsided thanks to political headwinds that included McCarthyism, the hegemony of the pluralist view of American politics, and the successful decades-long project of the corporate sector to reestablish its legitimacy and rehabilitate its public image (and that of capitalism) following the wreckage of the Great Depression.[11] The dearth of good databases on the nature and extent of crime in the suites was another contributing factor.

The surge in law-and-order politics and spike in the homicide rate in the mid-to-late 1960s spurred a surge in public attention to street crime.[12] The reigning consensus among scholars and opinion leaders at the time was that the public was indifferent to crime in the suites.[13] Politicians and policymakers invoked that alleged indifference to justify ramping up a war on crime that centered on street crime and that set in motion the gears of mass incarceration. The monumental final report of President Lyndon B. Johnson's crime commission, released in 1967, devoted just two pages to the subject of "white-collar offenders and business crimes."[14] The report concluded that "the public tends to be indifferent to business crime or even to sympathize with the offenders when they have been caught."[15] But the limited data available on public opinion and white-collar crime around that time suggested that the commission's claims were overdrawn.[16]

With passage of the Omnibus Crime Control and Safe Streets Act of 1968, criminology departments and programs proliferated at colleges and universities, thanks to a huge infusion of federal funding.[17] Their research and teaching agendas tended to reflect the concerns of government officials and policymakers, who fixated on street crime, not corporate crime, and who controlled key streams of funding.[18]

In the mid-to-late 1970s, scholarly and public interest in corporate crime and the political power of business in American politics briefly surged thanks to growing skepticism toward government and business. That skepticism had several sources, including the US defeat in Vietnam; Watergate and other major scandals; the civil rights movement's success in drawing public attention to issues of equal justice; growing interest in the rights of victims, including victims of corporate malfeasance; and the advent of a golden era for investigative journalism.[19] But by the early 1990s, interest in the role of business in politics and the criminal activities of the corporate sector had diminished. Criminology journals, textbooks, and courses continued to overrepresent street violence and underrepresent or ignore corporate violence and corporate crime despite massive corporate crime waves, including the S&L scandal of the 1980s and the financial and foreclosures crises of the aughts, which rocked the country's political and economic systems.[20] Likewise, the subject of business and politics failed to become a central concern of political scientists. The dearth of high-quality databases on corporate crime reinforced this deep and long-standing bias toward focusing on street crime, not crime in the suites.

Dearth of Corporate Crime Data

Researchers and journalists interested in corporate crime face a data desert compared to the quantity and quality of governmental and nongovernmental statistics that track and analyze street crime.[21] White-collar crime and corporate malfeasance barely exist, according to the FBI's Uniform Crime Reporting (UCR) program, which was established a century ago and until recently was the premier database for tracking crime in the United States.[22] The UCR has been a highly imperfect barometer of trends in all kinds of crime for many reasons.[23] In the case of corporate crime, it served to keep crime in the suites out of sight while keeping the public focused on street crime.[24] The central role that police departments and other law enforcement agencies played in establishing and administering the UCR and modifying it over the years help explain why. Furthermore, the UCR was developed during the 1920s, before many of the statutes that criminalized certain corporate activities had been enacted.[25] The National Crime Victimization Survey (NCVS), which was developed in the 1980s and became the country's other major database for tracking crime, also failed to capture the extent of corporate and white-collar crime.[26]

Since its inception, the UCR focused on collecting and analyzing data about types of offenses, not types of offenders or organized criminal activities. The UCR did not collect socioeconomic or occupational data on people who were arrested. It also did not gather data on corporate structures that might facilitate organized or systemic criminal activities.[27]

For decades, the official crime rate was calculated based on trends in the eight so-called part 1 or index crimes (murder, forcible rape, robbery, aggravated assault, burglary, larceny theft, motor vehicle theft, and arson), not trends in part 2 offenses, such as fraud or environmental crimes.[28] Thus, jaw-dropping cases of fraud, such as the gigantic Ponzi scheme engineered by Bernie Madoff with the help of knowing winks, nods, and tacit assistance from top financial institutions, had no significant impact on the official national crime rate. (Madoff was arrested in 2008 after his sons turned him in to the authorities.) Madoff's $20 billion grand theft was equal to about three and a half times the total yearly losses due to all robberies, burglaries, larcenies, and motor vehicle thefts in the United States.[29] His decades-long scheme also left no mark on the UCR's fraud data, which tallied the number of arrests, not the magnitude of the financial losses.

Likewise, the subprime mortgage scandal of the aughts robbed millions of people of their homes and life savings and saddled taxpayers with trillions of dollars in costs as the government bailed out the largest banks and other financial institutions, as detailed in chapters 7 to 9. But as far as the official national crime statistics and the UCR's fraud data were concerned, this epic fraud never happened. In another notable example, the deadly Flint, Michigan scandal a decade ago killed at least a dozen people and injured thousands more thanks to contaminated water and lead pipes. But this scandal left no trace on the US crime statistics.

Another factor contributing to the relative invisibility of corporate crime is that corporations are more impervious to outside scrutiny. Corporations, unlike government entities, are not subject to Freedom of Information Act (FOIA) requests. Civil lawsuits and criminal cases lodged against corporations have been important mechanisms to pry loose corporate documents and subject corporations and their executives to greater scrutiny. But the mounting legal barriers to filing and winning class-action suits and the proliferation of binding arbitration agreements, nondisclosure agreements, deferred prosecution agreements (DPAs), and nonprosecution agreements (NPAs) have fortified the veil of secrecy that shields corporations and their executives from outside accountability and scrutiny.[30]

Criminology's long-standing bias toward quantitative studies has also hampered research on corporate criminal behavior. Criminologists treat quantitative analyses as the gold standard in findings about crime and punishment. But studies of corporate criminal behavior have more difficulty meeting that gold standard compared to research on street crime because of the limitations of statistical data on crime in the suites, as well as definitional disputes over what constitutes corporate and white-collar crime.[31]

If we widen the lens to include qualitative studies of corporate malfeasance, including ethnographic research, historical accounts, case studies of individual corporations and specific corporate sectors, high-quality investigative journalism, and congressional and other government reports, a rich body of work on corporate criminal behavior comes into view.[32] These studies and investigations provide compelling evidence that, while the United States was constructing the carceral state by ramping up penalties for drug and street crimes over the last five decades, a de facto decriminalization of corporate crime was underway. In the wake of the financial and foreclosure crises, this corporate misconduct continued to rise, as did the political and economic clout of business led by the financial sector.[33]

The State and the Privileged Position of the Financial Sector

The "way a state punishes (or does not punish) capitalist offenders" hinges on "the nature of the relationship between the state and capital and the degree to which the offenses in question jeopardize that relationship."[34] In the late 1970s, a growing number of scholars of American politics began to question the predominant view that the US political system was fundamentally a pluralist one in which no single group, including business, holds disproportionate political power. The publication of *Politics and Markets* in 1977 by Charles E. Lindblom, a Yale professor who had been closely identified with pluralism, served to legitimize the study of the privileged position of business in the United States, bringing it from the Marxist and neo-Marxist fringes to the perimeter of the mainstream for a time. Scholars debated whether the political clout of business was overwhelming or whether its political fortunes fluctuated depending on various factors, including how the national economy and global economy were organized; how the business sector and individual firms were structured; the strategic choices and capacity of business associations such as the Chamber of Commerce and Business Roundtable; the relative power of potentially countervailing forces, including organized labor and public interest groups; and public perceptions of how well the economy was performing.[35]

Some scholars argued that the state was largely captured by business in all major public policy areas central to the corporate sector. Others contended that the privileged position of business was contingent. Under certain conditions, the government had the capacity to act autonomously from corporations, especially when their behavior fundamentally threatened the overall health and stability of the economy. In those instances, state actors would mobilize to rein in corporate activities that put at risk the interests of capital more broadly because a teetering economy threatened their own political fortunes.[36]

In assessing whether the political fortunes of business fluctuated, scholars of the US political economy tended to focus on policymaking in key areas related to regulation and redistribution. A parallel body of research in criminology dating from the 1970s and 1980s established that the privileged position of business was selective with respect to criminally prosecuting corporations and levying administrative sanctions on them. Corporations that violated labor laws, environmental laws, and health and safety standards for food, pharmaceuticals, consumer products, and the workplace seldom faced serious legal consequences. But if the criminal activities of the business sector gravely threatened the economy, a coalition of state actors, including law enforcement, would eventually spring into action, as in the case of the S&L debacle of the 1980s and early 1990s.[37]

But between the dawn of the new era of deregulation in the late 1970s and the eruption of the financial and foreclosure crises three decades later, a radical transformation of the financial industry spurred a radical transformation of the US economy and polity. This financialization of the United States further circumscribed the already limited autonomy that state officials had vis-à-vis the privileged position of business. The main preoccupation of commercial banks shifted from the old-fashioned business of lending to industrial and commercial enterprises, especially small businesses, to a preoccupation with speculative activities, including gaming the markets in real estate, consumer debt, and securities.[38] From 1978 to 2007, the amount of debt held by the financial sector skyrocketed from $3 trillion to $36 trillion.[39] Investment banks and other financial institutions became fixated on buying and selling securities using sophisticated mathematical models programmed to exploit or engineer small shifts in share prices.

Speculation thrives on instability, unpredictability, misinformation, falsehoods, big risk taking (all the better if it is with other people's money), and the lure of making a quick killing before the house of cards collapses. Heretofore, government officials had enjoyed some autonomy from business because the overall interests of capital depended on having a reasonably stable and predictable economic environment. But that formula broke down as speculation and financial gimmickry became the main drivers of finance—and increasingly the main drivers of the US economy.

Between 1970 and the eve of the financial crisis in 2007, the US financial sector grew to an unprecedented size. As a percentage of the GDP, it roughly doubled to about 8 percent. This figure surpassed the prior peak of 6 percent on the eve of the Depression and was quadruple the modern low of 2 percent in the mid-1940s.[40]

These figures understate the size and significance of finance. Leading nonfinancial firms now derive much of their revenue and profits from financial engineering as opposed to manufacturing and production. This financial engineering includes stock buybacks, direct loans to consumers to purchase their products, speculation in the oil and natural gas markets, and creative accounting to stash cash in overseas tax shelters.[41] Furthermore, figures for corporate profits do not include the supersized compensation packages that top executives rake in. These packages are deducted from reported profits and tend to be much larger than executive compensation in other sectors of the economy.[42] Since the late 1970s, compensation for chief executive officers has increased more than 900 percent after accounting for inflation compared to just a 12 percent rise for the typical worker.[43]

The financial industry favors investing in sectors that have the potential for quick, short-term gains, notably real estate and construction. It also specializes in so-called financial engineering, including financial gimmicks that incentivize companies to juice their stocks at the cost of investing in research and de-velopment (R&D) and other items critical to raising productivity and produc-ing jobs over the long run. Countries with large and fast-growing financial sectors tend to have weaker gains in productivity.[44] An overweening financial sector is deleterious to those sectors of the economy most vital for long-term economic growth and job creation, notably advanced manufacturing. An un-named economist who won a Nobel Prize for his innovations in financial en-gineering reportedly confessed to Paul Volcker, former chairman of the Federal Reserve, that these financial gimmicks do nothing to enhance the economy, including its productivity. Their main function is to move "around the rents in the financial system." And besides that, financial engineering "was a lot of intel-lectual fun," he told Volcker.[45]

A revolution in executive compensation helped to propel the revolution in financial engineering. Citibank was a pioneer beginning in 1977 in transform-ing the compensation structure for Wall Street by tying compensation to stock options.[46] Since then, stock options, shares of stock, and earnings from invest-ments have displaced salaries as the primary source of compensation for top corporate executives, hedge fund managers, and other major financiers. Tying compensation to share prices, stock options, and rates of return from invest-ments provided an enormous incentive for executives at Citi and then other financial institutions to pursue riskier deals to jigger their stocks and conceal bad assets and losses. Manipulation of a company's share price through stock buybacks and other gimmicks often hurt lower-level employees and other stakeholders and jeopardized the stability of the economy.[47] (These new forms of compensation were costly in other ways, for they are generally taxed at a lower rate than income from salaries.)[48]

Prior to 1982, companies were not permitted to repurchase their own stocks.[49] As US firms slashed jobs and cut investments in R&D and other items that boost productivity, spending on buybacks soared.[50] Even Apple, widely lauded for its visionary technology, disproportionately relied on finan-cial engineering, rather than the "old-fashioned kind" of engineering, to boost its bottom line and the value of its shares.[51] Its financial engineering included purchasing stock buybacks with low-interest bonds and stashing billions of dollars in offshore tax havens.[52] As of 2023, firms were spending an estimated 90 percent of their earnings on buybacks and dividends. Efforts to ban buy-backs or significantly tax them have faced daunting obstacles. The Inflation Reduction Act of 2022 included a minuscule 1 percent excise tax on stock buy-backs by publicly traded corporations.[53]

As financialization bolstered the privileged position of business, it also fostered a radical transformation of the criminal legal system with respect to corporate crime. Fraud and other financial crimes emerged as much more significant components of corporate crime as finance and real estate displaced manufacturing to become leading sectors of the economy. With the accelerated financialization of the US economy, financial crimes that enriched executives and managers but jeopardized a firm's long-term viability and the health and stability of the economic system proliferated.[54]

Origins of the S&L Scandal

The kid-glove approach to corporate malfeasance was decades in the making. As deregulation took off in the 1980s, so did the view that free markets were an antidote to financial fraud and that the best way to reform corporate criminal misconduct was to offer carrots to change corporate culture. The massive S&L scandal of the 1980s and early 1990s was a fundamental challenge to these claims.

In response to the S&L scandal, regulators, lawmakers, and the administration of George H. W. Bush belatedly installed some important guardrails. During the Clinton and George W. Bush administrations, everything they did "was undone," according to a lead regulator.[55] Not only were the guardrails removed, but new legislation accelerated the deregulation of the financial industry and thus hastened the financialization of the United States. All this occurred as the criminal legal system was undergoing a sea change in its approach to investigating, prosecuting, and penalizing corporate crime.

Explanations for the S&L and related junk-bond scandals of the 1980s emphasize the wave of financial deregulation that the Carter administration set in motion in the late 1970s and that the Reagan administration turbocharged with strong congressional support in the 1980s. The focus on deregulation overshadows the moderately successful acts of reregulation that occurred in response to the S&L crisis under Ronald Reagan's successor George H. W. Bush. Thanks to these measures, the losses from the S&L scandal totaled hundreds of billions of dollars rather than trillions of dollars. During the S&L scandal, the criminal legal system did not step aside as it would two decades later in response to the financial and foreclosure crises. More than one thousand people were convicted in felony cases characterized as major.[56] Furthermore, in a rare exception, the National Institute of Justice, the research arm of the Department of Justice (DOJ), which almost never funds studies of elite white-collar crime or corporate crime, funded a comprehensive autopsy of the S&L debacle. The NIJ study concluded that "collective embezzlement" perpetrated by S&L owners and executives was a major cause of the scandal.[57]

At the time, some public interest groups, members of Congress, and other critics complained that the Justice Department and other arms of law enforcement did not do enough to prosecute criminal behavior in the S&L crisis. They also charged that the bailout was constructed to enrich Wall Street at the expense of average taxpayers.[58] They faulted lawmakers for hastily drafting the S&L bailout legislation without adequate public scrutiny. Critics blasted the S&L bailout because it was opaquely designed to conceal its long-term costs; left average taxpayers, not the financial sector or wealthy people, to shoulder most of the costs; and enriched Wall Street thanks to the quasi-public bonds sold by the financial sector to pay for the bailout.[59] Critics also charged that many of the small fish went free as regulators working with law enforcement focused on catching the big fish. And some of the big ones escaped anyway.[60] Yet compared to the anemic response to the epic fraud in mortgage-backed securities that brought on the Great Recession two decades later, the government's response to the S&L debacle looks more impressive.

From the 1930s to the 1970s, S&Ls, also known as thrifts, had been a central component of national housing policy and one of the most stable, some would say boring, sectors of banking. The thrifts raised large amounts of deposits that they used to finance long-term, fixed-rate mortgages at below-market rates. They thrived for decades thanks to several factors. Structural reforms of the banking sector dating back to the Great Depression brought the thrifts under the auspices of the Federal Home Loan Bank Board (FHLBB), established in 1932, and, two years later, under the umbrella of federal deposit insurance as part of the National Housing Act of 1934. Government regulations shielded the thrifts from competition with commercial banks and with one another. Favorable macroeconomic conditions and government policies that kept interest rates from rising substantially or fluctuating widely also kept the thrift sector solvent.[61]

That changed in the 1970s as the US economy was gripped for the first time by stagflation—stagnating growth and raging inflation. The Federal Reserve Bank's shock treatment under Chairman Paul Volcker in the late 1970s and early 1980s to curtail double-digit inflation by jacking up interest rates to double digits was devastating for the S&L industry. It also hurt the manufacturing sector as the dollar's strength skyrocketed, making US exports less competitive and fueling deindustrialization across the country.[62] Locked into low-interest, fixed-rate, long-term mortgages, the thrifts could not compete with commercial banks and other financial institutions that offered high interest rates and other more lucrative investments.[63]

The S&L lobby and its powerful political patrons convinced legislators that deregulation was the solution for their failing industry, which by 1982 had a massive negative net worth. A series of regulatory and statutory changes, some explicitly aimed at S&Ls and others at the banking industry more generally, radically deregulated the thrift industry. They set in motion what has been called the "greatest-ever bank robbery" and the "cure that killed."[64] These measures opened the door to a "whole new world of variable-rate mortgages, ever more complex securities, derivatives to hedge them all, and the rapidly swelling financial institutions that would make vast fortunes on them."[65]

The FHLBB substantially loosened its restrictions on thrifts, including drastically reducing the net worth requirement for S&Ls (which meant they might have only razor-thin margins to cover any losses); allowing highly permissive accounting practices that enabled troubled and insolvent S&Ls to appear healthy on paper; and permitting S&Ls to grant loans to developers based on the appraised value of a property. In 1980, Congress, with the support of the Carter administration, enacted legislation that for the first time was aimed at bolstering S&L profits "rather than using the industry to promote housing."[66] The measure phased in the elimination of ceilings on interest rates for S&Ls and other financial institutions; permitted the thrifts to expand into riskier ventures, including consumer loans, credit cards, and corporate debt; raised the federal deposit insurance limit on deposits; and relaxed rules on bank mergers.[67]

Two years later, the Garn–St. Germain Depository Institutions Act enacted during the Reagan administration effectively abolished all ceilings on interest rates; granted S&Ls even wider latitude to invest in areas other than home mortgages; and eliminated some restrictions on how much S&Ls were permitted to lend developers. A leading analyst of the S&L debacle described the Garn–St. Germain Act as "the financial equivalent of a nuclear attack on the deposit insurance fund."[68] President Reagan, however, lauded it as a "home run" when he signed the legislation.[69]

The lifting of regulations on interest rates was a key catalyst for the S&L scandal. The thrifts began a rash of speculation using depositors' savings that were insured by the government. Moreover, at the same time that the FHLBB and Congress were radically deregulating the thrifts, they were also subjecting them to less supervision and oversight.

A Critical Realignment

The thrift industry benefited from a critical realignment engineered by the Reagan administration that bolstered public alarm about street crime while fostering public quiescence about corporate crime. President Reagan vilified risk taking on city streets to justify ratcheting up the penalties for street crimes and redirecting law enforcement resources away from policing crime in the suites. Meanwhile, he valorized risk taking by corporate executives to justify not only deregulation but also less rigorous oversight of financial institutions. During the Reagan years, thousands of federal agents tasked with investigating white-collar financial crimes were transferred to waging the war on drugs.[70]

This critical alignment had been decades in the making and had many powerful patrons—first on the margins and then in the mainstream of the Democratic and Republican Parties, academia, and the corporate sector.[71] In 1969, James Buchanan, who received his PhD in economics from the University of Chicago, established the Center of Public Choice at Virginia Polytechnic Institute. In 1983, he transferred the center to George Mason University, a public university just outside Washington, DC, in Fairfax, Virginia. Wealthy patrons, including energy czar Charles Koch, helped turn George Mason University into a powerful hothouse to incubate and spread "public choice theory" and "free-market absolutism."[72] Buchanan and other proselytizers wielded public choice theory to push for the wholesale privatization of nearly all government functions and programs, including schools, Medicare, and Social Security. Buchanan also deployed public choice theory to bolster opposition to integration in Virginia as he advocated for publicly funded vouchers for private schools to circumvent the US Supreme Court's 1954 *Brown v. Board of Education* decision. Buchanan and other public choice disciples disparaged civil servants and elected officials as little more than self-serving rational actors who were preoccupied with their own interests, not the public good. Indeed, Buchanan and his disciples were contemptuous of the idea that there could even be such a thing as the "public good."[73]

At this time, the burgeoning public interest movement—sparked by consumer advocate Ralph Nader, the new wave of environmental activism, and other developments—was attacking government but from a different direction. Members of the public interest movement charged that the government had failed to protect consumers, patients, the environment, and others because the private sector had captured government agencies. Their attacks on government from the left unwittingly contributed to public doubts about government and regulation that Buchanan and other free-market zealots had been stoking.[74]

In August 1971, a relatively unknown corporate lawyer representing the tobacco industry wrote what became a famous (some would say infamous) memo imploring the business community to mobilize against what he charged was a left-wing attack on corporations. In a confidential thirty-four-page memo to an official at the US Chamber of Commerce that became public a year later, Lewis Powell called on business to forge a united front against the growing public interest movement and organized labor.[75] Galvanized by the Powell memo, wealthy individuals and corporate executives established powerful and well-endowed think tanks and other organizations to press their interests, including the Cato Institute, founded by Charles Koch, and the Heritage Foundation, established by Joseph Coors of Coors Beer.[76]

The Powell memo called for rolling back the power of public interest groups, employees, and individuals to challenge corporations in court. A central pillar of this effort was to remake the judiciary, which Powell said "may be the most important instrument for social, economic and political change."[77] Weeks after Powell penned his manifesto, Richard Nixon nominated him for the US Supreme Court, which he joined in January 1972. A decade later, a group of law students at Yale, Harvard, and the University of Chicago founded the Federalist Society, which became the juggernaut of a decades-long project to transform the judiciary by seeding it with archly conservative judges who, among other things, turbocharged its procorporate tendencies.[78] The conservative Olin Foundation provided vital seed money for the Federalist Society.[79]

Powell's memo helped propel a sharp turn toward business with the help of generous support from conservative and mainstream foundations funded by leading corporations and banks. Economists centered at the University of Chicago supplied key intellectual firepower to justify a radical reconception of corporations.[80] They claimed that corporations had no obligations to stakeholders, including employees, communities, consumers, or the wider society. Their sole obligation was to maximize financial value for their shareholders. As University of Chicago economist Milton Friedman famously declared, the "one and only one social responsibility of business" is "to increase its profits."[81] The Chicago school proselytized that the best way to protect the interests of shareholders was through laissez-faire policies that liberated markets from government regulation and intervention.[82]

The Brain Drain to the Financial Sector

The financial sector and corporate law firms specializing in white-collar crime became a giant brain drain, siphoning off talent from other sectors of the economy and society. New graduates flocked to careers in finance and corporate law in unprecedented numbers as a huge pay gap opened up between careers in finance and careers in other sectors of the economy and government.[83] By the eve of the financial crisis in 2006, nearly three-quarters of graduating seniors from Princeton and over 40 percent of new Harvard graduates were taking jobs in finance or consulting.[84]

The business school at the University of Chicago emerged as the epicenter for a radical transformation in business education that propelled the financialization of the United States. Aided by Nobel laureates, hefty donations from business and conservative interests, sophisticated mathematical models, and quantum leaps in computer science, Chicago's B-school was a pioneer for a new kind of MBA education primarily focused on "finance, not business—a major distinction."[85] The key tenets of that education included that "markets know best," and that companies should be explicitly managed for the benefit of the short-term "interests of shareholders, and shareholders alone."[86]

As the financial sector emerged as a major funder of business schools and departments of economics, influential academics often neglected to reveal their conflicts of interest or affiliations with the private sector. These conflicts included lucrative consulting contracts with financial institutions.[87] (In a memorable scene from the 2010 Oscar-winning documentary *Inside Job*, Glenn Hubbard, a former top economic adviser to George W. Bush and then dean of Columbia University's business school, was asked about his role as a hired gun for financial institutions, including Bear Stearns, that were deeply implicated in the subprime fiasco and Great Recession. Hubbard answered by abruptly demanding that the filmmakers turn off their cameras.)

MBA programs in the United States, unlike those in Europe, began downplaying manufacturing, industry-specific expertise, ethics, and solving practical, real-world problems. Their emphasis shifted toward mathematical finance and financial engineering in the service of how best to increase gains for shareholders and corporate executives holding stock options. Lending for R&D and other activities to raise productivity and ensure a corporation's health over the long term were not priorities. Case studies, the staple of a B-school education, generally did not concern themselves with "the social, moral, and even larger macroeconomic consequences of corporate actions."[88] American MBA programs began mass producing traders fixated on how to game the stock market over the short term. These traders devised "financial weapons of mass destruction" that fueled the dizzying rise and fall of numerous dot-coms at the turn of the twenty-first century and then, a few years later, the financial and foreclosure crises that crashed the US and global economies.[89]

The reach of the Chicago school's radical take on markets and rational actors was expansive. The claim by Nobel prize–winning economist Gary Becker that people are rational actors who will desist from crime if the penalties are ratcheted up high enough so that the costs outweigh the benefits had an enormous impact on crime policy.[90] It helped to justify the prison boom in the name of reducing crime despite a growing pile of evidence that people are often irrational—not rational—actors when they commit street crimes. People frequently do not know what the actual penalty is or do not think they will get caught. Their judgment is often impaired because of drugs, alcohol, or mental illness. Not surprisingly, young people tend to be more irrational and more crime prone (when it comes to street crime, that is). They are swayed more by the moment they are in than by the future they cannot imagine. Experts on crime have demonstrated, contrary to the claims of the Chicago school and its acolytes, that longer sentences do not necessarily deter crime (and might actually be criminogenic).[91]

The Chicago school's radical take on corporate crime, which has received far less public attention, helped to legitimize the widespread decriminalization of criminal behavior by corporate executives. As the United States was embarking on an epic prison-building boom by ratcheting up punishments for both major and trivial infractions in the case of street crime, economists centered at the Chicago school were proselytizing magical thinking about corporate fraud. They claimed that free markets were the best protection against fraud because they provide perfect information about value through prices that automatically self-correct. As Alan Greenspan, chairman of the Federal Reserve from 1987 to 2006, once declared, laws against fraud were unnecessary because "if a floor broker was committing fraud, the customer would figure it out and stop doing business with him."[92]

The Reagan Administration and the S&L Scandal

The S&L debacle proved otherwise. Deregulation, coupled with the pullback in supervision and oversight, "created powerful incentives and opportunities for insolvent and weakly capitalized S&Ls to use insured deposits to grow rapidly and engage in speculative, imprudent, and sometimes fraudulent activities," according to the National Commission on Financial Institution Reform, Recovery, and Enforcement (NCFIRRE).[93] "Weak regulation and lax enforcement" at the federal level and "virtually nonexistent regulation and supervision" in some states, notably Texas, Florida, and California, "encouraged the equivalent of 'ponzi' schemes in which rapid growth guaranteed accounting profits and the capacity to loot S&Ls through dividends, perks, bonuses, and payments to developer-owners," the commission concluded.[94]

In some cases, outright corruption was to blame for the disappearance of deposits in government-insured and other thrifts. In other instances, incompetence, foolishness, and bad luck were to blame as local real estate markets collapsed.[95] The "S&L lambs" fell prey to more sophisticated Wall Street operatives, who sold them complex financial products that were a "far cry" from the heretofore stable, predictable, locally based market in home mortgages that they had been more accustomed to.[96] Savings and loans, once the most staid sector of the banking industry, were transformed into vehicles to hide and launder vast sums of dark money, including from organized crime figures, arms dealers, drug traffickers, and even Central Intelligence Agency (CIA) operatives involved in off-the-books missions.[97]

Senior executives of failing S&Ls and others who preyed on the thrifts became wealthy, sometimes fabulously so. Some of them lined their pockets with kickbacks they received for approving shady loans for dubious projects, many of them ridden with conflicts of interest. Some banking executives were developers of the risky projects they were approving loans for. Savings and loan executives also became rich thanks to the dawning of a new age in executive compensation based increasingly on sales volume and stock values, not annual salaries. As the volume of loans soared, the fees that their institutions received also skyrocketed. The short-term profits were enormous, at least on paper, which propelled the liftoff in executive compensation. As S&L executives gambled with other people's money and became rich, their institutions were careening toward insolvency. The pile of bad loans mounted, and the government and ultimately the public would be left holding the bag for these losses.[98]

The S&L debacle was also a windfall for Wall Street. Investment bankers helped investors acquire thrifts and then make the most of their new assets by, among other things, facilitating mergers and acquisitions so the S&Ls would grow rapidly. Wall Street reaped a second windfall as it profited from sweetheart deals negotiated with the government to unwind the debacle.[99] Regulators on the front lines were not blind to what was happening.

Early on they began warning that a disaster was in the making. But the S&L industry was able to convince the public and Congress, at least for a time, that the situation was under control. In 1983, Ronald Reagan appointed Edwin Gray, a close, longtime associate and member of his administration, to join the FHLBB. Gray became chair of the board in 1984. A strong advocate of deregulation, Gray had persuaded the White House to back the Garn–St. Germain Depository Institutions Act of 1982. But after taking over as head of the FHLBB, Gray began sounding the alarm that the S&L industry was in crisis.[100]

This Reagan loyalist became the bête noire of the S&L industry and its political patrons as he sought to stem the looting by imposing new regulations and more supervision.[101] Gray acted in the face of vigorous objections and outright threats from the industry, the White House, and powerful members of Congress, including Speaker Jim Wright (D-TX) and the "Keating Five," five US senators accused of improperly intervening with regulators on behalf of Charles Keating, chairman of the troubled Lincoln Savings and Loan Association.[102] Keating, who eventually served four and a half years in prison on charges related to the S&L scandal, had friends in other high places, including Alan Greenspan. Between his stint as chair of the Council of Economic Advisers under President Gerald Ford and then chair of the Federal Reserve beginning in 1987, Greenspan served as a business consultant. During that time, he received $40,000 from Keating for writing fawning letters to regulators and for testifying before Congress on his behalf.[103]

Congress essentially encouraged the FHLBB "to keep insolvent S&Ls open, operating, and growing."[104] In a letter to Ronald Reagan's chief of staff, Keating denounced Gray as a "Nazi" who was "diametrically opposed to everything your administration stands for."[105] Reagan's Office of Management and Budget (OMB) threatened to make a criminal referral against Gray on the grounds that he had closed too many S&Ls. Operators of some of the biggest S&Ls sued members of Gray's staff for hundreds of millions of dollars, hired private detectives to investigate them, and eventually succeeded in getting some of them fired.[106]

Deregulation under Reagan consisted not only of eliminating regulations but also of lopping off regulators charged with enforcing the regulations that remained. In 1981, David Stockman, Reagan's first OMB director, imposed a hiring freeze on regulators. When Gray implored an OMB official in 1985 to double the number of bank examiners as the S&L scandal was spinning out of control, the official rebuffed his request, saying it went against the administration's philosophy.[107] The S&L industry succeeded in blocking Gray's reappointment as chair of the FHLBB. Gray's successor sought "to appease Keating," which "set off a civil war within the Bank Board" and stymied the push initiated by Gray for greater regulation of the thrift industry.[108]

In the face of fierce opposition and threats, the FHLBB under Gray nonetheless succeeded in containing the crisis but not resolving it. Had it not been contained early on, the eventual tab for the S&L bailout would likely have been trillions of dollars rather than hundreds of billions.[109] The debacle would likely have rivaled the cost and swath of destruction of the subprime mortgage crisis decades later.

By 1986, many S&Ls were insolvent, and the insurance fund for federally insured thrifts was bankrupt. But during the 1988 presidential campaign, both George H. W. Bush and his Democratic rival Governor Michael Dukakis avoided the S&L issue since the causes of the debacle were deeply bipartisan.[110] Sparse media attention on the S&L crisis at the time helped them bury the issue. Behind the scenes, the outgoing Reagan administration and banking regulators were brokering sweetheart deals to "rescue" the thrifts that amounted to another massive giveaway to some of the country's richest people, including Ronald Perelman, proprietor of the Revlon fortune and protégé of junk-bond king Michael Milken, who served time in prison for his role in the S&L and associated junk-bond scandals.[111] Some members of Bush's "Team 100"—individuals who contributed at least $100,000 to his presidential campaign—were parties to these sweetheart deals to rescue the thrifts.[112] In one of the most notorious deals, which became public only in 1990, James M. Fail, an indicted securities trader, successfully contrived to acquire around $3.5 billion in Texas assets by putting up only $1,000 of his own cash. The intervention of a former aide to then Vice President George H. W. Bush was crucial in Fail's success.[113]

Cleaning Up the S&L Mess

After the election, the media and others began reporting that the S&L crisis was spinning out of control, putting the overall health and stability of the financial system and wider economy at risk. A broader set of state actors, including not just regulators but also Congress, the president, and law enforcement, belatedly sprang into action. Shortly after taking office in 1989, President Bush announced a plan to clean up the S&L mess. Vast infusions of public money were eventually needed—an estimated $500 billion—to cover the government-insured deposits that had disappeared because of "unprecedented fraud."[114] This sum was about twice the total cost in inflation-adjusted dollars of the US war in Korea or nearly ten times the cost of the Marshall Plan to rebuild Europe after World War II.[115] With Bush's support, Congress enacted the Financial Institutions Reform, Recovery, and Enforcement Act (FIRREA) in 1989, which established the Resolution Trust Corporation to shut down insolvent thrifts; adequately fund depositors' accounts covered by federal insurance; roll back some of the lax regulation and supervision of thrift industry; and rejigger federal agencies to protect government entities from being captured by the industry they were supposed to oversee.[116]

The FIRREA authorized tougher civil and criminal penalties for financial crimes and included a major infusion of funding for the Justice Department to investigate and prosecute financial fraud. Confronted with the worst epidemic of financial fraud in US history up to that point, Bush vowed in 1990 to "throw the crooks in jail."[117] But his administration initially dragged its feet about pursuing the culprits and refused to spend funds authorized by Congress to pursue financial crimes.[118]

In late 1990, the sprawling Crime Control Act of 1990, sponsored by Senator Joe Biden (D-DE), sailed through Congress. It included numerous get-tough measures for street crimes and other offenses.[119] President Bush lamented that the bill did not go far enough to penalize street crimes but lauded its provisions to enhance the prosecution and punishment of financial crimes in the wake of the S&L debacle.[120] The legislation increased the civil and criminal penalties for bank fraud, embezzlement, and other crimes. The 1990 act authorized nearly $500 million over the next three years for law enforcement to investigate and prosecute financial crimes and established a special task force to spearhead these efforts. It also created NCFIRRE, an independent advisory commission, to examine the causes of the S&L debacle and make recommendations to avoid a similar scandal.[121]

Between fiscal 1990 and fiscal 1991, the FBI's budget and personnel to investigate financial fraud roughly doubled. Although many smaller fish escaped, the extent to which the legal system held the S&L scandal's bigger fish accountable "was extraordinary."[122] Nicknamed the "sherpas" for law enforcement, regulators made more than thirty thousand criminal referrals, as well as about eight hundred civil actions and over three thousand enforcement actions. They worked closely with the Justice Department and FBI to identify and then prioritize the biggest S&L fraud schemes. Counting only cases categorized as "major," more than one thousand people were convicted of felonies, and many of them were sent to prison.[123] Some high-rolling business titans were convicted, including Michael Milken and Ivan Boesky, who served about two and three years respectively in federal prison. Gordon Gekko in Oliver Stone's 1987 film *Wall Street* was reportedly a composite of Boesky, Milken, and a couple of other financiers. In the film, Gekko, played by Michael Douglas, gives his "greed-is-good" speech, which was likely based on a 1986 commencement address Boesky delivered at Berkeley's B-school. Thanks to the film, "Greed is good" became an epithet for the 1980s and the financial sector.[124]

The 1990 crime act included the officially named Financial Kingpin Statute. Modeled on the drug kingpin provision in the Drug Control Act of 1970, it mandated sentences of ten years to life for masterminds of major financial crime operations. However, the Financial Kingpin Statute had more bark than bite. Since the 1990s, virtually no one has been sentenced to life in prison for financial crimes under this statute. Meanwhile, the number of people receiving life sentences and life sentences without the possibility of parole (LWOP) for street and drug crimes has skyrocketed.[125] People have been sentenced in record numbers to "the other death penalty" or "death by incarceration" for serious violent crimes, such as homicide, as well for minor infractions. (For example, under California's draconian three-strikes law enacted in 1994, people drew life sentences for third strikes that included such minor offenses as stealing videotapes, pilfering pizza, or taking change from a parked car.)[126]

Around this time, reinvigorated regulators staunched another potential scandal that would have dwarfed the S&L debacle and that foreshadowed the epidemic of subprime mortgage fraud that began infecting the economy a dozen or so years later. In 1990–91, regulators became alarmed about the spread of so-called toxic waste, which was later nicknamed "liar's loans." These are loans in which lenders conduct shabby underwriting. Lenders abdicate their most basic and important obligation—accurately assessing how risky a potential loan is by using standard yardsticks, such as verifying a borrower's income, assets, and liabilities.[127]

As liar's loans mushroomed, regulators soon became concerned that this "toxic waste" would be "exceptionally criminogenic" and potentially catastrophic for the economy.[128] Regulators quickly cracked down, alerting their examiners to be on the lookout for the telltale signs of sham underwriting. They also put lenders on notice that systematic failure to abide by the government's underwriting requirements amounted to fraud and would entail serious sanctions.[129] Some banks continued to flout the federal underwriting requirements, but federal overseers generally succeeded in cracking down on this fraudulent lending practice before it inflicted wider damage on the economy.[130]

The NCFIRRE's final report called for additional measures to ensure that wrongdoing in the S&L industry and financial sector more broadly was "aggressively prosecuted."[131] It castigated Congress for doing the "industry's bidding" for many years in the face of mounting alarms about the escalating costs of the S&L debacle.[132] The NCFIRRE recommended creating specialized antifraud units and appointing inspectors general in federal agencies who would be responsible for regulating institutions that receive federal insurance or guarantees. It also recommended that Congress and regulatory agencies develop better accounting standards to stem the abuses that allowed failing S&Ls to appear healthy—at least on paper.[133] The commission also called on the legal and accounting professions to establish specialized rules of professional responsibility that would hold lawyers and accountants responsible if they knowingly helped abusive and corrupt operators conceal their actions.[134]

Most of these recommendations were not implemented. That should not detract from the fact that, in response to the S&L debacle, regulators and prosecutors belatedly spun into action to staunch the losses, criminally prosecute the perpetrators, and reinstall some guardrails to prevent another such scandal. They pushed back despite enormous political pressures and outright threats not to do so.

Clinton and Financial Deregulation

The Clinton administration tore down key guardrails put in place during the Bush administration in response to the S&L fiasco. It also hastened the deregulation of the financial services industry and the decriminalization of corporate malfeasance. The Clinton administration did not act alone. Key accomplices included the US Sentencing Commission (USSC), the US Supreme Court, the Federal Reserve under Alan Greenspan's leadership, and US business and law schools, which mainstreamed what had once been fringe ideas about markets and corporate fraud. The critical backdrop to these developments was the accelerating financialization of not only the US economy, but also the US political system and American society. Together these developments enhanced the privileged position of the financial industry at the expense of manufacturing, other sectors of the economy, and the broader society as wealth, income, and political power became more unevenly distributed.

After Bill Clinton took office in 1993, it was back to the future as his admin-istration picked up where Reagan's antiregulatory regime had left off. Clinton deregulated the financial sector far beyond what Carter and Reagan had engi-neered. His administration set the stage for the epidemic of fraud in the subprime mortgage market that imperiled the economy during the adminis-trations of George W. Bush and Barack Obama. The Clinton administration's key props included nonchalance toward fraud; disregard for liar's loans; ardent support for dismantling the firewall between commercial and investment banking that dated back to passage of the Glass–Steagall Act in 1933; and fierce opposition to regulating financial derivatives.

The Clinton administration was dismissive of fraud as a problem. As one of the people charged with spearheading Vice President Al Gore's signature campaign to "reinvent government" explained, "don't waste one second going after fraud."[135] Some of the reinventors were also overtly disdainful of government.[136]

Legal scholars centered at, you guessed it, University of Chicago's law school were instrumental around this time in mainstreaming a dismissive stance toward fraud and other corporate crimes. Frank Easterbrook, a federal judge appointed by Ronald Reagan, and Daniel Fischel, who went on to be-come dean of Chicago's law school, contended that the main responsibility of firms, with some exceptions, was to maximize profits. These authors of a popular textbook on corporate law argued that "managers not only may but also should violate the rules when it is profitable to do so."[137]

The conservative Olin Foundation spent $68 million bankrolling the estab-lishment of law and economics programs at Chicago and other leading law schools.[138] These programs, which also received funding from Charles Koch and other figures on the far right, were ostensibly neutral vehicles. But they were actually designed to promote conservative ideas about the Constitution, the free market, and limited government.[139]

In a major reversal at the beginning of the Clinton administration, the White House essentially resurrected liar's loans. It replaced the loan under-writing rule that had been imposed during the Bush administration "with a deliberately unenforceable 'guideline' that did not prohibit liar's loans."[140] A former top banking regulator during the S&L crisis described this move as "the single most destructive act of deregulation by the Clinton and Bush (II) administrations," which is saying a lot.[141]

The Clinton administration also dynamited the firewall between commercial and investment banking that had been erected decades earlier in response to the

Great Depression and a series of periodic and devastating financial panics dating back to before the Civil War. Widespread speculation in securities by banks was a major cause of Black Tuesday, the stock market crash in 1929 that heralded the start of the Great Depression and spurred a run on banks. Over the next four years, more than four thousand banks closed permanently, pummeling depositors with nearly $400 million in losses.[142] A Senate investigation helmed by prosecutor Ferdinand Pecora "unearthed massive evidence of recklessness, cronyism, and fraud both in the use of depositor funds and in the promotion of securities for sale to the public."[143] His investigation implicated, among others, banks that eighty years later would once again play central roles in marketing toxic securities, foisting them off on unsuspecting investors, and enriching their executives by short selling a company's stock as the market crashed.[144]

In the years leading up to the Great Depression, banks had been wildly misrepresenting the value and riskiness of the securities they were promoting. They were also shorting their clients—that is, trading against them to reap money for the bank. The Glass–Steagall Act, officially named the Banking Act of 1933, was a seminal piece of legislation that changed all that. It severed commercial banking (the relatively stable business of accepting deposits and providing business and consumer loans) from the riskier but potentially more lucrative business of investment banking (which involves issuing stocks and bonds and brokering large, complex investments, including corporate mergers and acquisitions and initial public offerings, better known as IPOs).[145]

Glass–Steagall also established the concept of deposit insurance and created the Federal Deposit Insurance Corporation (FDIC), which insured deposits in commercial banks for a fixed amount ($5,000 in 1933; $250,000 today) to head off a run on banks in case of a financial crisis. To ensure that banks did not use the cushion of government-insured deposits and access to low-interest credit through the Federal Reserve to speculate in risky investments, Glass–Steagall also regulated the amount of interest that banks could offer to attract deposits. Commercial banks would have access to low-interest credit through the Federal Reserve to cover short-term liquidity crunches, but investment banks generally would not.[146]

By the 1970s, commercial banks were chafing at Glass–Steagall's restrictions and sought to circumvent them.[147] Their model was First National City Bank (which became Citibank in 1976). Since the 1960s, First National had been a pioneer in developing financial products that skirted restrictions on interest rates and that engaged in more speculative activities with government-insured deposits—and then dared regulators to call foul.[148] As discussed earlier, thrifts and commercial banks secured major victories in the early 1980s when Congress relaxed rules on bank mergers and deregulated interest rates, permitting banks to offer essentially whatever rates they wanted to attract depositors.

The Federal Reserve also was instrumental in chiseling away at Glass–Steagall. In spring 1987, it voted 3–2 to permit commercial banks to engage in certain underwriting activities. Fed Chairman Paul Volcker cast one of the dissenting votes. He was fearful that commercial banks would engage in selling risky securities, offloading the risk to the government and ultimately to taxpayers thanks to federal deposit insurance and their privileged access to low-interest credit through the Federal Reserve's discount window.[149] Alan Greenspan, Volcker's successor, and officials in the George H. W. Bush administration endorsed steps that further enfeebled Glass–Steagall. In 1991 they made a failed attempt to get it repealed.[150]

In 1998, Citibank dealt the coup de grâce to Glass–Steagall when it merged with Travelers Group, joining what had been a commercial bank with an insurance and investment firm to create Citigroup, the world's largest financial conglomerate. The merger was in apparent defiance of Glass–Steagall and the Bank Holding Company Act of 1956, which permitted banks to sell insurance but not underwrite it.[151] The Clinton administration did not seriously push back against the merger. In July 1999, Robert Rubin resigned as Treasury secretary. Three months later, Citigroup announced that Rubin would be the chair of its executive committee (with a reported annual salary of $40 million).[152]

In November 1999, Clinton signed the Financial Services Modernization Act of 1999, which essentially repealed Glass–Steagall.[153] As a sweetener to hasten its passage, the bill also included a measly expansion of the Community Reinvestment Act, which sets rules for lending in poor communities.[154] Nicknamed the "Citigroup Authorization Act," the measure sailed through Congress, ushered along by the financial services industry's massive and expensive lobbying campaign. The repeal of Glass–Steagall facilitated the expansion of commercial banks into the business of buying and selling mortgage-backed securities, credit default swaps, and other toxic investments, which would be the tinder for the financial crisis that exploded several years later.

The Clinton administration also resuscitated the private equity industry, which had temporarily collapsed in the wake of the leveraged buyout scandals and the prosecution of corporate raider Michael Milken in the late 1980s. The little-noted National Securities Market Improvement Act of 1996, which sailed through Congress, included a provision that eliminated limits on how many investors a hedge fund could have and "still be exempt from strict rules that reduce risky, speculative activities."[155] This provision opened the way for private equity firms to amass and invest trillions of dollars without requiring them to register with the Securities and Exchange Commission (SEC) and be subject to reporting and other requirements under the Investment Company Act of 1940.[156] In the decades since, private equity firms have delivered outsized returns to investors while bankrupting companies; slashing jobs, wages, pensions, and other benefits; and pursuing other cost-cutting measures that put the health, safety, and livelihoods of workers, patients, consumers, and communities at risk.[157]

Top officials in the Clinton administration and Fed Chair Alan Greenspan also championed the Commodity Futures Modernization Act (CFMA) of 2000, which prohibited the federal government and states from regulating financial derivatives. Derivatives are securities whose price is derived from one or more underlying assets, and their value is determined by the fluctuations in the value of that asset. The underlying asset can be anything from agricultural commodities to gasoline to interest rates to bundles of mortgages or student loans. By 1998, the global market for customized over-the-counter derivatives—that is, financial derivatives traded in private, opaque deals that are not listed on public exchanges like the New York Stock Exchange—had grown to over $70 trillion in face value (or about ten times the entire GDP) from virtually nothing a decade earlier.[158] As the opaque market in financial derivatives was taking off, a leading financial journalist warned in 1994, "Like alligators in a swamp, derivatives lurk in the global economy. Even the CEOs of companies that use them don't understand them."[159]

Brooksley Born, chair of the Commodity Futures Trading Commission (CFTC), warned that the exploding market in these derivatives and other unregulated financial instruments posed serious risks to the economy. But Clinton's leading economic policymakers strongarmed Born and thwarted her efforts to regulate financial derivatives as part of the mandate of the Commodity Exchange Act, which had created her agency in 1974.[160] In an infamous phone call in 1998, Larry Summers, who was deputy secretary of the Treasury at the time, reportedly warned Born: "I have thirteen bankers in my office, and they say if you go forward with this you will cause the worst financial crisis since World War II."[161]

The wave of megabillion-dollar scandals at the time involving derivatives and other new financial instruments did not derail the CFMA. Neither did

Born's opposition.[162] In another parting shot to regulation during Clinton's final year in office, the federal Office of Thrift Supervision succeeded in pre-empting state regulation of underwriting—and then proceeded to dispense with its own underwriting regulations.[163]

The dismantling under President Bill Clinton of the firewall between commercial and investment banking, together with the federal government's abandonment of antitrust enforcement, propelled the consolidation of the financial sector. As financialization swept the US economy, waves of consolidations and mergers swept the United States, enriching the financial institutions and corporate law firms that brokered these deals. While large companies became only slightly bigger in Europe, they became gigantic in the United States thanks to the increasingly permissive stance toward mergers and acquisitions by US courts, the Justice Department, and regulators.[164] The new age of oligopoly stifled economic competition, fueling higher prices and lower wages. It also stifled political competition as the two main political parties sought to aggressively court financial and corporate interests. Thanks to financialization, firms, executives, and the uberwealthy had gigantic resources that they could invest in lobbying and electoral politics as the courts stripped away restrictions on campaign finance.

Clinton and the Decriminalization of Crime in the Suites

The Clinton years were a transformative time not only for the deregulation of finance but also for the punitive turn in the criminal legal system when it came to crime in the streets and drug offenses. Clinton was a pivotal figure in fueling the largest run-up in the country's prison and jail population and other punitive measures. Less well known is that the Clinton years were a transformative moment in the federal government's approach to corporate crime. As Clinton and other policymakers spurned the rehabilitative ideal and were hellbent on ratcheting up penalties for street crimes, they were pivoting toward a kinder, gentler approach to crime in the suites.

In the 1970s, some leading liberal groups and individuals had become disenchanted with the rehabilitative ideal—that is, the belief that the primary purpose of incarceration and other sanctions was to change the antisocial and criminogenic attitudes and behavior of people convicted of street crimes. They contended, without much evidence to support their views, that indeterminate sentences perpetuated class and especially racial discrimination and yielded too much power to judges and parole boards to determine who was considered rehabilitated and worthy of release.[165] Their disillusion with indeterminate sentences provided a huge political opening for conservatives to push penalties for street crimes in a more punitive direction. The federal government and many states eliminated indeterminate sentences and replaced them with tough mandatory minimums, three-strike laws, and determinate sentencing statutes. At the federal level, the highly politicized US Sentencing Commission, which was established in 1984, began imposing tougher guidelines for street and drug crimes. In 1987, parole was eliminated for federal crimes.

As the rehabilitative ideal was falling out of favor with respect to street crime, a new rehabilitative ideal was germinating for corporate criminal misconduct. In the 1980s, academics and others began contending that the best way to deter crime in the suites was not by punishing corporations, individual executives, and other corporate employees. The better alternative was to inculcate law-abiding corporate cultures through improved internal compliance and training programs.[166] In 1991, the USSC adopted the first sentencing guidelines for corporations (four years after the guidelines for individuals went into effect). The commission singled out the overall adequacy of a company's internal compliance programs as the single most important factor in reducing the size of fines (by as much as 60 percent) imposed for corporate criminal misconduct in a federal case.[167] After adoption of the guidelines, the mean sentence for fraud in federal court nearly doubled, increasing from about one year to nearly two years between 1996 and 2011.[168] But white-collar defendants continued to draw much lower sentences than people convicted of drug and street crimes, and many major corporate and white-collar cases never ended up in court as deferred prosecution and nonprosecution agreements proliferated.

The US Sentencing Commission's view on corporate compliance complemented a new perspective on corporate criminal misconduct that was emerging in the Justice Department under Clinton and that contributed to the proliferation of corporate DPAs and NPAs under his successors. For the DOJ, the presence or absence of an adequate internal compliance program would become a central factor in determining whether corporations would even be charged or prosecuted in the first place.[169]

The original concept of "deferred prosecution" dates back to the 1930s when prosecutors began embracing pretrial diversion for juveniles apprehended for criminal activities. They agreed to defer and then eventually drop the charges for juveniles who successfully completed rehabilitation programs. In the case of corporate DPAs, prosecutors and companies enter into essentially a contract.[170] Typically, prosecutors consent to drop the charges (or not file any charges at all in the case of NPAs) if a corporation cooperates with investigators; acknowledges responsibility for certain criminal behavior and agrees to refrain from it; and implements a compliance program to prevent repeat misconduct. The absence of a good compliance program was equated with a lax corporate attitude toward corporate criminal misconduct. To secure a DPA or NPA, corporations do not have to plead guilty because they technically have not been charged with a crime. In some cases, they do not even have to admit responsibility for the criminal behavior.

Key officials in the Clinton administration were instrumental in laying the ideological and institutional groundwork for this monumental shift in how the federal government deals with criminal misconduct by large corporations that became entrenched under his successors. Mary Jo White, US attorney for the Southern District of New York, consummated the first DPA with a major corporation in 1994 to settle a case involving Prudential Securities.[171] After that, complaints escalated from white-collar lawyers that the DOJ lacked explicit guidelines for prosecuting corporations, a charge that career prosecutors grumbled was unsubstantiated.[172]

Bowing to these pressures, the Justice Department issued the Holder memo, named after Eric Holder, who was then the deputy attorney general under Janet Reno.[173] The 1999 memo conceded that the government was not seeking to routinely indict corporations as long as they cooperated with investigators. The memo also called for greater leniency for corporations that cooperated, including, "if necessary," their willingness to waive corporate attorney-client and other privileges. In laying out the rationale for seeking a corporate DPA, the memo called on prosecutors to consider the "adequacy of non-criminal remedies, such as civil or regulatory enforcement actions." It noted that government officials could also consider certain "collateral consequences" in determining whether to press charges against a corporation, including "disproportionate harm to shareholders and employees not proven personally culpable."

This sympathetic stance toward corporate malfeasance was starkly at odds with the Clinton administration's stance toward people accused of street and drug crimes. Clinton was a leading voice, along with Senator Biden, in the chorus of politicians, public officials, policymakers, and experts on crime and punishment who were spurning rehabilitation as a central goal of the criminal legal system. As Clinton once boasted, "I can be nicked a lot but no one can say I'm soft on crime."[174] In a grimly choreographed moment from the 1992 primary trail, Clinton made a show of flying back to Arkansas to sign the execution warrant of Ricky Ray Rector, a mentally disabled African American man.[175] Clinton championed the draconian 1994 crime bill and presided over a roughly 40 percent increase in the US incarceration rate during his eight years in office.[176] His administration also pushed for ratcheting up the collateral consequences for people convicted of drug offenses and street crimes. These measures included a vast expansion of bans on public housing, public assistance, and student loans for people convicted of drug-related crimes.[177]

During the twilight of the Clinton administration, corporate fraud emerged as a leading story as the dot-com bubble burst. Banks and financial services firms had made huge amounts of money from fees that they charged to arrange IPOs and from their preferential access to shares of companies that were about to go public.[178] At the same time, these banks and financial institutions were providing potential investors with analyses of the future risks and value of these companies. The result was a huge conflict of interest, with analysts under pressure to be overly bullish on the future potential of the very stocks their firms were marketing.

The stock market reeled as dozens of internet companies that had "spent lavishly, paid lavishly, told lies," and gone public were going bankrupt.[179] Wall Street firms and their star analysts had hyped these startups, bestowing stellar investment ratings and extraordinary valuations to attract their lucrative IPO business. In private, their analysts would deride these startups as junk—or "pos," which was short for *piece of shit*, not *positive*, as one up-and-coming star analyst clarified in a private email to a colleague.[180]

Many of the new dot-com companies were losing gigantic sums of money and were unlikely to ever become profitable. Under Clinton, the Justice Department and SEC did little to ferret out and punish the rampant fraud that fueled the dot-com bubble. Instead, they helped set in motion a radical shift in the approach to corporate criminal misconduct. The DOJ would cease charging high-level executives with crimes, focusing on their firms instead. The department would eschew indicting these corporations, preferring to seek DPAs and NPAs that were subject to little outside scrutiny or enforcement, as detailed in the next three chapters. These developments helped set the stage for how George W. Bush, Barack Obama, Congress, regulators, and law enforcement would respond to the epic fraud in the subprime mortgage market that set off the Great Recession. In short, the Clinton years were the dawn of a new era of crime and no punishment for major corporations, banks, and their executives.

7

Greed Is Not So Good

GEORGE W. BUSH AND THE FINANCIAL AND FORECLOSURE CRISES

"Bill, is what you're doing legal? I don't see how it can be."

—FATHER OF BILL WINTERS,
FORMER TOP JPMORGAN EXECUTIVE[1]

CORPORATE CRIMINALITY was a leading news story as George W. Bush took office in January 2001. Even after the 9/11 attacks and the launch of the war on terror in fall 2001, corporate crime remained a major issue during President Bush's first term. Initially the Bush administration took a tougher stance than the Clinton White House had toward investigating and prosecuting corporate criminality. But over time, the administration's approach to major cases of corporate crime shifted toward leniency and turning a blind eye. Deferred prosecution agreements (DPAs) and nonprosecution agreements (NPAs) were institutionalized under Bush. Their wide-scale use beginning in the early aughts signaled the federal government's retreat from the pursuit of elite-level corporate crime. These opaque get-out-of-jail-free contracts, which have no parallel in other countries, spared corporations from major penalties. Federal prosecutors also began backing off from filing charges against individual executives and corporate officers, focusing instead on corporations as the main defendants. After Bush's reelection in 2004, his task force on corporate crime sputtered, and prosecutions and investigations of corporate crime plummeted.[2]

Blowback from the government's 2002 prosecution of the accounting firm Arthur Andersen for its role in the Enron scandal helped turn the tide against

Bush's tougher stance toward corporate crime. So did a series of corporate-friendly court rulings and a counteroffensive by corporate law firms and lobbyists. Two other important factors were the deepening financialization of the US economy and the impact of 9/11 on the government's priorities and resources.

As the Bush administration mobilized to fight the global war on terror, it did not retreat from waging the wars on drugs, street crime, and immigrants that had propelled the US incarceration rate to record heights. But it made no sustained effort to increase the number of federal prosecutors and investigators charged with pursuing corporate crime. The administration also did not bolster the system of federal regulators empowered to make criminal referrals, which had atrophied under Clinton. Despite loud warnings early on from the Federal Bureau of Investigation (FBI) and elsewhere, the Bush administration, the Federal Reserve, and other key regulators were complacent about reports of burgeoning fraud in the market for mortgage-backed securities, which would spark a financial crisis at the tail end of his presidency.

The "Andersen Effect"

In early September 2001, amid allegations of cooked books and multibillion-dollar grand theft by its executives and accountants, the energy giant Enron imploded in the largest bankruptcy in US history up until then. The Texas-based Enron had close ties to the Republican Party and to George W. Bush in particular. Enron CEO Kenneth Lay was one of Bush's top fundraisers and was affectionately nicknamed Kenny Boy when Bush was governor of Texas. At the time of Enron's collapse, senior adviser Karl Rove worried that Bush might be a one-term president if Enron's implosion continued to dominate the headlines.[3] The meteoric rise and fall of Enron were due to a combination of "corporate greed, accounting scandals, public influence mongering, banking scandals, deregulation, and the free market mantra."[4] Leading banks, other financial institutions, and accounting firms were implicated in helping Enron and several other large firms in creating artificial profits and concealing liabilities so as to lure investors to buy their stock for a premium price.[5]

Months after Enron went bankrupt, Bush summoned Deputy Attorney General Larry Thompson and FBI Director Robert Mueller to the White House. They showed the president some of the evidence they had amassed in the Enron investigation and similar cases. Stunned by what they showed him, Bush reportedly said, "Bobby and L.T., continue what you are doing."[6]

In June 2002, the main stock indexes plummeted as reports surfaced that executives at the telecommunications giant WorldCom had committed fraud totaling $3 billion. Investors started "panicking about which public company holding their retirement funds might topple next."[7] In July, WorldCom went bankrupt. At the time, Citigroup and other top financial institutions were implicated in a rash of sweetheart deals and conflicts of interest that enriched World-Com executives and their bankers but ultimately brought down the firm.

That month, Congress enacted the Sarbanes-Oxley Act in response to Enron and other accounting-related scandals. This major legislation, among other things, upgraded accounting requirements for corporations; increased criminal penalties for accounting offenses; enhanced whistleblower protections; obligated CEOs and CFOs to certify that their companies' books were accurate and complete; and accorded prosecutors more oversight authority and power. Around this time, Bush also signed an executive order to establish the Corporate Fraud Task Force. Weeks later, he told a group of prosecutors that the "high-profile acts of deception in corporate America have shaken people's trust in corporations, the markets and the economy." He declared that the public needed to know that "we're acting. We're moving, and we're moving fast."[8]

How fast was not easy to discern because the Department of Justice (DOJ) does not collect comprehensive data on corporate crime or most other serious white-collar crimes, as discussed in chapter 6. But a major 2007 investigation by the American Lawyer concluded that Bush's task force had not been just window dressing but rather a serious "top-down strategy that encouraged local prosecutors to charge both corporations and individual defendants with fraud."[9] Hundreds of people were convicted, and some top executives were sentenced to lengthy prison terms, including corporate officers from Enron, WorldCom, and Adelphia, a leading telecommunications company.

In March 2002, the DOJ indicted the accounting firm Arthur Andersen, accusing it of stonewalling the government's investigation of Enron. The department charged that Arthur Andersen had hastily destroyed tens of thousands of documents as trucks worked around the clock to cart away documents related to its audits of Enron while the accounting firm was under investigation by the Securities and Exchange Commission (SEC). Arthur Andersen had been at the center of some of the biggest corporate scandals of the 1990s and had a history of violating SEC agreements.[10] Nonetheless, the DOJ offered the accounting firm a DPA to settle charges related to the Enron scandal.

The company spurned the DOJ's offer and decided to fight the obstruction of justice charges in court. To sway public opinion, the accounting firm embarked on an aggressive PR campaign, including demonstrations, full-page newspaper ads, and tales of employees "emotionally and financially crippled" by the indictment.[11] Its legal team accused the Justice Department of "a gross abuse of government power."[12] After Arthur Andersen was found guilty in June 2002, the accounting firm dissolved, and twenty-eight hundred employees lost their jobs.

Prodded by several high-profile lawsuits filed by New York State Attorney General Eliot Spitzer against leading banks involved in the dot-com scandal, the SEC belatedly stirred into action.[13] In late 2002, ten banks agreed to a $1.4 billion settlement for "fraudulent research reports," "supervisory deficiencies," and subjecting analysts to "inappropriate influence."[14] No corporate officers of leading banks or other financial firms faced serious criminal charges in these cases, however. Citigroup paid the largest single penalty, which totaled $400 million. The SEC gave Sandy Weill, the head of Citigroup, a slap on the wrist. It admonished him to never again speak one-on-one with his bank's analysts without a Citigroup lawyer present. As part of the SEC settlement, the banks agreed to new rules forbidding their supposedly independent analysts from being involved in soliciting initial public offerings (IPOs) and other investment banking business. But the banks continued to flout these and other laws and rules.

Three years after Arthur Andersen was convicted, the US Supreme Court overturned the verdict, citing faulty instructions to the jury. The prosecution of Arthur Andersen and the Supreme Court's reversal of the verdict were fodder for the narrative that an abusive, intrusive government had destroyed an innocent company and was unfairly going after other firms. Corporations and their powerful allies, including business groups, think tanks, lobbyists, and corporate lawyers who cycled back and forth between the public and private sectors, propagated what became known as the "Andersen effect." They claimed that prosecuting large corporations amounted to a "death sentence" that unfairly put firms out of business and victimized innocent employees and shareholders. They promoted this view despite extensive evidence that corporations rarely collapsed after being convicted. The handful of firms that have, including Arthur Andersen, had underlying problems that had jeopardized their viability even before they were indicted.[15]

Corporations strategically stoked public sympathy for innocent employees who might lose their jobs if a firm were indicted. Arthur Andersen was their exhibit A. Meanwhile, corporations and their political patrons were indifferent to the millions of innocent workers who were losing their livelihoods as financialization spurred private equity firms and corporations to ruthlessly slash jobs, wages, benefits, and costs; sell off assets; relocate production overseas; and put the interests of shareholders above all else. The heightened concern in elite political, business, and legal circles about the potentially negative collateral consequences of criminally prosecuting top corporations and their executives also stood in sharp contrast to the lack of concern about the collateral consequences for people convicted of drug or street crimes as the US incarceration rate soared. After serving their time, these less prominent defendants were increasingly subjected to "civil death" as courts, lawmakers, and policymakers began heaping more punishments and restrictions on people with criminal records. These sanctions included taking away their right to vote; rescinding their driver's licenses; banning them from receiving welfare, student loans, and public housing; and prohibiting them from numerous jobs and occupations.[16]

The Contested Right to Counsel

Seven months after Arthur Andersen was found guilty, Deputy Attorney General Larry Thompson issued a memo that revised the Clinton-era Holder memo and hastened a sea change in the DOJ's approach to prosecuting corporate crime.[17] The Thompson memo issued in January 2003 was binding on all federal prosecutors, unlike the 1999 Holder memo, which was a set of guidelines. The new memo elevated "collateral consequences" (including employee job losses) to a central consideration in deciding whether to indict a corporation.[18] The memo proffered the carrot of leniency, but only if a corporation genuinely cooperated with federal prosecutors and investigators.

Thompson charged that corporations often claim to be cooperating while actually impeding investigations. His memo spelled out the benchmarks to gauge cooperation, including a firm's willingness to waive attorney-client and other privileges; to share relevant documents and other materials; to forgo paying the legal expenses of employees suspected of job-related criminal activities; and to spurn joint defense agreements (in which attorneys representing various clients share information and legal strategies).[19] Thompson became the lightning rod for corporations, the corporate bar, and business groups charging that the Justice Department was abusive and unfair to them. Meanwhile, his department was coming under fire from the opposite direction for what some charged was a slow and flatfooted pursuit of the culprits in the Enron, WorldCom, and other headline-grabbing accounting and dot-com scandals.

The American Bar Association helped establish a coalition of powerful business and legal organizations, including the Business Roundtable, the US Chamber of Commerce, the National Association of Criminal Defense Lawyers, and even the American Civil Liberties Union, to wage a campaign against the Thompson memo in the name of defending the rights of corporations.[20] The coalition portrayed asking corporations under investigation to waive attorney-client privilege and forgo paying the legal expenses of their employees suspected of job-related criminal activities as direct attacks on the constitutional right to counsel enshrined in the Sixth Amendment. The coalition's opponents characterized payment of these legal expenses (and the costs of the golden parachutes for executives departing under a cloud) as a form of hush money. Years later Thompson would lament: "If you sit there and think these corporations are paying for the employees' choice of lawyer, and not sometimes simply to keep the employees quiet, then you believe in the tooth fairy."[21]

In a seminal setback for prosecutors on the question of legal fees, a federal judge excoriated federal prosecutors in a 2006 ruling for violating the due process and Sixth Amendment rights of partners and employees of the accounting firm KPMG. The firm had been accused of conspiring with numerous wealthy clients to conceal billions of dollars in fraudulent tax shelters. The judge in the case castigated prosecutors for bullying KPMG during the DPA negotiations to cease paying the legal fees of the executives implicated in the scheme, charges that prosecutors vehemently disputed.[22]

At the time, courts and lawmakers were bending over backward to ensure that corporate defendants had access to financial resources to purchase the best defense money could buy. Meanwhile, they were expanding the powers of the police and prosecutors to seize and keep the homes, cars, and assets of people accused of street and drug crimes. The expansion of civil asset forfeitures robbed these other defendants of the means to pay for their defense. Even people who were found not guilty had trouble retrieving their seized assets.[23]

The judge's caustic remarks in the KPMG case and the ongoing fallout from the reversal of the Arthur Andersen verdict buoyed the push by legal and business groups to eviscerate the Thompson memo. Congress got into the act in fall 2006 as the Senate Judiciary Committee held hearings on the Thompson memo and allegations that the Justice Department was abusing corporations. Senator Patrick Leahy (D-VT), ranking member of the committee, called for a voluntary rollback of the Thompson memo while Senator Arlen Specter (R-PA), the chair, repeatedly introduced legislation to enfeeble some of its key provisions.[24]

Succumbing to those pressures, Paul McNulty, the new deputy attorney general, issued a memo in December 2006 that greatly restricted the latitude of frontline prosecutors to waive attorney-client and other privileges. Months later, in another major win that boosted the campaign by corporations and their advocates to clip the DOJ's wings, the judge in the KPMG case threw out the charges against thirteen of the sixteen indicted partners and employees. He castigated prosecutors for their "intolerable" behavior in "deliberately or callously" preventing these executives from securing funds for their defense. Such an outcome, in his view, was "intolerable in a society that holds itself out to the world as a paragon of justice."[25]

A year later, in August 2008, the Second Circuit of Appeals upheld the judge's decision to dismiss the indictments. The chummy world of powerful white-collar law firms extracted its own revenge on the lead prosecutors in the KPMG case, ostracizing them and helping to dead-end their careers.[26] To borrow from a well-known Chinese proverb, they succeeded in killing the chicken to scare the monkey.

The Justice Department declined to appeal the decision and made a major retreat that month.[27] Mark Filip, McNulty's successor, issued a memo that barred prosecutors from even requesting that corporations waive their attorney-client privileges and from asking whether firms were covering any of their employees' legal expenses. The Filip memo "fully endorsed DPAs and NPAs as central to DOJ prosecution strategy" just a month before the September 2008 collapse of Lehman Brothers, which set off the financial panic.[28] The Filip memo also accorded even greater weight to considerations of "collateral consequences" in deciding whether to indict or pursue alternatives to prosecution in corporate cases.[29]

As the courts, lawmakers, and top officials at the Justice Department bent over backward to construct an expansive shield of Sixth Amendment protections for corporate executives, the right to counsel for indigent defendants was disintegrating. Lawmakers and public officials were slashing budgets for public defenders even as the demand for court-appointed lawyers was escalating because of skyrocketing arrest and incarceration rates for street and drug crimes. These developments pushed legal services for indigent defendants past the breaking point in many jurisdictions.[30]

The courts were also setting a low bar for the quality of legal representation that indigent defendants were entitled to under the Sixth Amendment. Just because your court-appointed attorney showed up to court drunk or dozed through the trial or made major legal errors did not necessarily mean you were entitled to a reconsideration of your case or a new trial. The courts also determined that capping fees for court-appointed counsel at a measly $1,000 was constitutional, even in death penalty cases.[31] On the fiftieth anniversary of the landmark 1964 *Gideon v. Wainwright* decision, which upheld the right to counsel for indigent defendants, one knowledgeable observer lamented: "There is no meaningful right to counsel for Americans too poor to afford their own attorney."[32]

DPAs, NPAs, and Get Out of Jail Free

The widespread use of DPAs and NPAs since the early aughts was a game changer in the United States and an exceptional development compared to how other countries address corporate malfeasance. These agreements are essentially a kind of probation, except that corporations and their senior officers are rarely punished for violating the terms of the agreements and are permitted to essentially police themselves. Previously, the DOJ typically would settle major corporate cases with plea agreements after the charges had been filed in court.[33] The focus had been on prosecuting individuals, not corporations, in cases of corporate crime. Trials were (and remain) exceedingly rare.[34]

Corporate DPAs and NPAs are largely an American invention. They did not result from an act of Congress but rather were devised by corporate lawyers and federal prosecutors who cycle back and forth between the private and public sectors. As sociologist Edwin Sutherland once observed, "The inventive geniuses for the lower-class criminals are generally professional criminals, while the inventive geniuses for many kinds of white-collar crime are generally lawyers."[35]

Ironically, DPAs, which were originally conceived in the 1930s in the United States to spare poor and young defendants the stain of a criminal record, emerged over the last two decades as the primary mechanism to handle major cases of corporate crime. These include multibillion-dollar cases of money laundering, kickbacks, bribes, mortgage-securities fraud, collusion in fixing interest rates, and so on. Or what bootlegger Al Capone would have characterized as the "legitimate rackets."[36]

In exchange for cooperating with prosecutors and investigators, vowing to enact reforms, and paying a fine, corporations procure a DPA or NPA. Under a DPA, the government files formal charges but agrees not to prosecute unless the corporation or individual violates the agreement. In the case of NPAs, no charges are filed in court. Because corporations are rarely prosecuted for violating the agreement, DPA is really a misnomer. With federal prosecutors increasingly relying on DPAs and NPAs to settle charges of corporate crimes, they were able to "succeed" without learning how to develop important prosecutorial and investigative skills to successfully pursue criminal charges against corporations and senior executives.[37]

Before 2003, DPAs and NPAs were seldom used for corporations, with the Justice Department entering into fewer than five each year. After that, these settlements surged for large corporations, amounting to dozens each year. Meanwhile, federal prosecutions of corporations declined to record lows.[38] Between 2006 and 2018, the number of NPAs and DPAs offered to corporations to settle criminal enforcement actions by the DOJ skyrocketed to nearly one in five. As DPAs and NPAs proliferated for corporations and shielded more of their executives from prosecution, federal prosecutors were becoming even more stingy about granting pretrial diversion in noncorporate cases.[39]

Thanks to the explosion in corporate DPAs and NPAs, crime has now been "defined as price rather than punishment" for the wealthiest firms and their executives, laments one expert on corporate law.[40] Often corporations do not even have to admit guilt or pay a fine to secure an agreement. Prosecutors essentially consent to defer indicting the corporation as long as it abides by the terms of the agreement, which typically lasts a couple of years. Since corporations are not obliged to plead guilty, they are spared the stain of a criminal record, which could jeopardize their access to government contracts and participation in lucrative government programs, such as Medicare and Medicaid. If found guilty, a corporation could also lose its charter to operate, but that almost never happens.[41]

Deferred prosecution agreements and nonprosecution agreements are essentially get-out-of-jail-free cards that deputize corporations to investigate themselves and absolve themselves of wrongdoing.[42] These agreements are typically finalized based on internal investigations conducted by the corporation itself, usually with the help of outside corporate law firms, rather than by law enforcement or public regulators. A negotiated agreement allows companies to "take charge of" or curtail a criminal investigation by "self-reporting" offenses that law enforcement or regulators might have inevitably uncovered on their own.[43] Prosecutors essentially agree to suspend their investigation until the corporation has completed its own investigation—which usually takes only a few months. Thus, these agreements transform "potential corporate criminals into corporate cops."[44]

What constitutes cooperation is in the eye of the beholder. In one notorious example, after Walmart got word in 2012 that the *New York Times* was working on a major investigation of the retail giant's shady business practices overseas, including widespread bribery of foreign government officials, the company preemptively came forward to the Justice Department.[45] The retail giant was richly rewarded in 2019 with a minuscule fine and a three-year nonprosecution agreement in which the parent company did not admit any guilt. (A Brazilian subsidiary of Walmart took the fall and entered a guilty plea.)[46]

The terms of DPAs and NPAs are the result of secret negotiations between prosecutors and well-paid corporate lawyers.[47] A quickly negotiated agreement in which many of the details of the offense and settlement remain secret allows firms to avoid the costs to their reputation and bottom line (including a hit on share prices) of a lengthy criminal investigation. Prosecutors and corporate lawyers jealously guard the details of these agreements. The public typically finds out about an agreement only after it is a done deal, and both sides propagate mutually approved press releases. The government does not maintain a public clearinghouse for DPAs and NPAs, which is yet another example of the widespread failure to track corporate crime. The most comprehensive information on these settlements is the Corporate Prosecution Registry, a joint project of the law schools at Duke University and the University of Virginia.[48]

A comprehensive analysis of hundreds of DPAs and NPAs in the United States between 2001 and 2012 concluded that these settlements obfuscate who was personally responsible for the company's criminal misconduct. They also have failed to deter corporate criminal behavior.[49] In most instances, no individual executives or corporate officers were indicted or penalized.[50] In the relatively few cases in which an individual was charged and found guilty, the sentence they received was typically lower than average, even when compared to similar crime categories.[51] As corporate prosecutions and convictions have dropped steadily, the number of DPAs and NPAs and size of fines have generally increased.[52] Larger firms tend to receive larger fines. But once the fines are scaled to a company's assets or number of employees, they are relatively small.[53]

Deferred prosecution agreements and nonprosecution agreements require prosecutors to devise corporate structural reforms, a task that they do not have the expertise or necessarily the statutory authority to carry out successfully.[54] The Justice Department trusts companies to largely police themselves. But the internal compliance measures are often "little more than window-dressing."[55] Companies are usually subject to little or no meaningful independent monitoring to determine whether they are abiding by the DPA or NPA. Outside monitors are seldom appointed to oversee implementation of the agreements. In cases in which monitors have been appointed, their findings are rarely released to the public. Monitoring can be a lucrative gig, and some monitors have had troubling conflicts of interests.[56] But until very recently, there were virtually no guidelines for appointing or selecting monitors, who are paid for by the corporations.[57]

The typical person on parole or probation, even for a relatively minor crime, is saddled with far more intrusive restrictions and state supervision than the typical multibillion-dollar company that has signed a DPA or NPA. People on parole or probation are routinely subjected to lengthy periods of state surveillance and numerous restrictions that micromanage all aspects of their lives—where they live, whom they may associate with, even whether they are permitted to carry a mobile phone. Hundreds of thousands of people convicted of drug or street crimes are sent back to prison or jail each year for minor technical violations of their parole or probation, such as a missed appointment with a parole officer or a failed drug test.[58] Meanwhile, corporations routinely violate their DPAs and NPAs and yet almost never face serious consequences.

One reason DPAs and NPAs do not deter corporations and their executives from reoffending is because these agreements are not credible threats that firms or their executives will be prosecuted if they violate the agreements. The sanction for breaching a DPA is supposed to be prosecution for the charges filed; in the case of violations of an NPA, charges are supposed to be filed. But this almost never happens.[59] Large corporations are much more likely than smaller ones to be offered the DPA or NPA option in the first place and to be treated more leniently when they violate an agreement.[60]

Corporate DPAs and NPAs perpetuate a double standard in how we view crime in the suites and crime in the streets with respect to recidivism and what weight to put on prior criminal misconduct in determining sanctions for new crimes. For decades, the DOJ has invested heavily in tracking recidivism rates for people convicted of street crimes and drug crimes. It has valorized recidivism rates for individuals, viewing them as an important barometer to measure how well the criminal legal system is performing, even though many recidivism studies are deeply flawed.[61] Meanwhile, the DOJ has been indifferent to tracking recidivism by large corporations and investigating whether DPAs and NPAs are meaningful deterrents to corporate crime.

In the United States, an individual's prior criminal record is cause to ratchet up the penalties for new crimes, unlike in many other countries. But the Justice Department routinely offers new DPAs or NPAs to large companies that have extensive histories of serial criminal misconduct.[62] Furthermore, corporations often maneuver to have their subsidiaries take the fall in DPAs and NPAs, thus absolving parent companies of blame or penalties.[63] This practice stands in sharp contrast to the expansive standard of culpability that prosecutors wield in cases of street crime. The most notorious example is the persistence of the so-called felony murder rule in the United States, which other common-law countries have largely abolished. In many states, an accomplice may be considered as culpable as the trigger person under US felony murder statutes. And the definition of accomplice can be quite capacious. A person who lends his or her car to a friend who uses it in connection with a homicide can end up in prison for life even though the lender knew nothing about the friend's plans.[64]

Deferred prosecution agreements are filed in court, but nonprosecution agreements are not. In the absence of enabling legislation or an official rule-making process to formalize how they operate, DPAs and NPAs generally are not subject to judicial review or judicial oversight, unlike plea agreements. There is no statutory or legal standard by which to evaluate them, assert a public interest, make the details of the agreements public, or otherwise subject these settlements to wider scrutiny by the courts or the public. Judges who have attempted to assert a right to review the substance of a DPA (including whether it is fair or serves the public interest) have been rebuked by the appellate courts in nearly all instances.[65] Bills introduced in Congress to subject DPAs and NPAs to more judicial oversight and public accountability have not gained much traction.[66]

Several other countries have begun to deploy DPAs, but generally on a much more limited basis. Unlike in the United States, DPAs in other countries did not emerge through a closed process developed by prosecutors and corporate lawyers. Rather, other countries typically enacted legislation to authorize DPAs only after extensive public debate. Furthermore, their lawmakers included provisions for judicial review or oversight. Nonprosecution agreements are largely unheard of in other countries.[67]

Department of Justice officials and other apologists for the failure to aggressively investigate and, if need be, prosecute corporations and their executives for major criminal activities proffer many excuses for the wide use of DPAs and NPAs. They claim prosecutors are outgunned by the flotilla of highly paid corporate lawyers with seemingly unlimited resources to fight back. They bemoan how these cases are exceedingly complex and thus require deep expertise in accounting, complex financial instruments, management of massive amounts of documents, and even math and computer science. They also contend that cases involving fraud by high-level executives can be hard to substantiate because the government must prove intent. Furthermore, if an accountant or lawyer advises that something is legal, executives can claim that they had a reasonable belief that it was indeed legal.[68]

Critics of the kid-glove treatment of corporations and their executives counter that the difficulty of pursuing elite-level corporate cases is often exaggerated. Shortly after George W. Bush appointed him US attorney for the Southern District of New York in 2002, James Comey denounced what he derisively called "the Chickenshit Club." He faulted federal prosecutors for pursuing the easier targets and ducking valid and compelling cases involving the biggest injustices for fear of losing in court. (Once he became deputy attorney general in 2002, Comey did side with the chickenshits in several notable instances, to the dismay of some career prosecutors in his office.)[69]

Federal District Judge Jed S. Rakoff, an outspoken critic of DPAs and NPAs, characterizes many of these agreements as "lax and dubious."[70] A former chief of business and securities fraud prosecutions in the US Attorney's Office for the Southern District of New York, Rakoff is dismissive of claims that DPAs and NPAs were often the only recourse because these cases were too complex and demanding, especially for a resource-strapped government agency outgunned by the most powerful corporate law firms. Rakoff observes that many similar objections were raised in other major cases of corporate financial fraud that were successfully prosecuted nonetheless, notably Enron and WorldCom.[71] He also notes that the Justice Department does not shy away from taking on cases involving organized crime networks or foreign narcotics cartels that are at least as complex and demanding.

United States criminal laws and procedures accord prosecutors many advantages vis-à-vis corporate offenders. Corporations do not enjoy Fifth Amendment protections and are required to turn over information or documents that may incriminate the firm or its officers.[72] Corporations also "often have their own affirmative disclosure obligations."[73] In addition, the United States has a far more sweeping standard for corporate criminal liability compared to many other countries. Federal statutes grant US prosecutors expansive powers to hold corporations criminally responsible for the behavior of their officers, employees, and others acting on behalf of the corporation, even if these individuals were disregarding corporate rules or policies.[74] Under US federal law, corporations may be held criminally responsible for the criminal behavior of a single employee. They also may be charged with nearly any crime for which an individual is subject to prosecution. (By contrast, state-level statutes in the United States, as well as statutes in other Western countries, typically restrict criminal prosecution of companies to instances of criminal behavior that were sanctioned or tolerated by senior officers of the firm.)[75]

Until recently, many other countries did not even recognize corporate criminal liability. They "viewed holding an artificial entity criminally liable as odd and morally problematic."[76] More countries have begun to adopt some form of corporate criminal liability, but their conception of it still tends to be narrowly drawn compared to the expansive standard in US federal law.[77]

The Racketeer Influenced and Corrupt Organizations Act, commonly known as RICO, is another potentially powerful tool for prosecuting corporate crimes. This 1970 statute was intended to cover not only violent criminal organizations but also organized financial crime.[78] This law has been used to successfully prosecute a wide range of criminal activities, including those of organized crime groups such as the Mafia, as well as gangs, labor unions, and even the sex abuse scandals involving the Catholic Church. But prosecutors have seldom wielded RICO in major cases of organized corporate crime.

Department of Justice officials and other champions of DPAs and NPAs promoted them as a win-win way to deal with the government's limited resources to pursue corporate crime.[79] By contrast, as politicians and government officials embarked on unprecedented law-and-order campaigns to ramp up punishments for drug and street crimes and immigration violations, they did not treat capacity as a major obstacle. They found the resources they needed to build hundreds of new prisons, jails, and immigration detention facilities and to expand the country's apparatus to closely monitor people serving probation and parole.[80] But in the case of corporate criminal misconduct, limited resources have been a major rationale for promoting workarounds like DPAs and NPAs.

As NPAs and DPAs were being institutionalized, white-collar defense work was in the midst of a sea change. This work was once considered a legal backwater best handled by small regional boutique law firms and well-regarded solo practitioners. Over the past four decades, it has morphed into the most lucrative revenue stream for big corporate law firms and their partners as law transformed from a profession into an industry.[81] The intensified federal focus on corporate crime beginning in the 1970s coincided with a burst of consolidation as the top law firms grew rapidly and became expansive national and then international firms. Big Law gobbled up small firms and solo practitioners specializing in white-collar cases.[82]

With the proliferation of DPAs and NPAs and the growing importance of corporate compliance measures in determining sanctions and the terms of these agreements, the demand for corporate lawyers with experience as federal prosecutors escalated. Lateral moves from government (especially from the Justice Department) to private practice upended the traditional career ladders to partnership in top corporate law firms. These former prosecutors cashed in on their network of connections with the Justice Department and their intimate knowledge of how DPAs and NPAs are hammered out.[83]

As they aggressively defended an expansive Sixth Amendment right to counsel for corporate officers and other employees, corporate law firms were also defending what had become their most profitable revenue stream. For corporations, stratospheric legal expenses were an expensive but invaluable down payment to control the direction of government investigations and their final outcomes. And besides, insurance companies often reimbursed corporations for their costly legal expenses.[84]

Origins of the Financial and Foreclosure Crises

The institutionalization of DPAs and NPAs in the early aughts was an important backdrop to how the criminal legal system would respond to the epidemic of subprime mortgage fraud that sparked the Great Recession and the financial and foreclosure crises. These get-out-of-jail-free cards helped delegitimize the criminal legal system and the government more broadly.

The DOJ prosecuted hundreds of individuals for fraud associated with the financial and foreclosure crises. But the defendants were mostly low-level players, such as mortgage brokers, real estate agents, borrowers, and minor bank employees. The large financial firms and their senior executives emerged unscathed. Once he was "safely out of office," Ben Bernanke, who had presided over the crises when he was chairman of the Federal Reserve, conceded that more bankers should have been sent to prison.[85]

Only one bank was indicted in connection with the financial crisis—a small institution in New York City's Chinatown that served the local community. The Manhattan district attorney's office filed charges against Abacus and its senior officers, who were acquitted after a jury trial. The title of the 2016 Academy Award–nominated documentary based on this case said it all: *Abacus: Small Enough to Jail.*[86]

Once you look past the confusing alphabet soup of new financial products that Wall Street devised—CDOs, CDSs, SPVs, SIVs, and so on—the origins and development of the epidemic of fraud in the mortgage market are not that difficult to understand. Banks, hedge funds, other financial firms, insurance companies, credit rating agencies, accounting firms, and property appraisers colluded in a giant pyramid scheme. Unlike in the case of the savings and loan (S&L) fiasco, the subprime mortgage fraud metastasized into the financial sector, wreaking havoc on the US economy and the global economy.[87]

The financial crisis hit in the summer of 2007 and became a financial panic in fall 2008 when Lehman Brothers, the storied 164-year-old investment bank, collapsed. With the onset of the Great Recession in late 2007, the economy contracted at an alarming annual rate of about 6 percent, with monthly job losses averaging 750,000 people.[88] The worst economic downturn in the United States in eight decades resulted in an estimated $6 trillion to $14 trillion loss in economic output between 2007 and 2009—or about $50,000 to $120,000 for every US household, according to conservative estimates.[89] Trillions of dollars in household wealth evaporated as home prices plummeted and financial assets, including stocks and pension plans, tanked. Median household wealth fell by almost half between 2007 and 2010.[90] During the "lost decade of the 2000s," median income for the middle class decreased by 5 percent, and wealth fell by 28 percent.[91]

The US economy shed jobs at a record pace.[92] The official US unemployment rate peaked at 10.1 percent in November 2010, but the "real" unemployment rate was 17.4 percent, the highest level since 1994, when the government first began calculating this alternative measure.[93] The Great Recession devastated tax revenues, forcing state and local governments to slash public services just as the demand for them was skyrocketing as millions of people lost their jobs, homes, and health insurance. The unemployment rate soared in many other countries, prompting a surge in austerity politics across the globe as governments slashed social welfare spending.

Top executives of the financial industry and leading government officials claimed that they were blindsided by a crisis that was an act of God or an act of nature that could not have been foreseen. But the two definitive government-sponsored studies of the financial and foreclosure crises show in exhaustive detail that the warnings were everywhere but went unheeded, allowing the crisis to fester.[94]

Prior decisions by the Clinton administration were pivotal in setting the stage for the crisis and the subsequent failure of regulators and the criminal legal system to hold the main culprits accountable.[95] The Clinton administration's reversal of the underwriting rules and regulations imposed by George H. W. Bush's administration was patient zero for the subprime mortgage epidemic. The originators of these loans included "a new breed of largely unregulated mortgage banks," as well as big, established commercial banks that were entering the mortgage market that had once been dominated by local S&Ls.[96] These mortgage originators misrepresented the riskiness of the liar's loans. They were not forthcoming that these mortgages had not been properly underwritten, and that they would likely have high default rates.[97]

The mortgage originators made their money by maximizing the fees they collected for originating and refinancing the mortgages, not by holding on to the loans and servicing them, as mortgages lenders had traditionally done. Their business model was premised on rapidly selling off the mortgages, so they had little stake in whether the borrower could pay back the loan or would default. Mortgage originators were told or pressured to do whatever it took to get the loans approved. They dispensed with the most central task of lending—conducting meaningful underwriting to assess the borrower's ability to repay the loan.

To secure these liar's loans, they intentionally inflated the borrower's income and net worth, often without the applicant's knowledge or approval, and falsified documentation in other ways. Many of these mortgages were deceptively structured such that the monthly payments were initially low and enticing but soon became large and onerous. Appraisers were pressured to inflate property values because higher selling prices commanded larger mortgages and thus larger fees and commissions for lenders, realtors, and appraisers. In 2005, just before the crash of the real estate market, more than half of the mortgage applicants steered toward the more expensive subprime market would have qualified for prime mortgages that had less onerous monthly payments.[98]

Two major culprits were Clayton Homes, the country's largest mobile-home builder, and Vanderbilt Mortgage, its companion lender. Clayton and Vanderbilt were among the dozens of subsidiaries owned by billionaire Warren Buffett's Berkshire Hathaway. Journalistic exposés in 2015 revealed that these two companies deployed high-pressure tactics to sell loans loaded with hidden fees and higher interest rates that were targeted at African American, Latino, and Indigenous borrowers. Saddled with mortgages carrying higher interest rates and fees than the mortgages granted to white people who earned less, these groups of borrowers were at greater risk of defaulting. When they did, Clayton Homes foreclosed on the properties, resold the homes, and reaped more fees. Its foreclosure rate was three times the national average.[99]

The subprime lending fraud resulted in an unprecedented net loss of an estimated 240,000 homes for African American people and eroded the value of properties in Black neighborhoods. These losses reinforced a recurring and misleading narrative that Black people seeking home mortgages are risky bets. These losses fostered "the pretext for mortgage lenders to, once again, engage in exclusionary practices that marginalize potential Black homeowners."[100]

Leading mortgage servicers and mortgage insurers had created the Mortgage Electronic Registration System (MERS) in the mid-1990s. It was an alternative means of tracking mortgage ownership through an electronic database rather than by publicly registering new mortgages the traditional way in local county clerks' offices. With the help of some of the most powerful corporate law firms, mortgage servicers and banks thus established a complex and opaque system that facilitated the quick sale and securitization of mortgages. The MERS reportedly saved the servicers and banks billions of dollars in recording fees as they transferred mortgages multiple times and tracked predatory loans. The MERS made it harder to stem foreclosure abuses and for homeowners to figure out who even owned their mortgages.[101]

Investment banks, some of which were subsidiaries of the banking conglomerates that originated the loans (thanks to the demise of Glass–Steagall), bought up these mortgages. They then bundled them into complex and opaque securities that they sold off to investors.[102] These mortgage-backed securities were a mishmash of debt. Sometimes they contained just mortgages. But often they were composed of all kinds of debt, including mortgages, consumer loans, credit card debt, and corporate bonds, all of which had varied and opaque repayment schemes. These securities were considered derivatives because their value was derived from some underlying asset or rate—in this case, mortgages and other types of debt.

Financial derivatives had become the wild west of finance, thanks to the Commodity Futures Modernization Act enacted in late 2000 under Clinton, which prohibited federal agencies from regulating or tracking them.[103] In its final report in 2011, the Financial Crisis Inquiry Commission (FCIC) would single out the 2000 ban on federal or state regulation of financial derivatives as "a key turning point in the march toward the financial crisis."[104] Between late 2000 and June 2008, the face value of the market in over-the-counter derivatives increased sevenfold, "peaking at $672.6 trillion—ten times larger than the GDP of the entire global economy."[105]

Banks and other financial institutions created quasi shell companies or holding companies to repackage and resell these bundles of debt, which were known as collateralized debt obligations (CDOs) and collateralized loan obligations (CLOs). These shell companies, called special purpose vehicles (SPVs) or structured investment vehicles (SIVs), allowed the banks to evade rules about how much capital they had to hold in reserves to cover any losses. These vehicles essentially enabled banks to move their risky mortgage and other debt off the books. In their marketing pitches, remarks to the media, and mandatory public filings and disclosures, the banks represented themselves (and other firms) as solid and healthy, knowing they were sitting on piles of toxic assets that threatened to bankrupt them.[106]

To shield themselves from potential losses in these high-risk securities, banks, hedge funds, and other financial firms purchased credit default swaps (CDSs), another type of unregulated derivative. The CDSs were insurance-like contracts. But they were not subject to many of the rules and regulations of traditional insurance, including engaging in credible underwriting and maintaining adequate reserves to cover any losses. Hence their nickname "insurers without reserves."[107] Because the credit swaps market was not regulated, these contracts could be bought and sold—that is, swapped—between investors without any independent entity assessing whether the riskiness of the security had been concealed and whether adequate reserves were available to cover any losses should the security go sour. A brisk trade in buying and selling these derivatives emerged beginning in the late 1990s. By mid-2007, the CDS market had exploded to $45 trillion. This figure exceeded how much was invested in the US stock market, mortgages, and US Treasury bonds combined.[108]

Credit default swaps are essentially sophisticated bets. This kind of wagering over the value of mortgages, student loans, or the future price of fuel is considered legal and is widely accepted. By contrast, small-scale betting over dice in the street or poker in a private home is illegal in most jurisdictions in the United States.[109]

Insurance companies, hedge funds, and banks were the fulcrum of the CDS market as they collected regular premiums on these contracts in exchange for guaranteeing that they would cover any outstanding debt if the borrower defaulted. With a wink and a nod, these financial institutions agreed to contracts in which the initial value of the assets was overinflated. The lure of large individual bonuses and other compensation propelled employees to look the other way as they exposed their companies and the wider economy to great risk due to poor or outright fraudulent underwriting.[110]

Investors purchased CDSs as insurance for their own investments. But a secondary market emerged in CDSs in which the purchasers of these contracts had no direct relationship with the underlying investment—sort of like how people bet on racehorses or sports teams. Investors would speculate on whether a particular credit default swap contract was priced too high (or too low) and on the creditworthiness and viability of companies and other investors that had purchased the contract.[111]

Major banks and hedge funds even got into the business of deliberately putting together packages of securities designed to fail. They would then sell them to so-called dumb money—often less sophisticated small and midsized banks overseas—which spread the subprime epidemic to the global economy. The large banks and other financial institutions profited twofold from these schemes. They reaped fees for putting together these deals for the dumb money. But the even bigger payoff came from the smart money—the sophisticated investors at hedge funds and elsewhere. These investors sought out topflight investment banks to custom design securities that were doomed and then to sell them off to dumb money. These investors would then make a killing by placing sure bets against these securities (and sometimes against the viability of the firms that bought these toxic assets) in the derivatives market. Goldman Sachs and Deutsche Bank became notorious for unloading these toxic assets on their unsuspecting customers and for putting together packages of securities they knew would fail or were even deliberately designed to fail, as discussed further in chapter 8.[112]

Grade Inflation

During this time, Wall Street coined a new term: IBGYBG, short for "I'll be gone, you'll be gone." The phrase referred to large deals that reaped big upfront fees but were likely to incur huge losses for someone else later down the line. The major banks and financial services firms marketed these mortgage-backed securities as high-grade investments to unsuspecting clients, knowing that they were junk. This giant pyramid scheme was predicated on the cooperation of Moody's, Standard & Poor's, and Fitch, the three credit rating agencies, which together controlled 95 percent of the market. The FCIC concluded in 2011 that these private-sector rating agencies were "key enablers of the financial meltdown" because they granted high-grade AAA ratings to securities that were bundles of junk mortgages and other risky debt.[113]

The rating agencies had an extensive record of poor performance that predated the 2007–9 financial crisis. They were implicated in the Enron and World-Com scandals of the early aughts and in the 1997 East Asian financial crisis.[114] In the runup to the financial crisis, credit rating agencies colluded to an extraordinary degree with banks, hedge funds, and mortgage lenders to disguise and then market nearly worthless packages of loans as high-grade AAA securities that were unlikely to default.[115] The credit rating agencies also awarded AAA ratings to banks that were actually at great risk of going bust.[116]

As financial products became more complex and opaque, securing high credit ratings had become a decisive factor in marketing them.[117] Without AAA ratings, Wall Street firms would have had a much tougher time selling these complex financial instruments. Potential investors would have had to perform their own due-diligence review to assess the riskiness and value of the financial product. Furthermore, federal and state regulations forbid or limit certain institutional investors, such as pension funds and insurance companies, from purchasing low-grade financial products that are not rated AAA.

In a blatant conflict of interest, credit rating agencies made most of their revenues through fees they received from the very financial institutions whose securities they were rating. The agencies received the entire fee only if the deal for the security was ultimately consummated, which ratcheted up the incentives for grade inflation in the rating business. As one Bear Stearns partner remarked, this system of self-regulation by the private sector was akin to "cattle ranchers paying the Department of Agriculture to rate the quality and safety of their beef."[118] He added that subprime credit had become "the mad cow disease of structured finance."[119]

Previously, credit rating agencies made most of their money by selling subscriptions to investors—that is, to the potential buyers of the financial products, not the issuers and sellers of them.[120] With the shift in how the agencies were compensated and with the proliferation of opaque financial instruments, revenues for the three top credit rating agencies soared in the early aughts. So did their conflicts of interest.[121] In public, the rating agencies promiscuously awarded AAA ratings to risky securities. In private, their analysts often conceded that there was no scientific basis to justify their high ratings, and their executives ruminated about the imminent meltdown of the subprime market.[122] In a revealing email exchange, a Standard & Poor's analyst confessed that a deal the company had rated was "ridiculous," and that their model had not captured "half of the risk."[123] As one senior executive at a rating company remarked, "Let's hope we are all wealthy and retired by the time this house of card[s] falters."[124]

Early Warnings of the Crises

The shakiness of the house of cards was no secret. As one Nobel Prize–winning economist later observed, "The only surprise about the economic crisis of 2008 was that it came as a surprise to so many."[125] As early as 2002, some prominent financiers and economists were warning of a growing bubble in the housing market as toxic, deceptive subprime mortgages proliferated. Between 1998 and 2006, housing prices increased nationwide by 67 percent. Total mortgage debt nearly doubled, rising from $5.3 trillion in 2001 to $10.5 trillion in 2007. Consumer and other public interest groups and some law enforcement officials were also sending out alarms. Furthermore, appraisers had been alleging for years that mortgage originators were pressuring them to appraise properties for more than they were worth, and that honest appraisers were being blacklisted and cut out of the lucrative mortgage business.[126] Between 1996 and 2005, the number of suspicious activity reports (SARs) related to mortgage fraud that were filed by federally insured banks rose twentyfold and then doubled again over the next four years.[127]

At the 2005 Jackson Hole conference, an annual gathering of the world's central bankers and leading economists, Raghuram Rajan, the International Monetary Fund's chief economist, warned of the growing "possibility of a catastrophic meltdown." At the conference, Larry Summers, Bill Clinton's former Treasury secretary who was then president of Harvard University (with a lucrative hedge fund gig on the side), took on the task of dressing down Rajan for his paper's "largely misguided" and "Luddite premise."[128]

Key regulators were also dismissive of the signs of the coming crisis. As late as spring 2007, with the real estate market in freefall and homeowner defaults escalating, Fed Chair Ben Bernanke and Treasury Secretary Hank Paulson remained confident that the problem in the subprime market could be contained.[129] Meanwhile, Timothy Geithner, president of the Federal Reserve Bank of New York (FRBNY), was lauding "financial innovation," such as CDSs and mortgage-backed securities, that had fortified the "resilience of the market in the face of the latest shocks." He also proclaimed that "the major banks are larger and stronger today" and less vulnerable to economic shocks.[130]

In July 2007, the credit rating agencies suddenly downgraded hundreds of subprime mortgage-backed securities, which set off a scramble to sell off these securities, marking what some identify as the start of the financial crisis. By late 2007, it was an open secret on Wall Street that the growing financial bubble was getting closer to bursting. The big question then became not if, but when, the bubble would burst, what money could be made in the meantime by shorting the market in toxic assets, and how to clean up the mess left behind.[131]

The Big Short, the 2015 film based on the best-selling book by Michael Lewis, portrays Wall Street "blindly running itself off a cliff" while a handful of wild and crazy loners became fabulously wealthy by shorting the mortgage market as the bubble burst.[132] In reality, the "Big Short was seriously big business, and much of Wall Street was ruthlessly good at it." At some firms, "senior management was indeed disconnected and clueless," allowing their employees to destroy their firms (Lehman Brothers and Bear Stearns) or put them in mortal danger (Citigroup and Merrill Lynch). But others, including Goldman Sachs, JPMorgan, and Morgan Stanley, continued to game the system by devising fraudulent schemes that prolonged the financial bubble even as the housing bubble was bursting and threatening to take the economy off the cliff. With the market in mortgage-backed securities looking increasingly perilous, prescient insiders at some major financial firms stepped up their machinations to quietly unload their portfolios of toxic assets on "dumb money." They also got into the business of deliberately devising bundles of toxic assets at the behest of "smart money" at hedge funds that sought to bet against the "dumb" investors that naively purchased these doomed assets. Financial firms also manipulated the value of the toxic assets they were still holding to maximize their payouts from the credit default swaps they had purchased.[133]

Regulators and Resources

Under the 1934 Securities and Exchange Act, intentionally misleading or deceiving investors about the value of a security to sway their investment decisions and cause them losses is considered fraud. The 1934 law permits the SEC to take civil actions and to refer criminal complaints to the DOJ. It also allows the Justice Department to take civil or criminal actions and permits defrauded parties to file lawsuits.[134] State attorneys general also have broad authority to bring charges against large financial institutions that operate in their jurisdictions.

The FBI, which is the major law enforcement agency responsible for investigating financial and other white-collar crimes, began publicly warning as early as 2004 that fraud in the mortgage market was threatening to become an epidemic. Chris Swecker, an assistant director of the FBI, sounded the alarm on numerous occasions, including in congressional testimony, that a financial crisis would result if something was not done to contain it.[135] But FBI agents were handicapped by inadequate resources, uncooperative regulators, and the lack of support at the highest reaches of the FBI and DOJ. The few prosecutors and regulators who dared to take on the large firms and corporations often ended up getting blackballed or sidelined in their careers. As for corporate whistleblowers, they often ended up divorced, financially ruined, and unemployable in their profession.[136]

On the eve of the 9/11 attacks, about a million people were employed in law enforcement in the public sector. Of those million, only about twenty-three hundred FBI agents were assigned to investigating white-collar crimes.[137] After 9/11, resources to pursue white-collar crimes, already inadequate to begin with, plummeted as the United States ramped up the global war on terror.[138] Between 2001 and 2009, the number of agents reassigned to counterterrorism work doubled, while the number of white-collar investigations declined steeply.[139] The DOJ under George W. Bush rebuffed the FBI's requests to replace the reassigned agents.

Another drain on law enforcement resources was the escalation in the war on immigrants and migrants that blurred the line between immigration enforcement and law enforcement.[140] As criminal prosecutions for immigration-related offenses soared, federal prosecutions for other offenses, including white-collar crimes, fell.[141] The new US Department of Homeland Security, which was created in 2003 and absorbed the Immigration and Naturalization Service, soon began referring more cases to the Justice Department for prosecution than all the other major law enforcement agencies combined. Federal spending on immigration enforcement greatly exceeded funding for all principal federal law enforcement agencies combined.[142]

Despite a sharp downward trend in net migration from Mexico and in apprehensions at the border, prosecutions for immigration violations (mostly illegal entry and reentry) exploded in the aughts. Beginning in 2004, immigration prosecutions topped the list of federal criminal prosecutions nationwide. Requiring assistant US attorneys along the border to focus most of their time and energy on low-level immigration prosecutions came at the expense of developing the skills necessary to successfully investigate and prosecute more serious crimes, such as complex financial schemes and drug cartels.[143]

There was some support within the ranks of the FBI and in Congress during the Bush administration to beef up federal resources to combat mortgage fraud.

But FBI Director Robert Mueller and top officials at the DOJ and Office of Management and Budget were not strong advocates of additional funding.[144] By mid-2005, according to a former top FBI official, the bureau "realized we were going to have to pull out of some areas—bank fraud, investment fraud, ID theft—cases that protect the financial infrastructure of the country."[145]

Alberto Gonzales, Bush's attorney general from early 2005 to late 2007, later defended the DOJ's stance. "I don't think anyone can credibly argue that [mortgage fraud] is more important than the war on terror," he testified before the FCIC in November 2010. "Mortgage fraud doesn't involve taking [sic] loss of life so it doesn't rank above the priority of protecting neighborhoods from dangerous gangs or predators attacking our children."[146] His successor Michael B. Mukasey echoed this view, telling the commission that terrorism, gang violence, and southwestern border issues were more pressing problems.[147]

Federal banking regulators posed another major obstacle to holding financial firms and their executives accountable to the criminal legal system during the subprime mortgage scandal. Claims that regulators were outgunned by the financial sector because they were understaffed, underpaid, and underfunded are valid—up to a point. Between 1990 and 2000, the total number of staffers for federal agencies that regulate business and finance contracted by 13 percent. Over the next decade, the number rebounded by only 3 percent.[148] During those two decades, federal spending on agencies regulating business and finance rose by 50 percent in inflation-adjusted dollars.[149] But in the years leading up to the financial crisis, criminal referrals from these agencies plummeted even though they had more staff and money compared to what they had had in the 1990s.

Criminal cases against banks and other financial institutions are difficult to pursue without assistance and documentation provided by the "sherpas"— that is, regulators from the Office of the Comptroller of the Currency (OCC), the Federal Reserve, the Federal Deposit Insurance Corporation, and the Office of Thrift Supervision (OTS), which became part of the OCC in 2011.[150] During the S&L debacle of the 1980s, federal regulators worked closely with law enforcement. At that time, the Federal Home Loan Bank Board and its successor, the OTS, made more than thirty thousand criminal referrals.[151] Regulators sent detailed reports about suspicious activity to prosecutors and the FBI. These reports were indispensable for pursuing criminal cases. "Only the regulators can make a lot of these cases," as one former top regulator during the S&L crisis explained in 2010. "The FBI can make a few, but the regulators are the ones that understand the industry."[152]

Between the mid-1990s and the onset of the financial crisis, the number of cases that bank regulators referred to the Justice Department for criminal prosecution each year dried up—from 1,837 in 1995 to just seventy-five in 2006 to an average of seventy-two annually over the next four years.[153] "When regulators don't believe in regulation and don't get what is going on at the companies they oversee, there can be no major white-collar crime prosecutions," explained one expert on corporate crime.[154]

Between summer 2007 and the end of 2008, a string of banks overseen by the OTS, which together held assets totaling $355 billion, went under. But the OTS did not refer a single case to the Justice Department during the aughts, even though it was responsible for regulating the financial institutions that were at the center of the subprime scandal, including American International Group (AIG), Countrywide, IndyMac, and Washington Mutual. The OCC, which is part of the Treasury Department, made only three referrals over that period.[155] "As a bank regulatory agency, our job is to, one, identify the problems and then mandate they get fixed," said Thomas Curry, head of the OCC from 2012 to 2017, in defense of his agency's record. "I don't think it's our role to avenge or to punish per se."[156] The OCC and the OTS also maneuvered to preempt state bank regulators who wanted to take a more aggressive approach to containing the mushrooming fraud.[157] John Snow, Bush's Treasury secretary, later recollected that he was surprised that federal regulators he met with in late 2004 or early 2005 did not consider the proliferation of poor lending practices to be a problem at the institutions they oversaw.[158]

Despite numerous warnings from Swecker of the FBI and others about rampaging fraud in the mortgage market, none of the more than five thousand bank regulators followed up with the FBI.[159] Because law enforcement and prosecutors did not have the cooperation of regulators, they had to rely on SARs filed by the banks themselves. In the five years prior to the financial panic in 2008, the number of SARs filed by banks skyrocketed.[160] Banks fingered borrowers, independent mortgage originators, appraisers, and others, but not themselves or their own top executives.

With regulators not making any criminal referrals despite warnings of an epidemic of mortgage fraud, few FBI agents were assigned to investigate fraud in the mortgage market—just 120 as of 2007, compared to nearly one thousand agents who worked on the S&L scandal at the peak of the thrift crisis.[161] These agents were spread so thin across the country that they did not have the capacity to systematically pursue major fraud cases. They also were overwhelmed by tens of thousands of small cases, in many instances involving a single house loan.[162] In 2006, the FBI pressed Attorney General Mukasey to establish a national task force empowered with more resources and personnel to target major cases involving the biggest home lenders. But Mukasey refused, dismissing the mortgage fraud cases as trivial; in his words, the equivalent of "white-collar street crimes."[163] As the crisis deepened in the spring of 2008, the FBI scaled back a plan to allocate more field agents to investigate mortgage fraud, and the DOJ once again rejected calls to establish a special task force focused on mortgage-related investigations.[164]

As for the Federal Reserve, its top leadership thwarted efforts by its examiners to compel banks to provide accurate and comprehensive data on subprime loans. Information provided voluntarily by the banks had revealed that risky subprime loans constituted a huge and growing portion of their portfolios. In the face of what one Fed supervisor described as "very alarming" reports, the Fed refused to step in to contain the damage.[165] It did not wield the considerable statutory powers it already possessed to regulate mortgage lenders under the 1994 Home Ownership and Equity Protection Act (HOEPA). In 2004, Federal Reserve Chairman Alan Greenspan rebuffed pleas to use these powers to staunch the liar's loans, including reinstating stricter underwriting regulations. That same year, Robert Shiller, a Yale economist and leading expert on the real estate market, had warned Timothy Geithner, president of the FRBNY, that the financial system rested dangerously on a volatile housing bubble. Geithner quickly purged Shiller from the FRBNY's inaugural advisory board and ignored his warning.[166]

A 2005 study by the Fed and other regulators raised serious concerns about the "very rapid increase" in "irresponsible loans, very risky loans" by the nation's largest banks that together originated $1.3 trillion in mortgages that year—or nearly half of the nation's total. The Fed gingerly responded by issuing nonbinding guidelines for risky mortgages. The banking industry was immediately "up in arms." Opposition from the industry, regulators, and some members of Congress delayed implementation of the guidelines and succeeded in watering them down.[167] Finally in July 2008, Ben Bernanke, Greenspan's successor, invoked the Fed's powers under HOEPA to essentially ban liar's loans. But by that point "such lending had virtually ceased."[168] Yet "to avoid inconveniencing any fraudulent lenders who were still operating," Bernanke "delayed the effective date of the rule for fifteen months."[169]

Months later, Greenspan confessed to a congressional committee that the financial crisis had revealed a "flaw" in his ideology. "Those of us who looked to the self-interest of lending institutions to protect shareholders equity—myself included—are in a state of shocked disbelief," he told lawmakers in October 2008.[170] In his appearance before the FCIC in April 2010, Greenspan defended his record as head of the Fed. "I was right 70% of the time but I was wrong 30% of the time," the former Fed chair testified.[171] That comes to barely a C minus.

A 2009 confidential self-critique by the FRBNY conceded that the Fed's assumption that "markets will always self-correct" fostered its inadequate supervision of banks and the mortgage industry in the lead-up to the financial crisis. So was the related belief that banks could be counted on to police themselves. These two mistaken beliefs kept the Fed from using its considerable powers to oversee the banks and curtail certain activities. The report noted that, within the ranks of the FRBNY, the growing problems with toxic assets were recognized. But no one acted on them because of the bank's culture of intense deference to superiors. Furthermore, the Fed did not view financial stability as a central mission on par with combatting inflation.[172] Sheila Bair, who headed the FDIC during the financial crisis, was scathing about the regulatory failures of the FRBNY and the OCC, the primary watchdogs of the largest banks. She accused them of exercising "virtually no meaningful supervisory measures" over Citigroup and doing nothing "as that sick bank continued to pay major dividends and pretended that it was healthy."[173]

In its final report, the FCIC charged that major federal regulators, including the Fed, OTS, and OCC, held back "because of interagency discord, industry pushback, and a widely held view that market participants had the situation well in hand." The commission faulted the Fed for its "pivotal failure" to staunch the flow of "toxic mortgages." The FCIC concluded that the Fed and other regulators, including the SEC, "had ample power in many arenas" but "chose not to use it." And where they lacked the power, they failed to seek it because of a lack of fortitude and political will "to critically challenge the institutions and the entire system they were entrusted to oversee."[174] One of the Fed's governors conceded that the Fed had behaved in the crisis like "a city with a murder law but no cops on the beat."[175]

TARP and the Banana Republic to the Rescue

On September 15, 2008, Lehman Brothers came tumbling down in the biggest corporate bankruptcy in US history up until then. The demise of the country's fourth-largest investment bank set off a liquidity crisis as consumers and businesses, big and small, struggled to secure loans and credit. Three days after

Lehman collapsed, US Treasury Secretary Hank Paulson called for an emergency Thursday night meeting with leaders of Congress and Ben Bernanke, the head of the Federal Reserve. Prior to joining the Bush administration, Paulson had been CEO of Goldman Sachs, where he had been employed for over three decades. While at Goldman, Paulson was a central player in the subprime mortgage-backed securities market. At that meeting in Speaker Nancy Pelosi's office, Paulson and Bernanke fostered a sense of panic. The chair of the Federal Reserve reportedly warned, "If we don't do this tomorrow, we won't have an economy on Monday."[176]

The next day Paulson sent congressional leaders an audacious three-page proposal to bail out the banks. The draft legislation granted sweeping powers to the executive branch, including handing over $700 billion to the Treasury Department to rescue the banks with few strings attached, even though their complicity in the subprime fraud was an open secret. Alternatives—such as using the Treasury Department and Federal Reserve to boost consumer demand and lending to businesses in distress or putting the large banks under the conservatorship of the FDIC so as to protect government-insured deposits—were kept off the table.[177]

Paulson's and Bernanke's hyperbolic remarks that the economy would be mortally wounded unless Congress acted immediately to approve their proposal—without conducting hearings or soliciting wider input—spooked investors. The Treasury secretary and chairman of the Federal Reserve "helped create a self-fulfilling prophecy," with the Dow Jones dropping nearly eight hundred points after the House spurned their legislative proposal on September 29, 2008.[178] Four days later, Congress ended up quickly approving a slightly modified version of the Emergency Economic Stabilization Act of 2008, better known as TARP (Troubled Asset Relief Program), on October 3.

To secure passage of the legislation, the White House and Treasury Department agreed to distribute the $700 billion in installments subject to congressional approval. Over the objections of the administration, Senator Max Baucus (D-MT), chair of the Finance Committee, and Senator Chuck Grassley (R-IA), the ranking Republican on the committee, insisted on establishing a special inspector general for TARP (SIGTARP). In doing so, lawmakers accorded this new position not only broad oversight authority but also significant law enforcement powers and capacity, which is unique for an inspector general.[179]

The TARP ceded enormous power to the Treasury Department, including wide discretion over how to dispense the hundreds of billions of dollars in bailout funds and how to deal with the foreclosure crisis. The full extent of government support for the largest banks thanks to TARP and other measures remained secret until years later. The TARP ended up being a windfall for the largest and most powerful banks and other financial institutions.[180]

Fears stoked by Paulson and Bernanke that the economy was about to go over the cliff had not enhanced the government's autonomy to act independently of the banks in order to serve the interests of the wider public and other business sectors. But they did enhance the privileged position of some of the largest banks and their patrons in the government. Reflecting years later on the hastily drawn up bailout legislation, economist Joseph Stiglitz said he worried at the time that, as "the United States slipped into crisis," he would witness here what he had seen happen so often in developing countries: "Bankers, who had in large part precipitated the problem, took advantage of the panic that resulted to redistribute wealth—to take from the public purse to enrich their own."[181] Simon Johnson, former chief economist of the International Monetary Fund, put it more starkly: the United States was "becoming a banana republic" with an oligarchy that the government "seems helpless, or unwilling" to act against.[182]

Back to the Future

The swift, coordinated, and massive response by US policymakers and legislators headed off what looked like the second coming of the Great Depression in the immediate weeks after Lehman Brothers collapsed in September 2008.[183] Recognizing early on the global dimensions of the crisis, the Federal Reserve and Treasury Department sprang into action. The Fed in particular deserves credit for taking on the role of lender of last resort not only for banks and financial institutions in the United States but also for numerous central banks in Europe. It wielded established and innovative tools to bring the panic under control relatively quickly by flooding the global financial sector with liquidity.[184]

But as policymakers administered the equivalent of mouth-to-mouth resuscitation to the financial sector, they treated the emergency as an act of God or nature that was unpredictable and for which they, the banks, and other financial institutions were largely blameless.[185] They, along with the mainstream of the economics profession, underestimated or ignored the lasting consequences of the financial panic and Great Recession for the broader economy and the political system. They also mistakenly assumed that, by quickly saving Wall Street, Main Street would bounce back.

The political stars rarely line up to create an opening to rein in capital. But 2008 appeared to be one of those moments. By the time of the November election, the Bush administration had been thoroughly discredited. President Bush's approval rating was 20 percent, the lowest on record for any president.[186] Voters delivered a decisive rebuke to Bush, choosing Senator Barack Obama (D-IL) over Senator John McCain (R-AZ) by wide margins in the popular vote and Electoral College. As comedian Chris Rock observed, Bush "fucked up so bad that it's hard for a white man to run for president."[187] The Democrats increased their majority in the House by twenty-one seats and by July had secured a filibuster-proof Senate.[188] Public opinion polls indicated that wide swaths of the public, thrashed by the Great Recession and the decades-long erosion in living standards and quality of life, supported reining in Wall Street.

At the time, major fissures had opened up in public among leading economic policymakers, as discussed in the next two chapters. In private, these differences looked more like chasms. Some top Democrats were pressing to restructure the financial industry and hold Wall Street accountable to the criminal legal system. So were some leading Republican lawmakers, economists, and former government officials.

In short, the Obama administration had plenty of political cover and support to break with the policies and policymakers that had exacerbated economic inequality in the United States and delivered the biggest economic downturn since the Great Depression. Instead, Obama backed economic policies that, like his foreign policies, added up in many ways to the third term of the Bush administration. Treasury Secretary Hank Paulson, Federal Reserve Chair Ben Bernanke, New York Federal Reserve President Timothy Geithner, and Wall Street executives had hammered out these policies in fall 2008 with Obama's intimate knowledge and blessing before he was even elected president, as shown in the next chapter. Furthermore, the Obama administration did not dislodge the kid-glove treatment of the corporate sector that had been institutionalized with the proliferation of deferred prosecutions agreements and nonprosecution agreements over the previous two decades. Instead, the administration bolstered the de facto decriminalization of major corporate malfeasance.

8

Hope, Change, and Wall Street

DECRIMINALIZATION OF CRIME
IN THE SUITES UNDER OBAMA

Three tours in Iraq but no bailout for people like us.

—GRAFFITI IN A DEPRESSED RURAL TOWN IN EASTERN TEXAS[1]

BARACK OBAMA was elected president at an exceptional political moment. The first African American president in US history, he won a higher proportion of white voters in 2008 than had Bill Clinton in 1992, Al Gore in 2000, and John Kerry in 2004.[2] Public outrage toward Wall Street and suspicion of big business were high. So was public support for holding Wall Street accountable to the criminal legal system for the financial and foreclosure crises. Leading economists, policymakers, and lawmakers, many of whom had once championed financial deregulation, now favored major structural reforms of the financial sector. But during the 2008 campaign and then once he took office, Obama accommodated the financiers in key areas, including appointments, investigation and prosecution of the leading culprits, and regulation of the financial sector. At his swearing-in ceremony on February 3, 2009, Attorney General Eric Holder vowed to "drill down" into the role of Wall Street in the financial crisis and hold the perpetrators accountable.[3] But during Obama's eight years in office, the Justice Department did not prosecute a single major bank or leading financial services firm, and only one corporate executive was sent to prison in connection with the widespread fraud that had crashed the economy. Holder would show passion when it came to civil rights and national security issues but never demonstrated much interest in pursuing the masterminds behind the financial and foreclosure crises.[4]

The Obama administration failed to reverse the remarkable inversion in the criminal legal system of the last five decades—that is, the vast expansion of the carceral state to punish street crimes, drug offenses, and immigration violations since the 1970s and the accelerating de facto decriminalization of high-level crime in the suites since the 1990s. As nonprosecution agreements (NPAs) and deferred prosecution agreements (DPAs) proliferated to settle cases stemming from the financial and foreclosure crises, these get-out-of jail-free cards became even more deeply legitimized and institutionalized to deal with all kinds of corporate crime under Obama and his successors. Furthermore, Obama's mortgage relief program ended up being a boondoggle for leading banks and mortgage servicers, who turbocharged the foreclosure crisis, turning millions of people out of their homes and illegally repossessing many properties. An estimated nine to ten million families would end up losing their homes, about two-thirds of them to foreclosures.[5] Many people "simply walked away from their devalued properties, returning the keys to the banks—an action that would destroy families' credit for years."[6]

The financial crisis created historic opportunities to restructure the financial system and to mitigate the savage inequities and inequalities of the economic and criminal legal systems that have fostered widespread structural violence in the United States. The Obama administration foreclosed these opportunities. At key junctures, it surrendered without putting up much of a fight. Obama came down on the side of modest regulation—not law enforcement or financial restructuring—as the best vaccine to protect against another financial crisis. But Obama's modest quest for regulatory reform was a disappointment, as detailed in the next chapter.

In failing to indict Wall Street and its top executives in the courts or in the court of public opinion, the Obama administration indicted itself. It provided jet fuel for the antigovernment rage that conservative groups and their billionaire benefactors had been funding for decades. These groups channeled that rage into the incipient Tea Party movement that shellacked Obama and the Democrats in the 2010 midterm elections as the GOP gained sixty-three seats in the House and six in the Senate, the largest swing since 1948.

The "Free-Market Guy" and His Appointees

In late 2006 as Obama was consulting with his closest advisers and Michelle Obama about why and whether to run for president, a desire to reverse the country's large and growing economic inequalities did not appear to be a driving motivation. Asked by Michelle what he was "uniquely hoping" to accomplish if he became president, Obama raised a consistent theme of his—identity and, implicitly, how it was bound up with race.[7] During his quest for the White House, a narrative about identity remained his leitmotif, even as the economy suffered its worst downturn in eight decades.

With the economy unraveling in 2007 and 2008, Obama campaigned for president on a gauzy platform of hope and change knitted into a narrative about identity. He talked in broad strokes about restoring fairness and equity but seldom singled out Wall Street for umbrage. Indeed, Senator John McCain (R-AZ), his Republican opponent, emerged at times as a more caustic critic of Wall Street.[8]

Obama's worldview and political ambitions, shaped by his formative years in Chicago, help explain why he did not champion deep structural reforms of the financial industry despite an economic crisis that looked for a time like the second coming of the Great Depression. Before he became a US senator in 2005, Obama taught for about a dozen years at the law school of the University of Chicago. The university was the epicenter of the counterrevolution launched by the so-called Chicago school of economics to bludgeon the New Deal.[9] Just three days after Senator Hillary Clinton (D-NY) conceded the Democratic presidential nomination to Obama in June 2008, the presumptive Democratic nominee said famously, "Look. I am a pro-growth, free-market guy. I love the market."[10] Obama would go on to regularly praise the "power of the free market" during his presidency.[11]

As he was making a name for himself in Chicago, Obama strategically cultivated the city's top financiers, who would serve as critical springboards for his political career.[12] During his successful quest for the presidency, Wall Street emerged as a vital source of money, personnel, and advice. The focus on Obama's revolution in fundraising as he tapped into the power of the internet to attract campaign contributions from small donors obscured his dependence on Wall Street and large donors.[13] In the early days of his quest for the White House, Wall Street provided pivotal seed money that enhanced Obama's credibility as a candidate.

After he had locked up the Democratic nomination in June 2008, Obama announced that he would be opting out of the public campaign finance system, the first presidential candidate to do so in the general election since 1976. A year earlier Obama had vowed he would not abandon the federal system of financing presidential campaigns, which was instituted in the wake of the Watergate scandal to insulate candidates from the corrupting influence of private money.[14] Obama's momentous and controversial decision to opt out allowed him to raise unlimited amounts of money for the general election.

McCain, a champion of campaign finance reform, chose not to ditch the public system. Limited to $84 million in public money, the Republican nominee was outspent nearly three to one by Obama during the general election.[15] Obama's haul from large donors and Wall Street dwarfed what he collected from small contributors.[16] By Election Day, three megabanks in New York City—Goldman Sachs, Citigroup, and JPMorgan Chase—were among the top seven institutions in terms of bundled donations for Obama, with Morgan Stanley close behind.[17] No corporation gave more money to the Obama campaign than Goldman Sachs.[18]

The Chicago school orthodoxy cast a spell over Obama's appointments on the campaign trail and in the White House. Many of his key campaign advisers were veterans of the Clinton administration's wave of deregulation and disciples of Robert Rubin, who served as Treasury secretary from 1995 to 1999.[19] His chief economic adviser was Austan Goolsbee, a University of Chicago economist. The head of his economic team was Jason Furman, who was close to Larry Summers, another former Treasury secretary of Bill Clinton. Furman shepherded Summers—described by one Washington insider as having "a deist's conviction in a clockwork economy that runs efficiently without government intervention"—into a key advisory role in the Obama campaign.[20] Obama's national finance chair was Penny Pritzker, scion of a banking family and head of Superior Bank, a Chicago-area savings and loan institution that was a pioneer in predatory lending. Another key supporter was Chicago-based billionaire Kenneth Griffin, CEO of the hedge fund Citadel. Obama selected Jim Johnson, the former CEO of Fannie Mae, the troubled government-backed mortgage firm, to head his vice-presidential search committee. Within days, Johnson was forced to step aside in June 2008 after coming under fire from McCain and others for his financial ties to Angelo Mozilo, the controversial and embattled CEO of Countrywide Financial, a central player in the subprime mortgage scandal.[21]

During the campaign, Obama marinated himself in the worldview of the titans of finance in numerous phone calls and intimate meetings brokered by Wall Street operatives who were instrumental in his campaign.[22] Just days after he was elected, the *Wall Street Journal* pronounced, "Obama Builds Ties to 'Chicago School.'"[23] If there were any doubts about what hope and change would mean for Obama's policies to stem the financial crisis and who the winners and losers would be, the unveiling of the president-elect's Transition Economic Advisory Board and then his most senior economic appointments should have dispelled them. The board included champions of financial deregulation in the 1990s and major players in the subprime mortgage market, including Robert

Rubin (by then an influential director and senior adviser at Citigroup); Larry Summers; Penny Pritzker; William M. Daley (a senior executive at JPMorgan Chase); and billionaire Warren Buffett of Berkshire Hathaway.[24] But Obama also selected Paul Volcker, who had emerged as a leading critic of Wall Street's role in the financial crisis and of the government's response.

Volcker had served as chairman of the Federal Reserve under Jimmy Carter and Ronald Reagan. His record on economic policy did not track neatly to the left or right. Two decades earlier, Volcker took a page from the playbook of economist Milton Friedman, the best-known guru of the Chicago school, as he sought to tame inflation by pursuing a radical contraction of the monetary supply, as discussed in chapter 6. The so-called Volcker shock sent interest rates and unemployment soaring and decimated US exports and the country's manufacturing base thanks to the stronger US dollar. The contraction of the money supply spurred deindustrialization, enfeebled organized labor, and contributed to wage stagnation.[25] More households turned to loading up on debt and betting on the real estate market to maintain their standard of living, which provided the raw materials for the subprime mortgage scandal years later.[26]

The reverberations from the Volcker shock contributed to Ronald Reagan's win over Carter in 1980. But Volcker was not a zealot for deregulation, which helps explain why Reagan refused to renominate him in 1987. As the financial crisis unfolded two decades later, Volcker warned that without serious "rules of the road" enforced by the law, companies would ferret out ways to make a profit that put the market, the economy, and ultimately the general welfare of society at great risk.[27] In a high-profile appearance at the Economic Club of New York in April 2008, Volcker denounced the Federal Reserve Bank of New York's hastily brokered sweetheart deal the month before to prop up the investment firm Bear Stearns and then sell it off to JPMorgan Chase. With FRBNY President Timothy Geithner looking on from the audience, Volcker accused the Fed of taking "actions that extend to the very edge of its lawful and implied powers." He warned that the FRBNY's actions would be interpreted as "an implied promise" to bail out other troubled and reckless financial institutions.[28]

During the 2008 campaign, Volcker had anchored Obama's A-Team of economic advisers, which favored measures that echoed some of the New Deal's vision and audacity to restructure banking and finance. But by the time the president-elect announced his Transition Economic Advisory Board in late November, Volcker was a marginalized moose-head.[29] By then, the so-called

B-Team of economic advisers—a cadre of Clinton administration alumni with deep ties to Wall Street whose titular head was Larry Summers—had triumphed over the A-Team.[30]

Some leading economists and policymakers had joined Volcker in calling for a major overhaul of the financial sector to avoid another catastrophe.[31] But none of them were tapped to serve in the most consequential economic policymaking positions in the new administration. Instead, many of the top economic and regulatory appointments, as well as leading national security, foreign policy, and Justice Department positions, were filled by bankers and executives from hedge funds and private equity firms, including financiers who had fomented the crisis and profited from it.

A common saying in politics is that personnel is policy. Emails released in October 2016 by Wikileaks from the hacked email account of John Podesta, head of Obama's transition team and a longtime confidant of Bill and Hillary Clinton, revealed the intimate and outsized role that top Citigroup executives, including Robert Rubin, played in advising Obama's team about personnel and strategy.[32] As they were firing off emails from their Citigroup addresses in late 2008 to Obama's transition team, their megabank was in a death spiral. Its market value had plummeted by November to $20.5 billion, less than one-tenth what it had been two years earlier. Citigroup executives were busy negotiating with the outgoing Bush administration to secure yet another in a series of monster bailouts, the full extent of which remained secret at the time.[33]

Some of Obama's advisers were "downright giddy" when they heard that Rubin might reprise his role as Treasury secretary in the new administration.[34] When he served under Clinton, Rubin had been a radical deregulator, pushing policies that seeded the Great Recession and financial crisis, as discussed in chapter 6. As Obama was putting together his administration in late 2008, the media were reporting that Rubin had been extravagantly paid at Citigroup while playing a central role in the megabank's downfall with its reckless bets on mortgage-related securities.[35] "Don't you realize that half the country wants to tar and feather Bob Rubin?" warned Jeff Connaughton, a close aide of Ted Kaufman, Joe Biden's chief of staff who was chosen to fill the vice president–elect's Senate seat.[36]

Obama ended up passing over Rubin for Treasury, selecting instead Geithner of the FRBNY, who once worked under Rubin at the Treasury Department.[37] The president chose Summers to be director of the National Economic Council. Obama filled out his top three economic appointments with Christina Romer, a professor of economics at UC-Berkeley, who was selected to chair the Council of Economic Advisers. Romer shared the A-Team's sensibilities and ended up frequently sidelined in the Obama administration.[38] As for Volcker, he was appointed chair of the President's Economic Recovery Advisory Board. Established in early 2009, the board was ridiculed as a place to park Obama's "second-tier donors and campaign advisers who hadn't 'made the cut.'"[39] A remarkable number of Rubin's other protégés and associates staffed Obama's transition team and were chosen for his administration.[40] After serving under Clinton, many of them had gone to Wall Street to rake in their millions before returning to work in the Obama administration.

Goldman Sachs was well represented at the highest reaches of the Obama administration, as it had been in those of his immediate predecessors. Geithner selected a full-time lobbyist from Goldman Sachs as his chief of staff. His other key advisers at Treasury included the former head of Tricadia, a hedge fund that made billions of dollars by working with banks to create doomed securities that the firm could then short; and two top executives from private equity firms, including Matthew Kabaker of Blackstone, the country's largest private equity firm. As deputy assistant secretary for capital markets and housing finance in the Treasury Department, Kabaker would be the point person to address the collapse of the housing market just as private equity firms were swooping in to buy up hundreds of thousands of foreclosed properties, turning them into rental properties and charging crushing rates.[41]

Financiers were tapped to serve in top regulatory positions in the Treasury Department and elsewhere. Notably, Robert Khuzami, who was Deutsche Bank's general counsel for the Americas, was appointed director of enforcement for the Securities and Exchange Commission (SEC). Deutsche Bank was a major player in the fraudulent subprime market and in putting together securities that duped its own clients.[42] It also was Donald Trump's banker of choice over the years as he secured more than $2 billion in loans backed up with shaky collateral.[43]

The Department of Justice was thoroughly financialized under Obama. Eric Holder returned to the DOJ, this time as attorney general. A veteran of the Clinton administration, he was the author of the 1999 Holder memo, which pried open the door to the wide-scale use of DPAs and NPAs, as detailed in chapter 6. After leaving the Clinton administration, Holder had spent eight years as a partner at Covington & Burling, a powerhouse law firm that specialized in corporate lobbying & representing white-collar clients. Some of the biggest players in the subprime mortgage market fraud, including Bank of America, Citigroup, and JPMorgan Chase, were clients of the firm. Covington

& Burling also represented executives from Enron (the energy giant that imploded, as discussed in chapter 7); Blackwater (the mercenary and private security firm); Philip Morris (the tobacco company); and Halliburton (the military contractor and former Vice President Dick Cheney's old firm). Covington & Burling had been instrumental in creating the Mortgage Electronic Registration System (MERS), which New York's attorney general would sue for foreclosure abuses in 2012.[44]

Covington alums filled other key positions at the Justice Department. Lanny Breuer, cochair of the law firm's white-collar and investigations practice, was tapped to head DOJ's criminal division. Top deputies of Holder and Breuer hailed from Covington. After serving for a short time in the Obama administration, these aides returned to Covington to lobby their former colleagues in government on behalf of the financial industry.[45]

As Obama was putting together his administration in late 2008, ire toward Wall Street and the Troubled Asset Relief Program (TARP) bailouts was escalating.[46] Lawmakers of both parties were outraged at reports that Treasury had not put significant conditions on the banks and other financial institutions receiving TARP money or even required them to reveal how they spent the funds. In pressing the case for the TARP legislation in late September and early October, Treasury Secretary Hank Paulson and other government officials had assured lawmakers that the banks would use the funds to funnel loans to businesses and consumers to thaw the frozen credit markets. They also assured members of Congress that the legislation would assist homeowners at risk of foreclosure. In late 2008 and early 2009, lawmakers were irate as bankers started boasting about using the taxpayer windfall for stock buybacks, shareholder dividends, purchasing other banks and firms, paying out large bonuses, and saving for a rainy day. They accused Treasury officials of being a "chump" for the banks, playing bait-and-switch, and outright lying to Congress and the public.[47] Legislators were also angry that the Treasury Department had done so little to assist homeowners threatened with foreclosure.

Some Democratic leaders were openly critical of Obama's selection of Geithner, Summers, and others deeply implicated in the financial and foreclosure crises. Geithner was a tarnished nominee not only because of his central role in the bank bailouts and his disregard for the brewing financial storm during his tenure at the New York Fed, but also because he owed $34,000 in back taxes and was a dismal public speaker.[48] In December 2008, Senator Byron Dorgan (D-ND) bluntly told the president-elect: "I don't understand how you could do this. You've picked the wrong people!"[49]

The TARP had ceded enormous power to the Treasury Department, and Obama would end up delegating a lot of informal authority to Geithner.[50] The Treasury secretary would go on to be the most important person steering the administration's response to the financial and foreclosure crises. Summers would take the lead in beating back calls for a more ambitious economic stimulus package. Obama would stick by Geithner despite regular calls from Democratic and Republican lawmakers and others for him to step down because of a series of policy, political, and personal blunders.[51]

"God's Work" and Executive Compensation

When Obama took office in January 2009, millions of households were struggling to avoid foreclosure. Pressure was growing in Congress and the general public for law enforcement to aggressively investigate the financial and foreclosure crises and hold the perpetrators accountable. Pressure was also mounting to restructure the financial sector so that the government and ultimately taxpayers would not once again be called on to bail out the largest banks and financial institutions because of their reckless and fraudulent behavior. The administration's response to these pressures was alternately flatfooted, contradictory, obstructionist, and duplicitous.

As president, Obama was not deeply engaged in reining in the disputes over economic policy among his top aides that fostered policy drift at critical moments. He kept Democratic and other lawmakers seeking more far-reaching reforms of the financial sector at arm's length.[52] In those rare moments when Obama appeared poised to support more comprehensive reforms and make a break with past policies, Summers or Geithner would walk him back or disregard his directives.[53] At the Justice Department, Attorney General Eric Holder and his top deputies modeled Treasury's hands-off stance toward Wall Street.

Obama has been lauded for his management style and was nicknamed "no drama Obama."[54] But his economic team was vexed with acute policy differences and personal animosities that encumbered breaking with the financial orthodoxy that spawned the financial and foreclosure crises. Geithner and Summers, skilled political operatives in simpatico with Wall Street, took advantage of Obama's inexperience and indecisiveness to thwart pressures coming from within and outside of the administration to restructure the financial sector and hold it accountable. Summers regularly told colleagues in the administration that they were "home alone," unlike when Bill Clinton was in the White House.[55] As Obama's top aides undermined or outright ignored his directives, the president failed to demand accountability from them, which further weakened his authority and exacerbated his management problems.[56]

From the start, the Obama administration forfeited an opportunity to knit together a compelling narrative to drive comprehensive reform and to hold Wall Street accountable to the public and the criminal legal system. The confirmation hearings for Obama's nominees were an important opportunity to showcase a new narrative about financial reform and to break with the policies of the past. Instead, Geithner and other nominees antagonized senators as they bobbed and weaved. They adhered to Summers's diktat that Obama's appointees, many of whom were veterans of the Clinton administration, not criticize or apologize for past policies (especially the wave of deregulation under the former president) or commit to new policy positions. "This was the height of stupidity," one aide to Obama later reflected. "The nominees could have been leading the charge to make the needed changes, rather than looking like they were testifying under duress."[57]

Soon after Obama took office, public ire against Wall Street exploded as news broke that financial companies in New York City had distributed $18 billion in end-of-the-year bonuses. Lawmakers and the public were outraged that these companies were handing out lavish bonuses while the government and ultimately taxpayers were providing hundreds of billions of dollars in TARP money and other assistance to rescue Wall Street from one of its most disastrous years.[58] Citigroup, the most troubled of the megabanks, shelled out $5.3 billion in bonuses for 2008. That year, the bank had lost tens of billions of dollars, received $45 billion in TARP funds and billions more in other assistance from US taxpayers to stay afloat, and announced layoffs totaling seventy-five thousand people.[59]

In fall 2008, the congressional Democratic leadership reportedly had met in Speaker Nancy Pelosi's office to discuss including limits on executive compensation for banks and other financial institutions that would be receiving money under the proposed TARP legislation. Treasury Secretary Hank Paulson warned at the time that the financiers would walk away from the bailout deal if their compensation was limited. Asked whether they could live with limiting their bonuses to several million dollars, Robert Rubin, who was participating by conference call, said, "No, they can't."[60] In the end, Democrats secured no significant limits on executive compensation in the original TARP legislation.

At a hastily called appearance in the Oval Office, with Geithner and Vice President Joseph Biden sitting at his side, Obama angrily denounced the bonuses.[61] But behind the scenes, the administration was deeply divided over the issue of executive compensation for TARP recipients. Senior adviser David Axelrod reportedly wanted the administration to stop the payments. Geithner, Summers, and Bernanke were generally untroubled by the bonuses, except for the political headaches they caused. Geithner and Summers contended that going after the bonuses would violate private contracts and "do irreparable damage to our market-based system," according to Obama's account in his memoirs. (Geithner did have his limits, however. When a bank ordered a new jet, he "browbeat" the CEO to cancel it.)[62]

Under pressure from outraged lawmakers, Senator Chris Dodd (D-CT) amended the American Recovery and Reinvestment Act, the administration's signature economic stimulus bill, to curtail bonuses for executives at firms that received TARP money. But after a call from Geithner's office, Dodd quietly modified his amendment, largely exempting TARP-related bonuses agreed on prior to enactment of the stimulus bill.[63] The conference committee for the economic stimulus bill, which Obama signed on February 17, 2009, killed off an amendment to cap compensation of bailed-out bank executives at $400,000, the salary of the US president.[64]

The US government poured cash into not only commercial banks holding federally insured deposits but also investment banks and even American International Group (AIG), the world's largest insurance company, which was imperiled because of its overexposure in credit default swaps (CDSs), which were discussed in chapter 7. In return, the government got a poor deal for taxpayers. The Treasury and Federal Reserve under Bush and Obama refused to wield much control over the bailed-out banks and other financial firms, even though the government and taxpayers became essentially major owners of them.

The interest on TARP loans was far lower than prevailing interest rates, so banks ended up with billions of dollars in government subsidies. The Treasury Department also vastly overpaid for some troubled assets, so banks ended up with another windfall. As the economy choked on all the toxic subprime mortgages and as credit dried up, fears grew that the market would freeze for business and consumer loans, turning the recession into a depression. The Federal Reserve responded by keeping interest rates at or close to zero, supposedly to unfreeze capital markets for businesses and consumers and get the economy going again.[65]

Instead, corporations borrowed billions of dollars at near-zero interest rates and then invested the money in higher-yield foreign financial instruments, not in activities that would reverse the contraction of the US economy, which was hemorrhaging jobs. The low-interest and no-interest rates also allowed banks and other corporations to go on shopping sprees to buy out their competitors. In a remarkable and obscure provision in TARP, the Fed was permitted to pay banks a higher rate of interest on deposits than what it could charge them to borrow money. Banks ended up borrowing from the Fed, then turning around and parking the money in Fed accounts, pocketing the difference without channeling new capital into the economy to stimulate it. Furthermore, during the financial crisis, "bank stock prices reflected implicit bailout expectations equivalent to around $100 billion, which dramatically reduced the pain of subprime-related losses"—at least for the megabanks and their shareholders.[66]

In March 2009, AIG became the bullseye for public and political wrath over the bailouts and bonuses for financiers. Thanks to a $182 billion lifeline in federal loans and other assistance from the Federal Reserve and Treasury Department, the government—and ultimately taxpayers—had ended up with an 80 percent stake in the troubled insurance company.[67] That month, AIG reported $62 billion in red ink for the final quarter of 2008, the largest loss in corporate history.[68] News also broke that the Treasury Department had greenlighted $165 million in "retention bonuses" for employees in AIG's Financial Products division.[69]

This AIG unit was the mastermind for the reckless CDSs that had put the company in mortal peril by selling what were essentially insurance policies backed by a promise to make up any losses if borrowers defaulted on their debts.[70] The hitch was that AIG did not remotely have enough money in reserves to cover these contracts. Lawmakers across the political spectrum piled on about the AIG bonuses. Senator Chuck Grassley (I-IA) called on AIG executives to quit or commit suicide.[71] The House overwhelmingly passed a measure to levy a 90 percent tax on bonuses for employees at AIG and some other TARP recipients, but this proposal died in the Senate.[72]

Treasury officials defended the high salaries and bonuses, arguing that they were critical to keeping the "uniquely" qualified executives at AIG and elsewhere in their jobs as they performed the delicate task of unwinding the enormous mess they had created.[73] The financial crisis had not shaken their view that the titans of finance were "preternaturally gifted supermen" who fully deserved their sky-high paychecks and bonuses.[74] Behind the scenes, Treasury officials put pressure on the "pay czar" charged with determining the pay packages for top executives of TARP recipients to be more generous.[75] Alan Krueger, a top economic aide in the Obama administration, later lamented: "We lost the country with those AIG bonuses."[76]

Lawmakers and the public were further incensed as more details of AIG's deal with the government trickled out, including the insurance company's "backdoor bailout" of Goldman Sachs and other banks. AIG had funneled about $46 billion of the $182 billion lifeline from taxpayers to Goldman Sachs and its other mortgage trading partners.[77] Poised at the brink of bankruptcy in fall 2008, AIG nonetheless paid the banks one hundred cents on the dollar for outstanding insurance contracts. Goldman recouped its entire investment of about $13 billion without making any concessions.

Ignoring recommendations from some of its own advisers in late 2008, the New York Fed, helmed by Geithner at the time, did not wield its considerable clout to pressure AIG to force concessions on the banks.[78] The Treasury Department also opposed compelling the banks to take a "haircut" on the amounts AIG owed them, as creditors often have to do in cases of bankruptcy.[79] "The rescue of AIG distorted the marketplace by transforming highly risky derivative bets into fully guaranteed payment obligations," the Congressional Oversight Panel (COP) for TARP would later conclude in its devastating 2010 report on the AIG bailout. "The result was that the government backed up the entire derivatives market, as if these trades deserved the same taxpayer backstop as savings deposits and checking accounts."[80] The panel was headed by Elizabeth Warren, who at the time was a Harvard Law School professor. Other unsavory details about the AIG bailout subsequently became public, including that AIG was forced by the government, as a condition of the bailout package, to forfeit its right to sue Goldman and other banks for misrepresenting their shady mortgage deals.[81]

In the case of the bailouts of AIG, Citigroup, and other financial institutions, the US government, acting through the Treasury Department, behaved as a "reluctant shareholder."[82] It eschewed claiming any voting rights or asserting other managerial prerogatives even though it had become a major shareholder of these firms. The COP report documented "the incestuous stew of private financial players in the AIG case, who switch their allegiance between public and private roles numerous times."[83] For example, Treasury's main negotiator for the AIG bailout was Dan H. Jester, a former Goldman Sachs executive. It was later revealed that Jester still owned Goldman stock at the time. But Jester did not have to disclose his holdings because he was hired as an outside contractor and was not an appointed official.[84] (In another troubling TARP conflict of interest, a lawyer representing JPMorgan was hired by the Federal Reserve while his firm continued to represent the investment bank.)[85]

The AIG disclosures in March 2009 fueled pressure in Congress and elsewhere to cap executive compensation, reconsider the terms of the bailouts, and restructure the financial industry. Concerned about these pressures, thirteen of the world's most powerful bankers orchestrated, with Geithner's help, a meeting with Obama in April 2009. The president warned the executives at the icy meeting: "My administration is the only thing between you and the pitchforks."[86] But Obama did not demand much in return from the bankers, satisfied at the meeting with their pledges to voluntarily limit executive compensation. Adhering to the script agreed to ahead of time with the White House, the relieved bankers each vowed "we are all in this together" as they left the meeting.[87]

Later that year, Lloyd Blankfein, CEO of Goldman Sachs, defended the large banks and their sky-high bonuses by saying they serve a social purpose, and that the bankers were doing "God's work."[88] John Whitehead, a legendary former chairman of Goldman, later excoriated Blankfein for his remarks, which had become infamous. "He never thought that if the public is losing their jobs and we're in a recession, it isn't a very good time to talk about the justification for a $60 million bonus," remarked Whitehead. "He doesn't get it."[89]

In short, TARP and other government bailout measures ended up recapitalizing the largest banks without recapitalizing the real economy. The five biggest banks emerged with even more economic and political clout.[90] The terms for US banks were far more generous than those the British and German governments hammered out when they rescued their own banks. In the United Kingdom, for example, the government threw out the old management, imposed restrictions on dividends and compensation, and included provisions to encourage lending.[91] By contrast, in the US case, taxpayers did not even get the right to know where the hundreds of billions of TARP dollars went and what the banks and financial firms used the money for.[92] No wonder one Nobel Prize–winning economist titled a chapter of his book on the US bailout "The Great American Robbery."[93]

The Foreclosure Crisis and Foaming the Runway for the Banks

Obama and some of his top economic advisers remained tone deaf to how their approach to the financial crisis, including their failure to hold any of the top financiers criminally accountable for the massive fraud, was inciting

the pitchforks. So was the administration's flatfooted response to the foreclosure crisis.

As Obama took office in January 2009, millions of people had already lost
their homes, and many more were at risk.[94] Meanwhile, hundreds of billions
of TARP dollars were flowing to bail out the banks, the insurance giant AIG,
and other financial firms. Many members of Congress stressed how they had
voted for TARP because it included $50 billion to modify mortgages. By early
2009, TARP had become so reviled that Treasury Secretary Geithner officially
rebranded it as the Financial Stability Plan when he announced four new initiatives, including a long-awaited program to stem the foreclosures.[95]

Presidents Bush and Obama eschewed creating a quasi–government entity
to stem the wave of foreclosures modeled on the New Deal's Home Owners'
Loan Corporation. Created during the Depression, the HOLC purchased
troubled mortgages and then worked with borrowers to modify these loans.[96]
Instead, the Obama administration turned to the private sector, expecting
many of the same banks and other mortgage servicers that ignited the foreclosure crisis to ameliorate it. As the Treasury Department developed the plan, it
shut out the Federal Deposit Insurance Corporation (FDIC), which had vastly
more experience in how to design successful mortgage modification programs
to head off foreclosures.[97]

On February 18, Obama unveiled his Home Affordable Modification Plan
(HAMP), vowing it would help an estimated three to four million homeowners avoid foreclosure by allowing them to modify the terms of their mortgages.
The next day, CNBC reporter Rick Santelli took to the floor of the Chicago
Mercantile Exchange to rant against Obama's plan. His tirade, in which he
called for a possible "Chicago tea party in July," is widely considered a founding moment for the Tea Party. As the Fed and US Treasury were shoveling
hundreds of billions of dollars to leading banks and other financial firms to
bail them out because of their risky and criminal behavior, Santelli was instrumental in shifting the narrative.[98] Santelli charged that Obama's plan would
promote "bad behavior" by homeowners who were "losers" who deserved to
lose their properties.[99]

Santelli contributed to what became a widespread and misleading narrative
that the foreclosure crisis was the result of subprime and low-income losers
living beyond their means and foolishly taking out mortgages they could not
afford. In reality, millions of people were at risk of foreclosure because of forces
beyond their control. In the run-up to the financial and foreclosure crises, the
rate of new mortgages escalated for borrowers across all income levels and

credit scores. After the real estate market tanked and the financial crisis hit, the proportion of middle-income, high-income, and prime borrowers unable to make their mortgage payments soared.[100]

Granted, some people had speculated on the real estate market and lost out when the bubble finally burst. But many more were struggling to make their monthly payments because they were unemployed or underemployed as the economy hemorrhaged jobs thanks to the Great Recession. Millions were also at risk because they had been duped by mortgage originators and banks, who fraudulently sold mortgages without proper underwriting, devised deceptively complex payment provisions that made the mortgages appear more affordable than they were, and used forged or counterfeit documents to get these loans approved, as discussed in chapter 7. The majority (56 percent) of families who lost their homes to foreclosure between 2007 through 2009 were white people. But the foreclosure rates were higher for African American and Latino households (nearly 8 percent for each group) compared to non-Hispanic white households (4.5 percent).[101]

After the real estate bubble burst in mid-2006, nearly one-quarter of all home mortgages were underwater, worth less than what they were purchased for.[102] In some states, the figure was more than half.[103] People who sought to sell their homes in the depressed housing market because they could no longer afford the monthly payments or because of a life change, such as a death, divorce, or new job, would still be left with a debt to pay off. Furthermore, people who walked away from their properties would have stains on their credit scores, impairing their financial prospects for years.

Thanks to landmark legislation enacted in 2005 over the objections of consumers' groups, unions, women's groups, and others, declaring bankruptcy would not necessarily protect these struggling homeowners from their creditors or allow them to keep their primary residence.[104] In enacting that legislation with strong bipartisan support, Congress had mobilized to fight a phantom created by the credit card industry. Since the late 1990s, the credit card industry had been promoting a false narrative that consumers were spending wildly on luxuries they could not afford and then fraudulently declaring bankruptcy to weasel out of paying their bills and debts.[105] But seminal research by Elizabeth Warren dating back years had established that personal mishaps—not luxury spending sprees—were the primary drivers of personal bankruptcies.[106] These mishaps included illnesses, divorces, deaths, and job losses. Banking conglomerates, including Citigroup, were central players in the credit card industry. As lawmakers moved to make declaring personal bankruptcy more punitive, they were complacent about the burgeoning epidemic of mortgage-based securities fraud that implicated Citigroup and other megabanks.

Foreclosures took their toll not only on individual homeowners but also on neighborhoods and municipalities. The tsunami of foreclosures hurt the property values of the homeowners left behind. It also eroded tax bases while straining government budgets with additional costs to board up abandoned buildings, evict squatters, respond to fires, and provide social services for people who had lost their homes. Rising rates of foreclosures in a neighborhood were a strong predictor of rising rates of violent crime.[107] In 2009, a New York City councilman who represented hundreds of blocks in Queens pockmarked by shuttered and abandoned homes lost to foreclosures lamented, "My district feels like ground zero." "In military terms," he said, "we are being pillaged."[108]

Foreclosures took their heaviest toll on counties with Black and Latino majorities, according to a 2009 Pew study.[109] The National Association for the Advancement of Colored People (NAACP) and city, state, and federal officials around the country filed lawsuits against leading banks, including Wells Fargo, JPMorgan Chase, and Citigroup. They charged that the banks deceptively steered Black and Latino homeowners toward subprime loans even though many of them would have qualified for less-expensive conventional mortgages.

Baltimore city officials claimed that Wells Fargo's reverse redlining was responsible for hundreds of foreclosures that eroded the city's tax base while increasing the demand for city services. In an affidavit, a top loan officer at Wells Fargo admitted that she and her colleagues "rode the stagecoach from hell" as they systematically steered African American homebuyers in Baltimore and suburban Maryland toward more expensive subprime loans. Wells Fargo reportedly created an emerging markets unit that specifically targeted Black churches to market what bank employees called "ghetto loans." Loan officers falsely claimed to bank underwriters that their clients had not supplied proof of income even though W-2 forms were available. They also cut and pasted credit scores between applicants.[110]

In 2010, a federal judge tossed out Baltimore's lawsuit against Wells Fargo, ruling that the city could not prove that the bank's lending practices had caused widespread damage to Baltimore neighborhoods.[111] Two years later, Wells Fargo reached a $234 million agreement with the DOJ to settle claims that the bank discriminated against African American and Latino borrowers in communities across the country as it steered them into subprime mortgages and charged them higher fees from 2004 through 2009.[112]

The Home Affordable Modification Plan was a poorly designed plan that
the Treasury Department had hastily put together. Neil Barofsky, the first special inspector general for TARP (SIGTARP), warned that HAMP rested on
troubling conflicts of interest and was highly vulnerable to widespread fraud
by the financial industry. The outgoing Bush administration had appointed
Barofsky, a former federal prosecutor for the Southern District of New York
who had headed its Mortgage Fraud Group, to be TARP's special inspector
general. Barofsky underscored that HAMP was not a remedy for the homeowners most in need of relief. These included people whose properties were
underwater; borrowers who faced crushing monthly mortgage payments
because of unscrupulous or fraudulent mortgage brokers; and the growing
ranks of unemployed and underemployed people unable to make their mortgage payments because of the Great Recession.[113]

Treasury Secretary Geithner was not supportive of using TARP money
designated for homeowner relief to reduce the principal that borrowers owed
in the depressed housing market. He also did not heed SIGTARP's recommendations to implement measures to protect homeowners from hucksters
charging huge upfront fees for what turned out to be false and fraudulent
promises to secure permanent modifications from HAMP that would make
their mortgages more affordable.

Instead of designing a cash-transfer program that would give vouchers to
borrowers so they could lower their mortgage payments, the Treasury Department essentially designated the largest mortgage servicers, including Bank of
America, Wells Fargo, JPMorgan Chase, and Citibank, to run the program.
These servicers did not have vast experience in mortgage modifications
nor the capacity to undertake a gigantic number of modifications.[114] Even
more troubling, given how Treasury had structured HAMP, the servicers
often stood to make the most money by dragging out the mortgage modification process, collecting fees and taxpayer-funded incentive payments along
the way, then foreclosing on the properties anyway, and collecting another
windfall in fees.

To expedite the foreclosures, banks engaged in widespread fraud, including
robo-signing counterfeit mortgage and other documents that they had not
read, let alone confirmed the veracity of. In one notorious example, OneWest,
a bank owned by Steve Mnuchin (who later became Treasury secretary in the
first Trump administration) foreclosed on more than seventy-seven thousand
properties. An investigation by the attorney general's office in California documented numerous foreclosure abuses by OneWest, including backdating false

paperwork and taking actions on foreclosure without proper legal authority. Kamala Harris, who was the state's attorney general at the time, chose not to bring charges against OneWest.[115]

Geithner and the Obama administration did not use the considerable powers they possessed to compel banks and mortgage servicers to refinance mortgages for borrowers rather than foreclose on their properties. They also facilitated the rapid expansion of the predatory single-family home rental market by auctioning off repossessed and unsold properties owned by the government without ensuring that the investors who bought them would maintain the properties and charge fair rents and fees. The Obama administration sought to attract new investors by selling off these delinquent properties at fire-sale prices that included sweetheart agreements that basically guaranteed that the investors would not lose money. These policies gave companies a financial incentive to seek foreclosures. Private equity groups and other wealthy investors, many of them cronies of Donald Trump, swooped in to buy up these properties and then rent them out at above-market rates. It was déjà vu all over again as Wall Street started bundling those rental streams into complex and opaque financial products and selling them off in the unregulated market for financial derivatives.[116]

The special inspector general for TARP and the media documented extensive abuses by the mortgage servicers. Barofsky described HAMP as a "dehumanizing process" that took a deep "psychic toll" on borrowers.[117] Many borrowers would have been better off if they never had attempted to modify their mortgages through HAMP.[118] Banks and other servicers routinely "lost" documents submitted by borrowers seeking mortgage modifications (on average, six times per borrower, according to one survey), which dragged out the process and put borrowers at greater risk of foreclosure.[119] Bank of America employees testified in a class-action suit that they were instructed to lie to homeowners, deliberately lose their documents, and deny their loan modifications without giving any explanation.[120]

With Treasury's encouragement, servicers deployed a version of the infamous no-doc liar's loans to expedite and increase the number of "trial" modifications of mortgages, many of which ended up in foreclosure anyway.[121] Servicers misleadingly advised homeowners who were current on their payments to begin skipping them so as to qualify for HAMP, which put these borrowers at higher risk of foreclosure as the servicers piled on whopping late fees. Reports of abuse flooded into SIGTARP's hotline, but the Treasury Department failed "to hold servicers accountable for their incompetence and abuse of home owners."[122]

The office of the special inspector general for TARP found itself engaged in a "game of whac-a-mole that we could never win" as it sought to root out the scams and hucksters without Treasury's support.[123] The Treasury Department was reluctant to punish servicers for widespread violations by withholding incentive payments, suing them for not fulfilling their contracts, or revising their contracts with the department. It also fought to keep audits of the servicers secret and even permitted the servicers to define for themselves which violations were significant enough to disclose.[124]

The Obama administration's mortgage relief program was grossly insufficient, poorly designed, and excessively complicated. When Obama unveiled the program in February 2009, he vowed it would help seven to nine million families restructure their mortgages.[125] But fewer than one million mortgages were modified under this federal program. Many of the modifications were temporary, not permanent, with interest rates permitted to rise after five years.[126] Banks reported an additional 3.4 million other loan modifications of various kinds. But many of these modifications simply rolled over missed payments into a new mortgage. As a result, hard-pressed homeowners ended up with even higher monthly payments, putting them at risk of eventual foreclosure.[127] By late 2011, the Treasury Department had spent just $3 billion of the promised $75 billion ($50 billion of that from TARP and the rest from other sources) to help millions of homeowners.[128] By way of comparison, the credit card company American Express received nearly $3 billion in TARP assistance.

Despite wide-scale evidence that loan servicers were abusing homeowners by disregarding HAMP contracts, the Treasury Department did little to hold them accountable. The Treasury Department finally agreed to withhold TARP payments from three of the largest mortgage servicers—Wells Fargo, Bank of America, and JPMorgan Chase—that were flouting HAMP's rules and fleecing homeowners. But in early 2012, the Justice Department, the Department of Housing and Urban Development, and forty-nine state attorneys general reached a settlement with five of the country's largest banks and mortgage servicers in the robo-signing scandal. As part of that settlement, Treasury released all the TARP payments. The banks also received broad immunity from future civil cases related to the robo-signing scandal and were not criminally charged.

The banks agreed to a $25 billion settlement, but that figure was grossly inflated through creative and misleading accounting. Under the agreement, the 750,000 people who lost their homes to foreclosure between September 2008 and late 2011 were to receive checks that averaged about $2,000. Hundreds of thousands of other people were supposed to have their mortgages modified so as to reduce their payments.[129] New York Attorney General Eric Schneiderman was unsuccessful in his efforts to sue banks for violating terms of the settlement.[130] In late 2013, the court-appointed monitor for the mortgage settlement accused Bank of America, Wells Fargo, and JPMorgan Chase of violating the agreement, but there were no serious repercussions for the banks.[131]

Geithner reportedly never intended to use HAMP to provide federal relief to keep people in their homes and actively undermined the program. In private meetings, the Treasury secretary confessed that HAMP's main purpose was to "foam the runway for the banks" by slowing the rate of foreclosures. Stretching out the pace of foreclosures would give the banks "more time to absorb losses while the other parts of the bailout juiced bank profits that could then fill the capital holes created by housing losses," Geithner explained at a private meeting.[132]

Obama's Justice Department and the Financial Crisis

At the dawn of the Obama administration, top officials at the Justice Department had promised to aggressively investigate and prosecute crimes stemming from the foreclosure and financial crises.[133] But in the robo-signing scandal and numerous other instances, the administration failed to hold Wall Street accountable to the criminal legal system, despite strong bipartisan support in Congress and elsewhere to do so.

Against the wishes of the Bush administration, Congress had inserted a provision in the October 2008 TARP legislation to create SIGTARP, a potentially powerful special inspector general with law enforcement authority to oversee the program. Weeks later, a Senate subcommittee led by Senator Carl Levin (D-MI) began what would be a vigorous and far-reaching two-year investigation of the financial crisis that had the power to make criminal referrals. Shortly after Obama took office, the Fraud Enforcement and Recovery Act (FERA) sailed through Congress. The legislation authorized $330 million over two years to hire more investigators and prosecutors to battle financial crime. It also created the Financial Crisis Inquiry Commission (FCIC), a bipartisan panel appointed by congressional leaders to investigate the causes of the finan-

cial crisis and make criminal referrals if need be. At the time, Senator Ted
Kaufman (D-DE), a champion of FERA, declared, "People know that if they
rob a bank, they will go to jail. Bankers should know that if they rob people,
they will go to jail too."[134] But the top bankers never went to jail. They were
never even seriously investigated or indicted by the DOJ, despite compelling
evidence of criminal behavior.

The Fraud Enforcement and Recovery Act was kneecapped from the start.
Obama signed the bill at a high-profile ceremony in May 2009. But his administration did not push back when Senator Barbara Mikulski (D-MD), a
member of the Appropriations Committee and cosponsor of the legislation,
supported appropriating a measly $35 million, less than one-fifth of what Con-
gress had authorized for fiscal 2010.[135]

In November 2009, the DOJ ranked financial crimes as fifth in its annual
top ten list of major challenges.[136] This was an improvement over a year earlier,
when financial crimes did not even make the top ten as the financial panic
gripped the country in the waning weeks of the Bush administration.[137] By
late 2009, lawmakers were chafing at the Obama administration's flatfooted
response to tackling financial crimes. To put pressure on the administration,
lawmakers scheduled oversight hearings on FERA.

Seeking to disarm critics, Attorney General Eric Holder hastily announced
formation of the interagency Financial Fraud Enforcement Task Force in November 2009. With other top officials at his side, including Treasury Secretary
Geithner and Khuzami of the SEC, the attorney general promised "an aggressive, coordinated, and proactive effort to investigate and prosecute financial
crimes."[138] But the task force lacked operational powers to bring forth cases
and had a much broader mandate than just the financial crisis.[139] The Justice
Department received no additional resources for the task force and struggled
to staff it. The task force was essentially a large coordinating committee, not a
major new investigative unit.[140] No wonder a former DOJ official disparaged
it as "the turtle."[141] Three years after it was formed, the unit had only about
fifty-five people assigned to it and had still not filed charges in a single case
that involved any of the country's six largest banks.[142]

Between the mid-1990s and the financial crisis, the number of cases that
bank regulators referred to the Justice Department for criminal prosecution
each year had dried up, which hampered its efforts to hold Wall Street accountable. Top officials at the DOJ regularly pleaded that they lacked sufficient resources, but all indications were that they had not made high-level financial
crimes a priority and lacked the political will to do so.[143] In 2009, the FBI

had only 240 agents assigned to mortgage fraud cases. With additional funding from Congress, that figure rose to 377 for 2010.[144] By way of comparison, one hundred FBI agents worked on the Enron case a decade earlier, and more than one thousand were assigned to the S&L scandal at its height.[145]

Prominent lawmakers of both parties, including Senator Grassley, regularly complained to Lanny Breuer, assistant attorney general and head of the criminal division, that the Justice Department had not prioritized investigating major financial crimes.[146] Breuer repeatedly sought to reassure Congress, the media, and the public that the department was aggressively investigating criminal activities related to the financial crisis. He would excuse the slow pace by explaining that the Justice Department was strapped for resources, and that these cases took time because they were exceedingly complex. But insiders working in the fraud section of the criminal division reported that no major investigations of Wall Street's role in the financial crisis were under way. Indeed, Wall Street and its top executives did not even remotely come up at the department's weekly indictment approval meetings.[147] Lawmakers were flabbergasted in spring 2010 when Ray Lohier, the assistant US attorney in charge of securities fraud for the Southern District of New York, which has jurisdiction over Wall Street, told them that his top priority was cybercrime.[148]

Inside critics charged that Breuer sought to remake the culture of the Justice Department by surrounding himself with loyalists who were young lawyers recruited from elite white-collar firms and top-ranked law schools. These recruits had little experience prosecuting anyone, let alone investigating complex financial cases.[149] According to one dismayed former federal prosecutor, the message that Breuer's overhaul efforts transmitted to career prosecutors was "you suck."[150] The so-called Breu Crew reportedly fomented a "careerist culture" that eschewed pursuing corporate cases where they felt "the person is 100 percent guilty but they are only 70 percent sure they can win at trial," explained a former prosecutor at the DOJ in Washington.[151] A disgruntled career prosecutor who had been a central figure in the Enron investigation took to needling Breuer by asking: "How many cases are you dismissing this week?"[152]

In November 2009, two former Bear Stearns hedge fund managers accused in the first major criminal case stemming from the financial crisis were acquitted after the prosecution presented a "sloppy and hasty" case.[153] Their acquittal reinforced the DOJ's reticence to bring criminal charges in other financial cases. Six months later, federal investigators abandoned a two-year probe of

AIG executives and their role in the lucrative CDS business that brought the insurance firm to the brink of bankruptcy.[154] And in early 2011, prosecutors surprised many observers when they ended the investigation of Angelo Mozilo, the former chief executive of the mortgage lender Countrywide Financial, without bringing any criminal charges against him. Mozilo, one of the best-known highflyers in the mortgage-backed securities market, had confessed in a series of emails that his company had misrepresented the quality of the mortgages it was writing. These loans were, in his words, "poison."[155]

Career prosecutors grumbled that Obama's political appointees in the Justice Department were clueless about how to investigate and prosecute complicated corporate cases. They also complained that these officials violated the hands-off norm of not interfering in the department's most important cases. They accused top Justice officials of dwelling "in the weeds of criminal justice investigations, following each development and questioning each decision" made by prosecutors working at the DOJ headquarters in Washington.[156]

Amid growing concern about the absence of any major prosecutions in the financial crisis, the "Breu Crew" turned to foreign bribery cases to help neutralize the political fallout.[157] The nine largest-ever bribery settlements (as of late 2016) occurred between 2009 and 2016, and two-thirds of them involved foreign companies.[158] As one lawyer remarked, "It's fucked up that one of our priorities is crime in other countries. It's an area no rational person would put precious resources."[159]

The Justice Department did not establish special task forces, each responsible for investigating a major firm or bank implicated in the subprime mortgage scandal, as it had done with the Enron scandal.[160] It also did not designate the Southern District of New York to take the lead in investigating the subprime mortgage scandal. That office had the most experienced and well-resourced federal prosecutors when it comes to unraveling complex financial crimes.

In another key development, Holder assigned the high-profile 9/11 cases to the Southern District, which drained that office's attention and resources away from investigating the financial crisis. Holder's decision in November 2009 reinforced the long-standing view that waging the global war on terror remained a higher priority than bringing the main culprits of the subprime securities scandal to justice and preventing another financial meltdown. (Faced with a public uproar over trying the 9/11 cases in a federal court in Manhattan rather than the extrajudicial system that the Bush administration had established in Guantánamo, Holder reversed his decision in April 2011.)[161]

When Preet Bharara took over the Southern District office in 2009, he chose to focus on insider-trading cases, racking up an impressive 85–0 record of prosecutions. But he eschewed cases arising from the financial and foreclosure crises, which were more time consuming and harder to investigate and win. *Time* magazine celebrated Bharara in a cover story proclaiming, "This man is busting Wall Street." Bharara later conceded that the insider-trading cases "made our careers, but they don't change the world." Several former prosecutors in his office confessed that pursuing the bankers was never a priority. "The government failed," said one of them. "We didn't do what we needed to do."[162]

The mortgage fraud cases were scattered among federal prosecutors' offices around the country, many of which were inexperienced in pursuing sophisticated financial frauds.[163] These offices investigated the subprime mortgage scandal and related criminal activities in a decentralized, desultory fashion. They brought charges against lower-level culprits, but did not have the will, capacity, or support from the DOJ to go after the Wall Street masterminds.

In the case of elite-level corporate malfeasance, the Justice Department and other government agencies regularly pursued a "lone gunman" theory. They would go after a single low-level employee while letting corporate officers and the firm off the hook.[164] By contrast, when it came to crime in the streets, the Justice Department and police had an exaggerated sense of the degree to which lethal gangs were driving crime. They permissively slapped the *gang member* label on numerous suspects and defendants. Law enforcement officials were obsessed with ferreting out so-called gang activity and ratcheting up punishments for being a member of a gang.[165]

"The Untouchables," a 2013 PBS *Frontline* documentary, revealed that no real investigation of the major Wall Street firms—"no subpoenas, no document reviews, no wiretaps"—was underway at the Justice Department.[166] Lanny Breuer, head of the criminal division, defended the DOJ's record. "When a case could be brought, we did," he said. "But when we cannot prove beyond a reasonable doubt that there was criminal intent, then we have a constitutional duty not to bring those cases."[167] But Breuer also conceded that, when determining whether to bring a case, the department considered the effect that its actions might have on the economy.[168]

Breuer's remarks drew sharp criticisms from lawmakers. In a letter to Holder, Senator Sherrod Brown (D-OH) and Senator Grassley said Breuer's comments raised "important questions about the Justice Department's prosecutorial philosophy." These included whether the "too big to fail" status of certain Wall Street megabanks was undermining the ability and willingness of

the government to prosecute them for criminal misconduct and impose meaningful penalties.[169] Days after the documentary aired in January 2013, Breuer
announced he would be resigning. After leaving the Justice Department, he
returned to Covington & Burling to serve as vice chairman of this top corporate law firm.[170]

The Justice Department not only failed to make even a pretense of investigating Wall Street but also stymied investigations by other agencies. In late
2013, the media reported that the DOJ refused a request from the Office of the
Comptroller of the Currency (OCC), which is part of the Treasury Department and oversees the largest banks, to enforce a subpoena against JPMorgan
Chase (JPMC), Bernie Madoff's principal bank. JPMorgan Chase was refusing to turn over documents that the OCC sought for its investigation of
Madoff's relationship with the bank, including allegations that for years it had
obstructed federal examiners seeking to ascertain what bank employees knew
about his Ponzi scheme. Madoff was one of the bank's biggest clients. In a related case, Irving Picard, trustee for the Madoff victims' fund, charged in a
lawsuit that evidence of Madoff's multibillion-dollar Ponzi scheme "perme-
ated every facet of JPMC."[171] Unable to obtain key documents, the OCC shuttered its investigation in October 2013.[172]

In early 2014, the Justice Department's own watchdog issued a damning
report about the department's efforts to crack down on mortgage fraud. The
DOJ's inspector general cast doubt on the administration's claims that it was
committed to holding people accountable for criminal misconduct that precipitated the financial and foreclosure crises. It revealed that the FBI treated
mortgage fraud "as the lowest ranked criminal threat in its lowest crime category" between 2009 and 2011. Despite an infusion of nearly $200 million during
that period to investigate mortgage fraud, the number of FBI agents assigned
to these cases and the number of pending cases fell. The inspector general criticized the Justice Department for substantially overstating the track record of
its multiagency Distressed Homeowners Initiative in charging people with
mortgage fraud (by a factor of five) and in tallying the estimated losses of their
schemes (by a factor of more than ten). After being made aware of the serious
flaws in its figures, the DOJ continued to promote these inaccurate statistics in
its press releases.[173] In 2013, the FBI, which is part of the Justice Department,
quietly declared that the agency's "primary function" was no longer "law enforcement," as it had been for years, but "national security."[174]

The response from the SEC was also desultory and misdirected. When the
financial crisis hit, investors were holding trillions of dollars in mortgage-

backed securities that were "issued with practically no SEC oversight."[175] In its final report, the FCIC charged that the SEC had "failed to adequately enforce its disclosure requirements governing mortgage securities, exempted some sales of such securities from its review, and preempted states from applying state law to them, thereby failing in its core mission to protect investors."[176] After consulting with the Treasury Department, in 2009 the SEC adopted a broad guideline to avoid levying large penalties on financial institutions that had received government bailouts. This guideline, which was not made public at the time, rendered investigators more cautious.[177] The SEC took a one-and-then-done approach to the major banks, typically choosing one case to settle up with each of them and then moving on.[178]

In late 2008, the spectacular decades-long Ponzi scheme run by Bernie Madoff with winks and nods from top financial institutions, including Citigroup and JPMorgan Chase, came to light after his sons turned him into the authorities.[179] The SEC's inspector general released a damning report in 2009 about the agency's spectacular failure to uncover the scheme, and an embarrassed SEC sought to deflect criticisms that it had been asleep at the switch.[180] The SEC moved to concentrate its resources on ferreting out similar Ponzi-like schemes rather than pursuing the epic fraud in mortgage-backed securities.[181] Facing budget cuts in Congress, SEC staff members focused on smaller cases that they could resolve quickly and easily. Doing so, they calculated, would burnish the agency's track record as it sought additional money from lawmakers.[182]

The SEC's abysmal record as an enforcer of violations in securities law predated the financial crisis. A 2011 *New York Times* investigation into the SEC's enforcement activities over the prior fifteen years found at least fifty-one cases in which nineteen Wall Street firms had settled cases involving securities fraud after previously having been caught violating the same law and vowing not to do so again.[183] In response to these findings, Robert Khuzami, the SEC's enforcement director, maintained nonetheless that these agreements served as deterrents. Senator Levin, who chaired the Senate's main investigation of the financial crisis, disagreed. "It's a green light to operate the same way without a lot of fear that the boom is going to be lowered on you," he remarked.[184] This was a far cry from the SEC's heyday in the 1970s when corporate America feared Stanley Sporkin, a predecessor of Khuzami's who was known as the "Father of Enforcement"; or when Richard Breeden, SEC chairman under George H. W. Bush and briefly under Bill Clinton, threatened that corporate executives who violated securities laws would be left "naked, homeless, and without wheels."[185]

The "TARP Cop"

The lackadaisical and forgiving approach of the SEC and DOJ toward high-end corporate criminality stood in sharp contrast to the activities of the special inspector general charged with overseeing TARP.[186] The war on inspectors general during Trump's first and second terms raised public awareness of the potentially vital role these watchdogs can play in keeping government entities accountable and keeping Congress and the public informed about their activities.[187] But this war did not begin with Trump.

Obama's Treasury Department, enabled at key junctures by the White House and the Justice Department, took an "openly adversarial approach" to SIGTARP.[188] Treasury officials routinely refused SIGTARP's requests for information; undermined its efforts to audit banks and other TARP recipients to find out how much government assistance they were receiving and how they spent it; disparaged and bullied SIGTARP in public and private; stymied its investigations of fraud in the bank bailouts, the sale of toxic assets, and the mortgage relief program for homeowners; ignored SIGTARP's recommendations to shield these government programs from criminal activities; and misled or outright lied to SIGTARP, lawmakers, and the public.[189] On numerous occasions, top Democrats and Republicans in Congress had to intercede to get Treasury, and in some cases the White House, to back down so that SIGTARP could carry out its duties.[190]

The Federal Reserve and Treasury Department were adamantly opposed to revealing what financial institutions received TARP funding, which totaled more than the annual discretionary funding of the US government. At nearly every turn, they fought the efforts of lawmakers, SIGTARP, the General Accounting Office, and COP to calculate the full extent of government assistance to the country's leading financial institutions.[191] Audits of the TARP bailouts revealed that "the bounteous terms delivered by the government seemed to border on being corrupt," according to Neil Barofsky, the first head of SIGTARP.[192]

With the help of Congress, and at times the Fed and FDIC, SIGTARP was able to install some guardrails to curtail fraud in the TARP-related programs that the Treasury Department and Obama administration rolled out. Barofsky was especially concerned about Treasury's so-called public-private plan to purchase $2 trillion in toxic assets that essentially had been "designed by Wall Street, for Wall Street."[193] Congress was so outraged at the plan that it agreed to give an additional $15 million to SIGTARP to investigate possible conflicts of interest and collusion.[194]

This public-private plan was vulnerable to many of the same conflicts of interest, collusion, and self-dealing that had fueled the financial crisis in the first place. It would potentially leave taxpayers on the hook for massive losses while generating huge profits for Wall Street. Geithner and other Treasury officials treated these and other objections "with condescension and outright anger." They contended that guardrails recommended by SIGTARP were un-necessary because financiers' concerns for their "reputational risk" would be enough to prevent them from straying over the line between what was legal and illegal as their firms managed the sell-off of the toxic assets. In the face of congressional and public outrage, Treasury finally modified the plan but ob-stinately refused to rectify fundamental flaws that rendered it vulnerable to fraud and abuse. The plan ultimately crumbled as the FDIC and the Fed pulled out because of its flaws.[195]

Barofsky established and chaired a special law enforcement task force that included representatives from the FBI, SEC, Internal Revenue Service (IRS), and other agencies.[196] Many of the criminal cases that SIGTARP built went forward without the DOJ's support. The Justice Department remained mostly on the sidelines, even when Barofsky forwarded it compelling evidence of criminal activities.[197] In the face of obstructionism from the Treasury Depart-ment and foot-dragging by the Justice Department, SIGTARP nonetheless racked up a string of civil and criminal convictions involving grand theft from TARP, including a handful of banking executives. Most of its other cases in-volved hucksters "who were exploiting Treasury's mismanagement of HAMP to prey on struggling homeowners."[198] The office under Barofsky also pre-vented the loss of and assisted in the recovery of hundreds of millions of dollars.[199] Major media reported that Wall Street executives were fearful of Barofsky, nicknamed the "TARP cop."[200] But SIGTARP's jurisdiction was limited. It did not have authority to investigate activities that predated enact-ment of the TARP legislation in October 2008, including possible criminal activities by the largest banks and their executives in the years leading up to the financial and foreclosure crises. By the time Barofsky was appointed in late 2008, hundreds of billions of TARP dollars had already been dispersed with minimal oversight of Treasury's actions.[201]

The Treasury Department also impeded the work of COP, which was man-dated by the October 2008 TARP legislation and was initially chaired by Eliza-beth Warren. In fall 2009, Geithner and his aides developed an "Elizabeth Warren strategy" to undercut her influence.[202] As for Obama, while he would express begrudging admiration for Warren's acumen and tenacity as she elucidated the roots of the financial crisis and the need for reform to lawmakers and the public, the president kept her at arm's length.[203] At the time, Senator Grassley praised Warren, who would later become one of his colleagues across the aisle in the Senate, for her watchdog role as COP's chair. He also intervened at critical moments when the White House and Treasury Department were undermining the work of her panel and SIGTARP.[204]

Oh, Nevermind!

In a March 2008 campaign speech, candidate Barack Obama laid out his vision to address the foreclosure crisis and the threatening financial crisis.[205] Speaking just a stone's throw away from Wall Street at Cooper Union college, he took a conciliatory stance toward the financial industry. Obama said nothing about addressing the criminal behavior that fueled the subprime market scandals and the financial crisis. Two years later, he returned to Cooper Union, this time as president to pitch legislation for financial reform.[206] Once again, he maintained his silence about crime in the suites even though his April 2010 Cooper Union speech was bookended by a series of blockbuster revelations about rampant fraud and other criminal activities by the country's leading banks and other financial institutions.

A month before that speech, the bankruptcy examiner in the Lehman case had released a devastating twenty-two-hundred-page report that detailed massive fraud and other probable criminal misconduct at the investment firm prior to its collapse in September 2008.[207] Nine days before Obama spoke, the Levin committee held congressional hearings that detailed the vast number of liar's loans that had been funneled through Washington Mutual, which collapsed in September 2008 in the biggest bank failure in US history. The Levin hearings revealed that frontline bank examiners at the Office of Thrift Supervision (OTS) had been identifying high levels of fraud and weak internal controls at the bank for years. But the leadership of the main overseer of the country's thrifts had failed to act. It had also stymied the FDIC's investigation of WaMu. The OTS continued to rate WaMu as financially sound until shortly before it imploded.[208]

The week before Obama spoke at Cooper Union, the Treasury Department's inspector general testified before Congress that the financial system was "a target-rich environment" for financial fraud.[209] That same week, the SEC sent shock waves through Wall Street when it accused Goldman Sachs of securities fraud in a civil lawsuit filed in federal court. The SEC claimed that the investment bank had designed and sold a mortgage security named Abacus at the behest of Paulson & Company that was secretly intended to fail so that the hedge fund could profit handsomely by betting on its collapse. The SEC's lawsuit was the first time regulators took action against Wall Street for scamming investors so as to profit from the collapsing housing market.[210]

Just days after President Obama's Cooper Union speech, the Levin committee held an eleven-hour hearing in which it grilled CEO Lloyd Blankfein and other top Goldman Sachs executives about the investment bank's role in the mortgage-backed securities market, including the Abacus deal. The hearings revealed that Goldman executives realized in late 2006 that the investment bank was overexposed in mortgage-related securities as the real estate market was poised to crash. But no worries—they could still make a killing by selling these toxic assets off to unsuspecting customers and then by betting against the securities in the derivatives market. To simplify, "Goldman was like a car dealership that realized it had a whole lot of cars with faulty brakes," explained a shrewd analyst of the financial crisis. "Instead of announcing a recall, it surged ahead with a two-fold plan to make a fortune: first, by dumping the dangerous products on other people, and second, by taking out life insurance against the fools who bought the deadly cars."[211]

At that hearing, Goldman executives were clearly on the defensive as senators from both parties decried the bank's actions, and members of the audience, including four people dressed in mock prison jumpsuits, jeered at them. At one point, Senator John Ensign (R-NV) declared that he took offense at comparisons being made between Wall Street and Las Vegas. The Nevada senator came to the defense of the casinos, declaring that, unlike the "guys on Wall Street," the casinos did not manipulate the odds while you were playing the game.[212]

In July 2010, Goldman reached a settlement with the SEC in the infamous Abacus case. The investment bank agreed to pay a $550 million penalty without admitting any wrongdoing. A low-level trader, but no top executives, was held liable for violating securities law in creating the doomed security. James Kidney, the longtime SEC lawyer assigned to the Abacus investigation, savaged the settlement. He castigated top SEC officials for thwarting efforts to thoroughly investigate—or even interview—senior executives at Goldman Sachs and Paulson & Company, which made about $1 billion from the deal, despite credible evidence of wide-scale fraud sanctioned from above. "This appears to be an unbelievable fraud," Kidney wrote at the time to his boss. "I don't think we should bring it without naming all those we believe to be liable." In curtailing a wider investigation, Reid Muoio, the head of the SEC team investigating complex mortgage securities, defended potential targets of SEC charges as "good people who had done one bad thing."[213] In reflecting on the Abacus settlement and the SEC's role, Kidney lamented, "For the powerful, we are at most a tollbooth on the bankster turnpike. We are a cost, not a serious expense."[214]

Public Silence

The Levin committee and FCIC issued damning final reports in early 2011 about Wall Street's role in the financial crisis and made criminal referrals to the Justice Department. They documented how lax or nonexistent government oversight had created a criminogenic environment in which mortgage fraud and other financial crimes thrived. Policymakers largely ignored the massive crime wave in the mortgage, housing, and securities markets, the Levin committee and FCIC charged, allowing it to fester.[215]

Both investigations were exhaustive. The FCIC's nearly two-year investigation included interviews with more than seven hundred people, a review of millions of pages of documents, and nineteen days of public hearings around the country. In its final report, the FCIC used "variants of the word 'fraud' no fewer than 157 times in describing what led to the financial crisis."[216] When the final report was released, the commission confirmed that it had made criminal referrals to the Justice Department but provided few other details and did not publicly name names.[217]

Little else was publicly known about these criminal referrals until five years later, in March 2016, when the National Archives released a massive cache of documents related to the FCIC's investigation, including heretofore confidential interview transcripts, memos, and minutes of the commission's private meetings. Two memos prepared by the commission's legal staff were bombshells. They revealed that the FCIC's legal staff had recommended eleven separate criminal referrals based on "serious indications of violation[s]" of federal securities or other laws. The memos named names, including a who's who of Wall Street.[218]

Specifically, FCIC lawyers identified suspected criminal activities at fourteen corporations (including five that were implicated in several of the referrals), among them Citigroup, UBS, Moody's, Goldman Sachs, Fannie Mae, and PricewaterhouseCoopers. The referrals also implicated nine top-shelf Wall Street executives (two of them twice), including Robert Rubin, Chuck Prince, and Gary Crittenden of Citigroup (for potential fraud and false certifications); CEO Daniel Mudd and CFO Stephen Swad of Fannie Mae (for potential accounting fraud and false certifications); CEO Martin Sullivan and CFO Steven Bensinger of the insurance giant AIG (for potential fraud); and CEO Stanley O'Neal and CFO Jeffrey Edwards of Merrill Lynch (for false and misleading representations).[219] The commissioners voted separately on each of these eleven referrals in meetings in September and October 2010. They agreed by overwhelming margins in every instance to refer the potential criminal violations to the Justice Department.[220]

After the National Archives released the trove of FCIC documents, Phil Angelides, who had chaired the commission, confessed that he had been disappointed years earlier with the DOJ's lackadaisical response to his commission's findings and criminal referrals. "At the very least," he said, the Justice Department owed "the American people the reassurance that they conducted a thorough investigation of individuals who engaged in misconduct."[221] In September 2016, Senator Elizabeth Warren (D-MA) formally requested that the DOJ's inspector general investigate how the Justice Department had handled the FCIC's criminal referrals. Warren characterized the DOJ's failure to bring any criminal charges in the nearly six years since the FCIC made its criminal referrals as "outrageous and baffling."[222]

In cataloging the DOJ's "abysmal failure," Warren noted that none of the executives named in the FCIC referrals had been criminally charged.[223] Neither had any of the fourteen corporations that the FCIC had referred to the DOJ. Five of the firms had reached settlements with the DOJ.[224] They paid fines that appeared eye-popping but were minuscule compared to the firms' assets, profits, and massive financial aid from the government to keep them afloat.[225] Moreover, the firms were able to deduct the fines from their taxes, minimizing their penalties even further.

At the time, Warren also asked FBI Director James Comey to release materials related to his agency's response to the FCIC's criminal referrals. In making her request, Warren referred to Comey's exceptional actions in the FBI's investigation of Hillary Clinton's use of a personal email server when she was secretary of State. Warren noted how Comey had broken precedent in July 2016 when he publicly released information about the Clinton investigation even though the FBI had closed the case without charging anyone. Warren noted that Comey had pointed to "intense public interest" to justify his decision.[226] (The FBI ended up reopening the Hillary Clinton email server case in late October and then closing it once again in a series of controversial decisions just days before the 2016 election.) Warren's request was met with public silence from the DOJ and the FBI.[227]

A year after Warren's request, the DOJ rebuffed a narrower Freedom of Information Act request from a Wall Street watchdog group seeking information about the FCIC's criminal referrals involving Rubin and the two other Citigroup executives. The Justice Department would not even confirm or deny that it had any relevant records. The DOJ characterized release of any information in this case as "an unwarranted invasion of privacy" since no one had been charged.[228]

In addition to Warren, Federal District Court Judge Jed Rakoff emerged as another leading critic of the DOJ's failure to aggressively pursue these cases. Rakoff shocked Wall Street and the political establishment in September 2009 by refusing to sign off on a remarkable settlement concerning the bailout of Merrill Lynch and its merger with Bank of America that the SEC and the two financial institutions had agreed on. He forced through a more equitable settlement after charging that the initial deal defrauded shareholders and absolved bank executives.[229]

Liar's Poker

Even if we accept the questionable claims by the DOJ's defenders and apologists that wide-scale fraud cases are just too hard to make and win, this does not explain why the department let corporate officers off the hook for more straightforward, garden-variety crimes, such as perjury. Lying under oath to Congress and federal investigators, such as the FCIC, is against the law, but the DOJ never aggressively pursued cases of suspected perjury. The DOJ's nonchalance about investigating Blankfein, Rubin, Prince, and other Wall Street figures for perjury sharply contrasted with its dogged pursuit around this time of athletes accused of lying to Congress and other authorities about their use of steroids and other performance-enhancing drugs. (The DOJ indicted star athletes, including pitcher Roger Clemens, home run king Barry Bonds, and Olympic track-and-field gold medalist Marion Jones, who ended up serving six months in federal prison in 2008 for lying to federal agents.)[230]

At the Levin committee hearing on April 27, 2010, Blankfein of Goldman Sachs, who had spent nearly his entire three-decade career at the investment bank in commodities and trading securities, testified that he was unaware of the major role that credit ratings played in institutional investors' buying decisions. An astute chronicler of the financial crisis dismissed Blankfein's claim and suggested he had committed perjury. "I am willing to bet that if you go through his [Blankfein's] e-mail carefully and depose everyone around him, there would be plenty of evidence that he knew perfectly well how important ratings are," he observed.[231]

Blankfein and other current and former executives and traders at Goldman Sachs denied under oath that the investment bank had shorted its unsuspecting customers. They denied unloading Goldman's toxic assets on clients as real estate prices were collapsing and then betting against the securities, which the bank had marketed as high-grade investments.[232] Levin and other senators were incredulous about these claims during the hearings. When the committee released its 650-page final report a year later, Levin highlighted how it had identified thirty-four hundred places in Goldman documents where the firm's officials had used the phrase "net short," a reference to negative bets.[233]

When he released the report, Levin implored federal prosecutors to consider possible perjury charges against Blankfein and other current and former employees who testified before his committee. He also sent his findings to the Justice Department.[234] Federal prosecutors initiated a probe into potential fraud by Goldman Sachs and perjury by Blankfein. But in August 2012, the DOJ announced it would not pursue any criminal charges against them.[235]

The DOJ also did not pursue perjury charges against top executives at Citigroup, including Robert Rubin and Charles Prince. At closed-door interviews and a public hearing with Rubin and Prince, the FCIC's staff and commissioners zeroed in on the firm's misleading disclosures that it had only $13 billion in subprime exposure at a time when corporate officers knew the true figure was closer to $55 billion. The FCIC also focused on Citigroup's creation of financial vehicles specifically designed to circumvent capital asset requirements. These vehicles helped the megabank conceal the extent of its exposure to toxic assets and thus how at risk it was.[236]

Rubin brought along half a dozen attorneys from two of the country's most powerful law firms to his March 11, 2010, appearance before the FCIC.[237] Clinton's former Treasury secretary had chaired the Executive Committee of Citigroup's board of directors for nearly a decade before leaving the firm in early 2009. He also briefly served as chairman of the company following CEO and Chairman Charles Prince's abrupt resignation in early November 2007 after Citigroup revealed massive losses due to its investments in subprime mortgages.[238] During his stint at the megabank, Rubin received a reported $126 million in compensation from Citigroup.[239] In his March appearance before the

FCIC, Rubin presented himself as a rainmaker, jetting around the world wooing heads of state, finance ministers, and other high-flying influencers, clients, and potential clients. Rubin repeatedly denied that he was involved in the operations of the firm, or what he frequently characterized as its "granular" activities.[240]

The FCIC staff presented Rubin with numerous documents and other evidence that appeared to suggest otherwise. They questioned him about his presence at key meetings and his involvement in major decisions regarding Citigroup's entanglements with toxic mortgage-backed securities that had brought the megabank to the brink of collapse by fall 2008. Dozens of times during the interview Rubin responded with some version of "I don't remember."[241] He even used that dodge for a warm-up softball question about deregulation during his tenure as Clinton's Treasury secretary. (Rubin told the committee, "I don't think that there was deregulation—if there was deregulation, I don't recollect. You may be right about that.")[242]

In his appearance before the FCIC, Richard Bowen, Citigroup's business chief underwriter, testified that for years he had been warning the bank's corporate officers about its highly risky practices in the mortgage market.[243] The day before Robert Rubin was named chairman of Citi's board, Bowen had sent him and other Citi executives an email marked "URGENT" documenting the massive fraud he had discovered in the bank's mortgage operations.[244] As for Charles Prince, the former Citi executive denied at the FCIC's public hearing on April 8, 2010 that the megabank had ever created special financial vehicles designed to avoid capital requirements. When one FCIC commissioner presented minutes from a meeting Prince attended that strongly suggested otherwise, he attempted to walk back his remarks.[245]

Fines and Fees: Pay to Play

In fall 2011, the Occupy Wall Street movement erupted in Lower Manhattan. The movement spread around the country and the world, drawing attention to how the richest 1 percent and 0.1 percent had become even wealthier in the aftermath of the Great Recession while the other 99 percent faced declining living standards and quality of life. Obama mostly kept his distance from the movement.[246] After the administration of billionaire New York City Mayor Michael Bloomberg crushed the epicenter of the Occupy Wall Street movement on November 15, 2011, during a heavy-handed police raid in the middle of the night on Zuccotti Park in Lower Manhattan, Obama was publicly silent about the crackdown.[247]

As the Occupy Wall Street movement sputtered in the face of police crack-downs and other obstacles, and as the 2012 race for the White House geared up, the administration's kid-glove treatment of Wall Street continued to draw public ire and scrutiny. Polls at the time showed strong public support for the grievances of the Occupy Wall Street movement and for redistributing wealth more evenly. Polls also revealed deep distrust of the government to do the right thing. Nearly all those polled reported being fearful that the economy was stagnating or deteriorating further even though the Great Recession was technically over by then.[248]

Looking ahead to the November election, Obama sought to project a tougher stance toward Wall Street. In his 2012 State of the Union address, he highlighted the establishment of a new financial crimes unit to investigate and prosecute "large-scale" financial fraud. The special unit that Holder had un-veiled in late 2009 to investigate Wall Street had been so "invisible or non-existent" that few people recalled that the administration supposedly already had such a special task force in place.[249] The new Residential Mortgage-Backed Securities Working Group was chaired by many of the same members of the administration who headed the old special unit. When the group began its work in early 2012, the DOJ reportedly had no mortgage securitization cases in the pipeline, which calls into question prior claims by Breuer, the former head of the criminal division, that the department had been aggressively in-vestigating major mortgage fraud cases.[250]

By then, the statute of limitations to bring fraud charges under federal se-curities law, which is typically five years, was rapidly approaching.[251] But this statute of limitations for fraud was not necessarily the definitive final chapter. A determined and sophisticated prosecutor could have explored levying charges under money-laundering, conspiracy, or racketeering laws that have longer statutes of limitations.[252]

In the end, only one corporate executive was sent to prison in connection with the financial crisis. A trader at Credit Suisse pleaded guilty and received a thirty-month sentence for hiding millions of dollars in losses in the bank's portfolio of mortgage-backed securities. In handing down the sentence in late 2013, the judge declared that the trader's crime was but "a small piece of an overall evil climate within the bank and with many other banks."[253]

The Justice Department levied charges of civil fraud against some top banks. But it did not pursue charges against their senior executives who mas-terminded these frauds. Department of Justice officials claimed that proving fraudulent intent was too difficult, even though the department had done so successfully in comparably complex cases, including Enron and WorldCom, which were discussed in chapter 7.[254]

The Obama administration enshrined fines as the punishment of choice for corporate criminal misconduct. The megabanks and other corporations considered these fines to be just another line item in the cost of doing business. The fines that an individual bank or other financial institution shelled out appeared colossal. But they typically paled in comparison to their quarterly profits. The fines were also minuscule compared to the TARP bailout and additional direct and indirect government subsidies that Wall Street received, which together totaled trillions of dollars.[255] Furthermore, the DOJ, SEC, and other agencies often never even bothered to collect billions in civil and criminal penalties levied at corporations.[256]

When confronted by Senator Warren in early 2013 about possible fines that JPMC might have to shell out, CEO Jamie Dimon arrogantly shot back, "So hit me with a fine. We can afford it."[257] Two months later, JPMC agreed to a $13 billion civil penalty to resolve multiple claims related to its role in the financial crisis. Most of that penalty was eligible for a tax deduction.[258]

Goldman Sachs, which received $10 billion in TARP bailout funds, as well as other government assistance, agreed in 2014 to pay the Federal Housing Finance Agency $1.2 billion to resolve claims that it had failed to disclose the risks in certain mortgage bonds it sold. Two years later, Goldman agreed to pay $5 billion to settle claims that it fraudulently marketed mortgage-backed securities to investors. The actual amount it shelled out was considerably less because of allowances for tax deductions and other creative accounting.[259] As part of the agreement, Goldman did not have to confess to any legal wrongdoing, though the statement of facts accompanying the settlement detailed extensive fraudulent activities.[260]

Between 2009 and 2014, government authorities agreed to nearly $83 billion in penalties to settle cases stemming from the financial and foreclosure crises that involved the country's six largest banks.[261] (During that same period, these banks earned more than $320 billion in profits.)[262] The banks actually shelled out far less than that in real money to settle the fines because of the way these settlements were structured, including stipulations that allowed them to deduct some of the penalties from their taxes.[263]

As fines against corporations (but not their executives) became the primary sanction for elite-level corporate criminality, fines and fees were proliferating as a supplemental sanction for people convicted of street and drug crimes and even for minor offenses such as driving without a license.[264] The

Justice Department appeared acutely sensitive to the possible negative impact that fines might have on a corporation. Meanwhile, the criminal legal system was cruelly indifferent to the harms caused by levying fines and other legal financial obligations (LFOs) on individuals who had no realistic means of paying them off. Jurisdictions ladled onerous fees on top of fines to cover court costs, mandatory drug tests, the expense of administering electronic monitoring, probation, and parole, and the list goes on and on. Unpaid fines were cause to add on more punitive fees and even to send people back to jail or prison.[265] It is unconstitutional to incarcerate people because they cannot pay their debts. But numerous people continued to cycle through jail or prison because they failed to pay their LFOs.[266]

The proliferating LFOs tethered millions of people to the criminal legal system and trapped them, and often their families, in a cycle of compounding debt. Unpaid fines and fees besmirched their credit ratings and their housing and employment prospects, sometimes for decades after individuals completed their sentences. Declaring personal bankruptcy usually does not absolve individuals of their LFOs.[267] But for corporations, bankruptcy laws have been a blessing. Corporations have increasingly been exploiting bankruptcy laws to thwart large judgments against them in civil lawsuits and other legal actions.[268]

Backing Down in Other Ways

The Justice Department's nonchalance toward crime in the suites was manifest in many ways. As the judiciary sought to narrow the definition of corruption, the DOJ forfeited opportunities to push back. For example, in June 2010, the Supreme Court narrowed the scope of the so-called honest-services fraud statute, which was enacted in 1988 and had been used to convict Enron CEO Jeffrey Skilling. The court determined that the law was too vaguely written and, for this reason, applied only to blatant cases of fraud, such as kickbacks and bribery. It did not cover subtler situations, such as manipulating the financial results of a company and misleading investors about them.[269] In *Skilling v. United States* and a series of other rulings, the courts established that currying favor—by, for example, keeping government officials on private retainers or showering them with gifts or selling government access or donating troves of money to election campaigns—is not necessarily a crime.[270] Such actions may have the "appearance" of possible corruption, as the court ruled in the 2010 *Citizens United* decision, explained one legal scholar. But they are not criminal, the court reasoned, as long as public officials made no direct and explicit quid pro quo deals "to act in exchange for something of value."[271]

When some members of Congress sought to revise the honest-services statute by making it less vague, the DOJ took a backseat in efforts to salvage it.[272] The department also failed to appeal a number of court decisions that stripped prosecutors of important tools to combat white-collar corporate crime. Furthermore, it ducked retrying key cases that it had lost on appeal.[273] In one of the most important securities fraud cases in years, the DOJ and SEC actually submitted briefs to the US Supreme Court in support of greatly restricting what constituted fraud involving secondary participants.[274]

The criminal legal system's nonchalance toward allegations of criminality ranging from massive securities fraud to perjury committed by the country's most powerful financiers had important spillover effects. As the Justice Department relied exclusively on DPAs and NPAs to settle up with Wall Street over the subprime mortgage scandal, these get-out-of-jail-free cards became more deeply institutionalized and legitimized for all sorts of major corporate criminality unrelated to the financial crisis or even the financial sector.

Once the financial sector and economy were no longer on life support during Obama's second term, the DOJ remained loath to indict leading banks and senior corporate executives for new instances of criminal misconduct. Deferred prosecution agreements and nonprosecution agreements continued to proliferate in the face of eye-popping criminal behavior by leading banks and corporations. These criminal activities included colluding to fix interest rates; running vast money-laundering operations for drug cartels and countries on the US government's terrorist list; brazenly engaging in some of the same suspect activities that brought on the 2007–9 financial and foreclosure crises; and unscrupulously and illegally mass marketing opioids at the cost of tens of thousands of lives each year in the United States, as detailed in chapters 10 and 11.

At a Senate hearing on March 6, 2013, Eric Holder candidly admitted that some banks had become "so large that it does become difficult to prosecute them" because of the "negative impact on the national economy."[275] Weeks later he tried to walk back that claim, vowing that there is no bank, institution, or individual "who cannot be investigated and prosecuted by the DOJ." He vowed that "banks are not too big to jail."[276] But the record of the Obama administration suggests otherwise.[277]

Between 2012 and 2014, the financial industry paid nearly $139 billion in penalties for everything from mortgage fraud ($113 billion), to insider trading, to colluding to manipulate the London interbank offered rate (LIBOR), which sets the rates for trillions of dollars in financial instruments.[278] During the Obama administration, several large banks and their executives were implicated in laundering money for drug cartels and for Libya, Sudan, Burma, Iran, North Korea, and other countries seeking to circumvent international sanctions levied for developing nuclear weapons or supporting terrorism. The banks—including Barclays, Lloyds, and Credit Suisse—and their executives dodged criminal charges by signing DPAs.[279] Judge Emmet Sullivan blasted the Justice Department for giving a "sweetheart deal" to Barclays in a "shocking" DPA to settle accusations that the bank had evaded US sanctions against Cuba, Iran, and Libya. "There's no paper trail of $500 million being funneled illegally to other countries? I mean, senior management . . . has to know who's responsible for it. . . . Someone had to mastermind this," he declared to the prosecutor in the case.[280]

Federal grand juries served Wachovia Bank nearly seven thousand subpoenas in their investigation of its role in laundering $378 billion—yes, billion—for the illegal drug trade, most of it in cash. For years, Wachovia had disregarded or quashed numerous internal warnings about highly suspicious financial transactions and had sidelined its compliance officers who issued the warnings. The DOJ settled in 2010 with a DPA that required Wells Fargo, which acquired Wachovia after it collapsed in 2008, to pay a measly fine of $160 million. No former Wachovia executives were fined or prosecuted.[281]

In 2012, after a six-year investigation, the Justice Department entered into a DPA with the British bank HSBC to settle charges of laundering money for Mexican drug cartels and violating economic sanctions against Iran. The $1.9 billion settlement amounted to about half of HSBC's quarterly profits, if that, and sparked a public outcry. At least $881 million in drug trafficking revenues passed through HSBC, yet neither the bank nor any of its employees was prosecuted, despite extensive evidence of brazen, large-scale money laundering. (To facilitate their massive cash deposits, the drug cartels "even designed 'specially shaped boxes' that fit the size of teller windows" at local HSBC branches in Mexico, according to federal court documents.)[282] Government officials, including Treasury Secretary Geithner, defended the failure to indict Europe's largest bank, arguing that doing so would amount to a "death sentence" for the bank that could send shock waves through the financial system.[283]

Jimmy Gurulé, a former US assistant attorney general and former top enforcement official in the Treasury Department, castigated the HSBC settlement. He said the United States could have brought criminal charges against the bank in a way that might have been disruptive to its operations but would not have put it out of business.[284] The DOJ's actions sent a signal that "if you want to engage in money laundering, make sure you're doing it within the context of your employment at a bank," Gurulé mournfully quipped. "And don't go small. Do it on a very large scale, and you won't get prosecuted."[285] Senator Grassley, the top Republican on the Judiciary Committee, called the DOJ's decision "inexcusable."[286] Just weeks after completing its five-year probationary period for the DPA in its money-laundering case, HSBC entered into another DPA agreement, this time for alleged manipulation of foreign exchange markets. Prosecutors agreed to a trivial fine of $101.5 million in that case because of the bank's "extensive remediation."[287]

And then there is the case of the "London Whale," a scandal nicknamed after a JPMorgan Chase trader in Britain who headed a unit renowned for its supersized bets in the financial derivatives market that resulted in a $6.2 billion loss. A three-hundred-page bipartisan Senate report on the scandal concluded in 2013 that traders at the country's largest bank ignored internal controls and manipulated documents, and that CEO Jamie Dimon withheld information from regulators and knowingly lowballed the size of the losses.[288] In September 2013, JPMorgan agreed to pay a $920 million penalty to regulators to settle civil charges in the London Whale case—or barely 8 percent of its profits for the first six months of that year. Buried in its settlement with the SEC was a rare admission that the bank violated federal securities law. The FBI was brought in to investigate, but none of JPMorgan's officers at the time, including Dimon, were penalized by civil regulators or faced criminal charges.[289]

In these money-laundering and other settlements, the Obama administration perpetuated the long-standing double standard with respect to punishing crime in the suites and crime in the streets. Repeat offending by corporations and their officers was no barrier to receiving lenient treatment in the future with another DPA or NPA. In one notorious case of corporate recidivism, Wells Fargo, the country's fifth largest bank, paid nearly $20 billion in fines imposed by the Justice Department, the Consumer Financial Protection Bureau, and other government entities for numerous violations between 2010 and late 2022.[290] Despite what one top regulator described as "Wells Fargo's rinse-repeat cycle of violating the law," which harmed millions of individuals and their families, the DOJ under several administrations did not file criminal charges against one of the country's worst-run banks or its top executives.[291]

Banks were not the only brazen serial offenders who continued to get off with a slap on the wrist under Obama. Between 2002 and 2009, the pharmaceutical giant Pfizer entered into a series of four DPAs related to separate instances of bribery and illegal marketing of its drugs. Each time, the company agreed to put in place mechanisms to avoid and detect similar criminal misconduct going forward. But then, oops, Pfizer did it again.[292]

Deputy Attorney General Sally Yates issued a memo in 2015 that appeared to take a harder line on corporate crime.[293] But the memo was largely symbolic.[294] It did not call for a fundamental rethinking of the DOJ's approach to corporate criminal misconduct by, for example, banning or severely restricting the use of DPAs and NPAs; pushing for major new resources to pursue corporate cases; and stopping the revolving door between the top positions at DOJ and the most powerful corporate law firms. Nonetheless, this softball memo came under attack. And former top officials from the Obama administration who had returned to elite corporate law firms led the charge against it.[295]

After the Yates memo was issued, not much changed. That fall, the Justice Department entered into two egregious DPAs. One involved an agreement with General Motors to settle claims that the company fraudulently concealed ignition switch problems in its vehicles, which caused at least 124 deaths and 275 injuries.[296] The other involved Education Management Corporation, the country's second largest for-profit education company. This firm had illegally deployed recruiters working on commission who used deceitful tactics to recruit students in a widespread scam that violated numerous federal statutes and left students mired in debt. The DOJ conceded that EDMC engaged in "egregious abuse" yet settled its claims against the company for a mere $95.5 million, a sum equal to less than 1 percent of the estimated $11 billion in student loan aid the company had reaped through its fraudulent behavior.[297] Senator Warren and other senators denounced the agreement and charged that it ran counter to the DOJ's "highly-touted" new policy on corporate crime that it had announced two months earlier with the Yates memo.[298] After the DOJ issued the Yates memo, white-collar prosecutions nonetheless continued to decline under Obama.[299]

Crony Capitalism

White-collar prosecutions plummeted to twenty-year lows under Obama in the face of arguably the largest corporate crime wave in US history. The largest banks, financial services firms, and their executives emerged from the Great Recession as "The Untouchables." They ended up with greater economic and political clout and further beyond the reach of the criminal legal system. The FCIC, Levin committee, SIGTARP, COP, and the media compiled troves of evidence implicating top Wall Street firms and their executives in wide-scale criminal activities. The criminal legal system responded with a shrug.

Paul Volcker, the former Fed chairman, faulted the regulators and criminal legal system for treating the purveyors of subprime mortgages and mortgage-backed securities with kid gloves. He characterized profiting from knowingly selling "some sucker" a "bad mortgage" as "old-fashioned fraud." Volcker also excoriated Summers and Geithner for their laissez-faire approach to the banking sector's malfeasance that sparked the financial crisis.[300]

Treasury Secretary Geithner and Attorney General Holder echoed Obama's view that what Wall Street had done may have been immoral or reckless but was not necessarily illegal.[301] Geithner spurned what he called the "public desire for Old Testament justice," saying it might be morally satisfying but would be "dramatically damaging" to economic recovery.[302]

Obama occasionally rebuked Wall Street in public but largely maintained a forgiving and sympathetic stance, even as evidence of widespread criminality piled up. He subscribed to the view that regulatory loopholes that wily financiers had legally exploited for profit were the primary culprits. The main remedy then was to plug these loopholes, not to restructure the financial sector or indict Wall Street's top executives. But Obama's modest quest for regulatory reform was disappointing, as detailed in the next chapter. It left the country vulnerable to many of the same pathogens that caused the financial crisis as the largest banks and financial firms emerged from the Great Recession with even more political and economic power.

9

"The Banks Own This Place"

REGULATION AND SAVING
PRIVATE CAPITAL UNDER OBAMA,
TRUMP, AND BIDEN

I attest to this: the world is not white; it never was white, cannot be white. . . .
White is a metaphor for power, and that is simply a way of describing Chase
Manhattan Bank.

—JAMES BALDWIN[1]

PRESIDENT BARACK Obama did not view the financial and foreclosure crises
as major crime scenes. He blamed the worst economic crisis since the Depression on lapses in regulation, not a collapse of regulation. The president eschewed cultivating the groundswell of support for structural reform of the
financial industry that was coming not just from people like Elizabeth Warren
and Bernie Sanders on the left but also from mainstream Democrats, corners
of the Republican Party, current and former top regulators, and the public.
Even though distrust of government was deep and growing, the public, including an overwhelming majority of Republicans, strongly favored stricter regulation of Wall Street.[2]

At a press conference in October 2011 as the Occupy Wall Street movement
was erupting, Obama continued to express begrudging admiration for the financial sector's creativity in exploiting regulatory loopholes to make money—
lots of it. Much of what the bankers did leading up to the financial crisis "was
just immoral or inappropriate or reckless," Obama contended, but not "necessarily illegal."[3] The president lauded the Dodd–Frank bill he signed in July 2010,
praising it as a landmark piece of legislation to regulate the financial sector that

would prevent another crisis. But the measure was a piece of Swiss cheese, ridden with loopholes that Wall Street successfully exploited.

During Obama's crucial first eighteen months in office, the administration failed to present a compelling or consistent narrative about the causes and culprits of the financial and foreclosure crises. It also dithered as financial reform legislation was incubating in Congress. In private conversations with Obama, Paul Volcker, the former chair of the Federal Reserve, reportedly implored the president to seize the moment in 2009–10. With the most powerful banks on the skids and their corporate officers widely discredited because of their reckless behavior, the time was ripe, Volcker argued, "to put a spear through the heart of all these guys on Wall Street that for years have been mostly debt merchants." Treasury Secretary Timothy Geithner and Larry Summers, director of the National Economic Council, countered that meaningful reform would have to wait until the financial system had stabilized. But as the system stabilized, the window for real reform, not just window dressing, was rapidly closing. And Wall Street's top executives acutely understood this.[4]

During that pivotal period leading up to the passage of Dodd–Frank in summer 2010, Obama occasionally appeared ready to side with Volcker and other top advisers, policymakers, and lawmakers pushing to restructure the financial sector. But his top lieutenants, especially Geithner and Summers, would rope him back. If persuasion did not work, they resorted to foot dragging or even ignoring Obama's directives.[5]

The government bailouts of the megabanks and passage of a lame version of Dodd–Frank left their imprint not only on the financial system but also on the criminal legal system. In delivering strong messages that these financial institutions were too big to fail, the bailouts and Dodd–Frank also bolstered the view that they were too big to jail. Ditto for the country's most prominent financiers and senior corporate executives.

Restructuring

Shortly after he took office, Obama set out to remake the health-care system as the United States was battered by the financial and foreclosure crises. The battle over the Affordable Care Act (ACA) has distorted our understanding of key features of the political terrain at that time. From the very start, the leadership of the Republican Party was determined to deny Obama a victory on health-care reform in hopes of killing off his reelection chances.[6] Aligned with the burgeoning Tea Party movement, it corralled every single Republican in Congress to oppose the measure, which Obama signed into law in March 2010. The Republican Party's dogged efforts to repeal the ACA in the years since then have cemented claims that Obama's political options were highly constrained from the outset of his presidency by an intransient, highly disciplined Republican Party and a sharply polarized polity. In other words, to borrow from a leading scholar of the American presidency, he took office in a bad place in political time because of deeper structural and political forces that had outlasted the George W. Bush administration and stood ready to vanquish Obama's policy prescriptions for hope and change.[7]

But in 2009 and early 2010, Republicans in Congress were not yet lining up in lockstep on all major issues. Thanks to the financial and foreclosure crises, a deep bipartisan vein of outrage toward Wall Street coursed through Congress and the public. These twin crises opened up exceptional political terrain.[8] They created rare political opportunities to secure deep, not just cosmetic, reforms of the financial sector. Overestimating the clout of Wall Street, the hegemony of neoliberalism, and the unity of the Republican Party obscures these opportunities and how and why they were squandered.

Despite the huge infusions of government assistance from the Troubled Asset Relief Program (TARP) and elsewhere, many of the largest banks and financial services institutions were still in precarious health in early 2009 as Obama took office, as shown in chapter 8. They remained highly dependent on continued assistance from the government (which was a major stockowner of some of them thanks to the bailouts) if they were to survive. This gave the new administration and lawmakers considerable clout vis-à-vis Wall Street, should they choose to wield it. Democrats and Republicans spanning the political spectrum in Congress were open to seeking far-reaching reforms of the financial industry, not just tinkering around the edges. They looked favorably on limiting the size of banks, imposing stricter capital requirements on them, upending the cozy relationship between the credit rating agencies and the financial industry, reinstating some barriers between commercial and investment banking, and regulating financial derivatives, among other things.

Geithner and Summers fiercely opposed granting Congress more statutory authority to oversee the financial industry at the expense of the prerogatives of federal regulators, especially the Treasury Department and the Federal Reserve. They also opposed restructuring the megabanks and other major financial institutions, including the insurance giant American International Group (AIG). Many opponents of restructuring misleadingly disparaged this option as an unprecedented case of nationalization. But restructuring was not something unheard of, and it did not necessarily entail permanent government control and ownership of the banking sector. Since it was established back in the 1930s, the Federal Deposit Insurance Corporation (FDIC) had been routinely restructuring banks that became insolvent. In these government-managed bankruptcies, the FDIC would typically replace the failed management, strip the bank of bad loans to clear up its balance sheets, and then sell it off to the private sector, with bondholders and shareholders, not taxpayers, absorbing most of the losses.[9]

Some of Obama's top advisers contended that the administration should begin restructuring the troubled megabanks. In the early months of his administration, Citigroup's ongoing dire straits momentarily created a wedge between Geithner and Summers over the question of restructuring. At the time, this megabank was trading at less than a $1 a share and was on the brink of collapse despite the massive government assistance.[10] Thanks to a third bailout in late February, the US government had a 36 percent equity stake in Citigroup.[11] At a pivotal White House meeting on March 15, 2009, Summers made a rare break with Geithner and sided with other top economic advisers calling for a restructuring of Citigroup. Obama decided to direct Geithner to draw up a proposal to restructure the megabank. The president envisioned Citigroup as a test case that, if successful, could be a model for dealing with other troubled banks.[12]

Geithner ended up defying Obama's directive. He plowed ahead with Treasury's plan to administer stress tests to the banks, a remedy that was widely criticized by the administration's inner circle and elsewhere. When Obama heard weeks later that Geithner had ignored his directive, the president did not insist that his Treasury secretary double down on drawing up a restructuring plan for Citigroup.[13]

Geithner's approach to the flailing automobile industry was markedly different. He had no compunction about insisting on a major restructuring of General Motors and Chrysler in exchange for TARP funds. A team of Wall Street veterans with little or no experience in the auto industry helmed that restructuring. They sought to shutter thousands of car dealerships despite little evidence that doing so would enhance the long-term viability of the automobile industry. Geithner and the TARP auto team expressed little concern about or interest in the estimated one hundred thousand jobs that would be lost by closing all these dealerships.[14] As part of the auto bailout, retiree pension and health-care benefits for thousands of autoworkers were slashed. Restoring some of those benefits was a major issue in the historic 2023 strike against the auto companies.[15]

Divisions over Financial Reform

On the question of financial reform, Geithner and Summers were more in sync. They were protective of the prerogatives that the Treasury Department and Federal Reserve had to oversee the largest banks and other financial institutions. The two of them contended that expanding these prerogatives was key to preventing another financial crisis. Geithner and Summers maintained this stance despite the pile of evidence that federal regulators had failed miserably to wield the considerable powers they already possessed to rein in the reckless behavior of banks and other financial institutions during the subprime mortgage debacle.[16] They echoed the views of Wall Street lobbyists and their sympathizers, who sought to fend off what they perceived as congressional interference by arguing that "issues related to high finance are so hopelessly complex that it is nearly impossible for mere mortals to understand the unintended consequences of legislation."[17]

Geithner and the Treasury Department were not only the main architects of financial and economic policy but also the administration's primary "legislative strategists and tacticians" on these issues.[18] Laying out general principles for financial reform in testimony before the House Financial Services Committee in late September 2009, Geithner called for granting greater authority to the Treasury Department and Federal Reserve to oversee banks and other financial institutions that were deemed "systemically important."[19] Testifying the following day, Paul Volcker, head of the President's Economic Recovery Advisory Board, took issue with Geithner's testimony. He declared that designating certain banks as "systemically important" would exacerbate the moral hazard and too-big-to-fail problem. It would bolster the presumption that the government would step in to protect the largest banks and other financial entities should they once again face "imminent failure," he testified. Furthermore, Volcker argued, the administration's proposed plan would not ameliorate the fundamental conflicts of interests that had arisen with the disintegration of Glass–Steagall's wall between commercial and investment banking.[20]

Volcker could be at times a caustic critic of the Federal Reserve's role in the financial crisis. But in his testimony, he defended the central bank as an apolitical institution that should retain a high degree of autonomy in supervising the banking and financial services sector. He expressed deep reservations about proposals to create a supercommittee headed by the Treasury secretary that would render the Fed's supervisory role subservient to the Treasury Department.[21] He did not side with critics of the central bank who denounced its cozy relationship with Wall Street (as exemplified by the board of directors of the Federal Reserve Bank of New York, which routinely includes corporate officers from the largest banks it is supposed to oversee).[22]

In fall 2009, Obama dithered about financial reform as the window for over-hauling Wall Street was rapidly closing. Meanwhile, Volcker kept up his criti-cism of Wall Street. He dismissed the praise that Geithner and others heaped on Wall Street for its "financial innovation." He scoffed that the ATM invented two decades earlier was the last financial innovation that significantly in-creased productivity and efficiency.[23] The former Fed chair was particularly incensed at what he viewed as a diabolical shift beginning in the early 1990s toward compensating executives primarily through stock options, not salaries. Volcker warned that having bankers and other financiers reaping "tens of mil-lions for activities of no social or really economic value—or, as the crash shows, negative value—just tears a society apart, at all levels, top to bottom. Well, maybe not top."[24]

In January 2010, the president finally weighed in on one of the key regula-tory issues. Obama publicly endorsed what he dubbed the Volcker Rule, which Geithner and Summers loathed. As originally conceived by Volcker, his epon-ymous rule would tightly restrict the ability of certain banking entities to en-gage in proprietary trading (that is, the buying and selling of securities), as well as some other financial activities, including investing in hedge funds and pri-vate equity funds.[25] The purpose of the rule was to prevent banking entities that enjoyed the twin cushions of FDIC-insured deposits and access to the Federal Reserve's discount window to gamble recklessly with other people's money, knowing the federal government and taxpayers would eventually pick up the tab for any major losses. (The discount window allows large banks to borrow from the Fed at below-market rates to cover liquidity shortages.)

Obama came out in favor of the Volcker Rule as his political support was hemorrhaging and anger at Wall Street was escalating. Days before Obama endorsed the Volcker Rule, the Democrats had lost their filibuster-proof Sen-ate when Republican Scott Brown scored an upset victory in a special election to fill the seat of liberal lion Ted Kennedy, the Massachusetts senator who had succumbed to brain cancer in August 2009. The Great Recession had techni-cally ended in June 2009. But wide swaths of the country, especially outside of the financial and high-tech corridors in major cities and on the coasts, were still reeling from foreclosures, unemployment, underemployment, and cutbacks in public services thanks to decimated tax bases. By late 2009, Wall Street was raking in record profits.[26] Meanwhile, four out of five people surveyed characterized economic conditions in the country as poor or very poor, and the proportion of respondents who primarily blamed the Democrats for the Great Recession was rapidly growing.[27]

As the public's lack of confidence in banks and financial institutions was escalating, its favorable view of the Fed was plummeting.[28] In late 2009, senators piled on at the renomination hearing for Fed Chair Ben Bernanke. Senator Jim Bunning (R-KY) joined Senator Bernie Sanders (I-VT) in putting a "hold" on Bernanke's reappointment. They castigated the Fed chair for being "the definition of moral hazard" and for perpetuating the failed "legacy of Alan Greenspan."[29] Senators grilled Bernanke on the AIG bailout as more details of the "backdoor bailout" of Goldman Sachs and other banks trickled out in late 2009.[30] Bernanke was reconfirmed by a 70-to-30 vote in January 2010, the weakest support for any chairman in the Fed's more than one-hundred-year history.[31]

Obama's Frenemies on Wall Street

Once the government and taxpayers had rescued the largest banks and financial firms without demanding much in return, Wall Street turned on the administration. No longer in mortal danger and once again raking in record profits and bonuses, Wall Street ended its bromance with Obama. Despite the administration's kid-glove treatment, top Wall Street executives became contemptuous of Obama, speaking of the president as if he were "an unholy alliance between Bernie Sanders and Eldridge Cleaver." Finance executives privately disparaged him as a "Chicago mob guy," a "vilifier," and a "thug."[32]

Obama's public admiration for Wall Street and praise for that mythical creature called the "free market" did not waver much even as Wall Street turned on him. In a rare moment of public pique, Obama denounced the "fat cat bankers" during a 60 Minutes interview in December 2009.[33] But in early 2010, Obama was once again declaring his admiration for Wall Street's "very savvy businessmen" and how he did not "begrudge" the latest sky-high bonuses issued for JPMorgan Chase CEO Jamie Dimon ($17 million) and Goldman Sachs CEO Lloyd Blankfein ($9 million).[34]

Days earlier, Obama had belatedly endorsed the Volcker Rule and floated the idea of imposing a new tax on Wall Street firms that had been bailed out by TARP. In a pointed message to Obama and the Democratic Party, his frenemies on Wall Street opened the spigots of campaign contributions to the Republican Party. The political action committee of JPMorgan Chase, which had been a stronghold of support for Obama and the Democrats, started shunning solicitation requests from the party's national campaign committees and began funding their Republican counterparts.[35] (A year later, Obama would choose William F. Daley, a senior JPMorgan Chase executive, to replace Rahm Emanuel as his chief of staff.)

Less than three months after endorsing the Volcker Rule, Obama was back at Cooper Union college in April 2010, this time as president, to promote passage of the Dodd–Frank bill. Wall Street was continuing to rebound, with Goldman Sachs and Citigroup announcing record quarterly profits the week Obama spoke.[36] By then, the version of the Volcker Rule included in Dodd–Frank had been greatly watered down. It was bound to be drowned by the drip, drip, drip of the rulemaking process and legal actions by the financial industry after it became law in July 2010, which is what happened.[37]

As the royalty of Wall Street looked on from the audience at Cooper Union, Obama once again took a conciliatory stance. He emphasized how there was "no dividing line between Main Street and Wall Street" and that each would rise and fall together.[38] The president attributed the financial crisis to anachronistic and inadequate regulatory powers and to a few bad apples. He did not mention the systemic failure of regulators to use the significant powers they already possessed. He also did not bring up the systemic criminality that had ensued and that had not been investigated, let alone punished, as discussed in chapter 8.[39]

Obama pitched Dodd–Frank as a sweeping restructuring of the financial sector. But by then the measure was actually a Trojan horse for the Obama administration. Geithner and Senator Chris Dodd (D-CT), head of the Banking Committee, held the reins as they sought to quell the mounting pressures for major structural reforms of the financial sector.[40] Dodd, one of the largest congressional recipients of campaign donations from the financial sector, eviscerated a string of proposals in early 2010 to get tougher with the banks.[41] These measures had drawn considerable bipartisan support from leading Democrats and Republicans, including not just the right and left edges of their parties.

The strategy of the Democratic leadership "was to make the Republicans look like they were against any Wall Street reform, while the Democrats were for effective reforms," one insider lamented. At the time, Stanley Greenberg, a longtime pollster for the Democrats, advised the party's congressional leaders that it would be best if they "passed any Wall Street reform bill (even a weak one) if just to prove they were capable of governing, rather than taking a strong stand against Wall Street and risk more gridlock." Dodd played along, using "the Republicans to negotiate with himself, apparently because he wanted to give his Wall Street patrons the weakest bill that would pass."[42]

Obama obliquely suggested in his Cooper Union speech that Republican intransigence was the main obstacle standing in the way of real financial reform. But by most accounts, Dodd–Frank was expected to pass. The main opposition was coming not from the Republican Party but from a broad spectrum of individuals and groups who thought it did not go far enough to rein in Wall Street.

Leading opponents of Dodd–Frank were demanding statutory changes to ensure that the largest banks and financial institutions no longer held the economy and the country at their mercy because they were "too big to fail."[43] These critics did not want to continue leaving it up to the discretion of regulators, especially the Treasury Department and Federal Reserve, to rein them in. They noted that regulators had an extensive history under both Democratic and Republican administrations of failing to use the considerable powers they already possessed to curtail the brewing subprime market scandal. They castigated the Federal Reserve for failing abysmally to oversee the banks, including neglecting to make sure the megabanks held sufficient capital reserves and to stem their predatory lending and their lax, possibly criminal, underwriting practices.

Ted Kaufman, who was appointed to fill Joe Biden's unexpired Senate term after he became vice president, cosponsored the SAFE Banking Act with Senator Sherrod Brown (D-OH). An amendment to Dodd–Frank, it statutorily limited the size of the largest banks. It also spelled out how much capital they were required to hold in reserve, and what financial activities they were permitted to engage in. The two senators spurned leaving it up to the discretion of the Federal Reserve and other regulators to decide these crucial issues, which was the polestar of the original Dodd–Frank.[44]

Kaufman had support in some powerful places for these far-reaching structural reforms of the financial sector. In late 2009, Senator John McCain (R-AZ), the Republican Party's standard-bearer in the 2008 election, had introduced a bill with Senator Maria Cantwell (D-WA), a tough critic of Wall Street, that would reinstate Glass–Steagall, which the Obama administration did not favor.[45] Regional Federal Reserve officials and analysts were raising concerns that the version of Dodd–Frank winding its way through Congress did not solve the too-big-to-fail problem and would likely make it worse.[46] Public anger at the bailouts remained high and was a rallying point for the burgeoning Tea Party movement. Three-term Republican Senator Robert Bennett of Utah, who had voted for one of the two TARP bills, was not re-nominated at a state party convention in May 2010. The crowd denounced him as "Bailout Bob" and heckled, "TARP, TARP, TARP."[47]

Even Alan Greenspan, the former chairman of the Federal Reserve and a free-market ideologue, had begun raising questions by this time about the megabanks. He noted that research by the Federal Reserve had been unable to substantiate claims that megabanks enjoyed economies of scale or that breaking them up would hurt the competitiveness of the US banking sector. Greenspan appeared regretful that the Federal Reserve had not done more under his watch a decade earlier to address the systemic risks that the mega-banks posed for the national and global economies.[48] "If they're too big to fail, they're too big," he mused in late 2009. "In 1911 we broke up Standard Oil—so what happened? The individual parts became more valuable than the whole. Maybe that's what we need to do."[49]

Three Republican senators—Richard Shelby of Alabama (the ranking Republican on the Senate Banking Committee and his party's leading voice on banking matters), John Ensign of Nevada, and Tom Coburn of Oklahoma—signed on to Kaufman and Brown's SAFE Banking Act.[50] To undercut the measure, Dodd outmaneuvered supporters of the measure by calling for a snap vote. These three senators joined thirty Democrats in voting for the measure. But dozens of other Democrats sided with most Republicans, which doomed it. As a senior official from the Treasury Department (probably Geithner) smugly commented, "If we'd been for it, it probably would have happened. But we weren't, so it didn't."[51]

As lawmakers debated Dodd–Frank, support was growing in Congress and elsewhere to bring the financial derivatives market out of the shadows and to begin regulating it. Arthur Levitt, who back in 2000 had supported prohibiting the Commodity Futures Trading Commission (CFTC) from regulating financial derivatives when he was chair of the Securities and Exchange Commission (SEC), had recanted in 2008 as the economy was melting down.[52] He conceded that the ban included in the controversial Commodity Futures Modernization Act of 2000 was a "mistake."[53]

The Obama administration was divided over the issue of regulating financial derivatives. Obama had tapped Gary Gensler to be chairman of the CFTC. Gensler was a Goldman Sachs alumnus who had helped dismantle Glass–Steagall and head off the regulation of financial derivatives when he served in the Clinton administration. But Gensler turned out to be one of the rare veterans of Wall Street and the Clinton administration who, upon his return to government under Obama, was keen to take on Wall Street. During his nomination hearings, Gensler did not follow Summers's script that called for denying that mistakes had been made under Bill Clinton.[54]

In a major about-face, Gensler conceded that regulating the massive and shadowy $400 trillion market in over-the-counter (OTC) derivatives market was essential to unwind the "Wall Street culture that has permeated" the United States at great cost. As chairman of the CFTC, Gensler pushed for transparent trading of financial derivatives in exchanges, which put him on a collision course with Geithner, Summers, and much of Wall Street. Establishing transparent exchanges for financial derivatives would cut out the five largest banks, which controlled 90 percent of this market, from their lucrative intermediary role in marketing these dangerous products. No wonder that Wall Street executives disparaged Gensler as "the most dangerous man in Washington."[55]

Gensler threw his support behind an amendment to Dodd–Frank sponsored by conservative Senator Blanche Lincoln (D-AK), the chair of the Agriculture Committee, to impose tougher rules on financial derivatives. Testifying before Congress on September 22, 2009, Gensler presented simple, compelling, color-coded pie charts showing how the untamed market in OTC derivatives remained a mortal threat to the economy. He underscored that more than half of all these derivatives lacked any collateral to back them up. In April 2010, the committee voted 13–8 in favor of Lincoln's amendment, with Senator Charles Grassley (R-IA) joining the Democratic majority. But the amendment crumbled weeks later in the Dodd–Frank conference committee, impaled by an army of Wall Street lobbyists, the White House's passive-aggressive opposition, and an about-face by Lincoln after she vanquished a challenger to her left in the primaries.[56]

During the conference committee meeting on Dodd–Frank, lawmakers also stripped the Volcker Rule of its few remaining teeth. The final decisions that defanged the Volcker Rule were made outside the glare of the televised Senate-House conference committee. One insider likened them to a "late night mugging" perpetrated by the Treasury Department, Dodd, Representative Barney Frank (D-MA), and Senator Chuck Schumer (D-NY).[57]

Dodd also succeeded in killing an amendment, which the Senate had passed with sixty-four votes, that would have tempered the conflicts of interest that plagued the credit rating agencies.[58] The final version of Dodd–Frank did not rectify the "issuer pays" model of compensation for the rating agencies that was ridden with conflicts of interest.[59] Five years later, the SEC reported that the rating agencies continued to pose a threat to the financial system.[60]

The final version of the Dodd–Frank bill was deeply flawed. This legislation bestowed more oversight authority on existing regulatory entities, most notably the Treasury Department and the Federal Reserve. But it did not compel these regulators to adhere to certain statutorily defined benchmarks, such as a mandate on how much banks must keep in capital reserves as a cushion against losses. The Federal Reserve retained expansive discretion to act as it thought best without wider input or even scrutiny from lawmakers and the public. Despite congressional and public outrage over how the Treasury Department and Fed had managed the financial crisis, including periodic calls for Geithner to resign, Dodd–Frank concentrated even more power, authority, and discretion in the Treasury Department and the Federal Reserve.[61]

The administration touted Dodd–Frank's establishment of a new Consumer Financial Protection Bureau (CFPB). While this was an important achievement, the final shape of the CFPB was a far cry from what Elizabeth Warren and other advocates for consumers pummeled and fleeced by the banking industry had envisioned.[62] Geithner and the Treasury Department succeeded in getting the proposed independent agency reduced to a less powerful bureau housed under the Federal Reserve.[63] Not surprisingly, Geithner did not push back against the banking industry's demand that Obama not appoint Warren as the inaugural head of the CFPB.[64]

After the fate of Dodd–Frank was sealed, Senator Richard Durbin (D-IL), number two in the Senate Democratic leadership, conceded, "The banks own this place."[65] Paul Volcker, the former chair of the Federal Reserve, pointedly faulted Obama and his administration. "They say they're for it, but their hearts are not in it," he lamented in June 2010. Without Obama's involvement and enthusiasm, he declared, large changes "just won't happen. It's that simple."[66]

Death by a Thousand Cuts

The year Dodd–Frank became law, compensation for the top twenty-five Wall Street firms soared to $135 billion, a record level.[67] The US poverty rate hit a fifteen-year high that year and did not begin to decline until 2015, six years after the Great Recession was officially declared over.[68] No wonder that nearly three-quarters of the respondents in a 2014 poll said they believed the country was still in a recession.[69]

As a result of the bailouts and consolidations fostered by the Treasury Department and Federal Reserve, the biggest banks had quickly become much larger.[70] Between 2007 and 2010, the assets of JPMorgan Chase and Bank of America grew by about a third, while Wells Fargo doubled in size.[71] By 2015, the five largest banks in the United States constituted half of the country's commercial banking industry.[72] In defense of the megabanks, Jamie Dimon smugly told Senator Durbin, "It was the small banks that failed."[73] The megabank's CEO conveniently ignored the fact that the largest US banks had been spared thanks to TARP and the Fed, which lavished bailout funds and other life preservers on them but not smaller institutions.

During the debate over Dodd–Frank, Geithner had assured lawmakers that the legislation had resolved the too-big-to-fail problem. Thus, bailouts of the largest financial institutions with taxpayer money would not be necessary in the event of another financial crisis.[74] But less than six months after the bill became law, Geithner acknowledged that government bailouts might be necessary once again in the future.[75] The credit rating agencies agreed. In the wake of the gigantic bailouts, these agencies had concluded that the government would once again come to the rescue of the largest banks should they hit the skids in the future. Factoring this privileged position into their ratings, the credit rating agencies inflated the credit scores for the megabanks. As a result, borrowing costs for the largest banks were considerably lower than those for smaller institutions, putting the megabanks at an even greater competitive advantage.[76]

After Dodd–Frank became law, a flotilla of Wall Street lobbyists laid siege to it. Taking advantage of the wide discretion the act gave regulators in the rule-writing phase, lobbyists further enfeebled the measure and delayed its implementation. Wall Street firms successfully inserted numerous exemptions to what remained of the Volcker Rule—and then complained it was too complicated to understand and too expensive to adopt.[77] In December 2014, Citigroup lobbyists scored a coup when they quietly secured repeal of a major plank of Dodd–Frank that had required federally insured banks to shift their financial derivatives to another unit of the bank holding company. The aim was to protect taxpayers from having to bail out the banks again should their highly risky toxic assets start blowing up once more.[78] Thanks to all the pushback from the banks, that shift had yet to occur even before this plank was repealed.[79]

As Wall Street eviscerated Dodd–Frank during the rulemaking process, pressure to break up the largest banks and hold their officers more accountable to the criminal legal system remained strong.[80] A number of regional Federal

Reserve presidents and a top FDIC official faulted Dodd–Frank for failing to solve the too-big-to-fail problem and for making the problem worse as the largest financial institutions emerged from the crisis with even more economic and political clout.[81] Some major conservative commentators, including George Will and Peggy Noonan, joined the chorus to break up the banks.[82] So did Sandy Weill, the founder and longtime head of Citigroup. Weill also called for reinstating Glass–Steagall's wall between commercial and investment banks.[83] In his quest for the 2012 Republican presidential nomination, former Utah Governor Jon Huntsman Jr. called for repealing Dodd–Frank, breaking up the too-big-to-fail banks, and pursuing "real reform that ends crony capitalism."[84]

In April 2013, Senator David Vitter (R-LA) and Senator Brown introduced legislation requiring the largest banks to keep much more capital in reserves as cushions against any losses. The American Bankers Association condemned the proposal, but the Independent Community Bankers of America, the primary trade group for smaller banks, endorsed the bill. This was the first time since the financial crisis that a major financial industry group took a public stand against the megabanks.[85] Four months later, Senator McCain joined Senators Cantwell, Angus King (I-ME), and Elizabeth Warren (D-MA), who became a US senator in 2013, in calling for legislation to reinstate a modernized version of the Glass–Steagall Act.[86] At the time, Jacob Lew, Geithner's successor and a former colleague of Robert Rubin's at Citigroup, acknowledged the long delay in implementing the rules for Dodd–Frank and how the measure may have been weakened along the way. But he did not endorse the growing calls to reinstate some version of Glass–Steagall and break up the megabanks.[87] Neither did Obama.

"Drain the Swamp"

When he first ran for president, Obama suggested that the United States might need to create major new regulatory structures and lauded the establishment of the FDIC and enactment of Glass–Steagall during the Great Depression. Once in the White House, his administration pursued a radically diminished vision. Unlike in the case of the Great Depression, the Great Recession did not yield legislative and regulatory reforms that fostered a more stable, equitable, and democratically accountable financial sector. The Obama administration came out of the near-death experience of the financial crisis even more convinced that the banks were too big to fail and too big to prosecute.

In September 2009, as President Obama traveled to Wall Street to give a speech marking the one-year anniversary of the collapse of Lehman Brothers and the start of the financial panic, the window for structural reform of Wall Street was already rapidly closing. By this time, Wall Street executives were feeling increasingly emboldened. (Some of them were so emboldened that they conspicuously did not attend Obama's speech.) Raking in near-record profits once again, they hastened to pay back the TARP money so they could shed the minimal restrictions the government program had placed on them. In his speech, Obama made vague calls for financial reform but did not present a concrete proposal or put much political capital on the line.[88] As one prominent banker conceded moments before the president spoke, "For Washington to not demand anything when it saved us, even stuff we know is for our long-term good, was one of the stupidest moves in modern times." The banker expected Obama to understand that. "But he didn't, and I don't know who to thank. I feel like I should go over and hug Tim [Geithner]. It's a shame we can't pay him, 'cause that's a guy who really earned a big-time bonus."[89]

The megabanks emerged from the financial crisis confident that they would be first in line to be rescued should their big bets stop paying off. If they found themselves once again barreling toward the edge of the cliff, they expected the government would step in once again to save them in the name of saving the economy. Washington excelled at rescuing and then enriching the titans of the financial industry while leaving the economic and political fault lines that crashed the economy in 2008 largely intact. It also failed to ameliorate the economic inequalities that predated the Great Recession and deepened in the wake of the so-called economic recovery.

During the financial crisis, hundreds of small and medium-sized banks failed in the United States. Though a couple of large banks went under, the ones that remained bounced back quickly with the help of troughs of unprecedented government assistance. The largest banks and financial services firms emerged from the Great Recession with even more power and wealth. By 2009, the securities industry in New York City was reporting near-record profits and distributing huge bonuses. In fall 2011, as the Occupy Wall Street movement spread across the United States and around the world, the rate of annual profits for the financial industry was $369 billion.[90] This figure was just slightly below the peak in 2006, with the gains concentrated at the larger firms.

Senator Bernie Sanders's calls to break up the big banks and Donald Trump's refrain to "drain the swamp" resonated loudly during the 2016 campaign.[91] Trump won the White House in the face of an unprecedented number of public defections by a who's who of the Republican establishment. Despite his attacks on Wall Street, the swamp, and the overextended US military, Donald Trump drew heavily from the military sector and corporate world, most notably from Goldman Sachs, to fill major economic and other positions in his first administration.[92] Soon after taking office, he told a White House meeting of CEOs, "For the bankers in the room, they'll be very happy."[93] And they were. As an analyst for the *Financial Times* quipped: "Imagine going to the races, betting 98 percent of your stake on the favourite [Hillary Clinton], which loses in the final stretch, and going home with huge winnings."[94]

All the hand-wringing about the reputed outbreak of crony capitalism during Donald Trump's first term occluded the fact that crony capitalism had been flourishing for years before he took office in 2017 and soared in the wake of the Great Recession. This earlier version of crony capitalism may have been more genteel than the crass hucksterism of Trump's first term and the in-your-face corruption of his second term. Nonetheless, the crony capitalism under Trump's predecessors was responsible for perpetrating enormous structural violence in the United States as poverty, economic inequality, homelessness, and drug overdoses soared; wages stagnated; life expectancy plummeted; and the so-called social safety net was shredded even further.

The dismemberment of Dodd–Frank continued under Trump with the help of complicit Democrats even though polls showed that Americans by large margins still considered Wall Street to be a "danger to our economy." Only a small minority believed "government intervention has gone far enough or poses a threat to innovation or economic growth."[95] A majority of the public, including many Trump voters, opposed efforts to weaken Dodd–Frank by, among other things, enfeebling or eliminating the Consumer Financial Protection Bureau. But in 2017, Congress overturned one of the CFPB's most important rules, which would have allowed millions of people to join in class-action lawsuits against the financial industry.[96]

Trump 1.0 and Crime in the Suites

During Donald Trump's first term, his administration barreled down the well-trodden path of lenient treatment of firms and their corporate officers despite massive criminality as the decades-long decline in federal white-collar prosecutions continued.[97] Rod Rosenstein, Trump's deputy attorney general from 2017 to 2019, contended that corporations were well equipped to police themselves and were generally law-abiding, in contrast to "the most dangerous categories of criminals."[98] By the end of Trump's first term, "virtually every part of the white-collar enforcement apparatus at the Justice Department" was broken, according to a former federal prosecutor who led major corporate crime investigations at DOJ from 2016 to 2020.[99] The DOJ under Trump rolled back key provisions of the Yates memo and weakened the DOJ's corporate-prosecution program in other ways.[100]

The Justice Department scuttled or backpedaled major investigations and prosecutions of large corporations, including Walmart, Barclays, Royal Bank of Scotland, and Merrill Lynch, to name just a few.[101] During the Covid-19 pandemic, the Trump administration ignored massive and coordinated schemes to defraud the government's Covid-19 aid programs.[102] Fines levied against corporations fell during Trump's first term.[103] Barclays, which had stalled in signing a $5 billion DPA with the outgoing Obama administration to settle charges related to the subprime mortgage scandal, agreed to a $2 billion civil penalty in March 2018. At the time, Barclays was also under investigation for manipulating foreign exchange markets. The DOJ gave it a pass on those allegations, apparently because Barclays reported the misconduct and cooperated with the prosecutors.[104]

The Justice Department agreed to two exceptionally egregious deferred prosecution agreements toward the end of Trump's first term.[105] In October 2020, Goldman Sachs signed a DPA to settle what the DOJ described as a "sweeping international corruption scheme" in which the firm, among other things, paid over $1.6 billion in bribes to high-ranking state officials in Malaysia and elsewhere.[106] In return, the bank was chosen to facilitate the sale of $6.5 billion in bonds that the country's prime minister, his family, and their associates and hangers-on looted from the county's sovereign wealth fund. These bonds were supposed to fund public investments in Malaysia's economic development. With the help of Goldman and its money-laundering operation, billions of dollars were diverted to purchase superluxury items; fund covert campaign-finance accounts; contribute to US political campaigns, including those of Obama and Trump; and invest in Hollywood films, including, no joke, *The Wolf of Wall Street*.[107]

Goldman Sachs, nicknamed the "great vampire squid" for its role in the financial crisis, stonewalled the Malaysia investigation and sought to put the blame on a handful of rogue employees. Journalists and federal prosecutors unearthed evidence that compliance officers and others at Goldman had raised numerous red flags about the company's dealings with Malaysia's sovereign wealth fund. But top executives at Goldman, including Lloyd Blankfein, the bank's chief executive at the time, audaciously ignored these warnings.[108]

The powerhouse law firm Kirkland & Ellis represented Goldman Sachs in the negotiations. William Barr, the attorney general and a former partner of the firm, was reportedly "directly immersed" in the DOJ's negotiations with Goldman Sachs.[109] Under the terms of the DOJ's sweetheart agreement with Goldman, its Malaysian subsidiary pleaded guilty, but not its parent company, which was fined $2.9 billion by US authorities and another $2.5 billion by Malaysia.[110] Goldman clawed back or slashed the compensation for top corporate officers involved in the Malaysia scandal but later rewarded them with giant retention bonuses.[111]

Barely two weeks before Trump left office in 2021, the DOJ signed off on one of the worst DPAs ever, according to an expert on corporate crime.[112] It settled up with Boeing on charges that the giant airline manufacturer had conspired to defraud the Federal Aviation Administration (FAA) about the safety of its new 737 MAX airliners. Boeing was implicated after two 737 MAX airliners crashed in 2018 and 2019 in Indonesia and Ethiopia, respectively, together killing 346 people.

The 737 MAX had been hastily developed and built on a series of outright lies about its safety.[113] Prior to the crashes, it had been "the subject of numerous ignored whistleblower reports, tormented confessions, and abrupt career changes" by employees who raised safety concerns.[114] The DOJ settled with Boeing without conducting a thorough investigation of its own or having a reputable outside law firm conduct one. The department accepted Boeing's claims that a few bad apples, not deeper structural problems at the company, were to blame. The Boeing DPA did not even require appointment of a compliance monitor. Boeing's defense counsel was Mark Filip of Kirkland & Ellis, Attorney General Barr's former law firm.[115] The airline manufacturer agreed to pay a $2.65 billion fine as part of a DPA. Most of this money would go to compensate the airlines, not the families of the crash victims. In the "Statement of Facts" attached to the DPA, Boeing fingered a single culprit, a low-level employee. In 2022, the Boeing worker was acquitted after jurors deliberated for just two hours. The jury likely made the reasonable assumption that Boeing had made him a scapegoat.[116]

During Trump 1.0, Senator Warren introduced "The Ending Too Big to Jail Act" in March 2018. Modeled after SIGTARP, it called for creating a permanent law enforcement unit to investigate crimes at financial institutions. It also mandated judicial oversight of DPAs to assure that the settlements are in the "public interest" and that firms comply with their terms.[117] But the measure died in Congress that year.

Joe Biden and Crime in the Suites

Joe Biden had campaigned for president in 2020 on a criminal justice reform agenda that included detailed proposals to address policing abuses, reduce racial discrimination in law enforcement, and improve the juvenile justice system.[118] But he said comparatively little about restoring the government's will and capacity to pursue white-collar and corporate crime, which had been eroding for decades prior to Trump. Once Biden was in office, his administration revitalized the moribund antitrust enforcement apparatus as it took some of the most powerful corporations to court—including Google, Amazon, Apple, private equity firms, and the largest meat producers—and pushed for increased funding for the DOJ's Antitrust Division. The Federal Trade Commission under Chair Lina Khan "started to use its full powers for the first time in decades." The commission supported imposing criminal penalties on individual executives who committed fraud or deception and filed dozens of legal challenges to proposed corporate mergers.[119] Biden also appointed Gary Gensler to head the SEC. Gensler had been the bête noire of Wall Street during the financial crisis when he chaired the CFTC, as discussed earlier.

Shortly after Biden took office, the DOJ declared that the Obama-era Yates memo would be reinstated.[120] Top DOJ officials, including Attorney General Merrick Garland, pledged to crack down on corporate crime and conceded that the failure to hold corporations and their executives accountable eroded public trust in the criminal legal system and American democracy more broadly. They vowed to scrutinize DPAs and NPAs more carefully, especially in cases of corporate recidivism; to be more transparent about these settlements; to press Congress for more resources to combat crime in the suites; and to prioritize indicting individuals, not just corporations, in cases of corporate criminality.[121] The number of deferred prosecution and nonprosecution agreements fell noticeably during the Biden administration, but this drop did not necessarily reflect a tougher stance on corporate malfeasance. Federal prosecutions of corporate crimes remained at or near record lows during his administration.[122]

On January 5, 2024, just days before Boeing's DPA was set to expire, a door plug blew off a 737 MAX minutes after the Alaska Airlines flight took off from Portland, Oregon. Six months later, Biden's Justice Department and Boeing agreed to a plea agreement to settle charges that Boeing had violated the 2021 DPA by failing to make the promised major safety changes. Boeing consented to plead guilty to one felony charge of conspiracy to defraud the FAA. It also agreed to pay a minuscule additional fine of $244 million in connection with the two fatal 737 MAX crashes. Critics of Boeing, including the families of the crash victims, slammed the plea agreement.[123] In a rare move, a federal judge raised questions about Boeing's plea agreement and rejected it in late 2024. Early on in Trump 2.0, the DOJ reached a new plea agreement with Boeing that dropped the criminal charges, which further outraged victims' families.[124]

During the Biden administration, financial restructuring remained mostly off the table even though the overweening megabanks were as dangerous as ever. Furthermore, the emerging wild west of cryptocurrency was adding fuel to the fire. Congress, the White House, and regulators appeared unwilling or unable to corral this new frontier in speculation, gambling, and blatant corruption. In 2022, the Federal Reserve was rocked by the largest ethics scandal in its history. Several Fed officials were forced to resign after reports surfaced that they appeared to be capitalizing on insider information with aggressive stock trading as the pandemic struck in 2020. At the time, Senator Warren denounced the Fed's "culture of corruption."[125] The following March, Silicon Valley Bank (SVB), which largely catered to the tech sector and venture capital, imploded in the second-largest bank failure in US history. Shortly thereafter, Signature Bank was shut down after a run on its deposits set off by SVB's collapse. Amid fears of another financial crisis and calls for tougher regulation of US banks, Fed Chair Jerome Powell personally intervened to delete mentions of how regulatory failures had contributed to these collapses. Treasury Secretary Janet Yellen denied that the government would bail out SVB. But with her blessing, FDIC officials agreed to insure all of SVB's deposits, even those above the government-insured threshold of $250,000, which was a kind of backdoor bailout. Since the collapse of SVB, the numerous calls to action for greater regulation of the banking sector have gone unheeded.[126]

In short, the Biden administration made some important gestures toward reversing decades of obsequiousness toward the corporate sector. But much of the lax regulatory and get-out-of-jail-free regimes for banks and other corporations that have perpetrated so much structural violence in the United States remained intact. Just as the financial sector has been largely untouchable for decades, so has Big Pharma, as cruelly evidenced by its complicity in the decades-long opioid epidemic, which is discussed in the next two chapters.

PART IV

Corporate Violence, State Violence, and Structural Violence

10

Killing Me Softly

BIG PHARMA, THE GOVERNMENT, AND THE OPIOID CRISIS

I believe the Sackler family should know what their greed has caused. They should know the name of Troy Lubinski and the many, many others that have lost their lives to OxyContin.

—STEPHANIE LUBINSKI[1]

We know of no other medication that's routinely used for a nonfatal condition that kills patients so frequently.

—DR. TOM FRIEDEN, DIRECTOR OF CENTERS FOR DISEASE CONTROL AND PREVENTION[2]

AS OPIOIDS cut a widening swath of destruction across the United States over the last three decades, the response was at best inadequate and misguided, and, at worst, cruel and lethal. Public figures and the media occasionally reached for kinder and gentler language to frame the opioid epidemic and its victims. But that did not spur a radical shift away from waging an aggressive war on people who illicitly use drugs. Policymakers and law enforcement redeployed punitive tools from previous wars on drugs and created some new ones, which bolstered the carceral state, exacerbated the opioid crisis, and contributed to the militarization of US foreign and domestic policies.

Nearly one in ten US adults says they have a family member who died of a drug overdose. In 2022 alone, almost 108,000 people in the United States succumbed to an overdose, and most of these fatalities involved opioids. This figure is about twice the *total* number of US fatalities during the decade-long

American war in Vietnam and more than twice the peak in annual deaths from HIV/AIDS in the late 1990s before the discovery of antiretroviral treatments (see figure 10.1).[3]

The death and destruction due to the opioid crisis are exceptional. But the causes of the opioid crisis are not. The opioid epidemic was "the nation's most preventable epidemic."[4] The Food and Drug Administration (FDA) failed to use the tools it had to keep dangerous and ineffective drugs off the market. Big Pharma flooded the country with billions of highly addictive pain pills, despite compelling evidence about their toxic effects, including high rates of addiction and fatal overdoses. The drug manufacturers and distributors that instigated the crisis emerged relatively unscathed. They were largely spared criminal charges, even though they inundated the country with opioid pain pills "through poorly-calibrated, inappropriate, or at times totally venal prescribing."[5] As in the case of the financial and foreclosure crises, pharmaceutical companies and their executives typically settled up by signing deferred prosecution and nonprosecution agreements (DPAs and NPAs). They admitted no wrongdoing and paid fines that were trivial compared to their revenues and profits and to the harm they caused. And then they went on doing business as usual.

Meanwhile the criminal legal system continued to wage war on people who illicitly use drugs and on low-level dealers, many of whom are in the drug retail business to support their own substance use. Politicians and other public figures deployed law-and-order rhetoric that at times rivaled the excesses of the crack era. Lawmakers and policymakers ratcheted up penalties for people who use and possess opioids. Faced with a public health catastrophe, they allocated minuscule amounts of money to expand effective treatment and prevention. They also opposed harm reduction policies that have headed off opioid epidemics in other countries. Overseas, the United States did not retreat from the forever wars on drugs, which complement the Washington rules and militarization of US foreign policy, as discussed in chapter 5.

The US opioid crisis is far reaching. Fatal overdose deaths in the United States increased more than fivefold between 2000 and 2022, which contributed to unprecedented declines in the country's life expectancy rate since World War II.[6] Drug overdoses are now the leading cause of accidental death in the United States, surpassing motor vehicle fatalities, and the top cause of death by far for people under the age of fifty.[7] The Joint Economic Committee of the US Congress estimated that the toll of the opioid crisis was $1.5 trillion in 2020.[8] Three in ten US adults report that they or a family member have been

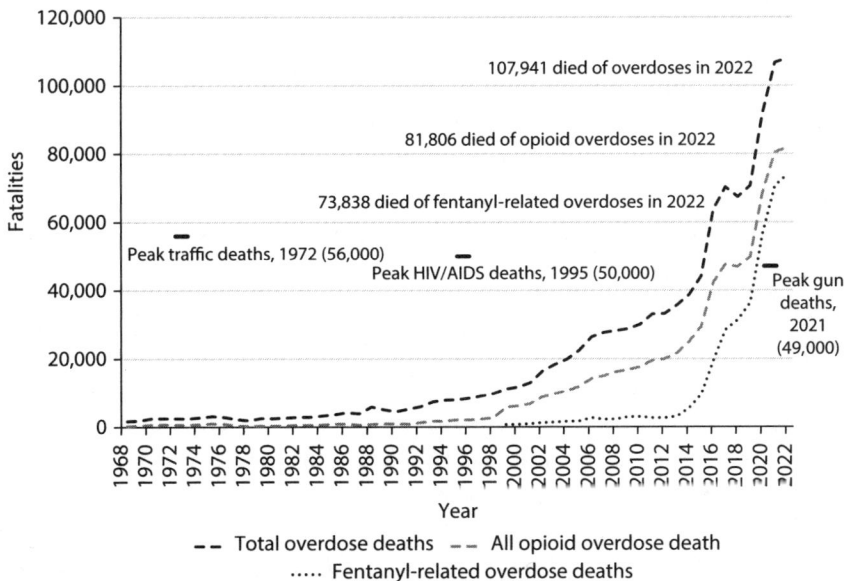

FIGURE 10.1. US Drug Overdose Deaths and Other Fatalities, 1968–2022. *Sources*: National Safety Council, "Motor Vehicle Deaths, United States, 1913–2022," n.d., https://injuryfacts.nsc.org/motorvehicle/overview /introduction/ (accessed August 17, 2024); "Update: Trends in AIDS Incidence, Deaths, and Prevalence—United States, 1996," *Morbidity and Mortality Weekly Report* (CDC) 46, no. 8 (February 28, 1997), https://www.cdc.gov/mmwr /preview/mmwrhtml/00046531.htm#00001188.gif; KFF, "Opioid Overdose Deaths and Opioid Overdose Deaths as a Percent of All Overdose Drug Deaths: 1999–2022," n.d., https://www.kff.org/other/state-indicator/opioid -overdose-deaths/?currentTimeframe=0&sortModel=%7B%22colId%22:%22 Location%22,%22sort%22:%22asc%22%7D (accessed February 23, 2025); US Congress, Joint Economic Committee, "Rate of Unintentional Drug Overdose Deaths, 1968–2015," August 1, 2017, https://www.jec.senate.gov/public/index .cfm/republicans/2017/8/the-rise-in-opioid-overdose-deaths; NIDA, "Drug Overdose Deaths," n.d., https://nida.nih.gov/research-topics/trends-statistics /overdose-death-rates (accessed February 23, 2025); and Ari Davis, Rose Kim, and Cassandra Crifasi, "U.S. Gun Violence in 2021: An Accounting of a Public Health Crisis," Johns Hopkins Bloomberg School of Public Health, Center for Gun Violence Solutions, June 2023, https://publichealth.jhu.edu/sites/default /files/2024-01/2023-june-cgvs-u-s-gun-violence-in-2021-v3.pdf. Gun deaths include both homicides and suicides.

addicted to opioids.[9] (The term *opioid* refers to a broad class of painkillers and mind-altering drugs. It includes prescribed medications and street drugs, among them, synthesized or semisynthesized drugs such as oxycodone [brand name OxyContin], hydrocodone, methadone, fentanyl, and fentanyl-like substances, as well as opiates that are naturally derived from opium poppies, notably opium, morphine, and heroin.)

Widespread claims that the United States has embraced harm reduction strategies and dialed back the war on drugs because the main victims of the opioid crisis are white people do not bear up under closer scrutiny. Government and other support for expanding access to the most effective treatments for opioid use disorder remains paltry given the scale of this public health catastrophe.[10] Law enforcement solutions directed at people who use and sell street drugs continue to far outpace public health and harm reduction solutions. As Ruth Wilson Gilmore, a leading expert on race and the criminal legal system, remarked about US drug policy: "People say, 'God knows they're not going to lock up white people,' and it's like, Yes, they *do* lock up white people."[11]

The mirage of a kinder, gentler approach must reckon with the mounting death toll of the opioid epidemic. If current trends continue, another million or so people in this country will succumb to fatal drug overdoses over the next decade. Furthermore, the demographics of opioid fatalities are changing. In the initial phases of the opioid epidemic, white people from nonurban areas were disproportionately victims of the crisis. But over the last decade or so, as potent fentanyl and fentanyl-like substances began coursing through and contaminating the illicit drug market, the opioid crisis entered a more lethal phase and reached a grim milestone as the racial gap in fatal overdoses closed. Promulgating claims that the United States has embraced kinder, gentler drug policies because the victims of the opioid crisis have been disproportionately white people robs the crisis of its urgency at a critical moment when the opioid death rate for African American people has raced past that of white people for the first time in decades.

Grieving families who have lost loved ones to an overdose are becoming a political force to be reckoned with. But a "great overdose grief divide" separates these families.[12] Some family members have aligned with sheriffs, prosecutors, and law-and-order politicians pushing to ramp up penalties for drug-related crimes. This emerging alliance is reminiscent of how the US victims' rights movement and the antirape and battered women's movements were co-opted by law enforcement beginning in the 1970s, which helped steer penal policy in a more punitive direction that fueled mass incarceration.[13] On the other side of the grief divide are families pressing the case that the wars on drugs were a failure and that the latest war on fentanyl will not reduce the overdose fatality rate and might actually fuel it. These families and their supporters have pressed for a shift toward investing in treatment and harm reduction, not law enforcement, to address the opioid epidemic.

This chapter is another episode in the continuing saga of the decriminalization of crime in the suites and the surge in structural violence in the United States. It first surveys the origins, development, and transformation of the opioid epidemic over the last three decades, including how Big Pharma, government regulators, medical providers, and various socioeconomic factors instigated, fostered, and exacerbated the opioid crisis. It then examines how public officials and the criminal legal system pushed for larger doses of punishment for people who use opioids and for people who sell them in the street-level illicit market. Meanwhile, Big Pharma has been mostly let off the hook despite flooding the United States with lethal, high-dosage pain pills.

This chapter challenges the widespread claim that a kinder, gentler approach to the opioid epidemic—one that stresses harm reduction, not law enforcement—has prevailed because the victims of the crisis are disproportionately white people. In fact, the United States responded to the opioid crisis by ramping up its law enforcement apparatus. Furthermore, as detailed in the next chapter, the United States has invested relatively little in harm reduction, public health, and other remedies that have stemmed the death toll of substance use disorder in other countries. Indeed, many US policymakers, lawmakers, and health-care providers have been contemptuous of such solutions.

Phase 1: Big Pharma and Government Regulators

The opioid crisis unfolded in three phases over the last three decades. In each phase, a changing mixture of racial, ideological, political, and institutional factors propelled the crisis and recast some of its consequences. The powerful pharmaceutical industry triggered the first phase. It was assisted by government regulators and public officials who were politically and financially beholden to Big Pharma thanks to its lobbying efforts, campaign donations, and other activities. Another key factor was the FDA's dependence on drug manufacturers as the main source of funding for the drug approval process thanks to a regulatory change in the 1990s.[14]

In 1995, against the recommendations of its own experts, the FDA greenlighted the sale and marketing of OxyContin, a new high-dosage opioid pain pill. Purdue Pharma's introduction of OxyContin, which "is basically heroin made in a lab," was a game changer for pharmaceutical makers, the medical profession, and patients.[15] As its patent for MS Contin—a long-acting version of morphine—was about to expire, Purdue sought approval for OxyContin.[16] The new drug, which was a reformulated version of oxycodone, was designed to be released more slowly to provide longer-lasting pain relief than shorter-acting rival drugs.

Oxycodone and other semisynthetic opioids are indispensable in treating some types of extreme pain such as end-of-life pain associated with metastatic cancer. But physicians had long eschewed prescribing opioids for more routine ailments and less extreme pain, such as aching backs, knee injuries, or tooth extractions, because of concerns about their risky side effects, including overdoses, dependence, and addiction.[17] Purdue claimed OxyContin would be less subject to abuse and addiction because people could not get a euphoric high from this timed-release drug. In a major case of regulatory failure, "based on this theory and little else," the FDA approved OxyContin in late 1995, permitting the new drug "to contain twice the usual dose of oxycodone."[18] It also allowed Purdue to initially label the drug with the unproven claim that delayed absorption was "believed to" reduce abuse of this pill.[19] Purdue executives "gushed in one internal report" that this labeling "could have easily served as OxyContin's 'principal selling tool.'"[20]

Soon after the drug was introduced in 1996, Purdue knew of "significant" abuse of OxyContin but hid that information.[21] Two decades later, a confidential memo from the Justice Department conceded that the approval process for OxyContin had been "'tainted' by Purdue's efforts to position the drug as less addictive and prone to abuse than other opioids."[22] (The FDA official who managed OxyContin's successful application in 1995 took a plum job at Purdue Pharma shortly thereafter.)[23]

To overcome the medical community's reluctance to prescribe OxyContin and other opioids more widely, Purdue Pharma launched an aggressive marketing campaign to persuade physicians that it "had the holy grail of a nonaddictive opioid" when the company rolled out the new drug.[24] The lucrative marketing even included providing free thirty-day OxyContin prescriptions for new patients.[25] An emergency room physician in western Virginia would later lament: "I can remember telling my residents, 'A patient can't get hooked on fourteen days' worth of [opioid] pills.' And I was absolutely wrong."[26]

Purdue deployed hundreds of sales representatives to promote OxyContin in doctors' offices and at fancy dinners. The company hosted physicians at conferences that were essentially junkets at luxury resorts. It also trained more than five thousand medical providers to be paid speakers to promote OxyContin. Deliberately downplaying the risks of drug addiction and overdoses was a key part of the message.[27]

A 2013 investigation by the *Milwaukee Journal Sentinel* revealed that FDA regulators and pharmaceutical executives had been regularly holding private, unpublicized meetings at expensive hotels for more than a decade. The investigation uncovered that the FDA agreed to greenlight the practice of "enriched enrollment," whereby drug companies cull from their studies patients who were not responding well to drugs that were being developed and tested. This practice enhanced—at least on paper—the apparent efficacy of new drugs.[28] Journalistic exposés of the FDA's complicity spurred a Senate investigation in 2012, the results of which have not been released despite periodic pressure to do so.[29]

Drugmakers also funded patient advocacy groups and, of course, researchers, which helped to "[align] medical culture with industry goals" and create "the necessary conditions for the U.S. opioids epidemic," according to a 2018 US Senate report.[30] While they were advocating for wider use of opioids to treat chronic pain, the American Pain Society and the American Academy of Pain Medicine were raking in millions of dollars from the pharmaceutical industry.[31] Research sponsored by the National Academy of Sciences (NAS), a premier advisory group for Congress and other policymakers, bolstered support for the wider use of prescribed opioids. An NAS report concluded that chronic pain afflicted 42 percent of American adults—or one hundred million people. This finding has since been widely discredited. But at the time, this grossly inflated figure helped legitimize the permissive use of OxyContin and other opioid pain pills even as the opioid death spiral was accelerating.[32] Research sponsored by NAS also influenced the FDA's 2013 decision to approve Zohydro, another controversial and highly potent opioid pain pill. A decade later, a *New York Times* investigation revealed that, since 2000, NAS had accepted donations totaling $19 million from the Sackler family, owners of Purdue Pharma.[33]

Purdue, Mallinckrodt, and other leading opioid manufacturers paid hundreds of millions of dollars in rebates to pharmacy benefit managers (PBMs), including Express Scripts, CVS Caremark, and Optum Rx, that together oversee prescriptions for more than two hundred million people, to propel sales of their powerful painkillers. Employers and insurance companies contract with PBMs, which supposedly constrain drug costs by, among other things, negotiating discounts with drug companies and determining which drugs will be reimbursed at what rates. The drugmakers struck backroom deals to ensure that these middlemen did not place restrictions on the use of opioids, including requiring prior authorization and imposing limits on daily dosages. For years, PBMs regularly "bargained away safeguards in exchange for rebates" from opioid makers, according to an investigation by the *New York Times*. Insurance companies and employers were slow to push back because they got a cut of the rebates.[34]

Purdue and other manufacturers of opioid pain pills targeted their marketing at rural and suburban whites to avoid the racialized stigmas associated with street drugs sold in urban markets that the police and politicians had been waging war against for decades.[35] Focusing on "deserving" white patients in need of pain relief was a way to neutralize the historic hostility of the Drug Enforcement Administration (DEA), other law enforcement groups, and government regulators to the expansion of opioid use.[36] Purdue's ads promoted OxyContin's "social identity as white" and played up stereotypical "markers of deservedness," including being elderly, female, or a military veteran.[37] Thanks to this racial and geographic targeting—as well as the structural advantages that white people have in health-care access and the medical profession's long-standing pattern of undertreating pain in African American people—the new opioids were disproportionately prescribed to white people complaining of or at risk of pain.[38] Purdue also shrewdly targeted its OxyContin marketing campaign at states that did not use so-called triplicate programs, an early and rudimentary form of prescription monitoring.[39]

Beginning in the late 1990s, opioid prescriptions to treat chronic pain surged "despite the absence of randomized trials showing clinically significant benefit from the long-term use of opioids."[40] Medical providers soon began prescribing OxyContin and other opioid pain pills such as Vicodin and Percocet not just for chronic pain like backaches and knee injuries, but also for routine acute pain, including wisdom tooth extractions and minor sports injuries. For some patients, a routine tooth extraction or sports injury was the road to opioid dependency for them—or friends and family members who used their leftover pain pills.[41] Many medical providers were unaware that there was little evidence from randomized control trials to support widespread claims that the benefits of opioid pain pills for all kinds of chronic and acute short-term pain outweigh the risks.[42] In fact, opioid pain pills are no more effective (and may be less effective) than less risky alternatives, such as physical therapy for chronic backaches, or nonopioid medications like acetaminophen and ibuprofen for short-term acute pain.[43]

Despite Purdue's and the FDA's claims to the contrary, OxyContin and other new formulations of oxycodone and hydrocodone were highly addictive and subject to misuse. People soon discovered that it was possible to get a quick high by crushing or liquifying the high-dosage pain pills and then snorting, injecting, or swallowing the drug. As early as 2000, medical providers, community activists, public health officials, and family members in southwestern Virginia were raising alarms about the burgeoning OxyContin crisis in their communities. They implored Purdue Pharma, the FDA, and other government officials to have OxyContin reformulated to make it more tamper resistant or to withdraw it from the market.[44] But Purdue Pharma stonewalled and boasted about its success at fending off civil suits.[45] As the number of overdoses began rising, Richard Sackler urged his company to heap the blame on patients. "We have to hammer on abusers in every way possible," Purdue's president and chairman implored in a 2001 email that became public years later. "They are the culprits and the problem. They are reckless criminals."[46]

In 2002, the FDA convened an advisory panel to reevaluate its policies on opioids. Eight of the ten panelists had been paid speakers or consultants for Purdue or other opioid makers. Not surprisingly, the panelists did not recommend any major changes to OxyContin's label or marketing.[47] In 2010, Purdue Pharma finally introduced a tamper-resistant formulation of its blockbuster drug—about fifteen years after the FDA first approved OxyContin. David Sackler defended the company's reported $1 billion investment in developing this new version of OxyContin as "a tremendously honest and ethical effort to fix a problem."[48] Left unsaid was that Purdue's patent for the original formulation was about to expire.[49] Purdue was seeking to thwart release of a generic version of OxyContin at the time by brazenly arguing "that the drug it had been selling for nearly fifteen years was so prone to abuse that generic manufacturers should not be allowed to copy it."[50]

Purdue remained incorrigible in other ways. In 2014, as the number of opioid overdoses continued to escalate, a Purdue executive proposed to reintroduce a super potent 160 milligram dose of OxyContin. Nicknamed "Oxy-Coffin," these high-dosage pills had been pulled from the market in 2001 after less than a year "due to safety concerns."[51] Company executives were also discussing a secret project code-named Tango, which would situate Purdue as an "end-to-end pain provider" by exploiting the link between pain treatment and the expanding (and lucrative) market in treating opioid addiction.[52]

OxyContin rapidly became a blockbuster drug with more than $1 billion in annual sales. Purdue Pharma and other manufacturers and distributors of

natural and semisynthetic opioids, most notably oxycodone and hydrocodone, saturated rural communities with high-dosage prescription pain pills.[53]
They created "a virtual opioid belt" of more than ninety counties stretching
from West Virginia to Kentucky.[54] Because of inadequate health care and
health insurance in rural areas, as well as the marketing prowess of drug manufacturers and distributors, prescription opioids became the treatment of
choice for people complaining of chronic pain. American insurance companies "were more likely to cover opioid pills, which were not only cheaper but
also considered a quicker fix," than alternatives such as physical therapy, bio-
feedback, acupuncture, and nonopioid drugs.[55]

In just two years in the mid-aughts, a single pharmacy in Kermit, West Virginia,
which had a population of barely four hundred, sold nearly nine million opioid
pain pills.[56] People drove hundreds of miles to get to the pharmacy. As they
waited in long lines at the drive-by window to purchase their pills, they munched
on hot dogs and popcorn, a profitable side business of the pharmacy.[57] William-
son, another town in West Virginia, was known locally as "Pilliamson."

A popular nonstop flight nicknamed the "Oxy Express," which shuttled between West Virginia and Florida, was a key link in the supply chain. It ferried
OxyContin and other opioids to the numerous pill mills in the Sunshine State
that were filling prescriptions for large quantities of pain pills without patients
ever having to see a physician. At one point, doctors in Florida were prescribing ten times more oxycodone pills than doctors were prescribing in all other
states in the country combined.[58]

A 2019 *Washington Post* investigation revealed that the number of opioid
pills sold in the United States far exceeded what had been previously reported
in public court documents and the news media. From 2006 through 2012, the
largest drug companies inundated the United States with seventy-six billion
oxycodone and hydrocodone pills—or thirty-six pills per year for every adult
and child in the country. Some states received astronomical numbers of pills,
with West Virginia leading at more than sixty-six pills per person per year.
Kentucky, South Carolina, Tennessee, and Nevada were close behind. Some
rural counties averaged hundreds of opioid pain pills per person per year.[59]

Additional Drivers of the Opioid Crisis

The opioid industry's marketing strategies that targeted white people and
states with laxer regulations for prescribing opioids do not entirely explain
why certain rural and Rust Belt communities were the initial epicenters of the

opioid crisis. In the United States and elsewhere, economic downturns and individual unemployment are associated with rising drug use.[60] Drug mortality rates for all types of drugs, not just opioids, are higher in counties with greater economic disadvantages, larger blue-collar and service sectors, and higher rates of opioid prescribing.[61] Opioid use and overdose deaths initially soared in US communities hit hardest by trade-related job losses and the shuttering of manufacturing plants, including communities in Appalachia, pockets of New England, and the desert Southwest.[62] American communities beset with "hopelessness, lack of opportunity, poverty, undertreated pain (both physical and emotional), and reduced access to medical care" were more vulnerable as legal and illegal suppliers inundated them with opioid pain pills.[63] The hollowing out of the social safety net and public services exacerbated the crisis in these communities.[64]

The global war on terror launched by President George W. Bush in 2001 was another driver of the opioid crisis. Compared to earlier eras, residents from rural areas now disproportionately serve in the military. As a consequence, American combat deaths and injuries from the US wars in Afghanistan, Iraq, and elsewhere were concentrated disproportionately among people in rural America, unlike during World War II and the US wars in Vietnam and Korea, as discussed in chapter 5. Thanks to medical and technical advances, soldiers with serious injuries are much more likely to survive today than during the American war in Vietnam. Many of these soldiers now return home with major injuries involving chronic pain, as well as significant mental health problems.[65]

The overdose death rate for veterans is nearly twice the rate for other adults. Members of the military and veterans are especially vulnerable to substance use disorder because of higher rates of chronic pain, post-traumatic stress disorder (PTSD), and other behavioral health problems.[66] The widespread stigma in the military about seeking treatment for mental health problems is another factor.[67] Veterans with PTSD and other behavioral health disorders were three times more likely to receive opioids for diagnoses of pain compared to other veterans.[68] The widespread use of opioids and other drugs may have contributed to the escalating suicide rate for military personnel and veterans.[69]

Pharmaceutical companies aggressively marketed prescription opioids to the military and the US Department of Veterans Affairs (VA), viewing veterans and active-duty military personnel as lucrative emerging markets.[70] Purdue Pharma even quietly sponsored publication of *Exit Wounds: A Survival*

Guide to Pain Management for Returning Veterans and Their Families, which was written by a former navy corpsman who had lost a leg in the battle of Fallujah in Iraq. The book was published by the "putatively independent" American Pain Foundation.[71]

Opioids were widely prescribed in war zones where US troops "were physically breaking down under the weight of the equipment they carried."[72] Veterans Health Administration (VHA) clinicians ignored or were pressured to disregard guidelines for safely prescribing opioids. Until recently, the VHA treated chronic pain almost exclusively with prescription opioids, despite their apparent dangers and limited effectiveness. Some VHA clinics became pill mills, with opioid prescription rates far exceeding the national average. One VHA doctor was nicknamed "The Candy Man" because his prescribing practices were so promiscuous.[73] The diversion of pain pills to friends, relatives, and acquaintances of military personnel fueled the opioid crisis in US communities with military bases nearby, such as Fayetteville, North Carolina, home to Fort Bragg, the country's largest military base.[74] These bases tend to be located away from major urban centers.

The first phase of the opioid crisis generated a reversal in geographic and racial disparities in fatal overdoses. In 1999, drug overdose rates for urban areas exceeded those in rural areas. By 2004, they had converged. Two years later, the rural rate surpassed the urban rate.[75] In 1999, the rate of opioid overdose deaths for African American people slightly exceeded the rate for white people and equaled the rate for Latino people. Two years later, the rate for white people began charging ahead. Over the next decade, the overdose death rate for African American and Latino people remained reasonably constant but continued to surge for white people. By 2010, white people were dying of overdoses at about three times the rate that African American and Latino people were succumbing.[76]

Phase 2: Another Fatal Mistake

After OxyContin had been on the market for nearly fifteen years, policymakers made a sudden push to restrict the supply as the toll of deaths, disabilities, and other harms from prescription pain pills was skyrocketing. With tens of thousands of people dying each year from opioid overdoses, government officials sought to abruptly choke off the supply of OxyContin and other semisynthetic opioid pain pills beginning around 2010. Their actions marked the start of the second phase of the opioid crisis. In a public policy failure of epic proportions, policymakers made this move without radically expanding access to proven treatments for substance use disorder and alternative means of pain management. As a result, many people dependent on prescribed opioids were forced to turn to illegal street drugs, notably heroin, to stave off withdrawal symptoms and cravings and to manage their pain. Furthermore, patients dying of cancer had difficulty securing prescribed opioids to relieve their severe pain as the DEA sought to choke off the production of pain pills.[77]

Policymakers did not make a major effort to address the underlying physical and mental health problems that contribute to substance use disorder. Furthermore, they did not make a concerted effort to bolster the social safety net and ameliorate the socioeconomic factors—including poverty, unemployment, low wages, and dangerous and unhealthy jobs—that render some people and communities more vulnerable to chronic pain and substance use disorder.

Toward the end of the Clinton administration, federal officials sought to crack down on prescription drug abuse by bolstering drug monitoring programs and shuttering pill mills. The George W. Bush administration intensified the crackdown despite widespread warnings that doing so would fuel a heroin epidemic as the black-market price of pain pills skyrocketed. As early as 2002, the Justice Department's drug intelligence unit was already warning that, as "initiatives taken to curb the abuse of OxyContin are successfully implemented, abusers of OxyContin . . . also may begin to use heroin, especially if it is readily available, pure, and relatively inexpensive."[78] Those projections did not prod the Bush or Obama administrations to treat the emerging opioid epidemic as a public health emergency. Neither did the growing number of governmental and nongovernmental reports and warnings that the United States was in the throes of an opioid crisis.[79]

To stem the supply of opioid prescription pills, doctors and other medical providers were prodded to write fewer opioid prescriptions, reduce the dosages, and follow other prescription limits and guidelines. In some cases, they were threatened if they did not.[80] States also implemented prescription drug monitoring programs to crack down on pill mill doctors and people who doctor shopped to secure numerous prescriptions for opioid pills.[81] Prosecutors began aggressively pursuing charges against physicians and succeeded in securing draconian sentences in some cases.[82] The VHA began mandating swift and drastic cutoffs of opioid prescriptions for veterans with chronic pain, regardless of the patient's condition and despite the acute shortage of substance use treatment programs for veterans and active-duty military personnel.[83]

These measures succeeded somewhat in reducing the number of opioid prescriptions and overdose deaths from prescribed pain pills, but they were a public policy disaster.[84] Pill mills and other avenues to receive prescribed opioids were shut down without ensuring that people who were dependent on opioids would have access to treatment. Cases of untreated pain and medically unsupervised withdrawal increased. So did the substitution of other more potent and dangerous opioids. As opioid pain pills became harder to obtain through legal and illegal means, their price soared on the black market. People in pain and people dependent on prescription opioids scrambled to find "cheaper, more accessible, and more potent black-market alternatives— including heroin—in unprecedented numbers."[85] Many people, including veterans and members of the military, were forced to turn to risky street drugs, where the quality, potency, and ingredients are unknown and vary greatly.

Producers and suppliers of heroin and fentanyl at home and abroad shrewdly targeted the US market to capitalize on the desperation of millions of people who "traded down" to heroin, which, adjusted for potency, cost about one-third as much as OxyContin on the street.[86] Almost 80 percent of heroin users reportedly used prescription opioids prior to heroin.[87] Overdose deaths from heroin spiked in 2010 after increasing only slightly over the previous decade.[88] So did rates of infection from blood-borne diseases, including hepatitis C, HIV/AIDS, syphilis, and other infectious diseases associated with unsafe use of injectable drugs.[89]

The Iron Law of Prohibition

This public disaster was entirely foreseeable. The so-called iron law of prohibition transformed the market for opioid pain pills, much as enforcement of the Eighteenth Amendment prohibiting sales of alcohol triggered a massive transformation of the liquor market a century ago. In the bootleg era of the 1920s, production and consumption of highly distilled spirits (like gin and bathtub moonshine, which were less bulky and more potent) soared while consumption of wine and beer fell. As the country learned during Prohibition, "*the more intense the law enforcement, the more potent the drugs will become.*"[90] With the supply of opioid pills shrinking and the price escalating, heroin became a cheaper and more attractive alternative. Furthermore, the crackdown on opioid pills occurred just as an influx of new heroin producers and new formulations of this illicit drug were reducing its street price to historic lows.

Policymakers were aware that suddenly stemming the supply of prescription opioids would have deadly consequences. In a chilling admission, Dr. Carrie

DeLone, who served from 2013 to 2015 as Pennsylvania's physician general under Republican Governor Tom Corbett, conceded, "We knew that . . . we were going to push addicts in a direction that was going to be more deadly. . . . But, we also know that you have to start somewhere."[91] A federal official from the US attorney's office in Orlando trumpeted Florida's success in cracking down on the misuse of opioid pain pills and reducing the number of fatal overdoses from them. But embedded in his account was a bleaker story: While fatal overdoses from opioid pills in Florida fell, deaths from heroin, morphine, and fentanyl skyrocketed.[92]

Even as some policymakers belatedly sought to clamp down on the supply of prescription opioids, the FDA was opening the door wider for the sale of opioid pain pills. In October 2013, the agency approved Zohydro, an extended-release version of hydrocodone that is up to ten times as potent as OxyContin. It overruled its own expert staff and advisory panel, which had voted in December 2012 by an overwhelming 11–2 margin against approval. Critics charged that Zohydro would be highly addictive and would cause problems like the ones created by OxyContin.[93] Attorneys general from dozens of states lambasted the FDA for approving a formulation of Zohydro that was not even tamper resistant.[94] In 2015, the FDA sanctioned the use of OxyContin in patients as young as eleven. Three years later, it approved Dsuvia, a fentanyl-like substance that is a thousand times more potent than morphine.[95]

As the FDA continued to do the bidding of Purdue and Big Pharma, the Centers for Disease Control and Prevention (CDC), alarmed by what it characterized as an opioid epidemic, attempted in 2011 to issue a set of voluntary guidelines to assist medical providers in determining when to prescribe opioids. The firestorm from Big Pharma delayed the guidelines for five years.[96] Two decades after OxyContin hit the market, the CDC finally issued nonbinding guidelines in 2016 that called on physicians to severely limit their use of opioids for chronic pain and to frequently reevaluate their use in instances where opioids are prescribed.[97] The guidelines spurred a remarkable backlash within and outside of the government as the Department of Health and Human Services attempted to countermand the CDC's prescription.[98]

Phase 3: Russian Roulette

About a decade ago, the United States entered the third and most lethal wave of the opioid crisis with the proliferation of fentanyl. This potent, fast-acting synthetic opioid delivers a high like heroin but is much cheaper to produce and distribute illegally. Suppliers of street drugs began lacing fentanyl into everything from heroin to Ecstasy to counterfeit prescription pills. Cheap and deadly fentanyl and fentanyl-like analogues coursed through the illegal drug market, radically transforming the market and turning drug use into a game of Russian roulette.

Fentanyl is completely synthetic, unlike heroin, which is manufactured from poppy plants. Developed in 1960, fentanyl was FDA approved in the early 1970s for medical use, typically for surgery and cancer patients.[99] Over the last decade or so, illicit drug labs and factories producing fentanyl and fentanyl analogues on an industrial scale have proliferated, especially in China and Mexico. These lab-made opioids are highly potent and toxic. They also are much cheaper to manufacture and smuggle than cocaine or heroin. Fentanyl can be fifty to one hundred times more powerful than morphine. Doses as small as two milligrams of fentanyl—equivalent to a few grains of table salt—can be fatal. Some other synthetic opioids are even more lethal.[100]

Overdose deaths involving fentanyl and other synthetic opioids, which had been gradually climbing between 2000 and 2013, began to soar (see figure 10.1). Around 2016, fentanyl became the leading cause of overdose deaths in the United States, far surpassing deaths from heroin, prescription drugs, or homicide.[101] Whereas a window of two or three hours may exist to respond to a heroin or prescription opioid pill overdose, death can occur in just minutes with fentanyl if the overdose-reversal drug naloxone (better known as Narcan) is not administered right away. Furthermore, fentanyl overdoses are harder to reverse, even with several doses of naloxone.[102]

Experts warn that a permanent transformation of the illegal drug market is well under way as fentanyl and fentanyl-like drugs are replacing or supplementing plant-based ones like heroin or are being laced into other drugs to bulk them up, including cocaine, methamphetamines, Ecstasy, and counterfeit pain pills nicknamed "fentapills." These pills often look nearly identical to the real thing, including OxyContin and other widely used prescription drugs, such as the antianxiety drug Xanax.[103] Users do not know whether the drugs they bought contain a lethal dose of fentanyl.[104] And drug dealers often do not know all the ingredients that are in the drugs they are selling illicitly.

As fentanyl and its analogues contaminated the street drug market in urban areas, the rural-urban and white-Black disparities in overdose deaths began to narrow.[105] Around 2016, urban overdose rates overtook those of rural counties for the first time in about a decade.[106] In many cities, overdose deaths began to outpace homicides by far.[107] In 2019, the overdose death rate for Black men surpassed that for white men for the first time in decades. The overdose fatality rate for Black women, which had lagged far behind that of white women for years, was nearly identical by 2020.[108]

The focus on the tens of thousands of opioid fatalities each year during this third phase of the opioid crisis has obscured that the country may be at the cusp of a real—not manufactured—crisis over methamphetamine and possibly cocaine. With overdoses from these two drugs skyrocketing and with growing numbers of people taking a cocktail of drugs, many of which have been laced with fentanyl, it may be an anachronism to continue talking about an opioid crisis.[109] The CDC warned in 2023 about the growing crisis of "polysubstance abuse."[110]

The Opioid Crisis and the Pursuit of Crime in the Suites

Purdue Pharma has been the designated corporate villain in the opioid crisis. But while Purdue played a critical role in securing FDA approval for new high-dosage opioids and in pioneering aggressive marketing strategies, several other drug companies were also major manufacturers of these pills.[111] And just a handful of firms, including CVS, Walgreens, and Walmart, were the distributors for three-quarters of the pills.[112]

The DEA brought civil enforcement cases against some of the largest drug distributors and pharmacies for not heeding the agency's warnings that they were required to report and halt all suspicious orders of painkillers. The fines these companies paid to settle these charges were tiny, while the revenues they earned were gigantic. Drug companies and distributors vowed to do a better job at reporting and halting suspicious orders, but they continued to produce, transport, and sell huge amounts of the pills in certain jurisdictions. Some DEA agents and officials reportedly sought to file more serious criminal charges against drug companies and their executives but were overruled by federal prosecutors.[113]

With the support of the Obama administration, the drug industry's champions in Congress successfully fought to curtail the DEA's ability to rein in the opioid industry. Representative Tom Marino (R-PA), whose district included predominantly white communities in northeastern and central Pennsylvania hard hit by the opioid crisis, was a leading defender of the opioid industry in Congress. In April 2016, President Barack Obama signed legislation dubbed the "Marino bill" that made it virtually impossible for the DEA to freeze dangerous and suspicious shipments by drug manufacturers and distributors. This measure, which the House and Senate approved by unanimous consent, upended four decades of DEA practice. The opioid industry donated troughs of money to Marino and other members of Congress and recruited dozens of former DEA officials to work for pharmaceutical firms, including D. Linden Barber, the agency's former associate chief counsel. While at the DEA, Barber had been instrumental in designing and implementing measures to target drug companies that failed to report suspicious orders of narcotics. After he went to work for the drug industry, Barber was a lead author of the Marino bill.[114]

Joseph Rannazzisi, who headed the DEA's diversion control office, reportedly accused members of Congress who cosponsored the Marino bill of "supporting criminals."[115] Marino and Representative Marsha Blackburn (R-TN), who cosponsored the bill and became a US senator in 2019, fought back. They demanded that the Justice Department's inspector general investigate Rannazzisi for intimidating members of Congress. The Department of Justice (DOJ) investigation did not amount to anything, but Rannazzisi was forced out of his position at the DEA and retired shortly thereafter.[116]

After he was pushed aside, Rannazzisi excoriated the opioid industry in a 2018 interview with *60 Minutes*. He accused the agency of allowing "millions and millions of drugs to go into bad pharmacies and doctors' offices, that distributed them out to people who had no legitimate need for those drugs."[117] Rannazzisi lamented the lack of congressional support to curtail these practices and faulted lawmakers for turning the tables on him, instead of the pharmaceutical industry. Rannazzisi was incredulous that President Donald Trump had nominated Marino in September 2017 to be the director of the Office of National Drug Control Policy (ONDCP). After reports surfaced about the congressman's pivotal role in hamstringing the DEA's efforts to contain the opioid crisis, Trump was forced to withdraw Marino's nomination as the country's next drug czar.[118]

Only a handful of pharmaceutical executives have been convicted of criminal charges related to the opioid crisis, including racketeering, bribing doctors, and misrepresenting the safety of their products. In spring 2019, executives of opioid manufacturer Insys Therapeutics were convicted in what is believed to be the first criminal trial of pharmaceutical executives involving the marketing of an opioid painkiller since the FDA had approved OxyContin nearly twenty-five years earlier.[119] Four years later, Laurence F. Doud III, former CEO of Rochester Drug Cooperative Inc., the country's seventh-largest drug wholesaler, was sentenced to twenty-seven months in prison for conspiring to distribute narcotics and defrauding the United States in connection with the opioid epidemic. This was a rare instance in which criminal charges against a drug executive in connection to the opioid epidemic resulted in a prison term.[120] For the most part, drug companies and their corporate officers have been spared. As in the case of the financial and foreclosure crises, DPAs and NPAs shielded them from criminal charges and major sanctions.[121] Drug companies, including Purdue and Mallinckrodt, which manufactured more opioid pain pills than any other firm, also used bankruptcy procedures to weasel out of fines they had agreed to pay and to reduce what they had to shell out to settle civil lawsuits.[122]

For more than a decade after OxyContin hit the market in 1996, Purdue successfully fended off federal prosecutors. Capitalizing on the post-9/11 popularity of former New York City mayor Rudolph Giuliani, Purdue hired "America's mayor" and his consulting firm to convince "public officials they could trust Purdue because they could trust him."[123] Another key figure on Purdue's legal team was Mary Jo White, a former US attorney for the Southern District of New York and later chair of the Securities and Exchange Commission (SEC) under President Barack Obama.[124] "It pains me to look at somebody like Mary Jo White," said Massachusetts Attorney General Maura Healy, who tussled with White over the Purdue case. "Not that there isn't room to represent corporations, that's worthy work. But this corporation? These people? It's no different from representing a drug cartel in my mind."[125]

The federal government finally took some modest action against Purdue in 2007, at which point about eighteen thousand people in the United States were dying of opioid overdoses annually.[126] Federal prosecutors in western Virginia had recommended charging the company and three of its top executives with numerous felonies, including money laundering, conspiracy, misbranding, and fraud. But political appointees at the Justice Department during George W. Bush's administration overruled them. This was "a political outcome that Purdue bought," said one dismayed former DOJ official involved in the case.[127] In 2007, the Purdue Frederick Company (Purdue Pharma's holding company) and three top Purdue executives pleaded guilty to federal misdemeanor charges of misbranding. They were accused of "falsely claiming that OxyContin was less addictive, less subject to abuse, and less likely to cause withdrawal symptoms than other pain medication."[128] The executives were sentenced to four hundred hours of community service and three years of probation. They were also fined $34 million, which the company, not the executives, paid. Shortly after taking the fall, two of the Purdue executives were rewarded with millions of dollars in bonuses from the company.[129]

As for the company, it paid a $634 million fine as part of a nonprosecution agreement. This amount was trivial considering the billions of dollars that

OxyContin had earned for Purdue Pharma. As part of the five-year probation agreement, Purdue Frederick was banned from participating in Medicare, Medicaid, and TRICARE (the federal health program for military personnel). But Purdue Pharma was not banned, so it was able to continue selling Oxy-Contin to the major federal health-care programs.[130] Purdue Pharma followed a well-worn corporate practice of circumventing bans on participating in government programs by having a shell company, subsidiary, or holding company plead guilty and take the fall.[131] At the time of this agreement, the Sacklers were quietly establishing a new company called Rhodes to sell generic opioids as a hedge against the "possibility that they would need to start afresh following the crisis then engulfing OxyContin."[132]

Court papers and other documents revealed that McKinsey and Company had an extensive relationship with Purdue and other major manufacturers and distributors of opioid pain pills. Among other things, the world's most prestigious consulting firm had advised Purdue to "band together" with other opioid makers to forestall stricter FDA regulations. It also recommended finding ways "to counter the emotional messages from mothers with teenagers that overdosed" on OxyContin. McKinsey even proposed that Purdue issue rebates to CVS, other distributors, and insurers for each overdose or case of opioid use disorder attributable to prescribed OxyContin.[133]

While McKinsey was advising Purdue and other pharmaceutical companies on how to better market their addictive painkillers and minimize the political and reputational damage from the opioid crisis, the firm was contracting with state and local governments on how to address the damage done by the opioid epidemic. It was also simultaneously advising the FDA on how to, among other things, reorganize the agency's office responsible for approving new drugs. In its pitches to pharmaceutical companies, McKinsey would tout its "inside access" to government officials.[134]

McKinsey ended up paying nearly $900 million to settle lawsuits from state attorneys general, local governments, and school districts for its role in helping to "turbocharge" sales of OxyContin. In late 2024, it agreed to pay an additional $650 million as part of a DPA to settle federal criminal and civil charges related to its role in the opioid crisis. As part of that agreement, a former senior partner at McKinsey agreed to plead guilty to one felony charge of obstruction of justice for destroying company records with the intent to thwart the federal probe. More than two dozen McKinsey partners who worked with Purdue to aggressively boost sales of OxyContin as overdose deaths were surging were let off the hook.[135]

Less than two weeks before the 2020 election, the DOJ announced that Purdue Pharma had agreed to plead guilty to criminal and civil charges related to its aggressive and misleading marketing of OxyContin. Purdue was eager to settle the federal charges before the election, calculating it would get a better deal under Trump than under Joe Biden, should he unseat the president. The company agreed to $8 billion in criminal and civil penalties to be paid to the government, not the victims of Purdue's malfeasance. The Sackler family, whose net worth was estimated at $13 billion at the time, would shell out just $225 million as part of the settlement. The agreement did not preclude the Justice Department from later filing criminal charges against Purdue executives or members of the Sackler family, but it was widely understood that the DOJ was closing its case with this settlement.[136]

Family members of opioid victims and state attorneys general pursuing their own civil litigation against Purdue derided the DOJ's agreement, saying that it was premature and did not hold the company and the Sackler family accountable. State officials also charged that Sackler family members had siphoned off company assets into Swiss and other secret offshore bank accounts to shield their wealth from the thousands of pending lawsuits.[137] Furthermore, the company had filed for bankruptcy a year earlier, which meant the DOJ would likely receive just pennies on the dollar as it joined the line of claimants in bankruptcy court. According to a forensic audit commissioned by the company as part of the bankruptcy proceedings, the Sacklers had shifted at least $10.7 billion between 2008 and 2017 from the company to trusts and holding companies controlled by the family as Purdue Pharma faced growing public and legal scrutiny for its role in the opioid crisis.[138]

Opioid makers and distributors faced a cascade of civil lawsuits filed by individuals, states, cities, and other entities that accused them of fueling the epidemic. Thanks to the shroud of nondisclosure agreements, many of these initial cases were settled quietly without a public accounting of the extent of the epidemic or how drug companies and the government fomented it. That changed as more cities, towns, and counties devastated by the deluge of opioid pain pills started to fight back in court beginning around 2014. In 2017, a federal court in Cleveland consolidated thousands of lawsuits brought by state and local governments, tribal communities, and labor unions seeking to recover costs associated with the opioid epidemic.[139] In early 2022, AmerisourceBergen, McKesson, and Cardinal Health, the three largest opioid distributors, announced along with Johnson & Johnson that they had reached a $26 billion agreement to resolve many of the claims. Indigenous groups reached a separate

$665 million deal with the companies.[140] The firms admitted no wrongdoing and accepted no responsibility for the opioid epidemic. The day the agreement was announced, their stock prices rose by 3 percent or more. Cabell County and Huntington, West Virginia, often described as ground zero for the opioid crisis, did not join the settlement. Instead, these two jurisdictions took the three distributors to court, where a federal judge resoundingly absolved the drug companies of any blame.[141]

In 2021, Purdue agreed to a bankruptcy plan that would dissolve the company, transfer its assets to a new firm, and pay out $4.5 billion over several years to settle the opioid lawsuits. The company also consented to turn over tens of millions of internal company documents to archivists and to make them publicly available through an easy-to-use, text-searchable portal.[142] The agreement would also absolve the Sackler family from liability in opioid-related civil cases, thus shielding most of its wealth. Hundreds of Purdue's business associates, attorneys, lobbyists, subsidiaries, and other company-related entities would also be absolved.[143] Mary Jo White, who returned to private practice at Debevoise & Plimpton after serving as SEC chair under Obama, represented several members of the Sackler family during the bankruptcy proceedings. In a rare public interview about the case, White disparaged the plaintiffs' claims that the Sackler family was liable under the law of public nuisance.[144] White said the real culprit in the opioid crisis was the flood of illegal heroin and fentanyl flowing in from Mexico and China.

The judge in the Purdue bankruptcy case sidelined victims during the proceedings.[145] Most of the $4.5 billion settlement was earmarked for states and communities to fund opioid-related treatment and prevention efforts and, of course, to pay the massive attorneys' fees. Victims, including the families of people who died of opioid overdoses, would receive payments ranging from $3,500 to $48,000. The compensation to victims was so paltry that Ryan Hampton, who served as cochairman of a federally appointed watchdog committee of plaintiffs, resigned on the eve of the settlement. He went on to write a scathing account of the bankruptcy proceedings.[146]

A federal judge overturned the bankruptcy settlement in December 2021, ruling that the Sackler family, which had not declared bankruptcy, could not be shielded from civil lawsuits as part of the company's bankruptcy settlement.[147] But in May 2023, a federal appeals court approved the bankruptcy plan. Most of the parties who opposed the original bankruptcy agreement dropped their objections after the Sacklers consented to increase the payout by about $1.73 billion.[148] Under the revised terms, victims' families would still receive only token compensation.

The Justice Department appealed the decision to the US Supreme Court. The solicitor general characterized the Purdue settlement as "an abuse of the bankruptcy system." She argued that bankruptcy courts do not have the authority to immunize company owners from lawsuits if those owners have not personally declared bankruptcy.[149] In June 2024, the Supreme Court in a 5–4 decision rejected Purdue's maneuver that would have shielded the Sackler family and others from civil claims under the bankruptcy settlement. In early 2025, fifteen states reached a tentative deal with the Sacklers that would not immunize the family from future lawsuits. The settlement included a novel provision to set aside as much as $800 million from the $7.4 billion agreement in an account for the Sackler family to draw on in their legal fight against pending opioid-related claims.[150]

All the attention on Purdue has overshadowed other egregious settlements, including the case of Endo Health Solutions, a huge but lesser-known opioid maker. As its opioid business hummed along and the firm lavished tens of millions of dollars in bonuses on its executives, the Philadelphia-area company devised a corporate restructuring plan and used bankruptcy proceedings to weasel out of $7 billion it owed in civil and criminal penalties, back taxes, and other charges. In the end, the Justice Department settled for just $200 million.[151]

The Purdue and other opioid-related settlements are expected to total upward of $50 billion in payments over the next two decades or so. These settlements are unlikely to have a transformative effect on the opioid crisis, for reasons discussed in the next chapter. That sum is trivial given the scale of the crisis. An expert witness for the plaintiffs in one of the major opioid cases estimated that it would cost almost $500 billion to significantly mitigate the damage done by the opioid epidemic.[152] Furthermore, the opioid settlements promise to be boondoggles for state and local governments, including police departments seeking additional funds to pay for cop cars, scanners to detect drug use, overtime for narcotics detectives, and other law enforcement items, as detailed in chapter 11.

Not Necessarily Kinder or Gentler

The criminal legal system's kid-glove treatment of Purdue, the Sacklers, and other opioid manufacturers and distributors who triggered the opioid epidemic stands in sharp contrast to the hard-line stance of police, prosecutors, and other public officials toward people who illicitly use opioids or sell them on the street. Despite some slight gestures toward public health and harm reduction, the predominant response has been punitive and carceral in both words and deeds toward people dependent on opioids. The drug warrior mentality of previous drug scares has persisted and, in some instances, intensified. Politicians, policymakers, and police officers have once again engaged in "policy theater," pursuing actions that are "visible and noteworthy, regardless of their ultimate impact."[153] Their actions have had deadly consequences.

In a keynote address to the Drug Policy Alliance in 2017, Michelle Alexander, author of the best-selling *The New Jim Crow*, suggested that the United States has entered an era of "newfound tolerance and compassion" in drug policy because the public face of the opioid crisis is predominantly white.[154] When she was a first-term US senator from California, Democrat Kamala Harris echoed this view. She charged that people with opioid problems were treated with empathy, in contrast to the stigmatization and demonization years ago of Black and Latino people who used crack.[155] Other public officials and commentators have made similar claims that the country has deployed a racialized double standard in the opioid epidemic.[156] But an examination of media coverage, the response of law enforcement, the legislative and policy record, and the availability of treatment for substance use disorder casts doubt on claims that the policy and legal response to the opioid crisis has been kinder and gentler compared to that of previous drug scares.

Analyses of the opioid crisis often invoke the crack scare as a standard of comparison. Commentators and researchers frequently slip into talking about the crack scare as an "epidemic," which fosters misleading apples-to-oranges comparisons between the opioid and crack crises.[157] The crack scare was precipitated by a highly racialized moral panic fueled by fears that were out of proportion to the actual problem. Crack and so-called crackheads became the scapegoats. Politicians, other public figures, and even some residents of poor African American neighborhoods heaped much of the blame for urban decay on crack, as discussed in chapter 2. In doing so, they legitimized casting a massive dragnet over these neighborhoods while other culprits—disinvestment in public housing and education, the assault on organized labor and public-sector jobs, a failing health-care system, residential segregation, a shredded social safety net, and a regressive tax system— remained invisible or blameless. Hyperbolic claims about the threat crack purportedly posed to public health and safety unleashed a massive overreaction by police, prosecutors, politicians, and segments of the public that targeted poor urban communities and people of color. Crack propelled a law enforcement crisis as residents of these communities increasingly viewed the police as an illegitimate occupying army and the United States as a semi-authoritarian state, not a democracy.[158]

Unlike today's opioid crisis, the crack scare and many other prior drug scares in the United States were not public health crises or epidemics, even though they were portrayed as such. Fueled by fear, political opportunism, ignorance, and prejudice, these earlier drug scares were moral panics that singled out historically disadvantaged groups for blame, shame, and punishment.[159] By contrast, the opioid epidemic is a real public health crisis, not just a rhetorical one. Opioids kill more people each year than any other drug does.[160] The total number of opioid-related fatal overdoses in 2022 was more than tenfold the number of all drug overdose deaths during the height of the so-called crack epidemic in the mid-1990s (see figure 10.1). For years, this public health catastrophe received comparatively little media and public attention.[161] Compared to the so-called crack epidemic of the 1980s and 1990s, the opioid crisis has been "*under-* rather than overstated."[162] As one public health expert observed, "The scale of death here is really unprecedented, and so you have to judge the response against the scale of the problem."[163]

On occasion, depictions of the opioid crisis by the media, politicians, and other public figures have been kinder and gentler compared to the earlier depictions of the wars on opium, marijuana, heroin, crack, and methamphetamine—and on the people who used these substances. But tough law enforcement rhetoric has predominated. At times, it has rivaled the excesses of the crack era as lawmakers have excoriated people who sell fentanyl as "agents of death," likened fentanyl to a serial killer, and called for bringing back the guillotine and public executions for drug traffickers.[164]

Journalists tend to portray white users of prescription opioids more favorably than people of color who use heroin, according to some research findings.[165] That said, use of stigmatizing language, such as "addict" or "substance abuser," to refer to people with opioid use disorder has been pervasive in the news media and actually increased slightly over the course of the crisis.[166] As stigmatizing references to so-called addicts increased in the news media, the complicity of the pharmaceutical industry in fostering the crisis largely disappeared from view for a long period.[167]

Experts on public opinion and the news media agree that even small changes in wording in news coverage can shape public opinion and public policies. That is especially true in the case of public sentiment on crime and the wars on drugs, which is complex, often contradictory, highly malleable, and subject to sudden, dramatic shifts.[168] Negative views of people with opioid use disorder correlate with reduced support for public health and harm reduction approaches, as detailed in the next chapter, and with greater support for punitive measures, such as prosecuting people who doctor shop to secure multiple prescriptions for opioid pain pills.[169]

A comprehensive analysis comparing news coverage of the waves of drug scares since the so-called crack epidemic in the late 1980s concluded that a strong criminalization focus prevailed in reporting on crack while a medical model prevailed in later reporting on the opioid crisis. But that study had some serious shortcomings.[170] Furthermore, the study does concede that it is difficult to conclude from its findings that "the difference in narratives between the opioid epidemic and other substance use epidemics stems from the perception that the opioid epidemic is uniquely white."[171]

The White House, Congress, and "Silence = Death"

The evidence is overwhelming that tougher sentences and other punitive measures do not reduce the harms associated with substance use disorder and may actually increase them. Yet at the national, state, and local levels, draconian policies and laws directed at people who use and sell drugs on the street have "persisted and in many cases been expanded."[172] A fifty-state statistical analysis by the Pew Charitable Trusts concluded that tougher sentences for drug crimes do not reduce drug use, drug overdoses, or drug arrests.[173] Drug policy specialist Jonathan Caulkins estimates that more than one million people are involved in distributing illegal drugs in America.[174] Rounding up the many low-level sellers and giving them long penal sentences will not make much of a dent in the supply. It might even make the problem worse. Sweeps to arrest street-level drug dealers result in more 911 calls and overdoses as people are forced to seek out new and unfamiliar sources to illicitly purchase drugs.[175]

Between 2009 and 2019, the number of drug arrests in the United States remained steady at around 1.5 million per year even as the number of arrests overall fell by nearly a third. That said, the number of people admitted to and held in state prisons for drug crimes fell by about a third during that period.[176] Nearly 90 percent of drug arrests in 2019 were for possession, not for sale or manufacturing, and most of them involved small amounts.[177] The proportion of people incarcerated in state prisons for drug offenses varies enormously, from a high of 47 percent of the total state prison population in South Dakota to a low of just 6 percent in Alaska.[178]

Racial and geographic shifts in arrests and incarceration for drug crimes since the onset of the opioid crisis in the early aughts call into question claims that US policies toward opioid use are more lenient because white people are the poster child of the epidemic. African American people are still more likely than white people to be incarcerated for drug crimes. But their rate of incarceration for drug crimes has fallen considerably while the comparable rate for white people has not, as detailed in chapter 2.

As the carnage from the opioid crisis mounted in the aughts, the US Congress and executive branch continued to wage a punitive war on drugs in the United States and abroad.[179] Drug policy under President George W. Bush focused on the alleged dangers of marijuana, even though tens of thousands of people in the United States were dying of opioid overdoses by the time he left office in 2009.[180] The Obama administration engaged in a series of low-profile but significant guerilla actions in its war on drugs. The administration scaled up punishment for certain drug crimes while softening the drug warrior rhetoric. Faced with a near doubling of overdose deaths during his administration, Obama did not declare a national emergency. He did not speak out about the opioid epidemic until his final sixteen months in office.[181] His silence is reminiscent of President Ronald Reagan's prolonged and controversial silence in the early years of the AIDS epidemic. During that time, ACT UP and other groups fighting for more funding for research and treatment and for quicker approval of experimental drugs to combat AIDS popularized the slogan "Silence = Death." Reagan did not give a speech about AIDS until 1987 at the tail end of his administration.[182]

In his second term, Obama, along with his attorney general, Eric Holder, haltingly promoted the "Smart on Crime" initiative to reduce time served for federal drug offenses. But many of the US attorneys who served under Holder continued to pursue harsh penalties for fentanyl and other drug-related offenses even as they acknowledged that the "deterrent doesn't last a long time" and that they cannot arrest their way out of the fentanyl problem.[183] In late 2013, federal prosecutors openly revolted against Holder's support of the Smarter Sentencing Act, a modest sentencing reform bill.[184]

In his final full year in office, Obama sought to burnish his image with respect to the opioid epidemic. His surgeon general issued a report on substance abuse that emphasized the need for a public health approach to stem the opioid epidemic. The report included recommendations to rapidly scale up state-of-the-art treatment, curtail stigmas surrounding addiction, and expand access to naloxone, the opioid-overdose-reversal drug.[185] That July, Obama signed the Comprehensive Addiction and Recovery Act (CARA), which was hyped as "the first major federal addiction legislation in 40 years."[186] In reality, this was a modest bill with some admirable provisions, including expanding access to medication-assisted treatment (MAT) using methadone and buprenorphine (often marketed under the brand name Suboxone), the most proven and effective treatments for opioid use disorder. This measure was ultimately enacted with strong bipartisan support, but only after lawmakers had stripped the bill of much of its funding.[187]

Months later, legislation to address the opioid crisis got a second chance on Capitol Hill. The unlikely vehicle was the 21st Century Cures Act, whose original focus was regulation—or, more aptly, deregulation—of the drug and medical device industries. After the House approved the Cures Act in summer 2015, the bill came to a standstill for more than a year.[188] With public outrage mounting over the complicity of Big Pharma and the FDA in triggering the opioid crisis, it was not a politically auspicious moment to seek a radical deregulation of the drug industry.

The solution for Big Pharma and its supporters was to rebrand the Cures Act as a landmark piece of legislation to address the opioid crisis even though it was not. The original legislation did not include any provisions specifically related to opioid use disorder. The bill's champions added them to secure additional support in Congress.[189] In his final months in office, Obama embraced the Cures Act, which gave the bill critical momentum.[190]

The sprawling Cures Act was one of the most lobbied health-care bills in recent history.[191] The legislation included controversial provisions to radically relax federal requirements for drug approval and marketing that industry lobbyists had been seeking for years and that would save pharmaceutical companies billions of dollars. It also weakened the requirements for approval of medical devices—"an area long criticized for lack of rigor as compared with drug evaluations."[192] Knowledgeable critics of the bill, including scientific researchers and consumer advocates, argued that the legislation dramatically watered down the scientific standards of evidence used to evaluate the efficacy and safety of new drugs, new medical devices, and new uses for existing drugs.[193] They warned that this watering down would open the market to more drugs and devices that were ineffective or dangerous.[194]

The legislation also diminished the FDA's ability to challenge off-label claims made in marketing drugs to patients and doctors. This change would likely expand "the number of drugs physicians prescribe based on weaker evidence" about their safety and efficacy.[195] Furthermore, the measure shielded a wide swath of medical and health-care devices from government oversight and from requirements to protect patient and consumer privacy. It granted manufacturers more freedom to use, store, share, and possibly sell private health information without the knowledge, let alone the informed consent, of the patient or consumer.[196] The Cures Act also included a "grab bag of goodies" to overwhelm or disarm its opponents. Billions of dollars in new funding for the National Institutes of Health, for example, helped quell opposition in the scientific community to watering down standards for the approval of drugs and medical devices.[197]

Senate Majority Leader Mitch McConnell (R-KY) designated the Cures Act as a priority for the lame-duck Congress after the 2016 election. The legislation sailed through Congress, receiving only five nays in the Senate, including from Senators Elizabeth Warren (D-MA) and Bernie Sanders (I-VT). Warren railed against the bill, charging that it had been "hijacked" by the pharmaceutical industry.[198] Obama, however, lauded the bill, singling out the $1 billion in new funding over the next two years to treat the opioid crisis as the legislation's crowning achievement.[199] In reality, this was a trivial amount given the scope of the crisis. It was a far cry from the $100 billion in new spending in the 1990 Ryan White Comprehensive AIDS Resources Emergency Act (CARE), which helped staunch the AIDS epidemic.[200]

Numerous states planned to use Cures Act money not for treatment but to establish opioid task forces. Police, prosecutors, and judges dominated these task forces and promoted "carceral and wasteful responses to the crisis, especially in the hard-hit states."[201] States intended to use only a tiny proportion of the Cures Act money to mitigate the opioid crisis in prisons and jails.[202]

The Legislative War on Opioids

The successful string of ballot initiatives and other measures to decriminalize or legalize marijuana has prompted many commentators to prematurely declare that the beginning of the end of the wars on drugs is in sight. But even as many states and municipalities have been decriminalizing or legalizing marijuana and reducing penalties for some other substances, they have been increasing the already harsh penalties for the use and sale of opioids, notably heroin, fentanyl, and fentanyl analogues, and excluding these drugs from reform measures to lessen the penalties for drug offenses.[203] For example, in 2014, Louisiana lawmakers approved a ten-year mandatory minimum sentence for the sale of *any* amount of heroin.[204] Nine years later, Louisiana bolstered the state's already stiff penalties for drug crimes, including making more drug offenses subject to mandatory life sentences.[205] In early 2024, lawmakers in

Oregon rolled back the state's pioneering law to decriminalize possession of small amounts of drugs for personal use—including heroin and cocaine—and beefed up enforcement of drug-related offenses.[206]

As fentanyl infiltrated the illicit drug market, federal and state legislators and policymakers from both parties treated this synthetic opioid and its analogues as the new crack. They demonized fentanyl and the people who use and sell it. Many lawmakers who say they favor scaling back mass incarceration have nonetheless been supportive of "extremely harsh measures for fentanyl, undercutting the effectiveness of criminal justice reforms."[207] Since so much of the illegal drug market is now adulterated or contaminated with fentanyl, the potential reach of these new measures is enormous. As in previous drug wars, these tougher sanctions have ended up ensnaring primarily users and small-time dealers—not the promised drug "kingpins."[208]

After falling steadily for nearly two decades, federal drug convictions began rising in 2021 and continued to climb. With the sharp drop in federal marijuana convictions, fentanyl and meth cases drove most of the increases.[209] Sentences have eased for some federal drug crimes, but not for offenses involving opioids and methamphetamines.[210] Fentanyl was cause for the US Sentencing Commission (USSC) to backpedal on reducing penalties for drug crimes.[211] Tougher federal sanctions for fentanyl-related offenses have disproportionately ensnared African American and Latino people. Those convicted were overwhelmingly street-level dealers or mules, not major traffickers.[212]

Paralleling developments at the national level, state lawmakers have introduced hundreds of bills to toughen up penalties for fentanyl offenses and to explicitly exclude fentanyl from proposals to reduce penalties for drug violations. Many of these tough-on-fentanyl measures have attracted bipartisan support. Lawmakers have even pressed to have fentanyl declared a weapon of terrorism or mass destruction. State lawmakers have relaxed penalties for possession of many types of drugs while stiffening sanctions for drug distribution. But since many drug users are petty dealers who sell drugs to support their habit, enhancing penalties for distribution renders many users vulnerable to harsher punishments.[213]

Prosecution of Drug-Induced Homicides

A provision in the 1986 Anti–Drug Abuse Act, one of the signature pieces of drug warrior legislation from the Reagan era, has become a key weapon in today's war on people who use opioids. This landmark legislation, which Congress swiftly enacted after the cocaine-related death of Len Bias, a National Basketball Association recruit, is best known for its infamous 100-to-1 disparity in punishment for possession of powder cocaine compared to crack cocaine. But this legislation also included a provision that carries a mandatory minimum of twenty years in prison for illicit drug distribution "if death or serious bodily injury results from the use of such substance."[214]

During the 1980s, many states copied this federal statute and enacted so-called drug-induced homicide laws of their own. But for a quarter century, these federal and state measures lay moribund, with no or just a handful of such prosecutions each year in the 1980s and 1990s. In the early aughts, drug-induced homicide prosecutions began rising, totaling one or two dozen in most years.[215] Over the last decade or so, they have skyrocketed as local, state, and federal officials have championed lodging homicide charges against people who gave or sold drugs to someone who then died of an accidental overdose.[216] Under these statutes, prosecutors generally do not need to prove that the defendant intended to kill someone with the drug or that they knew about the drug overdose or were even present when it occurred.

After the US Supreme Court upheld the conviction of Marcus Burrage in a federal drug-induced homicide case in 2014, the Justice Department under Eric Holder pointedly recommended pursuing more such prosecutions.[217] Between 2010 and 2017, drug-induced homicide cases surged at least tenfold at the state level, numbering over seven hundred in 2017 alone. Some of the states hit hardest by the opioid crisis, notably Pennsylvania and Ohio, have led the nation in these prosecutions.[218] As of 2023, some thirty states had specific drug-induced homicide laws on the books, and at least three dozen states had used these statutes or various felony murder or manslaughter laws to prosecute accidental overdose deaths as criminal homicides.[219] In 2018, Florida revised its drug-induced homicide statute to make distribution of fentanyl and fentanyl-like substances that results in an overdose death a first-degree homicide offense punishable by death or life imprisonment.[220]

Drug-induced homicide laws are selectively enforced. They disproportionately target people of color, but many white people have also been prosecuted under them. As more police officers and prosecutors treat overdoses as crime scenes, the defendants they typically ensnare with these laws are not big-time drug dealers. Finding family members, partners, friends, coworkers, or acquaintances who may have used or purchased drugs with the overdose victim is key to successfully prosecuting drug fatalities as homicides, according to prosecutors. "You want to get them while the teardrops are warm," one New Jersey prosecutor advised colleagues in a chilling comment.[221]

There is not a "*shred of evidence*" that drug-induced homicide statutes and prosecutions are stemming the tide of overdose deaths.[222] Indeed, these measures have exacerbated the opioid crisis. Pursuing homicide charges in drug overdose cases is resource intensive. As police, prosecutors, and the courts devote more personnel and other resources to these cases, public health agencies, nonprofit organizations, and medical personnel tasked with providing treatment and other services, including distributing the overdose-reversal drug naloxone, are operating "in an environment of extreme scarcity."[223] Drug-induced homicide prosecutions also undermine "Good Samaritan" laws that provide some criminal immunity for people who seek emergency assistance for an overdose victim.[224]

Pregnant Women, New Parents, and the Opioid Crisis

As in prior wars on drugs, pregnant women with substance use issues are once again widely viewed as criminals deserving severe sanctions.[225] The practice of prosecuting women for substance abuse during pregnancy began in earnest during the moral panic over crack in the late 1980s and disproportionately affected Black women. More recently, given the racial disparities of opioid use disorder, white women have been more likely to be arrested and prosecuted for substance abuse during pregnancy.[226]

District attorneys have deployed child abuse and chemical endangerment laws to prosecute pregnant women who use opioids and other drugs. Their efforts discourage pregnant women from seeking treatment "even in the 19 states where a publicly funded drug-treatment program specifically for pregnant women exists."[227] Medical providers have referred thousands of new mothers under treatment for opioid use disorder with methadone or buprenorphine to child welfare authorities. Law enforcement and child protective services often put the lives of these new parents under a microscope. Judges and caseworkers pressure them to discontinue these and other medications. In some cases, new parents are forced to place their infants in foster care temporarily or even permanently after their parental rights are terminated.[228]

For years, federal drug laws required medical providers to inform the authorities if a newborn was "affected by" an illegal substance. The 2016 Comprehensive Addiction and Recovery Act upended this long-standing federal child welfare policy by requiring medical providers to notify the authorities when a newborn is "affected by" *any* substance, whether legal or illicit.[229] Law-makers claimed that the purpose of the change was to channel mothers with a prescription opioid problem into services and treatment. The CARA did not require that these referrals to child welfare services trigger child abuse investigations. But it did grant states leeway to implement the law as they saw fit. Many states chose to expand their child abuse reporting mandate to include use of any prescribed medicines, including drugs approved for treating substance use disorder, as well as other drugs, including antidepressants and antianxiety medications. Some women even found themselves under state scrutiny for suspected fentanyl use after receiving an epidural with fentanyl to relieve pain during labor.[230]

Scientific and medical authorities agree that MAT with methadone or buprenorphine is generally safe for pregnant women and their fetuses, and that the withdrawal symptoms for newborns are modest if properly managed. They also agree that forcing pregnant women to discontinue MAT puts them and their fetuses at greater risk because withdrawal can trigger miscarriages, premature births, and other complications. Furthermore, discontinuation of MAT during pregnancy or after birth can destabilize women's lives, putting them at greater risk of relapsing and losing their jobs and homes.[231]

Parents of infants and toddlers who are Black, Indigenous, or of mixed race are more likely to have their parental rights permanently terminated.[232] White people are more likely to regain custody because they tend to have greater financial and other resources to challenge the legal system and meet the conditions demanded by caseworkers. But even if new parents do not lose custody permanently of their children, investigations by child protective services and law enforcement are traumatic ordeals that cause some of them to relapse. "It's like a sick game," said one mother whose infant was removed for eight months. "They don't want you on illicit street drugs, so here, we're going to give you this medication. But then if you take this medicine, we are going to punish you for it and ruin your family."[233]

In another punitive turn, prosecutors and policymakers have intensified their efforts to forcibly institutionalize pregnant women and other people with substance abuse problems under civil commitment statutes, a practice opposed by the Association of Addiction Personnel.[234] Many women incarcerated in state prisons and jails have been "involuntarily committed to treatment, either by family or themselves in order to avoid a criminal charge" or to access scarce treatment services.[235] Family members are often unaware that involuntarily committing their loved ones frequently results in incarceration because of the lack of community-based treatment beds. Compulsory treatment does not necessarily ameliorate opioid use disorder or reduce recidivism and may even put people with drug problems at a greater risk of a fatal overdose.[236]

Involuntary commitment is highly punitive. In some cases, drug courts and other legal authorities are permitted to force people who have not even been charged with any drug crime into involuntary treatment. Some involuntary commitment centers for substance abuse are located inside local jails. Florida's involuntary commitment statute is technically not a criminal statute, yet police officers have deployed "full coercive force" to serve warrants issued under the law, which has had "severe consequences."[237]

At the municipal level, eviction proceedings are another noncriminal but highly popular punitive weapon in the latest war on drugs and people who use them. So-called drug house ordinances set in motion eviction proceedings based on allegations of drug activity, which can include a report of a single overdose. A drug arrest—not just a conviction—can be cause enough to evict a tenant. These so-called drug nuisance ordinances have contributed to a rise in homelessness.[238]

The Drug Trade and Business as Usual

For decades, an overriding goal of the many US wars on drugs has been to reduce the number of drug users by shutting down the supply of illicit drugs. But the illegal drug distribution system at home and abroad "is not a centrally controlled hierarchy vulnerable to decapitation."[239] Eliminating the supply of an extremely lucrative product that can be readily produced with sophisticated technology and easily moved across borders through regular ports of entry is next to impossible.[240] As interdiction efforts disrupt the supply chains in a neighborhood, city, country, or region, others quickly form to take their place.[241] A militarized border wall costing billions of dollars would be no match for stopping all the heroin imported from Mexico each year, which "could fit in about 2,000 pieces of luggage." And the fentanyl supply is "even more compact and harder to interdict."[242]

Despite hundreds of billions of dollars spent on interdicting drugs from overseas, the supply of illicit drugs has remained steady in the United States. The plummeting price of many street drugs over the last few decades is compelling evidence that interdiction has not done much to stem supply. But the forever wars on drugs grind on. Longtime drug warriors continue to promise light at the end of the tunnel as they push for more weapons and personnel to interdict the supply, rather than for investing more in treatment and harm reduction to stem the demand and mitigate the destruction. In a 2017 article published in a mainstream foreign policy journal, two directors of drug policy under President George W. Bush applauded how poppy production in Afghanistan fell as US troop levels surged more than threefold between 2007 and 2012. They ignored, however, that opioid overdose deaths in the United States continued to surge during those years as well.[243]

American-led interdiction efforts in Mexico, Afghanistan, and elsewhere have had only minimal impact on the supply of illegal drugs in the United States but have had brutal consequences in drug-producing countries.[244] They have fueled violence and corruption and enriched armed groups, including drug cartels and local militias. Agricultural and economic development programs intended to get drug producers to switch to other livelihoods have not been that successful. Programs that seek to eradicate crops of opium poppies and coca plants have failed to stem the supply of illegal drugs but have hastened environmental degradation and destabilized local economies.

In 1971, President Richard Nixon became the first president to officially declare a war on drugs. But the country has been fighting a series of wars on drugs at home and abroad since the late nineteenth century. Nixon, who singled out drug abuse as "public enemy number one," was a complicated drug warrior.[245] He was instrumental in passage of the Controlled Substances Act in 1970 (which stiffened penalties for drug crimes and fostered the federalization of drug policy) and in the establishment of the DEA to ramp up interdiction efforts. But he also earmarked two-thirds of his drug policy budgets for treatment and prevention and only one-third for law enforcement and interdiction.[246] No US president since Nixon has designated such a large portion of federal resources to address the demand side, not the supply side, of the drug problem.[247]

As the opioid epidemic took off in the early aughts, President George W. Bush called for more treatment slots. But federal drug dollars continued to flow disproportionately to law enforcement and interdiction, not treatment and harm reduction, during his administration.[248] In 2004, the United States even threatened to stop funding the UN Office on Drug Control if its executive director did not vow to stop supporting harm reduction programs.[249] Under Obama, federal spending on drug treatment and prevention increased, but federal spending on drug control, including interdiction, increased even more.[250] Only in 2016, Obama's final full year in office, did the White House propose to spend, for the first time in decades, more money on treatment and research than on enforcement and interdiction.[251] Five years later, for the first time in decades, the ONDCP allocated slightly more money for prevention and treatment than for law enforcement and interdiction.[252]

American interdiction efforts to cut off the illegal drug supply from overseas and at home remain the "eternal hope" that drives US drug policy.[253] These militarized policies rob the United States of money and other resources that could be better spent on treatment, prevention, and addressing the underlying socioeconomic conditions that have fostered the opioid crisis, as discussed in the next chapter. They also deflect political and public attention from how the US domestic drug cartel—that is, the US drug companies that manufacture and distribute opioids—has committed social murder on a grand scale and, like the culprits in the financial and foreclosure crises, has not suffered the consequences.

Leading culprits in the opioid crisis have carried on business as usual. The White House, lawmakers, and regulators have failed to rein in the pharmaceutical companies, curb the conflicts of interest, or strengthen the weak regulatory regime that triggered and fostered the opioid epidemic. Faced with a public health catastrophe, lawmakers and policymakers have approved trivial amounts to expand treatment and harm reduction programs, as detailed in the next chapter. They have not deployed their fiscal and regulatory might to compel states, local governments, health-care providers, and insurers to significantly improve access to the most proven and effective treatments for opioid use disorder. "The crisis we face is not opioids," laments Dr. Kimberly Sue, medical director of the Harm Reduction Coalition. "The crisis we face is a war on people who use drugs and on our reliance on incarceration as a catch-all policy solution."[254]

11

Undertreated and Mistreated

THE OPIOID CRISIS AND A NATION IN PAIN

You can't put a dead person into recovery. It doesn't work that way.

—ROSALIND PICHARDO[1]

THE SURGE in law enforcement to stem the opioid crisis has not been matched by a surge in access to proven treatments in the United States. If current trends continue, about a million people in this country will succumb to fatal drug overdoses over the next decade. And millions more will be at greater risk of major health issues, including renal failure, heart problems, pulmonary infections, and cognitive disorders, after surviving a drug overdose.[2]

The United States is leagues behind Canada and Western Europe in embracing harm reduction strategies that save lives and help repair families and communities, including access to the overdose-reversal drug naloxone, needle exchange programs to reduce the spread of infectious diseases, safe drug consumption sites, and medication-assisted (MAT) treatment with methadone and buprenorphine. A bleak marker of this failure is that the US overdose death rate was eighteen times that of the European Union in 2021. Had the US rate matched that of Portugal, the number of US drug fatalities in 2021 would have been around twenty-three hundred instead of nearly 107,000 fatalities.[3]

The harm reduction approach centers on providing wide access to effective treatments for substance use disorder and on mitigating the harms caused to people who use drugs and to their families and communities. Harm reduction approaches recognize that some people are unable or unwilling to stop using drugs; others are struggling to stop using but will likely experience several relapses on the road to recovery.[4]

Unlike during the early stages of the HIV/AIDS epidemic in the 1980s and 1990s, experts know what works to treat opioid use disorder and to stem its dangerous and lethal consequences for individuals and communities. Yet millions of people with opioid problems do not have access to high-quality treatment.[5] Despite a marked rise in treatment capacity since the early aughts, opioid use disorder goes largely untreated in the United States. Federal, state, and local funding for treatment is grossly inadequate.[6]

Pervasive and multiple stigmas associated with substance use disorder keep people from seeking treatment, let alone proven and effective treatments such as MAT.[7] Survey respondents overwhelmingly characterize individuals who use opioids as worthless and not deserving.[8] High rates of public stigma toward people who use drugs illicitly are also major obstacles to forging solutions based on harm reduction and not higher doses of law enforcement and punishment.[9] In the face of the country's deadliest drug crisis, journalists persisted in portraying opioid use disorder as primarily a criminal matter rather than as a treatable medical condition. Frames that emphasize prevention, harm reduction, and MAT have only recently been gaining ground on ones that emphasize criminality and law enforcement.[10] In states with high opioid overdose rates, local news coverage still tends to emphasize the negative rather than the positive aspects of MAT for opioid use disorder.[11]

Lack of health insurance is a formidable barrier to treatment despite passage of the Affordable Care Act (ACA) in 2010 and the subsequent expansion of Medicaid. Shortages of providers and programs keep timely and efficacious care out of reach. So do cumbersome insurance and government rules.[12] Public misinformation about and ideological opposition to treating opioid use disorder with methadone or buprenorphine are additional hurdles. An estimated half of all Americans, including many substance use counselors, are unaware that proven treatments, notably MAT, exist for this disorder.[13] Even though opioid use disorder has been a major issue for the US military, veterans and active-duty personnel face insurance and other barriers to receiving MAT that mimic those faced by the general population.[14]

Medical training in substance use disorder is shockingly lacking in medical schools and residency programs. Consequently, physicians feel unprepared to diagnose and treat this disorder and do not view themselves as critical players in providing treatment for it. Furthermore, doctors share many of the wider public's stigmas about people with substance use disorder and the use of MAT to treat opioid use disorder.[15]

The Affordable Care Act, nicknamed Obamacare, fostered access to treatment for substance use disorder in critical ways. Thanks to the ACA, millions of people without health insurance gained coverage through private insurance policies subsidized by the government. Millions more became eligible for Medicaid because of a provision in the ACA that required states to expand the country's primary government-funded health-care program for low-income people. The ACA also strengthened existing requirements that insurance policies cover mental health problems on par with other health problems, such as diabetes or high blood pressure. Obamacare also forbade insurers from denying coverage based on a known drug or alcohol problem. Under the Biden administration, the Labor Department finally began enforcing these legal requirements.[16]

Although the ACA requires state Medicaid programs and private insurers to cover substance use disorder, it grants them wide leeway to determine which specific services are covered. Many states do not cover all levels of care required for effective treatment of opioid use disorder as defined by the American Society of Addiction Medicine.[17] Residents of states that chose to expand Medicaid coverage under the ACA have better access to treatment for substance use disorder but not necessarily access to MAT with methadone or buprenorphine.

Long-term use of methadone or buprenorphine is considered the gold standard of care for treatment of opioid use disorder.[18] Outpatient treatment with these medications is more effective and considerably cheaper than long-term inpatient treatment at a residential facility.[19] The research is compelling that people prescribed methadone or buprenorphine are more likely to stay in treatment, to reduce their use of other drugs (such as heroin and prescription pain pills), and to refrain from criminal activities compared to people undergoing other kinds of treatment.[20] They also have better interpersonal relations, higher rates of employment, and lower rates of relapses, overdoses, and transmission of infectious diseases. If properly administered, these medications cut the death rate from opioid use disorder by half.[21]

Methadone and buprenorphine are known as opioid agonists, for they bind to, rather than shield, the receptors in the brain that crave opioids. If properly prescribed and monitored, opioid substitution treatment with these drugs reduces withdrawal symptoms and cravings for opioids without getting people high or making them groggy, allowing them to stabilize and rebuild their lives. While MAT has a better record than abstinence-based or residential treatment programs in reducing relapses and fatal overdoses, relapse is still common.

Medication-assisted treatment is based on the recognition that opioid use disorder is a chronic and relapsing condition that often requires long-term or even lifelong treatment with maintenance drugs in ways similar to treating diabetes with insulin. Good MAT programs typically supplement these medications with mental health counseling.

Medication-assisted treatment has a controversial history. When the Food and Drug Administration (FDA) approved methadone for the treatment of addiction in the early 1970s, it imposed arguably the strictest regulations for any medication distributed on an outpatient basis.[22] President Richard Nixon endorsed methadone maintenance programs as key artillery in his war on drugs and in his efforts to address reportedly high rates of heroin addiction among US military personnel returning home after serving in Vietnam.[23] Between 1970 and 1973, the number of people in treatment for opioid addiction rose eightfold nationally. But infighting among federal agencies, escalating law-and-order rhetoric by politicians and other public figures, and a public backlash against methadone spurred a drop in government and public support for methadone treatment programs.[24] A quarter century later, a National Academy of Sciences (NAS) report lamented how the strict federal and local regulations on methadone put "too much emphasis on protecting society *from* methadone, and not enough on protecting society from the epidemics of addiction, violence, and infectious diseases that methadone can help reduce."[25]

The roots of the early public backlash against methadone were complex and had racial overtones. In the 1960s and 1970s, the long history of abuse or neglect of African American people in federally funded health and research programs—including forced sterilizations, the decades-long Tuskegee syphilis study, and the neglect of sickle cell anemia—came to light. These revelations fostered distrust in government-sponsored health programs, including methadone treatment, among African American people.[26] Some Black people in urban areas, where most pilot methadone programs were located, viewed methadone with skepticism or outright hostility, denouncing it "as a tool of social control and oppression."[27] Black politicians and journalists castigated methadone as "chemical slavery" that was "honky's way of keeping black men hooked." The Congressional Black Caucus raised concerns about the long-term effects of methadone and characterized it as an "alternative" to addiction, not a "cure."[28] Egged on by politicians staking out tough, racially charged law-and-order stances, some members of the public falsely blamed methadone clinics that were sprouting up in urban areas for surges in crime and immoral behavior.[29]

Until recently, methadone was available only through highly regulated clinics that "often resemble Soviet breadlines." People were forced to endure long public lines to receive their daily doses at bleak, specialized clinics with limited hours and services.[30] Methadone was nicknamed "orange handcuffs" because of the orange juice people typically drank it with during mandated daily visits that disrupted their work and family lives.[31]

The restrictions on prescribing and dispensing methadone contrasted sharply with the loose regulations placed on OxyContin and other new high-dosage opioid pain pills that began hitting the market in the late 1990s. Doctors, nurse practitioners, and physician assistants were permitted to prescribe these highly addictive pills without any specialized training or certification in their use (or abuse). As one state official in New York explained, if you want prescription pain pills, "limp into the ER and when they ask you how much pain you have say seven and you'll get it. But if you want methadone it's regulated as if it were weapons-grade plutonium."[32]

In 2002, the FDA approved buprenorphine for substance use treatment under the brand names Suboxone and Subutex. This marked the first approval of an opioid for this purpose since methadone was sanctioned in 1972. Physicians were required to receive extensive training and be certified by the Drug Enforcement Administration in order to prescribe buprenorphine. The DEA also placed strict limits on the number of opioid patients a physician was allowed to treat with buprenorphine.[33]

Lack of access to MAT with methadone or buprenorphine remains a huge problem in the United States, especially for residents in rural and remote areas, low-income people, and individuals without health insurance.[34] African American people are more likely to be channeled into community methadone clinics that operate outside of the main health-care system while white people are more likely to receive a prescription for buprenorphine, which allows them to take the pill on their own.[35] People residing in small rural communities are more reluctant than urban residents are to seek treatment of any kind for opioid use disorder because they are more likely to know medical providers in other contexts.[36]

Not only do most substance abuse treatment centers neglect to offer MAT, but they "often actively dissuade patients from accessing these medications."[37] Some programs even refuse to admit people already taking buprenorphine or methadone.[38] Insurers and government programs, notably Medicaid, have been reluctant to stop reimbursing drug treatment programs and facilities that do not offer MAT maintenance using methadone or buprenorphine and that do not provide patients with informed consent about the effectiveness of these medications. The clinics and doctors' offices that treat substance use disorder with methadone or buprenorphine often have long wait lists.

Ideological and political opposition to MAT is fierce in the United States, including in states and communities with major opioid and overdose problems. Some public officials and members of law enforcement even oppose providing the police and public with Narcan, the overdose-reversal nasal spray. One sheriff in a county in Ohio hard hit by the opioid crisis declared that his deputies would never carry Narcan. "I'm not the one that decides if people live or die. They decide that when they stick the needle in their arm," he remarked.[39] A city councilman in that same county proposed a kind of three-strikes-and-you're-out policy for people who repeatedly overdose. One too many overdoses and the authorities would not send an ambulance to revive them.[40] West Virginia, which has one of the country's highest rates of fatal drug overdoses, prohibited Medicaid coverage of methadone; set a lifetime cap on access to buprenorphine; blocked establishment of new methadone clinics; and, as HIV/AIDS infections surged, made it more difficult for programs to supply clean syringes.[41]

There is a widespread misperception that prescribing methadone or buprenorphine is just replacing one addiction with another. Although people undergoing MAT for opioid use disorder do become physically dependent on methadone or buprenorphine, "this is distinct from addiction—which is defined as compulsive use of a drug despite harm."[42] Many critics of MAT view "abstinence as the only true recovery—even though abstinence treatment has not been shown to reduce mortality and is less effective than medication at preventing relapse."[43] Abstinence-only programs—including Narcotics Anonymous, founded on the twelve-step method pioneered by Alcoholics Anonymous—predominate in many public and private treatment programs. These twelve-step programs often shun people who are taking medications to treat their opioid use disorder.[44]

The tight restrictions on buprenorphine and even tighter restrictions on methadone partly stem from outsized concerns that people with opioid use disorder will divert these medications to the illegal drug market. Companies that specialize in the lucrative business of providing inpatient or residential treatment have exploited such concerns to thwart the expansion of outpatient MAT programs. But the reality is that many people who turn to the black market to secure buprenorphine often do so out of a desperate need to avoid withdrawal symptoms, not to get high. Lacking health insurance or access to medical providers, they are unable to secure a legitimate prescription for the medication.[45] For people accustomed to heroin or oxycodone, the high provided by buprenorphine is generally a letdown.

Some poorly run clinics that were little more than mass pill dispensaries gave buprenorphine and well-run clinics a bad name. These shoddy providers did not drug test clients or mandate counseling, and they coprescribed benzodiazepines, which can give people a potentially dangerous "Cadillac high."[46] Some cash-only clinics oversubscribed buprenorphine, "fully knowing" that patients "would sell some on the black market so they could afford to return for the next visit."[47] As a result, buprenorphine became stigmatized as "just another pill being sold on the street."[48]

The 2016 Cures Act expressed a clear intention to prioritize increased access to methadone and buprenorphine and evidence-based treatments.[49] But it did not mandate access by, for example, requiring state Medicaid programs to include MAT as a covered benefit.[50] The grant program of the Cures Act did not specifically prohibit funding "abstinence-based or other unscientific treatment approaches."[51] As a consequence, some of the states hardest hit by the opioid crisis used their Cures Act money to fund treatment services and programs that did not appear "to align with the spirit (or, in some cases, the letter)" of the legislation and that were potentially harmful.[52]

Thanks to provisions in the 2016 Comprehensive Addiction and Recovery Act (CARA) and the 2018 SUPPORT Act, the number of clinicians authorized by the DEA to administer buprenorphine more than doubled between December 2017 and July 2020. But access is still a major issue.[53] The SUPPORT Act also included important changes in Medicaid to make MAT more available but did not substantially increase funding to address the opioid crisis.[54] In many states, the various pools of federal money allocated for opioid treatment went unused.[55] After the pandemic struck, federal authorities further eased some of the rules for administering buprenorphine and methadone. They have since made some of these changes permanent. But many states have retained more stringent regulations than those required by federal law. By the end of 2023, the total number of people on buprenorphine had barely budged.[56]

The obstacles to timely and efficacious treatment for opioid use disorder are formidable even in well-resourced states that have made some of the greatest strides in reducing the insurance, financial, and other barriers to treatment. For example, treatment is still "difficult or impossible" to access in New York State because of underlying obstacles, including severe staffing shortages, lack of access to transportation, providers' refusal to treat people with co-occurring substance abuse and mental health disorders, and the lack of detox facilities in many hospitals.[57] In one promising state-level development, North Carolina established a pilot program that permits local pharmacists to oversee the ongoing care of people stabilized on buprenorphine with the initial help of physicians.[58]

Methadone and buprenorphine have been much more widely available in other Western countries. Doctors in Britain, Australia, and Canada have been prescribing methadone to be taken at home since the 1960s.[59] Facing a widespread heroin problem, in 1995 France became the first European Union country to approve buprenorphine for the treatment of opioid use disorder. Opioid overdose deaths plummeted in France as buprenorphine became widely available through general practitioners and community pharmacies.[60]

Party Politics and Treatment and Prevention

The US opioid crisis fostered a major policy and political dilemma for the Republican Party. The rate of fatal opioid overdoses was generally higher in states that Donald Trump won in 2016, and residents of those states favored more federal spending to address the epidemic.[61] Furthermore, Republican-led states at the epicenter of the opioid crisis have faced growing pressures to expand Medicaid to treat the epidemic. At the same time, these states have had to contend with strong political headwinds from national leaders of the Republican Party and their wealthy network of donors, including the billionaire Koch brothers, who staunchly opposed the ACA and Medicaid expansion. Since passage of the ACA in 2010, the Republican Party and its supporters have turned to the courts and Congress numerous times to repeal this legislation outright or, that failing, to dismember it through a war of attrition. In their most significant legal victory to date, the US Supreme Court ruled in 2012 that the Medicaid mandate was unconstitutional, rendering expansion voluntary, not mandatory, for states.[62]

States under Republican control have enacted comparatively more opioid-related legislation and appropriated more money for prevention and treatment initiatives than Democratic-led ones.[63] The opioid crisis has also been a crucial driver for at least sixteen Republican-led states to break ranks and participate in Medicaid expansion under the ACA.[64] On the surface, these actions suggest that the Republican Party is tending to its base, taking a more sympathetic stance toward the opioid crisis because its white constituents are most at risk.

But a closer look reveals that this is another instance of policy theater in which there has been a lot of motion but no real movement to expand access to state-of-the-art treatment for opioid use disorder to curtail the crisis.

Although Republican-led states enacted more legislation related to the treatment and prevention of opioid use disorder than Democratic ones did between 2014 and 2018, these measures tended to be low-hanging fruit that was not politically or fiscally costly. They included bills to raise public awareness of the opioid crisis, implement prescription drug monitoring programs, and increase access to naloxone, the overdose-reversal drug. None of these initiatives substantially expanded access to treatment, let alone to the most effective and proven treatments. In short, the policy response was "active but meager."[65] Republican-controlled states did devote a higher proportion of their state spending to these opioid initiatives than Democratic-controlled ones did, but the total amounts were trivial, averaging well below $1 million per year.[66] By comparison, state spending on treatment for opioid use disorder in states that opted to expand Medicaid coverage has been much higher than in states that did not. So are the rates of Medicaid recipients receiving MAT.[67]

Republican states that opted into Medicaid expansion under the ACA pursued "expand and retrench" strategies, seeking to put a conservative stamp on their actions.[68] Republican states, including those that did not choose to expand Medicaid under the ACA, also jiggered their existing Medicaid programs to collect more federal dollars for the treatment of opioid use disorder—but again with a conservative imprimatur. They traveled a path of "hidden politics" that allowed them "to target the needs of their base and other key patient and provider stakeholders, without suffering any political repercussions from using a program they otherwise condemn."[69] These states channeled the extra federal money they received into treatment programs that were in sync with the dominant ideology of the Republican Party, but that were not the most efficacious means to treat substance use disorder.

For example, in response to the opioid crisis, the federal government added "recovery support" to the list of services eligible for federal reimbursement under Medicaid. Federal administrators defined recovery support to encompass a wide range of services, including practical support for housing and employment, as well as emotional support provided by individual mentors and peer-led support groups. (People who are homeless are at a much higher risk for fatal and nonfatal overdoses, as well as other health problems associated with substance use disorder.)[70] Republican-led states were more likely than Democratic-led ones to add recovery support services to their Medicaid programs. But they eschewed adding those recovery services, notably housing and employment support, that address major structural problems that impede successful treatment for drug dependency and addiction.

Instead, they embraced peer-led recovery services, which tend to focus on individual behavior, personal responsibility, and faith-based recovery. The peer-centered approach is more compatible with a conservative view of substance use disorder as primarily an individual failing rather than a problem with societal or biological roots. Furthermore, centering recovery support on peers is relatively inexpensive and serves to delegitimize formal substance use disorder services that require expertise, notably medication-assisted treatment.[71]

Republican-led Florida provides one of the most egregious examples of playing to your base of conservative voters and wealthy and corporate patrons at the cost of people desperate for good treatment for their substance use problems. Republican lawmakers in Florida staunchly opposed expanding Medicaid under the ACA. But they have found other ways to channel billions of federal dollars to the state for substance use programs, many of which are not effective.

The Sunshine State was a pioneer decades ago in developing the "Florida model" of treatment centered on sober homes rather than more expensive residential rehab programs. People from around the state and the country would flock to these "recovery residences," where they would attend outpatient therapy—often modeled on a twelve-step program—after a stint of detox and inpatient rehab.[72] In 2019, Florida succeeded in securing a federal waiver to be permitted to use federal dollars to cover residential treatment services for Medicaid recipients with substance use disorder.[73] (The Social Security Amendments of 1965, which established Medicaid, had excluded residential treatment for substance use disorder from federal reimbursement.)

That Medicaid waiver, together with the ACA's requirement that insurers include substance use disorder as a basic benefit and provide comparable coverage for behavioral health and physical ailments, turbocharged the recovery industry in the Sunshine State and elsewhere. So did legal decisions that interpreted the mental parity requirement in the ACA and earlier legislation in expansive ways. Furthermore, the growth in public funding for health care thanks to the ACA spurred a significant rise in profits for the private health-care industry. Private equity firms rapidly expanded into the health-care sector, targeting nursing homes and behavioral health and treatment programs, which are highly lucrative and subject to little government regulation and oversight.[74]

Treatment centers for substance use disorder and other behavioral health problems, such as eating disorders, are not federally licensed and are often only loosely regulated, if at all, by the states. In Florida and many other states, these facilities are not even required to register with the authorities or to have mandatory certifications or inspections. Their counselors tend to have minimal training and experience, and their medical directors may not even be on-site. "Sober" or "safe" homes (which have been springing up in other states besides Florida) are largely unregulated.[75]

The explosive growth of loosely regulated treatment centers and unregulated sober or safe homes has been wracked with rampant fraud in Florida and elsewhere. A brisk business in patient brokering emerged in the Sunshine State, even though offering bribes, kickbacks, and commissions for referrals are first-degree felonies, punishable by up to thirty years in prison under state law. "Many patient-brokers pick up young drug users from the street," according to a firsthand account in the New Yorker about the lucrative treatment industry in Florida. "The castaways of treatment centers are easy to spot as they walk around, their bedrolls wrapped in black garbage bags, wild and disconsolate from loitering all day in the heat."[76] To pay for the kickbacks, treatment facilities and brokers push patients toward "expensive private insurance (often government subsidized)" and "may even pay insurance premiums for the duration of the treatment."[77] In Arizona, the proliferation of hundreds of unregulated and fraudulent government-funded sober homes has had a devastating impact on Indigenous people with substance use disorder, resulting in dangerous relapses and even death.[78]

In another widespread scam—the so-called liquid gold rush—treatment facilities receive kickbacks for channeling patients to expensive urine-testing labs. These labs bill insurers hundreds—or in some cases thousands—of dollars for high-tech urine drug tests even though effective lower-tech alternatives are readily available for $5 a pop. Testing a patient three times weekly can generate upward of $20,000 a month in charges to insurers.[79]

Local and state law enforcement agencies have been slow to investigate the unseemly and illegal practices of the recovery industry in Florida and elsewhere. The FBI and Justice Department eventually spun into action in one Florida case, which in 2018 resulted in the country's largest ever crackdown on health-care fraud.[80] The problem of patient brokering and kickbacks has been so extensive in Florida that, when he served in the US Senate, Marco Rubio (R-FL) was an original cosponsor of the Eliminating Kickbacks in Recovery Act (EKRA), which was part of the 2018 SUPPORT Act. The EKRA targets patient brokers who receive kickbacks and the lucrative multibillion-dollar business in "liquid gold."[81]

Substance Use Disorder in Prisons and Jails

The problem of lack of access to substance abuse treatment, let alone efficacious treatment, is especially acute for incarcerated people. Most of them do not receive good—or indeed any—treatment for their drug or alcohol problems.[82] The World Health Organization (WHO) declared in 2009 that incarcerated people with opioid use disorder should have access to methadone and buprenorphine to reduce opioid dependency, the risk of overdoses, and the harm caused by drug use, as well as to stem the cycle of incarceration and addiction.[83] A 2019 NAS report concluded that withholding MAT for any reason (including incarceration, other involvement in the criminal legal system, or the lack of supplemental behavioral therapy) is unethical.[84] Yet the overwhelming majority of jails and prisons in the United States do not provide incarcerated people with access to ongoing MAT programs.[85]

What passes for substance abuse treatment in prison can be shockingly punitive and unscientific. For example, one so-called therapeutic community in a state prison for women convicted of drug offenses deployed "confrontational and coercive tactics" that "effectively collapsed the distinction between treatment and punishment." It sought to "break down" the women, who were disproportionately African American women, claiming they suffered from "diseased selves." This program "fundamentally destabilized" how these women "understood their experiences with poverty, violence, and social marginalization" as it "shattered their sense of themselves as 'good' and 'respectable' people." The program left most of the women "worse off than they would have been had they simply done their time in the main prison," not the facility's therapeutic wing.[86]

Most county jails and prisons prohibit the use of methadone, buprenorphine, and naltrexone, the three FDA-approved pharmaceuticals for treatment of opioid use disorder.[87] Even though jails have become de facto detox centers, many of them do not even provide methadone or buprenorphine for detox, let alone for MAT maintenance programs. In about half of the country's jails, incarcerated people must endure the wrenching symptoms of opioid withdrawal without any significant medical assistance.[88]

Resource constraints, security concerns, the strong bias against harm reduction approaches, and the deep stigma surrounding MAT help explain the lack of methadone or buprenorphine treatment in prisons and jails.[89] Administrators of jails and prisons say they do not have sufficient staff to ensure that people properly take their methadone or buprenorphine and do not sell or give these medications to other incarcerated people.[90] Methadone clinics must be federally licensed, which entails a mountain of red tape and expenses for jails and prisons seeking to establish on-site treatment. Transporting incarcerated people to outside clinics for their daily dose of methadone is expensive, and many local communities lack methadone clinics anyway. Most rural areas do not have even one doctor who is certified to prescribe buprenorphine, according to an official of the National Sheriffs' Association.[91]

Most MAT programs in prisons and jails are limited to the controversial injectable drug naltrexone. Better known by its brand name, Vivitrol, naltrexone is more appealing than methadone or buprenorphine to moralistic, hardline prison administrators, politicians, and law enforcement officers because they consider it more punitive.[92] Vivitrol, which was available in an estimated three hundred jails as of 2022 or so, is typically administered to incarcerated people just as they are about to be released. It is classified as an "opioid antagonist."[93] Taken as a monthly shot, Vivitrol acts like a helmet, blocking the opioid receptors in users' brains so they do not experience feelings of euphoria associated with opioids, such as heroin, pain pills, and fentanyl (but not nonopioids like cocaine and methamphetamine). Prior to starting a Vivitrol regimen, people with opioid use disorder must undergo detoxification, thus forcing an abrupt exit rather than a more gradual one from drug dependency and addiction.[94]

Vivitrol is not popular with people with opioid use disorder because it gives them the worst of both worlds. It blocks opioids from producing feelings of euphoria and yet does not stave off withdrawal symptoms, which can be intense and even life threatening. It also does not alleviate the cravings that are obstacles to stabilization and recovery.[95] Many specialists in opioid use disorder also do not favor Vivitrol, which costs about $1,200 a month for the drug and associated services, or more than twice the cost of maintenance treatment with methadone or buprenorphine.[96] Critics charge that Vivitrol is not only more expensive than these other treatments but also less effective and more harmful.[97]

Alkermes, which manufactures Vivitrol, has aggressively marketed this drug. The company has focused its efforts on law enforcement and public officials, rather than medical providers. Alkermes has been a main sponsor of key conferences and professional meetings, including the National Association of Drug Court Professionals. Its sales representatives have targeted sheriffs managing jails and judges overseeing drug courts. In promoting Vivitrol, Alkermes executives have denigrated methadone and buprenorphine, stigmatizing them as "black market" or "street" drugs. The company has wooed sheriffs and drug court judges by portraying Vivitrol as a "miracle drug" and a "cleaner alternative," which has incensed specialists in public health and opioid use disorder.[98] The company's sales representatives have persuaded hundreds of judges overseeing drug courts to favor monthly Vivitrol injections as the main line of treatment. Alkermes has even provided free starter shots of Vivitrol for people leaving jail and for defendants in drug court, banking on Medicaid or insurance companies to pick up the expense of future monthly shots.[99]

This relatively small company has lavished campaign contributions on both political parties and made controversial marketing claims that Vivitrol is more effective than other MAT drugs.[100] The company's generous campaign contributions and aggressive marketing strategies have paid off. In May 2017, Health and Human Services Secretary Tom Price lauded Vivitrol as the future of addiction treatment during his visit to its Ohio plant. His remarks alarmed seven hundred experts in addiction, who signed a letter complaining that the company's marketing tactics and Price's remarks ignored widely accepted science.[101] In March 2018, the Trump administration announced its support of Vivitrol but not any other MAT drugs, and the stock price of Alkermes soared. Alex Azar, Price's successor, was more supportive of a wider range of MAT drugs as he likened treating opioid use disorder without medication to treating an infection without antibiotics.[102]

Incarcerated people have eked out a handful of legal victories that have forced some jails and prisons to provide methadone or buprenorphine in individual cases or in limited class-action lawsuits.[103] But no general right of access to these medications for incarcerated people has been established.[104] Federal officials have sent mixed messages on whether denying incarcerated people MAT violates the landmark 1990 Americans with Disabilities Act (ADA).[105] The Justice Department has investigated state prisons for failing to provide MAT for opioid use disorder. Meanwhile, the federal Bureau of Prisons (BOP), which is under its jurisdiction, continues to severely limit access to methadone or buprenorphine for people incarcerated in federal facilities. The 2018 First Step Act mandated that the BOP expand access to MAT and authorized tens of millions of dollars for implementation. But the mandate was vague and included no enforcement mechanism. As of mid-2021, only 268 individuals of the nearly 172,000 people incarcerated in federal prisons were receiving medications to treat opioid dependence, according to a BOP official.[106] In 2023, the Biden administration announced changes in the Medicaid program to encourage more jails and prisons to facilitate medication-assisted treatment for opioid use disorder.[107]

For people dependent on opioids, a stint in prison or jail can be a death sentence. It is harder to procure drugs in prison or jail than on the outside but far from impossible. A brisk black market for drugs—some smuggled in by visitors, most brought in by staff and outside contractors—exists in most penal facilities. As overdose deaths have soared across the country, prisons and jails have not been spared.[108] Despite skyrocketing overdose fatalities, sheriffs and guards in many jails and prisons do not have ready access to Narcan and in some cases are prohibited from carrying the overdose-reversal drug.[109]

In the first few weeks after release from prison or jail, formerly incarcerated people face an astronomical risk of a fatal overdose.[110] People discharged from state prisons in North Carolina were forty times more likely than the general population (after adjusting for age and other factors) to suffer a fatal opioid overdose during the first two weeks after they were released.[111] Only one-quarter of US jails supply overdose-reversal medicine to people who are being discharged.[112] People are at such great risk upon release because their tolerance for opioids typically plummets while they are incarcerated. Furthermore, after they get out, they often lack critical supports to reintegrate into the community and receive treatment. Many of them are ineligible for health-care services or cannot afford health insurance. Others face delays in getting enrolled in Medicaid and other health programs.[113] Providing buprenorphine treatment to incarcerated people while they are on the inside dramatically reduces their risk of overdose and death after they get out. Overdoses of people recently released from Rhode Island's penal facilities plummeted after the state made all three MAT options available in its prisons and jails.[114]

Punitive Drug Courts

Many people single out the proliferation of drug courts in the United States as evidence that the country is winding down its wars (yes, wars) on drugs. But US drug courts "serve not as an alternative, but as an *adjunct* to incarceration" as they merge criminal and therapeutic approaches in ways that have "complex and often damaging effects."[115] Drug courts, which date back to the 1980s, were once a tiny part of the criminal legal system. Since then, they have mushroomed across the country, despite little evidence that they reduce problematic drug use or crime.

A vast network of at least thirty-one hundred drug courts, which are governed by few regulations or standard procedures, operate in about half the counties in the United States.[116] These specialized courts tend to resemble community-based probation programs but include intensive court supervision, drug testing, and mandated treatment programs. Most drug courts require defendants to plead guilty as a condition of participation. If someone successfully completes the program, the plea may be removed from their records. Judges and other court personnel monitor defendants' treatment plans and compliance with the program. Drug courts have wide discretion to impose sanctions and to dictate treatment. Sanctions include short-term, or flash, incarcerations for relapses or failure to comply with the program requirements or treatment plan devised by the court.

Drug courts are one of the most studied institutions in the criminal legal system in recent years. But much of the research has major methodological flaws that cast doubt on claims that drug courts are an alternative to incarceration that saves money, reduces crime, and lowers drug use. Developers of drug court programs rather than independent researchers have conducted many of the evaluations. Studies often fail to account for how drug courts cherry-pick defendants, selecting people deemed most likely to succeed. Drug courts tend to exclude individuals charged with more serious crimes; people with high levels of addiction; defendants more likely to reoffend; and people who have struggled to succeed in other treatment programs.

Thanks to net-widening, defendants who might previously have had their cases dismissed or been sentenced to probation now end up in drug court.[117] People diverted to drug court who use drugs but are not drug dependent (such as individuals arrested for recreational use of marijuana) take up scarce treatment slots needed by people with serious substance abuse problems. The National Association of Drug Court Professionals recommends that drug courts focus their efforts on defendants who are high risk and high need.[118] But many drug courts continue to exclude whole categories of defendants, partly because prosecutors usually have the final say in who is allowed to participate in drug court.[119]

A 2013 comprehensive analysis of drug courts concluded that they reduced the number of times people were incarcerated but did not significantly reduce the amount of time they spent in custody. The widespread practice of punishing drug relapse with incarceration explains why.[120] Thanks to flash incarcerations, drug court participants do appear to have lower rates of pretrial detention but not necessarily lower rates of incarceration.[121] Individuals who successfully complete the program typically have lower rates of criminal offending, drug use, and incarceration going forward. But the longer sentences meted out to people who drop out of drug court cancel out the decreases in incarceration for people who successfully finish. "People who fail tend to do no better, or maybe even worse, than people who don't participate at all," explains one expert on drug courts.[122]

Claims that drug courts significantly reduce crime are overstated. The level of self-reported minor offenses is lower for drug court participants, but the amount of self-reported major crimes is not, according to one of the most comprehensive analyses of drug courts. Furthermore, there was no statistically significant reduction in rearrests for drug court participants.[123] Drug court participants tend to be people whose primary crime is petty possession or sale of drugs to maintain their drug habits (or both). Since many drug courts screen out drug users charged or convicted of serious or violent crimes, it is no wonder that drug courts have not yielded major reductions in serious or violent crime.

Studies claiming that drug courts save money tend to focus on two narrow measures: reductions in pretrial detention and recidivism. They do not include the full range of costs associated with drug courts, including net-widening, the use of incarceration to detox people before they are admitted to drug court, the flash incarcerations imposed by drug courts, and the harsher sentences meted out to people who drop out or are forced out of drug court.[124] They also do not include the burdensome expenses of extensive court-mandated drug testing. These expenses routinely fall on the shoulders of drug court participants, many of whom cannot afford them. Furthermore, cost-benefit studies typically compare the expense of sending someone with a substance use disorder to drug court versus the cost of incarcerating that person. These studies do not compare the cost of handling an individual's legal case and treatment through drug court to the expense of diverting that person out of the criminal legal system altogether and providing community-based treatment instead. An analysis by the Washington State Institute of Public Policy found that community-based drug treatment yielded $21 in benefits in terms of reduced crime for every dollar spent compared to drug courts, which produced only $2 in benefits for every dollar spent.[125]

Substance use specialists cast doubt on claims that drug courts represent a major turn toward harm reduction approaches to problematic drug use.[126]

Drug courts are built on a fundamental contradiction: people are reportedly being "treated" through a medical model, but the symptoms common to substance use disorder—relapses and the struggle to maintain abstinence—are treated through a penal one.[127] People who relapse while under the supervision of a drug court risk being sent to jail or prison, where they are not likely to receive adequate drug treatment or medical care.[128] People are punished not only for relapsing but also for minor infractions, such as missing therapy appointments and otherwise not following rules laid down by the drug court. And defendants who do not successfully complete drug court may face longer sentences than if they had been conventionally sentenced—up to two to five times longer, according to one study.[129]

"Courts are a good place to do" drug treatment, according to one supportive state legislator in Ohio. "You have a black robe and the threat of jail time."[130] But experts on treatment of alcohol and drug problems disagree, arguing that the threat of jail time increases the risk of relapse. "The very definition of substance-use disorder is continued and compulsive use despite negative consequences," explained one expert. It does not make sense, he said, to threaten jail for people "whose disorder by definition makes them less responsive to those consequences."[131]

Legal experts testifying before a special session of the United Nations to review global drug policy urged the international community to reject drug courts because most of them fail to follow the "best practices" in substance treatment.[132] By training, temperament, and resources, many drug courts are not well equipped to diagnose substance abuse problems, direct people to the best treatment, monitor their progress, and adjust their treatment accordingly. "In what other medical situation do judges prescribe specific treatments from the bench?" asked one substance abuse specialist. "If you get in a car crash because you're diabetic, do they prescribe a specific medication from the bench? This is the only area in medicine or health care where judges think they know more than doctors."[133]

Judges trained in law, not social work, medicine, or substance abuse, helm the drug courts. Overcrowded dockets, high staff turnover, and lack of expertise in substance abuse treatment hamper drug courts.[134] Drug court staff members are routinely called "treatment teams," even though they often lack qualified health providers with medical backgrounds, such as physicians or nurse practitioners.[135] A survey of judges and other drug court personnel revealed widespread ignorance about buprenorphine and methadone treatment, for example.[136]

Most drug court programs are founded on a model designed for treating adult white men with alcohol problems. They are inattentive to the special needs of women, teenagers, Black and Latino people, and other demographic groups.[137] Health insurance—or the lack thereof—and the availability of court-approved treatment slots often dictate the type of treatment, even if the assigned program is not the most suitable one for a drug court participant.[138] Some drug courts require participants to detox before starting treatment, forcing people to go through withdrawal in jail with no or only minimal medical supervision. Detox under these conditions subjects people to a grueling and dangerous process that puts their health at risk and can even be fatal.[139] Suing judges and court personnel for ineffective or damaging mandated treatments is an option, but few defendants do so.[140]

Drug courts run roughshod over norms and protections that are bedrocks of medical care, including privacy, confidentiality, and meaningful consent to treatment, all of which raise serious human rights concerns. Medical treatment providers typically must adhere to federal confidentiality regulations, but drug court personnel are exempt.[141] Drug courts, mental health courts, and other so-called problem-solving courts flout the norm of consent, let alone informed consent. Defendants in drug court do not receive the information they need "to understand the health consequences of both treatment and refusal of treatment."[142] The enthusiasm of drug court judges for mandatory injections of Vivitrol raises particularly troubling issues about consent. "They make you an offer you can't refuse," explains a psychiatrist who specializes in substance abuse. "People are being forced to take medication with jail over their heads."[143]

Drug court judges, who are often elected officials, tend "to reflect local cultural biases about addiction, viewing it as a moral weakness that called for tough paternalism."[144] Many drug courts prohibit medication-assisted treatment with methadone or buprenorphine for the same reasons that lawmakers and corrections officials balk at providing these medications to incarcerated people.[145] Many judges and court personnel consider MAT programs to be another form of addiction and favor an abstinence-only approach.[146] With mixed success, participants have sued drug courts to be allowed to take methadone, buprenorphine, medical marijuana, and other prescribed medications. Some drug courts prohibit participants from receiving prescribed medications for other medical conditions, including anxiety, attention deficit hyperactivity disorder (ADHD), and other chronic health problems.[147] In 2015, the federal government moved to deny some funding to drug courts that forced people already on drug maintenance therapy to stop using these medications.[148] Judges who do permit buprenorphine often impose arbitrary time limits of just weeks or months even though specialists in MAT say people with opioid use disorder typically need long-term treatment measured in years.[149]

Drug courts are a sign of just how far the United States has moved away from understanding addiction and substance use disorder as illnesses, not crimes. It is hard to imagine, but in 1962, the US Supreme Court struck down a California law that criminalized addiction, invoking the Eighth Amendment's prohibition against cruel and unusual punishments.[150] Six years later, the court reversed course somewhat but by a narrow 5–4 vote. The dissenting judges reaffirmed that criminally penalizing people for the disease of addiction violated the Eighth Amendment.[151]

Drug courts and other problem-solving courts are one of many examples of the fusion of the therapeutic and law enforcement apparatus. Parole and probation are another.[152] People with an alcohol or drug problem are often required to enroll in a treatment program in addition to all the other conditions that the criminal legal system ladles on people serving parole or probation. But treatment slots are frequently unavailable, and many people do not have health insurance or Medicaid to cover the costs. Frequent, often unannounced, drug tests are a common condition of parole and probation. So are bans on MAT, medical marijuana, and other prescribed medications. Failure to meet the conditions can land someone back in jail or prison. "They wouldn't punish a diabetic or someone with cancer, so why punish a person with a drug problem when what they really need is help and ongoing treatment?" asked one man in Philadelphia. The authorities had sent this man back to state prison for violating parole because he relapsed after arriving too late to get his drug test one day and feared being arrested under zero-tolerance policies.[153]

Treatment and Prevention in Other Countries

The United States has eschewed harm reduction strategies, including sterile needle exchange programs, supervised drug consumption sites, and wide access to good MAT, that have spared other Western countries from deadly opioid epidemics. For decades, US policymakers and lawmakers have opposed needle exchange programs even though specialists in substance abuse and public health, including the Centers for Disease Control, have championed them to curtail the spread of HIV/AIDS and other needle-borne diseases. In 1998, President Bill Clinton rejected the recommendation of Health and

Human Services Secretary Donna Shalala to rescind the nine-year-old ban on needle exchanges. He took this stance despite compelling evidence that supplying sterile needles saves lives and does not spur drug use.[154]

Faced in 2015 with a massive outbreak of HIV/AIDS among intravenous drug users, lawmakers in Congress quietly inserted a provision in an omnibus spending bill to allow the use of federal money to pay for staff and counseling to operate needle exchanges but not to purchase sterile needles.[155] In early 2022, the Biden administration's proposal to expand funding of sterile needle programs set off a political firestorm. Conservative groups falsely charged that Washington was preparing to distribute "crack pipes" paid for with tax dollars.[156] A bipartisan stampede of lawmakers introduced legislation that would bar federal funding of "drug paraphernalia."[157]

State and local prescription laws, drug paraphernalia statutes, and so-called drug free ordinances force many needle exchanges to operate illicitly or quasi-legally.[158] The few needle exchanges that do exist tend to be concentrated in large urban areas, and even there they are politically vulnerable. Shortly after taking office in 2024, Philadelphia mayor Cherelle Parker pointedly withdrew city funding for needle exchanges despite warnings from the Centers for Disease Control and Prevention (CDC) and elsewhere that an increase in HIV/AIDS and other infectious diseases would likely result.[159] Philadelphia's elected officials also pushed to curtail the operations of mobile vans and other vital programs that deliver health care and social services to people with drug-related problems in Kensington, the epicenter of the city's opioid crisis. They even pressed a landlord to stop renting space to a storefront harm reduction program.[160]

Officially sanctioned drug consumption sites have been another political and legal flashpoint in the United States.[161] At these sites, people administer their street drugs under medical supervision and receive referrals for treatment, health care, and social services without fear of being arrested. For years, federal prosecutors and other public officials have battled against such sites in court and in the court of public opinion despite compelling evidence that these sites slash the number of fatal overdoses.[162] Numerous underground safe injection sites have been operating and saving lives for years in the United States.[163] The United States had only three officially sanctioned drug consumption sites as of early 2025. Two of them are in New York City. The third one is in Providence, Rhode Island, and is the first such facility sanctioned by a state, not a municipality.[164]

More than a hundred supervised consumption sites or safe injection facilities operate in at least eleven other countries. Some of these programs have been operating for decades. These facilities have been credited with preventing the spread of infectious diseases, reducing overdose fatalities, improving the health of people who use drugs, and mitigating the harm caused by public drug consumption, including streets littered with discarded syringes and lined with people injecting drugs.[165] Heroin-assisted treatment, in which people unable to stop using heroin after exhausting all types of treatment receive prescribed heroin, has been a harm reduction strategy available for decades in several European countries and Canada. But it is a nonstarter in discussions of US drug policy even though prescribed heroin programs reduce crime and over-doses and improve the quality of life for people dependent on heroin.[166] With fentanyl and its potent analogues now coursing through the illicit drug market, Canada and some other countries have recently doubled down on harm reduc-tion. Since 2020, medical professionals in Canada have been permitted to pro-vide thousands of people with full-strength prescription opioid pain pills free of charge to protect them from the toxic risk of adulterated street drugs.[167]

Decriminalization and Legalization

The costly failures of the forever wars on drugs have bolstered the movement to legalize or at least decriminalize drugs in the United States. Calls for de-criminalization or legalization might sound good on bumper stickers or t-shirts, but they obfuscate a messier reality. After all, the opioid crisis was triggered by drugs sanctioned by government regulators, aggressively mar-keted by pharmaceutical companies, and prescribed legally—for the most part—by medical providers.

If not properly managed and regulated, legalization could be harmful, even lethal, in the context of a for-profit health-care system in which powerful drug manufacturers and distributors freely push their products with ads to consumers and inducements to medical providers; in which government regulators are docile, underresourced, and captured by the industries they are supposed to monitor; in which insurers are empowered to dictate quick, cheap fixes (such as prescribing drugs rather than talk therapy or physical therapy for mental health problems or chronic pain) that are less efficacious and have troubling, even fatal, side effects and consequences; in which so many people lack access to afford-able, high-quality health care and state-of-the art treatment for substance abuse; and in which the public health system is a skeleton of what it once was.

Scholars of drug policy generally agree that drug use increases in the wake of legalization.[168] The effects of decriminalization on drug use are less clear-cut.[169]

If the United States were to widely legalize substances such as marijuana, co-caine, and heroin, consumption of and dependence on these substances would likely increase—at least for a time. More people would experiment with these formerly illicit substances as the price fell and the social stigma attached to using them diminished. Most people would remain casual users, but for some, experimentation would result in dependency or addiction.

Some advocates of legalization argue that tight regulation of cannabis and other formerly illicit substances through government monopolies, perhaps modeled after state-controlled liquor stores, would offset some of this increase in drug use and dependency. So would imposition of high taxes on these sub-stances. That was the hope when the manufacture and sale of alcohol were legalized after Prohibition ended nearly a century ago. But the alcohol example is a sobering one. In the decades after Prohibition ended, taxes on alcohol plummeted in the United States. Today alcohol is taxed at a much lower rate in the United States than it is in much of Western Europe.[170] Many of the initial controls on alcohol in the United States, which were quite restrictive, have since been lifted under pressure from the powerful alcohol industry.[171] State-controlled stores lost out to private ones as this powerful and well-connected industry asserted itself. Well-heeled and sophisticated advertising campaigns helped make alcohol a widely popular and abused drug.

Tobacco and alcohol have done enormous harm to individuals and society. Yet proposals to substantially increase taxes on these two legal drugs and regu-late them to reduce consumption and abuse have been uphill battles. The al-cohol and tobacco industries seek to "maintain consumption, regardless of problem use" because their revenues and profits come overwhelmingly from their heaviest users, not from casual drinkers and smokers.[172] The FDA's abys-mal record in protecting teenagers and young adults from vaping since e-cigarettes came on the market nearly two decades ago is one more example of the government's abdication in the game of whac-a-mole with Big Tobacco, a major purveyor of smokeless nicotine devices.[173]

Many public health advocates contend "that alcohol and other drugs ought to be provided grudgingly by the government, not marketed aggressively by private enterprise."[174] Otherwise, the risk is great that legalization will em-power new for-profit drug producers and distributors bent on increasing con-sumption through Madison Avenue–style marketing techniques. We already have witnessed that in states that have legalized marijuana. Proposals to struc-ture the cannabis market around consumer-oriented co-ops and users growing marijuana for personal use have been losing out to Big Weed and the lure of billions of dollars in projected tax revenues from cannabis sales. So far, legal-ization of marijuana has provided some tax relief for cash-strapped states, but it has not been the promised windfall.[175]

Furthermore, the strategic use of medical marijuana as a wedge to pry open the legal market for weed has obscured mounting research document-ing marijuana's potentially harmful effects, especially for teenagers and young adults, whose brains are still developing.[176] A 2017 report sponsored by NAS concluded that marijuana use likely increased "the risk of developing schizophrenia, other psychoses, and social anxiety disorders, and to a lesser extent depression," and exacerbated other behavioral health problems in cer-tain users. The report also documented possible damage to learning, memory, and attention spans, even after people stopped using marijuana, as well as physical harms, including respiratory problems.[177]

Contrary to popular perceptions, millions of people have become addicted to cannabis and experience serious side effects from frequent use, including debilitating nausea, vomiting, and pain, and, in rare instances, even death, from cannabinoid hyperemesis syndrome. Just two of the dozens of states that have legalized cannabis have capped the level of THC permitted in most rec-reational marijuana products. (THC is the main psychoactive ingredient that produces a "high.") Only ten states require warning labels that cannabis can be habit forming, and even fewer mandate warnings about the risk of severe side effects, including cannabinoid hyperemesis syndrome and psychosis. None of these states "are monitoring—or even equipped—to assess the full scope of health outcomes."[178] As one expert on psychosis remarked, "There is no other quote-unquote medicine in the history of our country where your doctor will say, 'Go experiment and tell me what happens.'"[179]

Claims that shifting resources from law enforcement to prevention pro-grams would stem the expected increase in drug consumption and abuse that would come with legalization (and possibly decriminalization) are question-able. Prevention sounds good in theory, but the reality is that even the best prevention programs have only a modest impact on stemming substance use disorder.[180] They do not address the underlying socioeconomic and other risk factors for problematic use of alcohol and drugs.[181]

The case of Portugal illustrates the complexities of the decriminalization and legalization question. Almost twenty-five years ago, Portugal became the first country in the world to decriminalize use and possession of small amounts of all drugs. The country's across-the-board decriminalization has been cred-ited with dramatic reductions in overdose deaths, blood-borne infectious diseases, and problematic drug use. But a closer look reveals that Portugal's success hinged on numerous factors, not just decriminalization.[182]

The 2001 law that decriminalized drugs in Portugal essentially codified what had been existing practice for years. By then, drug consumption had already been de facto decriminalized in Portugal, with fines serving as the main sanction for personal drug use and possession. Despite this de facto decriminalization, Portugal still had a major drug problem at the turn of the twenty-first century, including high rates of drug-related HIV/AIDS infections, rising overdose fatalities, and one of Europe's largest open-air drug markets. At the time, the Portuguese public ranked drug issues, including flagrant drug use in public spaces, as the country's main social problem.[183]

When Portugal formally decriminalized drugs, it dramatically scaled up funding and other resources for "prevention, treatment, harm reduction and the social integration of drug users," including housing and employment support.[184] Thanks to these and other reforms—not just the decriminalization law alone—Portugal has been a pioneer in drug policy reform. The number of people voluntarily entering treatment in Portugal has risen substantially over the last two decades or so, and HIV/AIDS infections from drug use have plummeted. Problematic drug use and overdose deaths have dropped, while incarceration for drug trafficking has fallen significantly.[185]

US Public Health System on Life Support

Maintaining a robust public health system is vital for heading off and containing epidemics and implementing effective harm reduction, treatment, and prevention programs. The successful efforts beginning in the 1990s to slash the death and infection rates for HIV/AIDS in the United States occurred at a time when the country had a strong public health system to implement the 1990 Ryan White Act and other pioneering measures. Since then, the US public health system, once the envy of the world, has been starved for personnel and other resources. With the onset of the pandemic, it came under vicious political attacks, impeding the response not only to Covid-19 but also to the opioid crisis.

The US public health system suffers from chronic underfunding, great disparities in resources, and extreme fragmentation. Spending on public health, which doubled as a percentage of total health expenditures between 1960 and 2003, has been declining almost steadily since then. The losses are gigantic. In 2017, spending on public health equaled just 2.5 percent of all money spent on health care in the United States—or about $274 per person.[186]

The public health system was still reeling from the blows of the Great Recession when the pandemic struck.[187] Between 2008 and 2016, local and state health departments shed more than fifty thousand jobs—or about one-quarter of their workforce.[188] The budget of the CDC, the country's leading public health agency, fell by 10 percent between 2010 and 2019 after adjusting for inflation.[189] The hiring freeze during Trump's first term, which left seven hundred CDC positions unfilled, further imperiled the public health system. So did the administration's decision to shutter the White House office charged with preparing for pandemics.[190] Centers for Disease Control and Prevention funding specifically aimed at addressing the opioid epidemic increased significantly in 2018 and 2019 compared to 2017—but the overall increase was trivial. Furthermore, much of that money was targeted at punitive supply-side interventions, such as prescription drug monitoring programs. Trump 2.0 has compounded these problems in every which way, including the administration's first proposed budget, which called for cutting CDC funding by nearly half.[191]

In a prepandemic survey, almost half of public health workers reported that they planned to retire or leave their current jobs within five years. Low pay was the top reason given. Public health workers are so underpaid that many of them qualify for public programs for low-income people, such as Medicaid and nutritional support. Even prior to the pandemic, public health workers "received so little support that they found themselves without direction, disrespected, ignored, even vilified."[192] During the pandemic, these problems intensified as public health workers were further disparaged, received death threats, and quit in droves or were laid off.

On his return to the White House, Donald Trump immediately ramped up the assault on public health. The administration announced plans to withdraw from the WHO and ordered the CDC to cease working with this UN agency. The CDC's public portal for health data went dark for a time, and its website was scrubbed of vital public health information on everything from the prevention of sexually transmitted infections to a national survey that tracks adolescent health.[193]

The National Opioid Settlements

The payouts from the opioid lawsuits are Band-Aids on a failing health-care system in the United States. Drug companies and distributors are projected to pay out upward of $50 billion to the states over the course of about two decades—or about one-tenth of what is needed to address the opioid crisis.[194]

These funds will supply vital tourniquets to some communities to staunch overdose deaths and get some people into treatment. But they will not be game changers in the prevention and treatment of opioid use disorder. When he ran for president in 2020, Joe Biden vowed that the White House would take an active role in the opioid settlements. But his administration did not wield the federal government's considerable clout to press states to use the funds for prevention, harm reduction, and effective treatments.[195]

The opioid settlements are at risk of repeating the pitfalls of Big Tobacco's 1998 settlement to pay out $246 billion to the states over a twenty-five-year period.[196] Only about 3 percent of the tobacco settlement, which was the largest public health settlement in US history, ended up going to support anti-smoking programs.[197] Lawmakers siphoned off most of the money to plug holes in state budgets and pay for items like filling potholes, building sports stadiums, and even subsidizing tobacco farmers.[198]

To avoid the tobacco settlement's shortcomings, the national opioid agreements stipulate that states must spend at least 85 percent of the funds they receive on treatment and prevention. But enforcement was left up to the drug companies, and Big Pharma has little incentive to ensure adherence to the 85 percent benchmark. For these multibillion-dollar companies, the "money is committed already," and "the settlements are chump change." For example, Johnson & Johnson (J&J) agreed to pay out $5 billion over nine years. In 2022, J&J reported total sales of nearly $95 billion.[199]

The settlements did not include rigorous reporting mandates on how the money is spent. As of 2023, less than a third of the states had committed to transparent, publicly accessible means of tracking the opioid money. In many states, the money has ended up in black holes where it is hard to trace, even by the mandated state-level councils set up to manage the opioid settlements. In states that promised transparency, many of the reports were "difficult, if not impossible, for the average person to decipher."[200]

Another problem is that the 85 percent stipulation is subject to wide interpretation.[201] For some states, purchasing police cruisers, paying overtime for narcotics detectives, and funding body scanners to detect drugs in prisons and jails are considered treatment and prevention and thus permissible under the settlements. Some state councils are stocked with representatives from law enforcement; others explicitly forbid police, sheriffs, and prosecutors from serving. Urban areas are overrepresented on many councils. Not surprisingly, formulas for distributing the funds favor cities even though the need is greater in some rural areas.[202] Pamlico County, a rural county in North Carolina that for years had the state's highest overdose death rate, is expected to receive annual payouts of about $43,000 over nearly two decades. This is not even enough to fund a single qualified outreach worker.[203] Councils are unrepresentative in other ways. For example, one-third of Louisiana's population is African American, but not a single African American person was initially chosen to serve on its opioid council.[204]

The sums of the opioid settlements are trivial given the scale of the problem, how the money will be distributed and used, and the enfeebled state of the US public health system. Some of the opioid money is flowing to programs that deny people access to methadone and buprenorphine, the gold standards for treatment of opioid use disorder. Almost half a million dollars of settlement money has already gone to the Drug Abuse Resistance Education (DARE) program, the controversial youth drug prevention program that lives on despite decades of research documenting its ineffectiveness.[205]

Philadelphia, which has the highest overdose fatality rate of any major US city, expects to receive about $200 million over the course of eighteen years from the $26 billion national opioid settlement inked in October 2021.[206] This sum averages out to about $11 million a year—or less than 0.002 percent of the city's nearly $6 billion operating budget in 2022–23. The city chose to distribute some of the money to community-based organizations through a grant program run by a local foundation and community representatives.[207] In the first round of grants, the program awarded $1.9 million in grants ranging from $20,000 to $100,000 to twenty-seven organizations.[208]

Philadelphia's let-a-hundred-flowers-bloom approach is admirable. These grants will provide vital resources for some groups doing critical work on the front lines of the epidemic. But such grants will not propel the comprehensive, radical new direction in treatment and prevention that is urgently needed. The sums of money are too tiny. There will not be economies of scale. And it will be difficult and costly to monitor whether the money was well spent or wasted, as has been the case with the numerous community-based antiviolence programs the city has funded.[209] Furthermore, despite some inroads, resistance to harm reduction approaches remains fierce in Philadelphia and elsewhere. Mayor Cherelle Parker banned using opioid settlement money to fund sterile syringe programs and has emphasized the need for more doses of police and law enforcement, not harm reduction, to stem the epidemic.[210]

Donald Trump, Joe Biden, and the War on Opioids

The war on drugs was a linchpin of Donald Trump's nativist, anti-immigrant campaign in 2016 as he promoted the fiction that undocumented migrants crossing the US border with Mexico were the main couriers of the illegal drug trade. But Trump also vowed that, if elected, he would declare a national emergency to address the opioid crisis. Trump's focus on the opioid crisis helped him secure an important primary victory in New Hampshire, a state hit hard by the epidemic. On the campaign trail in 2016, Trump mentioned heroin at least fifty-seven times. During the primaries, Hillary Clinton unveiled a plan to combat the opioid crisis that was billed as a public health solution and "one of the most progressive anti-drug plans in decades." But after she secured the Democratic Party's nomination for president, she mentioned the opioid crisis less frequently.[211] Notably, in counties with higher rates of death from drugs, alcohol, and suicide, Trump's vote totals in the 2016 election exceeded those of Republican nominee Mitt Romney in 2012.[212]

In his first term, Trump leaned heavily toward framing the opioid crisis as a law-and-order problem. Trump's attorneys general—first Jeff Sessions and then William Barr—were seasoned drug warriors who remained committed to law enforcement and military solutions to the country's drug problems.[213] In early 2017, Sessions reversed the 2013 memo issued by Eric Holder, which had directed federal prosecutors to stop charging people accused of low-level drug offenses with crimes that triggered long mandatory sentences. Sessions also pushed for ramping up federal prosecutions for fentanyl offenses and dispatched additional prosecutors to ten jurisdictions around the country with the highest number of overdose deaths.[214] Edwin Meese III, who had served as Ronald Reagan's attorney general, hailed Sessions for his "extraordinary" and "largely unnoticed" efforts to "create a Reaganesque resurgence of law and order."[215]

Trump did not honor his campaign promise to declare a national emergency to address the opioid crisis, which would have rapidly released federal disaster relief funding for states and municipalities.[216] Instead, in October 2017, he declared that the opioid epidemic was a "public health emergency" and made available an additional $57,000—less than a dollar for each overdose death in the United States that year.[217] As a result, very little changed in terms of funding and resources for prevention and treatment, according to a report by the US Government Accountability Office.[218]

Trump established the President's Commission on Combatting Drug Addiction and the Opioid Crisis chaired by Governor Chris Christie (R-NJ), which lambasted the FDA's abysmal record in the regulation and oversight of prescription opioids. The commission's final report, released in November 2017, faulted the FDA for accepting unsupported claims that OxyContin and other semisynthetic opioids were not addictive.[219] More than two decades after OxyContin first hit the market, the commission concluded that many patients and their families were still not being "fully informed regarding whether their prescriptions are opioids, the risk of opioid addiction or overdose, control and diversion, dose escalation, or use with alcohol or benzodiazepines."[220] Patients were also unaware of the lack of high-quality evidence that opioid pain pills were efficacious in treating most chronic and acute pain.

The commission echoed many of the recommendations of the surgeon general's report on substance abuse issued under Obama. Its public health and law enforcement proposals were not pioneering and did not add up to a new coherent strategy to combat the opioid epidemic. The commission acknowledged that substance use disorder is a disease and recommended the expansion of treatment. But it also called for enhanced law enforcement, including stiffer penalties for trafficking fentanyl and its analogues. The Trump administration did not use the report to press Congress for major guaranteed long-term funding to fight the opioid epidemic.[221]

In a March 2018 speech in Manchester, New Hampshire, a state hit hard by the opioid epidemic, Trump, with Sessions by his side, vowed once again to build a border wall to stem the flow of illegal drugs into the United States. He repeated the false claim that undocumented migrants trekking through the desert and sagebrush to enter the United States were flooding the country with illegal drugs. (In fact, most illegal drugs from overseas arrive through legal ports of entry or the mail and overnight express services.) Several times during that speech, Trump enthusiastically called for sentencing drug traffickers to death as some other countries do.[222]

Trump signed the SUPPORT Act in October 2018, which was a hodgepodge of modest measures to expand access to treatment of opioid use disorder, bolster prescription drug monitoring programs, beef up law enforcement at the border, and enhance penalties for overprescribing opioids. The SUPPORT Act authorized $3.3 billion over the next decade to stem the opioid crisis, a paltry sum compared to the streams of guaranteed long-term federal funding to fight HIV/AIDS, including the 1990 Ryan White Act and George W. Bush's Emergency Plan for AIDS Relief.[223] Furthermore, the

Trump administration remained committed to killing off the Affordable Care Act and severely cutting funding for Medicaid, which are two of the most important sources of government support for the treatment of substance use disorder.[224]

Trump's hard-line stance had considerable bipartisan support in Congress and elsewhere, including the support of Senator Charles Grassley (R-IA), chair of the Senate Judiciary Committee, and Senator Dianne Feinstein (D-CA), its ranking member. Both senators favored tougher sanctions for fentanyl-related offenses and designating methamphetamine as an emerging drug threat.[225] The federal First Step Act, which Trump signed into law in December 2018, reflected this hard line on fentanyl. Leaders of both parties and a wide range of groups stretching from the American Civil Liberties Union to the Koch brothers hailed the measure, which reduced penalties and time served for some drug offenses. But the measure excluded people convicted of fentanyl-related offenses and sex offenses. The First Step Act also included a sentencing enhancement for selling fentanyl.[226]

During Trump's first administration, the ONDCP did not have a permanent director until January 2019, when the Senate confirmed James Carroll, a former counsel to the Ford Motor Company and Trump's deputy chief of staff.[227] After Carroll took over, the ONDCP released a twenty-page sketch of drug policy that was largely a throwback to the Reagan administration's "Just Say No" campaign and that identified the border wall and increased interdiction overseas as critical to staunching the opioid epidemic.[228]

William Barr, who had served as attorney general under George H. W. Bush, succeeded Sessions in early 2019. The George H. W. Bush administration was bookended by the racially incendiary Willie Horton ad in the 1988 campaign and, four years later, by the "The Case for More Incarceration," a Justice Department report released with Barr's blessing.[229] How Barr would handle Robert Mueller's investigation of possible Russian interference in the 2016 campaign on behalf of Trump was the central preoccupation during his Senate nomination hearings in early 2019, as well as during his first year in office. The focus on the Mueller investigation overshadowed the fact that Barr presented himself at the hearings as an unapologetic drug warrior who was incorrigible on the question of mass incarceration.

During Barr's Senate testimony, it was back to the law-and-order 1980s and 1990s. Egged on by some Republican and Democratic senators, Trump's nominee invoked images of marauding gangs, predatory repeat offenders, and blood "running on the streets all over the United States" as he characterized fentanyl as the "new crack."[230] Barr credited escalating incarceration rates with the historic drop in the US crime rate and ignored a mountain of research—some of it funded by the Justice Department—that had concluded otherwise.[231]

Once in office, Barr championed legislation that would grant permanent new powers for the attorney general—and by extension the DEA—to schedule drugs and thus determine penalties.[232] Barr wielded misinformation and scare tactics as he pushed for this radical change in drug policy.[233] Dozens of civil rights and other groups warned that granting this power to the DEA would exacerbate "already disturbing trends in federal drug prosecutions and incarceration levels and excise public health authorities from their critical role in promulgating drug policy."[234] Some drug experts argued against permanently designating certain fentanyl-like substances as schedule I drugs before much is known about their potential medical benefits. Doing so, they contended, would make it harder to get approval for research on these synthetic drugs, including the development of more effective drugs to reverse fentanyl overdoses.[235] The drug policy reform movement succeeded in blocking measures to permanently grant this rescheduling power to the DEA under Trump but was unable to block a series of temporary extensions.

Biden campaigned in 2020 for an end to mandatory minimums and a greater emphasis on harm reduction to stem the opioid epidemic. But once in office, he signed legislation extending the emergency scheduling of fentanyl analogues. The Biden administration also supported legislation that would permanently reclassify certain fentanyl-related drugs as schedule I substances, even as it was moving to reclassify marijuana from schedule I to a less restricted schedule III substance.[236] With strong support from Democrats, the Republican-led Congress passed versions of the HALT Fentanyl Act soon after Donald Trump returned for a second term. The measure permanently categorizes all fentanyl-related substances as schedule I drugs and ratchets up mandatory minimum prison terms for offenses involving these substances.[237]

In 2019, a spokesperson for the FDA conceded that the agency had "missed opportunities" to stem the opioid crisis and was partly to blame for this public health tragedy.[238] Nonetheless, after Biden took office, Janet Woodcock, who had directed the FDA's Center for Drug Evaluation and Research for more than two decades and played a central role in the approval and regulation of OxyContin and other opioid prescription pills, was a top candidate to head the agency. Dozens of groups successfully mobilized to derail her nomination.[239] After months of turmoil at the FDA, Biden ended up choosing Robert M. Califf, who had briefly directed the agency under Obama and had close ties with the pharmaceutical industry.[240]

Like Donald Trump in his first term, President Biden singled out enemies abroad as the top villains in the opioid crisis at home. Both Trump and Biden were united in the mistaken belief that the solution to the opioid epidemic lies overseas, not at home. They excoriated China and Mexico for allegedly allowing producers of illegal fentanyl and its analogues to flood the United States with these dangerous drugs. Their attacks complemented the larger strategy to isolate China as part of the Washington rules and the new cold war discussed in chapter 5. Some Republicans supported more radical changes in US drug policy, including bombing and invading Mexico to vanquish its drug cartels.[241]

Just hours after being sworn into office for a second term, President Trump ratcheted up the war on drugs. He issued an executive order that broadly labeled all Mexican drug cartels as Foreign Terrorist Organizations, a move that could foreshadow direct military action, including drone strikes and targeted killings by American special forces. The CIA expanded the covert program begun under the Biden administration to patrol cartel territory in Mexico with US drones. Green Berets were reportedly training Mexican troops, the first US soldiers on Mexican soil since the controversial American invasion of that country more than a century ago under President Woodrow Wilson.[242]

Trump opened another new front in the war on drugs by weaponizing tariffs. In justifying his plans to impose sweeping tariffs on Canada, Mexico, and China, he blamed these three countries for the US opioid crisis. The president falsely accused drug cartels of "killing 250,000 [or] 300,000 Americans per year," grossly overstating the already grim annual toll of US drug overdoses by more than twofold. Trump included Canada even though experts on drug policy and law enforcement agree that Canada's role in drug smuggling is negligible. In short, it was another Groundhog Day in America's forever wars on drugs. The United States once again chased the mirage of interdiction and choking off the fentanyl supply to stem the crisis. It shunned mobilizing on behalf of harm reduction and proven solutions to reduce demand and provide good treatment on demand.[243]

Social Murder and the Opioid Crisis

The harm reduction movement is slowly making headway in the United States. As part of the $1.9 trillion American Rescue Plan Act of 2021, Congress for the first time specifically appropriated funds for evidence-based harm reduction services, but the amount was trivial—just $30 million.[244] Growing acceptance of the view that addiction is form of disease has helped propel this movement.[245] This biological framework is preferable to ideological explanations of substance use disorder that emphasize a person's moral and other shortcomings. But in developing drug policies that save and repair lives and prevent problematic drug use in the first place, we need to keep in mind the wide array of situational and environmental factors that render some people more vulnerable to drug dependence and addiction.

People take opioids "as a refuge from physical and psychological trauma, concentrated disadvantage, isolation, and hopelessness."[246] Biological factors predispose some people to becoming dependent on drugs or alcohol but so do political, socioeconomic, and environmental ones. We also must keep in mind the political and economic interests that catalyzed the crisis in the United States and have gone largely unpunished.[247]

Scaling up MAT and other harm reduction strategies is desperately needed to save lives. For "harm reduction to work, maintenance drugs need to be almost as accessible as street drugs," one expert on substance abuse noted.[248] But in scaling up, we need to reject treating the opioid epidemic as primarily a medical problem. Providing good treatment on demand and embracing harm reduction treats the symptoms, not the causes, of the opioid epidemic. It does not address why so many people in the United States are gripped with such lethal despair. Or why they turn to drugs, alcohol, or suicide for some relief because the economic system, the health-care system, and the social safety net have forsaken them.[249]

"The United States is a nation in pain," as one expert on the opioid epidemic observed.[250] The US consumption of illegal and legal drugs tops world rankings.[251] With just under 5 percent of the world's population, the United States consumes an estimated 30 percent of the global supply of opioid drugs.[252] The overprescribing of opioid medications is "emblematic of a health care system that incentivizes quick, simplistic answers to complex physical and mental health needs."[253] Physical and emotional ailments in the United States are far more likely to be treated with pharmaceuticals, "even if that means being on multiple medications with complex, poorly-understood, and risky interactions."[254]

Improving treatment and reducing the harms caused by opioid use do not address the fact that the opioid crisis was iatrogenic—that is, induced by the pharmaceutical industry and medical providers, who were aided and abetted by lax, self-interested, and under-resourced government regulators at the FDA and elsewhere. As one drug policy expert told Congress in 2018, as "long as we continue putting countless Americans in 'heroin prep school' each year by over-prescribing opioids, the next generation of users will soon replace those who exit the heroin market."[255] In one promising development, in late 2022, Congress enacted the Non-Opioids Prevent Addiction in the Nation Act (NO-PAIN) to expand access to alternatives to opioids in nonsurgical outpatient settings.[256]

Drug overdose deaths in the United States fell by nearly 22 percent between August 2023 and August 2024 as the United States experienced its first major decline in the decades-long opioid epidemic. But the scale of the death and destruction remains massive—nearly ninety thousand overdose fatalities during that twelve-month period. Furthermore, this drop "might reflect what epidemiologists call a depletion of susceptibles, a grim term that can describe the waning of an epidemic because the most vulnerable people have perished," explains Maia Szalavitz, one of the sharpest analysts of the opioid crisis. And while overdose fatalities among white people have begun to decline after decades of outpacing other demographic groups, overdose deaths are skyrocketing among Black people and Indigenous people.[257]

Having created a vast, powerful, and highly militarized apparatus to wage the forever wars on drugs at home and abroad over the last six decades, the United States is still not ready to kick the habit. The exceptional lethalness of the political, economic, social, and criminal legal systems in the United States is ultimately to blame for the grim toll of the opioid epidemic. Among Western countries, the United States remains unequaled in the punitiveness of its drug policies and its indifference to addressing the pain and suffering of wide swaths of its people who are victims of what Friedrich Engels called social murder.[258]

PART V

Conclusion

12

Fraught

WHERE DO WE GO FROM HERE?

Not everything that is faced can be changed;
but nothing can be changed until it is faced.

—JAMES BALDWIN[1]

IN AUGUST 1967, Martin Luther King Jr. declared that the "triple evils" of racism, economic exploitation, and war were "all tied together." And he asked, "Where do we go from here?"[2] These triple threats are embedded in the "true front end of violence"—that is, the corporate, tax, military, social welfare, economic, and environmental policies that radically redistribute wealth upward, prop up the US empire, and render so many people, and even the planet, in peril.[3]

The building blocks for peaceful, livable, healthy, and thriving communities are no mystery. Low levels of political and economic inequality. A robust social safety net. Vibrant community and neighborhood groups that foster feelings of efficacy and belonging. Political and economic institutions widely perceived as legitimate. The absence of a heavily armed citizenry. No permanent state of war. No global empire

The Washington rules, the costly forever wars, the fallout from the financial and foreclosure crises, the government's regulatory retreat, and the privatization of everything from public schools to sewer systems have plundered the United States. They destabilized its political institutions and fostered polarization and violence. Not just interpersonal violence but also state and structural violence. In short, social murder. Meanwhile, an oligarchy—sanguine about gaping economic and other inequalities and contemptuous of elections and democracy—is consolidating.

The path to a more peaceful, dignified, and equitable future in which prosperity is widely shared is not out of reach. Major shifts in corporate, tax, and military policies are necessary to free up resources to underwrite living-wage jobs; revitalize organized labor; provide affordable housing; establish a good, universal health-care system; rein in the power of corporations and the wealthy; and head off a climate catastrophe. The resources are there. So is public sentiment. A large majority of Americans blame structural obstacles, not personal shortcomings, for poverty. They believe the rich are rich because of unfair advantages. By surging margins, they support organized labor and raising the minimum wage to a living wage. They have favorable views of the military but unfavorable views of the forever wars. They want to raise taxes on corporations and the rich and to hold oil and gas companies criminally responsible for incinerating the planet. They favor universal health care. And they loathe health insurance companies, as evidenced by the public scorn heaped on them after a UnitedHealthcare executive was gunned down in late 2024.[4]

Retribution, the Carceral State, and Corporate Crime and Punishment

So-called good people do bad things all the time. And many so-called bad people are redeemable. Vilifying and dehumanizing corporate executives or public officials who commit social murder will not significantly reduce violence in America. Neither will sending them away to prison for decades or a lifetime. Likewise, some people should not be police officers. Period. But vilifying individual officers who wantonly use excessive force and kill their fellow citizens will not make US police departments much safer and less lethal. Corporate executives, police officers, and public officials need to be held accountable for causing violence, just like people who commit street crimes must be held accountable. But, more importantly, the political, institutional, economic, and social structures that are petri dishes for such high levels of social murder and interpersonal and state violence in America must be identified, held accountable, and remediated. There are no shortcuts.

In addressing the true front end of violence, we need to dispense with the notion that the primary solution—whether we are talking about crime in the streets or crime in the suites—should be a carceral one. The number of victims of corporate malfeasance is vast. So is the urge for retribution. But as prison abolitionist Angela Davis warns, we must resist the "retributive impulses" that politicians and other public figures have inscribed on our very being thanks to the decades of punitive policies that fueled the prison boom.[5] These impulses call out like sirens on the rock, demanding that the state impose harsh carceral punishments in the name of furthering justice and reducing crime. But revenge is a wild kind of justice, as philosopher Francis Bacon once said.[6] Donald Trump rode that urge into the White House in 2016 and then again in 2024 with his calls to lock up Hillary Clinton and deport millions of migrants.[7]

Victims of crime want accountability, as Danielle Sered and other experts on restorative justice and crime in the streets have shown.[8] They want restitution. They want to heal the harm caused and to ensure that no one else is victimized like they were. But they do not necessarily want the person who hurt them to receive a life-destroying prison sentence.

When asked if she was relieved when a teenage boy who had assaulted her received a lengthy prison sentence, an older woman told Sered, "Oh yes, honey, of course I was." When asked how long the relief lasted, the woman said, "Oh, baby, at least three or four hours." After she got home from court that day, the woman was still poor, afraid, unable to sleep, and gripped by nightmares. The next morning, the woman lamented that she "could not shake the image of that boy's mother's face in court when those guards took her baby from her for good. Because that is my face."[9]

Throwing a handful of prominent CEOs in prison might satisfy, at least momentarily, some populist urges for retribution in the face of so much corporate lawlessness. But it would not transform the "current culture of immunity and lax enforcement" of corporate crime, as legal scholar Brandon Garrett argues.[10] It also would not ameliorate the harm that these executives inflicted or the deeper structural problems that perpetrate social murder in the United States.

Corporations are well schooled in the occasional need for a ritual sacrifice of an executive—the "vice presidents responsible for going to jail"—so that they can continue doing business as usual.[11] The criminal legal system and the regulatory system are also well schooled in such ritual sacrifices. They made a spectacle of sentencing Bernie Madoff to essentially die in prison while ignoring the willful blindness of regulators and leading bankers that allowed his multibillion-dollar Ponzi scheme to flourish for decades.[12] The twenty-five-year prison sentence handed down in 2024 to Sam Bankman-Fried, the young founder of the crypto exchange FTX, was a similar ritual sacrifice that will do little to restrain the unregulated wild west of cryptocurrency. Political operatives from both major parties are already cashing in as lobbyists for the crypto industry, including David Plouffe, a senior adviser to Kamala Harris's 2024 presidential campaign and architect of Obama's winning 2008 campaign.[13]

An overemphasis on the criminal legal system to stem corporate and other malfeasance impoverishes the public discourse. Discussions of a public figure's behavior often "degenerate into arguments about whether the behavior constitutes a 'crime,' with the implication that what's not criminal is acceptable."[14] But in many realms of life—from friendships to work to marriage to parenting—we hold people accountable to not only criminal standards but also moral and ethical ones. Just because you are legally permitted to do something does not mean you *should* do that thing. Many top corporate executives in the pharmaceutical and financial industries likely committed criminal fraud, perjury, and other crimes in connection with the opioid epidemic and the financial and foreclosure crises. But much of what they did was not technically criminal. The reflexive recourse to the criminal legal system undermines the development of noncriminal norms to stem the violence and other harms that corporations inflict.[15]

Relying on the penal system and law enforcement as the main line of defense against crime in the suites runs the risk of further legitimizing the massive carceral state.[16] The evidence is compelling that prisons and jails do not significantly reduce crime and are often incubators of crime.[17] Furthermore, US penal institutions are sites of intense brutality, violence, dehumanization, and racial and sexual degradation that we should not cavalierly subject anyone to—not even the "worst of the worst."[18] As prison abolitionist Ruth Wilson Gilmore warns, imposing "violent and self-annihilating" punishments on people who hurt people "is not a solution." This holds true whether we are talking about the financiers who unleashed the financial and foreclosure crises or the C-suite drug dealers at Purdue Pharma or the person who robbed the local 7-Eleven. In short, "where life is precious, life *is* precious," Gilmore poignantly observes.[19]

The criminal legal system has untapped powers short of incarceration to curtail deadly and destructive corporate behavior. Treating carceral punishments as a last resort to address corporate criminality does not mean eschewing serious legal and other consequences. For corporate executives, these consequences could include significant clawbacks of ill-gotten gains; lifetime bans on working in their profession; public apologies; truth and reconciliation commissions; and imposition of fines or restitution that eject guilty corporate executives from their Learjet and yacht-sized lifestyles (and perhaps leave them to get by on what the average American household earns). Furthermore, corporate capital punishment, such as revoking drug manufacturing licenses or banning participation in Medicaid, Medicare, and other government programs, needs to be a real, not a theoretical, threat for criminal corporations.

Credible threats of criminal enforcement and sanctions are necessary for a robust regulatory system to thrive.[20] The certainty that major corporate crimes will be detected and that corporate executives will be personally sanctioned may be a more powerful deterrent than expectations about the severity of punishment.[21] But the wars waged over the last half century or so against crime in the streets, terrorism, immigrants, and so-called street drugs have drained resources away from the pursuit of elite-level corporate crime. So have the wars that the corporate sector and lawmakers from both parties have waged against regulation. Weak, corporate-friendly deferred prosecution and nonprosecution agreements (DPAs and NPAs) proliferated over the last twenty-five years for many reasons, including the growing clout of the corporate sector and the revolving door between the Justice Department, the major regulatory agencies, and top law firms. But they also mushroomed because they appealed to underresourced prosecutors and regulators who faced pressure to settle cases fast with a splash to ensure that their budgets would not be slashed.[22]

Fixating on prisons, jails, and penal policies runs the risk of marginalizing other institutions and public policies that are better able to stem corporate crime and social murder. The need is great for constructing robust regulatory institutions that cannot be captured by private interests. In the case of the financial sector, this would include regulatory bodies that have the authority, capacity, and political will to impose meaningful and enforceable caps on the size of financial institutions; to put troubled banks and other financial institutions, including the largest ones, into temporary state receivership, restructure their management, and sell them off at a fair price to more responsible parties if necessary; and to unwind executive compensation schemes that reward Wall Street and Fortune 500 executives at great risk to Main Street and the rest of society.

In the case of the pharmaceutical industry, a "massive dose of criminal deterrence cannot begin" to curtail its predatory behavior.[23] A ritual penal sacrifice of a Purdue executive or a Sackler family member would not end the opioid epidemic or head off a similar one in the future. Furthermore, individual corporate officers, even members of the Sackler family who became fabulously rich peddling OxyContin, do not have the resources to repair the enormous damage they have caused. Reinstituting the ban on direct-to-consumer advertising of drugs and imposing hefty taxes on other drug advertising would be far more consequential than jailing some Sacklers.[24] So would restructuring the patent system to close loopholes that allow drug companies to profit by keeping safer, cheaper, more efficacious drugs out of the market while they disinvest in research and development. So would liberating the Food and Drug Administration (FDA) from the clutches of Big Pharma by ending its financial dependence on drug companies, among other things. But Donald Trump's appointment of Robert Kennedy Jr. to head the Department of Health and Human Services (HHS) in his second term may lead to the de facto death of the FDA—a vital but troubled agency—all in the name of reforming it.[25]

Reinvigorating the tort system is another pressing need. The decades-long tort revolution waged by business groups and their sympathizers in Congress, state legislatures, and the courts has decimated the public's ability to sue corporations for criminal and other misconduct. The proliferation of strategic corporate bankruptcies, secret nondisclosure agreements, mandatory arbitration provisions, legal barriers to corporate discovery, and limits on class-action suits has denied more people their day in civil court to seek redress for harms caused by corporations. These developments have also shielded corporations from legal and public scrutiny, as has the growing use of private investigators and threats of legal action to keep whistleblowers and other critics silent.[26]

Whistleblowers, activists, and journalists play a key role in exposing corporate and government wrongdoing. They often do so at great risk to their families, jobs, financial security, mental and physical health, and even their lives, as evidenced by the cases of Julian Assange, Edward Snowden, Chelsea Manning, journalist James Risen, and lesser-known whistleblowers.[27] The patchwork of federal whistleblower laws and protections, some of which reward people financially for blowing the whistle, are complex, inconsistent, highly circumscribed, and hard to navigate.[28] The risks of blowing the whistle have escalated in the face of an intensified government and private war to stem leaks and keep information secret. The weapons in this war include increased restrictions on Freedom of Information Act (FOIA) requests; greater use of the draconian Espionage Act of 1917 to prosecute whistleblowers and journalists as spies; and widespread intimidation of and disdain for the press. These trends predate Donald Trump's rise to power but ramped up during his presidencies as he and his supporters charged that the media were an "enemy of the people" and attacked scientific expertise of all types.[29]

Financialization and the internet are also suffocating the watchdog role of the news media. Relaxation of antitrust enforcement and other policies accelerated the corporate consolidation of the media. The rise of the internet decimated advertising revenues for newspapers and magazines, jeopardizing their economic viability. The billionaire class and private equity firms swooped in to buy up many struggling news outlets at fire-sale prices. A frenzy of cost cutting, layoffs, and asset sell-offs ensued, killing off many publications or leaving them on life support. Over the last two decades, about three thousand newspapers have closed.[30] Premier publications that have survived the bloodletting are under enormous pressure to do the bidding of their billionaire owners. Amazon's Jeff Bezos, who bought the *Washington Post* in 2013, and physician and tech mogul Patrick Soon-Shiong, who purchased the *Los Angeles Times* in 2018, created uproars with their newsrooms and the public as they pushed their publications to toady up to Donald Trump during the 2024 campaign and afterward.[31]

The belated efforts of the philanthropic world to prop up local newspapers and support nonprofit news operations have slowed some of the death spiral. Nonprofit ownership has transformed some struggling papers, such as the *Philadelphia Inquirer*, into first-rate news operations once again. But foundations and nonprofit groups do not have the resources to revitalize the news industry on their own. And AI may kill off what's left of the independent news media. It is going to take major government action, such as levying taxes on internet advertising and restrictions on AI's use of copyrighted materials in machine learning, to maintain a thriving news media that fulfills its watchdog role.

The Police and State Violence

With the proliferation of smart phones, security cameras, and body-worn and dashboard cameras, disturbing recordings of Black men killed by the police are now ubiquitous in the news media and on social media. These graphic deaths overshadow the less graphic social murders caused by economic, corporate, and state violence that occur more slowly and are less visible to the wider public.[32] The shocking scenes of police officers shooting and suffocating Black men foster what political scientist Lester K. Spence describes as a politics of spectacle in which mass demonstrations and other protest activities create their own kind of spectacle in response.[33]

This politics of spectacle has been invaluable in generating public awareness of police use of excessive and deadly force. But it is not well suited to exposing the underlying reasons why law enforcement in the United States is so lethal and publicly unaccountable, or why the problem of excessive state violence has been framed as a problem affecting almost exclusively Black people, especially Black men. Framing it as such "cuts off potential constituencies," explains political scientist Cedric Johnson.[34] Furthermore, the politics of spectacle or episodic revolt is not well-equipped for the long haul, including overcoming the immense challenges to forging successful broad-based coalitions to right-size and demilitarize the police and also curtail the less visible structural violence that victimizes so many African American and other people in the United States.[35]

The US judiciary has been obsequious to the police. But the problem runs much deeper than that. When it comes to governing the police, lawmakers and policymakers have abdicated. States have extensive rules and statutes to govern everything from licensing hair stylists to classifying citrus fruits to harvesting oysters. But they have little or nothing to say about more consequential matters involving the police, including what the limits are on police use of force, warrantless searches, roadside body cavity searches, SWAT teams, stop and frisk, qualified immunity, and high-tech surveillance, to give but a few examples. In the case of policing, "the ordinary rules of democratic governance seem to evaporate."[36] Police mostly police themselves. They decide on their own how to enforce the law. The rules governing their behavior are often not public and are seldom adopted with public input, especially from the communities and individuals that are harmed the most by abusive and lethal police officers. When things go wrong with policing, "we try to fix things *after the fact*," with civilian review boards, inspectors general, and the courts, all of which are not up to the task.[37]

The United States needs to demilitarize its police forces and make them more democratically accountable by reducing their firepower, raising the bar for use of force, and reining in the power of police unions to shield their members from investigations, disciplinary actions, criminal charges, and civil lawsuits. It also needs to rein in hot-spots policing, stop and frisk, excessive traffic stops, and other practices that have eroded the legitimacy of the police in the eyes of the communities they are supposed to protect. But calls to defund or eliminate the police are politically vexing. Residents in poor, marginalized Black and brown communities have deep concerns about being under protected and overpoliced as homicides and shootings go unsolved, and the police don't show up when called.[38] Many residents of these communities have an "all of the above approach" to policing. They favor spending more on law enforcement, but they also want to change how police operate. Their top spending priority is not law enforcement but rather more money to remediate the social and economic conditions that are the root causes of street crime.[39]

Calls to defund the police are vexing for other reasons. Police, the National Guard, and federal troops have sided with violent, reactionary forces numerous times in American history. But state coercion at select moments has also been critical in furthering social and economic justice and protecting the public from political violence. Federal troops were the backbone of Reconstruction after the Civil War. Federalized National Guard troops shielded Black students attending formerly all-white schools in Little Rock, Arkansas, and elsewhere after the 1954 *Brown v. Board of Education* decision. Today, as paramilitary groups have become commonplace at demonstrations, political rallies, and elsewhere in public life, the need is great for well-trained, nonpartisan police forces to show up and keep the peace. One of the most disturbing images from the 2014 protests in Ferguson, Missouri, was of rifle-toting members of the far-right Oath Keepers positioned on rooftops and ready to take the law into their own hands. At the 2017 "Unite the Right" rally in Charlottesville, Virginia, local police failed to protect peaceful counterprotesters from armed white nationalist groups. And on January 6, 2021, the skeletal police force was no match for the militias and their supporters who stormed the Capitol.

Taxation and the Politics of Entitlement

When we think about violence in America, we don't usually think about the tax system. But as US Supreme Court Justice Oliver Wendell Holmes declared in 1927, "Taxes are what we pay for civilized society."[40] The average American is paying more in taxes today but getting less in return as the building blocks for "thick public safety" continue to erode.[41] Bridges, highways, streets, and water systems are decaying and unsafe. The social safety net is threadbare or nonexistent. Public services—from public education to public transit to public health to public housing—are under siege.

The United States must restore the progressivity of its tax system, plug the gaping tax loopholes for corporations and wealthy individuals, and capture the personal and corporate wealth siphoned off to tax shelters and other dodges. The comprehensive tax gap—that is, the difference between what should be and what is collected in tax receipts—was $630 billion in 2019, according to US Treasury estimates.[42] Tax evasion and avoidance by individuals and corporations directly cost the United States $177 billion in lost tax revenues in 2018, according to conservative estimates.[43] To put that figure in some perspective, sociologist Matthew Desmond estimates that ending poverty in America would roughly cost that much in additional spending each year.[44]

We are now living in the "golden age of tax avoidance."[45] Law firms, accountants, and financial institutions shield trillions of dollars of personal and corporate wealth from tax authorities worldwide in what one critic characterizes as "havens against democracies."[46] A brief stint serving in a senior position at the Treasury Department has become the career fast track for tax lawyers at the largest US accounting firms. During their sabbatical at Treasury, these lawyers "write policies that are frequently favorable" to their former corporate and other clients, "often with the expectation they will return to their old employers."[47]

Corporations and wealthy individuals no longer consider it shameful to not pay their fair share of taxes. They have largely exited from the US tax system thanks to waves of tax cuts and to the machinations of the "wealth management industry," which helps them avoid or evade paying taxes. Between 1952 and 2019, the corporate proportion of the federal government's total tax revenues fell from one-third to less than 7 percent, and corporate income tax revenue as a percentage of the GDP fell from 6 percent to 1 percent.[48] Since the 1970s, the average tax rate for the top 0.01 percent has shrunk by more than half (to about 30 percent) while rates for the bottom 90 percent have increased slightly (to an average of 25 percent).[49]

Some years, the richest people in the United States, and indeed the world, including Jeff Bezos, Elon Musk, Michael Bloomberg, and George Soros, have not paid a single cent in federal income taxes.[50] The twenty-five richest Americans paid a true federal tax rate of just 3.4 percent between 2014 and 2018—or barely a quarter of the 14 percent in federal taxes paid by the median American household, according to a *ProPublica* investigation.[51] Between 2014 and 2018, folksy billionaire Warren Buffett paid a true federal tax rate of just 0.1 percent.[52] Note that the decimal point in this figure is not a typo.

The Panama Papers, the trove of millions of documents leaked from a Panamanian law firm and published in 2016, revealed how the vast "wealth defense industry" assists the uber-rich in finding safe, stable havens overseas to park their wealth and circumvent the rules, laws, and regulations of their home countries.[53] Many of the tax avoidance activities described in the Panama Papers are not technically illegal. But the line between tax avoidance (legal) and tax evasion (illegal) is thin.[54]

Major corporations pay little or no taxes thanks to various tax avoidance schemes, including artificially booking their profits in countries with low corporate tax rates.[55] In 2017, Apple booked $246 billion offshore and avoided nearly $77 billion in US taxes on those earnings.[56] In 2018, Amazon paid no corporate taxes on $11 billion in profits and even received a $129 million tax rebate from the Internal Revenue Service (IRS).[57] The United States and other wealthy OECD (Organisation for Economic Co-operation and Development) countries have thwarted growing efforts in the United Nations and elsewhere to impose a global wealth tax on the billionaire class and an enforceable global corporate minimum tax.[58]

Donald Trump's signature tax legislation enacted during his first term, which slashed the US federal corporate tax rate from 35 to 21 percent, had only a minor impact on luring corporate profits back home to the United States where they could be taxed.[59] The Congressional Budget Office estimated in 2018 that the 2017 tax measure would cost government coffers nearly $2 trillion by 2029. The legislation disproportionately lavished tax benefits on corporations and wealthy individuals.[60] The cuts for low earners "were so small as not to be noticed."[61]

United States officials have periodically made a show of pushing for laws and treaties to force foreign governments and financial institutions to be more transparent about the assets that US investors and wealthy Americans hold overseas. Meanwhile, the federal government and many states grant tax breaks and other sweeteners to foreign corporations and individuals so as to, among other things, attract foreign capital and protect the value of the US dollar.[62] As federal and state laws have become more protective of private wealth from overseas, the United States has emerged as the number one country in the world for nonresidents to conceal their identity and their wealth from tax and legal authorities.[63] Hundreds of billions of dollars have poured into South Dakota. This tiny state has become "the best place in the world to *stay* rich" because it does not tax income, inheritance, or capital gains and shields many assets from legal proceedings.[64] The financial industry has captured South Dakota's part-time legislature, helping to turn the home state of Senator George McGovern, the Democratic presidential nominee in 1972, from blue to deep red.[65]

Even though wealthy people are more likely to evade or avoid paying taxes (and have a lot more money to hide), the country's poorest households have often been just as likely to be audited as the top 1 percent.[66] Lobbyists and their friends in Congress decimated a 2009 IRS initiative to create a crack team of hundreds of tax specialists to claw back tax revenues from the nation's wealthiest people.[67] Crippling budget cuts to the IRS under Barack Obama and then during Donald Trump's first term contributed to major drops in tax audits and in criminal investigations of tax evasion.[68] The IRS even lost the capacity to go after billions of dollars of so-called low-hanging fruit—back taxes owed by people who filed their tax returns but had not yet paid what they owed.[69]

By the end of Trump's first term, audit rates were at their lowest level in four decades.[70] The Biden administration faced an uphill battle to increase funding for the IRS and crack down on tax cheating. It even had a hard time curtailing the widespread practice of writing off personal use of corporate jets as a business expense.[71] But the Biden administration's efforts to modernize the IRS and compel rich delinquent taxpayers to pay up had some success, yielding at least a $1 billion for the government's coffers.[72] With Trump's return to the White House, it's open season on the IRS. Billy Long, Trump's pick to lead the IRS, repeatedly sponsored legislation to abolish the agency when he served in Congress. After entering the private sector in 2023, Long worked with a company that helped clients claim a pandemic-related tax credit that the IRS described as a "magnet for fraud," according to a *New York Times* investigation.[73]

After Trump was reelected, companies and wealthy individuals immediately geared up for a "taxapalooza." They eagerly anticipated that the new administration would kneecap the IRS and lavish another round of deep tax cuts on the uberwealthy.[74] When Trump returned to the Oval Office in 2025, plans were already well under way to decimate vital pieces of the government, slash the social safety net, and jack up tariffs to pay for another round of tax cuts for the wealthiest Americans. The centerpiece of Trump 2.0's One Big Beautiful Bill Act (OBBBA), which Congress passed by a razor-thin margin in July 2025, was $4 trillion in tax cuts that favor the wealthy. The annual after-tax incomes of top earners are projected to increase by about 2.3 percent over the next decade, while the bottom fifth would see a 2.3 percent drop. People making more than $3 million would reap on average a $118,000 tax windfall by 2034. Those with little or no income would lose $560 on average. To cover the expense of these trickle-up policies, the OBBBA slashes government programs and will necessitate borrowing trillions of dollars. The legislation includes an unprecedented retrenchment for Medicaid, food stamps, and other pieces of the social safety net. Nearly 12 million people are estimated to be at risk of losing their health-care coverage thanks to the Beautiful Bill's curtailment of Medicaid and the Affordable Care Act. Borrowing trillions of dollars to pay for the tax cuts threatens to send the US economy and thus the country into a death spiral. As for Trump 2.0's first proposed budget, like the OBBBA, it hits poor and working-class people the hardest. But the administration's budget proposal puts nearly everyone at greater risk due to breathtaking plans to slash spending on everything from clean water to public health to the arts to weather forecasting to public transportation to renewable energy to infectious disease prevention programs.[75]

Elon Musk's so-called Department of Government Efficiency (DOGE) was hellbent on lopping off vital pieces of the government and the social safety net for ideological reasons and to pay for the tax cuts. The Consumer Financial Protection Bureau (CFPB), the brightest light of the Dodd–Frank legislation, was an early target of the new administration as its acting director ordered the federal agency to stop almost all its work. Core pieces of the social safety net were also on the chopping block, including Medicaid and the Children's Health Insurance Program (CHIP). These two government health-care programs together cover about seventy-nine million people in the United States, including nearly half of all children. Another major target was the Supplemental Nutrition Assistance Program (SNAP), more commonly known as food stamps, which one in eight people in the United States depends on to stave off hunger. Musk's chainsaw will not make much of a dent in offsetting the tax cuts unless it goes after Social Security and Medicare benefits, among other items.[76]

These tax policies fly in the face of public opinion. Proposals to institute a wealth tax on the ultrarich are hugely popular with Democratic and Republican voters.[77] But public sentiment is no match for the "stealth politics" of the Learjet class.[78] Superrich individuals tend to remain publicly silent about upwardly redistributive issues such as ladling more tax cuts on corporations and wealthy people, slashing spending on social programs, privatizing Social Security, and eliminating the estate tax. But behind the scenes in Washington and state capitals, they pursue their politics of entitlement and push their shovel-up agenda. They also generously contribute to candidates, political action committees (PACs), think tanks, and other organizations that champion these causes. Indeed, 40 percent of all federal political donations in the United States came from the top 0.01 percent in 2012.[79]

Although a few prominent wealthy individuals publicly lament the country's economic inequality, they generally do not actively lobby for tax and other policies that would reduce their massive piece of the economic pie. Instead, they support small-bore solutions that are not likely to work and that may make the problem worse, including public-private partnerships in which the private sector clearly has the upper hand.[80] These partnerships—whether for housing (such as tax abatements and set-asides for affordable housing), health care (notably Medicare Advantage plans), the criminal legal system (such as social impact bonds and privatized, fee-for-service parole, probation, and electronic monitoring), or public education (notably charter schools and vouchers)—entail giving private entities "sweetheart, low-risk" deals "in exchange for helping out a little."[81] Likewise, corporate social responsibility programs are feel-good exercises. They do not challenge the tax, labor, economic, and military policies that generate the fundamental maldistribution of income and wealth and that fuel the many strands of violence in America.[82]

Major foundations are part of this "elite charade of changing the world." That charade leaves in place the underlying political and economic system "that has allowed the winners to win and fostered many of the problems they seek to solve."[83] Foundations and their wealthy patrons overwhelmingly favor solutions that are anchored in the private or nonprofit sector and are not democratically accountable. They tend to marginalize the role of government and eschew the redistribution of wealth downward through tax reform and other measures. As one critic of philanthropy-led solutions asks: "What does it mean for a rich person to extract money that should be going to the country's tax base and then decide for themselves how to donate it to the public again?"[84]

Give Peace a Chance

Along with the regressive tax system, the US military budget is a huge obstacle to forging a more peaceful path for the United States at home and abroad in which its prosperity is widely shared. "Every gun that is made, every warship launched, every rocket fired signifies, in the final sense, a theft from those who hunger and are not fed, those who are cold and are not clothed," warned Republican President Dwight D. Eisenhower in 1953. "This world in arms is not spending money alone. It is spending the sweat of its laborers, the genius of its scientists, the hopes of its children," declared the former World War II commander of US forces in Europe.[85]

For much of US history, the military did not drive the US economy and polity, and national defense consumed a minor portion of America's resources compared to what European countries shelled out. That changed radically in the aftermath of World War II with the launch of the Cold War and the construction of the national security state.[86] Throughout US history, major figures—from Alexander Hamilton to Theodore Roosevelt to publisher Henry Luce—sought to link national greatness with military glory and global domination. But their efforts did not go unchallenged. Other public figures—including Thomas Jefferson, Congressman Abraham Lincoln during the Mexican-American War, two-time presidential candidate William Jennings Bryan, Jane Addams, W.E.B. Du Bois, Mark Twain, Booker T. Washington, President Eisenhower, and Martin Luther King Jr.—raised unsettling questions about how an outsized military poses a threat to democratic institutions and society. At important junctures in the past, prominent industrialists, including Henry Ford and Andrew Carnegie, castigated America's imperial ambitions. Some of them even supported the vibrant, broad-based pacifist and anti-imperialist movements that emerged in the United States in response to the US war in the Philippines and then the coming of World War I. These movements were political forces to be reckoned with for decades thereafter.[87]

Prominent African Americans have periodically been at the forefront of drawing scorching connections between US warmaking overseas and deepening inequalities and violence back home. Booker T. Washington and Ida B. Wells were major figures in the anti-imperialist movement at the turn of the twentieth century. W.E.B. Du Bois and A. Philip Randolph, who later became president of the Brotherhood of Sleeping Car Porters, campaigned against US entry into World War I, castigating the munitions industry for what they charged was warmongering for profit. As the United States threw itself into the Cold War, singer, actor, and activist Paul Robeson directed international attention to the widespread human rights abuses of the Jim Crow era and denounced US entry into the Korean war. The US government responded by blacklisting him, confiscating his passport, and making him a pariah.[88]

Martin Luther King Jr.—the real version, not the canonized version celebrated each January with a day of service and T-shirts pockmarked with corporate logos—was a leading critic of the US war in Southeast Asia. As the 1960s unfolded, King publicly aligned himself more closely with the worldview of Malcom X, a strident critic of US imperialism whose deep influence on King has gone largely unacknowledged until recently.[89] The US war in Vietnam was an "inflection point" for King's "radicalization on matters of global justice."[90]

On April 4, 1967—a year to the day before he was assassinated—King threw down the gauntlet in a bitter break with President Lyndon B. Johnson over the US war in Vietnam. King did not just criticize the war. He excoriated US imperialism for the violence, oppression, and racial and economic injustice it spawned overseas and in the United States. The civil rights leader declared that he "could never again raise my voice against the violence of the oppressed in the ghettos without having first spoken clearly to the greatest purveyor of violence in the world today—my own government."[91] In breaking with LBJ, King challenged claims that the United States could deliver both guns and butter. He bulldozed the wall that the political and economic establishment strategically uses to separate domestic and foreign policies. Many of his longtime supporters assailed King for his indictment of Johnson and American imperialism.

Today, guns are clearly winning out over butter. More than half of the federal government's discretionary budget goes toward spending on defense overall, including outlays for the Department of Defense (DOD), nuclear weapons programs, veterans, and the Department of Homeland Security (DHS). And about half of the DOD's allocation ends up in the pockets of private defense contractors.[92] In inflation-adjusted dollars, the United States is spending hundreds of billions of dollars more on the military than at the height of the US war in Vietnam or the peak of the Cold War.[93] The lifetime cost to US taxpayers of Lockheed's F-35 fighter program, the country's most expensive weapons program, is projected to be $2 trillion—a sum that could fund two years of free community college for all students for nearly two decades or universal pre-K for all three- and four-year-olds for at least four decades.[94]

Lawmakers and military contractors have strategically spread the military largesse and wielded the threat of job losses and reduced tax revenues to bulletproof the defense budget.[95] Communities throughout the country have become increasingly dependent on the warfare state for jobs and government revenues as decades of exorbitant spending on the military have impaled the country's capacity to invest in core functions—including disaster relief, education, health care, infrastructure, public works programs, and economic development—that provide genuine security and the essentials for decent lives.[96] High levels of spending on the military and defense contractors have also impaired non-defense-related manufacturing. Military spending does create jobs. But dollar for dollar, it creates far fewer jobs than money spent on education, health care, infrastructure, clean energy, and other sectors of the economy. A million dollars spent on education creates about three times as many jobs as $1 million spent on defense.[97]

Today it is not enough to rail against each misguided war and the outsized Pentagon budget, implores analyst Robert Borosage. Rolling back the empire must be an "integral part of the reform agenda."[98] Unwinding the warfare state hinges on forging broad coalitions supportive of investing in a just transition in which people and communities dependent on the military-industrial complex receive government assistance to engineer a soft landing for them. This includes unemployment compensation, retraining and relocation assistance, and additional financial and other supports.[99] Ditto for communities economically dependent on their local jails and prisons if we are to significantly cut the nation's incarceration rate.

As civilian leaders increasingly seek to bask in the military's glow, they have become less capable or willing to confront how metastasizing militarization in the United States has been deforming democratic institutions and making the country and world less safe. Military figures have invaded civilian realms once considered largely off-limits—as handsomely paid talking heads in the media, as political appointees to the most powerful civilian positions in government, as partisans publicly allied with the Democrats or the Republicans, and as political activists. To shore up their own political fortunes, presidents of both parties and other civilian leaders have taken to deferring to military figures and extolling their reportedly superior wisdom and expertise.[100] (As Sarah Huckabee Sanders, President Trump's press secretary in his first term, brashly declared in 2017, Chief of Staff John Kelly was beyond reproach because it is "highly inappropriate" to question a four-star general.)[101]

Global Warming and Planetary Violence

The United States has a long history of discrediting people and movements that object to the American empire, and today is no exception. Calling for an end to the US empire and for slashing the US military budget runs the risk of being maligned as a simple, naive isolationist or a so-called American Firster sympathetic to Trump. It's as if the only path for US foreign policy is a choice between empire or isolation rather than a multipolar world of "discerning internationalism."[102]

The US military and Washington rules are now existential problems for the United States and the world. They are culpable in the two greatest threats of violence that the United States and the world now face: nuclear war and global warming. The US empire has fostered the destabilization of US political institutions and robbed the country of the political will and resources to mitigate global warming. For decades, Democratic and Republican administrations have cultivated close ties with authoritarian leaders and waged numerous wars and other military actions to ensure US access to fossil fuels in the Middle East and elsewhere. In the quest to be the "indispensable nation," in the memorable words of Madeleine Albright, Bill Clinton's secretary of State, the United States created the world's largest military.[103] The US military is the single largest consumer of energy in America and the largest institutional emitter of greenhouse gases in the world.[104]

For years, US military leaders have acknowledged in their war plans that global warming is a fact, even as many other government officials and public figures dismissed it as science fiction. The US military has been preparing for a hotter planet, including the possibility of climate-related wars as conditions on Earth become more extreme.[105] But US military doctrine and foreign policy remain wedded to the Washington rules. Thus, a dramatic reduction in the size and reach of the US military to help cool the planet is not on the table.[106]

Every person, animal, and plant on Earth today is "living in a crime scene" thanks to the crime of global warming.[107] "There should be a word when you commit treason against a whole planet," declared climate activist Bill McKibben.[108] Scholars associated with the burgeoning field of green criminology characterize global warming as a crime against humanity that the fossil fuel industry and its enablers in government have perpetrated with impunity.[109] That crime, they claim, has brought the planet to the brink of "ecocide"—the deliberate destruction of the natural environment.[110]

Heat is the leading cause of weather-related deaths. Higher heat indexes are associated with increases in self-harm, aggression, conflict, suicide, and gun violence.[111] With the rise in global temperatures, interpersonal violence will likely increase as individuals, communities, and governments face greater strains; as social controls and social supports erode; and as beliefs and traits conducive to crime proliferate.[112]

The link between global warming and the carceral state is especially lethal. Many jails and prisons are built on flood plains and lack air-conditioning. Incarcerated people are more susceptible to becoming ill or dying from the heat because they tend to be in poorer health and to have higher incidences of chronic health problems that excessive heat exacerbates, including obesity, diabetes, and hypertension. Medications prescribed for these ailments can interfere with the body's ability to regulate its temperature, raising the risk of heat-related problems.[113]

Global warming is an exceptional crime, as measured by the unprecedented harm and violence it has already perpetrated and by the existential threat it poses to the planet. But in many other ways, it is a mundane and familiar crime. Since the late 1950s, "scientists have been seriously investigating the subject of human-made climate change." Political leaders, including US presidents, have been aware of their alarming findings for nearly as long.[114] By the late 1970s, scientists at Exxon and other fossil fuel companies had concluded that global warming was real, and that the continued burning of fossil fuels could "indeed be catastrophic," according to internal company documents.[115] But oil executives remained silent about these findings and continued to expand production.

As global warming emerged as a major public issue in the 1980s and 1990s, the fossil fuel industry mimicked Big Tobacco's response to the 1964 surgeon general's report on the harms of smoking. The oil, gas, and coal industries became "merchants of doubt" as they financed an expansive and sophisticated public relations campaign "to reposition global warming as theory not fact."[116] Their efforts to sow doubts in the public's mind about climate change became part of a larger onslaught against what a top adviser to George W. Bush famously derided as the "reality-based community."[117]

A growing number of US cities and states have joined the wave of civil lawsuits and pursued criminal actions against Big Oil for lying to the public and defrauding investors and consumers about the threat of fossil fuels.[118] In 2023, a handful of senators, including Elizabeth Warren (D-MA) and Bernie Sanders (I-VT), publicly urged Attorney General Merrick Garland to hold the fossil fuel industry criminally liable for knowingly destroying the planet. In May 2025, the Trump 2.0 Justice Department announced it was filing lawsuits against New York and Hawaii "to prevent each state from suing fossil fuel companies in state court to seek damages for alleged climate change harms."[119]

An internal JPMorgan Chase report on climate change leaked to the press in 2020 predicted that policymakers will likely take the path of "business as usual" to deal with global warming in the years ahead, increasing the chances of a "catastrophic outcome." The report did not discuss JPMorgan's culpability in the climate emergency, including its role as the leading financier of the fossil fuel industry.[120] Oil and gas companies have so far escaped serious legal or other consequences for global warming for many of the same reasons why the financial industry and Big Pharma are more powerful than ever despite the wide-scale harms they have inflicted.

The planetary violence caused by global warming is a fundamental social justice and civil rights issue. As in the case of other environmental and health threats, the most marginalized communities, including many low-income, Indigenous, Black, and Latino people, are the most vulnerable to the harms and violence of global warming. But being a rung or two up on the ladder—or even several rungs higher—will be scant protection as the sea waters begin to boil, the wildfires burn out of control, and more of the Earth becomes uninhabitable.

Advocates of a Green New Deal have characterized global warming as a "world war" that "we are losing" and have extolled the rapid and massive mobilization for World War II as a model to cool the planet.[121] But the time is long past to retire war as a model, metaphor, and inspiration for transformative public policies. In his first inaugural address, President Franklin D. Roosevelt "invoked war as a metaphor for the nation's economic crisis and a model for its solution."[122] As he pursued rearmament during the 1930s in anticipation of entering the war in Europe, he sought to legitimize a greater role for the state at home by linking it to the war overseas. Roosevelt and other New Dealers embraced war mobilization as a means to foster the state's capacity and the public's temperament to put the New Deal's social welfare and other programs on a permanent footing. Roosevelt dismissed considerable fears at the time, stemming from the US experience in World War I, of the power of corporate-military institutions "to manipulate or corrupt the nation."[123] Celebrating war as a model in policymaking impedes taking a critical look at how the warfare state and national security state born out of World War II and the Cold War are major impediments to stemming all kinds of violence in the United States and abroad today, including the planetary violence of the climate emergency.

The Pandemic, Social Murder, and the US Health-Care System

The country's exceptionally dysfunctional health-care system has compounded the problems of violence and social murder in America. And it will compound the lethalness of global warming. The United States has the world's most expensive medical system. Health care constitutes about 18 percent of the US GDP or nearly twice what other high-income countries spend on average. Yet people in the United States are more likely to die at a younger age and suffer from chronic health problems and preventable diseases.[124] United States spending on clinical care is disproportionately high compared to spending on other items that do a better job at improving a nation's health.[125] These items include education; disability, sickness, and unemployment benefits; public housing; income support for families; jobs programs; and public health departments.[126]

The time is long overdue for creating an affordable system of universal health care in the United States that sucks the profit motive out of keeping people healthy and treating their ailments. Universal health care must be the polestar. In the meantime, there are many intermediate steps the United States should take to make the health-care system less lethal and harmful. These include getting private equity firms out of the health-care business; restoring the public health system to its former glory; and establishing a public system of pharmaceutical development and manufacturing, which California has been exploring.[127]

The drug companies are a deadweight on the US health-care system. Medications are far costlier in the United States than in other high-income countries, despite the proliferation of generics.[128] Less than one-third of new drugs approved in recent years by the FDA and the European Medicines Agency, its

European counterpart, have "high therapeutic value," according to outside experts.[129] The FDA, lawmakers, medical providers, and the criminal legal system have done remarkably little to curtail aggressive marketing of unproven, ineffective, or dangerous drugs; misrepresentation and suppression of clinical results; and the manipulation of patent laws and loopholes that keeps safer, cheaper, and more efficacious drugs off the market. And these problems in the drug industry appear to be getting worse.[130]

The pandemic was a godsend for Big Pharma, allowing it to bask in the glow of the lifesaving Covid-19 vaccines just as the opioid lawsuits were battering its reputation.[131] Big Pharma used the megadose of good publicity from the Covid-19 vaccines as an opening to aggressively raise drug prices and push back on price controls, including controls on the cost of the Covid-19 vaccines. Pharmaceutical companies touted their central role in developing the Covid-19 vaccines and downplayed the government's more consequential role. In fact, decades of prior government spending on seminal research powered the Covid-19 vaccine breakthroughs. So did the Trump administration's Operation Warp Speed, which provided billions of dollars in government subsidies, patent deals, and other sweeteners to select pharmaceutical companies to ensure that the "free" market did not get in the way of rapidly developing a vaccine.[132]

The pandemic provided numerous opportunities to fleece the government and ultimately taxpayers. Thanks to decades of disastrous budgetary decisions (including defunding the Strategic National Stockpile) and the deep bias toward investing in private, not public, solutions, the government turned to unscrupulous brokers to rustle up masks and other medical necessities as the pandemic struck. These brokers gouged the government and the public. The government also channeled billions of dollars in Covid relief through privately run programs, notably the Paycheck Protection Program, that initially had few antifraud and other guardrails, resulting in hundreds of billions of dollars in fraud.[133]

The pandemic fueled a short-lived surge in public spending on social welfare, economic supports, and public health. This spending soon subsided despite its proven success in lowering the child poverty rate by one-third and reducing the rate of health-care uninsurance to a record low of 8 percent.[134] Unfortunately, after a bold reassertion of the need for public solutions to the pandemic in the wake of the Trump administration's failures, the Biden administration retreated to a private-led, individualistic, "you do you" approach to Covid-19 and future pandemics.[135] And it was shockingly nonchalant in the face of the growing deadly threat of H5N1, better known as avian or bird flu.[136]

As it precipitated a "catastrophic loss of life," the Covid-19 pandemic laid bare the exceptional lethalness of the United States.[137] The death rate from Covid-19 infections was far higher in America than in Canada and Western Europe. Covid-19 was indirectly more lethal in the United States as well. As the pandemic descended, the US homicide rate soared by nearly a third between 2019 and 2020. This was the largest single-year rise in nearly a century and included huge increases in homicide deaths for residents in both rural and urban areas. But homicide rates did not surge in Western Europe after Covid-19 struck.[138] Neither did traffic deaths and drug overdoses, unlike in the United States.[139]

A New Deal and a New Kind of State

Exceptional levels of violence in the United States, including interpersonal, state, structural, and, increasingly, political violence, have undermined the government's legitimacy. This violence has fueled antigovernment sentiments at a time when more state intervention, not less, is needed in many areas.[140] State power was essential to shrinking economic inequality, poverty, and violence in the past and must be so in the future. Thanks to the New Deal, the GI bill, and the Great Society, rates of poverty and income inequality fell, life expectancy increased, more African American and other historically disadvantaged people joined the burgeoning middle class, and corporate power was somewhat corralled.

The legacy of the New Deal looms large at this fraught political moment. For nearly a century, business interests and the far right have been on a long march to impale the New Deal and bury it. They have sought to kill off its social programs and those of its heir, the Great Society, including welfare, Social Security, Medicare, and Medicaid. They also have been on a mission to cripple the government's capacity to carry out functions considered the sine qua non of a modern, developed, democratic state, including collecting taxes; protecting people from infectious diseases; ensuring the safety of foods, drugs, and other products; facilitating free and fair elections; and keeping the water safe to drink and the air safe to breathe. In short, they have sought to shrink the government "down to the size where we can drown it in the bathtub," as Grover Norquist, the antitax, antigovernment zealot, once declared.[141] Their long march has succeeded in mainstreaming what were once considered fringe ideas on the far right.

More recently, the New Deal has been assailed from a different direction, condemned as a hopelessly racist project that did not significantly improve the lives of African American people in the United States. But the racial scorecard for the New Deal is complex.[142] The 1935 Social Security Act exempted agricultural and domestic workers, including an estimated 3.5 million African American people, from receiving public old-age and unemployment benefits. But it also exempted an estimated 11.4 million white sharecroppers, tenant farmers, and domestic servants, all at the behest of powerful Southern lawmakers who were doing the bidding of the region's economic and agricultural elite.[143] Over the decades, the various expansions of Social Security transformed this program into a bulwark against poverty for older people, individuals who are disabled, and other marginalized groups. Discriminatory policies were embedded in the New Deal's Civilian Conservation Corps (CCC) and the Works Progress Administration (WPA). But these signature public works programs became more egalitarian over time and provided large numbers of African American people, as well as members of other historically disadvantaged groups, with employment that staunched their poverty.[144]

The wave of unionization spurred by the New Deal opened up living-wage jobs and better work conditions to millions of people, including African American people. Organized labor "emerged from decidedly imperfect beginnings to become America's most potent democratizing force."[145] The Congress of Industrial Organizations (CIO) broke away from the notoriously racist American Federation of Labor (AFL) in 1938 and set its sights on organizing millions of unskilled workers. Unions were rife with discriminatory practices, but the activities of CIO organizers in the South and elsewhere dating back to the 1930s laid important political groundwork for the blossoming of the civil rights movement decades later.[146]

The New Deal's racial scorecard on housing is more checkered. The Federal Housing Administration (FHA), established in 1934, opened up homeownership to millions of white families. But it also sanctioned the long-standing discriminatory practices of the real estate and banking sectors. The FHA's policies kept safe, affordable housing out of reach for many African American households and devastated Black communities with redlining and other practices, as historian Keeanga-Yamahtta Taylor masterfully documents.[147]

The New Deal's racial shortcomings are significant but not cause for the wholesale dismissal of its social, economic, and regulatory achievements. Casting out the New Deal plays into the far right's efforts to drown public faith in government and its potential to better people's lives.[148] It also fuels fatalism about the utility of politics, including a surge of what has been called Afro-pessimism.[149] On a related point, writing off corporations and their executives as congenitally criminal and infinitely more powerful than the government and the public fosters political passivity, disabling pessimism, and ultimately defeat. For anyone who cares about stemming violence in America, recognizing how and why corporate power and corporate criminality have waxed and waned is vital.[150]

To borrow from the social reformer John Dewey, we need to understand how history is a series of plastic junctures.[151] We need a fine-tuned understanding of the political, institutional, social, racial, and economic context of the past and present so as to perceive when important opportunities open up to override pieces of the historical terrain or to build on accomplishments from the past.[152]

Teddy Roosevelt, Joe Biden, Bernie Sanders, and Donald Trump

The financial and foreclosure crises yielded strands of populism on the right and left that crisscrossed in the candidacies of Donald Trump and Bernie Sanders in 2016 and 2020. As veterans of the 2011 Occupy Wall Street movement "gradually developed a foothold in the Democratic Party," they tussled with the old guard to pull the party leftward during Obama's second term.[153] The leadership of the Democratic Party fired back in 2016, closing ranks and putting the party's apparatus behind Hillary Clinton to stop Sanders.[154] Four years later, the insurgent Democrats were deeply divided between Sanders and Senator Elizabeth Warren, allowing the party's leadership and its financial patrons, with former President Barack Obama at the helm, to circle the wagons and propel Joe Biden forward despite his early stumbles in the 2020 primaries.[155] Veterans of Occupy Wall Street and the Warren and Sanders campaigns became a force to be reckoned with in the Democratic Party. They were part of an explosion in grassroots energy and organization that prodded President Biden to be less obsequious toward the corporate sector.[156]

Biden had a lot in common with President Theodore Roosevelt. To varying degrees, they both did much more than their immediate predecessors to curb corporate power, especially monopolistic power. In his first annual message to Congress in 1901, Roosevelt implored, "Great corporations exist only because they are created and safeguarded by our institutions." Roosevelt went on to declare that "it is therefore our right and our duty to see that they work in harmony with these institutions."[157] Just months after taking office, Biden signed a sweeping executive order that featured seventy-two initiatives— everything from net neutrality to cheaper hearing aids—to curb corporate power. At the time, Biden declared, "Capitalism without competition isn't capitalism; it's exploitation."[158]

Biden's record on curbing corporate power and reviving rural America was mixed but considerably stronger than that of Bill Clinton, Barack Obama, or Donald Trump. His three signature pieces of legislation—the Infrastructure Investment and Jobs Act, the CHIPS and Science Act, and the Inflation Reduction Act—appropriated nearly half a trillion dollars in spending for "many projects that could be particularly relevant to the economic revival of rural communities."[159]

The Biden administration did not significantly curtail the de facto decriminalization of crime in the suites.[160] But Biden's appointees in the Justice Department and Federal Trade Commission (FTC) pursued a slew of antitrust and other actions to break up concentrated corporate power that is harming workers, consumers, and the public in myriad ways. No wonder that one of the first orders of business for the Democratic Party's megadonors—after Biden was pushed aside in July 2024—was trying to persuade Vice President and Democratic nominee Kamala Harris to replace FTC Chair Lina Khan should she win the White House.[161] The second order of business was to pressure Harris to distance herself from the promised tax hikes for corporations and wealthy Americans that Biden had campaigned on. And Harris obliged, selecting corporate tax policy as one of the few issues that distinguished her from Biden.[162]

On the issue of curbing state violence meted out by the carceral state, the police, and the US military, Biden's record was more troubling. Trump and his supporters seized on the Covid-related spike in homicides and shootings to torpedo the billowing movement to end mass incarceration and make the police more accountable and less powerful. In response, Biden and many top Democrats endorsed a kinder, gentler form of tough law-and-order politics. They backed larger budgets for law enforcement, opposed even modest reforms to make the criminal legal system fairer and less punitive, and enlisted in another war on drugs, this time against fentanyl and fentanyl-like substances.[163]

As he went on the offensive toward corporate power, Biden, like Teddy Roosevelt before him, remained steadfast in his commitment to the US global empire. During the 2016 presidential campaign, Trump and Sanders were the only major candidates who seriously questioned why the United States has been on a permanent war footing worldwide since 9/11. Four years later, Sanders made opposition to the war on terror, and the mindset that generated it, a centerpiece of his campaign. And the hawkish old guard in the Democratic Party declared war on him.[164] The entire Democratic field in 2020, including Joe Biden, gave lip service to the promise to "end endless wars." But after Biden secured the nomination, he and his allies "opted to regress to familiar 9/11-era patterns."[165]

Biden eagerly sought and received the endorsements of top Republican and Democratic figures in the global war on terror and the forever wars, including John Brennan and James Clapper, who had positioned themselves as leaders of the resistance to Trump and as champions of democracy. This was a remarkable feat given that Brennan and Clapper were deeply implicated in some of the most egregious human and civil rights violations of the war on terror when they served in the Bush and Obama administrations, including the torture of "enemy combatants" and the illegal mass surveillance of American citizens.[166]

The high-profile involvement of Brennan, Clapper, and other former intelligence officers in electoral politics raised troubling questions about whether the intelligence community, in an unprecedented development, had become an organized political faction.[167] But mainstream commentators and the media mostly ignored these questions, despite the US intelligence community's long and troubling history of undermining democracy in the United States and elsewhere. Brennan, Clapper, and other members of the foreign policy establishment promoted the spy agencies and massive warfare state as the bulwark of American democracy, which, in their view, was under siege from a growing list of threats from abroad and at home.[168]

As president, Biden declared that the forever wars were over even as the fighting raged. In September 2021, the month following the US withdrawal from Afghanistan, Biden told the United Nations: "I stand here today, for the first time in 20 years, with the United States not at war. We've turned the page."[169] But at the time, the United States was involved in wars in Syria, Somalia, Libya, Niger, and other undeclared war zones. Barely six months later, the United States entered a proxy war against Russia in Ukraine as part of the new cold war with Russia and China. Spending on the US military and US arms sales surged under Biden. And defense contractors celebrated their bonanza. "We went through six years of Stingers in 10 months," brayed Gregory J.

Hayes, the chief executive of Raytheon, in late 2022. Raytheon manufactures the shoulder-fired anti-aircraft missiles that have been a game changer in the war in Ukraine.[170]

The fixation on waging the forever wars and a new cold war against Russia, China, or both of them occluded the far more consequential threat from the new nuclear arms race stoked by the multitrillion-dollar modernization of the US nuclear arsenal and the raging arms race in space.[171] In March 2023, the Biden administration proposed the largest nuclear weapons budget in history. Two months later, Biden laid a wreath in Hiroshima to commemorate the seventy thousand people killed by a single nuclear bomb dropped by the United States on August 6, 1945, which destroyed the Japanese city.[172]

The US military, defense contractors, and the Washington rules remained largely unassailable in the eyes of the foreign policy and military establishment, Fortune 500 executives, and the ultrawealthy during Trump's first term and then during the Biden administration.[173] But there were some exceptions. The odd couple of billionaires Charles Koch on the right and George Soros on the left backed the new Quincy Institute for Responsible Statecraft. The institute's stated mission is to rethink the "practical and moral failures of US efforts to unilaterally shape the destiny of other nations by force."[174]

Senator JD Vance (R-OH) and Governor Tim Walz (D-MN) were another such odd couple. The Republican and Democratic nominees for vice president in 2024 could not be more different in many ways. But they both shared profound unease over the forever wars. Walz retired from the National Guard in 2006 to make a run for Congress centered on opposition to the war in Iraq. And he won his longshot bid in a heavily Republican district. Vance, who served in the US Marine Corps in Iraq, was a harsh critic of the US war there. In a 2023 speech to the Heritage Foundation, Vance deplored how those who were the "most wrong" about Iraq "suffered no consequences." He lambasted the US foreign policy establishment for learning "zero lessons from what is perhaps the most unforced and catastrophic error in the history of this country."[175]

On the presidential campaign trail, Kamala Harris did not put any distance between herself, the Washington rules, and the US military. In her acceptance speech at the 2024 Democratic National Convention, she vowed to "ensure America always has the strongest, most lethal fighting force in the world."[176] Harris warmly embraced not only former Representative Liz Cheney (R-WY), the most outspoken Republican critic of Donald Trump and the January 6 insurrection, but also her father, Dick Cheney. As vice president in the George W. Bush administration, her father was a mastermind of the US global war on terror and its unprecedented civil liberties and other abuses at home and abroad.

As for Donald Trump, his critique of the forever wars has been, not surprisingly, acerbic but shifty. When he ran for president in 2024, Trump struck a familiar note from his 2016 campaign as he railed against the "warmongers" in government who "want to fight everybody" in places "we've never heard about before."[177] Trump 2.0's Big Beautiful Bill funds state violence at record levels. The Pentagon will reap about a 13 percent increase in spending, which amounts to an additional $150 billion and will push its official budget over $1 trillion for the first time.[178] Shortly after becoming the new Defense secretary in Trump's second term, Pete Hegseth ordered the Pentagon to slash $50 billion in DOD spending from "so-called 'climate change' and other woke programs, as well as excessive bureaucracy." The savings would be redirected to pay for "securing the border" and building the Iron Dome missile defense system Trump proposed for America.[179]

On the campaign trail, and then when he was back in the White House, Trump frequently lashed out at the forever wars and vowed to purge the "woke" generals in the military. His targets included military officials who reportedly had opposed deploying the armed forces to quash the George Floyd protests, undo the 2020 election results, and curb the growing white power movement in the ranks. Barely a month into his second term, Trump initiated an extraordinary purge of the Pentagon.[180]

During the 2024 campaign, Trump called for opening a new warfront, this one back home in the United States. He declared that the country's "greatest danger" was not "our enemies from the outside" but rather "the destruction of our nation from the people from within."[181] At the start of his second term, Trump quickly moved to, in his words, "root out the communists, Marxists, fascists and the radical-left thugs that live like vermin within the confines of our country." The US bombing of Iran in June 2025 revealed the shallowness of Trump's commitment to ending the forever wars overseas. For a strongman like Trump, attacking Iran and other military adventures are irresistible opportunities to silence domestic dissent, cripple a free press, and accelerate the US descent into authoritarianism.[182]

Imperfect Coalitions and Partners

Franklin D. Roosevelt became president at an exceptional moment in 1933. Four years into the Depression, the Hoover administration was thoroughly discredited, as was the business sector. Roosevelt recognized that the country was ready for a break with the past as he symbolically and substantively cultivated that sentiment. But the break did not come from Roosevelt alone. Massive numbers of Americans mobilized in unions, women's organizations, veterans' groups, senior citizen associations, and civil right groups to ensure that the country switched course to rein in corporations and banks and alleviate economic and other inequalities. And without congressional lawmakers to lay the groundwork and then to lead the charge, there might have been no New Deal.[183]

The prevalence today of zero-sum thinking—that is, the widespread belief that gains for Black people and other historically marginalized racial and ethnic groups will inevitably come at the expense of white people and vice versa—is a major impediment to forging broad, durable, and successful political coalitions to stem the many strands of violence in America today.[184] It is possible to recognize how the United States has been exceptionally toxic for many African American people throughout US history while also acknowledging how the country has been toxic for poor and working-class people, many of whom are white, and for growing numbers of middle-class people who lead precarious lives.

Martin Luther King Jr. stressed the imperative "to attack the evil system rather than individuals who happen to be caught in the system" and to win over rather than humiliate one's political opponents.[185] If King were alive today, legal scholar Randall Kennedy speculates, "it is hard to imagine him 'writing off' even deplorable Trump voters."[186] As the 1960s unfolded, King became even more insistent about the connection between wide-scale economic justice and racial justice. He identified higher wages, low unemployment, and robust unionization as key to containing the surges of racial animus that political and economic elites have historically stoked to keep poor and working-class people divided and weak.[187] King's chosen slogan was "Power for poor people." At the time of his death in April 1968, his "Poor People's Campaign" had brought him to Memphis to support striking sanitation workers. A week before he was assassinated, King told a reporter, "In a sense you could say we are engaged in the class struggle."[188]

Fighting racism and discrimination are important battles that cannot be abandoned. But discourses and political strategies centered primarily on antiracism and antidiscrimination risk impoverishing the language and strategies for addressing inequality in its many forms, as sociologist Karen Fields and historian Barbara Fields show. They can render invisible or incidental the political and economic structures and the interlocking domestic and foreign policies that perpetrate state violence, interpersonal violence, and social murder in America. When racism is compartmentalized into an exceptional category all its own and defined primarily by individual traits and prejudices, racism and "other forms of inequality are rarely tackled together because they rarely come into view together." This "racecraft," as Fields and Fields demonstrate, conceals the "affiliation between racism and inequality in general" and how "they work together and share a central nervous system."[189] Racecraft thus stymies the formation of durable, broad-based, multiracial, multiethnic, cross-class coalitions that bridge the divide between urban and rural communities; between poor people, working-class people, and the precarious middle class; between people with and without college degrees; and between people who have served in the military and those who have not.[190]

Today rising numbers of white people are at risk of premature death or other serious harms because they are uninsured, underinsured, underpaid, underemployed, incarcerated, unhoused, damaged by the forever wars, or dependent on opioids. Charging them with the crime of white privilege is a self-defeating political strategy. So is decrying the privilege of college students who have put themselves on the front lines of opposing the US-backed war in Gaza and defending free speech and peaceful dissent. At this fraught political moment, justifiable concerns over relative privilege and relative oppression risk morphing into titanic concerns that threaten to debilitate economic, social, and racial justice organizations with internecine battles.[191]

Twilight for Democracy in America?

Democracy in America is far from immortal. It could shatter or succumb to death by a thousand cuts. Donald Trump has put US democracy in peril, but neither he nor the Republican Party, which opportunistically hitched its future to his roller coaster, is singularly to blame. Trump's return to the White House in 2025—with his crass cronyism, government of grifters, weaponization of the FBI and Justice Department to settle scores, and promiscuous pardoning of wealthy people convicted of fraud, bribery, and cheating on their taxes—will likely make the Clinton, Bush, and Obama years look once again like a golden era. But that golden era is a mirage. The way forward to a more peaceful and democratic future in which prosperity is widely shared begins by recognizing how the leaders of the Republican and Democratic parties, including revered figures like Bill Clinton, Barack Obama, and their wealthy patrons, were deeply culpable in the rise of Trumpism.

In the United States and elsewhere, financial crises have periodically been combustible fuel for bursts of racist and nativist scapegoating, the emergence of demagogic politicians, and surges in extreme-right parties.[192] Donald Trump's quests for the White House spurred vigorous debates about whether cultural and identity politics trumped economic interests or vice versa in driving his supporters.[193] But the formation of political preferences is complex. Material interests are often deeply entangled with factors related to culture and identity, including racism, nativism, anti-elitism, and status anxiety. Material factors include anxieties about economic hardship for oneself, one's family, and one's community, as well as class cleavages defined not just by income and wealth but also by education, occupation, geography, and historical experience.[194]

Singling out virulent racism and nativism as the primary reasons for Trump's electoral success cannot account for the fact that the white working-class voters critical to his victory in 2016 had twice voted in droves for Obama.[195] Or that in 2016 Trump performed comparatively better with Black and Latino voters than John McCain did in 2008 or Mitt Romney did in 2012.[196] Polling data suggest that Trump's supporters in 2016 were "not particularly down on their luck."[197] But the specific subset of working-class voters in Wisconsin, Michigan, and Pennsylvania that delivered the White House to Trump in 2016 lived "in communities that are literally dying" thanks to the economic and health crises, including the opioid epidemic, unfolding across working-class America.[198] And a potentially consequential portion of Sanders voters in these states moved over to Trump in the general election.[199]

Some commentators have suggested that winning back just a small fraction of the Trump voters, notably those who were once attracted to Bernie Sanders, "could be the beginning of the marginalization of the far right."[200] But this assumes that the main political arena is still electoral politics. That may have been true a decade ago when Trump was still a political punchline. But the full-frontal assault since then on the electoral apparatus, the media, universities, unions, governing institutions, and civil society has delegitimized the electoral process and put democracy in America at great risk.

The United States is exceptional today among Western countries for its "persistent levels of pernicious polarization."[201] Furthermore, America is awash in guns thanks to the US Supreme Court's radical reinterpretation of the Second Amendment, which has transformed the country into a lock-and-carry nation over the last two decades.[202] With just 4 percent of the world's population, the United States has nearly half of its civilian firearms.[203] Brandishing a weapon has become a critical marker of political identity for some groups, especially on the right. Furthermore, as fears grow that political violence is becoming an endemic rather than an episodic feature of American politics, more people across the political spectrum are arming themselves.[204]

Today there is a wistful belief in the mainstream media, the Democratic establishment, and the remnants of the old Republican establishment that somehow the US military is the secret weapon that will save democracy in America if all else fails.[205] But President Eisenhower would have seen through the folly of such thinking. In his nationally televised farewell address to the nation three days before he left office in 1961, Eisenhower warned of the "grave implications" of the emerging "military-industrial complex."[206] In short, any democracy expecting the military to save it is no longer much of a democracy.

The consolidation of an oligarchy of multimillionaires, billionaires, and decabillionaires in the United States with burgeoning ties to plutocrats in other countries poses a mortal threat to democracy in America and elsewhere. Big business is highly compatible with authoritarianism, fascism, and the warfare state. Just look at Mussolini and Italy in the 1920s and 1930s, or Pinochet and Chile in the 1970s and 1980s, or Germany in the 1930s and 1940s. Germany's leading corporations, including Allianz, Daimler, Deutsche Bank, and Siemens, profitably made their peace with Hitler and his National Socialist Party and emerged from World War II even larger and more powerful.[207]

Today, the dark money of the uber-rich has been funding orchestrated attacks on democracy in America, including the efforts to overturn the results of the 2020 election and the assaults on academic freedom and scientific inquiry at colleges and universities.[208] Right after the January 6 insurrection, hundreds of corporations announced that they would suspend their contributions to Republican lawmakers who voted against certifying the election of Joe Biden. But as the 2022 midterm elections were gearing up, most of these companies resumed their contributions.[209]

Once it became apparent that Donald Trump would be the 2024 Republican nominee, the country's corporate titans not only made peace with him but also embraced him.[210] During the 2024 campaign, Trump gestured in public toward economic populism as he promoted higher tariffs and sweet-talked workers and unions. But in private meetings, he reassured business leaders of his fealty to cutting more of their taxes and disemboweling more regulations.[211] After Trump was reelected, the country's oligarchs—including Tim Cook, Bill Gates, Mark Zuckerberg, Jeff Bezos, and Sundar Pichai—jetted off to Mar-a-Lago to pledge their allegiance to him and Elon Musk, the richest person in the world, who was auditioning to be copresident. Other members of the US oligarchy, notably Jamie Dimon of JPMorgan Chase, were bonding with Trump behind the scenes.[212]

During the pandemic, billionaire wealth saw its biggest increase ever. The ten richest people in the world—all of whom are men and seven of whom are from the United States—own more wealth than the 3.1 billion people at the bottom, according to a 2022 report by Oxfam.[213] The new American dream of the superrich "is to make enough money so that you can insulate yourself from the damage you're creating," observes one chronicler of the billionaire class. "It's as if they want to build a car that goes fast enough to escape from its own exhaust."[214]

But the uber-rich's version of the American dream is as illusionary as other versions. Some of the world's richest people irrationally believe they can opt out should the apocalypse arrive—be it a bloody civil war, or a cold war that turns nuclear hot, or the wrath of global warming that drowns and immolates large parts of the planet. They can imagine themselves safely waiting out the civil war in luxury homes in New Zealand. Or hunkering down in five-star bunkers under the desert as the seas drown the shores. Or sipping martinis on Mars.[215] What they cannot imagine is that they would be reduced to wandering the barren postapocalyptic terrain like the father in Cormac McCarthy's *The Road*, trying to save his son, the only precious possession he has left.

ACKNOWLEDGMENTS

WHEN ASKED how he worked, Albert Einstein replied, "I grope." As I wrote this book, I groped a lot. I am indebted to the many scholars, policymakers, researchers, and journalists—some of whom I know personally, most of whom I don't—who helped show me the way.

A sweeping, synthetic book like this would not be possible without the extraordinary research of numerous colleagues in history, sociology, law, political science, criminology, public health, and other fields. My many citations of your work are testimony to how much I relied on your important research. I also depended on the growing number of nonprofit organizations and publications that have been churning out indispensable data and articles on the carceral state, corporate criminality, and violence in America, including The Sentencing Project, the Prison Policy Initiative, *Prison Legal News*, the Vera Institute, the *Appeal*, Public Citizen, the Marshall Project, the American Civil Liberties Union, and the financial news website Wall Street on Parade, to name but a few. The outstanding investigative and other reporting of the *Philadelphia Inquirer*, my hometown newspaper, was a powerful daily reminder of the many ways that violence manifests itself in the lives of people in my city and beyond.

I am grateful to the anonymous reviewers of my manuscript for their thoughtful, tough, constructive suggestions, which made this a much better book. A special thanks to Keeanga-Yamahtta Taylor, who provided extensive comments on the manuscript. Our lively lunchtime discussion was one of the highlights of this project. I am also indebted to John Hagan, another reviewer of the manuscript, for his sharp comments and encouragement, and to Sara Doskow.

The team at Princeton University Press was wonderful to work with. Bridget Flannery-McCoy kept this project moving in the right direction. After speaking with her, I always felt uplifted and encouraged. I am thankful to Eric

Crahan, David McBride, and especially Alena Chekanov for seamlessly stepping in and keeping the project on track after Bridget left the press. Natalie Baan and the rest of the production team treated my book with care as they spun their magic.

I am thankful to David Garland and Daniel Nagin for inviting me at an opportune moment to contribute an essay on the opioid epidemic to the *Annual Review of Criminology* 6 (2023). Portions of chapters 10 and 11 draw on that essay, which appeared in volume 6 (copyright 2023 Annual Reviews, https://www.annualreviews.org). Barry Eidlin and Michael McCarthy's invitation to contribute to "Rethinking Class and Social Difference," a special issue of *Political Power and Social Theory*, also came at a fortunate time. Their incisive comments on my contribution helped refine my analysis of the relationship between race, class, and the carceral state. Portions of chapter 2 draw on that essay (© 2020 Emerald Publishing Limited). The 2017 conference "Tracing the Relationship Between Inequality, Crime and Punishment," sponsored by the British Academy and organized by Leonidas Cheliotis, Nicola Lacey, David Soskice, and Sappho Xenakis, moved this project along before I even knew it was a project. Niki and David's comments on my draft for the edited volume sharpened my thinking, as did the contributions of other conference participants. Chapters 2 and 5 draw on that essay (© 2020 The British Academy). I am humbled and deeply appreciative that civil rights attorney Riley H. Ross III took time out from fighting the good fight to read and comment on chapter 3.

Karen Heimer, Sarah E. Malone, and Stacy De Coster graciously allowed me to use two graphs from their 2023 *Annual Review of Criminology* article on shifts in the imprisonment rates of women. Gabriel Zucman, whose research is transforming the conversation about economic inequality and tax policy in the United States and globally, generously shared his data on shifting wealth inequality in the United States that was the basis for the striking graph in chapter 1.

Over the years, my students and research assistants at Penn have been invaluable in showing me the way. A special thanks to my RAs for going the extra mile for me numerous times and for saving me from many embarrassing errors. I am indebted to Penn's Christopher H. Browne Center for a timely grant for this project, and to my students and colleagues for their helpful suggestions on the appendix.

My wonderful colleagues on the board and staff of ACLU-PA have been a deep source of sustenance and inspiration for nearly a decade now. I remain in awe of their political acumen, respect for divergent viewpoints, and well-spring of optimism and good humor despite the odds.

To Glaciey, thank you for always making me laugh and for reminding me how much little creatures and little things matter as we wrestle with the big picture. To Atul and Tara, thank you for the many ways you shaped this book (most of which remain unknown to you) and for helping me grope through life with your love and compassion.

On Use of Language and Data

LANGUAGE IS imperfect and evolving. Certain words and phrases fall out of use. They are rehabilitated. Words or terms that were once reviled or dismissed as oddities, such as Ms. in place of Miss or Mrs., go mainstream.

With the explosion in public awareness of the problem of mass incarceration, terms like *felon, ex-felon, offender,* and *ex-offender* have been falling out of favor. More journalists, professional associations, policymakers, and activists have been choosing language that does not define individuals primarily by their legal status, physical or mental health problems, race, ethnicity, or other broad categories.[1]

Whenever possible, I sought to use person-centered language in this book. For example, *incarcerated person* rather than *inmate* or *prisoner*; *person with opioid use disorder* rather than *addict*; *people convicted of sex offenses* rather than *sex offenders*; and *Black people* and *white people*, not *Blacks* and *whites*. Some of these terms and phrases are more cumbersome and may sound discordant, at least initially. But that is a small price to pay for recognizing the dignity, humanity, and complexity of all people. Likewise, I decided to use the term *criminal legal system* rather than *criminal justice system* because the law enforcement apparatus does not always deliver justice and often perpetrates injustice.

In everyday conversation, we tend to use the words *jail* and *prison* interchangeably, but these words are technically different. Jails are run by local authorities, typically cities or counties. They hold people who have been arrested but have not made bail or who have been denied bail; people awaiting trial, other disposition of their cases, or sentencing; and people serving a short sentence (usually a year or less). Prisons confine people who were convicted and received longer sentences. Unless otherwise specified, *incarceration*, as used in this book, is a comprehensive term that refers to the total level of confinement—that is, the total number of people or rate of people locked up in local jails, state prisons, and federal penitentiaries. *Imprisonment* refers to a smaller subset of confinement that includes confinement in state or federal prisons, but not local jails.

How best to categorize or refer to people whose ethnicity is Hispanic or Latin American is a vexing question. Except when using data from official sources such as the Justice Department's Bureau of Justice Statistics (BJS) that use the terms *Hispanic* and *non-Hispanic*, I decided to mostly use the term *Latino* to refer to people of Hispanic and Latin American origin. For a variety of reasons, I chose *Latino*, rather than *Latinx* or the newer term *Latine*, which is more promising but even less familiar than *Latinx*.[2] I recognize that the term *Latino* is still problematic. It is not technically gender inclusive. Furthermore, many Latin American and Hispanic people "identify as mixed race, indigenous, or Afro-Latino," and "Hispanic or Latino ethnicities can be split further by country of origin."[3]

How best to refer to the descendants of the original inhabitants of the land that became the United States is another challenging issue. I ended up choosing to use the term *Indigenous people*, while recognizing its shortcomings.[4] When specifically referencing BJS statistics on Indigenous people, I use the terms *American Indian/Alaskan Native*, the bureau's chosen category.

The BJS is the principal federal agency for collecting and analyzing data on incarceration and other penal sanctions, as well as conditions in the country's prisons and jails. The agency's incomplete, inconsistent, or missing demographic and other data about people ensnared in the criminal legal system, including their ethnicity, race, gender, class background, and sexuality, is a perennial problem. Chronic underfunding of the BJS has contributed to these data problems. More recently, escalating political attacks on all kinds of government statistical databases, which are part of a wider political assault on expertise and scientific evidence, have exacerbated these data difficulties.[5]

Data limitations make it more difficult to track trends in key indicators such as incarceration, parole, and probation. For example, beginning in the early 1990s, BJS data on people incarcerated in local jails stopped separating out "gender-specific numbers by race and ethnicity," which, among other things, hampered tracking trends in the rates of Black and white women in jail.[6] The BJS did not begin routinely collecting comprehensive data on the ethnicity of incarcerated people until about twenty-five years ago. Up until then, it deployed only two racial categories—Black and white. Today the BJS uses five ethnic/racial categories: non-Hispanic Black people, non-Hispanic white people, Hispanic people, American Indian/Alaskan Native people, and Asian people.

The BJS is dependent on the quality of the data that individual states and counties collect, which varies enormously. Data on the ethnicity and race of people serving time in state prisons tend to be more accurate and comprehensive than racial and ethnicity data collected on arrests, the jail population, and people on probation and probation.[7]

In compiling and reporting data on the criminal legal system, many jurisdictions do not follow even the minimal guidelines of the US Census Bureau: to collect race and ethnicity data separately, but report them "as combined categories such as 'non-Hispanic white' or 'Hispanic Black.'"[8] Jurisdictions that continue to use only two categories—Black and white—to enumerate people involved in the criminal legal system likely categorize Latino people as white, which artificially inflates the number of white people, obfuscates white/ Black disparities, and makes it more difficult to track the involvement of Latino people (the country's largest and fastest-growing ethnic group) in the US criminal legal system.[9]

The data of states and counties that do include Hispanic or Latino as a separate category can still be problematic. For example, Miami–Dade County in Florida, Dallas County in Texas, and Harris County in Texas, which includes the city of Houston, "have in recent years reported either no or very low numbers of Hispanic or Latino people" in their jails and "correspondingly large increases" in jailed white people.[10] Instances in which government employees determine someone's race or ethnicity, rather than permit individuals to declare their race or ethnicity to the authorities, create additional data problems. People are "boxed into identities they do not claim as their own" and that are "inconsistent with Census Bureau data collection standards."[11]

NOTES

Preface

1. For the direct quotations in this preface, see John Kenneth Galbraith, "Power and the Useful Economist," *American Economic Review* 63, no. 1 (1973): 2; Shirley Hazzard, "The Flowers of Sorrow," *NY*, October 17, 1964, 52; and the archived recording of James Baldwin in "James Baldwin's Fire," *Throughline*, September 17, 2020, NPR, https://www.npr.org/transcripts /912769283. On Trump's racism and misogyny, see, for example, David Leonhardt and Ian Prasad Philbrick, "Donald Trump's Racism: The Definitive List, Updated," *NYT*, January 15, 2018, https://www.nytimes.com/interactive/2018/01/15/opinion/leonhardt-trump-racist. html; and Michael Barbaro and Megan Twohey, "Crossing the Line: How Donald Trump Behaved with Women in Private," *NYT*, May 14, 2016, https://www.nytimes.com/2016/05/15/us /politics/donald-trump-women.html.

1. Social Murder: Wealth, Power, and Violence in America

1. Mary Harris Jones, *Autobiography of Mother Jones*, ed. Mary Field Parton (Chicago: Charles H. Kerr, 1925), 81.

2. Friedrich Engels, *The Condition of the Working-Class in England in 1844*, trans. Florence Kelley Wischnewetzky (London: George Allen and Unwin, 1892), https://www.gutenberg.org /cache/epub/17306/pg17306-images.html, 95–96.

3. On the criminality of notable founders, including George Washington and Alexander Hamilton, and the failure to sanction them, see Scott Christianson, *With Liberty for Some: 500 Years of Imprisonment in America* (Boston: Northeastern University Press, 1998), 101–2.

4. As David Garland notes, "there is a whole body of research showing that penal institutions and welfare institutions are tightly coupled and mutually reinforcing." David Garland, "The Current Crisis of American Criminal Justice: A Structural Analysis," *Annual Review of Criminology* 6 (2023): 51.

5. Paul Butler, "The Problem of State Violence," *Daedalus* 151, no. 1 (Winter 2022): 24. Johan Galtung and liberation theologians coined the term *structural violence* in the 1960s. See "Violence, Peace and Peace Research," *Journal of Peace Research* 6, no. 3 (1969): 167–91. See also Paul E. Farmer et al., "Structural Violence and Clinical Medicine," *PLOS Medicine* 3, no. 10 (2006): 1686–91.

6. Butler, "Problem of State Violence," 24. See also Cecilia Menjívar, "A Framework for Examining Violence," in *Gender Through the Prism of Difference*, 6th ed., ed. Maxine Baca Zinn et al. (Oxford: Oxford University Press, 2020), 485–500.

7. Anne Case and Angus Deaton, *Deaths of Despair and the Future of Capitalism* (Princeton, NJ: Princeton University Press, 2020).

8. Matthew Desmond, *Poverty, by America* (New York: Crown, 2013), 37.

9. Ruth Wilson Gilmore, *The Golden Gulag: Prisons, Surplus, and Opposition in Globalizing California* (Berkeley: University of California Press, 2007), 245.

10. Émile Durkheim, *The Division of Labor in Society* (New York: Free Press, 1964), 77–78.

11. For an incisive analysis of the United States as a failed state, see Lisa Miller, *The Myth of Mob Rule: Violent Crime and Democratic Politics* (New York: Oxford University Press, 2016).

12. There are of course some important exceptions. On the impact of the carceral state on rural areas, see, for example, Gilmore, *Golden Gulag*; John Eason, *Big House on the Prairie: Rise of the Rural Ghetto and Prison Proliferation* (Chicago: University of Chicago Press, 2017); Travis Linnemann, *Meth Wars: Police, Media, Power* (New York: New York University Press, 2016); William Garriott, *Policing Methamphetamine: Narcopolitics in Rural America* (New York: New York University Press, 2011); Judah Schept, *Coal, Cages, Crisis: The Rise of the Prison Economy in Central Appalachia* (New York: New York University Press, 2022); and Kirstine Taylor, *Sunbelt Capitalism and the Making of the Carceral State* (Chicago: University of Chicago Press, 2025). On the impact of the carceral state on groups other than Black men, see, for example, Karen Heimer, Sarah E. Malone, and Stacy De Coster, "Trends in Women's Incarceration Rates in US Prisons and Jails: A Tale of Inequalities," *Annual Review of Criminology* 6 (2023): 85–106; Andrea J. Ritchie, *Invisible No More: Police Violence Against Black Women and Women of Color* (Boston: Beacon, 2017); Kimberlé Crenshaw and the African American Policy Forum, *#SayHerName: Black Women's Stories of Police Violence and Public Silence* (Chicago: Haymarket Books, 2023); Beth Richie, *Arrested Justice: Black Women, Violence, and America's Prison Nation* (New York: New York University Press, 2012); Joey Mogul, Andrea J. Ritchie, and Kay Whitlock, *Queer (In)Justice: The Criminalization of LGBT People in the United States* (Boston: Beacon, 2012); Lynn A. Haney, *Offending Women: Power, Punishment, and the Regulation of Desire* (Berkeley: University of California Press, 2010); Anna Lvovsky, *Vice Patrol: Cops, Courts, and the Struggle over Urban Gay Life Before Stonewall* (Chicago: University of Chicago Press, 2021); Shatema Threadcraft and Lisa L. Miller, "Black Women, Victimization, and the Limitations of the Liberal State," *Theoretical Criminology* 21, no. 4 (2017): 478–93; and Susan Dewey et al., *Outlaw Women: Prison, Rural Violence, and Poverty in the New American West* (New York: New York University Press, 2019).

13. On trends in US incarceration rates, see Jeremy Travis, Bruce Western, and Steve Redburn, eds., *The Growth of Incarceration in the United States: Exploring Causes and Consequences* (Washington, DC.: National Academies Press, 2014), 35, fig. 2.1.

14. Jonathan Simon, *Governing Through Crime: How the War on Crime Transformed American Democracy and Created a Culture of Fear* (New York: Oxford University Press, 2009).

15. According to a landmark study by the NAS, "the increase in incarceration may have caused a decrease in crime, but the magnitude of the reduction is highly uncertain and the results of most studies suggest it was unlikely to have been large." Travis et al., *Growth of Incarceration in the United States*, 4. See also chap. 5; and Bruce Western, *Punishment and Inequality in America* (New York: Russell Sage Foundation, 2006), chap. 7.

16. For more on the crime drop, see pp. 20–21.

17. Travis et al., *Growth of Incarceration*; and Jordan T. Camp, *Incarcerating the Crisis: Freedom Struggles and the Rise of the Neoliberal Carceral State* (Berkeley: University of California Press, 2016).

18. Nicola Lacey and David Soskice, "Crime and Punishment in the U.S.: Political Systems and Technology Regime Change," Working Paper No. 16 (London School of Economics Legal Studies, 2019), 1–31.

19. William J. Sabol, Thaddeus L. Johnson, and Alexander Caccavale, *Trends in Correctional Control by Race and Sex* (Washington, DC: Council on Criminal Justice, 2019), 4.

20. Jacob Kang-Brown et al., *The New Dynamics of Mass Incarceration* (New York: Vera Institute of Justice, 2018), 22 and 33, appendix table 1. See also Jacob Kang-Brown and Ram Sub-

ramanian, *Out of Sight: The Growth of Jails in Rural America* (New York: Vera Institute of Justice, 2017).

21. Keeanga-Yamahtta Taylor, *From #BlackLivesMatter to Black Liberation*, rev. ed. (Chicago: Haymarket Books, 2021), 167.

22. Daniela Oramas Mora, William Terrill, and Jacob Foster, "A Decade of Police Use of Deadly Force Research (2011–2020)," *Homicide Studies* 27, no. 1 (2023): 17.

23. For more on trends in police killings of civilians in rural areas, see pp. 60–61, 87, 90, 126–27.

24. Laura Hein, "Revisiting America's Occupation of Japan," *Cold War History* 11, no. 4 (2011): 585–86.

25. My use of the term *militarization* encompasses the social and political processes by which "civil society organizes itself for the production of violence" at home and overseas and the consequences of those arrangements. See Michael Geyer, "The State in National Socialist Germany," in *Statemaking and Social Movements: Essays in History and Theory*, ed. Charles Bright and Susan Harding (Ann Arbor: University of Michigan Press, 1984), 193–232, as quoted in John R. Gillis, ed., *Militarization of the Western World* (New Brunswick, NJ: Rutgers University Press, 1989), 1. Those consequences include how "war and national security" have become "consuming anxieties" that shape wide areas of state and society, including what is thought to be politically feasible; and how they have perpetuated various types of violence in the United States. Michael S. Sherry, *In the Shadow of War: The United States Since the 1930s* (New Haven, CT: Yale University Press, 1995), xi. Following Sherry's lead, I chose to use *militarization* rather than *militarism* because the latter is an older, "more politically charged" term that is "evocative of Prussia, Nazi Germany, or imperial Japan" and that "refers more to a static condition than to a dynamic process." Sherry, *In the Shadow of War*, xi.

26. On how blowback from the global war on terror has imperiled US democracy, see Spencer Ackerman, *Reign of Terror: How the 9/11 Era Destabilized America and Produced Trump* (New York: Viking, 2021); and Karen J. Greenberg, *Subtle Tools: The Dismantling of American Democracy from the War on Terror to Donald Trump* (Princeton, NJ: Princeton University Press, 2021).

27. David Vine, "Lists of U.S. Military Bases Abroad, 1776–2021," American University Digital Research Archive, 2021, https://doi.org/10.17606/7em4-hb13.

28. David Vine, "Build Back (Much, Much) Worse," *Progressive*, August/September 2023, 8.

29. Nick Turse, "Will the Biden Administration Shine Light on Shadowy Special Ops Programs?," *Intercept*, March 20, 2021, https://theintercept.com/2021/03/20/joe-biden-special-operations-forces/; and Mark Bowden, "How Special Ops Became the Solution to Everything," *Atlantic*, April 2021, 62–69.

30. Nan Tian et al., "Trends in World Military Expenditure, 2023," Stockholm International Peace Research Institute, Fact Sheet, April 2024, https://www.sipri.org/sites/default/files/2024-04/2404_fs_milex_2023.pdf, 2; and Gisela Cernadas and John Bellamy Foster, "Actual Military Spending Reached $1.537 Trillion in 2022—More Than Twice Acknowledged Level," *Monthly Review* 75, no. 6 (November 2023): 18–26.

31. James Mann, "The Adults in the Room," *NYRB*, October 16, 2017, https://www.nybooks.com/articles/2017/10/26/trump-adult-supervision/.

32. This project resulted in seven edited volumes, none of which included a chapter on the US military or post-9/11 wars. Cambridge University Press, "Anxieties of Democracy," n.d., https://www.cambridge.org/core/series/ssrc-anxieties-of-democracy/C0E49C4EEC82DF-BA3169708C32199A71 (accessed November 4, 2024).

33. See, for example, Ned Blackhawk, *The Rediscovery of America: Native Peoples and the Unmaking of U.S. History* (New Haven, CT: Yale University Press, 2023); Ned Blackhawk, *Violence over the Land: Indians and Empires in the Early American West* (Cambridge, MA: Harvard University Press, 2008); Michael John Witgen, *Seeing Red: Indigenous Land, American Expansionism, and the Political Economy of Plunder in North America* (Chapel Hill: University of North

Carolina Press, 2022); and Paul Frymer, *Building an American Empire: The Era of Territorial and Political Expansion* (Princeton, NJ: Princeton University Press, 2017).

34. Stephen Wertheim, *Tomorrow, the World: The Birth of U.S. Global Supremacy* (Cambridge, MA: Belknap Press of Harvard University Press, 2020).

35. Andrew J. Bacevich, *Washington Rules: America's Path to Permanent War* (New York: Metropolitan Books, 2010). Some other historians place the date earlier. Michael Sherry identifies the 1930s as the decisive decade. Michael Kazin singles out the peace movement's failure to keep the United States out of World War I and Woodrow Wilson's about-face entry into the war as formative moments for the worldview that Bacevich characterizes as the Washington rules. Sherry, *In the Shadow of War*; and Michael Kazin, *War Against War: The American Fight for Peace, 1914–1918* (New York: Simon and Schuster, 2017).

36. Bacevich, *Washington Rules*, 182–83.

37. Bacevich, 182–83.

38. David Garland, "Introduction: The Meaning of Mass Imprisonment," *Punishment and Society* 3, no. 1 (2001): 5–7.

39. One notable exception is the subfield of critical criminology, which emerged around 1980 and treats corporate crime as a central concern. See Anthony Grasso's important new book, *Dual Justice: America's Divergent Approaches to Street and Corporate Crime* (Chicago: University of Chicago Press, 2024).

40. David Garland, *The Culture of Control: Crime and Social Order in Contemporary Society* (Chicago: University of Chicago Press, 2001), especially 20, 38–39, 53, 132–33.

41. John Hagan, *Who Are the Criminals? The Politics of Crime Policy from the Age of Roosevelt to the Age of Reagan* (Princeton, NJ: Princeton University Press, 2010), 135.

42. Franklin Zimring, *The Great American Crime Decline* (New York: Oxford University Press, 2007).

43. "White Collar Prosecutions for October 2024," TRAC Reports, Syracuse University, December 17, 2024, https://tracreports.org/tracreports/bulletins/white_collar_crime/monthlyoct24/fil/; "Corporate and White-Collar Prosecutions Hit New All-Time Lows in FY 2022," TRAC Reports, Syracuse University, January 19, 2023, https://trac.syr.edu/reports/708/; PricewaterhouseCoopers, "Fighting Fraud: A Never-Ending Battle," 2020, https://www.pwc.com/gx/en/forensics/gecs-2020/pdf/global-economic-crime-and-fraud-survey-2020.pdf; and Ann Tenbrunsel and Jordan Thomas, "The Street, the Bull and the Crisis: A Survey of the US and UK Financial Services Industry," University of Notre Dame and Labaton Sucharow LLP, May 2015, https://www.corporatecrimereporter.com/wp-content/uploads/2015/05/Labaton+2015+Survey+report_11–1.pdf.

44. Dorothy S. Lund and Natasha Sarin, "Corporate Crime and Punishment: An Empirical Study," *Texas Law Review* 100, no. 2 (2021): 285, 295; Keith B. Anderson, *Mass-Market Consumer Fraud in the United States: A 2017 Update* (Washington, DC: FTC Bureau of Economics, 2019), ii; Keith B. Anderson, *Consumer Fraud in the United States, 2011: The Third FTC Survey* (Washington, DC: FTC Bureau of Economics, April 2013), https://www.ftc.gov/sites/default/files/documents/reports/consumer-fraud-united-states-2011-third-ftc-survey/130419fraudsurvey_0.pdf, i; and "Scam Inc.," *Economist*, February 8–14, 2025, 9, 15–17, and 65–66.

45. Mary Dodge, "A Black Box Warning: The Marginalization of White-Collar Crime Victimization," *JWCCC* 1, no. 1 (January 2020): 24–25; Danielle McGurrin et al., "White Collar Crime Representation in the Criminological Literature Revisited, 2001–2010," *Western Criminology Review* 14, no. 2 (2013): 3–19; and Russell Mokhiber, "Corporate Crime Excised from the Mainstream," *Common Dreams*, July 6, 2007, https://www.commondreams.org/views/2007/07/06/corporate-crime-excised-american-mainstream. For one notable recent exception, see Zephyr Teachout, *Corruption in America: From Benjamin Franklin's Snuff Box to Citizens United* (Boston: Harvard University Press, 2014).

46. Russell Mokhiber, "20 Things You Should Know About Corporate Crime," *Harvard Law Record*, March 24, 2015, http://hlrecord.org/20-things-you-should-know-about-corporate -crime/.

47. Mokhiber.

48. For more on the shortcomings of data on white-collar and corporate crime, see chap. 6.

49. AFL-CIO, *Death on the Job: The Toll of Neglect*, 31st ed. (Washington, DC: AFL-CIO, 2022), 5; and FBI, "Crime Data: 2021 Nationwide Crime Statistics, Bulletin Highlights," December 7, 2022, https://leb.fbi.gov/bulletin-highlights/additional-highlights/crime-data-2021 -nationwide-crime-statistics.

50. Mokhiber, "20 Things You Should Know."

51. Brady Meixell and Ross Eisenbrey, "An Epidemic of Wage Theft Is Costing Workers Hundreds of Millions of Dollars a Year," Economic Policy Institute, Issue Brief no. 385 (September 11, 2014), https://files.epi.org/2014/wage-theft.pdf, 2.

52. Stephen M. Rosoff, Henry N. Pontell, and Robert Tillman, *Profit Without Honor: White-Collar Crime and the Looting of America*, 7th ed. (Hoboken, NJ: Pearson 2020), 454.

53. Adam Tooze, *Crashed: How a Decade of Financial Crises Changed the World* (New York: Viking, 2018), 156.

54. Tooze, 7, 43, 116.

55. Tooze, 157.

56. John Braithwaite, "In Search of Donald Campbell: Mix and Multimethods," *Criminology and Public Policy* 15, no. 2 (May 2016): 418; and Graham Dukes, John Braithwaite, and J. P. Maloney, *Pharmaceuticals, Corporate Crime and Public Health* (Cheltenham, UK: Edward Elgar, 2014).

57. Dodge, "Black Box Warning," 27; John Braithwaite, *Corporate Crime in the Pharmaceutical Industry*, 1984, Routledge Revivals (New York: Routledge, 2013); and Gerald Posner, *Greed, Lies, and the Poisoning of America* (New York: Avid Reader / Simon and Schuster, 2020).

58. The drugmaker Gilead, for example, delayed for years the release of a newer version of an HIV drug that executives knew could be less toxic so as to continue making money on the older version of their patent-protected drug. Rebecca Robbins and Sheryl Gay Stolberg, "How a Drugmaker Profited by Slow-Walking a Promising H.I.V. Therapy," *NYT*, July 22, 2023, https://www .nytimes.com/2023/07/22/business/gilead-hiv-drug-tenofovir.html. See also Rebecca Robbins, "How a Drug Company Made $114 Billion by Gaming the U.S. Patent System," *NYT*, January 28, 2023, https://www.nytimes.com/2023/01/28/business/humira-abbvie-monopoly.html.

59. The overdose fatality rate skyrocketed from about 6 per 100,000 people to nearly 33 per 100,000 people between 2000 and 2022. KFF, "Drug Overdose Death Rate (per 100,000 Population)," n.d., https://www.kff.org/other/state-indicator/drug-overdose-death-rate-per-100000 -population/?dataView=0&activeTab=graph&currentTimeframe=0&startTimeframe =22&selectedRows=%7B%22wrapups%22:%7B%22united-states%22:%7B%7D%7D%7D& sortModel=%7B%22colId%22:%22Location%22,%22sort%22:%22asc%22%7D (accessed November 8, 2024).

60. National Safety Council, "Preventable Deaths: Odds of Dying," n.d., https://injuryfacts .nsc.org/all-injuries/preventable-death-overview/odds-of-dying/ (accessed April 7, 2021); and Our World in Data, "Causes of Deaths for 15 to 49 Year Olds, United States, 2017," https:// ourworldindata.org/grapher/causes-of-death-in-15-49-year-olds?country=~USA.

61. US Joint Economic Committee, "The Economic Toll of the Opioid Crisis Reached Nearly $1.5 Trillion in 2020," n.d., https://www.jec.senate.gov/public/_cache/files/67bced7f -4232-40ea-9263-f033d280c567/jec-cost-of-opioids-issue-brief.pdf (accessed December 30, 2023). Between 1999 and 2018, the opioid epidemic cost state governments an estimated $125 billion in increased health-care expenses, including rising Medicaid costs and lost tax revenues. These figures exclude the added costs for private insurers, the criminal legal system, individuals

and their families, the federal government, and the broader economy. "Opioid Crisis Cost Pa. Justice System Millions," *PI*, August 2, 2019, A10.

62. On how the carceral state was built by fits and starts, see Marie Gottschalk, *The Prison and the Gallows: The Politics of Mass Incarceration in America* (Cambridge: Cambridge University Press, 2006).

63. Margaret Thatcher, quoted in David Frum, "Context for Margaret Thatcher's 'There Is No Such Thing as Society' Remarks," *Daily Beast*, April 8, 2013, https://www.thedailybeast.com /context-for-margaret-thatchers-there-is-no-such-thing-as-society-remarks.

64. Wendy Brown, *Undoing the Demos: Neoliberalism's Stealth Revolution* (New York: Zone Books, 2015).

65. Alan Greenspan, "Ich bin im falschen Jahrhundert geboren," *Zücher Tages-Anzeiger*, September 19, 2007, quoted in Tooze, *Crashed*, 574.

66. Christopher Leonard, *Kochland: The Secret History of Koch Industries and Corporate Power in America* (New York: Simon and Schuster, 2019), 5.

67. In recent years, direct federal subsidies to the fossil fuel industry have totaled about $20 billion annually at a time when the natural gas and oil sectors have been hauling in record profits. If tax and other indirect subsidies are included, the figure may be closer to $50 billion. That figure does not include the billions spent by the US military and State Department to ensure that US companies have access to energy markets and supplies that are overseas. The Stockholm Environment Institute calculated that as much as half of all gas and oil development would not be profitable without the cushion of direct government subsidies. The International Monetary Fund estimated that global subsidies, including the unpaid social and environmental costs of burning fossil fuels, totaled $5.2 trillion in 2017, or about 6.5 percent of global GDP. See Environmental and Energy Study Institute, "Fact Sheet: Fossil Fuel Subsidies: A Closer Look at Tax Breaks and Societal Costs," July 29, 2019, https://www.eesi.org/papers/view/fact-sheet -fossil-fuel-subsidies-a-closer-look-at-tax-breaks-and-societal-costs; Lisa Friedman, "Why Fossil Fuel Subsidies Seem Impossible to Banish," *NYT*, March 18, 2024, B1; Stockholm Environment Institute, "US Subsidies Boost the Expected Profits and Development of New Oil and Gas Fields," press release, July 29, 2021, https://www.sei.org/about-sei/press-room/us-subsidies -boost-profits-oil-gas-fields/; David Roberts, "Friendly Policies Keep US Oil and Coal Afloat Far More Than We Thought," *Vox*, July 26, 2018, https://www.vox.com/energy-and-environment /2017/10/6/16428458/us-energy-coal-oil-subsidies; and David Coady et al., "Global Fossil Fuel Subsidies Remain Large: An Update Based on Country-Level Estimates," Working Paper (International Monetary Fund, May 2, 2019), https://www.imf.org/en/Publications/WP /Issues/2019/05/02/Global-Fossil-Fuel-Subsidies-Remain-Large-An-Update-Based-on -Country-Level-Estimates-46509, 2.

68. Julia Ott, "Words Can't Do the Work for Us," *Dissent*, January 22, 2018, https://www .dissentmagazine.org/blog/neoliberalism-forum-julia-ott.

69. Barrington Moore, *Social Origins of Dictatorship and Democracy: Lord and Peasant in the Making of the Modern World* (Boston: Beacon, 1967), 486.

70. Gerald Davis, *Managed by the Markets: How Finance Reshaped America* (New York: Oxford University Press, 2009), 5.

71. For an elaboration of what constitutes financialization, see Greta R. Krippner, *Capitalizing on Crisis: The Political Origins of the Rise of Finance* (Cambridge, MA: Harvard University Press, 2011), 27–28.

72. Krippner, 28. See also Rana Foroohar, *Makers and Takers: The Rise of Finance and the Fall of American Business* (New York: Crown Business, 2016), 7–8; Thomas Philippon, "The Evolution of the U.S. Financial Industry from 1860 to 2007: Theory and Evidence," National Bureau of Economic Research, November 2008, https://pages.stern.nyu.edu/~tphilipp/papers/finsize _old.pdf, 37, fig. 1.

73. For more on the brain drain to the financial sector, see pp. 177–78.

74. Thomas Piketty, Emmanuel Saez, and Gabriel Zucman, "Economic Growth in the United States: A Tale of Two Countries," Washington Center for Equitable Growth, December 6, 2016, https://equitablegrowth.org/economic-growth-in-the-united-states-a-tale-of-two-countries/, fig. 2.

75. Ben Fountain, *Beautiful Country, Burn Again: Democracy, Rebellion, and Revolution* (New York: Ecco/Harper Collins, 2018), 359.

76. Both *Forbes* and Bloomberg characterize their estimates of billionaire wealth as conservative. Willy Staley, "How Many Billionaires Are There, Anyway?," *NYT*, April 7, 2022, https://www.nytimes.com/2022/04/07/magazine/billionaires.html#:~:text=And%20in%20fact%2C%20there%20exists,about%20these%20203%20unnamed%20billionaires.

77. Katherine Stewart, "The Claremont Institute: The Anti-Democracy Think Tank," *NR*, August 10, 2023, https://newrepublic.com/article/174656/claremont-institute-think-tank-trump.

78. Quoted in Ben Stein, "In Class Warfare, Guess Which Class Is Winning," *NYT*, November 26, 2006, https://www.nytimes.com/2006/11/26/business/yourmoney/26every.html.

79. Martin Gilens and Benjamin I. Page, "Testing Theories of American Politics: Elites, Interest Groups, and Average Citizens," *Perspectives on Politics* 12, no. 3 (2014): 564–81. See also Christopher Witko et al., *Hijacking the Agenda: Economic Power and Political Influence* (New York: Russell Sage Foundation, 2021); Jeffrey A. Winters and Benjamin Page, "Oligarchy in the United States?," *Perspectives on Politics* 7, no. 4 (2009): 731–51; and Jacob S. Hacker and Paul Pierson, *Winner-Take-All Politics: How Washington Made the Rich Richer—and Turned Its Back on the Middle Class* (New York: Simon and Schuster Paperbacks, 2010).

80. Thanks to *Citizens United*, corporations and unions are permitted to make independent expenditures from their own general funds on behalf of or against candidates. They also are allowed to make unlimited contributions to super PACs, political action committees that are supposed to operate independently of federal candidates (though in practice often do not). Adam Winkler, *We the Corporations: How American Businesses Won Their Civil Rights* (New York: Liveright, 2018), 372 and chap. 10. The 2014 *McCutcheon* decision struck down caps on the total amount individuals may contribute to federal candidates and national parties in an election cycle.

81. Lee Epstein, William M. Landes, and Richard A. Posner, "How Business Fares in the Supreme Court," *Minnesota Law Review* 97, no. 5 (2013): 1431–72; and Jesse Eisinger, *The Chickenshit Club: Why the Justice Department Fails to Prosecute Executives* (New York: Simon and Schuster, 2017), 306–8.

82. Teachout, *Corruption in America*, chaps. 3 and 4.

83. Mark Sherman, "The Supreme Court Weakens Federal Regulators, Overturning Decades-Old Chevron Decision," AP, June 28, 2024, https://apnews.com/article/supreme-court-chevron-regulations-environment-5173bc83d3961a7aaabe415ceaf8d665.

84. Quoted in Randall D. Eliason, "The Supreme Court Has a Corruption Problem," *NYT*, May 19, 2023, A23.

85. Teachout, *Corruption in America*.

86. Quoted in Daniel I. Weiner and Eric Petry, "Supreme Court Weakens Safeguards Against State Public Corruption," July 2, 2024, https://www.brennancenter.org/our-work/analysis-opinion/supreme-court-weakens-safeguards-against-state-public-corruption.

87. Laura Antonini and Harvey Rosenfield, *Reboot Required: The Civil Justice System Has Crashed* (Los Angeles: #Represent, 2022), https://www.representconsumers.org/wp-content/uploads/2022/02/2022.02.15_Reboot-Required.pdf; and Winkler, *We the Corporations*.

88. Joe Walsh, "U.S. Has at Least 20 Million Assault Weapons: A Ban Wouldn't Reduce That Number," *Forbes*, March 25, 2021, https://www.forbes.com/sites/joewalsh/2021/03/25/us-has

-at-least-20-million-assault-rifles-a-ban-wouldnt-reduce-that-number/. See also Cameron Mc-Whirter and Zusha Elinson, *American Gun: The True Story of the AR-15* (New York: Farrar, Straus and Giroux, 2023).

89. Desmond King, "American Political Violence (The *Government and Opposition*/Leonard Shapiro Lecture 2023," *Government & Opposition*, January 14, 2025: 1–24.

90. Michael Corkery, "Fighting Soaring Suicide Rate with Gun Locks and Leaflets," *NYT*, June 11, 2024, A1.

91. In 2019, the suicide rate for non-Hispanic white people was 17.6 per 100,000. The 2019 homicide and suicide rates for Black people were, respectively, 21.3 per 100,000 and 7.1 per 100,000. As of 2020, white males made up nearly seven out of ten of all suicides. The mountain West states have some of the country's highest suicide rates. "KHSB: Suicide Rates High in Middle-Aged White Men," Saint Luke's Health System, September 21, 2022, https://www.saintlukeskc.org/about/news/kshb-suicide-rates-high-middle-aged-white-men; CDC, "Health, United States—Data Finder," table SlctMort., "Age-Adjusted Death Rates for Selected Causes of Death, by Sex, Race, and Hispanic Origin: United States, Selected Years 1950–2019," 2020–21, https://www.cdc.gov/nchs/data/hus/2020-2021/slctmort.pdf, 3; and Corkery, "Fighting Soaring Suicide Rate with Gun Locks and Leaflets."

92. California Department of Justice, Office of Gun Violence Prevention, "Data Report: The Impact of Gun Violence in California," August 2023, https://www.oag.ca.gov/system/files/media/OGVP-Data-Report-2022.pdf, 15.

93. See, for example, Krippner, *Capitalizing on Crisis*; Tooze, *Crashed*; Thomas Piketty, *Capital in the Twenty-First Century* (Cambridge, MA: Belknap Press of Harvard University Press, 2017); Foroohar, *Makers and Takers*; and Nolan McCarty, Keith T. Poole, and Howard Rosenthal, *Political Bubbles: Financial Crises and the Failure of American Democracy* (Princeton, NJ: Princeton University Press, 2013).

94. See, for example, see Lily Geismer, *Don't Blame Us: Suburban Liberals and the Transformation of the Democratic Party* (Princeton, NJ: Princeton University Press, 2014); Daniel T. Rogers, *Age of Fracture* (Cambridge, MA: Belknap Press of Harvard University Press, 2012); Paul Sabin, *Public Citizens: The Attack on Big Government and the Remaking of American Liberalism* (New York: W. W. Norton, 2021); Joshua Green, *The Rebels: Elizabeth Warren, Bernie Sanders, Alexandria Ocasio-Cortez, and the Struggle for a New American Politics* (New York: Penguin, 2024), chaps. 1 and 2; Nelson Lichtenstein and Judith Stein, *A Fabulous Failure: The Clinton Presidency and the Transformation of American Capitalism* (Princeton, NJ: Princeton University Press, 2023); and Brent Cebul, *Illusions of Progress: Business, Poverty, and Liberalism in the American Century* (Philadelphia: University of Pennsylvania Press, 2023).

95. On lease revenue bonds, see Gilmore, *Golden Gulag*, 98–102, 116, 120–21. For more on privatization of the penal system, social impact bonds, lease revenue bonds, and the three R's, see Marie Gottschalk, *Caught: The Prison State and the Lockdown of American Politics*, rev. ed. (Princeton, NJ: Princeton University Press, 2016).

96. Barack Obama, *A Promised Land* (New York: Crown, 2020), 338.

97. Obama implored, "Now that the worst of the recession is over, we have to confront the fact that our government spends more than it takes in. That is not sustainable. Every day, families sacrifice to live within their means. They deserve a government that does the same." Barack Obama, "State of the Union Address," January 25, 2011, Obama White House Archives, https://obamawhitehouse.archives.gov/the-press-office/2011/01/25/remarks-president-state-union-address.

98. Jed S. Rakoff, *Why the Innocent Plead Guilty and the Guilty Go Free and Other Paradoxes of Our Broken Legal System* (New York: Farrar, Straus and Giroux, 2021), as quoted in Brandon Garrett, "How Biden Should Prosecute Corporate Crime," *TAP*, January 29, 2021, https://prospect.org/culture/books/how-biden-should-prosecute-corporate-crime/.

99. Franklin E. Zimring and Gordon Hawkins, *Crime Is Not the Problem: Lethal Violence in America* (New York: Oxford University Press, 1997).

100. The homicide rate for African American people fell from 36.3 per 100,000 in 1990 to 21.3 per 100,000 in 2019. CDC, "Health, United States—Data Finder," table SlctMort., 2.

101. Calculated from C. Puzzanchera, G. Chamberlin, and W. Kang, "Easy Access to the FBI's Supplementary Homicide Reports: 1980–2020," Victim Cross Tabs, 2021, https://ojjdp.ojp.gov /statistical-briefing-book/data-analysis-tools/ezashr/victim-crosstabs.

102. CDC, "Nonfatal Injury Reports," Web-Based Injury Statistics Inquiry and Reporting System (WISQARS), http://www.cdc.gov/injury/wisqars/nonfal.html cited in Rhonda Bryant, "Taking Aim at Gun Violence," CLASP [Center for Law and Social Policy], April 2013, http://www.clasp.org/admin/site/publications/files/Taking-Aim-at-Gun-Violence.pdf.

103. Jody Miller, *Getting Played: African American Girls, Urban Inequality, and Gendered Violence* (New York: New York University Press, 2008), 8; Janet L. Lauritsen, "How Families and Communities Influence Victimization," OJJDP [Office of Juvenile Justice and Delinquency Prevention], *Juvenile Justice Bulletin*, November 2003, https://www.ncjrs.gov/pdffiles1/ojjdp /201629.pdf; Threadcraft and Miller, "Black Women, Victimization"; and Treva B. Lindsey, *America, Goddam: Violence, Black Women, and the Struggle for Justice* (Oakland: University of California Press, 2022).

104. Karen F. Parker, *Unequal Crime Decline: Theorizing Race, Urban Inequality, and Criminal Violence* (New York: New York University Press, 2008).

105. In 2019, the homicide rates for New York City and Los Angeles were 3 per 100,000 and 6 per 100,000, respectively, while the rates for smaller cities, including East St. Louis (137 per 100,000), Camden (20 per 100,000), and New Orleans (30 per 100,000), were many times higher. FBI, "Offenses Known to Law Enforcement by State by City, 2019," *Crime in the United States, 2019*, n.d., https://ucr.fbi.gov/crime-in-the-u.s/2019/crime-in-the-US-2019/tables/table -8/table-8.xls/view (accessed September 14, 2023).

106. The average rate of criminal violence for Black urban neighborhoods is five times that for white urban neighborhoods; for minority areas, it is three and a half times that of white neighborhoods. Ruth D. Peterson and Lauren J. Krivo, *Divergent Social Worlds: Neighborhood Crime and the Racial-Spatial Divide* (New York: Russell Sage Foundation, 2010), 17.

107. David A. Weiner, Byron F. Lutz, and Jens Ludwig, "The Effects of School Desegregation on Crime," Working Paper No. 1530 (National Bureau of Economic Research, September 2009), 1.

108. For an overview of this work, see Patricia L. McCall, Kenneth C. Land, and Karen F. Parker, "An Empirical Assessment of What We Know About Structural Covariates of Homicide Rates: A Return to a Classic 20 Years Later," *Homicide Studies* 14, no. 3 (2010): 226–28; and Matthew R. Lee, "Concentrated Poverty, Race, and Homicide," *Sociological Quarterly* 41, no. 2 (2000): 189–206. As two leading experts on race, class, and crime explain, "regardless of whether a black juvenile is raised in an intact or single-parent family, or a rich or poor home, he or she will not likely grow up in a community context like that of whites with regard to family structure and income. Reductionist interpretations of race and social class camouflage this key point." Robert J. Sampson and William Julius Wilson, "Toward a Theory of Race, Crime, and Urban Inequality," in *Crime and Inequality*, ed. John Hagan and Ruth Peterson (Stanford, CA: Stanford University Press, 1995), 44.

109. Peterson and Krivo, *Divergent Social Worlds*, 62. See also Robert J. Sampson, "Urban Black Violence: The Effect of Male Joblessness and Family Disruption," *American Journal of Sociology* 93, no. 2 (1987): 354.

110. Philip J. Cook and Jens Ludwig, "Gun Violence Is THE Problem," *Vital City*, March 2, 2022, https://www.vitalcitynyc.org/articles/gun-violence-is-the-crime-problem; Steven F. Messner, "Economic Discrimination and Societal Homicide Rates: Further Evidence on the

Cost of Inequality," *American Sociological Review* 54, no. 4 (1989): 597–611; Parker, *Unequal Crime Decline*, 117–18; Patrick Sharkey, *Uneasy Peace: The Great Crime Decline, the Renewal of City Life, and the Next War on Violence* (New York: W. W. Norton, 2018); Robert J. Sampson, *Great American City and the Enduring Neighborhood Effect* (Chicago: University of Chicago Press, 2013); and McCall, Land, and Parker, "Empirical Assessment of What We Know," 219–43.

111. Joel Wallman, Richard Rosenfeld, and Randolph Roth, "The Opioid Epidemic and Homicide," HFG [Harry Frank Guggenheim] Research and Policy in Brief, May 2023, https://www.hfg.org/wp-content/uploads/2023/05/Opioids_HFG-Brief.pdf.

112. See Steven N. Durlauf and Daniel S. Nagin, "Imprisonment and Crime: Can Both Be Reduced," *Criminology and Public Policy* 10, no. 1 (2011): 13–54, and responses to this article in the same volume; see also, Franklin E. Zimring, *The City That Became Safe: New York's Lessons for Urban Crime and Its Control* (New York: Oxford University Press, 2012); Christopher S. Koper and Evan Mayo-Wilson, "Police Strategies to Reduce Illegal Possession and Carrying of Firearms: Effects on Gun Crime," *Campbell Systematic Reviews* 8, no. 1 (January 2012): 1–53; and Cynthia Lum, "Perspectives on Policing," *Annual Review of Criminology* 4 (2021): 23.

113. These programs encompass a grab bag of interventions, including small-scale employment and cognitive behavioral therapy programs; "violence interrupter" programs, in which cities enlist community residents, some of whom have criminal backgrounds, to use their street smarts, credibility, and contacts to de-escalate situations before someone is shot; and "focused deterrence," in which teams of police, prosecutors, and respected community members meet with young men identified as most likely to commit violent crimes and offer them the carrot of social services bundled with the threat of serious legal consequences if they engage in violent crime. For an excellent overview of "community violence intervention" programs and their mixed record in reducing violent crime, see Alec MacGillis, "Stopping the Violence," *NY*, February 6, 2023, 16–23.

114. See Durlauf and Nagin, "Imprisonment and Crime," and responses in the same volume.

115. Elliott Currie, "On the Pitfalls of Spurious Prudence," *Criminology and Public Policy* 10, no. 1 (2011): 113–14.

116. Currie, 113–14.

117. Bruce Western, *Homeward: Life in the Year After Prison* (New York: Russell Sage Foundation, 2018), 182. See also Elliot Currie, *The Roots of Danger: Violent Crime in Global Perspective* (Oxford: Oxford University Press, 2016), 45–86.

118. Ryan S. Johnson, Shawn Kantor, and Price V. Fishback, "Striking at the Roots of Crime: The Impact of Social Welfare Spending on Crime During the Great Depression," Working Paper No. 12825 (National Bureau of Economic Research, January 2007): 20–21n4; John R. Sutton, "The Political Economy of Imprisonment in Affluent Western Democracies, 1960–1990," *American Sociological Review* 69, no. 2 (2004): 170–89; David Downes and Kirstine Hansen, "Welfare and Punishment in Comparative Context," in *Perspectives on Punishment: The Contours of Control*, ed. Sarah Armstrong and Lesley McAra (Oxford: Oxford University Press, 2006), 33–54; and Tapio Lappi-Seppälä, "Trust, Welfare, and Political Culture: Explaining Differences in National Penal Policies," *Crime and Justice: A Review of Research* 37 (2008): 313–87.

119. CDC, "Health, United States—Data Finder"; and Miller, *Myth of Mob Rule*.

120. Calculated from United Nations Office on Drugs and Crime, "Victims of Intentional Homicide," n.d., https://dataunodc.un.org/dp-intentional-homicide-victims (accessed August 29, 2023).

121. Adrian Cherney, "Beyond Technicism: Broadening the 'What Works' Paradigm in Crime Prevention," *Crime Prevention and Community Safety* 4, no. 3 (2002): 52.

122. US poverty rates are higher and more extreme than the poverty rates of wealthy democracies. "America's Poor Are Worse Off Than Elsewhere," Confronting Poverty, n.d., https://confrontingpoverty.org/poverty-facts-and-myths/americas-poor-are-worse-off-than-

elsewhere/#:~:text=Source%3A%20OECD%20Data%2C%202019.,country%20average%20 of%2010.7%20percent (accessed April 24, 2023).

123. Adolph Reed Jr. and Merlin Chowkwanyun, "Race, Class, Crisis: The Discourse of Racial Disparity and Its Analytical Discontents," in *Socialist Register 2012: The Crisis and the Left*, ed. Leo Panitch, Gregory Albo, and Vivek Chibber (New York: Monthly Review Press, 2011), 151.

124. Adolph Reed Jr., "The Surprising Cross-Racial Saga of Modern Wealth Inequality," *NR*, June 29, 2020, https://newrepublic.com/article/158059/racial-wealth-gap-vs-racial-income -gap-modern-economic-inequality.

125. Cedric Johnson, *After Black Lives Matter: Policing and Anti-Capitalist Struggle* (London: Verso, 2023), 333.

126. See, for example, Jonathan Hopkin, *Anti-System Politics: The Crisis of Market Liberalism in Rich Democracies* (New York: Oxford University Press, 2020).

127. Majid Ezzati et al., "The Reversal of Fortunes: Trends in County Mortality and Cross-County Mortality Disparities in the United States," *PloS Med* 5, no. 4 (April 2008): 557–67.

128. WHO, "The Global Health Observatory: Life Expectancy at Birth (Years)," n.d., https:// www.who.int/data/gho/data/indicators/indicator-details/GHO/life-expectancy-at-birth -(years) (accessed September 2, 2023).

129. Laura Dwyer-Lindgren et al., "Inequalities in Life Expectancy Among US Counties, 1980 to 2014: Temporal Trends and Key Drivers," *JAMA Internal Medicine* 177, no. 7 (2017): 1003.

130. Experts disagree somewhat on whether a BA or a high school diploma is the big dividing line on premature death but do concur that less educated white people are increasingly at risk. Case and Deaton, *Deaths of Despair*; Paul Novosad, Charlie Rafkin, and Sam Asher, "Mortality Change Among Less Educated Americans," *American Economic Journal: Applied Economics* 14, no. 4 (October 2022): 1–34; Anne Case and Angus Deaton, "Accounting for the Widening Gap Between American Adults With and Without a BA," *Brookings Papers on Economic Activity*, Fall 2023, 1–44; and Dylan Matthews, "What a Striking New Study of Death in America Misses," *Vox*, October 4, 2023, https://www.vox.com/future-perfect/23895909/angus-deaton-anne -case-life-expectancy-united-states-college-graduates-inequality-heart-disease.

131. In Western countries, mortality rates for middle-aged people have been declining on average 2 percent annually since the late 1970s. The big exception is the United States, where they began to rise sharply after 2000. Case and Deaton, *Deaths of Despair*, 9 and 30, fig. 2.1.

132. Jacob Bor et al., "Missing Americans: Early Death in the United States—1933–2021," *PNAS Nexus* 2 (2023), https://doi.org/10.1093/pnasnexus/pgad173, 5, table 1.

133. Bor et al., 1.

134. Gottschalk, *Caught*, 7–8.

135. For a development of this point, see Gottschalk, 7–10 and chap. 2.

136. Gottschalk, chap. 5.

137. Jane Mayer, "New Koch," *NY*, January 17, 2016, https://www.newyorker.com/magazine /2016/01/25/new-koch. For an analysis of the First Step Act, see Marie Gottschalk, "Incorrigible: The First Step Act and the Carceral State," *Prison Legal News* 30, no. 4 (April 2019): 1–13; and Colleen P. Eren, *Reform Nation: The First Step Act and the Movement to End Mass Incarceration* (Stanford, CA: Stanford University Press, 2023).

138. Nancy MacLean, *Democracy in Chains: The Deep History of the Radical Right's Stealth Plan for America* (New York: Viking, 2017); Jacob S. Hacker and Paul Pierson, *American Amnesia: How the War on Government Led Us to Forget What Made America Prosper* (New York: Simon and Schuster Paperbacks, 2017); Jane Mayer, "Covert Operations," *NY*, August 23, 2010, https:// www.newyorker.com/magazine/2010/08/30/covert-operations; Julilly Kohler-Hausmann, *Getting Tough: Welfare and Imprisonment in 1970s America* (Princeton, NJ: Princeton University Press, 2017), chaps. 3 and 4; Theda Skocpol and Alexander Hertel-Fernandez, "The Koch Network and Republican Party Extremism," *Perspectives on Politics* 14, no. 3 (September 2016): 681–99; Alexander Hertel-Fernandez, *State Capture: How Conservative Activists, Big Businesses,*

and Wealthy Donors Reshaped American States—and the Nation (New York: Oxford University Press, 2019); and Nancy MacLean and Lisa Graves, "The Billionaire Kingmaker (Still) Dividing the Nation," *Progressive*, December 2022–January 2023, 43–46.

139. For more on the Texas case, see Marie Gottschalk, "No Star State: What's Right and Wrong About Criminal Justice Reform in Texas," *Seattle Journal for Social Justice* 19, no. 3 (May 2021): 927–1052.

140. Matt Ford, "Could a Controversial Bill Sink Criminal-Justice Reform in Congress?," *Atlantic*, October 26, 2017, https://www.theatlantic.com/politics/archive/2017/10/will -congress-reform-criminal-intent/544014/.

141. In his autobiography, Sutton denied saying this. See Willie Sutton and Edward Linn, *Where the Money Was* (New York: Viking Press, 1976), 120, cited in Quote Investigator, "I Rob Banks Because That's Where the Money Is," February 10, 2013, https://quoteinvestigator.com /2013/02/10/where-money-is/.

142. For a discussion of the relative weight of jails and prisons compared to other items in government budgets, see Gottschalk, *Caught*, 26–27; and Michelle S. Phelps, *The Minneapolis Reckoning: Race, Violence, and the Politics of Policing in America* (Princeton, NJ: Princeton University Press, 2024), 150–54.

143. Grace Manthey, Frank Esposito, and Amanda Hernandez, "Despite 'Defunding' Claims, Police Funding Has Increased in Many US Cities," ABC News, October 16, 2022, https://abcnews .go.com/US/defunding-claims-police-funding-increased-us-cities/story?id=91511971.

144. Lum, "Perspectives on Policing": 23.

145. William K. Black, *The Best Way to Rob a Bank Is to Own One: How Corporate Executives and Politicians Looted the S&L Industry*, updated ed. (Austin: University of Texas Press, 2013), 270.

146. Simon Johnson, "The Quiet Coup," *Atlantic*, May 2009, https://www.theatlantic.com /magazine/archive/2009/05/the-quiet-coup/307364/.

147. Quoted in Teachout, *Corruption in America*, 38.

148. See, for example, Steven Levitsky and Daniel Ziblatt, *How Democracies Die* (New York: Crown, 2018); "The Democracy Papers" (February 7, 2017, https://items.ssrc.org/category /democracy-papers/), part of the Anxieties of Democracy Project, funded by the Social Science Research Council; and Robert Kuttner, *Can Democracy Survive Global Capitalism?* (New York: W. W. Norton, 2018).

149. Barbara Walter, "Why Should We Worry that the U.S. Could Become an 'Anocracy' Again? Because of the Threat of Civil War," *WP*, January 24, 2022, https://www.washingtonpost .com/opinions/2022/01/24/why-should-we-worry-that-us-could-become-an-anocracy-again -because-threat-civil-war/; and Sheldon S. Wolin, *Democracy Incorporated: Managed Democracy and the Specter of Inverted Totalitarianism* (Princeton, NJ: Princeton University Press, 2008). On "zombie democracy," see David Runciman, *How Democracy Ends* (New York: Basic Books, 2018), 47.

150. Eric Zuesse, "Jimmy Carter Is Correct That the U.S. Is No Longer a Democracy," *HuffPost*, August 3, 2015, updated August 3, 2016, https://www.huffpost.com/entry/jimmy-carter-is -correct-t_b_7922788. See also Winters and Page, "Oligarchy in the United States?," 731–51; and the January/February 2024 special issue of *Mother Jones*, "American Oligarchy."

151. "Remarks by President Biden in a Farewell Address to the Nation," January 15, 2025, https://www.whitehouse.gov/briefing-room/speeches-remarks/2025/01/15/remarks-by -president-biden-in-a-farewell-address-to-the-nation/.

152. PRC, "Modest Declines in Positive Views of 'Socialism' and 'Capitalism' in U.S.," September 19, 2022, https://www.pewresearch.org/politics/2022/09/19/modest-declines-in -positive-views-of-socialism-and-capitalism-in-u-s/; Frank Newport, "Democrats More Positive About Socialism Than Capitalism," *Gallup News*, August 13, 2018, https://news.gallup.com /poll/240725/democrats-positive-socialism-capitalism.aspx; and Lydia Saad, "Do Americans

Like or Dislike 'Big Business?,'" *Gallup News*, July 27, 2022, https://news.gallup.com/poll/270296/americans-dislike-big-business.aspx.

153. Francis Cullen, Jennifer Hartman, and Cheryl Lero Jonson, "Bad Guys: Why the Public Supports Punishing White-Collar Offenders," *Crime, Law and Social Change* 51 (2009): 36.

154. They are especially troubled by illegal acts that involve clear culpability, recklessness, or great harm, such as violence to workers or consumers and large sums of misgotten money. Cullen et al., "Bad Guys," 36.

155. Cullen et al., 39.

156. Michael D. Shear and Gardiner Harris, "Trump Wants to 'Drain the Swamp,' but Change Will Be Complex and Costly," *NYT*, November 10, 2016, https://www.nytimes.com/2016/11/11/us/politics/trump-government.html. On the marginalization of Sanders, Warren, and others, see Green, *Rebels*.

157. Katie Reilly, "Read Hillary Clinton's 'Basket of Deplorables' Remarks About Donald Trump Supporters," *Time*, September 10, 2016, https://time.com/4486502/hillary-clinton-basket-of-deplorables-transcript.

158. See, for example, the spate of books over the last decade analyzing the politics of rural America and working-class people, including Elizabeth Catte, ed., *Left Elsewhere: Finding the Future in Radical Rural America* (Cambridge, MA: Boston Review, 2019); Anthony Harkins and Meredith McCarroll, eds., *Appalachian Reckoning: A Region Responds to "Hillbilly Elegy"* (Morgantown: West Virginia University Press, 2019); Steven Conn, *Lies of the Land: Seeing Rural America for What It Is—and Isn't* (Chicago: University of Chicago Press, 2023); Kathleen Cramer, *The Politics of Resentment: Rural Consciousness in Wisconsin and the Rise of Scott Walker* (Chicago: University of Chicago Press, 2016); Justin Gest, *The New Minority: White Working Class Politics in an Age of Immigration and Inequality* (New York: Oxford University Press, 2016); Nicholas Jacobs and Daniel Shea, *The Rural Voter: The Politics of Place and the Disuniting of America* (New York: Columbia University Press, 2023); and Arlie Russell Hochschild, *Stolen Pride: Loss, Shame, and the Rise of the Right* (New York: New Press, 2024).

159. On "mutant populism," see Green, *Rebels*, 208.

160. Almost one-quarter of Americans believe it's sometimes permissible to use violence against the government—and one in ten agree that such violence should be waged "right now." COVID States Project, "Report #80: Americans' Views on Violence Against the Government," January 2022, https://www.covidstates.org/reports/americans-views-on-violence-against-the-government; and Jennifer McCoy et al., "Reducing Pernicious Polarization: A Comparative Historical Analysis of Depolarization," Working Paper (Carnegie Endowment for International Peace, May 2022), https://carnegieendowment.org/files/McCoy_et_al_-_Polarization_final_3.pdf, 10, figs. 4 and 5. See also Nathan P. Kalmoe and Lilliana Mason, *Radical American Partisanship: Mapping Violent Hostility, Its Causes, and the Consequences for Democracy* (Chicago: Chicago University Press, 2022).

161. David Leonhardt and Ian Prasad Philbrick, "Donald Trump's Racism: The Definitive List, Updated," *NYT*, January 15, 2018, https://www.nytimes.com/interactive/2018/01/15/opinion/leonhardt-trump-racist.html); and Michael Barbaro and Megan Twohey, "Crossing the Line: How Donald Trump Behaved with Women in Private," *NYT*, May 14, 2016, https://www.nytimes.com/2016/05/15/us/politics/donald-trump-women.html.

162. "Donald Trump's Argument for America," *YouTube*, November 6, 2016, https://www.youtube.com/watch?v=vST61W4bGm8&t=120s; and Dave Johnson, "Trump Nominates Goldman Sachs 'Alligator' Jay Clayton to Run SEC," *TruthOut*, March 29, 2017, https://truthout.org/articles/trump-nominates-alligator-clayton-to-run-sec/.

163. Michael C. Dawson, *Not in Our Lifetimes: The Future of Black Politics* (Chicago: University of Chicago Press, 2011), 166; and Adolph Reed Jr., "The James Brown Theory of Black Liberation," *Jacobin*, October 6, 2015, https://jacobinmag.com/2015/10/adolph-reed-black-liberation-django-lincoln-selma-glory.

2. *Breaking Bad* in America: State Violence and the Changing Carceral State

1. James Baldwin, "Malcolm and Martin," *Esquire*, April 1, 1972, https://classic.esquire.com/article/1972/04/01/malcolm-and-martin.

2. Michelle Alexander's best-selling 2010 book *The New Jim Crow* and Ava Duvernay's 2016 documentary *13th* galvanized public interest in mass incarceration in the United States. Michelle Alexander, *The New Jim Crow: Mass Incarceration in the Age of Colorblindness* (New York: New Press, 2010). This book and this film bolstered the tendency to view penal policies and the carceral state through a racial disparities lens centered on cities, African American people, and the country's historical legacy of slavery. So did earlier research findings that mass incarceration fuels poverty and marginality and, vice versa, that poverty and marginality fuel mass incarceration. See, for example, Bruce Western, *Punishment and Inequality* (New York: Russell Sage Foundation, 2006); and Todd Clear, *Imprisoning Communities: How Mass Incarceration Makes Disadvantaged Communities Worse* (New York: Oxford University Press, 2007). For a list of more recent works that examine the impact of the carceral state in non-urban areas and on other groups in addition to African American men, see p. 408n12.

3. Relatively larger refers here to the relative size of Black populations among nonmetropolitan areas, not as compared to urban areas. Katherine Beckett and Lindsey Beach, "Understanding the Place of Punishment: Disadvantage, Politics, and Geography of Imprisonment in 21st Century America," *Law and Policy* 43, no. 1 (2021): 15–16.

4. Jeremy Travis, Bruce Western, and Steve Redburn, eds., *The Growth of Incarceration in the United States: Exploring Causes and Consequences* (Washington, DC: National Academies Press, 2014), chap. 4; see also Ruth Peterson and Lauren Krivo, *Divergent Social Worlds: Neighborhood Crime and the Racial-Spatial Divide* (New York: Russell Sage Foundation, 2012).

5. Jordan T. Camp, *Incarcerating the Crisis: Freedom Struggles and the Rise of the Neoliberal Carceral State* (Berkeley: University of California Press, 2016).

6. For an overview of the literature on the relationship between punishment and perceptions of social threat, see Bruce Western, Meredith Kleykamp, and Jake Rosenfeld, "Crime, Punishment, and American Inequality," in *Social Inequality*, ed. Kathryn Neckerman (New York: Russell Sage Foundation, 2004), 782–85.

7. David Garland, *The Culture of Control: Crime and Social Order in Contemporary Society* (Chicago: University of Chicago Press, 2001), 132–33.

8. Travis et al., *Growth of Incarceration in the United States*; Peterson and Krivo, *Divergent Social Worlds*.

9. Travis et al., *Growth of Incarceration*, chaps. 3 and 4.

10. Nicola Lacey and David Soskice, "Crime and Punishment in the U.S.: Political Systems and Technology Regime Change," Working Paper 22/2019 (London School of Economics, Society and Economy), n.d., https://papers.ssrn.com/sol3/papers.cfm?abstract_id=3492701 (accessed October 7, 2023).

11. Charles S. Aiken, "A New Type of Black Ghetto in the Plantation South," *Annals of the Association of American Geographers* 80, no. 2 (1990): 223–46; and John Eason, *Big House on the Prairie: Rise of the Rural Ghetto and Prison Proliferation* (Chicago: University of Chicago Press, 2017), 41.

12. Eason, *Big House on the Prairie*, 41.

13. Jacob Kang-Brown et al., *The New Dynamics of Mass Incarceration* (New York: Vera Institute of Justice, 2018), 2.

14. Kang-Brown et al., 22 and 33, appendix table 1. See also Jacob Kang-Brown and Ram Subramanian, *Out of Sight: The Growth of Jails in Rural America* (New York: Vera Institute of Justice, 2017).

15. Beckett and Beach, "Understanding the Place of Punishment": 5–29; and Ram Subramanian, Kristine Riley, and Chris Mai, "Divided Justice: Trends in Black and White Jail Incarcera-

tion, 1990–2013," Vera Institute of Justice, February 2018, https://www.vera.org/downloads/publications/Divided-Justice-full-report.pdf, 26.

16. Josh Keller and Adam Pearce, "This Small Indiana County Sends More People to Prison Than San Francisco and Durham, N.C., Combined: Why?," *NYT*, September 2, 2016, https://www.nytimes.com/2016/09/02/upshot/new-geography-of-prisons.html.

17. Keller and Pearce.

18. Two-thirds of white people with less than a high school degree have had an immediate family member incarcerated compared to 71 percent of Black people who lack a high school diploma. Elderbroom FWD.us, "Every Second: The Impact of the Incarceration Crisis on America's Families," December 2018, https://everysecond.fwd.us/downloads/everysecond.fwd.us.pdf, 10, 16, 27, 30.

19. Elderbroom FWD.us, 10, 16, 27, 30.

20. For white and Latino males born in the late 1970s, the risk of being sent to prison by the time they turned thirty-four was about four times what it was for their counterparts born three decades earlier. For Black males, it was two and a half times higher. For Black and Latino male high school dropouts born in the late 1970s, the risk was about five times higher than the risk for their counterparts born in the late 1940s; for white high school dropouts, it rose more than sevenfold. Calculated from Bruce Western and Becky Pettit, "Incarceration and Social Inequality," *Daedalus* 139, no. 3 (2010): 11, table 1.

21. Western and Pettit, 11, table 1.

22. William J. Sabol, Thaddeus L. Johnson, and Alexander Caccavale, *Trends in Correctional Control by Race and Sex* (Washington, DC: Council on Criminal Justice, 2019), 4.

23. These racial disparities are calculated from Allen J. Beck and Jennifer C. Karberg, "Prison and Jail Inmates at Midyear 2000," DOJ BJS, March 2001, https://bjs.ojp.gov/content/pub/pdf/pjim00.pdf https://www.bjs.gov/content/pub/pdf/pjim01.pdf; E. Ann Carson, "Prisoners in 2020," DOJ BJS, December 2021, https://bjs.ojp.gov/content/pub/pdf/p20st.pdf, 10, table 3, and 13, table 5; Todd D. Minton and Zhen Zeng, "Jail Inmates in 2020," DOJ BJS, December 2021, https://bjs.ojp.gov/content/pub/pdf/ji20st.pdf, 8, table 2, and 10, table 4; and William J. Sabol, Heather C. West, and Matthew Cooper, "Prisoners in 2008," DOJ BJS, December 2009, updated June 30, 2010, https://bjs.ojp.gov/content/pub/pdf/p08.pdf.

24. For historic trends, see Christopher Muller, "Northward Migration and the Rise of Racial Disparity in American Incarceration," *American Journal of Sociology* 118, no. 2 (2012): 281–326. On declining racial disparities in US jails, see Subramanian, Riley, and Mai, "Divided Justice."

25. Miltoneete Olivia Craig, Mijin Kim, and Dawn Beichner-Thomas, "Incarcerated in a Pandemic: How COVID-19 Exacerbated the 'Pains of Imprisonment,'" *Criminal Justice Review* 49, no. 2 (June 2024): 244–66. For a clearinghouse of information on the impact of Covid on US prisons and jails, see UCLA Law, Covid Behind Bars Data Project, n.d., https://uclacovidbehindbars.org (accessed August 31, 2024).

26. The trends in rates of incarceration and total numbers of people in prison and jail in this paragraph are calculated from Beck and Karberg, "Prison and Jail Inmates at Midyear 2000"; Carson, "Prisoners in 2020," 10, table 3, and 13, table 5; Minton and Zeng, "Jail Inmates in 2020," 8, table 2, and 10, table 4; and Sabol, West, and Cooper, "Prisoners in 2008." For a discussion of data lacuna in determining incarceration rates and trends by race, ethnicity, and gender, see the appendix.

27. Figures in this paragraph are calculated from Beck and Karberg, "Prison and Jail Inmates at Midyear 2000"; Carson, "Prisoners in 2020," 10, table 3, and 13, table 5; Minton and Zeng, "Jail Inmates in 2020," 8, table 2, and 10, table 4; and Sabol, West, and Cooper, "Prisoners in 2008."

28. The figures in this paragraph are from Subramanian, Riley, and Mai, "Divided Justice," 16, 18, and 20.

29. Calculated from Zhen Zeng and Todd Minton, "Jail Inmates in 2019," DOJ BJS, March 2021, https://bjs.ojp.gov/content/pub/pdf/ji19.pdf, 8, table 6; and E. Ann Carson, "Prisoners in 2019," DOJ BJS, October 2020, https://bjs.ojp.gov/library/publications/prisoners-2019, 9, table 5.

30. These ten states are Texas (768 per 100,000 residents), Oklahoma (767 per 100,000), Kentucky (705 per 100,000), Louisiana (675 per 100,000), New Mexico (659 per 100,000), Idaho (656 per 100,000), Georgia (640 per 100,000), Florida (626 per 100,000), Arizona (633 per 100,000), and West Virginia (622 per 100,000). Peter Wagner and Wendy Sawyer, "States of Incarceration: The Global Context 2018," June 2018, https://www.prisonpolicy.org/global/2018.html; and Prison Policy Initiative, "Visuals: Discover Your State," n.d., https://www.prisonpolicy.org/profiles/ (accessed September 26, 2023).

31. Ashley Nellis, *The Color of Justice: Racial and Ethnic Disparity in State Prisons* (Washington, DC: Sentencing Project, 2021). See also Richard Frase, "What Explains Persistent Racial Disproportionality in Minnesota's Prison and Jail Populations?," *Crime and Justice: A Review of Research* 38 (2009): 201–80.

32. Frase, "What Explains Persistent Racial Disproportionality?," 234.

33. Nellis, *Color of Justice*, 10, table 5.

34. The Black/white ratio for people imprisoned in Texas state prisons is 3.4 to 1. The national figure for state prisons is about 5 to 1. As for Latino people, Texas is locking them up in state prisons at nearly the same rates as non-Hispanic white people. Nellis, *Color of Justice*, 5, 7, table 1. See also Marie Gottschalk, "No Star State: What's Right and Wrong About Criminal Justice Reform in Texas," *Seattle Journal for Social Justice* 19, no. 3 (May 2021): 927–1052.

35. Aleks Kajstura, "States of Women's Incarceration: The Global Context 2018," Prison Policy Initiative, June 2018, https://www.prisonpolicy.org/global/women/.

36. Calculated from Kajstura.

37. Calculated from Kajstura.

38. In 2001, the chances of going to prison for women were six times greater than in 1974; for men, the increase was threefold. Calculated from Thomas Bonczar, *Prevalence of Imprisonment in the US Population, 1974–2001* (Washington, DC: DOJ BJS, 2003), 1. See also Karen Heimer, Sarah E. Malone, and Stacy De Coster, "Trends in Women's Incarceration Rates in US Prisons and Jails," *Annual Review of Criminology* 6 (2023): 87, fig. 1.

39. Heimer, Malone, and De Coster, "Trends in Women's Incarceration Rates," 88, fig. 1.

40. Calculated from Carson, "Prisoners in 2019," 4, table 2; Zeng and Minton, "Jail Inmates in 2019," 5, table 3; Meda Chesney-Lind, "Imprisoning Women: The Unintended Victims of Mass Imprisonment," in *Invisible Punishment: The Collateral Consequences of Mass Imprisonment*, ed. Marc Mauer and Meda Chesney-Lind (New York: New Press, 2004), 80–81.

41. Tiana Herring, "Since You Asked: What Role Does Drug Enforcement Play in the Rising Incarceration of Women?," Prison Policy Initiative, November 11, 2020, https://www.prisonpolicy.org/blog/2020/11/10/women-drug-enforcement/.

42. Samuel Myers Jr., William J. Sabol, and Man Xu, "The Determinants of Declining Racial Disparities in Female Incarceration Rates, 2000–2015," December 31, 2018, paper prepared for 2019 American Economic Association / National Economic Association Meetings, Atlanta, January 4–6, 2019, 8.

43. For more on the impact of the opioid crisis, see chaps. 10 and 11.

44. S. Jay Olshansky et al., "Differences in Life Expectancy Due to Race and Educational Differences Are Widening, and Many May Not Catch Up," *Health Affairs* 31, no. 8 (2012): 1807, exhibits 1 and 2.

45. Between 1980 and 2018, the white female incarceration rate increased sixfold (from about 10 to 60 per 100,000). Samuel L. Myers Jr., William J. Sabol, and Man Xu, "Determinants of Racial Disparities in Female Incarceration Rates, 2000–2018," *Review of Black Political Economy* 49, no. 4 (2022): 382–83.

46. See also Myers et al., 383, fig. 1.

47. Heimer, Malone, and De Coster, "Trends in Women's Incarceration Rates," 92; and Myers et al., "Determinants of Racial Disparities in Female Incarceration Rates, 2000–2018," 383.

48. Myers et al., "Determinants of Declining Racial Disparities in Female Incarceration Rates, 2000–2015," 4.

49. See also Myers et al., "Determinants of Racial Disparities in Female Incarceration Rates, 2000–2018," 383.

50. Myers et al., 381.

51. Marie Gottschalk, *Caught: The Prison State and the Lockdown of American Politics*, rev. ed. (Princeton, NJ: Princeton University Press, 2016), chap. 10.

52. "Federal Criminal Prosecutions Referred by DHS Continue to Fall," TRAC Reports, Syracuse University, June 14, 2017, https://trac.syr.edu/immigration/reports/472/.

53. Michael T. Light, Mark Hugo Lopez, and Ana Gonzalez-Barrera, *The Rise of Federal Immigration Crimes* (Washington, DC: PRC's Hispanic Trends Project, 2014), 9; Gottschalk, *Caught*, 225, fig. 10.2; National Immigrant Justice Center, "Fact Sheet: Immigration Prosecutions by the Numbers," November 2022, https://immigrantjustice.org/staff/blog/fact-sheet-immigration-prosecutions-numbers#:~:text=All%20told%2C%20prosecutions%20for%20immigration,charged%20category%20of%20federal%20crimes.

54. Doris Meissner and Julia Gelatt, *Eight Key U.S. Immigration Policy Issues: State of Play and Unanswered Questions* (Washington, DC: Migration Policy Institute, 2019), https://www.migrationpolicy.org/sites/default/files/publications/ImmigrationIssues2019_Final_WEB.pdf, 3.

55. Juliana Kim, "How Trump's Tax Cut and Policy Bill Aims to 'Supercharge' Immigration Enforcement," NPR, July 3, 2025, https://www.npr.org/2025/07/03/g-s1-75609/big-beautiful-bill-ice-funding-immigration.

56. Gottschalk, *Caught*, xv–xxi and 234–35.

57. BOP, "Inmate Ethnicity," December 28, 2024, https://www.bop.gov/about/statistics/statistics_inmate_ethnicity.jsp; and Mark Motivans, "Federal Justice Statistics, 2022," DOJ BJS, January 2024, rev. June 6, 2024, https://bjs.ojp.gov/document/fjs22.pdf, 13, table 8.

58. Gottschalk, *Caught*, 234.

59. Human Rights Watch, *Turning Migrants into Criminals: The Harmful Impact of US Border Prosecutions* (New York: Human Rights Watch, 2013), 5.

60. This paragraph is based on Jacqueline Stevens, "America's Secret ICE Castles," *Nation*, January 4, 2010, 13.

61. Gottschalk, *Caught*, 225, fig. 10. After Donald Trump was sworn in, deportations dipped in 2017. They rose from 2018 to 2020 but did not hit the highs of the Obama years. "Latest Data: Immigrations and Customs Enforcement Removals," TRAC Reports, Syracuse University, n.d., https://trac.syr.edu/phptools/immigration/remove/ (accessed September 21, 2023).

62. Daniel Kanstroom, *Aftermath: Deportation Law and the New American Diaspora* (New York: Oxford University Press, 2012).

63. "Immigration and Customs Enforcement Removal," TRAC, February 2024, https://trac.syr.edu/phptools/immigration/remove/; and ICE, *Annual Report 2024*, December 19, 2024, https://www.ice.gov/doclib/eoy/iceAnnualReportFY2024.pdf, 31, fig. 23.

64. Douglas S. Massey, testimony, US Senate Committee on the Judiciary, May 20, 2009, https://www.judiciary.senate.gov/imo/media/doc/massey_testimony_05_20_09.pdf, 2; and Wayne A. Cornelius et al., eds., *Mexican Migration and the U.S. Economic Crisis: A Transnational Perspective* (San Diego: Center for Comparative Immigration, 2010).

65. Lisa Sample, "The Social Construction of the Sex Offender" (PhD diss., University of Missouri, 2001).

66. Chrysanthi S. Leon, *Sex Fiends, Perverts, and Pedophiles: Understanding Sex Crime Policy in America* (New York: New York University Press, 2011), 100.

67. Lisa L. Sample and Colleen Kadleck, "Sex Offender Laws: Legislators' Accounts of the Need for Policy," *Criminal Justice Policy Review* 19, no. 1 (2008): 40–62.

68. This does not include "commercialized vice, morals, and decency offenses," which the BJS includes in a broader category of other public order offenses. Carson, "Prisoners in 2020," 28, table 14.

69. For overview of data on race and child pornography convictions, see Gottschalk, *Caught*, 368–69n6.

70. Corey Rayburn Yung, "The Emerging Criminal War on Sex Offenders," *Harvard Civil Rights–Civil Liberties Law Review* 45 (2012): 436.

71. The term *ritual exile* comes from Eric S. Janus, *Failure to Protect: America's Sexual Predator Laws and the Rise of the Preventive State* (Ithaca, NY: Cornell University Press, 2006), 89.

72. Dale Spencer, "Sex Offender as Homo Sacer," *Punishment and Society* 11, no. 2 (2009): 225.

73. Richard Nixon, "Remarks About an Intensified Program for Drug Abuse Prevention and Control," June 17, 1971, American Presidency Project, https://www.presidency.ucsb.edu /documents/remarks-about-intensified-program-for-drug-abuse-prevention-and-control.

74. David F. Musto, *The American Disease: Origins of Narcotic Control*, 3rd ed. (New York: Oxford University Press, 1999); David Farber, ed., *The War on Drugs: A History* (New York: New York University Press, 2022); and Michael Massing, *The Fix* (New York: Simon and Schuster, 1998).

75. Michael Tonry, *Punishing Race: A Continuing American Dilemma* (New York: Oxford University Press, 2011), 59–70; Marc Mauer, "The Changing Racial Dynamics of the War on Drugs," *Ethnicity and Race in a Changing World* 1, no. 2 (2009): 4; ACLU, "The War on Marijuana in Black and White: Billions of Dollars Wasted on Racially Biased Arrests," June 3, 2013, https:// www.aclu.org/publications/report-war-marijuana-black-and-white, 4; and Ojmarrh Mitchell and Michael S. Caudy, "Examining Racial Disparities in Drug Arrests," *Justice Quarterly* 32, no. 2 (2015): 288–313.

76. Alfred Blumstein, "Racial Disproportionality of U.S. Prison Populations Revisited," *University of Colorado Law Review* 64, no. 3 (1993): 743–60; and Alexander, *New Jim Crow*, 60–71.

77. Gottschalk, *Caught*, 85–87.

78. Craig Reinarman and Harry G. Levine, "Crack in the Rearview Mirror: Deconstructing Drug War Mythology," *Social Justice* 31, no. 1–2 (2004): 185.

79. Susan Okie, "The Epidemic That Wasn't," *NYT*, January 26, 2009, https://www.nytimes .com/2009/01/27/health/27coca.html; and Barry M. Lester, Lynne Andreozzi, and Lindsey Appiah, "Substance Use During Pregnancy: Time for Policy to Catch Up with Research," *Harm Reduction Journal* 1, no. 5 (April 20, 2004), https://www.ncbi.nlm.nih.gov/pmc/articles /PMC419718/.

80. James Forman, *Locking Up Our Own: Crime and Punishment in Black America* (New York: Farrar, Straus and Giroux, 2017). On Black support for the war on heroin in the 1960s and 1970s, see Michael Fortner, *Black Silent Majority: The Rockefeller Drug Laws and the Politics of Punishment* (Cambridge, MA: Harvard University Press, 2015); and Donna Murch, "Who's to Blame for Mass Incarceration?," *BR*, October 16, 2015, https://www.bostonreview.net/articles/donna -murch-michael-javen-fortner-black-silent-majority/.

81. Donna Murch, "Crack in Los Angeles: Crisis, Militarization, and Black Response to the Late Twentieth-Century War on Drugs," *Journal of American History* 102, no. 1 (June 2015): 162–73.

82. Tonry, *Punishing Race*, 59–60, figs. 3.1 and 3.2.

83. See, for example, Alexander, *New Jim Crow*, 101–2. A federal conviction for distributing five grams of crack cocaine—the equivalent of about one packet of sugar—triggered a mandatory five-year sentence. It took five hundred grams of powder cocaine to trigger the same penalty. In 2010, President Barack Obama signed the Fair Sentencing Act, which reduced the sen-

tencing disparity between crack and powder cocaine from 100:1 to 18:1. On court indifference to claims of racially biased drug policies, see Alexander, *New Jim Crow*, 60–71, 106–20, 128–36; and Doris Marie Provine, *Unequal Under the Law: Racism in the War on Drugs* (Chicago: University of Chicago Press, 2007), 140–61.

84. John F. Pfaff, "The Empirics of Prison Growth: A Critical Review and Path Forward," *Criminology* 98, no. 2 (2008): 559.

85. Franklin E. Zimring, "Imprisonment Rates and the New Politics of Criminal Punishment," *Punishment and Society* 3, no. 1 (2001): 161–66.

86. Franklin E. Zimring and Gordon Hawkins, *Incapacitation: Penal Confinement and the Restraint of Crime* (New York: Oxford University Press, 1995), chap. 5.

87. Zimring and Hawkins, 162.

88. Christopher Seeds, "Bifurcation Nation: American Penal Policy in Late Mass Incarceration," *Punishment and Society* 19, no. 5 (2017): 590–610; Gottschalk, *Caught*, chap. 8; and Christopher Seeds, *Death by Prison: The Emergence of Life Without Parole and Perpetual Confinement* (Berkeley: University of California Press, 2022).

89. Calculated from Sabol, West, and Cooper, "Prisoners in 2008," 6, table 7; and Carson, "Prisoners in 2020," 28, table 14.

90. Pew Charitable Trusts, "Drug Arrests Stayed High Even as Imprisonment Fell from 2009 to 2019," February 15, 2022, https://www.pewtrusts.org/-/media/assets/2022/02/drug-arrests-stayed-high-even-as-imprisonment-fell-from-2009-to-2019.pdf.

91. Calculated from Mauer, "Changing Racial Dynamics of the War on Drugs," 4, table 1; and Carson, "Prisoners in 2020," 29, table 15. The percentage of Black people among all drug arrests rose from 27 percent in 1980 to a peak of 42 percent in 1993 before falling back to 26 percent in 2019. Human Rights Watch, "Decades of Disparity," March 2009, https://www.hrw.org/reports/us0309web.pdf, 5, table 1; and FBI, "Uniform Crime Reports: Crime in the United States, 2019," table 43, "Arrests by Race and Ethnicity, 2019," n.d., https://ucr.fbi.gov/crime-in-the-u.s/2019/crime-in-the-US-2019/topic-pages/tables/table-43 (accessed August 31, 2024). Between 2000 and 2019, the number of Black people serving time in state prison for drug crimes fell by two-thirds; the number for Hispanic people was down 50 percent; and the number for white people was more than 10 percent higher. Calculated from Mauer, "Changing Racial Dynamics of the War on Drugs," 4, table 1; and Carson, "Prisoners in 2020," 29, table 15.

92. Human Rights Watch, "Decades of Disparity," 11, table 4.

93. See Naomi Murakawa, "Toothless: The Methamphetamine 'Epidemic,' 'Meth Mouth,' and the Racial Construction of Drug Scares," *Du Bois Review* 8, no. 1 (2011): 220.

94. William Garriott, *Policing Methamphetamine: Narcopolitics in Rural America* (New York: New York University Press, 2011); Jonathan Simon, *Governing Through Crime: How the War on Crime Transformed American Democracy and Created a Culture of Fear* (New York: Oxford University Press, 2009).

95. Quoted in Travis Linnemann, *Meth Wars: Police, Media, Power* (New York: Oxford University Press, 2016), 48–49.

96. Linnemann, 27–29; and Murakawa, "Toothless," 220.

97. Linnemann, *Meth Wars*, 88–90.

98. Linnemann, 74.

99. Linnemann, 154–57.

100. "President Signs USA Patriot Improvement and Reauthorization Act," March 9, 2006, George W. Bush White House Archives, https://georgewbush-whitehouse.archives.gov/news/releases/2006/03/20060309-4.html.

101. Eason, *Big House on the Prairie*, 2.

102. On some of these notable exceptions, see p. 408n12.

103. For an overview of this literature, see Gottschalk, *Caught*, 308n23–24.

104. Eason, *Big House on the Prairie*, 14, 164, 170; and John Eason, "Mapping Prison Proliferation: Region, Rurality, Race and Disadvantage in Prison Placement," *Social Science Research* 39, no. 6 (2010): 1015–28.

105. Eason, *Big House on the Prairie*, 14.

106. Eason, 173.

107. Robert D. Crutchfield, "From Slavery to Social Class to Disadvantage: An Intellectual History of the Use of Class to Explain Racial Differences in Criminal Involvement," *Crime and Justice* 44, no. 1 (2015): 38.

108. Crutchfield, 1.

109. Daniel P. Moynihan, *The Negro Family: The Case for Action* (Washington, DC: GPO, 1965).

110. Elizabeth Hinton, *From the War on Poverty to the War on Crime: The Making of Mass Incarceration in America* (Cambridge, MA: Harvard University Press), 57–61, 74–75.

111. Oscar Lewis, *Five Families: Mexican Case Studies in the Culture of Poverty* (New York: Basic Books, 1959).

112. These examples are from Michael Woodsworth, *Battle for Bed-Stuy: The Long War on Poverty in New York City* (Cambridge, MA: Harvard University Press, 2016), 129.

113. Woodsworth, 129.

114. Michael Harrington, *The Other America: Poverty in the United States* (New York: Macmillan, 1962).

115. Maurice Isserman, "50 Years Later: Poverty and the Other America," *Dissent*, Winter 2012, 86.

116. Isserman, 86. For more on the historical origins and development of these stereotypes, see Nancy Isenberg, *White Trash: The 400-Year Untold History of Class in America* (New York: Penguin Books, 2017).

117. Alice O'Connor, *Poverty Knowledge: Social Science, Social Policy, and the Poor in Twentieth Century U.S. History* (Princeton, NJ: Princeton University Press, 2001), 121–22, 150–51.

118. Woodsworth, *Battle for Bed-Stuy*, 131.

119. See Pam Fessler, "Kentucky County That Gave War on Poverty a Face Still Struggles," NPR, January 8, 2014, https://www.npr.org/2014/01/08/260151923/kentucky-county-that-gave-war-on-poverty-a-face-still-struggles.

120. Julilly Kohler-Hausmann, *Getting Tough: Welfare and Imprisonment in 1970s America* (Princeton, NJ: Princeton University Press, 2017), chaps. 3 and 4.

121. Barack Obama, "Text of Obama's Fatherhood Speech," *Politico*, June 15, 2008, https://www.politico.com/story/2008/06/text-of-obamas-fatherhood-speech-011094.

122. Charles A. Murray, *Coming Apart: The State of White America, 1960–2010* (New York: Crown, 2013).

123. Mona Charen, "What *Hillbilly Elegy* Reveals About Trump and America," *National Review*, July 28, 2016, https://www.nationalreview.com/2016/07/hillbilly-elegy-jd-vances-new-book-reveals-much-about-trump-america/; and J. D. Vance, *Hillbilly Elegy: A Memoir of a Family and Culture in Crisis* (2016), with a new afterword (New York: HarperCollins, 2018); page nos. in citations correspond to the 2018 edition.

124. Vance, *Hillbilly Elegy*, 363–64.

125. These include its winner-take-all, first-past-the-post electoral system, stingy social safety net, and high levels of autonomy for local governments, as well as the centrality of race-related factors in American political development. Lacey and Soskice, "Crime and Punishment in the U.S."

126. Pew Trusts, "'Lost Decade' Casts a Post-Recession Shadow on State Finances," June 4, 2019, https://www.pewtrusts.org/en/research-and-analysis/issue-briefs/2019/06/lost-decade-casts-a-post-recession-shadow-on-state-finances, figs. 1–7.

127. Beckett and Beach, "Understanding the Place of Punishment," 7. On deepening poverty in suburban communities, see Scott W. Allard, *Places in Need: The Changing Geography of Poverty* (New York: Russell Sage Foundation, 2017).

128. Deep poverty is commonly defined as households existing on cash income that is less than half of the federal poverty threshold. Tracey Farrigan, "Poverty and Deep Poverty Increasing in Rural America," DOA, Economic Research Service, March 4, 2014, https://www.ers.usda.gov/amber-waves/2014/march/poverty-and-deep-poverty-increasing-in-rural-america/.

129. DOA, Economic Research Service, "Rural Poverty and Well-Being: Poverty Rates by Metro/Nonmetro Residence, 1959–2019," n.d., https://www.ers.usda.gov/topics/rural-economy-population/rural-poverty-well-being/ (accessed September 15, 2023).

130. In counties with high rates of poverty, 20 percent or more of the residents live below the federal poverty line. Tracey Farrigan, "Extreme Poverty Counties Found Solely in Rural Areas in 2018," DOA, Economic Research Service, May 4, 2020, https://www.ers.usda.gov/amber-waves/2020/may/extreme-poverty-counties-found-solely-in-rural-areas-in-2018/.

131. Farrigan.

132. For more on the culture of control, see p. 10; and Gottschalk, *Caught*, 27–28.

133. John Gramlich, "Voters' Perceptions of Crime Continue to Conflict with Reality," PRC, November 16, 2016, https://www.pewresearch.org/short-reads/2016/11/16/voters-perceptions-of-crime-continue-to-conflict-with-reality/; and Gallup, "Crime," n.d., https://news.gallup.com/poll/1603/crime.aspx (accessed October 7, 2023).

134. Kang-Brown and Subramanian, *Out of Sight*, 18–20; and C. Holly Andrilla et al., "Geographic Variation in the Supply of Selected Behavioral Health Providers," *American Journal of Preventive Medicine* 54, no. 6 (2018): S-200.

135. Allard, *Places in Need*, 109.

136. Kei Kawashima-Ginsberg and Felicia Sullivan, "Study: 60 Percent of Rural Millennials Lack Access to a Political Life," *Conversation*, March 26, 2017, https://theconversation.com/study-60-percent-of-rural-millennials-lack-access-to-a-political-life-74513.

3. Tougher Than the Rest: State Violence and US Police Forces

1. Unless otherwise specified, the phrases *police killings* and *police homicides* are used here to refer to members of the public killed by the police and not to police officers who were killed in the line of duty.

2. Franklin E. Zimring, *When Police Kill* (Cambridge, MA: Harvard University Press, 2017), 143; and Lawrence Sherman quoted in David Kirkpatrick, "Split-Second Decisions: How a Supreme Court Shaped Modern Policing," *NYT*, April 25, 2021, https://www.nytimes.com/2021/04/25/us/police-use-of-force.html.

3. Calculated from World Population Review, "Police Killings by Country 2024," n.d., https://worldpopulationreview.com/country-rankings/police-killings-by-country (accessed November 23, 2024). The US rates are likely underestimates, given the incomplete collection of data on officer-involved deaths, as discussed in this chapter. See also Zimring, *When Police Kill*, 76, fig. 4.2.

4. Jamiles Lartey, "By the Numbers: U.S. Police Kill More in Days Than Other Countries Do in Years," *Guardian*, June 9, 2015, https://www.theguardian.com/us-news/2015/jun/09/the-counted-police-killings-us-vs-other-countries.

5. The United States ranked twenty-eight. See World Population Review, "Police Killings by Country, 2024," n.d., https://worldpopulationreview.com/country-rankings/police-killings-by-country (accessed September 2, 2024).

6. David M. Kennedy, "State Violence, Legitimacy, and the Path to True Public Safety," *CLN*, September 2020, 4.

7. Daniela Oramas Mora, William Terrill, and Jacob Foster, "A Decade of Police Use of Deadly Force Research (2011–2020)," *Homicide Studies* 27, no. 1 (2023): 21.

8. Joanna Schwartz as reported in Editorial Board, "End the Court Doctrine That Enables Police Brutality," *NYT*, May 22, 2021, https://www.nytimes.com/2021/05/22/opinion /qualified-immunity-police-brutality-misconduct.html.

9. Kennedy, "State Violence, Legitimacy," 4, emphasis in original.

10. Jill Lepore, "The Invention of the Police," *NY*, July 13, 2020, https://www.newyorker.com /magazine/2020/07/20/the-invention-of-the-police.

11. Kimberlé Crenshaw and the African American Policy Forum, *#SayHerName: Black Women's Stories of Police Violence and Public Silence* (Chicago: Haymarket Books, 2023).

12. Between 2013 and 2020, homicides by police fell by nearly a third in the country's thirty largest cities. Shane Bauer, "Letter from California: An Unstoppable Force," *NY*, November 23, 2020, 29.

13. Paul Hirschfield, "Lethal Policing: Making Sense of American Exceptionalism," *Sociological Forum* 30, no. 4 (December 2015): 1110.

14. Alysia Santo and R. G. Dunlop, "Where Police Killings Often Meet with Silence: Rural America," *NYT*, August 13, 2021, https://www.nytimes.com/2021/08/13/us/police-shootings -rural.html.

15. Jean Reith Schroedel and Roger Chin, "Whose Lives Matter: The Media's Failure to Cover Police Use of Force Against Native Americans," *Race and Injustice* 10, no. 2 (2020): 150–75.

16. Mora et al., "Decade of Police Use of Deadly Force Research," 17.

17. Stephanie Woodard, "The Movement for Native Lives," *In These Times*, October 2016, 20–27; and Schroedel and Chin, "Whose Lives Matter."

18. Hirschfield, "Lethal Policing": 1112.

19. Notably, in metropolitan areas where the rate of police killings of white civilians is high, Black-white and Latino-white disparities in the deadly use of force are lower compared to those in metro areas where the rate of police killings of white people is lower. Gabriel L. Schwartz and Jaquelyn L. Jahn, "Mapping Police Violence Across U.S. Metropolitan Areas: Overall Rates and Racial/Ethnic Inequities, 2013–2017," *PLOS ONE* 15, no. 6 (2020): 1–16.

20. These ten states, ranked in order from highest to lowest rate of shooting fatalities by police, are New Mexico, Alaska, Oklahoma, Arizona, West Virginia, Nevada, Colorado, Wyoming, Montana, and Louisiana. These figures are only for shooting fatalities. They do not include civilian deaths from other types of lethal force, including Tasers and car chases. Rankings were calculated based on figures from 2015 to 2017 in David Hemenway et al., "Variation in Rates of Fatal Police Shootings Across U.S. States: Role of Firearm Availability," *Journal of Urban Health* 96 (2019): 66, table 1; and Governing.com, "2017 State Population by Race, Ethnicity Data: State Percentage of Population by Race," n.d., https://www.governing.com/archive/state -minority-population-data-estimates.html (accessed July 3, 2021).

21. Santo and Dunlop, "Where Police Killings Often Meet with Silence." State variations calculated from Hemenway et al., "Variation in Rates of Fatal Police Shootings": 66, table 1. See also Rachel Aviv, "Your Son Is Deceased," *NY*, January 26, 2015, https://www.newyorker.com /magazine/2015/02/02/son-deceased.

22. Zimring, *When Police Kill*, 8–9.

23. On the problems with official government figures on police killings of civilians, see Zimring, chap. 2.

24. Quoted in Tessa Berenson, "FBI Head Calls Lack of Data on Police Shootings 'Embarrassing,'" *Time*, October 8, 2015, https://time.com/4066558/police-shootings-data-fbi/.

25. Barry Friedman, *Unwarranted: Policing Without Permission* (New York: Farrar, Straus and Giroux, 2017), 6–7, 9, 46–47, and chap. 1.

26. Angelica Hendricks, "Exposing Police Misconduct in Pre-Trial Criminal Proceedings," *NYU Journal of Legislation and Public Policy* 24, no. 1 (2021): 177–252.

27. Kenny Jacoby, "Police Use of Force Data 'a Huge Mess' Across the U.S.," USA Today Network, August 25, 2019, https://stories.usatodaynetwork.com/data_stories/police-use-of-force-data-a-huge-mess-across-the-u-s/.

28. Zimring, *When Police Kill*, 24, discusses how the FBI has an expansive and controversial definition of what constitutes a "justifiable" police homicide.

29. Ryan Gabrielson, Eric Sagara, and Ryann Grochowski Jones, "Deadly Force, in Black and White," *ProPublica*, October 10, 2014, https://www.propublica.org/article/deadly-force-in-black-and-white; and Ryan Gabrielson and Ryann Grochowski Jones, "Answering the Critics of Our Deadly Force Story," *ProPublica*, December 24, 2014, https://www.propublica.org/article/answering-the-critics-of-our-deadly-force-story.

30. Jerome Karabel, "Police Killings Surpass the Worst Years of Lynching, Capital Punishment, and a Movement Responds," *HuffPost*, November 4, 2015, updated December 6, 2017, https://www.huffpost.com/entry/police-killings-lynchings-capital-punishment_b_8462778.

31. Lepore, "Invention of the Police."

32. FBI National Press Office, "FBI Releases 2021 and First Quarter 2022 Statistics from the National Use-of-Force Data Collection," May 31, 2022, https://www.fbi.gov/news/press-releases/fbi-releases-2021-and-first-quarter-2022-statistics-from-the-national-use-of-force-data-collection. See also Aaron Miguel Cantú, "The FBI Is Supposed to Track How Police Use Force—Years Later, It's Falling Well Short," *Guardian*, May 17, 2021, https://www.theguardian.com/us-news/2021/may/17/fbi-police-use-of-force-data-records.

33. Reese Dunklin et al., "Lethal Restraint: When Police Tactics Go Wrong," *PI*, March 30, 2024, A1.

34. See www.GovTrack.us, "H.R. 1336—117th Congress: National Statistics on Deadly Force Transparency Act of 2021," 2021, https://www.govtrack.us/congress/bills/117/hr1336.

35. For an overview of the main open-source and government databases, see Mora et al., "Decade of Police Use of Deadly Force Research," 12–15.

36. Brian Karl Finch et al., "Using Crowd-Sourced Data to Explore Police-Related Deaths in the United States (2000–2017): The Case of Fatal Encounters," *Open Health Data* 6, no. 1 (2019): 1–8.

37. Mapping Police Violence, January 8, 2025, https://mappingpoliceviolence.org.

38. As reported in Dunklin et al., "Lethal Restraint."

39. Sexual assault and sexual misconduct constituted over 9 percent of all complaints. Victoria M. Massie, "Daniel Holtzclaw and the Limits of Community Policing," *Intercept*, January 25, 2016, https://theintercept.com/2016/01/25/daniel-holtzclaw-and-the-limits-of-community-policing/. Nearly half of these incidents involved police accused of forced, nonconsensual sexual misconduct while on duty, and over half involved incidents with minors. Philip Matthew Stinson et al., *Police Integrity Lost: A Study of Law Enforcement Officers Arrested* (Bowling Green, KY: Bowling Green State University, 2016), 105, 23.

40. Andrea J. Ritchie, "#SayHerName: Racial Profiling and Police Violence Against Black Women," *New York University Review of Law and Social Change: The Harbinger* 41 (2016), https://socialchangenyu.com/harbinger/sayhername-racial-profiling-and-police-violence-against-black-women/; and Kimberlé W. Crenshaw et al., *Resisting Police Brutality Against Black Women*, 2015, https://scholarship.law.columbia.edu/faculty_scholarship/3226.

41. Friedman, *Unwarranted*, 11.

42. Friedman, 25.

43. James Fyfe, "Shots Fired: An Analysis of New York City Police Firearms Discharges" (PhD diss., State University of New York at Albany, 1978), 32, quoted in David Klinger et al., "Race, Crime, and the Micro-Ecology of Deadly Force," *Criminology and Public Policy* 15, no. 1 (2015): 197, emphasis in the original.

44. CDC, "WISQARS Fatal and Nonfatal Injury Reports, 2022: Injury Counts and Rates," n.d., https://wisqars.cdc.gov/reports/?o=NFI&y1=2022&y2=2022&d=0&i=0&m=3000&g

=00&s=0&a=ALL&g1=0&g2=199&a1=0&a2=199&r1=INTENT&r2=NONE&r3=NONE&r4=NONE&adv=true (accessed September 7, 2024).

45. Matthew Hickman et al., "Police Use of Force and Injury: Multilevel Predictors of Physical Harm to Subjects and Officers," *Police Quarterly* 24, no. 3 (2024): 267–97.

46. Simone Weichselbaum et al., "Violent Encounters with Police Send Thousands to the ER Every Year," Marshall Project, June 23, 2021, https://www.themarshallproject.org/2021/06/23/violent-encounters-with-police-send-thousands-of-people-to-the-er-every-year.

47. Dunklin et al., "Lethal Restraint"; and John Seewer, Reese Dunklin, and Taylor Stevens, "When Restraint Becomes Lethal," *PI*, May 19, 2024, A6.

48. See the six-part series by Reuters, "Shock Tactics," August–December 2017, https://www.reuters.com/investigates/section/usa-taser/.

49. In 2014, TASER International quietly removed its best-selling and most powerful stun gun from the market because it posed a higher risk of cardiac arrest than its other models. Stephanie Nebehay and Jason Szep, "U.N. Watchdogs Call for Probe of Taser Assaults in U.S. Jails," Reuters, December 7, 2017, https://www.reuters.com/article/world/exclusive-un-watchdogs-call-for-probe-of-taser-assaults-in-us-jails-idUSKBN1E12GQ/.

50. Dunklin et al., "Lethal Restraint."

51. John Whitehead, "Don't Shoot the Dogs: The Growing Epidemic of Cops Shooting Family Dogs," *CLN*, June 2019, 6.

52. See, for example, Paul Butler, *Chokehold: Policing Black Men* (New York: New Press, 2017); Radley Balko, *Rise of the Warrior Cop: The Militarization of America's Police Forces* (New York: PublicAffairs, 2014), 309–16; Kristian Williams, *Our Enemies in Blue: Police and Power in America*, 3rd ed. (Oakland, CA: AK Press, 2015); and Alex Vitale, *The End of Policing* (London: Verso, 2018).

53. William Finnegan, "The Blue Wall," *NY*, August 3/10, 2020, 52; and Seth Stoughton, "Law Enforcement's 'Warrior' Problem," *Harvard Law Review Forum* 128 (2015): 227.

54. Michael Fortino, "Inadequate and Outdated Training Results in Wild West Policing," *CLN*, February 2021, 43.

55. Karabel, "Police Killings Surpass the Worst Years of Lynching," emphasis in the original.

56. Karabel.

57. Quoted in Karabel.

58. Holly Yan, "States Require More Training to Become a Barber Than a Police Officer," CNN, September 28, 2016, https://www.cnn.com/2016/09/28/us/jobs-training-police-trnd/index.html.

59. Paul Hirschfield, "Why Do American Cops Kill So Many Compared to European Cops?," *Conversation*, November 25, 2015, https://theconversation.com/why-do-american-cops-kill-so-many-compared-to-european-cops-49696.

60. DOJ BJS, "National Sources of Law Enforcement Employment Data," April 2016, updated October 4, 2016, https://bjs.ojp.gov/content/pub/pdf/nsleed.pdf, 1.

61. Peter Kraska, *Militarizing the American Criminal Justice System: The Changing Roles of the Armed Forces and the Police* (Boston: Northeastern University Press, 2001), 7.

62. Ron Barnett and Paul Alongi, "Critics Slam 'No-Knock' Police Raids," *USA Today*, February 14, 2011, https://www.police1.com/police-training/articles/critics-slam-no-knock-police-raids-lrIChncrFtHGcuta/; and Kraska, *Militarizing the American Criminal Justice System*, 506.

63. Peter Hermann, "Numbers Paint Portrait of SWAT Team Use," *Baltimore Sun*, February 24, 2010, https://www.baltimoresun.com/news/crime/bs-xpm-2010-02-24-bal-md-hermann24feb24-story.html.

64. Hermann.

65. David M. Reutter, "No-Knock Warrants Leave Trail of Terror, Property Damage, and Deaths," *CLN*, May 2021, 1–11.

66. Josiah Bates, "Breonna Taylor's Killing Sparked Restrictions on No-Knock Warrants: But Experts Say Those Rules Don't Actually Change Much," *Time*, March 11, 2022, https://time .com/6156590/breonna-taylor-no-knock-warrants/.

67. Jonathan Mummolo, "Militarization Fails to Enhance Police Safety or Reduce Crime but May Harm Police Reputation," *Proceedings of the National Academy of Sciences* 115, no. 37 (September 11, 2018): 9181–86.

68. Jennifer Levitz, "Towns Say 'No Tanks' to Militarized Police," *WSJ*, February 7, 2014, https://www.wsj.com/articles/SB10001424052702304450904579366963588434656. For more on the history of the transfer of military equipment to local police, see pp. 111–13.

69. Edward Lawson Jr., "Trends: Police Militarization and the Use of Lethal Force," *Political Research Quarterly* 72, no. 1 (2019): 177–89.

70. Shawn Musgrave, Tom Meagher, and Gabriel Dance, "The Pentagon Finally Details Its Weapons-for-Cops Giveaway," Marshall Project, December 3, 2014, https://www.themarshallproj ect.org/2014/12/03/the-pentagon-finally-details-its-weapons-for-cops-giveaway.

71. OpentheBooks.com, "The Militarization of Local Police Departments," May 2016, https:// www.openthebooks.com/assets/1/7/OTB_SnapshotReport_MilitarizationPoliceDepts.pdf.

72. OpentheBooks.com.

73. OpentheBooks.com; and Executive Office of the President, "Review: Federal Support for Local Law Enforcement Equipment Acquisition," December 2014, Obama White House Archives, https://obamawhitehouse.archives.gov/sites/default/files/docs/federal_support _for_local_law_enforcement_equipment_acquisition.pdf.

74. Anna Gunderson et al., "Counterevidence of Crime-Reduction Effects from Federal Grants of Military Equipment to Local Police," *Nature Human Behaviour* 5, no. 2 (2021): 194–204.

75. Stephen Semler, "The Flow of Military Equipment to Police Through Q2 of FY 2021," Speaking Security Substack, April 1, 2021, https://stephensemler.substack.com/p/the-flow-of -military-equipment-to; Catie Edmondson, "Senate Kills Broad Curbs on Military Gear for Police, Thwarting Push to Demilitarize," *NYT*, July 21, 2020, https://www.nytimes.com/2020 /07/21/us/politics/senate-police-military-equipment.html; and Gabrielle Gurley, "The Congressional Black Caucus: Necessary but Not Sufficient," *TAP*, September 14, 2020, https:// prospect.org/politics/congressional-black-caucus-necessary-but-not-sufficient/. For more on the Congressional Black Caucus's reluctance to respond to issues of police brutality, see Keeanga-Yamahtta Taylor, *From #BlackLivesMatter to Black Liberation*, rev. ed. (Chicago: Haymarket Books, 2021), 102–3.

76. Musgrave, Meagher, and Dance, "Pentagon Finally Details Its Weapons-for-Cops Giveaway"; AP, "Militarized Police Forces Come Under Congressional Scrutiny," CBS, September 9, 2014, https://www.cbsnews.com/news/militarized-police-forces-come-under-congressional -scrutiny/; and Allison McCartney, Paul Murray, and Mira Rojanaskul, "After Pouring Billions into Militarization of U.S. Cops, Congress Weighs Limits," Bloomberg, July 1, 2020, https://www .bloomberg.com/graphics/2020-police-military-equipment/.

77. For an overview of civil asset forfeitures, see Marie Gottschalk, *Caught: The Prison State and the Lockdown of American Politics*, rev. ed. (Princeton, NJ: Princeton University Press, 2016), 34–35.

78. Amnesty International, "Police Use of Lethal Force in the United States," May 2015, https://www.amnestyusa.org/wp-content/uploads/2015/06/aiusa_deadlyforcereportjune 2015-1.pdf.

79. Amnesty International, 1–3.

80. Amnesty International, 2.

81. Samuel E. Walker and Carol A. Archbold, *The New World of Police Accountability*, 3rd ed. (Los Angeles: Sage, 2020), 113.

82. Walker and Archbold.

83. This is based on data analyzed by criminologist Philip Matthew Stinson as cited in German Lopez, "Police Officers Are Prosecuted for Murder in Less Than 2 Percent of Fatal Shootings," *Vox*, April 21, 2021, https://www.vox.com/21497089/derek-chauvin-george-floyd-trial-police-prosecutions-black-lives-matter.

84. Philip Stinson quoted in Karabel, "Police Killings Surpass the Worst Years of Lynchings."

85. Kimberly Kindy and Kimbriell Kelly, "Thousands Dead, Few Prosecuted," *WP*, April 11, 2015, https://www.washingtonpost.com/sf/investigative/2015/04/11/thousands-dead-few-prosecuted/.

86. Teressa Ravenell, "Unidentified Police Officials," *Texas Law Review* 100 (2021–22): 891–939.

87. Angelica Hendricks, "Tolling Justice," *Ohio State Law Journal* 85, no. 3 (2024): 476.

88. Michael LaForgia and Jennifer Valentino-DeVries, "They Investigate Police Killings: Their Record Is Wanting," *NYT*, September 25, 2021, https://www.nytimes.com/2021/09/25/us/police-shootings-killings.html; and Tom Hogan, "After I-95 Shooting, Time to Stop State Police from Investigating Themselves," *PI*, June 9, 2023, A11.

89. Samuel Walker, "Police Reform Hasn't Failed, 'It's Alive and Growing,'" *CR*, July 19, 2022, https://thecrimereport.org/2022/07/19/police-reform-hasnt-failed-its-alive-and-growing/.

90. LaForgia and Valentino-DeVries, "They Investigate Police Killings."

91. Sarah Maslin Nir, Jonah E. Bromwich, and Benjamin Weiser, "A Special Unit to Prosecute Police Killings Has No Convictions," *NYT*, February 26, 2021, https://www.nytimes.com/2021/02/26/nyregion/new-york-police-accountability.html.

92. Chicago's Independent Police Review Authority was established in 2007 amid charges that the Office of Professional Standards, a unit of the police department that previously handled police-brutality complaints, was too close to the police. Between 2007 and 2014, the new agency, whose top three leaders were all former cops, investigated 374 police shootings of civilians, including at least 116 fatalities, and deemed that all of them were justified. Chip Mitchell, "Who Polices the Police? In Chicago, It's Increasingly Ex-Cops," WBEZ, n.d., https://www.wbez.org/stories/who-polices-the-police-in-chicago-its-increasingly-ex-cops/fbeca316-8b2a-4ef2-beb1-d07f8b6e3bef (accessed October 19, 2023).

93. Samuel Dunkle, "'The Air Was Blue with Perjury': Police Lies and the Case for Abolition," *New York University Law Review* 96, no. 6 (December 2020): 2048–93.

94. Walker and Archbold, *New World of Police Accountability*, 66.

95. Zimring, *When Police Kill*, 19.

96. *Tennessee v. Garner et al.*, 471 U.S. 1 (Supreme Court, 1985), 11, https://tile.loc.gov/storage-services/service/ll/usrep/usrep471/usrep471001/usrep471001.pdf.

97. Mitchell Zamoff, "Determining the Perspective of a Reasonable Police Officer," *Villanova Law Review* 65 (2020): 585.

98. Zamoff, 590.

99. Loggers, fishing and hunting workers, and roofers are the top three. US Bureau of Labor Statistics, "Civilian Occupations with High Fatal Work Injury Rates," n.d., https://www.bls.gov/charts/census-of-fatal-occupational-injuries/civilian-occupations-with-high-fatal-work-injury-rates.htm (accessed October 17, 2023).

100. Rosa Brooks, quoted in "Crime and Punishment: Can American Policing Be Fixed?," roundtable discussion, *HM*, April 2024, 30.

101. Zimring, *When Police Kill*, 99–100, 106–7.

102. FBI, Uniform Crime Report, "Law Enforcement Officers Killed and Assaulted," 2019 and various other years, https://ucr.fbi.gov/leoka/2019/resource-pages/about-leoka (accessed October 17, 2023).

103. Zimring, *When Police Kill*, 107.

104. Zimring, 110–11.

105. Zimring; and Hemenway et al., "Variation in Rates of Fatal Police Shootings," 78–80.

106. Nicholas J. Richardson, Kelle Barrick, and Kevin J. Strom, "Is Policing Safer Today? The Case for a More Comprehensive Definition of Dangerousness," *Criminology and Public Policy* 18, no. 1 (2019): 41; and Lepore, "Invention of the Police."

107. Zamoff, "Determining the Perspective," 590.

108. See the analysis of *Thompson v. City of Chicago* (2006) in Zamoff, 629–30.

109. Butler, *Chokehold*, 187–89. There is some dispute about whether Brown had his hands in the air or not. The courts have determined that advancing toward an officer—whether hands are raised or not—could be perceived as a threat that warrants use of deadly force.

110. Quoted in Thomas Frank, "High-Speed Police Chases Have Killed Thousands of Innocent Bystanders," *USA Today*, July 30, 2015, https://www.usatoday.com/story/news/2015/07/30/police-pursuits-fatal-injuries/30187827/.

111. See the discussion of *Scott v. Harris* in Jason Lee Steorts, "When Should Cops Be Able to Use Deadly Force?," *Atlantic*, August 27, 2015, https://www.theatlantic.com/politics/archive/2015/08/use-of-deadly-force-police/402181/.

112. Quoted in Steorts.

113. The actual numbers are probably higher because police reports sometimes fail to mention a chase. Frank, "High-Speed Police Chases."

114. Maria Cramer and Hurubie Meko, "N.Y.P.D. Bans High-Speed Chases for Low-Level Offenses," *NYT*, January 15, 2025, https://www.nytimes.com/2025/01/15/nyregion/nypd-bans-high-speed-chases-for-low-level-offenses.html.

115. Quoted in Steorts, "When Should Cops Be Able to Use Deadly Force?."

116. Quoted in Steorts.

117. Texas Medical-Legal Partnership Coalition, "Police De-Escalation: Warning Before Shooting Maps," n.d., https://www.txmlpc.org/resources/police/warning (accessed November 4, 2023); and Olevia Boykin, Christopher Desir, and Jed Rubenfeld, "A Better Standard for the Use of Deadly Force," *NYT*, January 1, 2016, A10.

118. The revised policy bars tactics such as firing weapons solely to disable fleeing vehicles. It also requires officers to intervene when colleagues use excessive or unconstitutional force and to render or seek medical assistance for people injured by law enforcement. Merrick Garland, "Department's Updated Use-of-Force Policy," Office of the Attorney General, memo, May 20, 2022, https://www.justice.gov/d9/pages/attachments/2022/05/23/departments_updated_use-of-force_policy.pdf. See also Boykin et al., "Better Standard for the Use of Deadly Force."

119. Zolan Kanno-Youngs and Luke Broadwater, "Many of Biden's Goals on Police Reform Are Still Incomplete," *NYT*, February 8, 2023, https://www.nytimes.com/2023/02/08/us/politics/biden-police-state-of-the-union.html.

120. Miriam Berger and Rick Noack, "From Guns to Neck Restraint: How Police Tactics Differ Around the World," *WP*, April 21, 2021, https://www.washingtonpost.com/world/2020/06/06/guns-neck-restraint-how-police-tactics-differ-around-world/; and Philip Alpers and Michael Picard, "Guns in the United States: Number of Privately Owned Firearms—World Ranking," Sydney School of Public Health, University of Sydney, GunPolicy.org, February 22, 2021, https://www.gunpolicy.org/firearms/compare/194/number_of_privately_owned_firearms_-_world_ranking/204.

121. Hirschfield, "Why Do American Cops Kill So Many?"

122. Hirschfield; and Berger and Noack, "From Guns to Neck Restraint."

123. Darwin Bond Graham, "In One California City, Police Kill with Near Impunity," *Appeal*, December 18, 2019, https://theappeal.org/vallejo-california-police-shootings/. See also Joanna Schwartz, *Shielded: How the Police Became Untouchable* (New York: Viking, 2023), chap. 6.

124. Zimring, *When Police Kill*, 57, fig. 3.6.

125. Mapping Police Violence, "2020 Police Violence Report," n.d., https://policeviolence report.org/2020/ (accessed January 24, 2025); and Jon M. Shane, Brian Lawton, and Zoë Swenson, "The Prevalence of Fatal Police Shootings by U.S. Police, 2015–2016: Patterns and Answers from a New Data Set," *Journal of Criminal Justice* 52 (2017): 105, table 3.

126. For more on the "21-foot rule" and the lack of evidence to support it, see Zimring, *When Police Kill*, 100–102.

127. Between 2008 and 2013, two police officers in the United States were killed with knives or other sharp instruments; 268 died after being shot. Zimring, 96, fig. 5.1.

128. Zimring, 102; and Hirschfield, "Why Do American Cops Kill So Many?"

129. Berger and Noack, "From Guns to Neck Restraint."

130. David Kirkpatrick, "Split-Second Decisions: How a Supreme Court Shaped Modern Policing," *NYT*, April 25, 2021, https://www.nytimes.com/2021/04/25/us/police-use-of-force .html; and DOJ, "Department of Justice Announces Department-Wide Policy on Chokeholds and 'No Knock' Entries," press release, September 14, 2021, https://www.justice.gov/opa/pr /department-justice-announces-department-wide-policy-chokeholds-and-no-knock-entries.

131. Garner's family reached a $5.9 million settlement with New York City in 2015. In 2019, five years after Garner's death, Pantaleo was fired from the NYPD for killing him and was stripped of his pension benefits.

132. Topher Sanders and Yoav Gonen, "Still Can't Breathe: How NYPD Officers Continue to Use Chokeholds on Civilians," *City* and *ProPublica*, January 21, 2021, https://www.thecity.nyc /2021/01/21/nypd-officers-chokeholds-still-cant-breathe/.

133. Lynda G. Dodd, "The Rights Revolution in the Age of Obama and Ferguson: Policing, the Rule of Law, and the Elusive Quest for Accountability," *Perspectives on Politics* 13, no. 3 (September 2015): 658–59.

134. Schwartz, *Shielded*, 1–6.

135. Charles Epp, *Making Rights Real: Activists, Bureaucrats, and the Creation of the Legalistic State* (Chicago: University of Chicago Press, 2009), 17.

136. *Kisela v. Hughes*, 138 St. Ct. 1148 (2018).

137. Schwartz, *Shielded*, 79; and Jay Schweikert, "Qualified Immunity: A Legal, Practical, and Moral Failure," *CLN*, March 2021, 8. Officers are often uninformed about binding court decisions regarding use of force, including "clearly established" laws. Teressa E. Ravenell and Riley H. Ross III, "Qualified Immunity and Unqualified Assumptions," *Journal of Criminal Law and Criminology* 112, no. 1 (Winter 2022): 1–35.

138. Schwartz, *Shielded*, 76.

139. This account of *Baxter v. Bracey* is based on Schweikert, "Qualified Immunity," 7.

140. The one dissenting judge argued against granting qualified immunity on the grounds that "no competent officer would fire his weapon in the direction of a nonthreatening pet while the pet was surrounded by children." This account of *Corbitt v. Vickers* (2019) is based on Schweikert, 7.

141. Editorial Board, "End the Court Doctrine That Enables Police Brutality."

142. Schweikert, "Qualified Immunity," 8.

143. Schwartz, *Shielded*, 79.

144. Schwartz, 77.

145. Madison Pauly, "Meet the Company That Writes the Policies That Protect Cops," *Mother Jones*, September/October 2020, https://www.motherjones.com/crime-justice/2020/08 /lexipol-police-policy-company/.

146. Carl Takei quoted in Pauly.

147. For example, Lexipol does not endorse requiring police to attempt de-escalation before resorting to force, even though the National Consensus on Use of Force, a collaboration of eleven law enforcement groups, including the Fraternal Order of Police, backs such a stance. Lexipol was reportedly instrumental in watering down California's 2019 Act to Save Lives. Pauly,

"Meet the Company"; and Jane Coaston, "California's New Law to Stop Police Shootings, Explained," *Vox*, August 2019, https://www.vox.com/2019/8/23/20826646/california-act-to-save-livespolice-shooting-ab-392-explained.

148. Schwartz, *Shielded*, 169–71.

149. Dodd, "Rights Revolution," 662.

150. As a result, plaintiffs in Section 1983 litigation "have a far higher hurdle to meet in order to hold the government itself responsible for police misconduct and other violations than they do in Title VII cases and Americans with Disabilities cases, where the business or government entity is typically held responsible for their employees' misconduct." Dodd, "Rights Revolution," 663.

151. Dodd, 659–60.

152. Joanna Schwartz, "Qualified Immunity's Boldest Lie," *University of Chicago Law Review* 88, no. 3 (2021): 605.

153. Walker and Archbold, *New World of Police Accountability*, 48.

154. Joanna Schwartz, "Police Indemnification," *New York University Law Review* 89, no. 3 (2014): 912–13.

155. Schwartz, 885–1003.

156. Schwartz, 885.

157. Joanna Schwartz, "How Governments Pay. Lawsuits, Budgets, and Police Reform," *U.C.L.A. Law Review* 63, no. 5 (2016): 1144–298.

158. Zimring, *When Police Kill*, 132–35.

159. Andrew Cockburn, "Blood Money: Taxpayers Pick Up the Tab for Police Brutality," *HM*, November 2018, https://harpers.org/archive/2018/11/blood-money-police-brutality-taxpayers/.

160. Zusha Elinson and Dan Frosch, "Cost of Police-Misconduct Cases Soars in Big U.S. Cities," *WSJ*, July 15, 2015, https://www.wsj.com/articles/cost-of-police-misconduct-cases-soars-in-big-u-s-cities-1437013834.

161. "Watching the Watchmen," *Economist*, March 21, 2019, https://www.economist.com/united-states/2019/03/21/chicagos-troubled-police-force-gets-federal-oversight.

162. Cockburn, "Blood Money," 65. See also John Rappaport, "How Private Insurers Regulate Public Police," *Harvard Law Review* 130, no. 6 (2017): 1539–614.

163. Alyxandra Goodwin, Whitney Shepard, and Carrie Sloan, "Police Brutality Bonds: How Wall Street Profits," Action Center on Race and the Economy, June 2020, rev., https://acrecampaigns.org/research_post/police-brutality-bonds/.

164. See, for example, the discussion of Chicago's regressive tax system and "police brutality" bonds in Goodwin et al., "Police Brutality Bonds."

165. Schwartz, "How Governments Pay," 1178.

166. Cockburn, "Blood Money," 65.

167. Dodd, "Rights Revolution," 664–65; and Sean Farhang, *The Litigation State: Public Regulations and Private Lawsuits in the U.S.* (Princeton, NJ: Princeton University Press, 2010).

168. Schwartz, *Shielded*, 172.

169. Kimbriell Kelly, Sarah Childress, and Steven Rich, "Forced Reforms, Mixed Results," *WP*, November 13, 2015, https://www.washingtonpost.com/sf/investigative/2015/11/13/forced-reforms-mixed-results/.

170. Cockburn, "Blood Money."

171. Kelly et al., "Forced Reforms, Mixed Results."

172. For an overview of research findings on police departments and consent decrees, see Butler, *Chokehold*, 191–95.

173. Stephen Rushin, *Federal Intervention in American Police Departments* (New York: Cambridge University Press, 2017), 254; Brentin Mock, "Ignoring Police Violence," *TAP*, Summer 2017, 12–15; and Li Sian Goh, "Going Local: Do Consent Decrees and Other Forms of Federal

Intervention in Municipal Police Departments Reduce Police Killings?," *Justice Quarterly* 37, no. 5 (2020): 900–929.

174. Rushin, *Federal Intervention*, 255; and Mock, "Ignoring Police Violence."

175. Dodd, "Rights Revolution," 665. Between 1994 and 2017, seventy federal investigations and forty agreements resulted. Mock, "Ignoring Police Violence," 12.

176. Dodd, "Rights Revolution," 665.

177. DOJ, *Federal Reports on Police Killings* (Brooklyn: Melville House, 2017).

178. DOJ, Civil Rights Division, *The Ferguson Report* (New York: New Press, 2015), 141. It is hard to say what that means in practice because "community policing" is a popular but ill-defined concept that critics disparage as not signifying much more than deploying more cops on bicycles. Josmar Trujillo, "Police and Media Agree: Cops Just Need to Be Nicer," Fairness and Accuracy in Reporting, February 12, 2016, http://fair.org/home/police-and-media-agree-cops-just-need-to-be-nicer/.

179. Steve Herbert, *Citizens, Cops, and Power: Recognizing the Limits of Community* (Chicago: University of Chicago Press, 2006).

180. Jim Salter and Eric Tucker, "Ferguson Missed Deadlines in Deal with Justice Department," *Press Democrat*, January 27, 2017, https://www.pressdemocrat.com/article/news/ferguson-missed-deadlines-in-deal-with-justice-department/.

181. DOJ, Civil Rights Division and US Attorney's Office Northern District of Illinois, "Investigation of the Chicago Police Department, 2017," n.d., https://www.justice.gov/opa/file/925846/download (accessed October 27, 2021), 5, 7.

182. For an excellent analysis of Obama and policing issues, see Taylor, *From #BlackLivesMatter*, chap. 5. See also Alec Karakatsanis, *Usual Cruelty: The Complicity of Lawyers in the Criminal Injustice System* (New York: New Press, 2019), 92 and 211–12n362.

183. David Cole, "Obama's Civil Rights Legacy—and Ours," *Nation*, December 8, 2015, https://www.thenation.com/article/archive/obamas-civil-rights-legacy-and-ours/.

184. "Watching the Watchmen."

185. Katie Benner, "Barr Says Communities That Protest the Police Risk Losing Protection," *NYT*, December 4, 2019, https://www.nytimes.com/2019/12/04/us/politics/barr-police.html.

186. Michael Wines, "'Looting' Comment from Trump Dates Back to Racial Unrest of the 1960s," *NYT*, May 29, 2020, https://www.nytimes.com/2020/05/29/us/looting-starts-shooting-starts.html.

187. Samantha Michaels, "The Infuriating History of Why Police Unions Have So Much Power," *Mother Jones*, September/October 2020, https://www.motherjones.com/crime-justice/2020/08/police-unions-minneapolis/.

188. Justin Tasolides, "Biden Signs Three Bills Benefitting Police, First Responders: 'In Valor, There Is Hope,'" *Spectrum News*, November 18, 2021, https://ny1.com/nyc/all-boroughs/news/2021/11/18/biden-law-enforcement-police-first-responder-bills.

189. Denise Lavoie, Tatyana Monnay, and Juliette Rihl, "States Struggle with Pushback After Wave of Policing Reforms," AP, November 1, 2022, https://apnews.com/article/death-of-george-floyd-amir-locke-richmond-minneapolis-86370ae1c735d44525e37eed80b293b2.

190. Daniele Selby, "New Mexico Is the Second State to Ban Qualified Immunity," Innocence Project, April 7, 2021, https://innocenceproject.org/new-mexico-bans-qualified-immunity-police-accountability/; and Jeffrey Mays and Ashley Southall, "It May Soon Be Easier to Sue the N.Y.P.D. for Misconduct," *NYT*, March 25, 2021, updated June 23, 2021, https://www.nytimes.com/2021/03/25/nyregion/nyc-qualified-immunity-police-reform.html.

191. Shaila Dewan, "Will Troubled Police Departments Escape Federal Accountability?," *NYT*, December 24, 2024, https://www.nytimes.com/2024/12/24/us/biden-police-departments-federal-accountability.html; and Jacey Fortin et al., "Justice Dept. to End Oversight of Local Police Accused of Abuses," *NYT*, May 21, 2025, https://www.nytimes.com/2025/05/21/us/trump-police-consent-decrees.html.

192. Kennedy, "State Violence," 4.

193. See, for example, Philip Foner, *Organized Labor and the Black Worker, 1619–1981* (Chicago: Haymarket Books, 2018); Robin Kelley, *Hammer and Hoe: Alabama Communists During the Great Depression* (Chapel Hill: University of North Carolina Press, 1990); and Paul Frymer, *Black and Blue: African Americans, the Labor Movement, and the Decline of the Democratic Party* (Princeton, NJ: Princeton University Press, 2007).

194. Ellen Schrecker, *Many Are the Crimes: McCarthyism in America* (Princeton, NJ: Princeton University Press, 1998).

195. Finnegan, "The Blue Wall," 48.

196. Katherine J. Bies, "Let the Sunshine In: Illuminating the Powerful Role Police Unions Play in Shielding Officer Misconduct," *Stanford Law and Policy Review* 28, no. 1 (January 2017): 112.

197. Joshua Page, Heather Schoenfeld, and Michael Campbell, "To Defund the Police, We Have to Dethrone the Law Enforcement Lobby," *Jacobin*, July 2020, https://jacobinmag.com /author/heather-schoenfeld; and Catherine Fisk and L. Song Richardson, "Police Unions," *George Washington Law Review* 85, no. 3 (2017): 747–59.

198. Rodney Stark, *Police Riots: Collective Violence and Law Enforcement* (Belmont, CA: Wadsworth, 1972), 192–93, in Williams, *Our Enemies in Blue*, 216.

199. Williams, *Our Enemies in Blue*, 222–23.

200. Williams, 223.

201. Williams, 208.

202. Williams, 216.

203. Flint Taylor, "Blood on Their Hands: The Racist History of Modern Police Unions," *In These Times*, January 14, 2015, https://inthesetimes.com/article/police-unions-racist.

204. Stephen Rushin, "Police Union Contracts," *Duke Law Journal* 66, no. 6 (March 2017): 1192. See also Fisk and Richardson, "Police Unions": 737–44; and Reade Levinson, "Across the U.S., Police Contracts Shield Officers from Scrutiny and Discipline," Reuters, January 13, 2017, https://www.reuters.com/investigates/special-report/usa-police-unions/.

205. Abdul N. Rad, "Police Institutions and Police Abuse: Evidence from the U.S." (PhD diss., University of Oxford, 2018), 30; and Jamein Cunningham, Donna Feir, and Rob Gillezeau, "Collective Bargaining Rights, Policing, and Civilian Deaths," Institute of Labor Economics Discussion Paper No. 14208, March 2021, https://docs.iza.org/dp14208.pdf, abstract.

206. "Former Houston Chief: 'We've Let Police Unions Go Too Far,'" *CR*, July 16, 2020, https://thecrimereport.org/2020/07/16/former-houston-chief-weve-let-police-unions-go-too -far/#:~:text=In%20one%20of%20the%20most,won't%20go%20for%20this.

207. Stephen Rushin, "Police Disciplinary Appeals," *University of Pennsylvania Law Review* 167, no. 3 (2018): 583–84; and Kimbriell Kelly, Wesley Lowery, and Steven Rich, "Fired/Rehired," *WP*, August 3, 2017, https://www.washingtonpost.com/graphics/2017/investigations /police-fired-rehired/.

208. Steven Greenhouse, "How Police Unions Enable and Conceal Police Power," *NY*, June 18, 2020, https://www.newyorker.com/news/news-desk/how-police-union-power-helped -increase-abuses.

209. Ben Grunwald and John Rappaport, "The Wandering Officer," *Yale Law Journal* 129, no. 6 (2020): 1676; and E. D. Cauchi, "Justice Department Shuts Down Federal Law Enforcement Misconduct Tracker," CBS News, February 21, 2025, https://www.cbsnews.com/news/ justice-department-shuts-down-federal-law-enforcement-misconduct-tracker/.

210. United Auto Workers Local 2865, "UAW Local Calls on AFL-CIO to End Ties to Police Unions," *New Politics*, July 29, 2015, https://newpol.org/uaw-local-calls-afl-cio-end-ties-police -unions/.

211. Quoted in Steven Cohen, "The Labor Movement Needs to Take a Side on Criminal Justice Reform," *NR*, September 8, 2015, https://newrepublic.com/article/122755/labor -movement-needs-take-side-criminal-justice-reform.

212. It also called for increasing diversity among officers, improving training in implicit bias, allocating more resources to address officers' mental health needs, and establishing a new model in which police are not dispatched in situations better handled by an EMT. Alex N. Press, "On Police Reform, the AFL-CIO Has a Lot of Catching Up to Do," *Jacobin*, June 2021, https://jacobinmag.com/2021/06/police-reform-unions-alf-cio-report-labor -movement.

213. A note at the top of the task force report explained that it was "written by and from the perspective of unionized law enforcement officers and leaders, and endorsed by the participating unions and the AFL-CIO Task Force on Racial Justice." Press, "On Police Reform, the AFL-CIO Has a Lot of Catching Up to Do"; and AFL-CIO, "Public Safety Blueprint for Change," May 2021, https://aflcio.org/sites/default/files/2021-05/PublicSafetyBlueprint-Final .pdf, 2.

214. "Bands of Blue," *Economist*, July 11, 2020, 19; Lisa Backus, "Police Accountability Taking Shape One Year Later," *Chicago Tribune News Junkie*, July 22, 2021, https://ctnewsjunkie.com /2021/07/22/police-accountability-taking-shape-one-year-later/; and Gary Craig, "Police Disciplinary Records Must Be Opened, NY Appellate Judges Determine," *Democrat and Chronicle*, November 4, 2022, https://www.democratandchronicle.com/story/news/2022/11/11 /police-disciplinary-records-must-be-opened-ny-appellate-court-judges-determine /69639952007/#:~:text=Laying%20the%20foundation%20for%20the,complaints%20 sealed%20from%20public%20view.

215. Elahe Izadi, "Louisiana Is the First State to Offer Hate Crime Protections to Police Officers," *WP*, May 26, 2016, https://www.washingtonpost.com/news/post-nation/wp/2016/05 /26/louisianas-blue-lives-matter-bill-just-became-law/.

216. In 2021, Maryland became the first state to repeal its powerful Law Enforcement Officers' Bill of Rights. Rui Kaneya, "States Urged to Repeal Cops' Special Legal Protections," publicintegrity.org, October 29, 2021, https://publicintegrity.org/inside-publici/newsletters /watchdog-newsletter/states-repeal-police-accountability-protections/.

217. Michaels, "The Infuriating History of Why Police Unions Have So Much Power"; and Page et al., "To Defund the Police."

218. As a US senator, Biden introduced the Police Officers' Bill of Rights in May 1991, two months after LAPD officers severely beat Rodney King, which had set off days of unrest in Los Angeles. Biden also worked closely with police unions in drafting the 1994 crime bill, which provided funds to hire one hundred thousand more officers. He later praised NAPO for its leading role in drafting this exceptionally punitive legislation. "You wrote the bill," he declared. Quoted in Finnegan, "The Blue Wall," 55.

219. Donald Trump Campaign, "National Association of Police Organizations Endorses President Donald J. Trump," July 24, 2024, https://www.donaldjtrump.com/news/9d7357aa -4731-4cf7-aade-640824fe94c1.

220. Lepore, "Invention of the Police"; Jonathan Swan, "Police Union: Clinton Snubbed Us," *Hill*, August 6, 2016, https://thehill.com/blogs/ballot-box/presidential-races/290586-police -union-clinton-snubbed-us/; and Jason Silverstein, "National Association of Police Organizations Endorses Trump," CBS News, July 16, 2020, https://www.cbsnews.com/news/national -association-of-police-organizations-endorses-president-trump/.

221. Tony Cheng, *The Policing Machine: Enforcement, Endorsements, and the Illusion of Public Input* (Chicago: University of Chicago Press, 2022).

222. Alec Karakatsanis, *Copaganda: How Police and the Media Manipulate Our News* (New York: New Press, 2025), 11–14.

223. Ronald Helms and S. E. Costanza, "Contextualizing Race: A Conceptual and Empirical Study of Fatal Interactions with Police Across US Counties," *Journal of Ethnicity in Criminal Justice* 18, no. 1 (2019): 43–71.

224. Cedric Johnson, *After Black Lives Matter: Policing and Anti-Capitalist Struggle* (London: Verso, 2024), 162.

225. Mora et al., 19–20. See also James Forman Jr., *Locking Up Our Own: Crime and Punishment in Black America* (New York: Farrar, Straus and Giroux, 2017), chap. 3.

226. DOJ, *Ferguson Report*, 137–38. See also DOJ, Civil Rights Division, Office of Justice Programs and US Equal Employment Opportunity Commission, "Diversity in Law Enforcement: A Literature Review," submission to President's Task Force on 21st Century Policing, 2015, 4nv; and David A. Sklansky, "Not Your Father's Police Department: Making Sense of the New Demographics of Law Enforcement," *Journal of Criminal Law and Criminology* 96, no. 3 (Spring 2006): 1124–25.

227. See Ari Feldman, "Activists Want Bias Training for Cops: ADL Provides It; But Does It Work?," *Forward*, June 17, 2020, https://forward.com/news/national/448948/police-george-floyd-protest-implicit-bias; Michael Hobbes, "'Implicit Bias' Trainings Don't Actually Change Police Behavior," *HuffPost*, June 12, 2020, https://www.huffpost.com/entry/implicit-bias-training-doesnt-actually-change-police-behavior_n_5ee28fc3c5b60b32f010ed48; and Jeremy Stahl, "The NYPD Paid $4.5 Million for a Bias Trainer: She Says She's Not the Solution," *Slate*, June 18, 2020, https://slate.com/news-and-politics/2020/06/lorie-fridell-implicit-bias-policing .html; and Tom James, "Can Cops Unlearn Their Unconscious Biases?," *Atlantic*, December 23, 2017, https://www.theatlantic.com/politics/archive/2017/12/implicit-bias-training-salt-lake /548996/. A growing body of research suggests that implicit bias training and other diversity, equity, and inclusion initiatives, depending on how they are conducted, may be ineffective or, even worse, may backfire, fostering racial and other stereotypes and additional negative consequences. Alexander Kalev and Frank Dobbin, *Getting to Diversity: What Works and What Doesn't* (Cambridge, MA: Harvard University Press, 2022); and Mahzarin Banaji and Frank Dobbin, "Why DEI Training Doesn't Work—and How to Fix It," *WSJ*, n.d., https://www.wsj.com /business/c-suite/dei-training-hr-business-acd23e8b (accessed January 1, 2024).

228. Michelle M. Duguid and Melissa C. Thomas-Hunt, "Condoning Stereotyping? How Awareness of Stereotyping Prevalence Impacts Expression of Stereotypes," *Journal of Applied Psychology* 100, no. 2 (2015): 343–59, https://pubmed.ncbi.nlm.nih.gov/25314368/; and Association for Psychological Science, "Ironic Effects of Anti-Prejudice Messages," July 6, 2011, https://www.psychologicalscience.org/news/releases/ironic-effects-of-anti-prejudice -messages.html.

229. Christopher Chapman, "Use of Force in Minority Areas Is Related to Police Education, Age, Experience, and Ethnicity," *Police Practice and Research* 13, no. 5 (October 2012): 421–36.

230. Mora et al., "Decade of Police Use of Deadly Force Research," 18.

231. "An Exit Interview with U.S. Chief Data Scientist DJ Patil," *Science Friday*, December 9, 2016, https://www.sciencefriday.com/segments/an-exit-interview-with-u-s-chief-data-scientist -dj-patil/#segment-transcript.

232. Simone Weichselbaum, "Police with Military Experience More Likely to Shoot," Marshall Project, October 15, 2018, https://www.themarshallproject.org/2018/10/15/police-with -military-experience-more-likely-to-shoot.

233. Jessica Katzenstein, "The Wars Are Here: How the United States' Post-9/11 Wars Helped Militarize U.S. Police," Watson Institute, Brown University, September 16, 2020, https://watson .brown.edu/costsofwar/files/cow/imce/papers/2020/Police%20Militarization_Costs%20of %20War_Sept%2016%202020.pdf.

234. For more on police officers who are veterans, see pp. 95–103, 113–16, 121, and 126.

235. Suzanne Gordon, Steve Early, and Jasper Craven, *Our Veterans: Winners, Losers, Friends, and Enemies on the New Terrain of Veterans Affairs* (Durham, NC: Duke University Press, 2022), 65–68.

236. Katzenstein, "Wars Are Here," 15.

237. For a review of this literature, see Mora et al., "Decade of Police Use of Deadly Force," 18. The racism index is determined by levels of segregation and by economic, employment, incarceration, and educational disparities. Mora et al., 18.

238. James J. Sobol, Yuning Wu, and Ivan Y. Sun, "Neighborhood Context and Police Vigor: A Multilevel Analysis," *Crime and Delinquency* 59, no. 3 (2013): 344–68; and William Terrill and Michael D. Reisig, "Neighborhood Context and Police Use of Force," *Journal of Research in Crime and Delinquency* 40, no. 3 (2003): 291–321.

239. Klinger et al., "Race, Crime, and the Micro-Ecology of Deadly Force," 193; and Mora et al., "Decade of Police Use of Deadly Force Research," 8.

240. Zimring, *When Police Kill*, 77.

241. Alpers and Picard, "Guns in the United States."

242. Mora et al., "Decade of Police Use of Deadly Force Research," 18–21.

243. Mora et al., 18–21.

244. Hemenway et al., "Variation in Rates of Fatal Police Shootings," 63.

245. Hemenway et al., 72; and David Swedler et al., "Firearm Prevalence and Homicides of Law Enforcement Officers in the United States," *American Journal of Public Health*, 105, no. 10 (2015): 2047.

246. Hemenway et al., "Variation in Rates of Fatal Police Killings," 63–73.

247. For a masterful account of the reasons for this shift, see Jennifer Carlson, *Policing the Second Amendment: Guns, Law Enforcement, and the Politics of Race* (Princeton, NJ: Princeton University Press, 2020).

248. J. H. Skolnick and J. J. Fyfe, *Above the Law: Police and the Excessive Use of Force* (New York: Free Press, 1994), 20; and Nancy Krieger et al., "Trends in US Deaths Due to Legal Intervention Among Black and White Men, Age 15–34 Years, by County Income Level, 1960–2010," *Harvard Public Health Review* 3 (January 2015): 3.

249. Mora et al., "Decade of Police Use of Deadly Force Research," 16. See also Krieger et al., "Trends in US Deaths Due to Legal Intervention," 1–5.

250. Walker and Archbold, *New World of Police Accountability*, 69–70.

251. Dylan Purcell, Aubrey Whelan, and Mark Fazlollah, "Report on Phila. Police: New Rules, Training Needed," *PI*, March 23, 2015, https://www.inquirer.com/philly/news/20150324 _DOJ_on_Philly_police_shootings__new_rules__training_needed.html#loaded.

252. These calculations exclude people who shot themselves to death when confronted by the Philadelphia police. Philadelphia Police Department, "Officer Involved Shootings," n.d., https://www.phillypolice.com/ois/ (accessed September 2, 2024); and Tom Beck, "Study: Philly 2nd Worst Big City for Fatal Police Shootings from 2010–2014," phillymag.com, July 31, 2015, https://www.phillymag.com/citified/2015/07/31/philadelphia-fatal-police-shootings/.

253. World Population Review, "Police Killings by Country."

254. Doris Fuller et al., "Overlooked in the Undercounted: The Role of Mental Illness in Fatal Law Enforcement Encounters," Treatment Advocacy Center, 2015, https://www .treatmentadvocacycenter.org/storage/documents/overlooked-in-the-undercounted.pdf, 1.

255. Fuller et al., 1.

256. Krishanna J. Prince and Ivan Y. Sun, "Examining Individual and Aggregate Correlates of Police Killings of People with Mental Illness: A Special Gaze at Race and Ethnicity," *Homicide Studies* 27, no. 1 (2023): 89.

257. Alisa Roth, *Insane: America's Criminal Treatment of Mental Illness* (New York: Basic Books, 2018); and Katherine Beckett and Steve Herbert, *Banished: The New Social Control in Urban America* (New York: Oxford University Press, 2010).

258. For the seminal article on "broken windows," see George L. Kelling and James Q. Wilson, "Broken Windows: The Police and Neighborhood Safety," *Atlantic*, March 1982, https://www.theatlantic.com/magazine/archive/1982/03/broken-windows/304465/. On the lack of

evidence to support the theory, see Bernard E. Harcourt, *Illusion of Order: The False Promise of Broken Windows Policing*, rev. ed. (Cambridge, MA: Harvard University Press, 2005); and Wesley Skogan and Kathleen Frydl, eds., *Fairness and Effectiveness in Policing: The Evidence* (Washington, DC: National Academies Press, 2004), 228–29.

259. Vitale, *End of Policing*, 81.

260. Roth, *Insane*.

261. Vitale, *End of Policing*, 82.

262. The rate of high-level resistance by people with mental health problems in arrest situations is still quite low (7 percent). Philip Mulvey and Michael White, "The Potential for Violence in Arrests of Persons with Mental Illness," *Policing: An International Journal of Police Strategies and Management* 37, no. 2 (2014): 414.

263. Mulvey and White, 404–19.

264. Mulvey and White, 404–19.

265. Vitale, *End of Policing*, 84.

266. Nicole Leonard and Kate Wolffe, "Cities Know the Way Police Respond to Mental Crisis Calls Needs to Change: But How?," NPR, November 9, 2023, https://www.npr.org/sections/health-shots/2023/11/09/1203342875/cities-know-the-way-police-respond-to-mental-crisis-calls-needs-to-change-but-ho; and Michelle S. Phelps, *The Minneapolis Reckoning: Race, Violence, and the Politics of Policing in America* (Princeton, NJ: Princeton University Press, 2024), 187–93.

267. Cynthia Lum, "Perspectives on Policing," *Annual Review of Criminology* 4 (2021): 22.

268. Vitale, *End of Policing*, 85.

269. Barbara Armacost, "Police Shootings: Is Accountability the Enemy of Prevention?," *Ohio State Law Journal* 80, no. 5 (2019): 907–86.

270. Armacost, 986, emphasis in the original. Armacost's analysis focuses on the case of Tamir Rice, a twelve-year-old African American boy shot to death in 2014 by a police officer while playing with a toy gun outside a Cleveland recreation center. Her review of the case reveals that a breakdown in communications was a major contributing factor to Tamir's tragic death.

271. Lum, "Perspectives on Policing": 20.

272. Lum, 20–21. See also Daniel Nagin, "Deterrence in the Twenty-First Century," *Crime and Justice* 42, no. 1 (August 2013): 199–263.

4. Deadly and Professional: The Origins and Development of US Police Forces

1. Quoted in "Crime and Punishment: Can American Policing Be Fixed," *HM*, April 2024, 35.

2. For good overviews of how colonialism, slavery, and their legacies, including Jim Crow, shaped law enforcement in the United States, see Kristian Williams, *Our Enemies in Blue: Police and Power in America*, 3rd ed. (Oakland, CA: AK Press, 2015), 63–83, 126–27; Elizabeth Hinton and DeAnza Cook, "The Mass Criminalization of Black Americans: A Historical Overview," *Annual Review of Criminology* 4, no. 1 (2021): 265–71. On patrols for enslavers, see Sally E. Hadden, *Slave Patrols: Law and Violence in Virginia and the Carolinas* (Cambridge, MA: Harvard University Press, 2001); and Larry H. Spruill, "Slave Patrols, 'Packs of Negro Dogs' and Policing Black Communities," *Phylon* 53, no. 1 (Summer 2016): 42–66. On the impact of Jim Crow, see Khalil Gibran Muhammad, *The Condemnation of Blackness: Race, Crime, and the Making of Modern Urban America* (Cambridge, MA: Harvard University Press, 2010). For an overview of literature on convict leasing, see Marie Gottschalk, *The Prison and the Gallows: The Politics of Mass Incarceration in America* (New York: Cambridge University Press, 2006), 48–52; and Marie

Gottschalk, *Caught: The Prison State and the Lockdown of American Politics*, rev. ed. (Princeton, NJ: Princeton University Press, 2016), 58–59. See also scholarship on gender, race, and convict leasing, notably Sarah Haley, *No Mercy Here: Gender, Punishment, and the Making of Jim Crow Modernity* (Chapel Hill: University of North Carolina Press, 2019); and Talitha LeFlouria, *Chained in Silence: Black Women and Convict Labor in the New South* (Chapel Hill: University of North Carolina Press, 2016).

3. These developments have been garnering increased scholarly attention, however. For a survey of the emerging historiography of police brutality, see David Ponton III, "A Protracted War for Order: Police Violence in the Twentieth Century," *History Compass* 16, no. 6 (2018): e12453.

4. This discussion of the early development of US police forces is based on Gottschalk, *Prison and the Gallows*, 52–55.

5. Gottschalk, 54–55.

6. Gottschalk, 54–55.

7. See, for example, Nell Irvin Painter, *Standing at Armageddon: A Grassroots History of the Progressive Era* (New York: Norton, 1989).

8. Nearly a century later, the first published court case interpreting this act concluded in 1977 that it largely applied specifically to what the Pinkertons were doing at the time the legislation was enacted. Therefore this measure was not relevant to the US government's extensive use of private security agencies and private military contractors a century hence. Milton J. Socolar, General Counsel, GAO, letter to Senator John Stennis (D-MS), March 6, 1980, https://www.gao.gov/assets/b-139965.pdf.

9. Thomas Reppetto, *American Police: The Blue Parade, 1845–1945; A History* (New York: Enigma Books, 2011), 43; and Samuel E. Walker and Carol A. Archbold, *The New World of Police Accountability*, 3rd ed. (Los Angeles: Sage, 2020), 41–42.

10. Muhammad, *Condemnation of Blackness*; Anne Gray Fischer, *The Streets Belong to Us: Sex, Race, and Police Power from Segregation to Gentrification* (Chapel Hill: University of North Carolina Press, 2022); and Anna Lvovsky, *Vice Patrol: Cops, Courts, and the Struggle over Urban Gay Life Before Stonewall* (Chicago: University of Chicago Press, 2021).

11. Alex Gourevitch, "Police Work: The Centrality of Labor Repression in American Political History," *Perspectives on Politics* 13, no. 3 (2015): 765.

12. Gourevitch: 765. See also Sidney L. Harring and Lorraine M. McMullin, "The Buffalo Police 1872–1900: Labor Unrest, Political Power and the Creation of the Police Institution," *Crime and Social Justice* 4 (Fall–Winter 1975): 5–14.

13. For an overview of the Pinkertons, see Gottschalk, *Prison and the Gallows*, 54–55.

14. Sarah Schulman, "Red Lights, Blue Lines," *NYRB*, March 23, 2023, 34.

15. Schulman, 34. See also Muhammad, *Condemnation of Blackness*; Fischer, *Streets Belong to Us*; and Lvovsky, *Vice Patrol*.

16. Samuel Bowles and Arjun Jayadev, "Garrison America," *Economist's Voice*, Berkeley Electronic Press, March 2007, http://www.bepress.com/ev/vol4/iss2/art3/.

17. Gourevitch, "Police Work": 762–77.

18. Steven Greenhouse, "How Police Unions Enable and Conceal Abuses of Power," *NY*, June 18, 2020, https://www.newyorker.com/news/news-desk/how-police-union-power-helped-increase-abuses; and Shane Bauer, "Letter from California: An Unstoppable Force," *NY*, November 23, 2020, 30.

19. Williams, *Our Enemies in Blue*, 239–46.

20. During the 1950s, police red squads supplied much of the information that Senator Joseph McCarthy (R-WI) and others used to blackmail, slander, and destroy the careers of people accused of being communists and to decapitate the left in the United States. Christopher J. Coyne and Abigail R. Hall, *Tyranny Comes Home: The Domestic Fate of U.S. Militarism* (Stanford, CA: Stanford University Press, 2018), 79–82.

21. Peter Reuter, "Why Has US Drug Policy Changed So Little over 30 Years?," *Crime and Justice* 42, no. 1 (August 2013): 79–80.

22. Stephen Kinzer, *The True Flag: Theodore Roosevelt, Mark Twain, and the Birth of American Empire* (New York: Henry Holt, 2017), 136, 142.

23. Kinzer, 150–51, 217, 222.

24. In language largely dictated by Bryan himself, the Democratic platform denounced militarism as a "strong arm" that is "fatal to free institutions" as it foments "conquest abroad and oppression at home." The platform also decried "seizing or purchasing distant islands to be governed outside the Constitution." Quoted in Kinzer, 170–71.

25. Kinzer, 168–70.

26. Quoted in Kinzer, 176.

27. Mark Twain, "To the Person Sitting in Darkness," *North American Review*, February 1901, quoted in Kinzer, *True Flag*, 182; see also 83–85, 135–36.

28. Quoted in Kinzer, *True Flag*, 138.

29. Quoted in Kinzer, 138.

30. Daniel Immerwahr, *How to Hide an Empire: A History of the Greater United States* (New York: Farrar, Straus and Giroux, 2019), 98–103; Kim A. Wagner, *Massacre in the Clouds: An American Atrocity and the Erasure of History* (New York: PublicAffairs, 2024); and Stuart Creighton Miller, *Benevolent Assimilation: The American Conquest of the Philippines, 1899–1903* (New Haven, CT: Yale University Press, 1982).

31. Coyne and Hall, *Tyranny Comes Home*, 142–45.

32. W.E.B. Du Bois, letter to Moorfield Storey, October 21, 1907, in *The Correspondence of W.E.B. Du Bois*, ed. Herbert Aptheker, vol. 1, *Selections, 1877–1934* (Amherst: University of Massachusetts Press, 1973), 136–37.

33. Erving Winslow, letter to W.E.B. Du Bois, October 25, 1907, in Aptheker, 1:137. See also Wagner, *Massacre in the Clouds*.

34. Alfred W. McCoy, *Policing America's Empire: The United States, the Philippines, and the Rise of the Surveillance State* (Madison: University of Wisconsin Press, 2009). See also Jeremy Kuzmarov, *Modernizing Repression: Police Training and Nation-Building in the American Century* (Amherst: University of Massachusetts Press, 2012), chap. 1.

35. Coyne and Hall, *Tyranny Comes Home*, 78–83.

36. Atul Kohli, *Imperialism and the Developing World: How Britain and the United States Shaped the Global Periphery* (New York: Oxford University Press, 2020), 240–43.

37. Greg Grandin, *The End of the Myth: From the Frontier to the Border Wall in the Mind of America* (New York: Metropolitan Books, 2019), 86. See also Bartholomew Sparrow, *The Insular Cases and the Emergence of American Empire* (Lawrence: University of Kansas Press, 2006).

38. Grandin, *End of the Myth*, chap. 8.

39. Grandin, 137.

40. Grandin, 139.

41. Grandin, 145–46.

42. Immerwahr, *How to Hide an Empire*, 85–87.

43. Ken De Bevoise, *Agents of the Apocalypse: Epidemic Disease in Colonial Philippines* (Princeton, NJ: Princeton University Press, 1995), 13, cited in Immerwahr, *How to Hide an Empire*, 103. De Bevoise concluded that about 775,000 Filipinos died between 1899 and 1903 because of the war.

44. Grandin, *End of the Myth*, 140, 143, and 162–63. See also Kelly Lytle Hernández, *Migra! A History of the U.S. Border Patrol* (Berkeley: University of California Press, 2010).

45. Julian Go, "The Imperial Origins of American Policing: Militarization and Imperial Feedback in the Early 20th Century," *American Journal of Sociology* 125, no. 5 (March 2020): 1213.

46. Stuart Schrader, *Badges Without Borders: How Global Counterinsurgency Transformed American Politics* (Oakland: University of California Press, 2019), 67.

47. Alfred E. Parker, *Crime Fighter: August Vollmer* (New York: Macmillan, 1961), 144, as quoted in Schrader, *Badges Without Borders*, 67.

48. Go, "Imperial Origins of American Policing": 1193–254.

49. Coyne and Hall, *Tyranny Comes Home*, 146–47.

50. Schrader, *Badges Without Borders*, 68–70.

51. Jill Lepore, "Invention of the Police," *NY*, July 13, 2020, https://www.newyorker.com /magazine/2020/07/20/the-invention-of-the-police.

52. Coyne and Hall, *Tyranny Comes Home*, 103.

53. Schrader, *Badges Without Borders*, 74.

54. Coyne and Hall, *Tyranny Comes Home*, 103.

55. Schrader, *Badges Without Borders*.

56. Naomi Murakawa, *The First Civil Right: How Liberals Built Prison America* (New York: Oxford University Press, 2014).

57. President's Committee on Civil Rights, *To Secure These Rights: The Report of the President's Committee on Civil Rights* (Washington, DC: GPO, 1947), vii.

58. Mary L. Dudziak, *Cold War Civil Rights: Race and the Image of American Democracy* (Princeton, NJ: Princeton University Press, 2000).

59. Murakawa, *First Civil Right*.

60. Vesla M. Weaver, "Frontlash: Race and the Development of Punitive Crime Policy," *Studies in American Political Development* 21, no. 2 (2007): 230–65.

61. Murakawa, *First Civil Right*.

62. The budget for the LEAA soared from $63 million in 1968 to nearly $1 billion a year during its heyday in the 1970s. Franklin E. Zimring, *The Contradictions of American Capital Punishment* (New York: Oxford University Press, 2003), 17.

63. Michael Sherry, *The Punitive Turn in American Life: How the United States Learned to Fight Crime Like a War* (Chapel Hill: University of North Carolina Press, 2020), 9.

64. See, for example, Michael Flamm, *Law and Order: Street Crime, Civil Unrest, and the Crisis of Liberalism in the 1960s* (New York: Columbia University Press, 2007); Elizabeth Hinton, *From the War on Poverty to the War on Crime: The Making of Mass Incarceration in America* (Cambridge, MA: Harvard University Press, 2016); and Gottschalk, *Prison and the Gallows*.

65. Schrader, *Badges Without Borders*, 86.

66. Schrader, 13 and 88–89. See also Micol Seigel, *Violence Work: State Power and the Limits of Police* (Durham, NC: Duke University Press, 2018), 28, 55–57.

67. Kuzmarov, *Modernizing Repression*, 53–56; and Schrader, *Badges Without Borders*, 91–94.

68. Schrader, *Badges Without Borders*, 14.

69. Schrader, 30. See also Seigel, *Violence Work*, chap. 2.

70. Schrader, *Badges Without Borders*; and Seigel, *Violence Work*.

71. Schrader, *Badges Without Borders*, 2; and Seigel, *Violence Work*, chap. 1.

72. Julilly Kohler-Hausmann, "Militarizing the Police: Officer Jon Burge, Torture, and War in the 'Urban Jungle,'" in *Challenging the Prison-Industrial Complex: Activism, Arts, and Educational Alternatives*, ed. Stephen John Hartnett (Urbana: University of Illinois Press, 2011), 47.

73. Quoted in Lepore, "The Invention of the Police." See also Seigel, *Violence Work*, 34.

74. William J. Stuntz, *The Collapse of Criminal Justice* (Cambridge, MA: Harvard University Press, 2011), 133, fig. 2.

75. Weaver, "Frontlash," 250. See also Hinton, *From the War on Poverty*, 57.

76. For more on the culture of poverty, see pp. 52–55. See also the discussion of James Q. Wilson's work in Henry Ruth and Kevin R. Reitz, *The Challenge of Crime: Rethinking Our Response* (Cambridge, MA: Harvard University Press, 2003), 80–91; and William J. Bennett, John J.

DiIulio Jr., and John P. Walters, *Body Count: Moral Poverty . . . and How to Win America's War Against Crime and Drugs* (New York: Simon and Schuster 1996), 191–208.

77. Lawrence D. Bobo, "Inequalities That Endure? Racial Ideology, American Politics, and the Peculiar Role of the Social Sciences," in *The Changing Terrain of Race and Ethnicity*, ed. Maria Krysan and Amanda E. Lewis (New York: Russell Sage Foundation, 2004), 13–42.

78. Loïc Wacquant, *Punishing the Poor: The Neoliberal Government of Social Insecurity* (Durham, NC: Duke University Press, 2009).

79. David Garland, *The Culture of Control: Crime and Social Order in Contemporary Society* (Chicago: University of Chicago Press, 2001).

80. Hinton, *From the War on Poverty*, 124–31.

81. See Schrader, *Badges Without Borders*, 5.

82. For more on the central role of LEAA in the development of the carceral state, see Gottschalk, *Prison and the Gallows*, 84–91 and 124–49; and Hinton, *From the War on Poverty*, especially chaps. 4 and 5.

83. Schrader, *Badges Without Borders*, 22, 142, and 260–61; and Seigel, *Violence Work*, 30, 42–44.

84. For a development of these points, see Murakawa, *First Civil Right*.

85. Murakawa, *First Civil Right*; and Hinton, *From the War on Poverty*, 135–38.

86. Schrader, *Badges Without Borders*, 235. See also Hinton, *From the War on Poverty*, 134–36.

87. Schrader, *Badges Without Borders*, 120. See also Seigel, *Violence Work*, chap. 2; and Hinton, *From the War on Poverty*, chap. 4.

88. Hinton, *From the War on Poverty*, 163–77.

89. For more on why the United States ended up with a zero-sum victims' rights movement anchored in jacking up penalties, see Gottschalk, *Prison and the Gallows*, chap. 4.

90. Schrader, *Badges Without Borders*, 141.

91. Kuzmarov, *Modernizing Repression*, 234–35.

92. Schrader, *Badges Without Borders*, 186.

93. Jack O'Dell, "The July Rebellions and the 'Military State,'" *Freedomways* 7, no. 4 (Fall 1967): 297.

94. Schrader, *Badges Without Borders*, 261–62.

95. Kuzmarov, *Modernizing Repression*, 236; and Seigel, *Violence Work*, 30 and 42–44.

96. Seigel, *Violence Work*, 30.

97. See, for example, Seigel, *Violence Work*, chaps. 3 and 4, on OPS's role in the establishment and training of public and private security forces to guard the oil industry in Alaska and the oil giant Aramco in Saudi Arabia.

98. Schrader, *Badges Without Borders*, 261–62.

99. Murakawa, *First Civil Right*, 14.

100. Murakawa, 14.

101. Schrader, *Badges Without Borders*; and Seigel, *Violence Work*, 45–47.

102. For more on these military equipment transfer programs, see pp. 65–66.

103. Sherry, *Punitive Turn in American Life*, 30.

104. Ads for "the Curdler" promised that it simulated an "ear-splitting" sound akin to "standing behind a jet fighter during take-off" and would disperse "the slogan-shouting, chanting, handclapping that unifies and hypnotizes a mob incited to riot." Quoted in Sherry, 27.

105. NACCD (Kerner Commission), *Report of the National Advisory Commission on Civil Disorders* (Washington, DC: National Advisory Commission on Civil Disorders, 1968), 3, 28, 68.

106. NACCD, 3, 66, 176–77.

107. NACCD, 9.

108. Schrader, *Badges Without Borders*, 195–97.

109. For more on the development of CS, see Schrader, *Badges Without Borders*, chap. 8. For a chronicle of OPS's role in distributing CS to numerous countries to quash internal dissent, see Kuzmarov, *Modernizing Repression*, especially part 2. The abbreviation "CS" refers to the initials of Ben Corson and Roger Stoughton, who first synthesized this crystalline powder with a pepper-like odor in 1928. Committee on Acute Exposure Guideline Levels, Committee on Toxicology, Board on Environmental Studies and Toxicology, Division of Earth and Life Sciences, and National Research Council, *Acute Exposure Guideline Levels for Selected Airborne Chemicals*, vol. 16 (Washington, DC: National Academies Press, 2014), chap. 7.

110. Schrader, *Badges Without Borders*, 200, 213.

111. Schrader, 210.

112. Quoted in Schrader, 201 and 328n40.

113. Schrader, 203–4.

114. Schrader, 213.

115. For more on SWAT units, see pp. 64–65.

116. Seigel, *Violence Work*.

117. Sherry, *Punitive Turn*, 20–22, 25, 48.

118. Sherry, 49. For more on the all-volunteer army and the recruitment of African American people, see chap. 5, below.

119. Sol Stern, "When the Black G.I. Comes Back from Vietnam," *NYT*, March 24, 1968, quoted in Beth Bailey, *America's Army: Making the All-Volunteer Force* (Cambridge, MA: Belknap Press of Harvard University Press, 2009), 111–12.

120. On Gerald Ford's pivotal role in the war on crime, see Sherry, *Punitive Turn*, chap. 3.

121. Between 1970 and 1980, the number of people on active duty in the armed forces shrank by one-third—or about one million people—despite a growing population of young adults. After an uptick during the Reagan years, it had fallen by half to 1.5 million people by the end of the 1990s. Sherry, 63.

122. Jeremy Kuzmarov, *The Myth of the Addicted Army: Vietnam and the Modern War on Drugs* (Amherst: University of Massachusetts Press, 2009); and Sherry, *Punitive Turn*, 24–25, 45 and 51.

123. Sherry, *Punitive Turn*, 51, 53–54.

124. Schrader, *Badges Without Borders*, 187–88.

125. Seigel, *Violence Work*, 140.

126. Lawrence W. Sherman et al., *The Quality of Police Education in San Francisco* (San Francisco: Jossey-Bass, 1978), quoted in Richard S. Allinson, "A Great LEEP Backward?," *Change* 12, no. 1 (1980): 16.

127. Joachim J. Savelsberg, "Knowledge, Domination, and Criminal Punishment," *American Journal of Sociology* 99, no. 4 (1994): 911–43; and Joachim J. Savelsberg, Ryan King, and Lara Cleveland, "Politicized Scholarship? Science on Crime and the State," *Social Problems* 49, no. 3 (2002): 327–48.

128. Coyne and Hall, *Tyranny Comes Home*, 150.

129. Coyne and Hall, 153.

130. During hearings in 1977 on the CIA's decades of experimentation on human subjects, often without their knowledge or informed consent, Senator Edward Kennedy (D-MA) lashed out that "no one—no single individual—could be found who remembered the details, not the Director of the CIA, who ordered the documents destroyed, not the official responsible for the program, nor any of his associates." Quoted in Coyne and Hall, *Tyranny Comes Home*, 160.

131. Coyne and Hall, 160–63.

132. Kohler-Hausmann, "Militarizing the Police," 57–63; and Coyne and Hall, *Tyranny Comes Home*, 163–66.

133. Flint Taylor, "Blood on Their Hands: The Racist History of Modern Police Unions," *In These Times*, January 14, 2015, https://inthesetimes.com/article/police-unions-racist.

134. Williams, *Our Enemies in Blue*, 256.

135. Paul Wolf et al., *COINTELPRO: The Untold American Story*, Civil Liberties Defense Center, September 1, 2001, https://cldc.org/wp-content/uploads/2011/12/COINTELPRO. pdf; Nelson Blackstock, *COINTELPRO: The FBI's Secret War on Political Freedom* (New York: Pathfinder, 1988); Donna Jean Murch, *Living for the City: Migration, Education, and the Rise of the Black Panther Party in Oakland, California* (Chapel Hill: University of North Carolina Press, 2010), 160–70 and 184–89; and Hinton, *From the War on Poverty*, 205–17.

136. Seymour Hersh, "Huge C.I.A. Operation Reported Against Antiwar Forces, Other Dissidents in Nixon Years," *NYT*, December 22, 1974, https://www.nytimes.com/1974/12/22 /archives/huge-cia-operation-reported-in-u-s-against-antiwar-forces-other.html.

137. US Senate, Select Committee to Study Government Operations with Respect to Intelligence Activities (Church Committee), *Foreign and Military Intelligence: Book One; Final Report of the Select Committee to Study Government Operations with Respect to Intelligence Activities* (Washington, DC: GPO, 1976).

138. Williams, *Our Enemies in Blue*, 258–62.

139. Williams, 262.

140. Williams, 258–63.

141. Jarret S. Lovell, *Crimes of Dissent: Civil Disobedience, Criminal Justice, and the Politics of Conscience* (New York. New York University Press, 2009); and Luis A. Fernandez, *Policing Dissent: Social Control and the Anti-Globalization Movement* (New Brunswick, NJ: Rutgers University Press, 2008).

142. David M. Reutter, "Police Misconduct Reform: Forcing Police Officers to Have 'Skin in the Game' by Creating Financial Incentives with Insurance Premiums," *CLN*, 6 no. 10 (October 2023): 3; and Haley Draznin, "New York to Pay $17.9 Million to 2004 Republican Convention Protestors," CNN, January 16, 2014, https://www.cnn.com/2014/01/15/politics/new-york -republican-convention-settlement/index.html.

143. Michael Greenberg, "New York: The Police and the Protesters," *NYRB*, October 11, 2012, 57–61; Michael Greenberg, "The Problem of the New York Police," *NYRB*, October 25, 2012, https://www.nybooks.com/articles/2012/10/25/problem-new-york-police/; and Jeff Madrick, "The Fall and Rise of Occupy Wall Street," *HM*, March 2013, https://harpers.org/archive /2013/03/the-fall-and-rise-of-occupy-wall-street/.

144. Mike German, *Disrupt, Discredit, and Divide: How the New FBI Damages Democracy* (New York: New Press, 2019), 218.

145. German, 247.

146. Hina Shamsi and Hugh Handeyside, "Biden's Domestic Terrorism Strategy Entrenches Bias and Harmful Law Enforcement Power," aclu.org, July 9, 2021, https://www.aclu.org/news /national-security/bidens-domestic-terrorism-strategy-entrenches-bias-and-harmful-law -enforcement-power/.

147. People on the watchlist are subject to detention, interrogation, extra screening at airports, and travel restrictions by US and foreign authorities. ACLU, "U.S. Government Watchlisting: Unfair Process and Devastating Consequences," March 2014, https://www.aclu.org/sites /default/files/assets/watchlist_briefing_paper_v3.pdf, 1; and Shamsi and Handeyside, "Biden's Domestic Terrorism Strategy."

148. Incidents that have generated suspicious activity reports include "Suspicious ME [Middle Eastern] Males" buying several large pallets of water; a "Middle Eastern male adult physician who is very unfriendly"; and people planning to demonstrate about the excessive use of force by law enforcement. Julia Harumi Mass and Michael German, "The Government Is Spying on You," aclu.org, September 13, 2013, https://www.aclu.org/blog/national-security /privacy-and-surveillance/government-spying-you-aclu-releases-new-evidence.

149. Radley Balko, *Rise of the Warrior Cop: The Militarization of America's Police Forces* (New York: PublicAffairs, 2014), 145.

150. Balko, 145.

151. The hacked data from hundreds of police websites, the so-called Blue Leaks, exposed the inner workings of the fusion centers and other constitutionally suspect law enforcement practices. See the series of *Intercept* articles on Blue Leaks, various dates, June 2020–April 2021, https://theintercept.com/series/blueleaks/ (accessed November 16, 2023).

152. International Network of Civil Liberties Organizations, "'Take Back the Streets': Repression and Criminalization of Protest Around the World," October 2013, https://www.aclu .org/sites/default/files/assets/global_protest_suppression_report_inclo.pdf.

153. The President's Task Force on 21st Century Policing, *The Final Report* (Washington, DC: Office of Community Oriented Policing Services, May 2015), 25.

154. Joseph Nunn, "Trump Wants to Use the Military Against His Domestic Enemies. Congress Must Act.," Brennan Center for Justice, November 17, 2024, https://www.brennancenter .org/our-work/analysis-opinion/trump-wants-use-military-against-his-domestic-enemies -congress-must-act.

155. Adam Federman, "The War on Protest," *In These Times*, May 2024, 15–23; and "US Protest Law Tracker," International Center for Not-for-Profit Law, n.d., https://www.icnl.org /usprotestlawtracker/?location=&status=enacted&issue=&date=&type=legislative# (accessed November 17, 2021).

156. Emily Scolnick, "Penn Executes Search Warrant as Pro-Palestinian Activists Allege 'Raid' of Student Organizers' House," *Daily Pennsylvanian*, October 22, 2024, https://www.thedp .com/article/2024/10/penn-police-off-campus-raid.

5. Enemies Here, There, and Everywhere:
Forever at War at Home and Abroad

1. Thomas Paine, *Common Sense* (Philadelphia: W. and T. Bradford, February 14, 1776), https://www.gutenberg.org/cache/epub/147/pg147-images.html, emphasis in the original.

2. Andrew J. Bacevich, *Washington Rules: America's Path to Permanent War* (New York: Metropolitan Books, 2010).

3. Bacevich, 14.

4. Bacevich, 182.

5. Karen J. Greenberg, *Rogue Justice: The Making of the Security State* (New York: Broadway Books, 2016), chap. 16.

6. When Obama was asked whether he was essentially developing a second air force with the expansion of drone operations, this one under the control of the CIA not the US military, the president declared, "The CIA gets what it wants." Mark Mazzatti, *The Way of the Knife: The CIA, a Secret Army, and a War at the Ends of the Earth* (New York: Penguin, 2013), 228. See also Bureau of Investigative Journalism, "Obama's Covert Drone War in Numbers: Ten Times More Strikes Than Bush," January 17, 2017, https://www.thebureauinvestigates.com/stories/2017-01 -17/obamas-covert-drone-war-in-numbers-ten-times-more-strikes-than-bush.

7. Chalmers Johnson, *Blowback: The Costs and Consequences of American Empire* (New York: Metropolitan Books, 2000); Chalmers Johnson, *The Sorrow of Empire: Militarism, Secrecy, and the End of the Republic* (New York: Verso, 2004); Chalmers Johnson, *Nemesis: The Last Days of the American Republic* (New York: Henry Holt, 2007); and Chalmers Johnson, *Dismantling the Empire: America's Last Best Hope* (New York: Henry Holt, 2010).

8. This figure includes costs for medical care and disability payments for veterans (likely to exceed $2.2 trillion in federal spending in coming decades) and interest payments on borrowing for war costs. Neta C. Crawford, "The U.S. Budgetary Costs of the Post-9/11 Wars," Costs of War Research Series, Watson Institute, Brown University, September 1, 2021, https://watson .brown.edu/costsofwar/files/cow/imce/papers/2021/Costs%20of%20War_U.S.%20Budget- ary%20Costs%20of%20Post-9%2011%20Wars_9.1.21.pdf.

9. Janet Reitman, "U.S. Law Enforcement Failed to See the Threat of White Nationalism: Now They Don't Know How to Stop It," *NYT*, November 3, 2018, https://www.nytimes.com /2018/11/03/magazine/FBI-charlottesville-white-nationalism-far-right.html; and Michael German, *Disrupt, Discredit, and Divide: How the New FBI Damages Democracy* (New York: New Press, 2019).

10. Neta C. Crawford, "Blood and Treasure: United States Budgetary Costs and Human Costs of 20 Years of War in Iraq and Syria, 2003–2023," March 15, 2023, Costs of War Project, Watson Institute, Brown University, https://watson.brown.edu/costsofwar/files/cow/imce /papers/2023/Costs%20of%2020%20Years%20of%20Iraq%20War%20Crawford%2015%20 March%202023%20final%203.21.2023.pdf, 14; and "Human and Budgetary Costs to Date of the U.S. War in Afghanistan, 2001–2022," Watson Institute, Brown University, August 2021, https://watson.brown.edu/costsofwar/figures/2021/human-and-budgetary-costs-date-us-war -afghanistan-2001-2022.

11. Stephanie Savell, "How Death Outlives War: The Reverberating Impact of the Post-9/11 Wars on Human Health," May 15, 2023, Watson Institute, Brown University, https://watson .brown.edu/costsofwar/files/cow/imce/papers/2023/Indirect%20Deaths.pdf.

12. David Vine et al., "Creating Refugees: Displacement Caused by the United States' Post- 9/11 Wars," Watson Institute, Brown University, August 19, 2021, https://watson.brown.edu /costsofwar/files/cow/imce/papers/2021/Costs%20of%20War_Vine%20et%20al_Displace ment%20Update%20August%202021.pdf.

13. See Jessica Pishko, *The Highest Law in the Land: How the Unchecked Power of Sheriffs Threatens Democracy* (New York: Dutton, 2024), chap. 7.

14. Dani Anguiano, "Inside the Remote California County Where the Far Right Took Over: 'Civility Went Out the Window,'" *Guardian*, July 23, 2022, https://www.theguardian.com/us -news/2022/jul/23/california-shasta-county-far-right-extremists-politics-pandemic.

15. Kathleen Belew, "Insurrection," in *Myth America: Historians Take on the Biggest Legends and Lies About Our Past*, ed. Kevin M. Kruse and Julian E. Zelizer (New York: Basic Books, 2023), 253.

16. Kathleen Belew, *Bring the War Home: The White Power Movement and Paramilitary America* (Cambridge, MA: Harvard University Press, 2018), 63.

17. For more on the red squads and infiltration by the CIA and FBI, see pp. 115–17.

18. Rory McVeigh and Kevin Estep, *The Politics of Losing: Trump, the Klan, and the Mainstreaming of Resentment* (New York: Columbia University Press, 2019).

19. Belew, *Bring the War Home*, 23; see also 2.

20. Belew, 60–61.

21. These included the acquittal of neo-Nazis and Klansmen who killed five people in 1979 at a "Death to the Klan" rally in Greensboro, North Carolina, and the 1988 acquittal of thirteen white power leaders in Fort Smith, Arkansas, on federal charges of sedition, conspiracy, and other offenses. Belew, chap. 3, 156–58, 170–84, and 190–91.

22. Belew, 111–12, 120–21, and 171.

23. Belew, 204; and Kyle Burke, *Revolutionaries for the Right: Anticommunist Internationalism and Paramilitary Warfare in the Cold War* (Chapel Hill: University of North Carolina Press, 2018).

24. Belew, *Bring the War Home*, chap. 5, 113, and 135–37.

25. For more on SWAT teams, see pp. 64–65 and 113.

26. Michael Coard, "MOVE 30: Inside the May 1985 Assault on Osage Avenue," *Philadelphia Magazine*, May 12, 2015, https://www.phillymag.com/news/2015/05/12/move-30-year -anniversary/.

27. Belew, *Bring the War Home*, 200, 207; and Jeffrey Toobin, *Homegrown: Timothy McVeigh and the Rise of Right-Wing Extremism* (New York: Simon and Schuster, 2023), chap. 6.

28. Weaver's fourteen-year-old son was also killed in the standoff, shot in the back by a federal agent. A US marshal was also killed in the siege. AP, "18 Months in Jail for Supremacist," *NYT*, October 19, 1993, https://www.nytimes.com/1993/10/19/us/18-months-in-jail-for-supremacist.html; George Lardner Jr. and Pierre Thomas, "U.S. to Pay Family in FBI Idaho Raid," *WP*, August 16, 1995, https://www.washingtonpost.com/archive/politics/1995/08/16/us-to-pay-family-in-fbi-idaho-raid/04d69f83-06c5-4bf0-a10c-d8aa76a21866/.

29. Louis R. Beam, "Leaderless Resistance," *Seditionist*, no. 12 (February 1992), as quoted in Belew, *Bring the War Home*, 204, emphasis in the original. For more on how and why the white power movement consolidated, see Vegas Tenold, *Everything You Love Will Burn: Inside the Rebirth of White Nationalism in America* (New York: Nation Books, 2018).

30. Amy Cooter, "Vietnam and the Rise of White Power," *Reason*, October 2018, https://reason.com/2018/09/06/vietnam-and-the-rise-of-white/printer/. See also Amy Cooter, *Nostalgia, Nationalism, and the US Militia Movement* (New York: Routledge, 2024), 16.

31. Steven Simon and Jonathan Stevenson, "How Can We Neutralize the Militias?," *NYRB*, August 19, 2021, 34. See also Cooter, *Nostalgia, Nationalism, and the US Militia Movement*, 11–12 and 114–15.

32. Donna Murch, *Living for the City: Migration, Education, and the Rise of the Black Panther Party in Oakland, California* (Chapel Hill: University of North Carolina Press, 2010), chap. 5, especially 131–36.

33. For more on OPS and US police forces, see pp. 105–9.

34. Stuart Schrader, *Badges Without Borders: How Global Counterinsurgency Transformed American Politics* (Oakland: University of California Press, 2019), 263–64.

35. Toobin, *Homegrown*.

36. Cameron McWhirter and Zusha Elinson, *American Gun: The True Story of the AR-15* (New York: Farrar, Straus and Giroux, 2023).

37. Mike Giglio, "A Pro-Trump Militant Group Has Recruited Thousands of Police, Soldiers, and Veterans," *Atlantic*, November 2020, https://www.theatlantic.com/magazine/archive/2020/11/right-wing-militias-civil-war/616473/.

38. Kathleen Belew, "White Power Never Disappeared," *NYT*, April 19, 2018, A27.

39. Belew, A27. See also Belew, *Bring the War Home*, chap. 9; and Spencer Ackerman, *Reign of Terror: How the 9/11 Era Destabilized America and Produced Trump* (New York: Viking, 2021), 1–12.

40. Bacevich, *Washington Rules*, 134.

41. "President Ronald Reagan's Speech Before the National Association of Evangelicals," Reagan Information Page, March 8, 1983, https://web.archive.org/web/20040609055415/http://www.presidentreagan.info/speeches/empire.cfm.

42. Noam Chomsky and Vijay Prashad, *The Withdrawal: Iraq, Libya, Afghanistan, and the Fragility of U.S. Power* (New York: New Press, 2022), especially chap. 2.

43. Daniel Wirls, *Irrational Security: The Politics of Defense from Reagan to Obama* (Baltimore: Johns Hopkins University Press, 2010).

44. Wirls, 141.

45. Henry R. Luce, "The American Century," *Life*, February 17, 1941, 61–65.

46. Quoted in Jordan Michael Smith, "Twenty Years On, Are We Any Smarter?," *NR*, September 2021, 24.

47. Smith, 24.

48. Andrew Bacevich, *The New American Militarism: How Americans Are Seduced by War* (New York: Oxford University Press, 2005), 51, 119.

49. Bacevich, *Washington Rules*, 101.

50. Bacevich, *New American Militarism*, 120–21; and Louis Fisher, *Presidential War Power*, 3rd ed. (Lawrence: University of Kansas Press, 2013), 174.

51. Fisher, *Presidential War Power*, chap. 8.

52. Fisher, 200.

53. For more on Clinton, deregulation, and the financial crisis, see pp. 184–99.

54. Wirls, *Irrational Security*, 84.

55. Wirls, 63–69.

56. Douglas Kriner and Francis Shen, *The Casualty Gap: The Causes and Consequences of American Wartime Inequalities* (New York: Oxford University Press, 2010), 28–29.

57. Kriner and Shen, 74–75.

58. Kriner and Shen, 74–75.

59. Kriner and Shen, 75.

60. Kriner and Shen, 61.

61. Casualties came "not just disproportionately from poor or less-educated *towns* and *cities* but also from less advantaged *neighborhoods* within those census places." Kriner and Shen, 80, emphasis in the original; see also 29, 31, and chap. 3.

62. Kriner and Shen, 4.

63. Kriner and Shen, 39.

64. Kriner and Shen, 38. Sensitive to charges during the early years of the US troop buildup in Vietnam that African American people were disproportionately dying in combat, the DOD adopted a new policy that sought to limit the number of Black soldiers sent to the front lines. Subsequent analyses suggest that there actually had been no racial casualty gap initially, but that one opened up with the DOD's policy shift. African American people began dying in combat at lower rates compared to white soldiers with the same socioeconomic characteristics. Kriner and Shen, 38–39.

65. Beth Bailey, *America's Army: Making the All-Volunteer Force* (Cambridge, MA: Belknap Press of Harvard University Press), 2009. See also David Fitzgerald, *Uncertain Warriors: The United States Army Between the Cold War and the War on Terror* (Cambridge: Cambridge University Press, 2024).

66. The US Army is the largest and least specialized of the armed forces and requires the highest number of recruits. Bailey, *America's Army*, 75.

67. Brian Gifford, "The Camouflaged Safety Net: The U.S. Armed Forces as Welfare State Institution," *Social Politics: International Studies in Gender, State, and Society* 13, no. 3 (Fall 2006): 372–99.

68. Jennifer Mittelstadt, *The Rise of the Military Welfare State* (Cambridge, MA: Harvard University Press, 2015), 86.

69. For more on the culture of poverty, see pp. 52–55.

70. Mittelstadt, *Rise of the Military Welfare State*, 95.

71. The actual costs of these benefits and social welfare programs are hard to calculate because they are spread out across the Defense Department's budget and are so vast. In 2009, the department conceded it could not accurately tabulate their total costs. Mittelstadt, 3.

72. David Armor and Curtis Gilroy, "Changing Minority Representation in the Military," *Armed Forces and Society* 36, no. 2 (2010): 229–30.

73. Bailey, *America's Army*, 116–18.

74. Mittelstadt, *Rise of the Military Welfare State*, 86.

75. Bailey, *America's Army*, 115. On the disproportionate impact of the US military on rural places and how the military repeatedly "turned rural landscapes into militarized ones by brute force" throughout US history, see Steven Conn, *Lies of the Land: Seeing Rural America for What It Is—and Isn't* (Chicago: University of Chicago Press, 2023), 39 and chaps. 2 and 3.

76. Mittelstadt, *Rise of the Military Welfare State*, chap. 4.

77. Mittelstadt, 66.

78. Bailey, *America's Army*, ix and chap. 3.

79. Bailey, 76.

80. Mittelstadt, *Rise of the Military Welfare State*, 95–96.

81. Mittelstadt, chap. 6, and 121, 166, and 168.

82. Mittelstadt, 118–19.

83. Critical factors include the unemployment rate, especially for young people, and military pay relative to civilian pay. For a review of the literature on the relationship between economic factors and propensity to enlist, see Kriner and Shen, *Casualty Gap*, 58–59.

84. Marie Gottschalk, *Caught: The Prison State and the Lockdown of American Politics*, rev. ed (Princeton, NJ: Princeton University Press, 2016), 52–53.

85. DOD, Office of Undersecretary of Defense, Personnel and Readiness, *Population Representation in the Military Services: Fiscal Year 2019 Summary Report*, n.d., https://www.cna.org/pop-rep/2019/appendixd/appendixd.pdf (accessed January 10, 2022), 21.

86. Deborah Cowen, "National Soldiers and the War on Cities," *Theory and Event* 10, no. 2 (2007), https://www.proquest.com/scholarly-journals/national-soldiers-war-on-cities/docview/210791454/se-2.

87. Mittelstadt, *Rise of the Military Welfare State*, 191.

88. Gottschalk, *Caught*, chap. 3.

89. Mittelstadt, *Rise of the Military Welfare State*, 184–85.

90. Bailey, *America's Army*, 173.

91. The state of the economy and labor market conditions are central in young people's decisions to join the military, a fact the DOD recognizes with the inclusion of a detailed table of trends in youth unemployment for sixteen-to-twenty-four-year-olds in its annual recruitment reports. The main reasons young people cite for enlistment are obtaining financial help for college and finding more meaningful employment than what is available in their hometowns. See DOD, *Population Representation in the Military Services*, appendix D, "Historical Data Tables," 6, table D-2; Armor and Gilroy, "Changing Minority Representation in the Military": 235–36; and Stuart Tannock, "Is 'Opting Out' Really an Answer? Schools, Militarism, and the Counter-Recruitment Movement in Post–September 11 United States at War," *Social Justice* 32, no. 3 (2005): 176.

92. Bailey, *America's Army*, 206.

93. Wirls, *Irrational Security*, 129.

94. Douglas L. Kriner and Francis X. Shen, "Invisible Inequality: The Two Americas of Military Sacrifice," *University of Memphis Law Review* 46, no. 3 (Spring 2016): 547.

95. Sarah Chayes, "Afghanistan's Corruption Was Made in America," *Foreign Affairs*, September 3, 2021, https://www-foreignaffairs-com.proxy.library.upenn.edu/united-states/afghanistans-corruption-was-made-in-america; and Fitzgerald, *Uncertain Warriors*, chap. 5.

96. Gottschalk, *Caught*, 51–52.

97. An amendment to the 2007 defense authorization bill mandated that future war funding be included as part of the regular budget process. When President George W. Bush signed the bill, he issued a signing statement declaring he could, in effect, ignore the amendment. Wirls, *Irrational Security*, 154 and 156.

98. Wirls, 134.

99. Wirls, 144–57.

100. Mike Lofgren, *The Deep State: The Fall of the Constitution and the Rise of a Shadow Government* (New York: Penguin Books, 2016), 101.

101. Wirls, *Irrational Security*, 154–56.

102. Wirls, 179.

103. Mona Lynch, *Sunbelt Justice: Arizona and the Transformation of American Punishment* (Stanford, CA: Stanford University Press, 2010), 171–73; and Gottschalk, *Caught*, 53–55.

104. Wirls, *Irrational Security*, 134, 136, fig. 5.3.

105. Wirls, 189.

106. Wirls, 189.

107. Wirls, 143, fig. 5.6

108. Quoted in Smith, "Twenty Years On, Are We Any Smarter?," 27.

109. Clifford D. Conner, *The Tragedy of American Science: From Truman to Trump* (Chicago: Haymarket Books, 2020).

110. Indigo Oliver, "A Bachelor's in Bomb Making," *In These Times*, August 2007, 20–31.

111. Oliver.

112. Gottschalk, *Caught*, 64–74.

113. Ori Swed and Thomas Crosbie, "Who Are the Private Contractors in Iraq and Afghanistan," *Military Times*, March 14, 2019, https://www.militarytimes.com/news/your-navy /2019/03/14/who-are-the-private-contractors-in-iraq-and-afghanistan/; Ori Swed and Daniel Burland, "Contractors in Iraq: Exploited Class or Exclusive Club?," *Armed Forces and Society* 48, no. 1 (2022): 3–24; and Andrea Mazzarino, "The Army We Don't See: The Private Soldiers Who Fight in America's Name," *TomDispatch*, May 9, 2023, https://tomdispatch.com/the-army-we -dont-see/.

114. These figures are from the State and Defense Departments and may be underestimates. Wirls, *Irrational Security*, 183; and T. Christian Miller, "Contractors Outnumber Troops in Iraq," *LAT*, July 4, 2007, https://www.latimes.com/archives/la-xpm-2007-jul-04-na-private4-story .html. Many of these contract workers were recruited from low-income countries by Halliburton and other defense contractors, "sometimes under false or misleading pretenses." They generally were paid less, had harsher living and working conditions, and were provided with less security compared to what US personnel in Iraq received. Ariana Eunjung Cha, "Underclass of Workers Created in Iraq," *WP*, July 1, 2004, https://www.washingtonpost.com/archive/politics/2004 /07/01/underclass-of-workers-created-in-iraq/73cdb7cf-e7ba-414c-96c8-1358dea0a5a7/. See also Sonni Efron, "Worry Grows as Foreigners Flock to Iraq's Risky Jobs," *LAT*, July 30, 2005, https://www.latimes.com/archives/la-xpm-2005-jul-30-fg-forhire30-story.html.

115. Mazzarino, "Army We Don't See."

116. Andrea Mazzarino, "The Privatization of War, American-Style," *TomDispatch*, May 9, 2023, https://tomdispatch.com/the-army-we-dont-see/.

117. Wirls, *Irrational Security*, 183.

118. Cited in Farah Stockman, "The War on Terror Was Corrupt from the Start," *NYT*, September 13, 2021, https://www.nytimes.com/2021/09/13/opinion/afghanistan-war-economy .html.

119. Wirls, *Irrational Security*, 184–85.

120. Wirls, 184.

121. Wirls, 191.

122. Gottschalk, *Caught*, 72–73.

123. See "Windfalls of War," August 2001–September 2011, https://publicintegrity.org/topics /national-security/defense-spending/windfalls-of-war/ (accessed October 30, 2023), a series of reports by the Center for Public Integrity that chronicled the flow of government money to US defense contractors in Iraq. See also Stockman, "War on Terror Was Corrupt from the Start."

124. Andrew Cockburn, "Why America Goes to War: Money Drives the US Military Machine," *Nation*, September 9, 2021, https://www.thenation.com/article/world/money-war -machine/.

125. Eric Schmitt, "Iraqi-Bound Troops Confront Rumsfeld over Lack of Armor," *NYT*, December 8, 2014, http://www.nytimes.com/2004/12/08/international/middleeast/iraqbound -troops-confront-rumsfeld-over-lack-of.html.

126. James Hosek, Jennifer Kavanagh, and Laura Miller, "How Deployments Affect Service Members," RAND, 2006, https://www.rand.org/pubs/monographs/MG432.html, xiii.

127. Bailey, *America's Army*, 257.

128. Jorge Mariscal, "The Poverty Draft: Do Military Recruiters Disproportionately Target Communities of Color and the Poor?," *Sojourners Magazine* 26, no. 6 (June 2007): 32–25.

129. Cowen, "National Soldiers and the War on Cities"; and Tyler Jeffrey Wall, "War-Nation: Military and Moral Geographies of the Hoosier Homefront" (PhD diss., Arizona State University, May 2009), chap. 4.

130. The No Child Left Behind Act has an opt-out provision for parents, but few of them are aware of it. Tannock, "Is 'Opting Out' Really an Answer?," 163–64.

131. Jonathan Lehrfeld, "How Would Project 2025 Impact Troops and Veterans?," *Military Times*, July 24, 2024, https://www.militarytimes.com/news/your-military/2024/07/24/how-would-project-2025-impact-troops-and-veterans/.

132. In some cases, they have taken the liberty to press their cause by, for example, replacing the periodic chart of the elements on the chalkboard with military recruiting posters. Wall, "War-Nation," 148.

133. Mittelstadt, *Rise of the Military Welfare State*, 226; and Fitzgerald, *Uncertain Warriors*, chap. 6.

134. The army's new creed replaced "I am a member of the United States Army." Creeds quoted in Bailey, *America's Army*, 249.

135. Fitzgerald, *Uncertain Warriors*, 216.

136. Bailey, *America's Army*, 252.

137. As of 2011, three-quarters of US soldiers had been sent to Afghanistan or Iraq, "with many clocking their second, third, or fourth deployments. Six or seven deployments were not unknown." Mittelstadt, *Rise of the Military Welfare State*, 223. See also Fitzgerald, *Uncertain Warriors*, 140–53.

138. David Kieran, *Signature Wounds: The Untold Story of the Military's Mental Health Crisis* (New York: New York University Press, 2019), 149.

139. Suzanne Gordon, Steve Early, and Jasper Craven, *Our Veterans: Winners, Losers, Friends, and Enemies on the New Terrain of Veterans Affairs* (Durham, NC: Duke University Press, 2022), 8.

140. Bacevich, *New American Militarism*, 39.

141. Bacevich, 39.

142. Darron Salzer, "Post 9/11: This Isn't Your Father's National Guard," US National Guard, September 9, 2023, https://www.nationalguard.mil/News/Article-View/Article/576443/post-911-this-isnt-your-fathers-national-guard/; and James Griffith, "After 9/11, What Kind of Reserve Soldier? Considerations Given to Emerging Demands, Organizational Orientation, and Individual Commitment," *Armed Forces and Society* 35, no. 2 (2009): 215.

143. Kieran, *Signature Wounds*, 87.

144. Armor and Gilroy, "Changing Minority Representation in the Military": 230, fig. 1.

145. Sarah Abruzzese, "Iraq War Brings Drop in Black Enlistees," *NYT*, August 22, 2007, A12.

146. Prior to the start of the US war in Iraq, public opinion was decidedly against invading Iraq. But once the US launched its attack in March 2003, public opinion shifted. Black people in the United States remained opposed to the war by large margins (seven out of ten against it) while white people strongly favored it (eight out of ten for it). Jeffrey Jones, "Blacks Showing Decided Opposition to War," Gallup, March 28, 2003, https://news.gallup.com/poll/8080/blacks-showing-decided-opposition-war.aspx. See also "Black America's Opposition to the Iraq War," NPR, October 27, 2005, https://www.npr.org/templates/story/story.php?storyId=4976905; and Abruzzese, "Iraq War Brings Drop in Black Enlistees."

147. Matt Kennard, *Irregular Army: How the US Military Recruited Neo-Nazis, Gang Members, and Criminals to Fight the War on Terror* (London: Verso, 2012), chap. 4.

148. Armor and Gilroy, "Changing Minority Representation in the Military": 230, fig. 2.

149. Armor and Gilroy: 230, fig. 1.

150. Undersecretary for Personnel and Readiness David S. C. Chu, as quoted in Kriner and Shen, *Casualty Gap*, 59.

151. DOD, *Population Representation in the Military Services*, 2.

152. Kriner and Shen, *Casualty Gap*, 63.

153. Recruitment rates for the US Army in rural and exurban counties were well above the national average. The rates for rural counties in the South were more than 44 percent higher than the national average. Tim Murphy and Bill Bishop, "Largest Share of Army Recruits Come from Rural/Exurban America," *Daily Yonder*, March 3, 2009, https://dailyyonder.com/largest-share -army-recruits-come-ruralexurban-america/2009/03/03/; Matthew Bloch, "Top Counties for Army Recruitment," *NYT*, 2018, https://www.nytimes.com/interactive/2018/admin /100000006278586.embedded.html; Kriner and Shen, *Casualty Gap*, 4, 40, 229–30; and Phil Klay, *Uncertain Ground: Citizenship in an Age of Endless, Invisible War* (New York: Penguin, 2022).

154. In rank order, the top ten are South Carolina, Hawaii, Alaska, Florida, Georgia, Colorado, Alabama, Texas, North Carolina, and Nevada. Stephanie Savell and Rachel McMahon, "Numbers and Per Capita Distribution of Troops Serving in the U.S. Post-9/11 Wars in 2019," Watson Institute, Brown University, n.d., https://watson.brown.edu/costsofwar/files/cow /imce/costs/social/Troop%20Numbers%20By%20State_Costs%20of%20War_FINAL.pdf (accessed November 3, 2023).

155. Kriner and Shen, *Casualty Gap*, 74; and Kriner and Shen, "Invisible Inequality."

156. Kriner and Shen, *Casualty Gap*, 115–16.

157. Kriner and Shen, 8; and Kriner and Shen, "Invisible Inequality," 554.

158. Kriner and Shen, "Invisible Inequality," 546.

159. Steven Casey, *When Soldiers Fall: How Americans Have Confronted Combat Losses from World War I to Afghanistan* (New York: Oxford University Press, 2014), chap. 7 and 238–48.

160. Kriner and Shen, *Casualty Gap*, 9.

161. Mazzarino, "Army We Don't See."

162. Hosek, Kavanagh, and Miller, "How Deployments Affect Service Members."

163. Kriner and Shen, "Invisible Inequality," 586.

164. Valerie Bauerlein and Arian Campo-Flores, "The VA Hooked Veterans on Opioids, Then Failed Them Again," *WSJ*, December 29, 2016, https://www.wsj.com/articles/the-va -hooked-veterans-on-opioids-then-failed-them-again-1483030270.

165. CBO, "Approaches to Reducing Federal Spending on Military Health Care," January 2014, https://www.cbo.gov/sites/default/files/113th-congress-2013-2014/reports/44993 -militaryhealthcare.pdf, 19.

166. Leo Shane III, "Congressmen Blast Marines over Helmet Padding," *Stars and Stripes*, June 17, 2006, https://www.stripes.com/news/congressmen-blast-marines-over-helmet -padding-1.50443.

167. Quoted in Robert H. Bauman and Dina Rasor, *Shattered Minds: How the Pentagon Fails Our Troops with Faulty Helmets* (Lincoln, NE: Potomac Books, 2019), 68.

168. Bauman and Rasor, 69; and Gordon et al., *Our Veterans*, 41.

169. Cockburn, "Why America Goes to War." See also Tariq Ali, "The War on Terror: 20 Years of Bloodshed and Delusion," *Nation*, September 7, 2021, https://www.thenation.com /article/world/9-11-war-terror/.

170. In August 2023, 3M agreed to pay $6 billion to settle numerous lawsuits stemming from claims by US service members that the company knowingly sold faulty earplugs that resulted in hearing loss or other serious injuries. AP, "3M Agrees to Pay $6 Billion to Settle Earplug Lawsuits from US Service Members," August 29, 2023, https://apnews.com/article/3m-earplug -lawsuit-settlement-us-military-f2b68a4222c77cfefef3608c70e62f6c.

171. Hannah Fischer, *Guide to US Military Casualty Statistics* (Washington, DC: CRS, 2015), 1, table 1; and 2, table 2.

172. The suicide rate for US service members and veterans overall after adjusting for age and sex was 1.5 times greater than that for the general public as of 2018. The real rate for military personnel is likely higher since this figure does not include members of the National Guard and Reserves. Thomas Howard Suitt III, "High Suicide Rates Among United States Service Members and Veterans of the Post-9/11 Wars," Costs of War Project, Watson Institute, Brown University, June 21, 2021, https://watson.brown.edu/costsofwar/files/cow/imce/papers/2021/Suitt_Suicides_Costs%20of%20War_June%2021%202021.pdf, 5, 8, fig. 1.

173. Kieran, *Signature Wounds.*

174. Suitt, "High Suicide Rates Among United States Service Members," 1–4, 18–19.

175. Kieran, *Signature Wounds,* 71.

176. Kieran, 94–95.

177. Kieran, 15 and chap. 4.

178. Linda J. Bilmes, "The Long-Term Costs of United States Care for Veterans of the Afghanistan and Iraq Wars," Costs of War Project, Watson Institute, Brown University, August 18, 2021, https://watson.brown.edu/costsofwar/files/cow/imce/papers/2021/Costs%20of%20War_Bilmes_Long-Term%20Costs%20of%20Care%20for%20Vets_Aug%202021.pdf, 2.

179. These costs include disability and related benefits and medical care already paid, as well as the future costs of those expenses for personnel who served in Afghanistan and Iraq. Bilmes, "Long-Term Costs of United States Care for Veterans of the Afghanistan and Iraq Wars," 1.

180. Gordon et al., *Our Veterans,* 4, 8, and 19–22.

181. Gordon et al., chap. 1.

182. Institute of Medicine, *Gulf War and Health,* volume 8, *Update of Health Effects of Serving in the Gulf War* (Washington, DC: National Academies Press, 2010); and Research Advisory Committee on Gulf War Veterans' Illnesses, *Gulf War Illness and the Health of Gulf War Veterans: Scientific Findings and Recommendations* (Washington, DC: GPO, November 2008), 1–2.

183. Joseph Hickman, *The Burn Pits: The Poisoning of America's Soldiers* (New York: Hot Books, 2016), xv.

184. Beau Biden's case is featured in Hickman, chap. 4.

185. CBO, "Approaches to Reducing Federal Spending on Military Health Care," January 2014, https://www.cbo.gov/sites/default/files/113th-congress-2013-2014/reports/44993-militaryhealthcare.pdf, 1–2, 10–11.

186. These figures understate the fiscal burden of health-care costs for military personnel because much of the funding for operations in Iraq and Afghanistan, including medical care in combat operations, has come from emergency and supplemental appropriations outside of the Defense Department's base budget. CBO, 8, 16–17.

187. CBO.

188. T. Christian Miller, "Foreign Interpreters Hurt in Battle Find U.S. Insurance Benefits Wanting," *LAT,* December 18, 2009, https://www.latimes.com/archives/la-xpm-2009-dec-18-la-fg-interpreters18-2009dec18-story.html.

189. Mittelstadt, *Rise of the Military Welfare State,* 226.

190. These included dilapidated, moldy buildings infested with insects and rodents, and patients with severe brain and other injuries languishing unattended. Dana Priest and Anne Hull, "Soldiers Face Neglect, Frustration at Army's Top Medical Facility," *WP,* February 18, 2007, https://www.washingtonpost.com/archive/politics/2007/02/18/soldiers-face-neglect-frustration-at-armys-top-medical-facility/c0c4b3e4-fb22-4df6-9ac9-c602d41c5bda/. In another high-profile incident, members of the National Guard and Reserves returning from the battlefront alleged that they were being denied vital care at military bases designated for their demobilization, which spurred congressional investigations. Leo Shane III, "Back from Combat, Guardsmen Feel Slighted by Army Medical Care," *Army Times,* November 9, 2017, https://www.armytimes.com/news/pentagon-congress/2017/11/09/back-from-combat-guardsmen-feel-slighted-by-army-medical-care/.

191. American Legion, "Pending Veterans Health Care Legislation," April 6, 2018, https://www.legion.org/legislative/testimony/241712/pending-veterans-health-care-legislation; Kriner and Shen, *Casualty Gap*, 231; and Mittelstadt, *Rise of the Military Welfare State*, 226–27.

192. Michelle Ye Hee Lee, Lisa Rein, and David Weigel, "How a Koch-Backed Veterans Group Gained Influence in Trump's Washington," *WP*, April 7, 2018, https://www.washingtonpost.com/politics/how-a-koch-backed-veterans-group-gained-influence-in-trumps-washington/2018/04/07/398b67c4-3784-11e8-9c0a-85d477d9a226_story.html.

193. Lee, Rein, and Weigel.

194. Jasper Craven, "How Trump's Old VA Cronies Are Plotting to Convince Voters That Joe Biden Is Leaving Veterans Behind," *NR*, December 2021, 5.

195. "Documents Reveal Extent of Koch-Funded VA Privatization Group's Influence," *American Insight*, June 4, 2019, https://www.americanoversight.org/documents-reveal-extent-of-koch-funded-va-privatization-groups-influence.

196. James LaPorta, Julia Ingram, and Katrina Kaufman, "GOP Insiders Sought Hegseth's Removal as Leader of Veterans' Group in 2016," CBS News, December 2, 2024, https://www.cbsnews.com/news/pete-hegseth-concerned-veterans-for-america-jessie-jane-duff/.

197. Recent studies, for example, have found that there have been no racial disparities in deaths among VA patients with Covid-19, and that veterans admitted by ambulance to VA facilities instead of private hospitals were far less likely to die. Craven, "How Trump's Old VA Cronies Are Plotting," 5–6. See also David Chan, David Card, and Lowell Taylor, "Is There a VA Advantage? Evidence from Dually Eligible Veterans," Working Paper, National Bureau of Economic Research, n.d., http://conference.nber.org/conf_papers/f145428.pdf (accessed February 12, 2022).

198. Suzanne Gordan and Steve Early, "Unhealthy Competition," *TAP*, April 17, 2023, https://prospect.org/health/2023-04-17-unhealthy-competition-veterans-care-privatization/. With passage of the Inflation Reduction Act of 2022, the government began for the first time to negotiate drug prices for people covered by Medicare, the government health insurance program for older Americans.

199. Craven, "How Trump's Old VA Cronies Are Plotting," 5.

200. Craven, 5.

201. This discussion of the VHA under Trump and Biden is based primarily on the excellent reporting by Suzanne Gordon that appeared in *TAP* from 2019 to 2022. Only direct quotes are specifically cited. See also Gordon et al., *Our Veterans*, chap. 6.

202. Editorial Board, "Exploiting Veterans for Profit," *NYT*, November 24, 2017, https://www.nytimes.com/2017/11/24/opinion/exploiting-veterans-profit.html?ref=todayspaper; and Gordon et al., *Our Veterans*, 89–93.

203. Jasper Craven and Suzanne Gordon, "Trump's War on Veterans," *TAP*, April 7, 2020, https://prospect.org/health/trump-war-on-veterans/.

204. Gordon et al., *Our Veterans*, 163. Many veterans' groups caved on the issue of privatization, thanks partly to inclusion of a long-sought sweetener in the VA Mission Act of 2018 that would expand financial assistance for family members caring for aging and disabled veterans at home.

205. Jory Heckman, "House Pulls Funding from VA Commission to Close Hospitals in FY 2023 Spending Bill," Federal News Network, July 21, 2022, https://federalnewsnetwork.com/veterans-affairs/2022/07/house-pulls-funding-from-va-commission-to-close-hospitals-in-fy-2023-spending-bill/.

206. The final proposed DOD budget at the end of the first Trump administration included over $2 billion in cuts in medical care for active-duty military personnel, military retirees, and dependents. Suzanne Gordon and Steve Early, "Under Trump's Presidency, Military Veterans and Service Members Have Been 'Losers,'" *TAP*, September 9, 2020, https://prospect.org/health/under-trump's-presidency-military-veterans-and-service-membe/; Craven and Gordon, "Trump's War on Veterans"; and Suzanne Gordon, "Trump's VA Legacy: Human Capital

Mismanagement," *TAP*, January 19, 2022, https://prospect.org/health/trumps-va-legacy-human
-capital-mismanagement.

207. Gordan and Early, "Unhealthy Competition"; Suzanne Gordon and Steve Early,
"$23 Billion Up for Grabs: Joe Biden's Embrace of VA Outsourcing Just Got Worse," *TAP*, Oc-
tober 25, 2023, https://prospect.org/health/2023-10-25-23-billion-up-for-grabs-va-outsourcing
/; Gordon, "Trump's VA Legacy"; and Suzanne Gordon and Steve Early, "Gunning for More
Privatization," *TAP*, August 2023, 10–12.

208. Kriner and Shen, *Casualty Gap*, 193–97.

209. Kriner and Shen, chap. 8.

210. Kriner and Shen.

211. Kriner and Shen, "Invisible Inequality."

212. As with other statistical analyses, this one controlled for other factors, such as ideology
and partisanship. Kriner and Shen, *Casualty Gap*, 130.

213. See, for example, Representative John Murtha (D-PA), "War in Iraq," press release,
November 17, 2005, https://www.sourcewatch.org/index.php?title=John_P._Murtha
_Statement_to_the_Press_November_17,_2005.

214. Kriner and Shen, *Casualty Gap*, 181.

215. Nancy Pelosi, "Bringing the War to an End Is My Highest Priority," *HuffPost*, November 17, 2006, https://www.huffpost.com/entry/bringing-the-war-to-an-en_b_34393.

216. "Exclusive: Pelosi Says Bush 'Has to Answer for This War,'" ABC News, January 18, 2007,
https://abcnews.go.com/GMA/story?id=2805714&page=1.

217. For more on the 2008 presidential campaign and the financial crisis, see chaps. 8 and 9.

218. Cowen, "National Soldiers and the War on Cities."

219. Quoted in AP, "Sarah Palin's speech," *Politico*, September 9, 2008, https://www.politico
.com/story/2008/09/sarah-palins-speech-013144.

220. Michael Crowley, "Hillary's War: The Real Reason She Won't Apologize," *NR*, April 2,
2007, https://newrepublic.com/article/64828/hillarys-war; and Jeff Gerth and Don Van
Natta Jr., "Hillary's War," *NYT*, May 29, 2007, https://www.nytimes.com/2007/05/29
/magazine/03Hillary-t.html. See also Peter Baker, "With Pledges to Troops and Iraqis, Obama
Details Pullout," *NYT*, February 27, 2009, https://www.nytimes.com/2009/02/28/washington
/28troops.html.

221. Heidi M. Peters, "Department of Defense Contractor and Troop Levels in Afghanistan
and Iraq: 2007–2020," CRS, updated February 22, 2021, https://sgp.fas.org/crs/natsec/R44116
.pdf, 6, fig. 1.

222. Jonathan Stevenson, "Owned by the Army: Has the President Lost Control of the Generals?," *HM*, May 2011, 34–40.

223. Quoted in Helene Cooper, Eric Schmitt, and David E. Sanger, "Debating Exit from
Afghanistan, Biden Rejected Generals' Views," *NYT*, April 17, 2021, updated April 23, 2021,
https://www.nytimes.com/2021/04/17/us/politics/biden-afghanistan-withdrawal.html.

224. In the words of John Sopko, the inspector general who released the Afghanistan Papers:
"The American people have been constantly lied to." Quoted in Timothy Kudo, "Blame the
Generals for Our Defeat in Afghanistan," *NR*, July 12, 2021, https://newrepublic.com/article
/162955/afghanistan-war-generals-failed-america. See also Craig Whitlock, *The Afghanistan
Papers: A Secret History of the War* (New York: Simon and Schuster, 2021).

225. Quoted in Maureen Dowd, "Biden Ditches the Generals, Finally," *NYT*, April 17, 2021,
https://www.nytimes.com/2021/04/17/opinion/sunday/biden-afghanistan-war.html.

226. Samuel Moyn, "America Is Giving the World a Disturbing New Kind of War," *NYT*,
September 3, 2021, https://www.nytimes.com/2021/09/03/opinion/us-war-afghanistan.html.

227. "Barack Obama Says Libya Was 'Worst Mistake' of His Presidency," *Guardian*, April 11,
2016, https://www.theguardian.com/us-news/2016/apr/12/barack-obama-says-libya-was
-worst-mistake-of-his-presidency.

228. See the five-year, Pulitzer Prize–winning *NYT* investigation of civilian casualties from the US air wars conducted in Afghanistan, Iraq, and Syria in Azmat Khan et al., "The Civilian Casualty Files," *NYT*, December 18, 19, and 31, 2021, https://www.nytimes.com/interactive/2021 /us/civilian-casualty-files.html?action=click&module=RelatedLinks&pgtype=Article. See also Phil Klay, "America Kills Its Enemies in Our Name: And Then Keeps It Secret," *NYT*, May 27, 2022, https://www.nytimes.com/2022/05/27/opinion/us-military-targeted-killings.html; and Norman Solomon, *War Made Invisible: How America Hides the Human Toll of Its Military Machine* (New York: Free Press, 2023).

229. Greenberg, *Rogue Justice*, especially chaps. 17 and 18; Ackerman, *Reign of Terror*, especially chap. 6; and Nancy Bilyeau, "Secret NSA Surveillance Program Operates with 'No Oversight,'" *CR*, July 2, 2021, https://thecrimereport.org/2021/07/02/nsa-surveillance-program -operates-with-no-oversight/.

230. DHS, Office of Intelligence and Analysis, "Rightwing Extremism: Current Economic and Political Climate Fueling Resurgence in Radicalization and Recruitment," April 7, 2009, https://irp.fas.org/eprint/rightwing.pdf.

231. DHS, Office of Intelligence and Analysis, 2.

232. Michael German, "Hidden in Plain Sight: Racism, White Supremacy, and Far-Right Militancy in Law Enforcement," Brennan Center for Justice, August 27, 2020, https://www .brennancenter.org/our-work/research-reports/hidden-plain-sight-racism-white-supremacy -and-far-right-militancy-law.

233. FBI, "Intelligence Assessment: (U) White Supremacist Recruitment of Military Personnel Since 9/11," July 7, 2008, https://documents.law.yale.edu/sites/default/files/FBI_WHITE _SUPREMACY-2008-ocr.pdf, 10.

234. Reitman, "U.S. Law Enforcement Failed to See the Threat"; DHS, "Rightwing Extremism"; and German, *Disrupt, Discredit, and Divide*, 237–39.

235. Ronald Newman, National Political Director, ACLU, and Manar Waheed, Senior Legislative and Advocacy Counsel, ACLU, letter to Representatives Jerrold Nadler and Doug Collins, September 3, 2019, https://www.aclu.org/letter/aclu-statement-opposing-hr-4192-confronting -threat-domestic-terrorism-act; and German, *Disrupt, Discredit, and Divide*, 237–38.

236. Office of the Inspector General, DOJ, *A Review of the FBI's Investigations of Certain Domestic Advocacy Groups* (*Redacted Version*), September 20, 2010, https://www.oversight.gov /sites/default/files/oig-reports/s1009r.pdf, 184–90.

237. Reitman, "U.S. Law Enforcement Failed to See the Threat."

238. German, *Disrupt, Discredit, and Divide*, 239–45; and Pishko, *Highest Law in the Land*, 209–10.

239. Corrinne Hess, "Lawsuit Alleges Police Assisted Rittenhouse, Armed Militia in Kenosha," Wisconsin Public Radio, October 15, 2021, https://www.wpr.org/lawsuit-alleges-police -assisted-rittenhouse-armed-militia-kenosha; and Anna Orso, Allison Steele, William Bender, and Vinny Vella, "Philly Police Stood By as Men with Baseball Bats 'Protected' Fishtown: Some Residents Were Assaulted and Threatened," *PI*, June 2, 2020, https://www.inquirer.com/news /fishtown-george-floyd-protests-philadelphia-bats-hammers-20200602.html.

240. Jennifer Steinhauer, "Veterans Fortify the Ranks of Militias Aligned with Trump's Views," *NYT*, September 11, 2020, https://www.nytimes.com/2020/09/11/us/politics/veterans-trump-protests-militias.html.

241. Giglio, "Pro-Trump Militant Group Has Recruited Thousands"; Jason Wilson, "US Militia Group Draws Members from Military and Police," *Guardian*, March 3, 2021, https://www .theguardian.com/us-news/2021/mar/03/us-militia-membership-military-police-american -patriot-three-percenter-website-leak; Tim Dickinson, "Oath Keepers Use a Dystopian Fever Dream to Snare Police Forces, Military Vets," *Rolling Stone*, October 28, 2021, https://www .rollingstone.com/politics/politics-features/oath-keeper-police-military-veterans-conspiracy -theories-1248772/; and Dan Mihalopoulos, Tom Schuba, and Kevin G. Hall, "Extremism in

the Ranks," parts 1–3, *Chicago Sun-Times* and WBEZ Chicago, October 22, 2023, https://graphics
.suntimes.com/extremism-ranks/2023/oathkeepers-investigation-chicago-police-extremism
-insurrection/.

242. Maurice Chammah, "Does Your Sheriff Think He's More Powerful Than the President?," Marshall Project, October 18, 2022, https://www.themarshallproject.org/2022/10/18
/does-your-sheriff-think-he-s-more-powerful-than-the-president.

243. Some states even permit members of law enforcement to receive continuing education
credits for attending these "trainings." Anti-Defamation League, "The Constitutional Sheriffs and
Peace Officers Association (CSPOA) and Richard Mack: How Extremists Are Successfully Infiltrating Law Enforcement," September 2021, https://www.adl.org/media/16889/download, 3.

244. Pishko, *Highest Law in the Land*, 19–23.

245. Charlie Sykes, "Militias with Badges," *Bulwark*, October 19, 2021, https://morningshots
.thebulwark.com/p/militias-with-badges. See also Pishko, *Highest Law in the Land*, 357–66.

246. Pishko, *Highest Law in the Land*, 25.

247. Simon and Stevenson, "How Can We Neutralize the Militias?," 35.

248. Southern Poverty Law Center, "Militia Movement," n.d., https://www.splcenter.org
/fighting-hate/extremist-files/ideology/militia-movement (accessed May 8, 2024).

249. Steinhauer, "Veterans Fortify the Ranks of Militias"; and Simon and Stevenson, "How
Can We Neutralize the Militias?," 35.

250. Alan Feuer, "Trump Grants Sweeping Clemency to All Jan. 6 Rioters," *NYT*, January 20,
2025, https://www.nytimes.com/2025/01/20/us/politics/trump-pardons-jan-6.html; and
Michelle L. Price, "Day Two: AI and 'You're Fired!,'" *PI*, January 22, 2025, A1.

251. Institute for Constitutional Advocacy and Protection, "Prohibiting Private Armies at
Public Rallies: A Catalog of Relevant State Constitutional and Statutory Provisions," 3rd ed.,
September 2020, https://www.law.georgetown.edu/icap/wp-content/uploads/sites/32/2018
/04/Prohibiting-Private-Armies-at-Public-Rallies.pdf, 5–6; and Pishko, *Highest Law in the Land*,
210–11.

252. Cooter, *Nostalgia, Nationalism, and the US Militia Movement*, 178–79. For a state-by-state
rundown of militia-related statutes, see Institute for Constitutional Advocacy and Protection,
Georgetown Law, "Prohibiting Private Armies at Public Rallies," 4th ed., January 2024, https://
www.law.georgetown.edu/icap/wp-content/uploads/sites/32/2024/02/50-state-survey-v4
-FIN.pdf.

253. Simon and Stevenson, "How Can We Neutralize the Militias?," 34.

254. Michael German, "Hidden in Plain Sight"; and Amanda del Castillo, "New CA Law
Requires Additional Police Screening for Ties to Hate Groups," ABC 7 News, October 1, 2022,
https://abc7news.com/clear-act-police-audit-biased-behavior-screening/12284169/#:~:text
=The%20CLEAR%20Act%20calls%20for,would%20include%20social%20media%20posts.

255. For example, in 2019, a counterterrorism official for the FBI testified before Congress
that, while he would be "suspect" of white supremacist police officers, their beliefs were protected by the First Amendment. His testimony was at odds with a 2006 FBI threat assessment
of white power groups that correctly summed up the relevant Supreme Court rulings: that the
government "can limit the employment opportunities" of members of white supremacist groups
"who hold sensitive public sector jobs, including jobs within law enforcement, when their memberships would interfere with their duties." German, "Hidden in Plain Sight," n. 7 and n. 8; and
FBI, Counterterrorism Division, "White Supremacist Infiltration of Law Enforcement," October 17, 2006, https://fromthegman.net/wp-content/uploads/2021/01/White_Supremacist
_Infiltration_of_Law_Enforcement.pdf, 6.

256. For example, prosecutors who have evidence of or suspect that arresting officers have ties
to extremist groups could question them about this during legal proceedings. An officer's membership in a hate group or expression of extremist beliefs is potentially exculpatory evidence that a
defendant has a constitutional right to know about. Vida B. Johnson, "KKK in the PD: White

Supremacist Police and What to Do About It," *Lewis and Clark Law Review* 23, no. 1 (2019): 205–61.

257. Quoted in Christopher Mathias, "The Military Says It's Confronting Extremism: A Prominent White Nationalist Just Finished Boot Camp," *HuffPost*, April 10, 2021, https://www.huffpost.com/entry/extremists-military-shawn-mccaffrey-white-nationalist_n_60706 a94c5b634fd437d8e09.

258. Dave Philipps, "White Supremacism in the U.S. Military, Explained," *NYT*, February 27, 2019, https://www.nytimes.com/2019/02/27/us/military-white-nationalists-extremists.html.

259. FBI and DHS, "White Supremacist Extremism Poses Persistent Threat of Lethal Violence," Joint Intelligence Bulletin, May 10, 2017, https://s3.documentcloud.org/documents /3924852/White-Supremacist-Extremism-JIB.pdf, 4.

260. Arie Perliger, "Police, Soldiers Bring Lethal Skill to Militia Campaigns Against US Government," *Conversation*, January 19, 2021, https://theconversation.com/police-soldiers-bring -lethal-skill-to-militia-campaigns-against-us-government-153369.

261. US House of Representatives, Committee on Oversight and Reform, Hearings on Confronting White Supremacy (Part I): The Consequences of Inaction, May 15, 2019, https://oversight.house.gov/legislation/hearings/confronting-white-supremacy-part-i-the-conse quences-of-inaction.

262. Jana Winter and Sharon Weinberger, "The FBI's Terrorist Threat: 'Black Identity Extremists,'" *Foreign Policy*, October 6, 2017, https://foreignpolicy.com/2017/10/06/the-fbi-has -identified-a-new-domestic-terrorist-threat-and-its-black-identity-extremists/.

263. Ken Klippenstein, "Leaked FBI Documents Reveal Bureau's Priorities Under Trump," Young Turks, August 8, 2019, https://tyt.com/stories/4vZLCHuQrYE4uKagy0oyMA /mnzAKMpdtiZ7AcYLd5cRR. For more on the role of the FBI in crushing political dissent in the 1960s and 1970s, see chap. 4.

264. Quoted in John M. Donnelly, "Pentagon Report Reveals Inroads White Supremacists Have Made in Military," *Roll Call*, February 16, 2021, https://www.rollcall.com/2021/02/16 /pentagon-report-reveals-inroads-white-supremacists-have-made-in-military/.

265. See Donnelly.

266. See Donnelly.

267. See Donnelly.

268. Kristin M. Hall et al., "Weapons Gone AWOL," *PI*, June 16, 2021, A3.

269. Most of the defendants with military ties were veterans, but a few were still serving in the armed forces. Veterans made up nearly 10 percent of those charged in the insurrection but compose only 6 percent of the US adult population. Marshall Cohen, "1 in 10 Defendants from U.S. Capitol Insurrection Have Military Ties," CNN, May 28, 2021, https://www.cnn.com/2021 /05/28/politics/capitol-insurrection-veterans/index.html.

270. Michael Biesecker, Jake Bleiberg, and James Laporta, "Capitol Riot Drew Former Military, Police," *PI*, January 16, 2020, A3.

271. Mathias, "Military Says It's Confronting Extremism."

272. See, for example, the case of Matthew Gebert, a US State Department official with high-level security clearance, who remained active in the white power movement, including organizing events for its leading figures. Hannah Gais, "How to Fight the Extreme Right," *NR*, June 2021, 40–41, 45.

273. DOD, Inspector General, "Evaluation of Department of Defense Efforts to Address Ideological Extremism Within the Armed Forces," May 10, 2022, https://media.defense.gov /2022/May/12/2002995443/-1/-1/1/DODIG-2022-095_REDACTED.PDF.

274. Kelly R. Buck et al., *Screening for Potential Terrorists in the Enlisted Military Accessions Process* (Monterey, CA: DOD, Defense Personnel Security Research Center, April 2005), 12.

275. Sara Swann, "Did Pete Hegseth's Tattoos Bar Him from National Guard Service in 2021?," *PolitiFact*, November 19, 2024, https://www.politifact.com/article/2024/nov/19/ask -politifact-did-pete-hegseths-tattoos-bar-him-f/.

276. Greg Myre, "An Old Debate Renewed: Does the U.S. Now Need a Domestic Terrorism Law?," NPR, March 16, 2021, https://www.npr.org/2021/03/16/976430540/an-old-debate-renewed-does-the-u-s-now-need-a-domestic-terrorism-law.

277. Hini Shamsi and Hugh Handeyside, "Biden's Domestic Terrorism Strategy Entrenches Bias and Harmful Law Enforcement Power," July 9, 2021, aclu.org, https://www.aclu.org/news/national-security/bidens-domestic-terrorism-strategy-entrenches-bias-and-harmful-law-enforcement-power.

278. Dana Milbank, "Merrick Garland Lets Domestic Terrorists Know There's a New Sheriff in Town," WP, February 22, 2021, https://www.washingtonpost.com/opinions/2021/02/22/merrick-garland-lets-domestic-terrorists-know-theres-new-sheriff-town/.

279. Joseph Biden Jr., "Statement by Joseph R. Biden, Jr. on the National Strategy for Countering Domestic Terrorism," June 15, 2021, https://www.whitehouse.gov/briefing-room/statements-releases/2021/06/15/statement-by-president-joseph-r-biden-jr-on-the-national-strategy-for-countering-domestic-terrorism/; and "National Strategy for Countering Domestic Terrorism," whitehouse.gov, June 2021, https://www.whitehouse.gov/wp-content/uploads/2021/06/National-Strategy-for-Countering-Domestic-Terrorism.pdf.

280. Hina Shamsi and Hugh Handeyside, "Biden's Domestic Terrorism Strategy Entrenches Bias and Harmful Law Enforcement Power," aclu.org, July 9, 2021, https://www.aclu.org/news/national-security/bidens-domestic-terrorism-strategy-entrenches-bias-and-harmful-law-enforcement-power/.

281. Will Bunch, "Why Are Texas and Florida Building Their Own Large, Sadistic Armies?," PI, July 25, 2023, A11.

282. David Firestone, "Governor Defiance Tries to Usurp Washington's Role," NYT, January 1, 2024, https://www.nytimes.com/2024/01/01/opinion/editorials/greg-abbott-immigration.html; and Alejandro Serrano, "If It Survives, Texas' Immigration Law Could Upend Immigration Enforcement Nationwide," Texas Tribune, October 24, 2024, https://www.texastribune.org/2024/10/24/texas-immigration-law-sb4-supreme-court-migrants-border/.

283. Nicole Gaouette, "The Democrats' Republican Moment," CNN, July 30, 2016, https://www.cnn.com/2016/07/29/politics/democratic-convention-gop-moment-national-security/index.html.

284. Key figures in the white power movement were attracted to Pat Buchanan for his outspoken criticism of the Gulf War and NAFTA as the former aide to Presidents Richard Nixon, Gerald Ford, and Ronald Reagan veered even more to the right. Buchanan left the Republican Party in 2000 to become the Reform Party's presidential candidate, running on a platform opposed to interventionism overseas, illegal immigration, and so-called free trade policies that have eroded the country's manufacturing base. For more on white nationalism and anti-imperialism, see the profile of Matthew Heimbach in Tenold, Everything You Love Will Burn, especially chap. 3.

285. Maggie Haberman and Richard A. Oppel Jr., "Donald Trump Criticizes Muslim Family of Slain U.S. Soldier, Drawing Ire," NYT, July 30, 2016, https://www.nytimes.com/2016/07/31/us/politics/donald-trump-khizr-khan-wife-ghazala.html.

286. Nicole Gaouette, "Trump's Attacks on the Military," CNN, November 20, 2018, https://edition.cnn.com/2018/11/19/politics/trump-military-insults-compliments/index.html; and CNN, "Exit Polls: 2016," November 23, 2016, https://www.cnn.com/election/2016/results/exit-polls/national/president; Geoffrey Skelley, "How Veterans Vote," Sabato's Crystal Ball, April 24, 2014, https://centerforpolitics.org/crystalball/articles/how-veterans-vote/.

287. CNN, "Exit Polls: 2016"; and Shiva Maniam, "U.S. Veterans Are Generally Supportive of Trump," PRC, May 26, 2017, https://www.pewresearch.org/short-reads/2017/05/26/u-s-veterans-are-generally-supportive-of-trump/.

288. Gordon et al., Our Veterans, 11–12.

289. General Raymond A. Thomas, quoted in Mark Bowden, "How Special Ops Became the Solution to Everything," Atlantic, April 2021, 69.

290. Amanda Macias, "Trump Signs $738 Billion Defense Bill: Here's What the Pentagon Is Poised to Get," CNBC, December 20, 2019, https://www.cnbc.com/2019/12/21/trump-signs-738-billion-defense-bill.html.

291. "Press Conference: Donald Trump Hosts an Event with Sergio Mattarella of Italy: October 16, 2019," Factbase, n.d., https://factba.se/transcript/donald-trump-press-conference-sergio-mattarella-italy-october-16-2019 (accessed October 31, 2023); and Michael Klare, "How to Make War, Twenty-First-Century-Style, and Lose a World," *TomDispatch*, December 6, 2020, https://tomdispatch.com/trumps-pernicious-military-legacy/.

292. According to exit polls, Trump won 54 percent of the veteran vote in 2020, down from 60 percent in 2016. CNN, "Exit Polls: 2020," n.d., https://www.cnn.com/election/2020/exit-polls/president/national-results (accessed February 12, 2022); and CNN, "Exit Polls: 2016." For more on veterans and the 2020 election, see Gordon et al., *Our Veterans*, chap. 8.

293. Jeffrey Goldberg, "Trump: Americans Who Died in War Are 'Losers' and 'Suckers,'" *Atlantic*, September 3, 2020, https://www.theatlantic.com/politics/archive/2020/09/trump-americans-who-died-at-war-are-losers-and-suckers/615997/.

294. In 2024, Trump took 65 percent of the veteran vote. CNN, "Election 2024: Exit Polls," n.d., https://edition.cnn.com/election/2024/exit-polls/national-results/general/president/0 (accessed December 3, 2024). See also Lehrfeld, "How Would Project 2025 Impact Troops and Veterans?"; Roni Caryn Rabin and Nicholas Nehamas, "Chaos at the V.A.: Inside the DOGE Cuts Disrupting the Veterans Agency," *NYT*, March 9, 2025, updated March 10, 2025, https://www.nytimes.com/2025/03/09/us/politics/veterans-affairs-doge-cuts.html; and Eric Umansky and Vernal Coleman, "Internal VA Emails Reveal How Trump Cuts Jeopardize Veterans' Care," *ProPublica*, May 6, 2025, https://www.propublica.org/article/trump-veterans-affairs-budget-staff-cuts-jeopardize-cancer-research.

295. For more on veterans and the opioid epidemic, see chaps. 10 and 11.

296. Ann Shortridge, "The U.S. War Twenty Years On: Public Opinion Then and Now," *Water's Edge* (Council on Foreign Relations), October 21, 2021, https://www.cfr.org/blog/us-war-afghanistan-twenty-years-public-opinion-then-and-now; Craig Whitlock, "Confidential Documents Reveal U.S. Officials Failed to Tell Truth About War in Afghanistan," *PI*, December 9, 2019, https://www.inquirer.com/news/nation-world/us-afghanistan-war-confidential-documents-failures-hidden-from-public-20191209.html#loaded; J. Baxter Oliphant, "The Iraq War Continues to Divide the U.S. Public, 15 Years After It Began," *PRC*, March 19, 2018, https://www.pewresearch.org/fact-tank/2018/03/19/iraq-war-continues-to-divide-u-s-public-15-years-after-it-began/; and William Ruger, "Public Realism on Afghanistan," RealClear Politics, October 8, 2018, https://www.realclearpolitics.com/articles/2018/10/08/public_realism_on_afghanistan_138280.html.

297. Lydia Saad, "Historically Low Faith in U.S. Institutions Continues," Gallup, July 6, 2023, https://news.gallup.com/poll/508169/historically-low-faith-institutions-continues.aspx.

6. The Banksters Hiding in Plain Sight: The Corporate Crime Waves from Carter to Clinton

1. C. Wright Mills, *The Power Elite* (New York: Oxford University Press, 1956), 95

2. Marie Gottschalk, *The Prison and the Gallows: The Politics of Mass Incarceration in America* (New York: Cambridge University Press, 2006), 55–70; and Lisa McGirr, *The War on Alcohol: Prohibition and the Rise of the American State* (New York: W. W. Norton, 2015).

3. Gottschalk, *Prison and the Gallows*, 59–70.

4. John Hagan, *Who Are the Criminals? The Politics of Crime Policy from the Age of Roosevelt to the Age of Reagan* (Princeton, NJ: Princeton University Press, 2010), 177–80.

5. Hagan, 176–80, 212.

6. Edwin H. Sutherland, "White Collar Criminality," *American Sociological Review* 5, no. 1 (February 1940): 1–12. See also Edwin H. Sutherland, *White Collar Crime* (New York: Dryden, 1949), 9.

7. "Jana Macfarlane Horn on Why We Don't Recognize Corporate Crime as Crime," *Corporate Crime Reporter*, August 2, 2022, https://www.corporatecrimereporter.com/news/200/jana-macfarlane-horn-on-why-we-dont-recognize-corporate-crime-as-crime/.

8. Sutherland, "White Collar Criminality": 8.

9. Sutherland: 8.

10. Gilbert Geis and Colin Graf, "Introduction," Edwin H. Sutherland, *White Collar Crime: The Uncut Version* (New Haven, CT: Yale University Press, 1983), xxx–xxxi.

11. These headwinds left their mark on *White Collar Crime*. Sutherland relented to pressure from his publisher and university to eliminate three case studies and remove the names of the corporate offenders discussed in his book. The publisher cited concerns about liability lawsuits, and Sutherland suspected Indiana University was worried about alienating wealthy donors. The uncut version of his book was published more than three decades after Sutherland's sudden and premature death in 1950. Geis and Graf, "Introduction," x–xi. On the calculated political resurgence of capital and pluralism in the wake of the Great Depression, see Robert M. Collins, *The Business Response to Keynes, 1929–1964* (New York: Columbia University Press, 1981); and Wendy L. Wall, *Inventing the "American Way": The Politics of Consensus from the New Deal to the Civil Rights Movement* (New York: Oxford University Press, 2008).

12. For more on the surge in law-and-order politics during this time, see pp. 106–7.

13. Francis T. Cullen, Jennifer L. Hartman, and Cheryl Lero Jonson, "Bad Guys: Why the Public Supports Punishing White-Collar Offenders," *Crime, Law and Social Change* 51, no. 1 (2009): 31–44.

14. According to a later scholar, the nine lengthy task force reports accompanying the main report devoted just seven pages to the issue. Stuart L. Hills, *Crime, Power, and Morality: The Criminal Law Process in the United States* (Scranton, PA: Chandler, 1971), 187. See also President's Commission on Law Enforcement and Administration of Justice, *Challenge of Crime in a Free Society* (New York: Avon, 1967).

15. President's Commission on Law Enforcement and Administration of Justice, *Challenge of Crime in a Free Society*, 48.

16. Cullen et al., "Bad Guys."

17. See pp. 113–17.

18. Joachim Savelsberg, "Knowledge, Domination, and Criminal Punishment," *American Journal of Sociology* 99, no. 4 (January 1994): 911–43; and Joachim Savelsberg, Ryan King, and Lara Cleveland, "Politicized Scholarship? Science on Crime and the State," *Social Problems* 49, no. 3 (2002): 327–48.

19. Francis T. Cullen and Michael L. Benson, "White-Collar Crime: Holding a Mirror to the Core," *Journal of Criminal Justice Education* 4, no. 2 (Fall 1993): 325.

20. Danielle McGurrin et al., "White Collar Crime Representation in the Criminological Literature Revisited, 2001–2010," *Western Criminology Review* 14, no. 2 (2013): 3–19; Stacy K. McGoldrick, "Fragmented to Death: The Study of Violence and the Utility of Criminology," *Sociology Compass* 9, no. 7 (2015): 542–49; Anne Alvesalo-Kuusi and Gregg Barak, "The Inaugural Issue of the Journal of White Collar and Corporate Crime," *JWCCC* 1, no. 1 (2020): 3–6; and Laureen Snider, "The Sociology of Corporate Crime: An Obituary (Or: Whose Knowledge Claims Have Legs?)," *Theoretical Criminology* 4, no. 2 (2000): 169–206.

21. Government data on corporate criminal activities are scattered across dozens of federal and state regulatory agencies and are in diverse formats. Standardizing this data and systematically collecting it in official government sources is not impossible, but so far, the political will to do so has been missing. Sally S. Simpson, "Reimagining Sutherland 80 Years After *White Collar Crime*," *Criminology* 57, no. 2 (2019): 194.

22. In the 1980s, the DOJ began developing a new system, the National Incident-Based Reporting System (NIBRS), to better track and measure crime, including white-collar and corporate crime, that would eventually replace the UCR decades later. Like the UCR, the NIBRS was conceived primarily as a tool to help law enforcement and perpetuated the criminal legal system's long-standing biases toward focusing on the problem of street crime, not crime in the suites. The FBI officially retired the UCR program in 2021. The NIBRS has had a rocky rollout that has called into question the reliability of national statistics on crime trends at a time when crime has become a leading political issue thanks to the spike in violent crime during the Covid-19 pandemic and other factors. Nearly one-third of the country's law enforcement agencies failed to submit any data for 2022, and many others submitted only partial data. Paul Wormeli, "Criminal Justice Statistics—an Evolution," *Criminology and Public Policy* 17, no. 2 (2018): 488–90; Kevin J. Strom and Erica L. Smith, "The Future of Crime Data: The Case for the National Incident-Based Reporting System (NIBRS)," *Criminology and Public Policy* 16, no. 4 (2017): 1034–36; Mary Dodge, "A Black Box Warning: The Marginalization of White-Collar Crime Victimization," *JWCCC* 1, no. 1 (2016): 26; Cynthia Barnett, "The Measurement of White-Collar Crime Using Uniform Crime Reporting (UCR) Data," DOJ, FBI, NIBRS Publications Series, March 6, 2002, https://ucr.fbi.gov/nibrs/nibrs_wcc.pdf, 6; Weihua Li and Jasmyne Ricard, "4 Reasons We Should Worry About Missing Crime Data," Marshall Project, July 13, 2023, https://www.themarshallproject.org/2023/07/13/fbi-crime-rates-data-gap-nibrs; and Weihua Li and Jasmyne Ricard, "DeSantis Claims Florida's Crime Is at a 'Record Low': But He's Using Incomplete Data," Marshall Project, June 20, 2023, https://www.themarshallproject.org/2023/06/20/desantis-florida-crime-rate-incomplete-data.

23. In 2016, a panel of the NAS concluded that the "lack of systematic information about non-street crimes makes it very difficult to develop sound judgments about whether adequate resources are being devoted to these types of problems." National Academies of Sciences, Engineering, and Medicine, *Modernizing Crime Statistics Report 1—Defining and Classifying Crime* (Washington, DC: National Academies Press, 2016), 11. See also Janet L. Lauritsen and Daniel L. Cork, "Expanding Our Understanding of Crime: The National Academies Report on the Future of Crime Statistics and Measurement," *Criminology and Public Policy* 16, no. 4 (2017): 1090–97. Channeling Edwin Sutherland, the NAS panel called for a broader definition of crime that would include not only crimes known to the police but also offenses that traditionally have not been categorized as criminal activities, such as violations of government regulations that are punishable by sanctions. The panel recommended a new and broader framework for categorizing crime that would include fraud, deception, corruption, acts against public order and authority (among them, tax evasion and voter intimidation), and acts against the environment.

24. This discussion of the early history of the Uniform Crime Reporting Program and its shortcomings is based primarily on FBI, *Uniform Crime Reporting Handbook*, rev. 2004, https://ucr.fbi.gov/additional-ucr-publications/ucr_handbook.pdf, 1–3; and Wormeli, "Criminal Justice Statistics," 483–96.

25. Barnett, "Measurement of White-Collar Crime," 2.

26. Like other victimization surveys, the NCVS is dominated by traditional law enforcement concerns with street crime while ignoring the "crimes of fraud and deceit" committed by people with more education, power, and money. Furthermore, many victims of financial and other corporate crimes are unaware that they have been victimized and therefore do not report anything to the NCVS or authorities. By some estimates, about two-thirds of corporate fraud goes undetected. See Callie Marie Rennison and Martin D. Schwartz, "Crime Victimization Survey Research," in *The Routledge International Handbook of Violence Studies*, ed. Walter S. DeKeseredy, Callie Marie Rennison, and Amanda K. Hall-Sanchez (London: Routledge, 2019), 14; and Alexander Dyck, Adair Morse, and Luigi Zingales, "How Pervasive Is Corporate Fraud," *Review of Accounting Studies*, January 5, 2023, https://link.springer.com/article/10.1007/s11142-022-09738-5. For more on ongoing redesigns of the NCVS, including the inclusion of supplements on

school crime and safety, stalking, identity theft, and the public's contact with the police, see Lynn Langton, Michael Planty, and James P. Lynch, "Second Major Redesign of the National Crime Victimization Survey (NCVS)," *Criminology and Public Policy* 16, no. 4 (2017): 1049–74.

27. Barnett, "Measurement of White-Collar Crime," 1.

28. In 2013, two categories of human trafficking were designated as part 1 or index crimes, bringing the total to ten. Local police departments and other law enforcement agencies that participated in the UCR were supposed to report to the FBI "offenses known" to them (whether they involved arrests or not) with respect to the part 1 or so-called index crimes. The UCR categorized offenses typically associated with corporate criminal behavior—including fraud, forgery, and embezzlement, as well as environmental, health and safety, and labor law violations—as part 2 offenses. The UCR treated part 2 violations as less serious infractions than crimes that it categorized as index crimes, beginning with significant differences in the reporting standard for these two categories of offenses. For example, if no one was arrested for a part 2 offense, the crime never happened as far as the UCR was concerned, even if the offense was reported to the police. Furthermore, the UCR lumped environmental, health and safety, and labor law violations together in a single part 2 catchall category called "all other offenses." It did not break them out into their own separate categories as it did for fraud, forgery, and embezzlement. FBI, "Crime in the United States, 2011: Offense Definitions," UCR, September 2012, https://ucr.fbi.gov/crime-in-the-u.s/2011/crime-in-the-u.s.-2011/11offensedefinitions_final .pdf; and FBI, "Human Trafficking in the Uniform Crime Reporting (UCR) Program," n.d., https://ucr.fbi.gov/human-trafficking (accessed February 1, 2025).

29. If the fake gains Madoff told investors they were earning are included, the losses from his Ponzi scheme rise to $65 billion. Aaron Smith, "Five Things You Didn't Know About Bernie Madoff's Epic Scam," CNN Business, April 14, 2021, https://www.cnn.com/2021/04/14 /business/bernard-madoff-ponzi-scheme/index.html. For more on the Madoff case, see pp. 249–50. On the toll of wage theft, see Brady Meixell and Ross Eisenbrey, "An Epidemic of Wage Theft Is Costing Workers Hundreds of Millions of Dollars a Year," Economic Policy Institute, Issue Brief No. 385, September 11, 2014, https://files.epi.org/2014/wage-theft.pdf, 2; and Alec Karakatsanis, *Usual Cruelty: The Complicity of Lawyers in the Criminal Injustice System* (New York: New Press, 2019), 50.

30. For more on these legal barriers, see pp. 17–18. For more on DPAs and NPAs, see the discussions later in this chapter and in chapters 7 to 9.

31. For example, when a group of researchers sought a few years ago to conduct a pioneering meta-analysis to determine "what works" to deter corporate criminal behavior, they discovered a dearth of good quantitative studies. As a result, their conclusions were tentative and narrow. They conceded that the central question—whether law and the criminal legal system have a deterrent effect on corporate offending—remained unresolved. By comparison, a landmark meta-analysis of "what works" to deter street crime had numerous high-quality studies to draw on. That meta-analysis decisively concluded that swift and certain apprehension and punishment—not ratcheting up penalties—have a significant deterrent effect on street crimes such as robbery. Natalie Schell-Busey et al., "What Works? A Systematic Review of Corporate Crime Deterrence," *Criminology and Public Policy* 15, no. 2 (February 2016): 387–416; and Daniel S. Nagin, "Deterrence in the Twenty-First Century: A Review of the Evidence," *Crime and Justice: A Review of Research* 42 (2013): 199–263. On definitional disputes, see Barnett, "Measurement of White-Collar Crime," 1.

32. John Braithwaite, "In Search of Donald Campbell: Mix and Multimethods," *Criminology and Public Policy* 15, no. 2 (May 2016): 417–37.

33. Dorothy S. Lund and Natasha Sarin, "Corporate Crime and Punishment: An Empirical Study," *Texas Law Review* 100, no. 2 (2021): 285–352.

34. Kitty Calavita and Henry Pontell, "The State and White-Collar Crime: Saving the Savings and Loans," *Law and Society Review* 28, no. 2 (1994): 298.

35. Charles Lindblom, *Politics and Markets: The World's Political-Economic Systems* (New York: Basic Books, 1977). For an overview of these debates about the privileged position of business, including key citations, see Marie Gottschalk, *The Shadow Welfare State: Labor, Business, and the Politics of Health Care in the United States* (Ithaca, NY: Cornell University Press, 2000), 36–38.

36. Gottschalk, *The Shadow Welfare State*, 36–38.

37. For an overview of this literature, see Calavita and Pontell, "State and White-Collar Crime," 300–305.

38. In the early 1980s, US commercial banks were providing almost as much in loans to industrial and commercial enterprises as they were providing in loans for real estate and consumers. By the late 1990s, they were providing only about half as much, and by 2005, barely one-quarter as much. Robert D. Atkinson and Stephen J. Ezell, *Innovation Economics: The Race for Global Advantage* (New Haven, CT: Yale University Press, 2012), 21.

39. FCIC, *Financial Crisis Inquiry Report*, January 2011, https://www.govinfo.gov/content /pkg/GPO-FCIC/pdf/GPO-FCIC.pdf, xvii.

40. Greta R. Krippner, *Capitalizing on Crisis: The Political Origins of the Rise of Finance* (Cambridge, MA: Harvard University Press, 2011), 28; Rana Foroohar, *Makers and Takers: The Rise of Finance and the Fall of American Business* (New York: Crown Business, 2016), 7–8; Thomas Philippon, "The Evolution of the U.S. Financial Industry from 1860 to 2007: Theory and Evidence," National Bureau of Economic Research, November 2008, 37, fig. 1, https://pages.stern .nyu.edu/~tphilipp/papers/finsize_old.pdf, 37, fig. 1; Thomas Philippon and Ariell Reshef, "Skill Biased Financial Development: Education, Wages and Occupations in the U.S. Financial Sector," Working Paper No. 13437 (National Bureau of Economic Research, September 2007), 3; and Paul Kedrosky and Dane Stangler, "Financialization and Its Entrepreneurial Consequences," Ewing Marion Kauffman Foundation, March 1, 2011, https://papers.ssrn.com/sol3 /papers.cfm?abstract_id=1798605, 2, fig. 1.

41. Krippner, *Capitalizing on Crisis*, 35.

42. Krippner, 28.

43. Lawrence Mishel and Julia Wolfe, "CEO Compensation Has Grown 940% Since 1978," Economic Policy Institute, August 14, 2019, https://files.epi.org/pdf/171191.pdf, 4.

44. Stephen G. Cecchetti and Enisse Kharroubi, "Why Does Financial Sector Growth Crowd Out Real Economic Growth?," Working Paper No. 490 (Bank for International Settlements, Monetary and Economic Department, February 2015), https://www.bis.org/publ /work490.pdf.

45. Paul Volcker, "The Only Useful Thing Banks Have Invented in 20 Years Is the ATM," *NYP*, December 13, 2009, https://nypost.com/2009/12/13/the-only-thing-useful-banks-have -invented-in-20-years-is-the-atm/.

46. Phillip Zweig, *Wriston: Walter Wriston, Citibank, and the Rise and Fall of American Financial Supremacy* (New York: Crown, 1995), 343.

47. Foroohar, *Makers and Takers*, 113.

48. Foroohar, 106.

49. Foroohar, 52.

50. Between 2010 and 2019, total spending on stock buybacks was $6.2 trillion. Lenore Palladino and William Lazonick, "Regulating Stock Buybacks: The $6.3 Trillion Question," Working Paper (Roosevelt Institute, May 2021), https://rooseveltinstitute.org/wp-content/uploads /2021/04/RI_Stock-Buybacks_Working-Paper_202105.pdf, 3.

51. Foroohar, *Makers and Takers*, 2–3.

52. See pp. 373–78.

53. Andrew Ross Sorkin et al., "Wall Street Doesn't Hate This Spending Bill," DealBook Newsletter, *NYT*, August 17, 2022, https://www.nytimes.com/2022/08/17/business/dealbook /inflation-reduction-act-stocks.html; Christina Wilkie, "Here's What the SEC Will Require Under Its Strict New Stock Buyback Disclosure Rules," CNBC, May 5, 2023, https://www.cnbc

.com/2023/05/05/sec-stock-buyback-disclosure-rules.html; Jesse Fried and Charles C. Y. Wang, "Buyback Critics Are Not Letting the COVID-19 Crisis Go to Waste," Harvard School Law Forum on Corporate Governance, April 2, 2020, https://corpgov.law.harvard.edu/2020/04/02/buyback-critics-are-not-letting-the-covid-19-crisis-go-to-waste/; and Jane G. Gravelle, "The 1% Excise Tax on Stock Repurchases (Buybacks)," CRS, February 15, 2023, https://crsreports.congress.gov/product/pdf/R/R47397.

54. Calavita and Pontell, "State and White-Collar Crime," 320.

55. William K. Black, *The Best Way to Rob a Bank Is to Own One: How Corporate Executives and Politicians Looted the S&L Industry*, updated ed. (Austin: University of Texas Press, 2013), 271.

56. Black, 260.

57. Quoted in Kitty Calavita, Henry N. Pontell, and Robert H. Tillman, *Fraud and Politics in the Savings and Loan Crisis* (Berkeley: University of California Press, 1997), 64; see also 66–67.

58. Calavita and Pontell, "State and White-Collar Crime," 303n4; US House, Subcommittee on Financial Institutions Supervision, Regulation and Insurance of the Committee on Banking, Finance and Urban Affairs, *When Are the Savings and Loans Crooks Going to Jail?*, 101st Cong., 2d Sess., June 28, 1990, 38–50; and US Senate, Subcommittee on Consumer and Regulatory Affairs, Committee on Banking, Finance and Urban Affairs, *Efforts to Combat Criminal Financial Institution Fraud*, 102nd Cong., 2d Sess., February 6, 1992, 9–17.

59. Michael Waldman, *Who Robbed America? A Citizen's Guide to the S&L Scandal* (New York: Random House, 1990), 146–49.

60. L. J. Davis, "Big Money Crime: Fraud and Politics in the Savings and Loan Crisis," *Washington Monthly* 29, no. 10 (October 1997): 53.

61. NCFIRRE, *Origins and Causes of the S&L Debacle: A Blueprint for Reform; A Report to the President and Congress of the United States* (Washington, DC: GPO, 1993), part 2.

62. Samir Sonti, "The World Paul Volcker Made," *Jacobin*, December 20, 2018, https://jacobin.com/2018/12/paul-volcker-federal-reserve-central-bank?mc_cid=172e6cd8c7&mc_eid=997d6d360e.

63. NCFIRRE, *Origins and Causes of the S&L Debacle*, part 3.

64. Martin Mayer, *The Greatest-Ever Bank Robbery: The Collapse of the Savings and Loan Industry* (New York: Charles Scribner's Sons, 1990); and Kitty Calavita and Henry N. Pontell, "'Heads I Win, Tails You Lose': Deregulation, Crime and Crisis in the Savings and Loan Industry," *Crime and Delinquency* 36, no. 3 (1990): 312.

65. Foroohar, *Makers and Takers*, 52.

66. NCFIRRE, *Origins and Causes of the S&L Debacle*, 33. The measure was named the Depository Institutions Deregulation and Monetary Control Act of 1980.

67. See the Depository Institutions Deregulation and Monetary Control Act of 1980, Pub. L. No. 96-221, 94 Stat. 132-93 (1980).

68. Mayer, *Greatest-Ever Bank Robbery*, 95.

69. Mayer, 95.

70. Hagan, *Who Are the Criminals?*, 28, 137–212.

71. Nancy MacLean, *Democracy in Chains: The Deep History of the Radical Right's Stealth Plan for America* (New York: Viking, 2017); and Naomi Oreskes and Erik M. Conway, *The Big Myth: How American Business Taught Us to Loathe Government and Love the Free Market* (New York: Bloomsbury, 2023).

72. Jane Mayer, *Dark Money: The Hidden History of the Billionaires Behind the Rise of the Radical Right* (New York: Doubleday, 2016), 149–51; and MacLean, *Democracy in Chains*, 188–89.

73. MacLean, *Democracy in Chains*, 66–67, 195–96.

74. Paul Sabin, *Public Citizens: The Attack on Big Government and the Remaking of American Liberalism* (New York: W. W. Norton, 2021).

75. Lewis F. Powell, "Attack on American Free Enterprise System," memo to Eugene B. Sydnor Jr., US Chamber of Commerce, August 23, 1971, https://www.reuters.com/investigates/special-report/assets/usa-courts-secrecy-lobbyist/powell-memo.pdf; and Fred P. Graham, "Powell Proposed Business Defense," *NYT*, September 29, 1972, https://www.nytimes.com/1972/09/29/archives/powell-proposed-business-defense-wrote-a-memo-for-chamber-before.html.

76. Mayer, *Dark Money*, 70–78.

77. Powell, "Attack on American Free Enterprise System," 26.

78. Michael Avery and Danielle McLaughlin, *The Federalist Society: How Conservatives Took the Law Back from Liberals* (Nashville, TN: Vanderbilt University Press, 2013); and Sohrab Ahmari, Patrick Deneen, and Chad Pecknold, "We Know How America Got Such a Corporate-Friendly Court," *NYT*, June 14, 2022, https://www.nytimes.com/2022/06/14/opinion/conservatism-federalist-society-populists.html.

79. Mayer, *Dark Money*, 110.

80. On how "market fundamentalism" came to dominate the economics profession after World War II and how the financial and foreclosure crises did not spur much rethinking in the profession, including how economics is taught at colleges and universities, see Philip Mirowski, *Never Let a Serious Crisis Go to Waste: How Neoliberalism Survived the Financial Meltdown* (London: Verso, 2013), especially chap. 4. See also Paul Krugman, "The Profession and the Crisis," *Eastern Economic Journal* 37 (2011): 307–12.

81. Milton Friedman, "The Social Responsibility of Business Is to Increase Profits," *NYT*, September 13, 1970, https://www.nytimes.com/1970/09/13/archives/a-friedman-doctrine-the-social-responsibility-of-business-is-to.html.

82. On the pivotal role of economists at the University of Chicago, with Milton Friedman leading the charge, in misrepresenting the work of Adam Smith in order to entrench their brand of market fundamentalism among US-trained economists and policymakers more broadly, see Angus Deaton, "How Misreading Adam Smith Helped Spawn Deaths of Despair," *BR*, August 2, 2023, https://www.bostonreview.net/articles/how-misreading-adam-smith-helped-spawn-deaths-of-despair/; Glory M. Liu, *Adam Smith's America: How a Scottish Philosopher Became an Icon of American Capitalism* (Princeton, NJ: Princeton University Press, 2022), especially chap. 6; and Angus Burgin, *The Great Persuasion: Reinventing Free Markets Since the Depression* (Cambridge, MA: Harvard University Press, 2012), especially chap. 5.

83. Financiers who attended elite colleges and universities earn by one estimate three times as much money as peers with comparable education and skills who were employed in other industries. Until the late 1970s, people employed in the financial sector were only slightly more educated and received only slightly higher wages that those employed in other sectors. Claudia Goldin and Lawrence Katz, "Transitions: Career and Family Life Cycles of the Educational Elite," *American Economic Review* 98, no. 2 (2008): 366–67; and Philippon and Reshef, "Skill Biased Financial Development," 8–19.

84. Catherine Rampell, "Out of Harvard, and into Finance," *NYT*, December 21, 2011, https://archive.nytimes.com/economix.blogs.nytimes.com/2011/12/21/out-of-harvard-and-into-finance/?_php=true&_type=blogs&_r=0. See also Francesca Mari, "What Do Students at Elite Colleges Really Want?," *NYT*, May 22, 2024, https://www.nytimes.com/2024/05/22/business/gen-z-college-students-jobs.html.

85. Foroohar, *Makers and Takers*, 94.

86. Foroohar, 107.

87. Jessica Carrick-Hagenbarth and Gerald Epstein, "Dangerous Interconnectedness: Economists' Conflicts of Interest, Ideology, and Financial Crisis," *Cambridge Journal of Economics* 36, no. 1 (January 2012): 43–63; and Charles Ferguson, *Predator Nation: Corporate Criminals, Political Corruption, and the Hijacking of America* (New York: Crown Business, 2012), chap. 8.

88. Foroohar, *Makers and Takers*, 96.

89. Foroohar, 113.

90. The most noteworthy example is James Q. Wilson, *Thinking About Crime* (New York: Basic Books, 1983). See also Gary S. Becker, "Crime and Punishment: An Economic Approach," *Journal of Political Economy* 76, no. 2 (1968): 169–217.

91. Jeremy Travis, Bruce Western, and Steve Redburn, eds., *The Growth of Incarceration in the United States: Exploring Causes and Consequences* (Washington, DC: National Academies Press, 2014), 150.

92. As recounted by Brooksley Born, chair of the Commodity Futures Trading Commission, in Manuel Roig-Franzia, "Brooksley Born Warned About the Risks of Derivatives," *Seattle Times*, May 31, 2009, https://www.seattletimes.com/business/brooksley-born-warned-about-the-risks -of-derivatives/.

93. NCFIRRE, *Origins and Causes of the S&L Debacle*, 3.

94. NCFIRRE, 48.

95. NCFIRRE, 3 and 47–48.

96. NCFIRRE, 48.

97. AP, "House Panel to Probe CIA-S&L Story," *LAT*, February 7, 1990, https://www.latimes .com/archives/la-xpm-1990-02-07-fi-294-story.html; and Steve Weinberg, "The Mob, the CIA, and the S&L Scandal: Does Pete Brewton's Story Check Out?," *Columbia Journalism Review*, November/December 1990, 28–35.

98. Mayer, *Greatest-Ever Bank Robbery*, chap. 2.

99. Waldman, *Who Robbed America?*; and Black, *Best Way to Rob a Bank*.

100. Mayer, *Greatest-Ever Bank Robbery*, chaps. 5 and 6.

101. NCFIRRE, *Origins and Causes of the S&L Debacle*, 55–56; and Waldman, *Who Robbed America?*, 57–59.

102. The five senators were Alan Cranston (D-CA), Dennis DeConcini (D-AZ), John Glenn (D-OH), John McCain (R-AZ), and Donald W. Reigle Jr. (D-MI).

103. See Alan Greenspan, letter to Thomas F. Sharkey, FHLBB, February 13, 1985, as reprinted in Mayer, *Greatest-Ever Bank Robbery*, 324–26; see also 140–41.

104. NCFIRRE, *Origins and Causes of the S&L Debacle*, 73.

105. Quoted in Black, *Best Way to Rob a Bank*, 297.

106. Black, 281.

107. Stephen Pizzo, Mary Fricker, and Paul Muolo, *Inside Job: The Looting of America's Savings and Loans* (New York: McGraw-Hill, 1989), 267–79.

108. Black, *Best Way to Rob a Bank*, xviii.

109. Black, 295–96.

110. Calavita and Pontell, "State and White-Collar Crime," 313n12.

111. Mayer, *Greatest-Ever Bank Robbery*, 256. Full disclosure: I am a distant beneficiary of Perelman's dealings. In 2013, he donated $25 million to establish the Ronald O. Perelman Center for Political Science and Economics at the University of Pennsylvania.

112. Michael M. Thomas, "The Greatest American Shambles," *NYRB*, January 31, 1991, https://www.nybooks.com/articles/1991/01/31/the-greatest-american-shambles/.

113. Jeff Gerth, "Misuse of Savings Bailout Reported in Texas Purchase," *NYT*, July 8, 1990, https://www.nytimes.com/1990/07/08/us/misuse-of-savings-bailout-reported-in-texas -purchase.html.

114. NCFIRRE, *Origins and Causes of the S&L Debacle*, 3 and 47–48. See also Franklin E. Zimring and Gordon Hawkins, "Crime, Justice, and the Savings and Loan Crisis," in *Crime and Justice: A Review of Research* 18 (1993): 253.

115. Calavita, Pontell, and Tillman, *Fraud and Politics in the Savings and Loan Crisis*, 1, 191n1. For comparisons with the US war in Korea and the Marshall Plan, see Zimring and Hawkins, "Crime, Justice, and the Savings and Loan Crisis," 253, fig. 2.

116. The FIRREA abolished the FHLBB and shifted regulation and oversight of thrifts to the new Office of Thrift Supervision, a bureau within the US Treasury. It also abolished the Federal Savings and Loan Insurance Corporation (FSLIC) and shifted deposit insurance for thrifts to the FDIC. Financial Institutions Reform, Recovery, and Enforcement Act of 1989, Pub. L. No. 101-73, 103 Stat. 183 (1989). See also Bruce A. Green, "After the Fall: The Criminal Law Response to the S&L Crisis," *Fordham Law Review* 59, no. 6 (May 1991): S155–S192.

117. Quoted in US House of Representatives, *When Are the Savings and Loans Crooks Going to Jail?*, 128.

118. Waldman, *Who Robbed America?*, 133–35; and Green, "After the Fall," S155–S192.

119. These included enhanced penalties for numerous crimes, including drug offenses and sexual and other abuse of children; increased resources for law enforcement, including drug enforcement in rural areas; the first sweeping federal ban on possession of child pornography; new rights for crime victims; and grants and other support to foster controversial penal innovations, notably boot camps for young people and military-style "shock incarceration." Crime Control Act of 1990, Pub. L. No. 101-647, 104 Stat. 4789 (1990), https://www.congress.gov/bill/101st-congress/senate-bill/3266/text.

120. George H. W. Bush, "Statement on Signing the Crime Control Act of 1990," November 29, 1990, American Presidency Project, https://www.presidency.ucsb.edu/documents/statement-signing-the-crime-control-act-1990.

121. The commission was terminated after release of its final report in 1993. NCFIRRE, *Origins and Causes of the S&L Debacle*.

122. Black, *Best Way to Rob a Bank*, 296.

123. Black, 296.

124. Monica Sager, "How Ivan Boesky, Infamous 1980s Wall Street Trader, Inspired Gordon Gekko," *Newsweek*, May 20, 2024, https://www.newsweek.com/ivan-boesky-michael-douglas-wall-street-trader-gordon-gekko-1902787.

125. Christopher Seeds, *Death by Prison: The Emergence of Life Without Parole and Perpetual Confinement* (Oakland: University of California Press, 2022), 5, fig. 4.

126. Seeds; Marie Gottschalk, *Caught: The Prison State and the Lockdown of American Politics*, rev. ed. (Princeton, NJ: Princeton University Press, 2016), chap. 8; and Ashley Nellis, *No End in Sight: America's Enduring Reliance on Sentences* (Washington, DC: Sentencing Project, 2021).

127. William K. Black, "When Liar's Loans Flourish," *NYT*, January 30, 2011, https://www.nytimes.com/roomfordebate/2011/01/30/was-the-financial-crisis-avoidable/when-liars-loans-flourish.

128. Black, *Best Way to Rob a Bank*, 278, 280.

129. Black, 279–80.

130. See, for example, the case of Long Beach Savings, renamed Ameriquest, and Roland Arnall, its CEO billionaire who emerged unscathed. A top fundraiser for George W. Bush, he was rewarded with an ambassadorship to the Netherlands. Black, *Best Way to Rob a Bank*, 280–81.

131. NCFIRRE, *Origins and Causes of the S&L Debacle*, 71.

132. NCFIRRE, 73, 76–77.

133. NCFIRRE, 76.

134. NCFIRRE, 71.

135. Black, *Best Way to Rob a Bank*, 278.

136. In making his successful pitch to join Gore's reinvention effort, one top official, Robert Knisely, described the US government as "the last bastion of communist management." Quoted in Bob Stone, *Confessions of a Civil Servant: Lessons in Changing America's Government and Military* (Lanham, MD: Rowman and Littlefield, 2004), 68.

137. Frank H. Easterbrook and Daniel R. Fischel, "Antitrust Suits by Targets of Tender Offers," *Michigan Law Review* 80, no. 6 (May 1982): 1177n57. For a good critical assessment of Easterbrook and Fischel's work, see Kent Greenfield, *The Failure of Corporate Law: Fundamental*

Flaws and Progressive Possibilities (Chicago: University of Chicago Press, 2007), especially chap. 4. A prominent review lauded their textbook, *The Economic Structure of Corporate Law*, as "arguably the most important . . . corporate law book ever." Robert Daines and Jon Hanson, "The Corporate Law Paradox: The Case for Restructuring Corporate Law," *YLJ* 102 (1992): 577.

138. On the growth of the field of law and economics in legal studies, see Jedediah Britton-Purdy et al., "Building a Law-and-Political-Economy Framework: Beyond the Twentieth-Century Synthesis," *YLJ* 129, no. 6 (April 2020): 1784–835.

139. Mayer, *Dark Money*, 73 and 107–10.

140. Black, *Best Way to Rob a Bank*, 282.

141. Black, 282.

142. James Lardner, "A Brief History of the Glass–Steagall Act," *Demos*, November 10, 2009, https://www.demos.org/research/brief-history-glass-steagall-act.

143. Lardner.

144. Lardner. These banks included National City Bank, which eventually morphed into Citigroup, and Chase National Bank, whose heir is JPMorgan Chase.

145. David H. Carpenter, Edward V. Murphy, and M. Maureen Murphy, "The Glass–Steagall Act: A Legal and Policy Analysis," CRS, January 19, 2016, https://crsreports.congress.gov/product/pdf/R/R44349, 3–8.

146. Carpenter et al., 3–8.

147. For an excellent (and colorful) overview of the demise of the Glass–Steagall Act, see Nelson Lichtenstein and Judith Stein, *A Fabulous Failure: The Clinton Presidency and the Transformation of American Capitalism* (Princeton, NJ: Princeton University Press, 2023), 407–19.

148. Foroohar, *Makers and Takers*, 45–47.

149. "The Long Demise of Glass–Steagall," *Frontline*, PBS, n.d., https://www.pbs.org/wgbh/pages/frontline/shows/wallstreet/weill/demise.html (accessed December 12, 2022).

150. Lardner, "Brief History of the Glass–Steagall Act."

151. Barry A. Abbott, James E. Scott, and Ford Barrett, "Banks and Insurance: An Update," *Business Lawyer* 43, no. 3 (May 1988): 1005–24.

152. Robert Kuttner, "Friendly Takeover," *TAP*, March 18, 2007, https://prospect.org/features/friendly-takeover/.

153. William Jackson, *Glass–Steagall Act: Commercial vs. Investment Banking* (Washington, DC: CRS, Economics Division, 1987), 2.

154. William C. Agpar and Mark Duda, "The Twenty-Fifth Anniversary of the Community Reinvestment Act: Past Accomplishments and Future Regulatory Challenges," *Economic Policy Review* 9, no. 2 (2003): 174; and Lichtenstein and Stein, *Fabulous Failure*, 416–17.

155. Eileen Appelbaum, testimony, US House of Representatives, Committee on Financial Services, "America for Sale? An Examination of the Practices of Private Funds," November 19, 2019, https://cepr.net/images/stories/testimonies/appelbaum-house-fin-ser-2019-11.pdf.

156. David Dayen, "Cut Off Private Equity's Money Spigot," *TAP*, August 2022, 19–21.

157. Eileen Appelbaum and Rosemary Batt, *Private Equity at Work: When Wall Street Manages Main Street* (New York: Russell Sage Foundation, 2014).

158. Lichtenstein and Stein, *Fabulous Failure*, 421; and Simon Johnson and James Kwak, *13 Bankers: The Wall Street Takeover and the Next Financial Meltdown* (New York: Vintage Books, 2011), 8.

159. Carol J. Loomis, "The Risk That Won't Go Away," *Fortune*, March 7, 1994, republished at CNN Money, September 25, 2008, https://money.cnn.com/2008/09/25/magazines/fortune/loomis_swamp.fortune/index.htm?postversion=2008092616. Fifteen years later, her verdict was still the same. Carol J. Loomis and Doris Burke, "Derivatives: The Risk That Still Won't Go Away (Fortune 2009)," republished May 20, 2012, https://fortune.com/2012/05/20/derivatives-the-risk-that-still-wont-go-away-fortune-2009/.

160. Lichtenstein and Stein, *Fabulous Failure*, 424–32.

161. As quoted in Manuel Roig-Franzia, "Credit Crisis Cassandra: Brooksley Born's Unheeded Warning Is a Rueful Echo 10 Years On," *WP*, May 26, 2009, https://www.washingtonpost.com/wp-dyn/content/article/2009/05/25/AR2009052502108_pf.html. Born ended up resigning in June 1999, the year before Clinton signed the CFMA.

162. Reuters, "Republican Elected to Head C.F.T.C.," *NYT*, June 3, 1999, https://www.nytimes.com/1999/06/03/business/republican-elected-to-head-cftc.html.

163. Jed S. Rakoff, *Why the Innocent Plead Guilty and the Guilty Go Free and Other Paradoxes of Our Broken Legal System* (New York: Farrar, Straus and Giroux, 2021), 96.

164. Thomas Philippon, *The Great Reversal: How America Gave Up on Free Markets* (Cambridge, MA: Harvard University Press, 2019), 86–96, 124.

165. Gottschalk, *Prison and the Gallows*, 37–39.

166. Jed S. Rakoff, "Justice Deferred Is Justice Denied," *NYRB*, February 19, 2015, 8.

167. Rakoff, 8.

168. Samuell W. Buell, *Capital Offenses: Business Crime and Punishment in America's Corporate Age* (New York: W. W. Norton, 2016), 229.

169. Compliance programs are internal policies and procedures to ensure that a company is adhering to laws and government regulations.

170. For more on how DPAs and NPAs operate, see pp. 200–207.

171. Scot J. Paltrow, "Prudential Firm Agrees to Strict Fraud Settlement," *LAT*, October 28, 1994, https://www.latimes.com/archives/la-xpm-1994-10-28-mn-55889-story.html; and Jesse Eisinger, *The Chickenshit Club: Why the Justice Department Fails to Prosecute Executives* (New York: Simon and Schuster, 2017), 95–96. Reflecting years later on the Prudential Securities settlement and the proliferation of DPAs in the decades since, White emphasized how indicting a firm could throw thousands of employees out of work and harm investors. Russell Mokhiber, "Interview with Mary Jo White, Debevoise, New York, New York" *Corporate Crime Reporter*, December 12, 2005, https://www.corporatecrimereporter.com/news/200/category/sampleinterviews/.

172. Eisinger, *Chickenshit Club*, 96.

173. Eric Holder, "Bringing Charges Against Corporations," DOJ, June 16, 1999, https://www.justice.gov/sites/default/files/criminal-fraud/legacy/2010/04/11/charging-corps.PDF.

174. Bill Clinton, quoted in Marc Mauer, "Bill Clinton, 'Black Lives,' and the Myths of the 1994 Crime Bill," Marshall Project, April 11, 2016, https://www.themarshallproject.org/2016/04/11/bill-clinton-black-lives-and-the-myths-of-the-1994-crime-bill.

175. Robert Jay Lifton and Greg Mitchell, *Who Owns Death? Capital Punishment, the American Conscience, and the End of Executions* (New York: HarperCollins, 2000), 100–101.

176. Travis, Western, and Redburn, *Growth of Incarceration in the United States*, 35, fig. 2–1.

177. Michelle Alexander, *The New Jim Crow: Mass Incarceration in the Age of Colorblindness* (New York: New Press, 2010), 142–43 and 153.

178. Foroohar, *Makers and Takers*, 59.

179. Ferguson, *Predator Nation*, 43.

180. Ferguson, 165.

7. Greed Is Not So Good: George W. Bush and the Financial and Foreclosure Crises

1. Winters's father reportedly asked him this question in 2007. Quoted in Ron Suskind, *Confidence Men: Wall Street, Washington, and the Education of the President* (New York: HarperCollins, 2011), 414.

2. As reported in Daphne Eviatar, "What's Behind the Drop in Corporate Fraud Indictments?," *American Lawyer*, November 1, 2007, https://www.law.com/almID/900005494886/.

3. David Miller, "The Downfall of Karl Rove," CBS News, August 15, 2007, https://www
.cbsnews.com/news/the-downfall-of-karl-rove/.

4. Joseph E. Stiglitz, *The Roaring Nineties: A New History of the World's Most Prosperous
Decade* (New York: W. W. Norton, 2003), 241.

5. For a good overview of the Enron, WorldCom, and dot-com scandals, see Stiglitz, chaps.
6 and 10.

6. The account of this meeting is from Jesse Eisinger, *The Chickenshit Club: Why the Justice
Department Fails to Prosecute Executives* (New York: Simon and Schuster, 2017), 101–2.

7. Eviatar, "What's Behind the Drop?"

8. George W. Bush, "Remarks at the Corporate Fraud Conference," September 26, 2002,
American Presidency Project, https://www.presidency.ucsb.edu/documents/remarks-the
-corporate-fraud-conference.

9. Quoted in Eviatar, "What's Behind the Drop?"

10. Stiglitz, *Roaring Nineties*, 135–36.

11. Kathleen F. Brickey, "Andersen's Fall from Grace," *Washington University Law Review* 81,
no. 4 (2003): 919. See also Brandon L. Garrett, *Too Big to Jail: How Prosecutors Compromise with
Corporations* (Cambridge, MA: Belknap Press of Harvard University Press, 2014), chap. 2.

12. Brickey, "Andersen's Fall from Grace," 919.

13. Charles Ferguson, *Predator Nation: Corporate Criminals, Political Corruption, and the
Hijacking of America* (New York: Crown Business, 2012), 166–67; and Nicholas Thompson, "The
Sword of Spitzer," *Legal Affairs*, May/June 2004, https://www.legalaffairs.org/issues/May-June
-2004/feature_thompson_mayjun04.msp. Morgan Stanley, with the support of the SEC,
sought unsuccessfully to secure congressional passage of the so-called Spitzer amendments,
which would have curtailed the power of the New York attorney general and other state attorneys general to police Wall Street.

14. SEC, "Ten of Nation's Top Investment Firms Settle Enforcement Actions Involving Conflicts of Interest Between Research and Investment Banking," April 28, 2003, https://www.sec
.gov/news/press/2003-54.htm.

15. Gabriel Markoff, "Arthur Andersen and the Myth of the Corporate Death Penalty: Corporate Criminal Convictions in the Twenty-First Century," *University of Pennsylvania Journal of
Business Law* 15, no. 3 (March 2013): 797–98.

16. For more on civil death and these collateral consequences, see Marie Gottschalk, *Caught:
The Prison State and the Lockdown of American Politics*, rev. ed. (Princeton, NJ: Princeton University Press, 2016), 96 and chap. 11.

17. John Power, "Show Me the Money: The Thompson Memo, Stein, and an Employee's
Right to the Advancement of Legal Fees Under the McNulty Memo," *Washington and Lee Law
Review* 64, no. 3 (Summer 2007): 1216. For more on the Holder memo, see p. 191.

18. Larry D. Thompson, "Principles of Federal Prosecution of Business Organizations," January 20, 2003, https://mlaus.org/wp-content/uploads/filebase/cle_papers/cle_2015_-
_scottsdale_papers/cle_2005_-_scottsdale_supporting_papers/DAG_-_Thompson_Memo
-Criminal-Prosecution-of-Pollution.pdf.

19. Christopher Modlish, "The Yates Memo: DOJ Public Relations Move or Meaningful Reform That Will End Impunity for Corporate Criminals?," *Boston College Law Review* 58, no. 2 (2017):
752.

20. Eisinger, *Chickenshit Club*, 106–7.

21. As quoted in Eisinger, 130.

22. Eisinger, 132–36.

23. Eisinger, 139. For an overview of the expansion of civil asset forfeitures, see Gottschalk,
Caught, 34–35.

24. Eisinger, *Chickenshit Club*, 140; and Charles D. Weisselberg and Su Li, "Big Law's Sixth Amendment: The Rise of Corporate White-Collar Practices in Large U.S. Law Firms," *Arizona Law Review* 53, no. 4 (2011): 1246.

25. *United States v. Stein* (Stein IV), 495 F. Supp. 2d 390, 32 (S.D.N.Y. 2007), https://casetext.com/case/us-v-stein-36.

26. Eisinger, *Chickenshit Club*, chap. 7.

27. Weisselberg and Li, "Big Law's Sixth Amendment": 1280.

28. Modlish, "Yates Memo": 752; Mark Filip, "Principles of Federal Prosecution of Business Organizations," August 28, 2008, https://www.justice.gov/sites/default/files/dag/legacy/2008/11/03/dag-memo-08282008.pdf.

29. Filip, "Principles of Federal Prosecution of Business Organizations," 4, 8, 17–18.

30. Gottschalk, *Caught*, 9–10.

31. See Weisselberg and Li, "Big Law's Sixth Amendment": 1223.

32. Andrew Cohen, "The Lies We Tell Each Other About the Right to Counsel," Brennan Center for Justice, March 18, 2013. https://www.brennancenter.org/our-work/analysis-opinion/lies-we-tell-each-other-about-right-counsel.

33. The rise in DPAs and NPAs after 2003 did not result in a decline in corporate plea agreements, for reasons that remain unclear. Cindy R. Alexander and Mark A. Cohen, "The Evolution of Corporate Criminal Settlements: An Empirical Perspective on Non-Prosecution, Deferred Prosecution, and Plea Agreements," *American Criminal Law Review* 52, no. 3 (Summer 2015): 567, fig. 2, 591.

34. Garrett, *Too Big to Jail*, 10.

35. Edwin H. Sutherland, "White Collar Criminality," *American Sociological Review* 5, no. 1 (February 1940): 11.

36. Quoted in Sutherland: 3.

37. Jesse Eisinger, "Why Only One Top Banker Went to Jail for the Financial Crisis," *NYT*, April 30, 2014, https://www.nytimes.com/2014/05/04/magazine/only-one-top-banker-jail-financial-crisis.html.

38. Garrett, *Too Big to Jail*, 82, fig. 4.1.

39. Between 2003 and 2018, the proportion of individuals granted pretrial diversion in non-corporate cases fell from 3 percent to less than 1 percent. Rick Claypool, *Soft on Corporate Crime: DOJ Refuses to Prosecute Corporate Lawbreakers, Fails to Deter Repeat Offenders* (Washington, DC: Public Citizen, 2019), 4, 11.

40. Kent Greenfield of Boston College quoted in William Greider, "How Wall Street Crooks Get Out of Jail Free," *Nation*, March 24, 2011, https://www.thenation.com/article/archive/how-wall-street-crooks-get-out-jail-free/.

41. The rare state revocations of corporations' charters have generally come for "ignoring legal formalities, such as failing to file annual reports, rather than as a penalty for criminal behavior." Kyle Noonan, "The Case for a Federal Corporate Charter Revocation Penalty," *George Washington Law Review* 80, no. 2 (2012): 614–15.

42. Samuel Buell, *Capital Offenses: Business Crime and Punishment in America's Corporate Age* (New York: W. W. Norton, 2006), xiv.

43. Frederick T. Davis, "Judicial Review of Deferred Prosecution Agreements: A Comparative Study," *Columbia Journal of Transnational Law* 60, no. 3 (2022): 762.

44. Quoted in Davis: 763n36.

45. Nandita Bose, "Walmart to Pay $282 Million to Settle Seven-Year Global Corruption Probe," Reuters, June 20, 2019, https://www.reuters.com/article/idUSKCN1TL27I/#:~:text=The%20Justice%20Department%20launched%20an,permits%20to%20build%20stores%20there.

46. Jennifer Taub, *Big Dirty Money: The Shocking Injustice and Unseen Cost of White Collar Crime* (New York: Viking, 2020), 38.

47. Davis, "Judicial Review of Deferred Prosecution Agreements": 760.

48. Brandon L. Garrett and Jon Ashley, Corporate Prosecution Registry, Duke University and University of Virginia School of Law, n.d., http://lib.law.virginia.edu/Garrett/corporate -prosecution-registry/index.html (accessed September 23, 2022).

49. Garrett, *Too Big to Jail*, 151, 276. See also Emily Homer and Michael Maume, "The Deterrent Effect of Federal Corporate Prosecution Agreements: An Exploratory Analysis," *JWCCC* 5, no. 1 (August 2022): 15–27.

50. Garrett, *Too Big to Jail*, 82–83.

51. Brandon L. Garrett, "The Corporate Criminal as Scapegoat," *Virginia Law Review* 101, no. 7 (November 2015): 1810.

52. Dorothy S. Lund and Natasha Sarin, "Corporate Crime and Punishment: An Empirical Study," *Texas Law Review* 100, no. 2 (2021): 295.

53. Lund and Sarin, 291.

54. Modlish, "Yates Memo": 756–58.

55. Jed S. Rakoff, "The Financial Crisis: Why Have No High-Level Executives Been Prosecuted?," *NYRB*, January 9, 2014, 8.

56. Claypool, *Soft on Corporate Crime*, 23.

57. On recent guidelines concerning monitors, see Lisa Monaco, "Further Revisions to Corporate Criminal Enforcement Policies Following Discussions with Corporate Crime Advisory Group," DOJ, Office of the Deputy Attorney General, September 15, 2022, https://www.justice .gov/opa/speech/file/1535301/download, 11–15.

58. Leah Wang, "Punishment Beyond Prisons 2023: Incarceration and Supervision by State," Prison Policy Initiative, May 2023, https://www.prisonpolicy.org/reports/correctionalcontrol2023 .html.

59. Claypool, *Soft on Corporate Crime*, 5.

60. Corporate attorneys often push prosecutors to delay the announcement of new charges or a new DPA or NPA until after a previous agreement has expired so that technically the company is not considered in violation of the earlier agreement. Claypool, *Soft on Corporate Crime*, 5. See also Garrett, *Too Big to Jail*, 165–66.

61. For more on the problems with using recidivism as a metric, see Gottschalk, *Caught*, 101–6.

62. Claypool, *Soft on Corporate Crime*, 5.

63. See, for example, details of the DPA settlement in the case of Goldman Sachs and the looting of Malaysia's sovereign wealth fund at pp. 284–85.

64. For an overview of the doctrine of felony murder, see Gottschalk, *Caught*, 178–79.

65. For an overview of the key court decisions, see Davis, "Judicial Review of Deferred Prosecution Agreements": 764–85.

66. Davis: 779n118.

67. Davis: 818. On DPAs in the United Kingdom, see Colin King and Nicholas Lord, *Negotiated Justice and Corporate Crime: The Legitimacy of Recovery Orders and Deferred Prosecution Agreements* (London: Palgrave Macmillan, 2018).

68. Jed S. Rakoff, *Why the Innocent Plead Guilty and the Guilty Go Free and Other Paradoxes of Our Broken Legal System* (New York: Farrar, Straus and Giroux, 2021), chap. 7; and Eisinger, *Chickenshit Club*, 317–18.

69. See Eisinger, *Chickenshit Club*, xiv. See also, for example, Comey's role in the prosecution of KPMG. Eisinger, 133–35.

70. Quoted in Brandon L. Garrett, "How Biden Should Prosecute Corporate Crime," *TAP*, January/February 2021, 60. See also Rakoff, *Why the Innocent Plead Guilty*.

71. Rakoff, *Why the Innocent Plead Guilty*, 88–89.

72. Lisa Zornberg, "What In-House Corporate Counsel Should Know About the Fifth Amendment, Part I: The Basics," *Corporate Counsel*, October 22, 2019, 1–7.

73. Davis, "Judicial Review of Deferred Prosecution Agreements": 761.

74. Davis: 761–62.

75. Jed S. Rakoff, "Justice Deferred Is Justice Denied," *NYRB*, February 19, 2015, 8–9.

76. Garrett, *Too Big to Jail*, 223.

77. Garrett, 223.

78. Ferguson, *Predator Nation*, 202.

79. Rakoff, *Why the Innocent Plead Guilty*, chap. 7; Eisinger, *Chickenshit Club*; and Garrett, *Too Big to Jail*.

80. Gottschalk, *Caught*, especially chaps. 1 and 3.

81. David Enrich, *Servants of the Damned: Giant Law Firms, Donald Trump, and the Corruption of Justice* (Boston: Mariner, 2022).

82. Weisselberg and Li, "Big Law's Sixth Amendment": 1225–35; and Enrich, *Servants of the Damned*.

83. More than four out of five partners at large law firms who specialize in white-collar cases are former government lawyers, especially federal prosecutors. Weisselberg and Li, "Big Law's Sixth Amendment": 1254; see also 1260–63.

84. Weisselberg and Li: 1268–73. See also Enrich, *Servants of the Damned*.

85. Eisinger, *Chickenshit Club*, xvii.

86. See Ronald Goldfarb, "No Big-Game Hunting at Justice," *TAP*, February 14, 2018, https://prospect.org/health/big-game-hunting-justice/.

87. For more on the S&L scandal, see chap. 6.

88. Alan S. Blinder and Mark Zandi, "How the Great Recession Was Brought to an End," July 27, 2010, https://www.princeton.edu/~blinder/End-of-Great-Recession.pdf, 2.

89. David Luttrell, Tyler Atkinson, and Harvey Rosenblum, "Assessing the Costs and Consequences of the 2007–09 Financial Crisis and Its Aftermath," *Economic Letter: Insights from the Federal Reserve Bank of Dallas* 8, no. 7 (September 2013): 1, 4.

90. Edward N. Wolff, "The Asset Price Meltdown and the Wealth of the Middle Class," Working Paper No. 18559 (National Bureau of Economic Research, November 2012), 10. Median household wealth plunged by 49 percent for African American people and a staggering 86 percent for Latino people, who were more likely to have bought homes just before the real estate crash and to be at greatest risk of foreclosure. Calculated from Wolff, "Asset Price Meltdown," 60, table 12; 62, table 13; and 36.

91. PRC, *Fewer, Poorer, Gloomier: The Lost Decade of the Middle Class*, https://www.pewresearch.org/social-trends/wp-content/uploads/sites/3/2012/08/pew-social-trends-lost-decade-of-the-middle-class.pdf, 2.

92. FCIC, *Financial Crisis Inquiry Report* (Washington, DC: GPO, January 2011), 389, 391–92.

93. This calculation includes people who are unemployed and actively looking for a new job; part-timers who would prefer full-time positions; and people who want to work but are too discouraged by the economic conditions to search for a job. FCIC, 390–92.

94. FCIC; and US Senate, Committee on Homeland Security and Governmental Affairs, Permanent Subcommittee on Investigations, *Wall Street and the Financial Crisis: Anatomy of a Financial Collapse*, April 13, 2011, https://www.hsgac.senate.gov//imo/media/doc/Financial_Crisis/FinancialCrisisReport.pdf.

95. For more on Clinton and deregulation, see pp. 172 and 189–99.

96. Ferguson, *Predator Nation*, 55.

97. William Black, testimony, FCIC, *Financial Crisis Inquiry Report*, 160.

98. Ric Brooks and Ruth Simon, "Subprime Debacle Traps Even Very Credit-Worthy," *WSJ*, December 3, 2007, https://www.wsj.com/articles/SB119662974358911035.

99. David Dayen, "The Dirty Secret Behind Warren Buffett's Billions," *Nation*, February 18, 2018, https://www.thenation.com/article/archive/special-investigation-the-dirty-secret-behind-warren-buffetts-billions/.

100. Keeanga-Yamahtta Taylor, "Against Black Home Ownership," *BR*, November 18, 2019, https://bostonreview.net/articles/keeanga-yamahtta-taylor-keeanga-excerpt/.

101. Robert Kuttner and Katherine V. Stone, "The Rise of Neo-Feudalism," *TAP*, March/April 2020, 35; FCIC, *Financial Crisis Inquiry Report*, 407–8; Reuters, "New York Sues 3 Big Banks over Mortgage Database," *NYT*, February 3, 2012, https://www.nytimes.com/2012/02/04/business/new-york-suing-3-banks-over-mortgage-database.html; and Basil Katz and Karen Freifeld, "Banks to Pay $25 Million to NY State over Mortgage System," Reuters, March 14, 2012, https://www.reuters.com/article/us-banks-mortgages/banks-to-pay-25-million-to-ny-state-over-mortgage-system-idUSBRE82D0A620120314.

102. FCIC, *Financial Crisis Inquiry Report*, 22. The total value of mortgage-backed securities issued between 2001 and 2006 hit an estimated $13.4 trillion.

103. For more on Clinton and the CFMA, see p. 188.

104. FCIC, *Financial Crisis Inquiry Report*, xxiv.

105. Nelson Lichtenstein and Judith Stein, *A Fabulous Failure: The Clinton Presidency and the Transformation of American Capitalism* (Princeton, NJ: Princeton University Press, 2023), 432.

106. FCIC, *Financial Crisis Inquiry Report*, 427, 429, and 543.

107. For more details on AIG and credit default swaps, as well as the government's dodgy bailout of the company, see FCIC, *Financial Crisis Inquiry Report*, chap. 19.

108. This figure is from the International Swaps and Derivatives Association as reported in Janet Morrissey, "Credit Default Swaps: The Next Crisis?," *Time*, March 17, 2008, https://content.time.com/time/business/article/0,8599,1723152,00.html.

109. Alec Karakatsanis, *The Complicity of Lawyers in the Criminal Injustice System* (New York: New Press, 2019), 20.

110. Ferguson, *Predator Nation*, 108–12.

111. Ferguson, 108–12.

112. Ferguson, 132 and chap. 5; and US Senate, *Wall Street and the Financial Crisis*, chap. 6.

113. FCIC, *Financial Crisis Inquiry Report*, xxv, 8.

114. Joseph E. Stiglitz, *Freefall: America, Free Markets, and the Sinking of the World Economy* (New York: W. W. Norton, 2010), 92.

115. FCIC, *Financial Crisis Inquiry Report*; and US Senate, *Wall Street and the Financial Crisis*, chap. 5.

116. Dayen, "Dirty Secret."

117. US Senate, *Wall Street and the Financial Crisis*, 29.

118. William Cohan, *House of Cards: A Tale of Hubris and Wretched Excess on Wall Street* (New York: Doubleday, 2009), 332.

119. Cohan, 332.

120. Matt Taibbi, "The Last Mystery of the Financial Crisis," *Rolling Stone*, June 19, 2013, https://www.rollingstone.com/politics/politics-news/the-last-mystery-of-the-financial-crisis-200751/.

121. US Senate, *Wall Street and the Financial Crisis*, 5–7, chap. 5.

122. Taibbi, "Last Mystery of the Financial Crisis."

123. Cohan, *House of Cards*, 331–32.

124. Taibbi, "Last Mystery of the Financial Crisis."

125. Stiglitz, *Freefall*, 1. See also Adam Tooze, *Crashed: How a Decade of Financial Crises Changed the World* (New York: Viking, 2018), chap. 1; and Nolan McCarty, Keith T. Poole, and Howard Rosenthal, *Political Bubbles: Financial Crises and the Failure of American Democracy* (Princeton, NJ: Princeton University Press, 2013), 12–13.

126. FCIC, *Financial Crisis Inquiry Report*, 5, 7, 18.

127. These eye-popping figures are likely gross underestimates of the extent of the fraud. Congress rebuffed calls to improve the data reporting system for fraud, including a mandate that all lenders participate, whether they were federally insured or not. FCIC, 161–62.

128. Ferguson, *Predator Nation*, 121–22.

129. Jeremy W. Peters and Edmund L. Andrews, "Manageable Threats Seen by Fed Chief," *NYT*, March 29, 2007, https://www.nytimes.com/2007/03/29/business/29fed.html. In his memoir, Paulson admitted that his belief in spring 2007 that the subprime mortgage problems were "largely contained" was "just plain wrong." Henry M. Paulson, *On the Brink: Inside the Race to Stop the Collapse of the Global Financial System* (New York: Business Plus, 2010), 66.

130. Timothy Geithner, "Liquidity Risk and the Global Economy," May 15, 2007, https://www.newyorkfed.org/newsevents/speeches/2007/gei070515.html. Reflecting years later on the Fed's mistakes, Geithner said, "At the start of any crisis, there's an inevitable fog of diagnosis." Timothy F. Geithner, *Stress Test: Reflections on Financial Crises* (New York: Crown, 2014), 13, 119.

131. Vikas Bajaj, "Ratings Agencies Downgrade Subprime Bonds and Tighten Standards," *NYT*, July 11, 2007, https://www.nytimes.com/2007/07/11/business/worldbusiness/11iht-mortgage.1.6611290.html.

132. Michael Lewis, *The Big Short: Inside the Doomsday Machine* (New York: W. W. Norton, 2010). This paragraph, including direct quotes, is based on Ferguson, *Predator Nation*, 123.

133. Ferguson, *Predator Nation*, 123, 132, and chap. 5; and US Senate, *Wall Street and the Financial Crisis*, chap. 6.

134. Krystyna Blokhina, "Securities Exchange Act of 1934," Legal Information Institute, Cornell Law School, June 10, 2019, https://www.law.cornell.edu/wex/securities_exchange_act_of_1934.

135. FCIC, *Financial Crisis Inquiry Report*, 15, 161–62, 164.

136. Eisinger, *Chickenshit Club*, 327–28.

137. William K. Black, *The Best Way to Rob a Bank Is to Own One: How Corporate Executives and Politicians Looted the S&L Industry*, updated ed. (Austin: University of Texas Press, 2013), 283. This figure includes only people directly employed by the public sector in law enforcement. It does not include the millions of people working in the private security industry.

138. Shortly after 9/11, the FBI reassigned more than eighteen hundred agents, or about one-third of its criminal investigative work force, to antiterrorism and national security work. Eric Lichtblau, David Johnston, and Ron Nixon, "F.B.I. Struggles to Handle Financial Fraud Cases," *NYT*, October 18, 2008, https://www.nytimes.com/2008/10/19/washington/19fbi.html.

139. Paul Shukovsky et al., "The Terrorism Trade-Off: Focus on National Security After 9/11 Means That the FBI Has Turned Its Back on Thousands of White-Collar Crimes," *Seattle Post-Intelligencer*, April 11, 2007, https://perma.cc/4KN8-HAK7; and Trung Nguyen, "The Effectiveness of White-Collar Crime Enforcement: Evidence from the War on Terror," *Journal of Accounting Research* 59, no. 1 (March 2021): 5, 6, 9. In 2000, FBI agents referred ten thousand white-collar criminal cases to federal prosecutors; by 2005, that number had plummeted to thirty-five hundred.

140. For more on immigration enforcement, see pp. 43–45.

141. Gottschalk, *Caught*, 225, fig. 10.2.

142. Doris Meissner and Julia Gelatt, *Eight Key U.S. Immigration Policy Issues: State of Play and Unanswered Questions* (Washington, DC: Migration Policy Institute, 2019), https://www.migrationpolicy.org/sites/default/files/publications/ImmigrationIssues2019_Final_WEB.pdf, 3.

143. Gottschalk, *Caught*, 224–25.

144. FCIC, *Financial Crisis Inquiry Report*, 162.

145. Shukovsky et al., "Terrorism Trade-Off."

146. Quoted in FCIC, *Financial Crisis Inquiry Report*, 163.

147. FCIC, 163.

148. Calculated from Mark Febrizio and Melinda Warren, "Regulators' Budget: Overall Spending and Staffing Remain Stable," Regulatory Studies Center, July 2020, https://regulatorystudies.columbian.gwu.edu/sites/g/files/zaxdzs4751/files/downloads/RegulatorsBudget/GW%20Reg%20Studies%20-%20FY2021%20Regulators%20Budget%20-%20MFebrizio%20and%20MWarren_Weidenbaum%20Center.pdf, 9, table 2. See also McCarty et al., *Political Bubbles*, 145–47 and chap. 4.

149. Calculated from Febrizio and Warren, "Regulators' Budget," 4, table 1.

150. These federal agencies do not have the authority to bring criminal cases, even though some of the laws they enforce have criminal and civil sanctions. Their regulators and investigators may refer cases of suspected criminal activity to law enforcement. William K. Black, "2011 Will Bring More De Facto Decriminalization of Elite Financial Fraud," *HuffPost*, December 28, 2010, https://www.huffpost.com/entry/the-role-of-the-criminal_b_802115.

151. William K. Black, "The OCC's Tragic Response to the *Frontline* Exposé: The Untouchables," *HuffPost*, January 26, 2013, https://www.huffpost.com/entry/frontline-banking-crisis_b_2557146.

152. William K. Black quoted in David Heath, "Too Big to Jail? Executives Unscathed as Regulators Let Banks Report Criminal Fraud," *HuffPost*, July 3, 2010, https://www.huffpost.com/entry/too-big-to-jail-executive_n_561961.

153. Gretchen Morgenson and Louise Story, "In Financial Crisis, No Prosecutions of Top Figures," *NYT*, April 14, 2011, https://www.nytimes.com/2011/04/14/business/14prosecute.html.

154. Henry N. Pontell of University of California, Irvine, quoted in Morgenson and Story.

155. Morgenson and Story.

156. Quoted in Black, "OCC's Tragic Response."

157. FCIC, *Financial Crisis Inquiry Report*, xiii.

158. FCIC, 72.

159. FCIC, 164.

160. Heath, "Too Big to Jail?"

161. John Pistole, deputy director, FBI, testimony, US Senate, Judiciary Committee, "The Need for Increased Fraud Enforcement in the Wake of the Economic Downturn," February 11, 2009, https://www.judiciary.senate.gov/imo/media/doc/pistole_testimony_02_11_09.pdf, 1.

162. Black, *Best Way to Rob a Bank*, 286.

163. Eric Lichtblau, "Mukasey Declines to Create a U.S. Task Force to Investigate Mortgage Fraud," *NYT*, June 6, 2008, https://www.nytimes.com/2008/06/06/business/06justice.html.

164. Morgenson and Story, "In Financial Crisis, No Prosecutions."

165. FCIC, *Financial Crisis Inquiry Report*, 20.

166. Suskind, *Confidence Men*, 56–57.

167. This 2005 study and the reaction to it are discussed in FCIC, *Financial Crisis Inquiry Report*, 172–73.

168. Black, *Best Way to Rob a Bank*, 278.

169. Black, 278.

170. Quoted in Ben Fountain, *Beautiful Country, Burn Again: Democracy, Rebellion, and Revolution* (New York: Ecco/Harper Collins, 2018), 356n40.

171. FCIC, *Financial Crisis Inquiry Report*, 23. Ironically, the Chinese Communist Party arrived at the same 70–30 split in its ambiguous posthumous reassessment in 1981 of Chairman Mao Zedong, whose record includes tens of millions of deaths from the Great Leap Forward and the Cultural Revolution.

172. David Beim and Christopher McCurdy, "FRBNY Report on Systemic Risk and Supervision," draft, FRBNY, September 10, 2009, https://info.publicintelligence.net/FRBNY-BankSupervisionReport.pdf, 2–3.

173. Sheila Blair, *Bull by the Horns* (New York: Simon and Schuster, 2012), 121.

174. Quoted in FCIC, *Financial Crisis Inquiry Report*, 171, 123, xvii, and xviii.

175. Edward Gramlich, quoted in FCIC, 95.

176. Mike Lofgren, *The Deep State: The Fall of the Constitution and the Rise of a Shadow Government* (New York: Penguin Books, 2016), 134.

177. Lofgren, chap. 7.

178. Lofgren, 136.

179. The legislation also created an independent bipartisan Congressional Oversight Panel for the bailouts and included $150 billion in special tax provisions to help constituents of the dozens of lawmakers who initially voted against the legislation. This account of Treasury's proposal and the final version of TARP is based primarily on Lofgren, 134–36; Suskind, *Confidence Men*, especially chaps. 5 and 6; Neil Barofsky, *Bailout: An Inside Account of How Washington Abandoned Main Street While Rescuing Wall Street* (New York: Free Press, 2012), 23; Dwight D. Murphey, "Review of *Freefall: America, Free Markets, and the Sinking of the World Economy,*" *Journal of Social, Political, and Economic Studies* 35, no. 2 (Summer 2010): 255–65; and US Treasury, "Troubled Asset Relief Program (TARP)," n.d., https://home.treasury.gov/data/troubled-asset-relief-program (accessed December 16, 2023).

180. For more on the TARP windfall, see chap. 8.

181. Stiglitz, *Freefall*, 41.

182. Simon Johnson, "The Quiet Coup," *Atlantic*, May 2009, https://www.theatlantic.com/magazine/archive/2009/05/the-quiet-coup/307364/.

183. This is a central argument of Tooze, *Crashed*. See also Raghuram Rajan, "Comment," *Brookings Papers on Economic Activity*, Fall 2018, 331–38.

184. One "spectacular" Fed innovation that flew below the public radar during the crisis was the revival of currency swaps by which the Fed pumped trillions of dollars into Europe's banking system. The Fed also provided trillions of additional dollars in liquidity and loan guarantees to US and foreign banks, and made massive purchases of mortgage-backed securities and US Treasury bonds through what became known as "quantitative easing." Tooze, *Crashed*, 9–12, 210–15, 483–84. For an overview of the Fed's actions by a staff member, see Michael J. Fleming, "Federal Reserve Liquidity Provision During the Financial Crisis of 2007–2009," FRBNY Staff Report no. 563 (July 2012), https://www.newyorkfed.org/medialibrary/media/research/staff_reports/sr563.pdf.

185. A decade after the collapse of Lehman Brothers, former Fed Chair Ben Bernanke still considered the "horrific" financial crisis to be the equivalent of an unpredictable sunspot. He also contended that the failure of the economics profession to foresee the crisis was not cause to fundamentally rethink its basic assumptions and approach. Ben S. Bernanke, "The Real Effects of Disrupted Credit: Evidence from the Global Financial Crisis," *Brookings Papers on Economic Activity*, Fall 2018, 251–322. For a gently dissenting view, see Rajan, "Comment," 331–38.

186. "Bush's Final Approval Rating: 22 Percent," CBS News, January 16, 2009, https://www.cbsnews.com/news/bushs-final-approval-rating-22-percent/.

187. Ed Pilkington, "Everybody Loves Chris," *Guardian*, January 7, 2008, https://www .theguardian.com/film/2008/jan/07/comedy.usa.

188. In April 2009, Senator Arlen Specter (R-PA) defected to the Democratic Party. The courts ruled in June 2009 that Democrat Al Franken had won the Senate race in Minnesota. For public opinion polls, see pp. 496n248 and 500nn27-28.

8. Hope, Change, and Wall Street: Decriminalization of Crime in the Suites under Obama

1. Reported by Paul Street, "Barack Obama's Neoliberal Legacy: Rightward Drift and Donald Trump," *Truthdig*, n.d., https://www.truthdig.com/articles/barack-obamas-neoliberal-legacy -rightward-drift-and-donald-trump-2/ (accessed December 16, 2023).

2. Obama won 43 percent of white voters in 2008. Bill Clinton won 39 percent of them in 1992 and 44 percent in 1996. The figures for Al Gore in 2000 and John Kerry in 2004 were 42 percent and 41 percent, respectively. Roper Center for Public Opinion Research, Cornell University, "How Groups Voted," various years, https://ropercenter.cornell.edu/how_groups _voted (accessed March 11, 2023).

3. James Vicini and Randall Mikkelsen, "Attorney General Vows No Wall St 'Witch Hunts,'" Reuters, February 2, 2009, https://www.reuters.com/article/us-obama-holder/attorney -general-vows-no-wall-st-witch-hunts-idUKTRE5116EL20090203.

4. Jesse Eisinger, *The Chickenshit Club: Why the Justice Department Fails to Prosecute Executives* (New York: Simon and Schuster, 2017), 173.

5. This figure included households who lost their homes to foreclosures or had to resort to a distress sale. Brooke Niemeyer, "There Have Been 6.3 Million Foreclosures in the U.S. in the Last Decade," *MarketWatch*, May 31, 2016, https://www.marketwatch.com/story/there-were-63 -million-foreclosures-in-the-last-decade-2016-05-31; Laura Kusisto, "Many Who Lost Homes to Foreclosure in Last Decade Won't Return—NAR," *WSJ*, April 15, 2015, https://www.wsj.com /articles/many-who-lost-homes-to-foreclosure-in-last-decade-wont-return-nar-1429548640; and Francesca Mari, "The Housing Vultures," *NYRB*, June 11, 2020, 12.

6. FCIC, *Financial Crisis Inquiry Report*, January 2011, https://www.govinfo.gov/content/pkg /GPO-FCIC/pdf/GPO-FCIC.pdf, 389-90.

7. Obama reportedly answered, "This I know. When I raise my hand and take that oath of office, I think the world will look at us differently. And millions of kids across the country will look at themselves differently." Ron Suskind, *Confidence Men: Wall Street, Washington, and the Education of the President* (New York: HarperCollins, 2011), 126.

8. Mike Allen, "McCain Wants to Limit Execs to $400,000," *Politico*, September 21, 2008, https://www.politico.com/story/2008/09/mccain-wants-to-limit-execs-to-400-000-013711; and Caren Bohan, "Obama Denounces Big Corporate Pay Packages," Reuters, April 11, 2008, https://www.reuters.com/article/us-usa-politics-obama-ceo/obama-denounces-big-corporate -pay-packages-idUSN1131749320080411.

9. For more details on the Chicago school, see chap. 6.

10. Barack Obama, "CNBC Exclusive," CNBC, June 10, 2008, https://www.cnbc.com/2008 /06/10/cnbc-exclusive-cnbcs-chief-washington-correspondent-john-harwood-sits-down-with -presidential-candidate-senator-barack-obama-transcript-included.html.

11. Barack Obama, "Remarks by the President on Financial Rescue and Reform at Federal Hall," September 14, 2009, Obama White House Archives, https://obamawhitehouse.archives .gov/the-press-office/remarks-president-financial-rescue-and-reform-federal-hall.

12. "Money can't guarantee victory—it can't buy passion, charisma, or the ability to tell a story," Obama wrote in his book *Audacity of Hope*. "But without money, and the television ads that consume all the money, you are pretty much guaranteed to lose. Absent great personal wealth, there is basically one way of raising the kind of money involved in a U.S. Senate race.

You have to ask rich people for it." Barack Obama, *Audacity of Hope: Thoughts on Reclaiming the American Dream* (New York: Vintage, 2008), quoted in John R. MacArthur, "You Can't Be President: The Decrepit State of American Democracy," *In These Times*, September 17, 2008, https://inthesetimes.com/article/you-cant-be-president.

13. Angie Drobnic Holan, "Obama Campaign Financed by Large Donors, Too," *PolitiFact*, April 22, 2010, https://www.politifact.com/factchecks/2010/apr/22/barack-obama/obama-campaign-financed-large-donors-too/; and Brooks Jackson, "Obama's Small Donations," Fact-Check.org, March 19, 2008, https://www.factcheck.org/2008/03/obamas-small-donors/.

14. Ryan Lizza, "The Obama Memos: The Making of a Post-Post-Partisan Presidency," *NY*, January 30, 2012, https://www.newyorker.com/magazine/2012/01/30/the-obama-memos.

15. Lizza. In 2008, Obama raked in $15 million from Wall Street compared to $8.7 for McCain. Ben White, "Obama and Wall Street: Still Venus and Mars," *Politico*, December 28, 2010, https://www.politico.com/story/2010/12/obama-wall-st-still-venus-mars-046839.

16. Holan, "Obama Campaign Financed by Large Donors, Too"; and Jackson, "Obama's Small Donations."

17. "Top Contributors, 2008 Cycle," Open Secrets, n.d., https://www.opensecrets.org/pres08/contrib.php?cycle=2008&cid=N0000963 (accessed March 5, 2023).

18. "Top Contributors, 2008 Cycle."

19. Jackie Calmes, "Rubinomics Recalculated," *NYT*, November 23, 2008, https://www.nytimes.com/2008/11/24/us/politics/24rubin.html.

20. Reed Hundt, *A Crisis Wasted: Barack Obama's Defining Decisions* (New York: Rosetta Books, 2019), 24.

21. Alex Koppelman, "James Johnson Resigns from Obama Team," *Salon*, June 11, 2008, https://www.salon.com/2008/06/11/johnson_8/.

22. For an engaging, granular account of the close nexus between Obama and key Wall Street figures during his campaign, see Suskind, *Confidence Men*.

23. Justin Lahart, "Obama Builds Ties to 'Chicago School,'" *WSJ*, November 8, 2008, https://www.wsj.com/articles/SB122610604643110229; and Naomi Klein, "Beware the Chicago Boys," *Guardian*, June 13, 2008, https://www.theguardian.com/commentisfree/2008/jun/14/barackobama.uselections2008.

24. One of Obama's closest longtime aides later confessed in his memoirs that seeing the new administration "filled with many of the people who we had run against" added up to "a punch in the gut." Ben Rhodes, *World as It Is: A Memoir of the Obama White House* (New York: Random House, 2018), 35. See also Edward J. Epstein, "Warren Buffett's Hidden Stake in Financial Weapons of Mass Destruction," *Vanity Fair*, February 2, 2009, https://www.vanityfair.com/news/2009/02/warren-buffetts-hidden-stake-in-financial-weapons-of-mass-destruction.

25. Samir Sonti, "The World Paul Volcker Made," *Jacobin*, December 20, 2018, https://jacobin.com/2018/12/paul-volcker-federal-reserve-central-bank?mc_cid=172e6cd8c7&mc_eid=997d6d360e.

26. The Volcker shock also exacerbated the debt crisis in Latin America and hastened the imposition of structural adjustment programs by the International Monetary Fund and World Bank that fueled economic inequality and deteriorating standards of living in the region. See Sonti.

27. Suskind, *Confidence Men*, 35.

28. Paul A. Volcker, Economic Club of New York, April 8, 2008, https://www.econclubny.org/documents/10184/109144/2008VolckerTranscript.pdf.

29. Jennifer Parker, "Obama Announces Transition Economic Advisory Board," ABC News, November 26, 2008, https://abcnews.go.com/Politics/story?id=6338011&page=1.

30. Suskind, *Confidence Men*, chap. 7. See also Hundt, *Crisis Wasted*, chap. 3.

31. Charles Ferguson, *Predator Nation: Corporate Criminals, Political Corruption, and the Hijacking of America* (New York: Crown Business, 2012), 300–301. The policymakers included

Simon Johnson (chief economist of the International Monetary Fund); Nobel–prize winning economists Paul Krugman and Joseph Stiglitz; economist Jeffrey Sachs of Columbia; Sheila Bair (chair of the FDIC); Brooksley Born (chair of the CFTC under Clinton); New York University economist Nouriel Roubini; Senator Carl Levin (D-MI), who for fifteen years had led major Senate investigations of money laundering, offshore tax abuses, and other corporate crimes; and public interest lawyer Robert Gnaizda, who had for years been warning Alan Greenspan and the Federal Reserve of the impending subprime mortgage crisis.

32. Pam Martens and Russ Martens, "WikiLeaks Bombshell: Emails Show Citigroup Had Major Role in Shaping and Staffing Obama's First Term," Wall Street on Parade, October 11, 2016, https://wallstreetonparade.com/2016/10/wikileaks-bombshell-emails-show-citigroup -had-major-role-in-shaping-and-staffing-obamas-first-term/.

33. The Citigroup bailout, which was the largest bank rescue in US history, ended up including $45 billion in TARP money; more than $300 billion in federal loan asset guarantees; and over $2 trillion in nearly interest-free loans from the FRBNY. See GAO, *Federal Reserve Bank Governance: Opportunities Exist to Broaden Director Recruitment Efforts and Increase Transparency* (Washington, DC: GAO, 2011), 96; and Pam Martens, "How Taxpayers Were Royally Screwed on the Citigroup Bailout," Wall Street on Parade, August 7, 2012, https:// wallstreetonparade.com/2012/08/how-taxpayers-were-royally-screwed-on-the-citigroup -bailout/.

34. Quoted in Jeff Connaughton, *The Payoff: Why Wall Street Always Wins* (Westport, CT: Prospecta, 2012), 17. Years later, hacked emails from Wikileaks revealed that Rubin envisioned himself taking on a "Harry Hopkins" role in the Obama administration, modeling himself after Franklin D. Roosevelt's close aide, who was nicknamed the "shadow president." David Dayen, "The Most Important Wikileaks Revelation Isn't About Hillary Clinton," NR, October 14, 2016, https://newrepublic.com/article/137798/important-wikileaks-revelation-isnt-hillary -clinton.

35. Eric Dash and Julie Creswell, "Citigroup Saw No Red Flags Even as It Made Bolder Bets," NYT, November 22, 2008, https://www.nytimes.com/2008/11/23/business/23citi.html.

36. Connaughton, *Payoff*, 17.

37. Obama's personal chemistry with Geithner was reportedly a critical factor in his choice. Suskind, *Confidence Men*, 146–47. See also Hundt, *Crisis Wasted*, 90–99.

38. Romer's differences with Geithner and Summers over economic and financial policy were only one reason why she was sidelined. A number of senior women in the Obama administration complained bitterly about how they were poorly treated by his top advisers, including Summers. Suskind, *Confidence Men*, 152–53, 275–77, 350–53.

39. Suskind, 340; and "President's Economic Recovery Advisory Board: The Sunset of PERAB [President's Economic Recovery Board]," n.d., Obama White House Archives, https:// obamawhitehouse.archives.gov/administration/eop/perab (accessed March 4, 2023).

40. Citigroup's grip on the executive branch is remarkable. See the list of Citi alumni with close ties to the White House compiled by Senator Elizabeth Warren in 2014. "Remarks by Elizabeth Warren on Citigroup and Its Bailout Provision," YouTube, December 12, 2014, https:// www.youtube.com/watch?v=DJpTxONxvoo. Lew was a veteran of the Clinton White House.

41. Ferguson, *Predator Nation*, 301; and Connaughton, *Payoff*, 17–21.

42. Ferguson, *Predator Nation*, 138.

43. David Enrich, *Dark Towers: Deutsche Bank, Donald Trump, and an Epic Trail of Destruction* (New York: HarperCollins, 2020).

44. Lee Fang, "Eric Holder Returns as Hero to Law Firm That Lobbies for Big Banks," Intercept, July 6, 2015, https://theintercept.com/2015/07/06/eric-holder-returns-law-firm -lobbies-big-banks/; Reuters, "New York Sues 3 Big Banks over Mortgage Database," NYT, February 3, 2012, https://www.nytimes.com/2012/02/04/business/new-york-suing-3-banks

-over-mortgage-database.html; and Basil Katz and Karen Freifeld, "Banks to Pay $25 Million to NY State over Mortgage System," Reuters, March 14, 2012, https://www.reuters.com/article/us -banks-mortgages/banks-to-pay-25-million-to-ny-state-over-mortgage-system-idUSBRE82 D0A620120314. For more on MERS, see pp. 210 and 231.

45. Steve Fagell, Breuer's chief of staff, was tasked at DOJ with coordinating its financial task force. After returning to Covington in 2010, he was the point person for a coalition of financial firms lobbying the SEC to weaken Dodd–Frank's whistleblower protections. Ferguson, *Predator Nation*, 303.

46. For more on TARP, see chap. 7.

47. Neil Barofsky, *Bailout: An Inside Account of How Washington Abandoned Main Street While Rescuing Wall Street* (New York: Free Press, 2012), 27; see also 72–73, 98–99.

48. The failure to pay his taxes would likely have sunk any other nominee to head the Treasury Department, which oversees the IRS. A close personal tie between Jim Messina, Obama's deputy chief of staff, and Senator Max Baucus (D-MT), head of the Finance Committee, saved his nomination. Suskind, *Confidence Men*, 165.

49. Quoted in Suskind, 164; see also 167.

50. See, for example, Jason M. Breslow's interview with former Senator Ted Kaufman (D-DE), "Ted Kaufman: Wall Street Prosecutions Never Made a Priority," *Frontline*, PBS, January 12, 2013, https://www.pbs.org/wgbh/frontline/article/ted-kaufman-wall-street-prose cutions-never-made-a-priority/.

51. Hundt, *Crisis Wasted*, chaps. 8–10.

52. Suskind, *Confidence Men*, 281.

53. For more on how they navigated around Obama, see chap. 9.

54. Paul J. Quirk, "Presidential Competence," in *The Presidency and the Political System*, 12th ed., ed. Michael Nelson (Los Angeles: Sage and CQ Press, 2020), 174–77.

55. Summers frequently repeated some version of "We're home alone. There's no adult in charge. Clinton would never have made these mistakes." Suskind, *Confidence Men*, 301.

56. Suskind, 458; and Jonathan Alter, *The Promise: President Obama, Year One* (New York: Simon and Schuster, 2010), 189–208.

57. Quoted in Suskind, *Confidence Men*, 280–81; see also 453.

58. This figure did not include stock options. Ben White, "What Red Ink? Wall Street Paid Hefty Bonuses," *NYT*, January 28, 2009, https://www.nytimes.com/2009/01/29/business /29bonus.html. A subsequent report revealed that the bonuses for 2008 were even higher than first reported. Louise Story and Eric Dash, "Bankers Reaped Lavish Bonuses During Bailouts," *NYT*, July 30, 2009, https://www.nytimes.com/2009/07/31/business/31pay.html; and Steve Eder and Ed Stoddard, "Wall St Bonuses Spark Outrage on Main Street USA," Reuters, September 8, 2009, https://www.reuters.com/article/us-compensation-anger/wall-st-bonuses -spark-outrage-on-main-street-usa-idUSTRE5874VE20090908.

59. Sarah Anderson et al., "America's Bailout Barons: Taxpayers, High Finance, and the CEO Pay Bubble," Institute for Policy Studies, September 2009, https://ips-dc.org/wp-content /uploads/2009/09/EE09final.pdf, 6, 11; and "Citigroup Prepares to Cut 53,000 Jobs," NPR, November 17, 2008, https://www.npr.org/2008/11/17/97084181/citigroup-prepares-to-cut-53 -000-jobs.

60. This account is from an interview with Representative Henry Waxman (D-CA), as reported in Hundt, *Crisis Wasted*, 75–76.

61. Sheryl Gay Stolberg and Stephen Labaton, "Obama Calls Wall Street Bonuses 'Shameful,'" *NYT*, January 29, 2009, https://www.nytimes.com/2009/01/30/business/30obama.html.

62. Barack Obama, *A Promised Land* (New York: Crown, 2020), 323, 327.

63. Suskind, *Confidence Men*, 181. See also Laura Thatcher, "Executive Compensation and Restrictions Under the American Recovery and Reinvestment Act of 2009," *Compensation and*

Benefits Review 41, no. 3 (2009): 25; and Colin Barr, "Clawbacks Can't Scratch AIG," CNN, March 18, 2009, https://money.cnn.com/2009/03/17/news/aig.bonusgate.fortune/index.htm ?postversion=2009031811.

64. The Obama administration ended up imposing a $500,000 cap on executive pay at financial institutions aided by TARP, but his directive had major loopholes. Cap Executive Officer Pay Act of 2009, S. 360. Introduced in 111th Cong., 1st Sess., n.d., https://www.congress.gov /bill/111th-congress/senate-bill/360/text (accessed December 21, 2022); and Anderson et al., "America's Bailout Barons," 7.

65. In 2011, the GAO reported that the Federal Reserve had secretly bestowed nearly $16 trillion in almost-zero-interest loans on Wall Street. *Federal Reserve System: Opportunities Exist to Strengthen Policies and Processes for Managing Emergency Assistance* (Washington, DC: GAO, July 2011), https://www.sanders.senate.gov/wp-content/uploads/GAO-Fed-Investigation-1 .pdf, 131.

66. Rana Foroohar, *Makers and Takers: How Wall Street Destroyed Main Street* (New York: Crown Business, 2016), 304; and Bryan T. Kelly, Hanno N. Lustig, and Stijn Van Nieuwerburgh, "Too-Systemic-to-Fail: What Option Markets Imply About Sector-Wide Government Guarantees," Working Paper No. 17149 (National Bureau of Economic Research, December 2011), https://www-nber-org.proxy.library.upenn.edu/papers/w17149, 3.

67. Edmund Andrews, "Fed Rescues AIG with $85 Billion Loan for 80% Stake," *NYT*, September 17, 2008, https://www.nytimes.com/2008/09/17/business/worldbusiness/17iht -17insure.16217125.html.

68. David Ellis, "US Takes Another Crack at AIG Rescue," CNN, March 3, 2009, https:// money.cnn.com/2009/03/02/news/companies/aig/index.htm.

69. This was on top of the $55 million that had already been paid and the $230 million yet to be paid in 2009, for a total of $450 million in bonuses to AIG executives. Suskind, *Confidence Men*, 213.

70. For more on CDSs, see pp. 211–12.

71. "Grassley: AIG Execs Should Quit or Commit Suicide," CNBC, March 17, 2009, https:// www.cnbc.com/id/29735786.

72. DealBook, "House Passes 90% Tax on Bonuses at Rescued Firms," *NYT*, March 19, 2009, https://archive.nytimes.com/dealbook.nytimes.com/2009/03/19/in-house-anger-over-aig -bonuses-turns-partisan/.

73. Barofsky, *Bailout*, 139.

74. Barofsky, 139.

75. Barofsky, 139–40.

76. Quoted in Suskind, *Confidence Men*, 268.

77. Barofsky, *Bailout*, 183–91; and Louise Story and Gretchen Morgenson, "In U.S. Bailout of A.I.G., Forgiveness for Big Banks," *NYT*, June 29, 2010, https://www.nytimes.com/2010/06 /30/business/30aig.html.

78. The New York Fed was keen to keep details of the AIG bailout secret not only from the public but also from other regulatory bodies. Reuters, "AIG's Bailout Disclosure Surprised NY Fed," January 22, 2010, https://www.reuters.com/article/us-aig-nyfed/aigs-bailout-disclosure -surprised-ny-fed-idUSTRE60L5V620100122. See also Story and Morgenson, "In U.S. Bailout of A.I.G., Forgiveness for Big Banks."

79. Neil Barofsky, statement, US House, Committee on Oversight and Government Reform, Subcommittee on TARP, Financial Services, and Bailouts of Public and Private Programs, March 30, 2011, https://oversight.house.gov/wp-content/uploads/2012/01/Barofsky_Testimony _3-30-11.pdf.

80. COP, "June Oversight Report: The AIG Rescue, Its Impact on Markets, and the Government's Exit Strategy," June 10, 2010, https://fraser.stlouisfed.org/title/aig-rescue-impact-mar kets-government-s-exit-strategy-5139, 3.

81. Story and Morgenson, "In U.S. Bailout of A.I.G., Forgiveness for Big Banks."

82. Barbara Black, "The U.S. as 'Reluctant Shareholder': Government, Business and the Law," *Entrepreneurial Business Law Journal* 5, no. 2 (2010): 561–96; and Steven M. Davidoff, "Uncomfortable Embrace: Federal Corporate Ownership in the Midst of the Financial Crisis," *Minnesota Law Review* 95, no. 5 (2011): 1736–44.

83. William Greider, "The AIG Bailout Scandal," *Nation*, August 6, 2010, https://www .thenation.com/article/archive/aig-bailout-scandal/.

84. Story and Morgenson, "In U.S. Bailout of A.I.G., Forgiveness for Big Banks."

85. Greider, "AIG Bailout Scandal."

86. Eamon Javers, "Inside Obama's Bank CEOs Meeting," *Politico*, April 3, 2009, https:// www.politico.com/story/2009/04/inside-obamas-bank-ceos-meeting-020871.

87. Suskind, *Confidence Men*, 233–37.

88. Reuters, "Goldman Sachs Boss Says Banks Do 'God's Work,'" November 8, 2009, https:// www.reuters.com/article/us-goldmansachs-blankfein/goldman-sachs-boss-says-banks-do -gods-work-idUSTRE5A719520091108.

89. Quoted in Suskind, *Confidence Men*, 425.

90. On the eve of the crash in 2008, their assets equaled 43 percent of the US gross domestic product; four years later, they constituted 56 percent. Mike Lofgren, *The Deep State: The Fall of the Constitution and the Rise of a Shadow Government* (New York: Penguin Books, 2016), 136.

91. Joseph E. Stiglitz, *Freefall: America, Free Markets, and the Sinking of the World Economy* (New York: W. W. Norton, 2010), 125. See also Adam Tooze, *Crashed: How a Decade of Financial Crises Changed the World* (New York: Viking, 2018), 198–99.

92. Stiglitz, *Freefall*, 125.

93. Stiglitz, chap. 5.

94. The historic foreclosure rate of less than 1 percent more than doubled to over 2 percent of all homes as of 2009. Another 9 percent of homeowners had fallen behind in their payments. FCIC, *Financial Crisis Inquiry Report*, 402.

95. Barofsky, *Bailout*, 122–23.

96. Aaron Glantz, *Homewreckers: How a Gang of Wall Street Kingpins, Hedge Fund Magnates, Crooked Banks, and Vulture Capitalists Suckered Millions Out of Their Homes and Demolished the American Dream* (New York: Custom House, 2019), 88.

97. Joe Nocera, "Sheila Bair's Bank Shot," *NYT*, July 10, 2011, 46.

98. "Rick Santelli Calls for Tea Party on Floor of Chicago Board of Trade," CNBC, February 19, 2009, *YouTube*, https://www.youtube.com/watch?v=wcvSjKCU_Zo; and Rick Ungar, "The Tea Party: R.I.P.; February 19, 2009–April 15, 2011," *Forbes*, April 27, 2011, https://www .forbes.com/sites/rickungar/2011/04/27/the-tea-party-r-i-p-february-19-2009-april-15-2011 /?sh=37a9781d5643.

99. "Rick Santelli Calls for Tea Party"; and Ungar, "Tea Party."

100. Manuel Adelino, Antoinette Schoar, and Felipe Severino, "Loan Originations and Defaults in the Mortgage Crisis: The Role of the Middle Class," *Review of Financial Studies* 29, no. 7 (March 2016): 1635–70.

101. Debbie Gruenstein Bocian, Wei Li, and Keith S. Ernst, "Foreclosure by Race and Ethnicity: The Demographics of a Crisis," Center for Responsible Lending, June 18, 2010, https:// responsiblelending.org/mortgage-lending/research-analysis/foreclosures-by-race-executive -summary.pdf, 2.

102. FCIC, *Financial Crisis Inquiry Report*, 23.

103. These states were Nevada, Florida, and Michigan. FCIC, 404, fig. 22.1.

104. The Bankruptcy Abuse Prevention and Consumer Protection Act of 2005 also exempted federal and student loans from being discharged in bankruptcy. Matthew Yglesias, "The 20-Year Argument Between Joe Biden and Elizabeth Warren over Bankruptcy, Explained," *Vox*,

September 12, 2019, https://www.vox.com/policy-and-politics/2019/5/6/18518381/baccpa-bankruptcy-bill-2005-biden-warren.

105. Bill Clinton killed an earlier version of this legislation in 2000 with a pocket veto, reportedly after Elizabeth Warren briefed First Lady Hillary Clinton on her research findings. See Yglesias.

106. David Himmelstein, Elizabeth Warren, Deborah Thorne, and Steffie Woolhandler, "Illness and Injury as Contributors to Bankruptcy," *Health Affairs* 24, no. 25 (2005): W5–63; and Elizabeth Warren, "The Bankruptcy Crisis," *Indiana Law Journal* 73, no. 4 (1998): 1079–110.

107. Ryan M. Goodstein and Yan Y. Lee, "Do Foreclosures Increase Crime?," Working Paper No. 2010-05 (FDIC Center for Financial Research, May 2010), https://www.fdic.gov/analysis/cfr/working-papers/2010/2010-05.pdf.

108. James Sanders Jr. quoted in Michael Powell and Janet Roberts, "Minorities Affected Most as New York Foreclosures Rise," *NYT*, May 15, 2009, https://www.nytimes.com/2009/05/16/nyregion/16foreclose.html.

109. PRC, "Foreclosures in the U.S. in 2008," May 12, 2009, https://www.pewresearch.org/hispanic/2009/05/12/v-foreclosures-in-the-u-s-in-2008/. Black households in New York City earning more than $68,000 annually were nearly five times as likely to have subprime mortgages as white households with similar or even lower incomes. Powell and Roberts, "Minorities Affected Most as New York Foreclosures Rise."

110. Michael Powell, "Bank Accused of Pushing Mortgage Deals on Blacks," *NYT*, June 6, 2009, https://www.nytimes.com/2009/06/07/us/07baltimore.html.

111. Michael Powell, "Federal Judge Rejects Suit by Baltimore Against Bank," *NYT*, January 8, 2010, https://www.nytimes.com/2010/01/09/business/economy/09baltimore.html; and Reuters, "Judge Dismisses Baltimore Lawsuit, Wells Fargo Says," September 14, 2010, https://www.reuters.com/article/wellsfargo-baltimore-lawsuit-idCNN1410755620100914.

112. DOJ, "Protecting Borrowers from Credit Discrimination in All Forms," https://www.justice.gov/archives/opa/blog/protecting-borrowers-credit-discrimination-all-forms; and "Wells Fargo Settles Discriminatory Lending Suit, Pays Tennessee Towns Memphis, Shelby $432 Million," *HuffPost*, May 29, 2012, updated July 29, 2012, https://www.huffpost.com/entry/wells-fargo-discriminatory-lending_n_1554533.

113. Barofsky, *Bailout*, 125–29.

114. Barofsky, 125, 133.

115. This account of the foreclosure crisis is based on Mari, "The Housing Vultures," 10–13.

116. Mari. For more on financial derivatives, see pp. 188–89 and 210–11.

117. Barofsky, *Bailout*, 155.

118. David Dayen, "Portrait of HAMP Failure: The Mother of All HAMP Failures," Firedoglake, February 9, 2011, https://shadowproof.com/2011/02/09/portrait-of-hamp-failure-the-mother-of-all-hamp-nightmares/.

119. Paul Kiel and Olga Pierce, "Homeowner Questionnaire Shows Banks Violating Gov't Program Rules," *ProPublica*, August 16, 2010, https://www.propublica.org/article/homeowner-questionnaire-shows-banks-violating-govt-program-rules.

120. David Dayen, "Obama Program That Hurt Homeowners and Helped Big Banks Is Ending," *Intercept*, December 15, 2018, https://theintercept.com/2015/12/28/obama-program-hurt-homeowners-and-helped-big-banks-now-its-dead/.

121. Barofsky, *Bailout*, 133. For more on liar's loans, see pp. 183–84.

122. Barofsky, 153, 156, 199.

123. Barofsky, 154.

124. Paul Kiel and Olga Pierce, "Govt's Loan Mod Program Crippled by Lax Oversight and Deference to Banks," *ProPublica*, January 27, 2011, https://www.propublica.org/article/loan-mod-program-crippled-by-lax-oversight-and-deference-to-banks.

125. Barack Obama, "Remarks by the President on the Mortgage Crisis," Obama White House Archives, February 18, 2009, https://obamawhitehouse.archives.gov/the-press-office/remarks-president-mortgage-crisis.

126. Barofsky, *Bailout*, 157.

127. FCIC, *Financial Crisis Inquiry Report*, 405.

128. This included $50 billion from TARP and $25 billion from Fannie Mae and Freddie Mac. US Treasury Department, "Homeowner Affordability and Stability Plan Fact Sheet," February 18, 2009, https://home.treasury.gov/news/press-releases/20092181117388144; and Barofsky, *Bailout*, 127.

129. The real amount banks shelled out was closer to $7 billion, including $1.5 billion to abused homeowners. As for the remaining $17 billion, it did not involve actual payments but rather government credits for certain tasks that banks performed as part of their normal business activities. Barofsky, *Bailout*, 226–28; Nelson Schwartz and Shaila Dewan, "States Negotiate $25 Billion Agreement for Homeowners," *NYT*, February 8, 2012, https://www.nytimes.com/2012/02/09/business/states-negotiate-25-billion-deal-for-homeowners.html; Patrick Rizzo, "US Files $25 Billion Settlement with Banks on Mortgage Abuses," NBC News, March 12, 2012, https://www.nbcnews.com/business/economy/us-files-25-billion-settlement-banks-mortgage-abuses-flna409683; and Shaila Dewan and Jessica Silver-Greenberg, "Foreclosure Deal Credits Banks for Routine Efforts," *NYT*, March 27, 2012, https://www.nytimes.com/2012/03/28/business/foreclosure-deal-gives-banks-credit-for-routine-activities.html. See also Kathleen Day, *Broken Bargain: Bankers, Bailouts, and the Struggle to Tame Wall Street* (New Haven, CT: Yale University Press, 2019), 275–76.

130. Mark DeCambre, "Wells Fargo in Hot Water with State Attorney General," *NYP*, October 2, 2013, https://nypost.com/2013/10/02/state-attorney-general-sues-wells-fargo-over-mortgages/; and Aruna Viswanatha and Karen Freifeld, "Judge Rules for Wells Fargo in NY Challenge over Mortgage Settlement," Reuters, February 2, 2015, https://www.reuters.com/article/us-wells-far-lawsuit/judge-rules-for-wells-fargo-in-ny-challenge-over-mortgage-settlement-idUKKBN0L628H20150202.

131. Shaila Dewan, "Banks Fail to Comply with Parts of Mortgage Settlement, Report Says," *NYT*, December 4, 2013, https://www.nytimes.com/2013/12/05/business/banks-fail-to-comply-with-parts-of-mortgage-settlement-report-says.html.

132. Barofsky, *Bailout*, 156–57, 199, 207, and 226–27.

133. Acting Assistant Attorney General Rita Glavin promised the Senate Judiciary Committee that law enforcement would mount a "comprehensive," "vigorous," and "aggressive" effort to address securities fraud. Rita Glavin, testimony before the House Judiciary Committee, April 1, 2009, https://www.justice.gov/sites/default/files/testimonies/witnesses/attachments/2009/04/01/2009-04-01-crm-glavin-protect-taxpayers.pdf.

134. Ted Kaufman, "Prosecuting Wall Street Fraud," Senate floor speech, February 23, 2009, https://exhibitions.lib.udel.edu/kaufman/home/22-months/financial-system-reform/financial-fraud/prosecuting-wall-street-fraud/.

135. For fiscal 2011, Congress authorized $150 million but appropriated barely $20 million. DOJ, Office of the Inspector General, Audit Division, "Audit of the Department of Justice's Efforts to Address Mortgage Fraud," March 2014, https://oig.justice.gov/reports/2014/a1412.pdf, 4; and Connaughton, *Payoff*, 35–36.

136. Glenn Fine, Inspector General, "Memorandum for the Attorney General," November 13, 2009, https://oig.justice.gov/sites/default/files/reports/2009.pdf.

137. Financial crime did not make the list between 2000 and 2008. In 2010, financial crime was number 7. It was number 8 in 2011 and 2012, and it was not on the list in 2013. DOJ, Inspector General, "Top Management and Performance Challenges Facing the Department of Justice," various years, https://oig.justice.gov/reports (accessed February 15, 2025).

138. DOJ, "Attorney General Eric Holder Speaks at the Financial Fraud Enforcement Task Force Press Conference," press release, November 17, 2009, https://www.justice.gov/opa /speech/attorney-general-eric-holder-speaks-financial-fraud-enforcement-task-force-press; and "Two Financial Crises Compared: The Savings and Loan Debacle and the Mortgage Mess," *NYT*, April 13, 2011, https://archive.nytimes.com/www.nytimes.com/interactive/2011/04/14 /business/20110414-prosecute.html.

139. Breslow, "Ted Kaufman"; and Eisinger, *Chickenshit Club*, 175.

140. Jesse Eisinger, "Why Only One Top Banker Went to Jail for the Financial Crisis," *New York Times Magazine*, April 30, 2014, https://www.nytimes.com/2014/05/04/magazine/only -one-top-banker-jail-financial-crisis.html.

141. Quoted in Eisinger.

142. Gregg Barak, *Theft of a Nation: Wall Street Looting and Federal Regulatory Colluding* (Lanham, MD: Rowman and Littlefield, 2012), 14.

143. For example, at a meeting in late 2009, some senators pressed Lanny Breuer on why the DOJ was not drilling down into investigating the financial crisis cases, as Holder had promised months earlier. The head of DOJ's criminal division dodged the issue, pleading that he was still struggling to get laptops for his prosecutors. Connaughton, *Payoff*, 69–71.

144. David Heath, "Too Big to Jail? Executives Unscathed as Regulators Let Banks Report Criminal Fraud," *HuffPost*, July 3, 2010, updated December 7, 2017, https://www.huffpost.com /entry/too-big-to-jail-executive_n_561961.

145. William K. Black, *The Best Way to Rob a Bank Is to Own One: How Corporate Executives and Politicians Looted the S&L Industry*, updated ed. (Austin: University of Texas Press, 2013), 285; and Michael Anderson, "A Retrospective on the Opening of the Enron Case 15 Years Later," LinkedIn, December 28, 2016, https://www.linkedin.com/pulse/retrospective-opening-enron -case-15-years-later-anderson-mba-cfe/. For more on the S&L and Enron cases, see chaps 6 and 7.

146. Jason M. Breslow, "Lanny Breuer: Financial Fraud Has Not Gone Unpunished," *Frontline*, PBS, January 22, 2013, https://www.pbs.org/wgbh/frontline/article/lanny-breuer-financial -fraud-has-not-gone-unpunished/?mod=article_inline.

147. Breslow; and Pam Martens and Russ Martens, "FOIA Response on Citigroup Justice Department Referrals: DOJ Draws a Dark Curtain Around Its Actions," Wall Street on Parade, November 17, 2017, https://wallstreetonparade.com/2017/11/foia-response-on-citigroup -justice-department-referrals-doj-draws-a-dark-curtain-around-its-actions/.

148. Connaughton, *Payoff*, 82–83.

149. Eisinger, *Chickenshit Club*, 177.

150. Quoted in Eisinger, 177.

151. Eisinger, "Why Only One Top Banker Went to Jail."

152. Kathy Ruemmler, principal associate deputy attorney, quoted in Eisinger, *Chickenshit Club*, 182.

153. Eisinger, 181. See also Frank James, "Bear Stearns Prosecution Backfired with Jurors," NPR, November 11, 2009, https://www.npr.org/sections/thetwo-way/2009/11/bear_stearns _prosecution_backf.html.

154. Christian Plumb, "U.S. Drops Criminal Probe of AIG Executives," Reuters, May 22, 2010, https://www.reuters.com/article/us-aig-doj-idUSTRE64L09W20100523. See also Eis-inger, *Chickenshit Club*, chaps. 6, 8, and 14.

155. Mozilo settled a separate SEC case in 2010 for $67.5 million without admitting or deny-ing the allegations against him. In 2016, the Justice Department dropped its civil fraud case against Mozilo. Jason M. Breslow, "As Deadline Looms for Financial Crisis Cases, Prosecutors Weigh Their Options," *Frontline*, PBS, January 22, 2013, https://www.pbs.org/wgbh/frontline /article/as-deadlines-loom-for-financial-crisis-cases-prosecutors-weigh-their-options/.

156. Eisinger, *Chickenshit Club*, 166–67; see also chap. 14.

157. Eisinger, 177.

158. Richard L. Cassin, "Och-Ziff Takes Fourth Spot on Our New Top Ten List," October 4, 2016, https://fcpablog.com/2016/10/04/och-ziff-takes-fourth-spot-on-our-new-top-ten-list/.

159. Eisinger, *Chickenshit Club*, 349.

160. For more on the Enron scandal, see chap. 7.

161. Charlie Savage, "Accused 9/11 Mastermind to Face Civilian Trial in NY," *NYT*, November 13, 2009, https://www.nytimes.com/2009/11/14/us/14terror.html; and Michael Muskal, "Obama Administration Does About Face on 9/11 Trials," *LAT*, April 4, 2011, https://www.latimes.com/archives/la-xpm-2011-apr-04-la-pn-terror-military-trial-20110405-story.html.

162. Eisinger, *Chickenshit Club*, 230–31; and "This Man Is Busting Wall St.," *Time*, February 13, 2012, https://content.time.com/time/covers/0,16641,20120213,00.html. On insider trading by members of Congress, see David Dayen, "Sen. Jeff Merkley Wants to Stop Congress Members from Insider Trading by Banning Them from Owning Stocks," *Intercept*, December 17, 2018, https://theintercept.com/2018/12/17/jeff-merkley-james-inhofe-ban-stock-trading/; and Kate Kelly, Adam Playford, and Alicia Parlapiano, "Stock Trades Reported by Nearly a Fifth of Congress Show Possible Conflicts," *NYT*, September 13, 2022, https://www.nytimes.com/interactive/2022/09/13/us/politics/congress-stock-trading-investigation.html.

163. Eric Lichtblau, "Mukasey Declines to Create a U.S. Task Force to Investigate Mortgage Fraud," *NYT*, June 6, 2008, https://www.nytimes.com/2008/06/06/business/06justice.html.

164. Eisinger, *Chickenshit Club*, 320.

165. Ruth Wilson Gilmore, *Golden Gulag, Prisons, Surplus, Crisis, and Opposition in Globalizing California* (Berkeley: University of California Press, 2007), 181–220.

166. Martin Smith in "The Untouchables," *Frontline*, PBS, transcript, May 21, 2013, https://www.pbs.org/wgbh/frontline/documentary/untouchables/transcript/.

167. Quoted in Jason M. Breslow, "Watchdog Calls Out DOJ for Mortgage Fraud Response," *Frontline*, PBS, March 13, 2014, https://www.pbs.org/wgbh/frontline/article/watchdog-calls-out-doj-for-mortgage-fraud-response/. See also *Frontline*, "Untouchables."

168. "Lanny Breuer Returns to Covington & Burling," *BLT: The Blog of Legal Times*, March 28, 2013, https://legaltimes.typepad.com/blt/2013/03/lanny-breuer-returns-to-covington-burling-in-new-leadership-role.html.

169. Senator Sherrod Brown and Senator Charles E. Grassley, letter to Attorney General Eric Holder, January 29, 2013, https://www.brown.senate.gov/newsroom/press/release/sens-brown-grassley-press-justice-department-on-too-big-to-jail.

170. "Lanny Breuer Returns to Covington and Burling."

171. Pam Martens, "Why Did the Justice Department Kill the Madoff Subpoena Against JP Morgan?," Wall Street on Parade, December 31, 2013, https://wallstreetonparade.com/2013/12/why-did-the-justice-department-kill-the-madoff-subpoena-against-jpmorgan/.

172. Jason J. Metrick, special agent in charge (acting), US Department of the Treasury, "JPMorgan Chase Bank, N.A.," memo, October 8, 2013, https://www.governmentattic.org/10docs/TreasuryOIG-OCCinvs_2012-2013.pdf; and David Cay Johnston, "JP Morgan Doesn't Want to Talk About Bernie Madoff," *Newsweek*, December 23, 2013, https://www.newsweek.com/jpmorgan-doesnt-want-talk-about-bernie-madoff-225067. See also Richard Behar, *Madoff: The Final Word* (New York: Avid Reader / Simon and Schuster, 2024).

173. DOJ, Office of the Inspector General, Audit Division, "Audit of the Department of Justice's Efforts to Address Mortgage Fraud," March 2014, https://oig.justice.gov/reports/2014/a1412.pdf, i–iii.

174. Quoted in John Hudson, "FBI Drops Law Enforcement as 'Primary' Mission," *Foreign Policy*, January 5, 2014, https://foreignpolicy.com/2014/01/05/fbi-drops-law-enforcement-as-primary-mission/.

175. FCIC, *Financial Crisis Inquiry Report*, 169.

176. FCIC, 187.

177. Morgenson and Story, "In Financial Crisis, No Prosecutions."

178. Eisinger, *Chickenshit Club*, 295.

179. Reuters, "Trustee Suit Says Citigroup Ignored Signs of Fraud in Madoff Scheme," *NYT*, February 22, 2011, https://www.nytimes.com/2011/02/23/business/23madoff.html.

180. SEC, Office of Investigations, *Investigation of Failure of the SEC to Uncover Bernard Madoff's Ponzi Scheme—Public Version*, 2009, https://www.sec.gov/news/studies/2009/oig -509.pdf.

181. John Coffee Jr., "The Regulatory Sine Curve," in *After the Crash: Financial Crises and Regulatory Responses*, ed. Sharyn O'Halloran and Thomas Groll (New York: Columbia University Press, 2019), 285.

182. Jed S. Rakoff, "The Financial Crisis: Why Have No High-Level Executives Been Prosecuted?," *NYRB*, January 9, 2014, 6.

183. Edward Wyatt, "Promises Made, and Remade, by Firms in S.E.C. Fraud Cases," *NYT*, November 7, 2011, https://www.nytimes.com/2011/11/08/business/in-sec-fraud-cases-banks -make-and-break-promises.html. The *New York Times* investigation was limited to SEC securities fraud cases. It did not include "any criminal cases, private lawsuits by victims, cases filed by state attorneys general, or any cases of bribery, money laundering, tax evasion, or illegal asset concealment, all areas in which the banks have numerous and major violations." Ferguson, *Predator Nation*, 162.

184. Quoted in Wyatt, "Promises Made, and Remade."

185. Quoted in Kevin G. Salwen and Laurie P. Cohen, "SEC Under Breeden Takes a Harder Line on Securities Crime," *WSJ*, May 10, 1990, https://www.proquest.com/docview/135518218 /FAC29C0E0E324E54PQ/1?accountid=14707.

186. Rakoff, "Financial Crisis," 6.

187. David Sanger and Charlie Savage, "Trump Takes Aim at Watergate Reform: The Independent Inspector General," *NYT*, May 23, 2020, https://www.nytimes.com/2020/05/22 /us/politics/trump-inspectors-general.html.

188. Barofsky, *Bailout*, 211.

189. Barofsky.

190. See, for example, Barofsky, 115, 119, 145–46, 224.

191. GAO, "Troubled Asset Relief Program: Additional Actions Needed to Better Ensure Integrity, Accountability, and Transparency," December 2, 2008, https://www.gao.gov/products /gao-09-161; Gretchen Morgenson, "TARP's Watchdog: A Tough Act to Follow," *NYT*, March 19, 2011, https://www.nytimes.com/2011/03/20/business/20gret.html; and David Weidner, "The Loneliest Voice in Washington Gets Company," *WSJ*, March 4, 2010, https:// www.wsj.com/articles/SB10001424052748703862704575100284135047828.

192. Barofsky, *Bailout*, 175.

193. Barofsky, 129.

194. Barofsky, 136–37; and US Treasury, Office of the Special Inspector General for TARP, "Congressional Budget Justification and Annual Performance Plan and Report, FY 2023," n.d., https://home.treasury.gov/system/files/266/10.-SIGTARP-FY-2023-CJ.pdf (accessed March 5, 2023).

195. Barofsky, *Bailout*, 129–33, 137, 170.

196. FBI, "Multiple Federal Agencies Form Term Asset-Backed Securities Loan Facility (TALF) Task Force to Deter, Detect, and Investigate Any Instances of Fraud and Abuse," press release, March 11, 2009, https://archives.fbi.gov/archives/news/pressrel/press-releases /multiple-federal-agencies-form-term-asset-backed-securities-loan-facility-talf-task-force-to -deter-detect-and-investigate-any-instances-of-fraud-and-abuse.

197. Barofsky, *Bailout*, 107.

198. Barofsky, 210.

199. Neil Barofsky, prepared testimony, US House, Committee on Oversight and Government Reform, Subcommittee on TARP, Financial Services, and Bailouts of Public and Private Programs, "Has Dodd Frank Ended Too Big to Fail?," March 30, 2011, https://oversight.house .gov/wp-content/uploads/2012/01/Barofsky_Testimony_3-30-11.pdf, 1.

200. Deborah Solomon and Liz Rappaport, "Mr. Barofsky, the TARP Cop, Gets into Role as Street Tough," WSJ, March 6, 2009, C1, https://www.wsj.com/articles/SB123629998582 046773.

201. Barofsky, Bailout, 61.

202. Suskind, Confidence Men, 4–5. See also Barofsky, Bailout, 205–7.

203. Suskind, Confidence Men, 4–5, 81, 312, 344–45.

204. Senator Chuck Grassley, "TARP Oversight Reveals Significant Program Shortcomings," US Senate Committee on Finance, July 21, 2010, https://www.finance.senate.gov/ranking -members-news/grassley-tarp-oversight-reveals-significant-program-shortcomings; and Barofsky, Bailout, 145–46.

205. For a transcript of the speech, see "Obama on 'Renewing the Economy,'" NYT, March 27, 2008, https://www.nytimes.com/2008/03/27/us/politics/27text-obama.html.

206. "Remarks by the President on Wall Street Reform," April 22, 2010, Obama White House Archives, https://obamawhitehouse.archives.gov/the-press-office/remarks-president-wall -street-reform.

207. The report concluded that Lehman had concealed $50 billion in toxic assets and characterized the firm's financial statements as "materially misleading." It also accused Lehman's executives of engaging in "actionable balance sheet manipulation." No law enforcement or regulatory agency ended up bringing any charges against Lehman or any Lehman executive. Quoted in Ben Protess and Susanne Craig, "Inside the End of the U.S. Bid to Punish Lehman Executives," NYT, September 8, 2013, https://archive.nytimes.com/dealbook.nytimes.com/2013/09 /08/inside-the-end-of-the-u-s-bid-to-punish-lehman-executives/. See also Michael de la Merced and Andrew Ross Sorkin, "Report Details How Lehman Hid Its Woes," NYT, March 11, 2010, https://www.nytimes.com/2010/03/12/business/12lehman.html.

208. US Senate, Committee on Homeland Security and Governmental Affairs, Permanent Subcommittee on Investigations, Wall Street and the Financial Crisis: Anatomy of a Financial Collapse, April 13, 2011, https://www.hsgac.senate.gov//imo/media/doc/Financial_Crisis /FinancialCrisisReport.pdf, 4–5. See also Sewell Chan, "U.S. Faults Regulators over a Bank," NYT, April 11, 2010, https://www.nytimes.com/2010/04/12/business/12wamu.html.

209. Eric Thorson, testimony, US Senate, Homeland Security and Government Affairs Subcommittee, April 16, 2010, https://www.c-span.org/video/?293040-1/2008-financial-crisis -banking-regulators-panel-1#!.

210. SEC, "SEC Charges Goldman Sachs with Fraud in Structuring and Marketing of CDO Tied to Subprime Mortgages," press release, April 16, 2010, https://www.sec.gov/news/press /2010/2010-59.htm.

211. Matt Taibbi, "The People vs. Goldman Sachs," Rolling Stone, May 11, 2011, https://www .rollingstone.com/politics/politics-news/the-people-vs-goldman-sachs-245191/.

212. Louise Story, "Panel's Blunt Questions Put Goldman on the Defensive," NYT, April 27, 2010, https://www.nytimes.com/2010/04/28/business/28goldman.html.

213. This account of Goldman and the Abacus deal, including direct quotes, is based on Jesse Eisinger, "Why the S.E.C. Didn't Hit Goldman Sachs Harder," NY, April 21, 2016, https://www .newyorker.com/business/currency/why-the-s-e-c-didnt-hit-goldman-sachs-harder.

214. Eisinger, Chickenshit Club, 267.

215. Gretchen Morgenson and Louise Story, "Naming Culprits in the Financial Crisis," NYT, April 13, 2011, https://www.nytimes.com/2011/04/14/business/14crisis.html; and Carrick

Mollenkamp and Liz Rappaport, "Senate Report Lays Bare Mortgage Mess," *WSJ*, April 14, 2011, https://www.wsj.com/articles/SB10001424052748703730104576261350208808130.

216. Rakoff, "Financial Crisis," 4.

217. Senator Elizabeth Warren, letter to Michael E. Horowitz, DOJ inspector general, September 15, 2016, https://www.warren.senate.gov/files/documents/2016-9-15_Referral_DOJ_IG_letter.pdf, 3–13.

218. David Dayen, "Elizabeth Warren Asks Newly Chatty FBI Director to Explain Why DOJ Didn't Prosecute Banksters," *Intercept*, September 15, 2016, https://theintercept.com/2016/09/15/elizabeth-warren-asks-newly-chatty-fbi-director-to-explain-why-doj-didnt-prosecute-banksters/.

219. This analysis and summary of the criminal referrals is based on Warren letter to Horowitz, which includes full citations for the relevant FCIC documents. The tally for individuals and corporations is likely higher because all the identifying and background information in one of the eleven referrals was redacted.

220. Warren letter to Horowitz, 3–13.

221. Quoted in Stephen Gandel, "Robert Rubin Was Targeted for DOJ Investigation by Financial Crisis Commission," *Fortune*, March 13, 2016, https://fortune.com/2016/03/13/robert-rubin-financial-crisis-commission-justice-department/.

222. Elizabeth Warren, "On 8th Anniversary of Lehman Bankruptcy, Senator Warren Calls for IG Review of DOJ's Failed Response to Financial Crisis Inquiry Commission Referrals," press release, September 15, 2016, https://www.warren.senate.gov/oversight/letters/on-8th-anniversary-of-lehman-bankruptcy-senator-warren-calls-for-ig-review-of-doj-and-039s-failed-response-to-financial-crisis-inquiry-commission-referrals.

223. One individual (former Citigroup CFO Gary Crittenden) was fined a measly $100,000 to settle a civil case brought by the SEC. A second (Daniel Mudd, former CEO of Fannie Mae) reached a civil settlement with the SEC in which he did not pay a personal fine or admit any wrongdoing. Warren letter to Horowitz, 15, table 1.

224. Some of the remaining nine firms were investigated or reached civil settlements, but none of them faced any criminal consequences for the offenses alleged by the FCIC. Warren letter to Horowitz, 1–2 and 14.

225. Warren letter to Horowitz, 1–2, 14, 18, table 2.

226. Senator Elizabeth Warren, letter to James Comey, Director of the FBI, September 15, 2016, Wall Street on Parade, September 2016, http://wallstreetonparade.com/wp-content/uploads/2016/09/Elizabeth-Warren-Letter-to-FBI-Director-James-Comey-September-15-2016.pdf.

227. Chris Isidore, "Elizabeth Warren Wants Feds to Answer for Lack of Wall Street Prosecutions," CNN, September 15, 2016, https://money.cnn.com/2016/09/15/news/economy/elizabeth-warren-fbi-wall-street/index.html; and Laura Wagner, "FBI Head Under Fire for Clinton Email Scrutiny Days Before Election," NPR, October 29, 2016, https://www.npr.org/sections/thetwo-way/2016/10/29/499868601/fbi-head-under-fire-for-restarting-clinton-email-investigation-days-before-elect.

228. The DOJ would not even confirm or deny the existence of any records on these three Citigroup executives. Martens and Martens, "FOIA Response."

229. The SEC had conducted a sham investigation in which the agency did not even take depositions from most of the executives involved. In February 2010, Judge Jed Rakoff approved a revised settlement of $150 million that he characterized as "half-baked justice at best." Eisinger, *Chickenshit Club*, 203–4, 215–26.

230. Clemens was acquitted in 2012 on all charges of lying to Congress after a ten-week trial. Bonds was found guilty of obstruction of justice, but his conviction was later overturned on appeal. The DOJ dropped all charges in 2015. Michael Schmidt, "Clemens Lied About Doping, Indictment Charges," *NYT*, August 19, 2010, https://www.nytimes.com/2010/08/20/sports

/baseball/20clemens.html; "Roger Clemens Found Not Guilty," ESPN, June 18, 2012, https:/ /www.espn.com/mlb/story/_/id/8068819/roger-clemens-found-not-guilty-all-six-counts -perjury-trial; and Rob Harms, "Justice Department Drops Case Against Barry Bonds," *NYT*, July 21, 2015, https://www.nytimes.com/2015/07/22/sports/baseball/justice-department -drops-case-against-barry-bonds.html.

231. Ferguson, *Predator Nation*, 197.

232. Louise Story, "Panel's Blunt Questions Put Goldman on the Defensive," *NYT*, April 27, 2010, https://www.nytimes.com/2010/04/28/business/28goldman.html.

233. Morgenson and Story, "Naming Culprits in the Financial Crisis." See also Ferguson, *Predator Nation*, 144–49 and 197.

234. Taibbi, "People vs. Goldman Sachs"; Bloomberg, "Goldman Sachs Misled Clients, Law-makers on CDOs, Senate Panel Says," April 13, 2011, https://www.washingtonpost.com/business /economy/goldman-sachs-misled-clients-lawmakers-on-cdos-senate-panel-says/2011/04/13 /AFhEv8ZD_story.html; and Peter J. Henning, "Finding Goldman at Fault in the Crisis," *NYT*, April 18, 2011, https://archive.nytimes.com/dealbook.nytimes.com/2011/04/18/finding -goldman-at-fault-in-the-financial-crisis/.

235. Susan Antilla, "Is There Justice for Goldman Sachs?," CNN, August 16, 2012, https:// www.cnn.com/2012/08/16/opinion/antilla-goldman-justice/index.html.

236. Charles Prince, testimony, FCIC, April 8, 2010, https://fcic-static.law.stanford.edu/cdn _media/fcic-testimony/2010-0408-Prince.pdf; and Robert Rubin, testimony, FCIC, April 8, 2010, https://fcic-static.law.stanford.edu/cdn_media/fcic-testimony/2010-0408-Rubin.pdf. For more on these special purpose financial vehicles, see pp. 211.

237. This account is based on Robert Rubin, interview, FCIC, March 11, 2010, https://fcic -static.law.stanford.edu/NARA.FCIC.2016-03-11/SCREENED%20Interviews/2010-03 -11%20Transcript%20of%20Interview%20with%20Robert%20Rubin%20(condensed%20 format)_1.pdf.

238. "Citibank Loses Billions, CEO Prince Resigns," NPR, November 5, 2007, https://www .npr.org/2007/11/05/15994978/citibank-loses-billions-ceo-prince-resigns.

239. DealBook, "Rubin Is Stepping Down at Citigroup," *NYT*, January 9, 2009, https:// archive.nytimes.com/dealbook.nytimes.com/2009/01/09/rubin-plans-to-step-down-at -citigroup/.

240. Rubin, interview, FCIC, 20, 65.

241. Pam Martens and Russ Martens, "Robert Rubin Exorcises Citigroup from His Career in Today's NYT Op Ed," Wall Street on Parade, May 1, 2018, https://wallstreetonparade.com /2018/05/robert-rubin-exorcises-citigroup-from-his-career-in-todays-nyt-oped/.

242. Rubin, interview, FCIC, 9.

243. Richard Bowen, testimony before FCIC, April 7, 2010, https://www.sec.gov/news /studies/2009/oig-509.pdf, 2.

244. Dick Bowen, "URGENT—READ IMMEDIATELY—FINANCIAL ISSUES," email to Robert Rubin et al., November 3, 2007, https://fcic-static.law.stanford.edu/cdn_media/fcic -docs/2007-11-03_Citi_Email_from_Dick_Bowen_to_Robert_Rubin_and_David _Bushnell_Re_concerns_financial_issues.pdf.

245. Prince told the FCIC at the time: "I have no way of responding without seeing the document and understanding the context of it." Quoted in Ferguson, *Predator Nation*, 198.

246. Devin Dwyer, "Obama: Occupy Wall Street 'Not That Different' from Tea Party Pro-tests," ABC News, October 18, 2011, https://abcnews.go.com/blogs/politics/2011/10/obama -occupy-wall-street-not-that-different-from-tea-party-protests.

247. The White House press secretary was dispatched to say that municipalities should de-cide how much force to use in breaking up the protests. John Cassidy, "Obama and Zuccotti Park: What He Didn't Say," *NY*, November 17, 2011, https://www.newyorker.com/news/john

-cassidy/obama-and-zuccotti-park-what-he-didnt-say. For more on police crackdowns on Occupy Wall Street and other protests, see pp. 117–20.

248. Jeff Zeleny and Megan Thee-Brenan, "New Poll Finds a Deep Distrust of Government," *NYT*, October 25, 2011, https://www.nytimes.com/2011/10/26/us/politics/poll-finds-anxiety-on-the-economy-fuels-volatility-in-the-2012-race.html.

249. Barak, *Theft of a Nation*, 14.

250. Breslow, "Lanny Breuer."

251. Breslow, "As Deadline Looms."

252. Daniel C. Richman, "Corporate Headhunting," *Harvard Law and Policy Review* 8, no. 2 (Summer 2014): 266.

253. Alvin Hellerstein, quoted in Eisinger, "Why Only One Top Banker Went to Jail."

254. Jed S. Rakoff, *Why the Innocent Plead Guilty and the Guilty Go Free and Other Paradoxes of Our Broken Legal System* (New York: Farrar, Straus and Giroux, 2021), 88–89.

255. In November 2011, Bloomberg reported that the previous estimates of $2–3 trillion in government assistance were widely off the mark, and that the actual figure, including loans, loan guarantees, purchases of securities, and other assistance, totaled an astounding $7.8 trillion. Phil Kuntz and Bob Ivry, "Fed's Once Secret Data Compiled by Bloomberg Released to Public," Bloomberg, December 23, 2011, https://www.bloomberg.com/news/articles/2011-12-23/fed-s-once-secret-data-compiled-by-bloomberg-released-to-public?leadSource=uverify%20wall.

256. Ezra Ross and Martin Pritikin, "The Collection Gap: Underenforcement of Corporate and White-Collar Fines and Penalties," *Yale Law and Policy Review* 29, no. 2 (Spring 2011): 453–526.

257. Elizabeth Warren, *A Fighting Chance* (New York: Picador, 2015), 284.

258. DOJ, "Justice Department, Federal and State Partners Secure Record $13 Billion Global Settlement with JPMorgan for Misleading Investors About Securities Containing Toxic Mortgages," press release, November 19, 2013, https://www.justice.gov/opa/pr/justice-department-federal-and-state-partners-secure-record-13-billion-global-settlement; and Jason M. Breslow, "How $80 Billion in Corporate Fines Can Become $48 Billion in Tax Breaks," *Frontline*, PBS, December 4, 2015, https://www.pbs.org/wgbh/frontline/article/how-80-billion-in-coporate-fines-can-become-48-billion-in-tax-breaks/.

259. Eric Levitz, "Goldman Sachs Admits It Defrauded Investors, Receives $5 Billion Fine—but Will Pay Much Less Than That," *NYM*, April 12, 2016, https://nymag.com/intelligencer/2016/04/goldman-sachs-admits-it-defrauded-investors.html.

260. DOJ, "Goldman Sachs Agrees to Pay More than $5 Billion in Connection with Its Sale of Residential Mortgage Backed Securities," press release, April 11, 2016, https://www.justice.gov/opa/pr/goldman-sachs-agrees-pay-more-5-billion-connection-its-sale-residential-mortgage-backed.

261. Jason M. Breslow, "How Bank of America's $16.65 Billion Settlement Compares," *Frontline*, PBS, August 21, 2014, https://www.pbs.org/wgbh/frontline/article/how-bank-of-americas-16-65-billion-settlement-compares/.

262. Breslow.

263. An analysis by the United States Public Interest Group of the ten largest settlements by government regulators between 2012 and 2015 found that at least $48 billion of the nearly $80 billion in penalties qualified for tax deductions. Breslow, "How $80 Billion in Corporate Fines Can Become $48 Billion in Tax Breaks."

264. Alexes Harris, Heather Evans, and Katherine Beckett, "Drawing Blood from Stones: Legal Debt and Social Inequality in the Contemporary United States," *American Journal of Sociology* 115, no. 6 (2010): 1769; and Alexes Harris, *A Pound of Flesh: Monetary Sanctions as a Punishment for the Poor* (New York: Russell Sage Foundation, 2016), 5.

265. Harris, *Pound of Flesh*.

266. Judges have creatively circumvented US Supreme Court decisions that have banned or restricted the imprisonment of people with outstanding debts. They have ruled that the individuals were being sent to prison or jail for contempt of court for failing to comply with the court order to pay their fines and fees—not because they had legal debts. In some cases, people are serving more time in jail for failing to pay court costs than they served in their original sentence. Gary Hunter, "Washington Jail a Modern Debtor's Prison," *PLN*, April 2010, 8–9.

267. Harris, *Pound of Flesh*, 3.

268. Lindsey D. Simon, "Bankruptcy Grifters," *YLJ* 131, no. 4 (February 2022): 1062–384; and William S. Laufer, *Corporate Bodies and Guilty Minds: The Failure of Corporate Criminal Liability* (Chicago: University of Chicago Press, 2006), chaps. 4–6. For more on how corporations have been using bankruptcy laws to skirt financial penalties in civil and other legal judgments, especially in the case of the opioid crisis, see pp. 309 and 311–13.

269. Adam Liptak, "Justices Limit Use of 'Honest Services' Law Against Fraud," *NYT*, June 24, 2010, https://www.nytimes.com/2010/06/25/us/25scotus.html.

270. See *United States v. Sun-Diamond Growers of California*, 526 U.S. 398 (1999); *Skilling v. United States*, 561 U.S. 358 (2010); *Citizens United v. FEC*, 558 U.S. 310 (2010); *McCutcheon v. FEC*, 572 U.S. 185 (2014); and *McDonnell v. United States*, 579 U.S. 550 (2016).

271. Randall D. Eliason, "The Supreme Court Has a Corruption Problem," *NYT*, May 19, 2023, A23. The expensive gifts that Harlan Crow, an archly conservative megadonor to the Republican Party, bestowed on Justice Clarence Thomas—including numerous luxury trips, private school tuition for his grandnephew, and sweetheart deals for real estate and a luxurious recreational vehicle—created a PR headache for the US Supreme Court when the gifts became public in 2023. But, explains Eliason, the court's own rulings suggest that the justices do not consider accepting gifts from a powerful individual with interests before the court to constitute corruption as long as there is no explicit quid pro quo, and there was no such exchange between the justice and Crow.

272. Eisinger, *Chickenshit Club*, 185.

273. Eisinger, 181–84.

274. The Supreme Court sided with the DOJ and SEC in *Stoneridge Investment Partners, LLC v. Scientific-Atlanta, Inc.*, a 2008 decision that raised the bar for suing companies in certain fraud cases and hemmed in prosecutors seeking to pursue civil or criminal charges in such cases. Eisinger, *Chickenshit Club*, 254–55.

275. Eric Holder, testimony, US Senate Judiciary Committee, March 6, 2013, https://www.c-span.org/video/?311311-1/justice-department-oversight#.

276. Mark Gongloff, "Eric Holder: Actually I Meant to Say No Banks Are Too Big to Jail," *HuffPost*, May 15, 2013, https://www.huffpost.com/entry/eric-holder-too-big-to-jail_n_3280694.

277. Hudson, "FBI Drops Law Enforcement."

278. Luigi Zingales, "Does Finance Benefit Society?," Working Paper No. 20894 (National Bureau of Economic Research, January 2015), 18.

279. Ferguson, *Predator Nation*, 176–78.

280. Quoted in Brandon L. Garrett, "The Corporate Criminal as Scapegoat," *Virginia Law Review* 101, no. 7 (November 2015): 1817; see also Reuters, "U.S. Judge Calls Barclays Settlement Sweetheart Deal," August 17, 2010, https://www.reuters.com/article/barclays-justice/us-judge-calls-barclays-settlement-sweetheart-deal-idUSWAT01460420100817.

281. Ferguson, *Predator Nation*, 178–79.

282. Carrick Mollenkamp, "HSBC Became Bank to Drug Cartels, Pays Big for Lapses," Reuters, December 11, 2012, https://www.reuters.com/article/business/hsbc-became-bank-to-drug-cartels-pays-big-for-lapses-idUSBRE8BA05N/.

283. Ben Protess and Jessica Silver-Greenberg, "HSBC to Pay $1.92 Billion to Settle Charges of Money Laundering," *NYT*, December 10, 2012, https://archive.nytimes.com/dealbook .nytimes.com/2012/12/10/hsbc-said-to-near-1-9-billion-settlement-over-money-laundering/ . See also Eisinger, *Chickenshit Club*, 283–85.

284. Mark Gongloff, "Obama Administration Essentially Admits That Some Banks Are Too Big to Jail, Which Is Troubling," *HuffPost*, December 11, 2012, updated December 12, 2012, https://www.huffpost.com/entry/hsbc-too-big-to-jail_n_2279439.

285. Quoted in Gongloff.

286. Quoted in Terry Friedman, "Attorney General Eric Holder Blasted for HSBC Settlement," CNN, December 13, 2012, https://www.cnn.com/2012/12/13/politics/holder-hsbc /index.html.

287. Dylan Tokar, "The Department of Justice Is Turning Back the Clock on Corporate Accountability," *Nation*, March 6, 2019, https://www.thenation.com/article/archive/financial -crisis-justice-department-corporate-prosecutions-yates-memo/.

288. DealBook, "Timeline: The London Whale's Wake," *NYT*, March 27, 2013, https:// archive.nytimes.com/www.nytimes.com/interactive/2013/03/27/business/dealbook /20130327-jpmorgan-timeline.html#/#time247_7298; and Chris Isidore and James O'Toole, "JPMorgan Fined $920 Million in 'London Whale' Trading Loss," CNN, September 19, 2013, https://money.cnn.com/2013/09/19/investing/jpmorgan-london-whale-fine/.

289. Isidore and O'Toole, "JPMorgan Fined."

290. Wells Fargo's offenses included signing up customers for millions of fake accounts; billing clients for unwanted insurance and warranties; falsifying records to raise the fees for mortgage applicants; secretly making changes to mortgage terms for homeowners in bankruptcy; overcharging foreign exchange clients to reap bonuses; improperly recording customer payments on home and auto loans; wrongfully repossessing cars and homes; and charging overdraft fees even when people had sufficient money in their accounts. David Dayen, "The Dirty Secret Behind Warren Buffett's Billions," *Nation*, February 18, 2018, https://www.thenation .com/article/archive/special-investigation-the-dirty-secret-behind-warren-buffetts-billions/; and Emily Flitter, "Wells Fargo to Pay $3.7 Billion over Banking Violations," *NYT*, December 20, 2022, https://www.nytimes.com/2022/12/20/business/wells-fargo-consumer-loans-fine.html.

291. Emily Flitter, "Price of Wells Fargo's Fake Account Scandal Grows by $3 Billion," *NYT*, February 21, 2020, https://www.nytimes.com/2020/02/21/business/wells-fargo-settlement. html.

292. This account of Pfizer's DPAs is based on Jed S. Rakoff, "Justice Deferred Is Justice Denied," *NYRB*, February 19, 2015, 10.

293. Sally Yates, "Individual Accountability for Corporate Wrongdoing," DOJ, September 9, 2015, https://www.justice.gov/archives/dag/file/769036/download.

294. Christopher Modlish, "The Yates Memo: DOJ Public Relations Move or Meaningful Reform That Will End Impunity for Corporate Criminals?," *Boston College Law Review* 58, no. 2 (April 3, 2017): 743–74; Tokar, "Department of Justice Is Turning Back the Clock"; and Brandon L. Garrett, "How Biden Should Prosecute Corporate Crime," *TAP*, January/February 2021, 59–60.

295. Eisinger, *Chickenshit Club*, 321–23.

296. Russell Mokhiber, "Critics Rip GM Deferred Prosecution Agreement in Engine Switch Case," *Common Dreams*, September 17, 2015, https://www.commondreams.org/views/2015/09 /17/critics-rip-gm-deferred-prosecution-agreement-engine-switch-case.

297. DOJ, "For-Profit College Company to Pay $95.5 Million to Settle Claims of Illegal Recruiting, Consumer Fraud and Other Violations," press release, November 16, 2015, https://www .justice.gov/opa/pr/profit-college-company-pay-955-million-settle-claims-illegal-recruiting -consumer-fraud-and; and Senators Elizabeth Warren, Richard Blumenthal, and Richard J.

Durbin, letter to Attorney General Loretta Lynch and Education Secretary Arne Duncan, November 30, 2015, https://www.warren.senate.gov/files/documents/2015-11-30_Letter_to_Depts_of_Edu_and_Justice_re_EDMC_Settlement.pdf.

298. Warren et al., letter to Lynch and Duncan.

299. "White Collar Crime Prosecutions for December 2016," TRAC Reports, Syracuse University, January 20, 2017, https://trac.syr.edu/tracreports/bulletins/white_collar_crime/monthlydec16/fil/; and "Federal White Collar Crime Prosecutions for 2021 Continue Long Term Decline," TRAC Reports, Syracuse University, August 9, 2021, https://trac.syr.edu/tracreports/crim/655/.

300. Quoted in Suskind, *Confidence Men*, 288.

301. Eric Holder, "Preventing and Combating Financial Fraud," prepared remarks, Columbia University Law School, February 23, 2012, https://www.justice.gov/opa/speech/attorney-general-eric-holder-speaks-columbia-university-law-school-preventing-and; and Reuters, "Financial Crises Caused by 'Stupidity and Greed': Geithner," April 25, 2012, https://www.reuters.com/article/us-usa-economy-geithner/financial-crises-caused-by-stupidity-and-greed-geithner-idUSBRE83P01P20120426.

302. Quoted in Peter Baker, "The White House Looks for Work," *NYT*, January 19, 2011, https://www.nytimes.com/2011/01/23/magazine/23Economy-t.html.

9. "The Banks Own This Place": Regulation and Saving Private Capital under Obama, Trump, and Biden

1. As quoted in Raoul Peck, "James Baldwin Was Right All Along," *Atlantic*, July 20, 2020, https://www.theatlantic.com/culture/archive/2020/07/raoul-peck-james-baldwin-i-am-not-your-negro/613708/.

2. Tim Alberta, "Pew Poll: Rage Against Government," *Politico*, April 19, 2010, https://www.politico.com/story/2010/04/pew-poll-rage-against-government-036007; and Jeff Connaughton, *The Payoff: Why Wall Street Always Wins* (Westport, CT: Prospecta, 2012), 135.

3. Barack Obama, "News Conference by the President," October 6, 2011, Obama White House Archives, https://obamawhitehouse.archives.gov/the-press-office/2011/10/06/news-conference-president.

4. Ron Suskind, *Confidence Men: Wall Street, Washington, and the Education of the President* (New York: HarperCollins, 2011), 285, 287, 390.

5. Suskind, 306.

6. Glenn Kessler, "When Did McConnell Say He Wanted to Make Obama a 'One-Term President?,'" *WP*, September 25, 2012, https://www.washingtonpost.com/blogs/fact-checker/post/when-did-mcconnell-say-he-wanted-to-make-obama-a-one-term-president/2012/09/24/79fd5cd8-0696-11e2-afff-d6c7f20a83bf_blog.html.

7. Stephen Skowronek, *Presidential Leadership in Political Time: Reprise and Reappraisal*, 3rd ed. (Lawrence: University Press of Kansas, 2020), especially chap. 6.

8. Nolan McCarty, Keith T. Poole, and Howard Rosenthal, *Political Bubbles: Financial Crises and the Failure of American Democracy* (Princeton, NJ: Princeton University Press, 2013), especially chaps. 8 and 9.

9. Joe Nocera, "Sheila Bair's Bank Shot," *NYT*, July 9, 2011, https://www.nytimes.com/2011/07/10/magazine/sheila-bairs-exit-interview.html; and Suskind, *Confidence Men*, 219.

10. Two years earlier it had been trading in the upper forties per share. Suskind, *Confidence Men*, 189.

11. SEC, Form 8-K, Citigroup Inc., February 27, 2009, http://edgar.secdatabase.com/642/95010309000421/filing-main.htm.

12. Suskind, *Confidence Men*, 234.

13. Suskind, 214–20, 246–49, 285–86, and 306.

14. Neil Barofsky, *Bailout: An Inside Account of How Washington Abandoned Main Street While Rescuing Wall Street* (New York: Free Press, 2012), 176–78, 200–208.

15. Alice Herman, "Striking Autoworkers Remember Broken Promises," *In These Times*, November 2023, 25–33.

16. For more on the failure of regulators, see chap. 8.

17. Barofsky, *Bailout*, 148. This is also a common theme in Suskind, *Confidence Men*.

18. John Heilemann, "Obama Is from Mars, Wall Street Is from Venus," *NYM*, May 21, 2010, https://nymag.com/news/politics/66188/.

19. US House, Committee on Banking and Financial Services, "The Administration's Proposals for Financial Regulatory Reform," September 23, 2009, 111th Cong., 1st Sess., https://financialservices.house.gov/media/file/hearings/111/printed%20hearings/111-76.pdf, 3, 26, 54.

20. Paul Volcker, prepared statement, US House, Committee on Banking and Financial Services, September 24, 2009, https://financialservices.house.gov/calendar/eventsingle.aspx?EventID=231809, 3–4, 6, 10–11. For more on Glass–Steagall, see pp. 185–87.

21. Volcker, prepared statement, 17–18.

22. Jake Bernstein, "Inside the New York Fed: Secret Recordings and a Culture Clash," *ProPublica*, September 26, 2014, https://www.propublica.org/article/carmen-segarras-secret-recordings-from-inside-new-york-fed.

23. Paul Volcker, quoted in "The Only Useful Thing the Banks Have Invented in 20 Years Is the ATM," *NYP*, December 13, 2009, https://nypost.com/2009/12/13/the-only-thing-useful-banks-have-invented-in-20-years-is-the-atm/.

24. Quoted in Suskind, *Confidence Men*, 287.

25. R. Rex Chatterjee, "Dictionaries Fail: The Volcker Rule's Reliance on Definitions Renders It Ineffective and a New Solution Is Needed to Adequately Regulate Proprietary Trading," *International Law and Management Review* 8 (Winter 2011): 34. See also Kimberly D. Krawiec and Guangya Liu, "The Volcker Rule: A Brief Political History," *Capital Markets Law Journal* 10 (2015): 510.

26. Zachery Kouwe, "Wall Street on Track for Record in Profits," *NYT*, November 17, 2009, https://www.nytimes.com/2009/11/18/business/18wall.html.

27. "Poll: Public Shifting Blame for Recession," CNN, November 20, 2009, https://www.cnn.com/2009/POLITICS/11/20/poll.recession/index.html.

28. Between 2006 and 2010, the public's lack of confidence in banks and financial institutions rose from 15 percent to almost 45 percent of respondents. Lane Kenworthy and Lindsay Owens, "Political Attitudes, Public Opinion and the Great Recession," Stanford Center on Poverty and Inequality, October 2012, https://inequality.stanford.edu/sites/default/files/PublicOpinion_fact_sheet.pdf. See also Mark Trumbull, "Ben Bernanke and Fed in Crosshairs of Left and Right," *CSM*, December 3, 2009, https://www.csmonitor.com/USA/Politics/2009/1203/ben-bernanke-and-fed-in-crosshairs-of-left-and-right.

29. Shahien Nasiripour, "Senator to Fed Chair Bernanke: 'You Are the Definition of Moral Hazard,'" *HuffPost*, March 18, 2010, updated May 25, 2011, https://www.huffpost.com/entry/senator-to-fed-chair-bern_n_378673. On Bernanke's inability to break with Greenspan and reckon deeply with the political consequences of the Fed's actions and the financial crisis, even after he was no longer in office, see Jonathan Kirshner, "The Education of Ben Bernanke," *BR*, August 18, 2022, https://www.bostonreview.net/articles/the-education-of-ben-bernanke/.

30. For more on the controversies swirling around the AIG bailouts and bonuses, see chap. 8, "'God's Work' and Executive Compensation."

31. Sewell Chan, "Senate, Weakly, Backs New Term for Bernanke," *NYT*, January 28, 2010, https://www.nytimes.com/2010/01/29/business/economy/29fed.html. Eleven Democrats

and independent Bernie Sanders joined eighteen Republicans in voting against Bernanke's reappointment. AP, "Senate Roll Call on Fed Chief Ben Bernanke," *San Diego Union-Tribune*, January 28, 2010, https://www.sandiegouniontribune.com/2010/01/28/senate-roll-vote-on-fed-chief-ben-bernanke/.

32. Heilemann, "Obama Is from Mars."

33. Quoted in "Transcript: President Barack Obama, Part 2," *60 Minutes*, CBS News, December 9, 2009, https://www.cbsnews.com/news/transcript-president-barack-obama-part-2-13-12-2009/.

34. Frank James, "Obama Flips on Wall St. Pay as Banker Cash Flows to GOP," NPR, February 10, 2010, https://www.npr.org/sections/thetwo-way/2010/02/obama_flips_on_wall_st_pay_as.html.

35. David D. Kirkpatrick, "In a Message to Democrats, Wall St. Sends Cash to G.O.P.," *NYT*, February 7, 2010, https://www.nytimes.com/2010/02/08/us/politics/08lobby.html?sq=obama%20wall%20street%20donations%20republicans&st=cse&scp=1&pagewanted=print.

36. Bill Lucey, "Obama Cooper Union Speech: Reforming Wall Street Is Good for Main Street," *HuffPost*, June 22, 2010, updated May 25, 2011, https://www.huffpost.com/entry/obama-cooper-union-speech_n_548357.

37. In one notable example, Dodd–Frank forbids banking entities from engaging in proprietary trading but grants regulators wide leeway to determine what constitutes "proprietary" trading. Chatterjee, "Dictionaries Fail," 50–55. Financial institutions and their trade groups and law firms together accounted for over 93 percent of all federal agency meetings on the rule. Public interest, labor, research, and advocacy groups and other organizations and individuals accounted for the rest. Kimberly Krawiec, "Don't 'Screw Joe the Plummer' [*sic*]: The Sausage-Making of Financial Reform," *Arizona Law Review* 55, no. 1 (2013): 59. See also Connaughton, *Payoff*, 214 and 215–32; Shahien Nasiripour, "Obama's Cooper Union Speech: President Urges Wall Street Support for Reform," *HuffPost*, June 22, 2010, updated May 25, 2011, https://www.huffpost.com/entry/obama-cooper-union-speech-financial-reform_n_547456; and Kevin Drawbaugh, "White House Recommits to 'Volcker Rule' Bank Trade Ban," Reuters, February 23, 2010, https://www.reuters.com/article/us-financial-regulation/white-house-recommits-to-volcker-rule-bank-trade-ban-idUSTRE61L3UL20100224.

38. "Remarks by the President on Wall Street Reform," April 22, 2010, Obama White House Archives, https://obamawhitehouse.archives.gov/the-press-office/remarks-president-wall-street-reform.

39. For more on Obama's April 2010 Cooper Union speech, see pp. 253–54.

40. Connaughton, *Payoff*, 239.

41. Dodd received more in Wall Street campaign contributions than any other member of the Senate Banking Committee. David Grant, "Chris Dodd: How Much Did Wall Street Give Him?," *CSM*, January 6, 2010, https://www.csmonitor.com/Business/2010/0106/Chris-Dodd-How-much-did-Wall-Street-give-him.

42. Connaughton, *Payoff*, 223, 214–15.

43. "Too big to fail" was a catchall phrase that referred to banks and other financial institutions whose collapse could wreak havoc on the financial sector and the wider economy.

44. See the discussion of the "Safe Banking Act of 2010," also known as the Brown–Kaufman amendment to Dodd–Frank, in Connaughton, *Payoff*, 227–32.

45. "Demos Applauds Introduction of New Banking Integrity Act by Senators Cantwell and McCain," *Demos*, December 16, 2009, https://www.demos.org/press-release/demos-applauds-introduction-new-banking-integrity-act-senators-cantwell-and-mccain.

46. Borys Grochulski and Stephen Slivinski, "Systemic Risk and Regulation and the 'Too Big to Fail' Problem," Federal Reserve Bank of Richmond, July 2009, https://www.richmondfed.org/publications/research/economic_brief/2009/eb_09-07; and Thomas Hoenig, "Keep the

Fed on Main Street," *NYT*, April 17, 2010, https://www.nytimes.com/2010/04/18/opinion/18hoenig.html.

47. Timothy Noah, "Why Conservatives Want to Break Up the Banks, Too," *NR*, March 16, 2013, https://newrepublic.com/article/112609/conservative-plan-break-banks.

48. Connaughton, *Payoff*, 234.

49. DealBook, "Greenspan Calls to Break Up Banks 'Too Big to Fail,'" *NYT*, October 15, 2009, https://archive.nytimes.com/dealbook.nytimes.com/2009/10/15/greenspan-break-up-banks-too-big-to-fail/.

50. Suskind, *Confidence Men*, 429.

51. Quoted in Heilemann, "Obama Is from Mars."

52. For more on financial derivatives, see pp. 188, 210–11, and 242.

53. Quoted in "Frontline Investigates the Roots of the Financial Crisis," *Frontline*, PBS, press release, October 20, 2009, https://www.pbs.org/wgbh/pages/frontline/press/2009/08/the-warning.html.

54. Paul West, "Obama Pick Gensler Grilled at Senate Hearing," *Baltimore Sun*, February 25, 2009, https://www.baltimoresun.com/bs-mtblog-2009-02-obama_pick_gensler_grilled_at-story.html. For more on the demise of Glass–Steagall, see p. 187.

55. Over-the-counter derivatives are private financial contracts that do not trade openly on an exchange, unlike, say, futures contracts for many agricultural commodities that are traded on the Chicago Mercantile Exchange. Derivatives listed on exchanges are more standardized and transparent. Suskind, *Confidence Men*, 298, 328–29, and 397.

56. Suskind, 399–400, 431–32.

57. Connaughton, *Payoff*, 248.

58. The "Restore Integrity to Credit Ratings" amendment would have created a federal board to select which credit rating agency would evaluate a given asset-backed security. Connaughton, *Payoff*, 245–46. For more on these conflicts of interest, see chap. 7, "Grade Inflation."

59. Alice Rivlin and John Soroushian, "Credit Rating Agency Reform Is Incomplete," Brookings Institution, March 6, 2017, https://www.brookings.edu/research/credit-rating-agency-reform-is-incomplete/.

60. SEC, *2015 Summary Report of Commission Staff's Examinations of Each Nationally Recognized Statistical Rating Organization* (Washington, DC: SEC, 2015), 8.

61. Dodd–Frank's centerpiece was the creation of the Financial Stability Oversight Council (FSOC), a supercommittee of ten regulators chaired by the Treasury secretary to determine and implement new rules regarding proprietary trading (the now gutless Volcker Rule); oversee and possibly regulate OTC derivatives; set bank capital requirements; and address the conflicts of interest that vex the credit rating agencies. Barofsky, *Bailout*, 218. See also Baird Webel, *The Dodd–Frank Wall Street Reform and Consumer Protection Act: Background and Summary*, CRS Report 41350, April 21, 2017, https://crsreports.congress.gov/product/pdf/R/R41350.

62. Elizabeth Warren, "Unsafe at Any Rate," *Democracy* 5 (Summer 2007), https://democracyjournal.org/magazine/5/unsafe-at-any-rate/. See also Consumer Federation of America, "One Year After: Progress Report on the Dodd–Frank Wall Street Reform and Consumer Protection Act," 2011, https://consumerfed.org/pdfs/Dodd–Frank-progress-report.pdf, 2.

63. Under Dodd–Frank, a two-thirds majority of the ten-member FSOC has the power to veto regulations promulgated by the CFPB. Consumer Federation of America, "One Year After," 2; and Brenden Soucy, "The Consumer Financial Protection Bureau: The Solution or the Problem," *Florida State University Law Review* 40, no. 3 (2013): 716.

64. Suskind, *Confidence Men*, 4–5.

65. Connaughton, *Payoff*, 232.

66. Suskind, *Confidence Men*, 433.

67. Aaron Lucchetti and Stephen Grocer, "On Street, Pay Vaults to Record Altitude," *WSJ*, February 2, 2011, https://www.wsj.com/articles/SB100014240527487041245045761184218 59347048.

68. In 2010, the poverty rate was 15.1 percent, up from 12.5 percent in 2007. US Census Bureau, "Poverty in the United States: 2021," September 13, 2022, fig. 1, https://www.census.gov /content/dam/Census/library/visualizations/2022/demo/p60-277/figure1.pdf.

69. "PRRI 2014 American Values Survey," Public Religion Research Institute, September 23, 2014, https://www.prri.org/wp-content/uploads/2014/09/AVS-Pre-election-2014-Topline -Final.pdf.

70. The five largest financial institutions controlled $8.6 trillion in assets by late 2010 or the equivalent of 60 percent of GDP. Thomas M. Hoenig, "Too Big to Succeed," *NYT*, December 1, 2010, https://www.nytimes.com/2010/12/02/opinion/02hoenig.html.

71. Barofsky, *Bailout*, 217.

72. Rana Foroohar, *Makers and Takers: The Rise of Finance and the Fall of American Business* (New York: Crown Business, 2016), 14.

73. Connaughton, *Payoff*, 241.

74. Timothy Geithner, "Hearing Before the Congressional Oversight Panel," June 22, 2010, https://www.congress.gov/event/111th-congress/senate-event/LC5209/text?s=1&r=7.

75. Barofsky, *Bailout*, 222–23.

76. This de facto government subsidy was worth an estimated $83 billion a year for the top ten US banks. Bloomberg, "Why Should Taxpayers Give Big Banks $83 Billion a Year?," February 20, 2013, https://www.bloomberg.com/opinion/articles/2013-02-20/why-should -taxpayers-give-big-banks-83-billion-a-year-#xj4y7vzkg; and Kenichi Ueda and Beatrice Weder di Mauro, "Quantifying Structural Subsidy Values for Systematically Important Financial Institutions," Working Paper (International Monetary Fund, May 2012), https://www.imf.org /external/pubs/ft/wp/2012/wp12128.pdf.

77. Regulators did not unveil the final version of the Volcker Rule until late 2013, and they set July 2015 as the date it would take effect. Editorial Board, "Finally, the Volcker Rule," *NYT*, December 12, 2013, https://www.nytimes.com/2013/12/13/opinion/finally-the-volcker-rule .html; and James B. Stewart, "Volcker Rule, Once Simple, Now Boggles," *NYT*, October 21, 2012, https://www.nytimes.com/2011/10/22/business/volcker-rule-grows-from-simple-to -complex.html.

78. See Senator Elizabeth Warren's scorching condemnation of the repeal and of Citigroup's "unprecedented" grip over economic policymaking in the executive branch. "Remarks by Elizabeth Warren on Citigroup and Its Bailout Provision," *YouTube*, December 12, 2014, https://www .youtube.com/watch?v=DJpTxONxvoo.

79. OCC, *Quarterly Report on Bank Trading and Derivatives Activities: Third Quarter 2022* (Washington, DC: Office of the Comptroller of the Currency, 2022), 20.

80. "50% Favor Breaking Up Nation's Largest Banks," Rasmussen Reports, March 21, 2013, https://www.rasmussenreports.com/public_content/business/general_business/march_2013 /50_favor_breaking_up_nation_s_largest_banks.

81. Michael Crittenden, "Regional Fed Presidents, FDIC Official Warn on Too Big to Fail," *WSJ*, June 25, 2013, https://www.wsj.com/articles/SB100014241278873236835045785681026 11838408?mod=rss_whats_news_us&mg=reno64-wsj; and Hoenig, "Too Big to Succeed."

82. Noah, "Why Conservatives Want to Break Up the Banks, Too."

83. "Wall Street Legend Sandy Weill: Break Up the Big Banks," CNBC.com, July 25, 2012, https://www.cnbc.com/2012/07/25/wall-street-legend-sandy-weill-break-up-the-big-banks .html.

84. Quoted in Kevin Derby, "Down in the Polls, Jon Huntsman Pushes Financial Reform," *Sunshine State News*, November 27, 2011, https://sunshinestatenews.com/story/down-polls-jon

-huntsman-pushes-financial-reform. See also Michael Brendan Dougherty, "Jon Huntsman Has a Radical Financial Reform Plan That Even Occupy Wall Street Will Love," *Business Insider*, November 28, 2011, https://www.businessinsider.com/how-jon-huntsman-would-end-the-economic-doom-loop-break-up-the-banks-sound-money-2011-11.

85. Kate Davidson, "A Split on 'Too Big to Fail,'" *Politico*, May 1, 2013, https://www.politico.com/story/2013/05/dodd-frank-too-big-to-fail-banks-090795; Jack Torry, "Brown Pushing Bill to Keep Taxpayers from Bailing Out Banks," *Dayton Daily News*, April 25, 2013, https://www.daytondailynews.com/news/national-govt--politics/brown-pushing-bill-keep-taxpayers-from-bailing-out-banks/ffDgv29g0wMVic1xMMM2LK/; and M. J. Lee, "Brown–Vitter Struggling for Support," *Politico*, June 10, 2013, https://www.politico.com/story/2013/06/brown-vitter-struggling-for-support-in-congress-092459.

86. Elizabeth Warren et al., "We Need to Rein in 'Too Big to Fail' Banks," CNN, July 17, 2014, https://edition.cnn.com/2014/07/17/opinion/warren-mccain-big-banks/.

87. Marcy Gordon, "Lew Says Delays on Rules May Mean Big Bank Risk," AP, July 17, 2013, https://apnews.com/article/f44e1a754f7d4d5fb6945e10497c9bde.

88. David Goldman, "Obama: 'Learn Lessons of Lehman,'" CNN, September 14, 2009, https://money.cnn.com/2009/09/14/news/economy/obama_wall_street_anniversary_speech/index.htm.

89. Quoted in Suskind, *Confidence Men*, 333.

90. FCIC, *Financial Crisis Inquiry Report* (Washington, DC: GPO, January 2011), 401.

91. Eric Bradner, "Conway Touts Trump's 'Drain the Swamp' Message, Admits 'We Are Behind,'" CNN, October 23, 2016, https://www.cnn.com/2016/10/23/politics/kellyanne-conway-trump-drain-the-swamp/index.html.

92. David Dayen, "Donald Trump Isn't Even Pretending to Oppose Goldman Sachs Anymore," *Intercept*, March 15, 2017, https://theintercept.com/2017/03/15/donald-trump-isnt-even-pretending-to-oppose-goldman-sachs-anymore/.

93. Jeff Mason and Sarah N. Lynch, "Trump's Message to Bankers: Wall Street Reform Rules May Be Eliminated," Reuters, April 12, 2017, https://www.reuters.com/article/economy/trumps-message-to-bankers-wall-street-reform-rules-may-be-eliminated-idUSKBN17D2QM/. See also Adam Tooze, *Crashed: How a Decade of Financial Crises Changed the World* (New York: Viking, 2018), 587.

94. John Dizard, "The Trump Era of Light-Touch Regulations," *Financial Times*, July 2, 2017, https://www.ft.com/content/72687184-5d6b-11e7-9bc8-8055f264aa8b.

95. Americans for Financial Reform, "How Americans View Wall Street and Financial Regulation," August 2017, https://ourfinancialsecurity.org/americans-view-wall-street-financial-regulation-august-2017/.

96. In another major change, dozens of Democrats joined Republicans in 2018 to enact a law that rolled back a critical provision of Dodd–Frank by raising the threshold from $50 billion to $250 billion or higher in assets before more stringent banking regulations would kick in. Jake Johnson, "Warren and Porter Lead SVB Act to Repeal Trump-Era Bank Deregulation Law," *Common Dreams*, https://www.commondreams.org/news/warren-porter-trump-bank-deregulation, March 15, 2023; and Jessica Silver-Greenberg, "Consumer Bureau Loses Fight to Allow More Class-Action Suits," *NYT*, October 24, 2017, https://www.nytimes.com/2017/10/24/business/senate-vote-wall-street-regulation.html.

97. Ankush Khardori, "There's Never Been a Better Time to Be a White-Collar Criminal," *NR*, July 23, 2020, https://newrepublic.com/article/158582/theres-never-better-time-white-collar-criminal.

98. Dylan Tokar, "Department of Justice Is Turning Back the Clock," *Nation*, March 6, 2019, https://www.thenation.com/article/archive/financial-crisis-justice-department-corporate-prosecutions-yates-memo/.

99. Khardori, "There's Never Been a Better Time to Be a White-Collar Criminal."

100. Tokar, "Department of Justice Is Turning Back the Clock." For more on the Yates memo, see p. 267.

101. Khardori, "There's Never Been a Better Time to Be a White-Collar Criminal."

102. For more on Covid-19 and fraud, see p. 385.

103. Ben Protess, Robert Gebeloff, and Danielle Ivory, "Trump Administration Spares Corporate Wrongdoers Billions in Penalties," NYT, November 3, 2018, https://www.nytimes.com /2018/11/03/us/trump-sec-doj-corporate-penalties.html.

104. Tokar, "Department of Justice Is Turning Back the Clock."

105. For more on DPAs, see chaps. 6, 7, and 8.

106. DOJ, "Goldman Sachs Charged in Foreign Bribery Case and Agrees to Pay over $2.9 Billion," press release, October 22, 2020, https://www.justice.gov/opa/pr/goldman-sachs -charged-foreign-bribery-case-and-agrees-pay-over-29-billion.

107. Andrew Cockburn, "The Malaysian Job: How Wall Street Enabled a Global Financial Scandal," HM, May 2020, 67–68.

108. Goldman CEO Lloyd Blankfein personally met several times with key figures in the scandal to discuss deals. Cockburn, 67–73.

109. Cockburn, 73. Other troubling conflicts of interest swirled around Barr, including one involving a yearslong DOJ criminal investigation of tax evasion by Caterpillar, the giant industrial company. Jesse Drucker, "How Trump's Justice Department Derailed an Investigation of a Major Company," NYT, March 9, 2024, updated March 11, 2024, https://www.nytimes.com /2024/03/09/business/caterpillar-tax-trump-barr.html.

110. Matthew Goldstein and Emily Flitter, "Goldman Sachs Malaysia Arm Pleads Guilty in 1MDB [1 Malaysia Development Berhad] Fraud," NYT, October 22, 2020, https://www.nytimes .com/2020/10/22/business/goldman-sachs-fraud-guilty-plea.html. For more on what has been called the heist of the century, see Tom Wright and Bradley Hope, Billion Dollar Whale: The Man Who Fooled Wall Street, Hollywood, and the World (New York: Hachette Books, 2018).

111. Lananh Nguyen, "Goldman Sachs Offers Big Retention Bonuses to Top Executives, a Year After Docking Their Pay," NYT, October 22, 2021, https://www.nytimes.com/2021/10/22 /business/goldman-sachs-executive-compensation.html.

112. "Columbia Law Professor John Coffee Says Boeing Deferred Prosecution Agreement One of the Worst," Corporate Crime Reporter, February 23, 2021, https://www.corporatecrimereporter .com/news/200/columbia-law-professor-john-coffee-says-boeing-deferred-prosecution -agreement-one-of-the-worst/.

113. Peter Robinson, Flying Blind: The 737 Max Tragedy and the Fall of Boeing (New York: Doubleday, 2021); Andy Pasztor and Andrew Tangel, "Internal FAA Review Saw High Risk of 737 Max Crashes," WSJ, December 11, 2019, https://www.wsj.com/articles/internal-faa-review -saw-high-risk-of-737-max-crashes-11576069202; and Maureen Tkacik, "Built to Lie," TAP, November/December 2021, 55–57.

114. Tkacik, "Built to Lie," 55–56.

115. Mark Filip was a top DOJ official in the George W. Bush administration and author of the Filip memorandum, which for years was the Justice Department's guidebook for DPAs. See p. 199.

116. DOJ, "Boeing Charged with 747 Max Fraud Conspiracy and Agrees to Pay over $2.5 Billion," press release, January 7, 2021, https://www.justice.gov/opa/pr/boeing-charged-737-max -fraud-conspiracy-and-agrees-pay-over-25-billion; and AP, "Former Boeing Test Pilot Mark Forkner Found Not Guilty of Deceiving FAA in 737 Max Fraud Case," CBS News, March 23, 2022, https:// www.cbsnews.com/news/boeing-test-pilot-mark-forkner-not-guilty-of-deceiving-faa/.

117. "On Tenth Anniversary of Financial Crisis, Warren Unveils Comprehensive Legislation to Hold Wall Street Executives Criminally Accountable," press release, warren.senate.gov, March 14, 2018, https://www.warren.senate.gov/newsroom/press-releases/on-tenth -anniversary-of-financial-crisis-warren-unveils-comprehensive-legislation-to-hold-wall-street -executives-criminally-accountable.

118. "The Biden Plan for Strengthening America's Commitment to Justice," JoeBiden.com, n.d., https://joebiden.com/justice/# (accessed January 16, 2023).

119. Rana Foroohar, "US Antitrust Has Reached a Turning Point," *Financial Times*, October 9, 2023, https://www.ft.com/content/6c550fd5-9a4a-45d1-a457-296c0a52e192.

120. DOJ, "Deputy Attorney General Lisa O. Monaco Gives Keynote Address at ABA's 36th National Institute on White Collar Crime," press release, October 28, 2021, https://www .justice.gov/opa/speech/deputy-attorney-general-lisa-o-monaco-gives-keynote-address-abas -36th-national-institute. For more on the Yates memo, see p. 267.

121. Harper Neidig, "Justice Pledging White-Collar Crackdown," *Hill*, April 24, 2022, https:// thehill.com/homenews/administration/3460007-justice-pledging-white-collar-crackdown/; DOJ, "Deputy Attorney General Lisa O. Monaco Delivers Remarks on Corporate Criminal Enforcement," press release, September 15, 2022, https://www.justice.gov/opa/speech/deputy -attorney-general-lisa-o-monaco-delivers-remarks-corporate-criminal-enforcement; and DOJ, Office of Public Affairs, "Attorney General Merrick B. Garland Delivers Remarks to the ABA Institute on White Collar Crime," press release, March 3, 2022, https://www.justice.gov/opa/speech /attorney-general-merrick-b-garland-delivers-remarks-aba-institute-white-collar-crime.

122. Rick Claypool, "Enforcement Uptick: In 2023, DOJ Corporate Crime Prosecutions Increased Slightly," Public Citizen, March 25, 2024, https://www.citizen.org/wp-content /uploads/enforcement-uptick-corporate-prosecutions-report-2023.pdf, 3.

123. Eileen Sullivan and Danielle Kaye, "Boeing Agrees to Plead Guilty to Felony in Deal with Justice Department," *NYT*, July 8, 2024, https://www.nytimes.com/2024/07/08/business /boeing-justice-department-plea-deal.html; and Ramishah Maruf and Chris Isidore, "US Department of Justice Finalizes Plea Deal with Boeing," CNN Business, July 24, 2024, https://www .cnn.com/2024/07/24/business/boeing-doj-plea-deal/index.html.

124. Mark Walker and Niraj Chokshi, "Federal Judge Rejects Boeing's Guilty Plea Related to the 737 Max Crashes," *NYT*, December 5, 2024, https://www.nytimes.com/2024/12/05/us /politics/boeing-max-guilty-plea-rejected.html; and Niraj Chokshi, "Boeing Strikes Deal to Avoid Criminal Responsibility for 737 Max Crashes," *NYT*, May 23, 2025, https://www.ny-times.com/2025/05/23/business/boeing-doj-737-max-crashes.html.

125. Michael S. Derby, "Sen. Elizabeth Warren Says Fed Suffers from 'Culture of Corruption,'" *WSJ*, October 5, 2021, https://www.wsj.com/articles/sen-elizabeth-warren-says-fed -suffers-from-culture-of-corruption-11633463527.

126. Pam Martens and Russ Martens, "The Fed's Trading Scandal Broadens into a Scandal with the Mega Banks It 'Regulates,'" Wall Street on Parade, October 24, 2022, https:// wallstreetonparade.com/2022/10/the-feds-trading-scandal-broadens-into-a-scandal-with-the -mega-banks-it-regulates/; Jim Tankersley, Jeanna Smialek, and Emily Flitter, "Fed Blocked Mention of Regulatory Flaws in Silicon Valley Bank Rescue," *NYT*, March 16, 2023, https://www .nytimes.com/2023/03/16/business/fed-regulation-svb.html; and Peter Coy, "Not Much Has Changed Since a Bank's Collapse," *NYT*, May 19, 2025, B4.

10. Killing Me Softly: Big Pharma, the Government, and the Opioid Crisis

1. Quoted in Jan Hoffman, "Purdue Pharma Is Dissolved and Sacklers Pay $4.5 Billion to Settle Opioid Claims," *NYT*, September 1, 2021, updated September 17, 2021, https://www.nytimes.com /2021/09/01/health/purdue-sacklers-opioids-settlement.html. Stephanie Lubinski was the widow of Troy Lubinski, who became addicted to OxyContin after being prescribed the drug for a back injury. He eventually lost his job and his family's home, then took his own life.

2. "Transcript for CDC Telebriefing: Guideline for Prescribing Opioids for Chronic Pain," CDC, March 15, 2016, https://archive.cdc.gov/www_cdc_gov/media/releases/2016/t0315 -prescribing-opioids-guidelines.html.

3. About three-quarters of these overdoses were opioid fatalities. KFF, "Opioid Overdose Deaths and Opioid Overdose Deaths of All Drug Overdose Deaths," n.d., https://www.kff.org /other/state-indicator/opioid-overdose-deaths/?currentTimeframe=0&sortModel=%7B%2 2colId%22:%22Location%22,%22sort%22:%22asc%22%7D (accessed August 16, 2024); Grace Sparks et al., "KFF Tracking Poll July 2023: Substance Use Crisis and Accessing Treatment," KFF News, August 15, 2023, https://www.kff.org/other/poll-finding/kff-tracking-poll-july-2023 -substance-use-crisis-and-accessing-treatment/; Josh Katz and Margot Sanger-Katz, "'The Numbers Are So Staggering': Overdose Deaths Set a Record," NYT, November 29, 2018, A11.

4. Beth Macy, "Failures That Fueled the Opioid Epidemic," NYT, February 24, 2021, A23.

5. Leo Beletsky, "21st Century Cures for the Opioid Crisis: Promise, Impact, and Missed Opportunities," American Journal of Law and Medicine, 44, nos. 2–3 (May 2018): 361. See also Beth Macy, Dopesick: Dealers, Doctors, and the Drug Company That Addicted America (New York: Little, Brown, 2018); and Barry Meier, Pain Killer: An Epidemic of Deceit and the Origin of America's Opioid Epidemic (New York: Random House, 2018).

6. KFF, "Drug Overdose Death Rate (per 100,000 Population)," n.d., https://www.kff.org /other/state-indicator/drug-overdose-death-rate-per-100000-population/?dataView =0&activeTab=graph&currentTimeframe=0&startTimeframe=22&selectedRows =%7B%22wrapups%22:%7B%22united-states%22:%7B%7D%7D%7D&sortModel=%7B%2 2colId%22:%22Location%22,%22sort%22:%22asc%22%7D (accessed November 8, 2024).

7. National Safety Council, "Preventable Deaths: Odds of Dying," n.d., https://injuryfacts .nsc.org/all-injuries/preventable-death-overview/odds-of-dying/ (accessed April 7, 2021); and Our World in Data, "Causes of Deaths for 15 to 49 Year Olds, United States, 2017," https:// ourworldindata.org/grapher/causes-of-death-in-15-49-year-olds?country=~USA.

8. US Joint Economic Committee, "The Economic Toll of the Opioid Crisis Reached Nearly $1.5 Trillion in 2020," n.d., https://www.jec.senate.gov/public/_cache/files/67bced7f-4232 -40ea-9263-f033d280c567/jec-cost-of-opioids-issue-brief.pdf (accessed December 30, 2023).

9. Grace Sparks et al., "KFF Tracking Poll July 2023: Substance Use Crisis and Accessing Treatment," KFF News, August 15, 2023, https://www.kff.org/other/poll-finding/kff-tracking -poll-july-2023-substance-use-crisis-and-accessing-treatment/.

10. Maia Szalavitz, "Sending People to Jail for Using Drugs Doesn't Help," NYT, September 4, 2023, A18.

11. Rachel Kushner, "Is Prison Necessary? Ruth Wilson Gilmore Might Change Your Mind," NYT, April 17, 2019, https://www.nytimes.com/2019/04/17/magazine/prison-abolition-ruth -wilson-gilmore.html.

12. Zachary Siegel, "The Great Overdose Grief Divide," NR, July–August 2023, 38–45.

13. For more on the relationship between the victims' rights movement, the women's movement, and mass incarceration, see Marie Gottschalk, The Prison and the Gallows: The Politics of Mass Incarceration in America (New York: Cambridge University Press, 2006), chaps. 4–6.

14. Graham Dukes, John Braithwaite, and James Maloney, Pharmaceuticals, Corporate Crime and Public Health (Cheltenham, UK: Edward Elgar, 2014), 287. Since 1998, the pharmaceutical industry has spent at least 50 percent more on lobbying than any other industry. Rhoda Feng, "The Pain Profiteers," TAP, June 2022, 58.

15. Quoted in "'Vanguard' Season Premiere: 'The OxyContin Express,'" HuffPost, October 14, 2009, updated December 6, 2017, https://www.huffpost.com/entry/vanguard-season -premiere_b_320867.

16. Patrick Radden Keefe, Empire of Pain: The Secret History of the Sackler Dynasty (New York: Doubleday, 2021), chap. 14.

17. Gary M. Franklin and the American Academy of Neurology, "Opioids for Chronic Noncancer Pain: A Position Paper of the American Academy of Neurology," Neurology 83, no. 14

(2014): 1277; and Stephen S. Hall, "How Much Does It Hurt?," *NYM*, June 8, 2014, https://nymag.com/health/bestdoctors/2014/zohydro-2014-6/.

18. Marcia Angell, "Opioid Nation," *NYRB*, December 6, 2020, 56. Purdue's claim that less than 1 percent of people taking OxyContin would become addicted was based on a five-sentence letter published in the *New England Journal of Medicine* in January 1980, not on a peer-reviewed study. Bethany McLean, "'We Didn't Cause the Crisis': David Sackler Pleads His Case on the Opioid Epidemic," *Vanity Fair*, June 19, 2019, updated August 2019, https://www.vanityfair.com/news/2019/06/david-sackler-pleads-his-case-on-the-opioid-epidemic?srsltid=AfmBOor UPBJuST-MPINOmiu5KdKHJec9SLGRzTZxycQzWZnpVMiLInbT.

19. Macy, "Failures That Fueled the Opioid Epidemic," A23.

20. Quoted in Macy, A23.

21. Barry Meier, "Origins of an Epidemic: Purdue Pharma Knew Its Opioids Were Widely Abused," *NYT*, May 29, 2018, https://www.nytimes.com/2018/05/29/health/purdue-opioids-oxycontin.html.

22. Quoted in Macy, "Failures That Fueled the Opioid Epidemic," A23.

23. Keefe, *Empire of Pain*, 194–97.

24. Angell, "Opioid Nation," 56; and Macy, *Dopesick*, chap. 2.

25. McLean, "'We Didn't Cause the Crisis.'"

26. Quoted in Macy, *Dopesick*, 29.

27. Angell, "Opioid Nation," 56. See also Scott E. Hadland et al., "Association of Pharmaceutical Industry Marketing of Opioid Products with Mortality from Opioid-Related Overdoses," *JAMA Network Open* 2, no. 1 (January 2019), https://jamanetwork.com/journals/jamanetworkopen/fullarticle/2720914.

28. John Fauber, "E-Mails Point to 'Troubling' Relationship Between Drug Firms, Regulators," *Milwaukee Journal Sentinel*, October 6, 2013, https://archive.jsonline.com/watchdog/watchdogreports/emails-point-to-troubling-relationship-between-drug-firms-regulators-b99113286z1-226692641.html/.

29. Macy, *Dopesick*, 40; and McLean, "'We Didn't Cause the Crisis.'"

30. US Senate, Homeland Security and Governmental Affairs Committee, "Fueling an Epidemic: Exposing the Financial Ties Between Opioid Manufacturers and Third Party Advocacy Groups," February 2018, https://www.hsgac.senate.gov/wp-content/uploads/imo/media/doc/REPORT-Fueling%20an%20Epidemic-Exposing%20the%20Financial%20Ties%20Between%20Opioid%20Manufacturers%20and%20Third%20Party%20Advocacy%20Groups.pdf, 1.

31. John Fauber and Ellen Gabler, "Doctors with Link to Drug Companies Influence Treatment Guidelines," *Milwaukee Journal Sentinel*, December 18, 2012, https://archive.jsonline.com/news/health/doctors-with-links-to-drug-companies-influencetreatment-guidelines-ki7pjr6-184041791.html/.

32. The CDC subsequently estimated that chronic pain affects 7 to 21 percent of American adults. S. Michaela Rikard et al., "Chronic Pain Among Adults—United States, 2019–2021," *Morbidity and Mortality Weekly Report* 72, no. 15 (April 2023): 379–85.

33. Christina Jewett, "Sacklers Gave Millions to Institution That Advises on Opioid Policy," *NYT*, April 23, 2023, updated May 1, 2023, https://www.nytimes.com/2023/04/23/health/sacklers-opioids-national-academies-science.html.

34. Chris Hamby, "Giant Companies Took Secret Payments to Allow Free Flow of Opioids," *NYT*, December 17, 2024, https://www.nytimes.com/2024/12/17/business/pharmacy-benefit-managers-opioids.html.

35. Donna Murch, "How Race Made the Opioid Crisis," *BR*, April 10, 2019, http://bostonreview.net/forum/donna-murch-how-race-made-the-opioid-crisis; Julie Netherland and Helena Hansen, "White Opioids: Pharmaceutical Race and the War on Drugs That Wasn't,"

BioSocieties 12, no. 2 (June 2017): 217–38; and David Herzberg, *White Market Drugs: Big Pharma and the Hidden History of Addiction in America* (Chicago: University of Chicago Press, 2020), 275–76.

36. Murch, "How Race Made the Opioid Crisis."

37. Helena Hansen, Jules Netherland, and David Herzberg, *Whiteout: How Racial Capitalism Changed the Color of Opioids in America* (Oakland: University of California Press, 2023), 125.

38. Nabarun Dasgupta, Leo Beletsky, and Daniel Ciccarone, "Opioid Crisis: No Easy Fix to Its Social and Economic Determinants," *American Journal of Public Health* 108, no. 2 (February 2018): 184; and Will Boggs, "Opioid Prescriptions, Overdose Deaths Most Common Among Low-Income Whites," Psychiatry and Behavioral Health Learning Network, February 12, 2019, https://www.psychcongress.com/news/opioid-prescriptions-overdose-deaths-most-common-among-low-income-whites.

39. Abby Alpert et al., "Origins of the Opioid Crisis and Its Enduring Effects," Working Paper No. 26500 (National Bureau of Economic Research, November 2019), 1–3, 8–9.

40. Asim Alam and David N. Juurlink, "The Prescription Opioid Epidemic: An Overview for Anesthesiologists," *Canadian Journal of Anesthesiology* 63, no. 1 (January 2016): 61.

41. Shweta Kapoor and Beverly Thorn, "Healthcare Use and Prescription of Opioids in Rural Residents with Pain," *Rural and Remote Health* 14, no. 3 (September 9, 2014): 2879; and Theodore J. Cicero, Matthew Ellis, and Hilary Surratt, "The Changing Face of Heroin Use in the United States: A Retrospective Analysis of the Past 50 Years," *JAMA Psychiatry* 71, no. 7 (2014): 821–26.

42. Irfan A. Dhalla, Navindra Persaud, and David N. Juurlink, "Facing Up to the Prescription Opioid Crisis," *BMJ* 343 (August 23, 2011), https://doi.org/10.1136/bmj.d5142.

43. Deborah Dowell, Tamara M. Haegerich, and Roger Chou, "CDC Guideline for Prescribing Opioids for Chronic Pain—United Sates, 2016," *Morbidity and Mortality Weekly Report* 65, no. 1 (March 18, 2016): 7; and President's Commission on Combating Drug Addiction and the Opioid Crisis, *Final Report* (Washington, DC: White House, 2017), 22.

44. Macy, *Dopesick*, 36–51.

45. Macy, 51 and 65.

46. Quoted in Danny Hakim, Roni Caryn Rabin, and William K. Rashbaum, "Lawsuits Lay Bare Sackler Family's Role in Opioid Crisis," *NYT*, April 1, 2019, https://www.nytimes.com/2019/04/01/health/sacklers-oxycontin-lawsuits.html.

47. Macy, "Failures That Fueled the Opioid Epidemic."

48. McLean, "'We Didn't Cause the Crisis.'"

49. Macy, *Dopesick*, 186.

50. Christopher Glazek, "The Secretive Family Making Billions from the Opioid Crisis," *Esquire*, October 16, 2017, https://www.esquire.com/news-politics/a12775932/sackler-family-oxycontin/.

51. Julia Marsh and Ruth Brown, "OxyContin Maker Wanted to Push Super-Potent Pills on Patients," *NYP*, February 1, 2019, https://nypost.com/2019/02/01/oxycontin-maker-wanted-to-push-super-potent-pills-on-patients/.

52. David Armstrong, "OxyContin Maker Explored Expansion into 'Attractive' Anti-Addiction Market," *ProPublica*, January 30, 2019, https://www.propublica.org/article/oxycontin-purdue-pharma-massachusetts-lawsuit-anti-addiction-market.

53. Brian Pitman and Stephen T. Young, "Deflecting a 'Crisis': The Opioid Epidemic in Appalachia as State Violence," *Contemporary Justice Review* 26, no. 3 (2023): 225–49.

54. Sari Horwitz, Steven Rich, and Scott Higham, "Opioid Death Rates Soared in Communities Where Pain Pills Flowed," *WP*, July 17, 2019, http://www.washingtonpost.com/investigations/opioid-death-rates-soared-in-communities-where-pain-pills-flowed/2019/07/17/f3595da4-a8a4-11e9-a3a6-ab670962db05_story.html.

55. Macy, *Dopesick*, 29.

56. Eric Eyre, "Drug Firms Poured 780M Painkillers into WV amid Rise of Overdoses," *Charleston Gazette-Mail*, December 17, 2016, https://www.wvgazettemail.com/news/health/drug-firms-poured-m-painkillers-into-wv-amid-rise-of/article_78963590-b050-11e7-8186-f7e8c8a1b804.html.

57. Dwight Garner, "How Painkiller Pushers Made the Pain Worse," *NYT*, April 7, 2020, C1.

58. Greg Allen, "The 'Oxy Express': Florida's Drug Abuse Epidemic," NPR, March 2, 2011, https://www.npr.org/2011/03/02/134143813/the-oxy-express-floridas-drug-abuse-epidemic.

59. Scott Higham, Sari Horwitz, and Steven Rich, "76 Billion Opioid Pills: Newly Released Federal Data Unmasks the Epidemic," *WP*, July 16, 2019, https://www.washingtonpost.com/investigations/76-billion-opioid-pills-newly-released-federal-data-unmasks-the-epidemic/2019/07/16/5f29fd62-a73e-11e9-86dd-d7f0e60391e9_story.html.

60. Gera Nagelhout et al., "How Economic Recessions and Unemployment Affect Illegal Drug Use: A Systematic Realist Literature Review," *International Journal of Drug Policy* 44 (June 2017): 69–83.

61. Shannon Monnat et al., "Using Census Data to Understand County-Level Differences in Overall Drug Mortality and Opioid-Related Mortality by Opioid Type," *American Journal of Public Health* 109, no. 8 (August 2019): 1084–91.

62. Adam Dean and Simeon Kimmel, "Beyond the Sacklers: Free-Trade Policies Contributed to the Opioid Epidemic," *STAT*, October 8, 2019, https://www.statnews.com/2019/10/08/free-trade-policies-opioid-epidemic/; Atheendar Venkataramani et al., "Association Between Automotive Assembly Plant Closures and Opioid Overdose Mortality in the United States," *JAMA Internal Medicine* 180, no. 2 (February 2020): 254–62; Monnat et al., "Using Census Data to Understand," 1084; Khary Rigg, Shannon Monnat, and Melody Chavez, "Opioid-Related Mortality in Rural America: Geographic Heterogeneity and Intervention Strategies," *International Journal of Drug Policy* 57 (July 2018): 119–29; and David J. Peters et al., "The Opioid Hydra: Understanding Overdose Mortality Epidemics and Syndemics Across the Rural-Urban Continuum," *Rural Sociology* 85, no. 3 (September 2020): 589–622.

63. NAS, *Pain Management and the Opioid Epidemic: Balancing Societal and Individual Benefits and Risks of Prescription Opioid Use* (Washington, DC: National Academies Press, 2017), 155.

64. Rigg et al., "Opioid-Related Mortality in Rural America," 120–25; Peters et al., "Opioid Hydra."

65. About 60 percent of veterans returning from Middle East deployments and about one-quarter of older veterans have chronic pain compared to about 30 percent of Americans nationwide. Carolyn Clancy, interim under secretary for Health, Veterans Health Administration, Department of Veterans Affairs, prepared testimony, US Senate, Committee on Veterans Affairs, March 25, 2015, https://www.veterans.senate.gov/imo/media/doc/VA%20Clancy%20Testimony%203.26.20151.pdf, 2.

66. NIDA, "Is Medication to Treat Opioid Use Disorder Available in the Military?," April 13, 2021, https://nida.nih.gov/publications/research-reports/medications-to-treat-opioid-addiction/medication-to-treat-opioid-use-disorder-available-in-military.

67. Center for Ethics and the Rule of Law, "The Intersection of Opioid Overuse and Veteran Mental Health Challenges," January 13, 2017, https://health21initiative.org/wp-content/uploads/2017/08/2017-CERL-Opioid-Addiction-and-PTSD-Report.pdf, 4–5.

68. James Dao, "For Veterans with Post-Traumatic Stress, Pain Killers Carry Risks," *NYT*, March 7, 2010, https://atwar.blogs.nytimes.com/2012/03/07/for-veterans-with-post-traumatic-stress-pain-killers-carry-risks/?mcubz=0&_r=0.

69. A. S. Bohnert et al., "Accidental Poisoning Mortality Among Patients in the Department of Veterans Affairs Health System," *Medical Care* 49, no. 4 (April 2011): 393–96. See also Hanna

Yakubi, Brian Gac, and Dorie E. Apollonio, "Marketing Opioids to Veterans and Older Adults: A Content Analysis of Internal Industry Documents Released from *State of Oklahoma v. Purdue Pharma LP, et al.*," *Journal of Health Politics, Policy and Law* 47, no. 4 (August 2022): 453, 465.

70. Yakubi et al., "Marketing Opioids," 453–72.

71. Keefe, *Empire of Pain*, 297.

72. By 2010, one-third of soldiers in the US Army were on prescription medications, and nearly half of those troops were on prescription opioids. Ann Jones, "How Veterans Are Losing the War at Home: Making America Pain-Free for Plutocrats and Big Pharma, but Not Vets," *New Labor Forum* 26, no. 1 (2017): 58.

73. Art Levine, "How the VA Fueled the National Opioid Crisis and Is Killing Thousands of Veterans," *Newsweek*, October 12, 2017, https://www.newsweek.com/2017/10/20/va-fueled -opioid-crisis-killing-veterans-681552.html.

74. Valerie Bauerlein and Arian Campo-Flores, "The VA Hooked Veterans on Opioids, Then Failed Them Again," *WSJ*, December 29, 2016, https://www.wsj.com/articles/the-va-hooked -veterans-on-opioids-then-failed-them-again-1483030270.

75. In 2015, the rural rate was 17 per 100,000, and the urban rate was 16.2 per 100,000. The respective rates for 1999 were 4 and 6.4. CDC, "CDC Reports Rising Rates of Drug Overdose Deaths in Rural Areas," press release, October 19, 2017, https://www.cdc.gov/media/releases /2017/p1019-rural-overdose-deaths.html.

76. Calculated from KFF, "Opioid Overdose Deaths by Race/Ethnicity: Rate," various years, 1999–2017, https://www.kff.org/other/state-indicator/opioid-overdose-deaths-by -raceethnicity/?dataView=2&currentTimeframe=0&selectedRows=%7B%22states%22:%7B %22all%22:%7B%7D%7D,%22wrapups%22:%7B%22united-states%22:%7B%7D%7D%7D&s ortModel=%7B%22colId%22:%22Location%22,%22sort%22:%22asc%22%7D (accessed June 18, 2019). See also Debra Furr-Holden et al., "African Americans Now Outpace Whites in Opioid-Involved Overdose Deaths: A Comparison of Temporal Trends from 1999 to 2018," *Addiction* 116, no. 3 (March 2021): 677–83.

77. Shravani Durbhakula, "The D.E.A. Should Get Out of Public Health," *NYT*, March 25, 2024, A23.

78. Jerry Markon and Alice Crites, "Experts: Officials Missed Signs of Prescription Drug Crackdown's Effect on Heroin Use," *WP*, March 6, 2014, https://www.washingtonpost.com /politics/experts-officials-missed-signs-of-prescription-drug-crackdowns-effect-on-heroin-use /2014/03/06/2216414a-9fc1-11e3-b8d8-94577ff66b28_story.html.

79. Brianna Ehley, "Federal Scientists Warned of Coming Opioid Crisis in 2006," *Politico*, August 21, 2019, https://www.politico.com/story/2019/08/21/federal-scientists-opioid-crisis -1673694.

80. Corey S. Davis and Amy Judd Lieberman, "Laws Limiting Prescribing and Dispensing of Opioids in the United States, 1989–2019," *Addiction* 116, no. 7 (July 2021): 1817–27.

81. Prescription Drug Monitoring Program and Technical Assistance Center, "State PDMP [Prescription Drug Monitoring Program] Profiles and Contacts," n.d., https://www.pdmpassist .org/State (accessed July 31, 2020).

82. Scott Glover, "Southern California Doctor Sentenced in Overdose Deaths of 3 Patients," CNN, February 5, 2016, https://www.cnn.com/2016/02/05/health/california-overdose-doctor -murder-sentencing/.

83. Levine, "How the VA Fueled the National Opioid Crisis."

84. Stephen W. Patrick et al., "Implementation of Prescription Drug Monitoring Programs Associated with Reductions in Opioid-Related Death Rates," *Health Affairs* 35, no. 7 (July 2016): 1324–32.

85. Leo Beletsky and Corey S. Davis, "Today's Fentanyl Crisis: Prohibition's Iron Law, Revisited," *International Journal of Drug Policy* 46 (2017): 156–57.

86. Keith Humphreys, testimony, US House Judiciary Subcommittee on Immigration and Border Security, Hearing on Immigration and the Opioid Crisis, February 18, 2020, https:// republicans-judiciary.house.gov/wp-content/uploads/2018/02/Witness-Testimony-Keith -Humphreys.pdf, 2; and Sam Quinones, *Dreamland: The True Tale of America's Opiate Epidemic* (New York: Bloomsbury, 2015).

87. NIDA, "Prescription Opioids and Heroin Research Report: Prescription Opioid Use Is a Risk Factor for Heroin Use," January 2018, https://nida.nih.gov/publications/research-reports /prescription-opioids-heroin/prescription-opioid-use-risk-factor-heroin-use.

88. Holly Hedegaard, Arialdi Miniño, and Margaret Warner, "Drug Overdose Deaths in the United States, 1999–2018," *NCHS Data Brief* 356 (January 2020): 3, fig. 3.

89. T. Jake Liang and John W. Ward, "Hepatitis C in Injection-Drug Users—a Hidden Danger of the Opioid Epidemic," *NEJM* 378, no. 13 (March 29, 2018): 1169.

90. Richard C. Cowan, "How the Narcs Created Crack," *National Review Magazine* 38, no. 23 (December 5, 1986): 27, emphasis in the original.

91. Quoted in Joshua Vaughn, "2016 Crime Review: Heroin Deaths Rise as Prescription Policies Go into Effect," *Sentinel*, February 12, 2017, https://cumberlink.com/news/local/closer _look/digital_data/crime-review-heroin-deaths-rise-as-prescription-policies-go-into/article _fcde5d45-676a-54d4-873e-aac9a79b2cb0.html.

92. Roger B. Handberg, "The Opioid Epidemic in Florida: 2000 to 2017," *Florida Bar Journal*, May/June 2020, 22–23.

93. David Pittman, "FDA Panel Gives Thumbs Down to Opioid," *MedPage Today*, December 7, 2012, https://www.medpagetoday.com/painmanagement/painmanagement/36334.

94. Stephen Hall, "How Much Does It Hurt?," *NY*, June 6, 2014, https://nymag.com/health /bestdoctors/2014/zohydro-2014-6/; and Pat Anson, "Addiction Experts Want FDA to Revoke Zohydro Approval," *National Pain Report*, February 26, 2020, http://nationalpainreport.com /addiction-experts-want-fda-revoke-zohydro-approval-8823113.html.

95. Macy, "Failures That Fueled the Opioid Epidemic."

96. Keefe, *Empire of Pain*, 345–48.

97. Dowell et al., "CDC Guideline for Prescribing Opioids."

98. The National Association of Attorneys General charged that it was "incomprehensible" that the HHS would water down CDC guidelines. McLean, "'We Didn't Cause the Crisis.'"

99. Patil Armenian et al., "Fentanyl, Fentanyl Analogs and Novel Synthetic Opioids: A Comprehensive Review," *Neuropharmacology* 134, part A (May 15, 2018): 121.

100. DEA, "DEA Issues Carfentanil Warning to Police and Public," September 22, 2016, https://www.dea.gov/press-releases/2016/09/22/dea-issues-carfentanil-warning-police-and -public.

101. Overdose deaths from fentanyl and its analogues increased from 1 per 100,000 in 2013 to 17.8 per 100,000 in 2020. This is more than four times the overdose death rates from heroin (4.1 per 100,000) or prescription pain pills (4 per 100,000) and more than twice the country's homicide rate in 2020 (7.8 per 100,000). Holly Hedegaard et al., "Drug Overdose Deaths in the United States, 1999–2020," *NCHS Data Brief* 428 (December 2021): 4; and John Gramlich, "What We Know About the Increase in U.S. Murders in 2020," PRC, October 27, 2021, https:// www.pewresearch.org/fact-tank/2021/10/27/what-we-know-about-the-increase-in-u-s -murders-in-2020/.

102. Michael Collins and Sheila P. Vakharia, "Criminal Justice Reform in the Fentanyl Era: One Step Forward, Two Steps Back," Drug Policy Alliance, January 2020, https://drugpolicy .org/wp-content/uploads/2023/05/Criminal_Justice_Reform_in_the_Fentanyl_Era _Report.pdf, 7.

103. In 2021, the DEA issued a public advisory that more than 40 percent of black-market prescription pills contained lethal amounts of fentanyl. Sarah Maslin Nir, "Inside Fentanyl's

Mounting Death Toll: 'This Is Poison,'" *NYT*, November 20, 2021, updated November 22, 2021, https://www.nytimes.com/2021/11/20/nyregion/fentanyl-opioid-deaths.html.

104. Joseph P. Williams, "Separate, Unequal and Overlooked," *U.S. News*, January 28, 2019, https://www.usnews.com/news/health-news/articles/2019-01-28/black-americas-opioid-crisis-separate-unequal-overlooked; and Ben Westhoff, *Fentanyl, Inc.: How Rogue Chemists Are Creating the Deadliest Wave of the Opioid Epidemic* (New York: Atlantic Monthly Press, 2019).

105. Calculated from KFF, "Opioid Overdose Deaths by Race/Ethnicity: Rate."

106. Hedegaard, Minino, and Warner, "Urban-Rural Differences in Drug Overdose Death Rates."

107. Katherine M. Keyes et al., "Understanding the Rural-Urban Differences in Nonmedical Prescription Opioid Use and Abuse in the United States," *American Journal of Public Health* 104, no. 2 (February 2014): e52–e59, https://ajph.aphapublications.org/doi/abs/10.2105/AJPH.2013.301709.

108. Keri N. Althoff et al., "Opioid-Related Overdose Mortality in the Era of Fentanyl: Monitoring a Shifting Epidemic by Person, Place, and Time," *Drug and Alcohol Dependence* 216 (November 1, 2020), https://www.sciencedirect.com/science/article/abs/pii/S0376871620304865. See also Furr-Holden et al., "African Americans Now Outpace Whites"; and Rachel Hoopsick et al., "Differences in Opioid Overdose Mortality Rates Among Middle-Aged Adults by Race/Ethnicity and Sex, 1999–2018," *Public Health Reports* 136, no. 2 (March/April 2021): 192–200.

109. National Institute of Health Care Management, "Charting the Stimulant Overdose Crisis and the Influence of Fentanyl," November 17, 2022, https://nihcm.org/publications/stimulant-drug-overdose-deaths-2022-update; and Hedegaard et al., "Drug Overdose Deaths in the United States, 1999–2020," 5, fig. 5.

110. Jan Hoffman, "'A Monster': Super Meth and Other Drugs Push Crisis Beyond Opioids," *NYT*, November 13, 2023, https://www.nytimes.com/2023/11/13/health/polysubstance-opioids-addiction.html.

111. Using creative accounting, the Sacklers claimed that Purdue was responsible for only 4 percent of the opioid market, but the real figure is likely between 27 percent and 30 percent if only high-dosage, highly addictive pain pills are counted. Keefe, *Empire of Pain*, 365.

112. Higham, Horwitz, and Rich, "76 Billion Opioid Pills."

113. Higham, Horwitz, and Rich; and Jan Hoffman, "CVS and Walgreens Near $10 Billion Deal to Settle Opioid Cases," *NYT*, November 2, 2022, https://www.nytimes.com/2022/11/02/health/cvs-walgreens-opioids-settlement.html.

114. Scott Higham and Sari Horwitz, *American Cartel: Inside the Battle to Bring Down the Opioid Industry* (New York: Twelve, 2022), chaps. 8 and 20–21.

115. Scott Higham and Lenny Bernstein, "Rep. Tom Marino: Drug Czar Nominee and the Opioid Industry's Advocate in Congress," *WP*, October 15, 2017, https://www.washingtonpost.com/investigations/rep-tom-marino-drug-czar-nominee-and-the-opioid-industrys-advocate-in-congress/2017/10/15/555211a0-b03a-11e7-9e58-e6288544af98_story.html.

116. Higham and Horwitz, *American Cartel*, chap. 24.

117. "Ex-DEA Agent: Opioid Crisis Fueled by Drug Industry and Congress," *60 Minutes*, CBS, June 17, 2018, https://www.cbsnews.com/news/60-minutes-ex-dea-agent-opioid-crisis-fueled-by-drug-industry-and-congress/.

118. Higham and Horwitz, *American Cartel*, chap. 35.

119. A key piece of evidence at the trial was a thumping rap video featuring two young salesmen wearing alternately hoodies and black suits that was used for training its sales force. Jonathan Saltzman and Maria Cramer, "Insys Defendants Bribed Doctors to Prescribe Painkillers to Those That Didn't Need It," *BG*, May 2, 2019, https://www.bostonglobe.com/metro/2019/05/02/jury-returns-verdict-insys-trial/KeiTKLXZnnBZnOulLED17M/story.html; and Gabrielle Emanuel and Vanessa Romo, "Pharmaceutical Executive John Kapoor Sentenced to 66

Months in Prison in Opioid Trial," NPR, January 23, 2020, https://www.npr.org/2020/01/23 /798973304/pharmaceutical-executive-john-kapoor-sentenced-to-66-months-in-prison-in -opioid.

120. Colin Moynihan, "Drug Wholesaler's Chief Is Sentenced to Prison for Opioid Conspiracy," *NYT*, March 9, 2023, A23. See also the case of Shaun Thaxter, former CEO of Indivior, a former subsidiary of Reckitt Benckiser Pharmaceuticals, who was sentenced to six months in federal prison. DOJ, "Suboxone Manufacturer Indivior's Former Chief Executive Sentenced to Jail Time in Connection with Drug Safety Claims," press release, October 22, 2020, https://www .justice.gov/usao-wdva/pr/suboxone-manufacturer-indiviors-former-chief-executive-officer -sentenced-jail-time.

121. See, for example, Jacqueline Howard, "Drugmaker to Pay $1.4 Billion in Largest US Opioid Treatment Settlement," CNN, July 12, 2019, https://www.cnn.com/2019/07/12/health /opioid-lawsuit-reckitt-benckiser-bn/index.html.

122. Dietrich Knauth, "Court OKs Mallinckrodt Restructuring, $1 Billion Cut to Opioid Settlement," Reuters, October 10, 2023, https://www.reuters.com/business/healthcare -pharmaceuticals/mallinckrodt-gets-approval-restructuring-1-billion-cut-opioid-settlement -2023-10-10/.

123. Barry Meier and Eric Lipton, "Under Attack, Drug Maker Turned to Giuliani for Help," *NYT*, December 28, 2007, https://www.nytimes.com/2007/12/28/us/politics/28oxycontin .html.

124. Meier and Lipton.

125. Quoted in Keefe, *Empire of Pain*, 381.

126. KFF, "Opioid Overdose Deaths."

127. Quoted in Keefe, *Empire of Pain*, 277; see also chap. 20.

128. Hall, "How Much Does It Hurt?"

129. Keefe, *Empire of Pain*, 279–82.

130. Macy, *Dopesick*, 97.

131. Keefe, *Empire of Pain*, 283–84.

132. Purdue senior manager quoted in Hakim et al., "Lawsuits Lay Bare."

133. Michael Forsythe and Walt Bogdanich, "McKinsey Settles for Nearly $600 Million over Role in Opioid Crisis," *NYT*, February 3, 2021, https://www.nytimes.com/2021/02/03 /business/mckinsey-opioids-settlement.html; and Keefe, *Empire of Pain*, 349.

134. Chris Hamby et al., "McKinsey Opened a Door in Its Firewall Between Pharma Clients and Regulators," *NYT*, April 13, 2022, https://www.nytimes.com/2022/04/13/business /mckinsey-purdue-fda-records.html.

135. Brian Mann, "McKinsey & Company to Pay $650 Million for Role in Opioid Crisis," NPR, December 13, 2024, https://www.npr.org/2024/12/13/nx-s1-5155962/mckinsey-purdue -opioid-prosecution-doj; and Walt Bogdanich and Michael Forsythe, "McKinsey to Pay $650 Million in Opioid Settlement With Justice Department," *NYT*, December 13, 2024, https://www .nytimes.com/2024/12/13/business/mckinsey-oxycontin-settlement.html.

136. Purdue pleaded guilty to felony charges related to marketing opioids to more than a hundred doctors it suspected of writing illegal prescriptions and then lying about this to the DEA and to paying illegal kickbacks to physicians and an electronic medical records company. The civil charges related to claims that Purdue used aggressive marketing tactics to persuade doctors to write unwarranted prescriptions for opioids. Jan Hoffman and Katie Benner, "Purdue Admits That It Pushed Deadly Opioid," *NYT*, October 22, 2020, A1; and Ryan Hampton, with Claire Rudy Foster and Hillel Aron, *Unsettled: How the Purdue Pharma Bankruptcy Failed the Victims of the American Overdose Crisis* (New York: St. Martin's, 2021), 248.

137. Danny Hakim, "New York Uncovers $1 Billion in Sackler Wire Transfers," *NYT*, September 13, 2019, https://www.nytimes.com/2019/09/13/health/sacklers-purdue-opioids.html.

138. Jan Hoffman and Danny Hakim, "Purdue Pharma Payments to Sackler Family Soared amid Opioid Crisis," *NYT*, December 16, 2019, updated October 21, 2020, https://www.nytimes .com/2019/12/16/health/sacklers-purdue-payments-opioids-.html.

139. Higham, Horwitz, and Rich, "76 Billion Opioid Pills."

140. Higham and Horwitz, *American Cartel*, 318–20. See also "Executive Summary of National Opioid Settlements," n.d., https://nationalopioidsettlement.com/executive-summary/ (accessed December 16, 2023).

141. Higham and Horwitz, *American Cartel*, chaps. 50–54.

142. Antoine Lentacker, "How the Purdue Opioid Settlement Could Help the Public Understand the Roots of the Drug Crisis," University of California, press release, September 2, 2021, https://www.universityofcalifornia.edu/news/how-purdue-opioid-settlement-could-help -public-understand-roots-drug-crisis.

143. Geoff Mulvihill, "Judge Rejects Purdue Pharma's Sweeping Opioid Settlement," AP, December 16, 2021, https://apnews.com/article/business-health-lawsuits-opioids-colleen -mcmahon-1e96ea41f783d8f5db0a024fbb304c1f; Alison Frankel, "Purdue's Sackler Family Wants Global Opioids Settlement," Reuters, April 22, 2019, https://www.reuters.com/article /world/purdues-sackler-family-wants-global-opioids-settlement-sackler-lawyer-mary-jo -idUSKCN1RZ01L/; and Lentacker, "How the Purdue Opioid Settlement Could Help."

144. Frankel, "Purdue's Sackler Family Wants Global Opioid Settlement."

145. Hampton et al., *Unsettled*.

146. Hampton et al.

147. Jan Hoffman, "Judge Overturns Purdue Pharma's Opioid Settlement," *NYT*, December 16, 2021, https://www.nytimes.com/2021/12/16/health/purdue-pharma-opioid-settlement.html.

148. Jan Hoffman, "An Appeals Court Gave the Sacklers Legal Immunity: Here's What the Ruling Means," *NYT*, May 31, 2023, https://www.nytimes.com/2023/05/31/health/sackler -family-immunity-opioids.html.

149. Brief quoted in Abbie VanSickle and Jan Hoffman, "Supreme Court Pauses Opioid Settlement with Sacklers Pending Review," *NYT*, August 10, 2023, https://www.nytimes.com /2023/08/10/us/supreme-court-purdue-pharma-opioid-settlement.html.

150. Jan Hoffman, "Sacklers Up Their Offer to Settle Purdue Opioids Cases, with a New Condition," *NYT*, January 23, 2025, https://www.nytimes.com/2025/01/23/health/sacklers -purdue-settlement-opioids.html.

151. Bob Fernandez and Craig R. McCoy, "Endo's End Around: How a Huge Philadelphia-Based Opioid Maker Escaped a $7 Billion Federal Penalty," *PI*, December 17, 2024, https://www .inquirer.com/business/endo-settlement-opioids-justice-department.

152. Frankel, "Purdue's Sackler Family Wants Global Opioid Settlement."

153. Leo Beletsky, "America's Favorite Antidote: Drug-Induced Homicide in the Age of the Overdose Crisis," *Utah Law Review* 4, no. 4 (2019): 883–84.

154. Sanya Singh, "Michelle Alexander Urges 'Victories for All of Us'—Complete Speech," newdrugpolicy.org, November 3, 2017, https://newdrugpolicy.org/2017/11/michelle-alexander -urges-victories-us-complete-speech/.

155. Jamilah King, "Senator Kamala Harris Blasts Racialized Double Standard of Crack and Opioid Epidemics," *Mic*, May 17, 2017, https://www.mic.com/articles/177298/senator-kamala -harris-blasts-racialized-double-standard-of-crack-and-opioid-epidemics.

156. See, for example, Dahleen Glanton, "Race, the Crack Epidemic and the Effect on Today's Opioid Crisis," *Chicago Tribune*, August 21, 2017, https://www.chicagotribune.com /columns/dahleen-glanton/ct-opioid-epidemic-dahleen-glanton-met-20170815-column.html; Kristina Peterson and Stephanie Armour, "Opioid vs. Crack: Congress Reconsiders Its Approach to Drug Epidemic," *WSJ*, May 5, 2018, https://www.wsj.com/articles/opioid-v-crack -congress-reconsiders-its-approach-to-drug-epidemic-1525518000; and Ekow N. Yankah,

"When Addiction Has a White Face," *NYT*, February 9, 2016, https://www.nytimes.com/2016 /02/09/opinion/when-addiction-has-a-white-face.html.

157. See, for example, Julie Netherland and Helena B. Hansen, "The War on Drugs That Wasn't: Wasted Whiteness, 'Dirty Doctors,' and Race in Media Coverage of Prescription Opioid Misuse," *Culture, Medicine, and Psychiatry* 40, no. 4 (December 2016): 669; Jin Woo Kim, Evan Morgan, and Brendan Nyhan, "Treatment Versus Punishment: Understanding Racial Inequalities in Drug Policy," *Journal of Health Politics, Policy and Law* 45, no. 2 (April 2020): 179; and Carmel Shachar et al., "Criminal Justice or Public Health: A Comparison of the Representation of the Crack Cocaine and Opioid Epidemics in the Media," *Journal of Health Policy, Politics and Law* 45, no. 2 (April 2020): 211–39.

158. Amy Lerman and Vesla Weaver, *Arresting Citizenship: The Democratic Consequences of American Crime Control* (Chicago: University of Chicago Press, 2014).

159. For more on moral panics and the so-called crack epidemic, see pp. 47–48.

160. This is true, of course, only if we do not categorize alcohol and cigarettes—which cause many more deaths each year than opioids do—as drugs. In the 2020–21 period, the average annual number of US deaths from excessive alcohol use was 178,000. Cigarette smoking (including secondhand smoke) causes more than 480,000 deaths each year in the United States. Marissa B. Esser et al., "Deaths from Excessive Alcohol Use—United States, 2016–2021," *Morbidity and Mortality Weekly Report* 73, no. 8 (February 29, 2024):154–61, https://www.cdc.gov/mmwr /volumes/73/wr/mm7308a1.htm; and HHS, *The Health Consequences of Smoking—50 Years of Progress: A Report of the Surgeon General*, 2014, https://www.ncbi.nlm.nih.gov/books /NBK179276/pdf/Bookshelf_NBK179276.pdf, chap. 12, table 12.4.

161. At the height of the so-called crack epidemic in 1989–90, the *New York Times* ran over four hundred front-page stories that mentioned crack. In 2017–18, only sixty-eight of its front-page stories mentioned opioids. Kim, Morgan, Nyhan, "Treatment Versus Punishment," 181. See also Katie Zezima and Colby Itkowitz, "Flailing on Fentanyl," *WP*, September 20, 2019, https:// www.washingtonpost.com/graphics/2019/investigations/fentanyl-epidemic-congress/.

162. Miriam J. Laugesen and Eric M. Patashnik, "Framing, Governance, and Partisanship: Putting Politics Front and Center in the Opioid Epidemic," *Journal of Health Politics, Policy, and Law* 45, no. 2 (April 2020): 366, emphasis in the original.

163. Joshua Sharfstein, vice dean of Johns Hopkins Bloomberg School of Public Health, quoted in Sari Horwitz et al., "Trump Administration Struggles to Confront the Fentanyl Crisis," *WP*, May 22, 2019, https://www.washingtonpost.com/graphics/2019/national/fentanyl -epidemic-trump-administration/.

164. Kelly Ayotte, "Fighting Fentanyl Dealers—Agents of Death," *Concord Monitor*, June 15, 2016, https://www.concordmonitor.com/Kelly-Ayotte-stronger-penalties-for-fentanyl-dealers -2836359; and Tal Kopan, "Maine Gov. Paul LePage: Bring Back the Guillotine for Drug Traffickers," CNN, January 27, 2016, https://www.cnn.com/2016/01/26/politics/paul-lepage -maine-guillotine/.

165. Netherland and Hansen, "War on Drugs That Wasn't"; Michael Shaw, "Photos Reveal Media's Softer Tone on Opioid Crisis," *Columbia Journalism Review*, July 26, 2017, https://www .cjr.org/criticism/opioid-crisis-photos.php; and Genevieve Johnston, "The Kids Are All White: Examining Race and Representation in News Media Coverage of Opioid Deaths in Canada," *Sociological Inquiry* 90, no. 1 (February 2020): 123–46.

166. Emma McGinty et al., "Stigmatizing Language in News Media Coverage of the Opioid Epidemic: Implications for Public Health," *Preventive Medicine* 124 (2019): 110–14; Fiona Webster, Kathleen Rice, and Abhimanyu Sud, "A Critical Content Analysis of Media Reporting on Opioids: The Social Construction of an Epidemic," *Social Science and Medicine* 244, no. 112642 (January 2020): 1–9; and Philip R. Kavanaugh and Jennifer L. Schally, "The Neoliberal Governance of Heroin and Opioid Users in Philadelphia City," *Crime, Media, Culture: An International Journal* 18, no. 1 (2022): 126–44.

167. Webster, Rice, and Sud, "Critical Content Analysis."

168. Gottschalk, *Prison and the Gallows*, 26–27, 33–34. For recent polling on public sentiment and the war on drugs, see ACLU, "Poll Results on American Attitudes Toward War on Drugs," June 9, 2021, https://www.aclu.org/documents/poll-results-american-attitudes-toward-war -drugs; Siegel, "Great Overdose Grief Divide," 41; and Taylor Orth, "Whom Do Americans Blame for the Problem of Fentanyl in the U.S.?," *YouGov*, April 26, 2023, https://today.yougov .com/politics/articles/45633-whom-do-americans-blame-problem-fentanyl-us.

169. Emma McGinty et al., "Public Support for Safe Consumption Sites and Syringe Services Programs to Combat the Opioid Epidemic," *Preventive Medicine* 111 (2018): 73–77; Alene Kennedy-Hendricks, "Social Stigma Toward Persons with Prescription Opioid Use Disorder: Associations with Public Support for Punitive and Public Health-Oriented Policies," *Psychiatric Services* 68, no. 5 (2017): 462–69. For more on safe consumption sites and other types of harm reduction, see chap. 11.

170. For example, it categorized drug courts and prescription monitoring programs as treatment and prevention interventions, yet these interventions are highly punitive and do not adhere to the core features of a medical model grounded in treatment and prevention, as discussed further in chap. 11. Shachar et al., "Criminal Justice or Public Health." For a more detailed critique of this study, see Marie Gottschalk, "The Opioid Crisis: The War on Drugs Is Over; Long Live the War on Drugs," *Annual Review of Criminology* 6 (January 2023): 369.

171. Shachar et al., "Criminal Justice or Public Health," 233.

172. Collins and Vakharia, "Criminal Justice Reform in the Fentanyl Era," 3.

173. Pew Charitable Trusts, "More Imprisonment Does Not Reduce State Drug Problems," March 8, 2018, https://www.pewtrusts.org/en/research-and-analysis/issue-briefs/2018/03 /more-imprisonment-does-not-reduce-state-drug-problems.

174. As reported by Chris McGreal, "War on Fentanyl as States Get Tough to Tackle Crisis," *Guardian Weekly*, August 4, 2023, 32c.

175. Bradley Ray et al., "Spatiotemporal Analysis Exploring the Effect of Law Enforcement Drug Market Disruptions on Overdose, Indianapolis, Indiana, 2020–2021," *American Journal of Public Health* 113, no. 7 (2023): 750–58.

176. Pew Charitable Trusts, "Drug Arrests Stayed High Even as Imprisonment Fell from 2009 to 2019," Issue Brief, February 15, 2022, https://www.pewtrusts.org/en/research-and -analysis/issue-briefs/2022/02/drug-arrests-stayed-high-even-as-imprisonment-fell-from -2009-to-2019.

177. FBI, "Crime in the United States, 2019," n.d., https://ucr.fbi.gov/crime-in-the-u.s/2019 /crime-in-the-US-2019/topic-pages/tables/table-29 (accessed November 16, 2020); and Susan Stellin, "Is the 'War on Drugs' Over? Arrest Statistics Say No," *NYT*, November 5, 2019, www .nytimes.com/2019/11/05/upshot/is-the-war-on-drugs-over-arrest-statistics-say-no.html. The FBI reported that drug arrests fell by nearly half between 2019 and 2022. This drop may have been because of the lockdown and pandemic or an artifact of new methods to collect and calculate crime data or the start of an enduring shift in drug law enforcement policy. FBI, Crime Data Explorer, National Incident-Based Reporting System, "Arrestees, 2022," n.d., https://cde .ucr.cjis.gov/LATEST/webapp/#Crimean the United States 2022-Arrests (accessed December 14, 2023).

178. The US average is 24 percent. Pew Charitable Trusts, "More Imprisonment Does Not Reduce State Drug Problems."

179. One of the most comprehensive analyses of congressional drug-related legislation concluded otherwise. But a closer look at that study casts some doubt on its central conclusions. Kim, Morgan, and Nyhan, "Treatment Versus Punishment." For a critique of this study, see Gottschalk, "Opioid Crisis," 369.

180. Peter Reuter, "Why Has U.S. Drug Policy Changed So Little over 30 Years?," *Crime and Justice* 42, no. 1 (2013): 84.

181. Jerry Mitchell, "Obama Gets D-Minus, Trump an F for Work on Opioid Epidemic, Expert Says," *Clarion Ledger*, February 9, 2018, https://www.clarionledger.com/story/news /2018/02/09/obama-gets-d-trump-f-work-opioid-epidemic-expert-says/1043205001/; and Scott Higham et al., "Obama Officials Failed to Focus as Fentanyl Burned Its Way Across America," *WP*, March 13, 2019, https://www.washingtonpost.com/graphics/2019/national/fentanyl -epidemic-obama-administration/.

182. Donald P. Francis, "Deadly AIDS Policy Failure by the Highest Levels of the US Government: A Personal Look Back 30 Years Later for Lessons to Respond Better to Future Epidemics," *Journal of Public Health Policy* 33, no. 3 (2012): 290–300; "President Reagan Delivers First Major Speech on AIDS Epidemic in 1987," ABC News, April 1, 1987, https://abcnews.go .com/Health/video/president-reagan-delivers-major-speech-aids-epidemic-1987-46492956; and "Silence = Death" ACT UP banner, 1987, stonewallforever.org, n.d., https://stonewallforever .org/monument/silence-death-act-up-banner-1987/ (accessed February 8, 2025).

183. Betsy Swan, "Law Enforcement Struggles with New Opioid Craze: Elephant Tranquilizers," *Daily Beast*, March 23, 2017, updated April 10, 2017, https://www.thedailybeast.com/law -enforcement-struggles-with-new-opioid-craze-elephant-tranquilizers.

184. Marie Gottschalk, *Caught: The Prison State and the Lockdown of American Politics*, rev. ed. (Princeton, NJ: Princeton University Press, 2016), 263.

185. HHS, *Facing Addiction in America: The Surgeon General's Report on Alcohol, Drugs, and Health* (Washington, DC: HHS, 2016).

186. Community Anti-Drug Coalitions of America (CADCA), "The Comprehensive Addiction and Recovery Act (CARA)," n.d., https://cadca.org/comprehensive-addiction-and -recovery-act-cara (accessed September 29, 2020).

187. Beletsky, "21st Century Cures": 372.

188. "'Cures' Act in Congress Heavily Influenced by Lobbyists," NBC News, November 29, 2016, https://www.nbcnews.com/health/health-news/cures-act-congress-heavily-influenced -lobbyists-n689531.

189. Beletsky, "21st Century Cures": 360.

190. Beletsky: 372–73.

191. The Pharmaceutical Research and Manufacturers of America (PhRMA), the primary trade group for major drug manufacturers, reported spending nearly $25 million on lobbying alone for the bill. "'Cures' Act."

192. Jerry Avorn and Aaron Kesselheim, "The 21st Century Cures Act—Will It Take Us Back in Time?," *NEJM* 372, no. 26 (2015): 2474.

193. Jerome P. Kassierer, "The 21st Century Cures Potpourri: Was It Worth the Price?," *American Journal of Law and Medicine* 44, no. 2–3 (Summer–Fall 2018): 158.

194. Double-blinded randomized controlled trials would no longer be the gold standard for drug approval. Companies now would be permitted to submit observational studies, summaries of the literature, and even case studies during the approval process. Previously such evidence had "been shunned . . . as insufficiently reliable." Kassierer, 159; see also Eleanor D. Kinney, "21st Century Cures Act and Medical Device Regulation: Departure from Principles or Catching the Wave?," *American Journal of Law and Medicine* 44, nos. 2–3 (Summer–Fall 2018): 280.

195. Sam F. Halabi, "Off-Label Marketing's Audiences: The 21st Century Cures Act and the Relaxation of Standards for Evidence-Based Therapeutic and Cost-Comparative Claims," *American Journal of Law and Medicine* 44, nos. 2–3 (Summer–Fall 2018): 182.

196. Anthony W. Orlando and Arnold J. Rosoff, "Fast-Forward to the Frightening Future: How the 21st Century Cures Act Accelerates Technological Innovation . . . at Unknown Risk to Us All," *American Journal of Law and Medicine* 44, nos. 2–3 (Summer–Fall 2018): 253–68.

197. The Cures Act authorized nearly $5 billion in new money for the National Institutes of Health over ten years, notably for research on brain disease and for the Beau Biden Cancer

Moonshot initiative, named in honor of Joe Biden's son who died of brain cancer in 2015. To help pay for these new initiatives, the measure slashed $3.5 billion from the Prevention and Public Health Fund established under the Affordable Care Act to invest in public health and disease prevention, including infectious diseases that could spark pandemics. Even before this, the fund was being drained for other purposes. Sydney Lupkin and Steven Findlay, "Grab Bag of Goodies in the 21st Century Cures Act," Kaiser Health News, December 7, 2016, https://khn .org/news/grab-bag-of-goodies-in-21st-century-cures-act/; Benjamin Hulac, "Oil Purchase to Fill Strategic Reserve Dropped from Stimulus," Roll Call, March 25, 2020, https://rollcall.com/2020 /03/25/oil-purchase-to-fill-strategic-reserve-dropped-from-stimulus/; and Jennifer Haber- korn, "The Prevention and Public Health Fund," Health Affairs: Health Policy Brief, February 12, 2012, https://www.healthaffairs.org/do/10.1377/hpb20120223.98342/full/healthpolicybrief _63.pdf.

198. Sheila Kaplan, "Who Wins and Loses with the 21st Century Cures Act?," Newshour, PBS, December 6, 2016, https://www.pbs.org/newshour/health/wins-loses-21st-century-cures -act.

199. "Statement by the President on Senate Passage of H.R. 34, the 21st Century Cures Act," December 7, 2016, Obama White House Archives, https://obamawhitehouse.archives.gov/the -press-office/2016/12/07/statement-president-senate-passage-hr-34-21st-century-cures-act.

200. German Lopez, "Elizabeth Warren's $100 Billion Plan to Fight the Opioid Epidemic, Explained," Vox, May 8, 2019, https://www.vox.com/future-perfect/2019/5/8/18535959 /elizabeth-warren-opioid-epidemic-2020-democratic-campaigns-trump.

201. Beletsky, "21st Century Cures": 381.

202. Beletsky: 384, table 1.

203. Nazgol Ghandnoosh and Casey Anderson, Opioids: Treating an Illness, Ending a War (Washington, DC: Sentencing Project, 2017), 15.

204. Lauren Krisai, "The Media Narrative Around Drug Use Is Shifting, but the Harsh Poli- cies for Drug Crimes Are Not," Reason, February 21, 2016, https://reason.com/2016/02/21/the -media-narrative-around-heroin/.

205. Sara Cline, "Here's a Look at Some of Louisiana's New 2023 Laws," AP, August 1, 2023, https://apnews.com/article/louisiana-laws-new-2023-07531f610ccb3b89501ab13ce1cfd661.

206. Mike Baker, "Oregon Is Recriminalizing Drugs, Dealing Setback to Reform Move- ment," NYT, March 1, 2024, https://www.nytimes.com/2024/03/01/us/oregon-drug -decriminalization-rollback-measure-110.html; and E. Tammy Kim, "Do No Harm," NY, Janu- ary 22, 2024, 20–25.

207. Collins and Vakharia, "Criminal Justice Reform in the Fentanyl Era," 8.

208. Collins and Vakharia, 8.

209. Between fiscal 2017 and fiscal 2021, the number of people convicted of fentanyl offenses under federal drug trafficking laws soared by 950 percent. USSC, "Quick Facts: Fentanyl Traf- ficking Offenses; Fiscal Year 2021," n.d., https://www.ussc.gov/sites/default/files/pdf/research -and-publications/quick-facts/Fentanyl_FY21.pdf (accessed December 26, 2023). See also "Federal Drug Enforcement Cracks Down on Meth and Fentanyl," TRAC Reports, Syracuse University, May 10, 2023, https://trac.syr.edu/reports/715/.

210. Alexander Testa and Jacqueline G. Lee. "Trends in Sentencing of Federal Drug Offend- ers: Findings from U.S. District Courts 2002–2017," Journal of Drug Issues 51, no. 1 (January 2021): 84–108.

211. In 2014, the USSC agreed to make some recent changes in its sentencing guidelines retroactive, rendering nearly fifty thousand people serving time for drug offenses in federal prisons eligible to seek reduced sentences. But four years later, it voted unanimously to ratchet up penalties for fentanyl-related offenses. Jerry Markon and Rachel Weiner, "Thousands of Felons Could Have Drug Sentences Lessened," WP, July 18, 2014, http://www.washingtonpost

.com/politics/thousands-of-felons-could-have-drug-sentences-lessened/2014/07/18
/4876209e-0eb1-11e4-8341-b8072b1e7348_story.html; and Collins and Vakharia, "Criminal
Justice Reform in the Fentanyl Era," 8.

212. USSC, "Public Data Presentation for Synthetic Cathinones, Synthetic Cannabinoids,
and Fentanyl and Fentanyl Analogues Amendments," January 2018, https://www.ussc.gov/sites
/default/files/pdf/research-and-publications/data-briefings/2018_synthetic-drugs.pdf, 25;
and USSC, "Quick Facts: Fentanyl Trafficking Offenses; Fiscal Year 2018," n.d., https://www
.ussc.gov/sites/default/files/pdf/research-and-publications/quick-facts/Fentanyl_FY18.pdf
(accessed November 4, 2020).

213. Collins and Vakharia, "Criminal Justice Reform in the Fentanyl Era," 3, 10; Jan Hoffman,
"Harsh New Fentanyl Laws Ignite Debate over How to Combat Overdose Crisis," NYT, June 21,
2023, updated June 22, 2023, https://www.nytimes.com/2023/06/21/health/fentanyl-overdose
-crisis.html; and Katherine Beckett and Marco Brydolf-Horwitz, "A Kinder, Gentler Drug War?
Race, Drugs, and Punishment in 21st Century America," Punishment and Society 22, no. 4 (October 2020): 519–20.

214. US Congress, Public Law 99-570, "Anti–Drug Abuse Act of 1986," congress.gov, https://
www.congress.gov/99/statute/STATUTE-100/STATUTE-100-Pg3207.pdf.

215. Action Lab, "Media Mentions of Drug Induced Homicide by Year (1974–2022)," n.d.,
https://www.healthinjustice.org/drug-induced-homicide (accessed December 16, 2024).

216. Daniel Nichanian, "DAs Increasingly Treat Overdoses as Homicides: Will November
Reel That In?," Appeal, October 24, 2019, http://www.appealpolitics.org/2019/drug-induced
-homicide-da-elections-pennsylvania-new-york/; and Jeremy Roebuck and Aubrey Whelan,
"Montco Woman, 24, Is Sentenced to 21 Years in Prison for Friend's Heroin Overdose Death,"
PI, May 29, 2019, www.inquirer.com/news/emma-semler-heroin-philly-jenny-werstler-drug
-distribution-involving-death-mandatory-minimum-20190529.html.

217. DOJ, National Heroin Task Force Final Report and Recommendations, December 31, 2015,
https://www.justice.gov/file/822231/download, 12.

218. Action Lab, "Media Mentions of Drug Induced Homicide."

219. Hoffman, "Harsh New Fentanyl Laws"; and Prescription Drug Abuse Policy System,
"Drug-Induced Homicide Laws, Map," January 1, 2019, http://pdaps.org/datasets/drug-induced
-homicide-1529945480-1549313265-1559075032. The United States is exceptional for the
persistence of the felony murder rule, which other common-law countries have largely abolished. Gottschalk, Caught, 178–80.

220. Claire Goforth, "Florida in Debate over Murder Charges for Drug Dealers Whose Buyers Die," CR, July 29, 2019, https://jjie.org/2019/07/29/florida-considers-murder-charge-for
-drug-dealers/; and Handberg, "Opioid Epidemic in Florida," 23.

221. Patricia Daugherty and Nick Stachula, "Drug-Related Homicides: Investigative and
Prosecutorial Strategies," National RX Drug Abuse and Heroin Summit, April 19, 2017, https://
vendome.swoogo.com/2017-rx-summit/Wednesday-April-19; Zachary A. Siegel, "'You Want
to Get Them While the Teardrops Are Warm': Prosecutors Swap Strategies for Turning Overdose Deaths into Homicides," Appeal, November 21, 2017, https://theappeal.org/you-want-to
-get-them-while-the-teardrops-are-warm-prosecutors-swap-strategies-for-turning-942a783
ae87c/; and Beletsky, "America's Favorite Antidote": 890, fig. 5.

222. Drug Policy Alliance, "An Overdose Death Is Not Murder: Why Drug-Induced Homicide Laws Are Counterproductive and Inhumane," November 2017, http://www.drugpolicy.org
/sites/default/files/dpa_drug_induced_homicide_report_0.pdf, 2, emphasis in the original.
See also Bradley Stein et al., America's Opioid Ecosystem: How Leveraging System Interactions Can
Help Curb Addiction, Overdose, and Other Harms (Santa Monica, CA: RAND, 2023), 237.

223. Beletsky, "America's Favorite Antidote": 882.

224. Beletsky: 862–63.

225. Alene Kennedy-Hendricks, Emma McGinty, and Colleen Barry, "Effects of Competing Narratives on Public Perceptions of Opioid Pain Reliever Addiction During Pregnancy," *Journal of Health Politics, Policy and Law* 41, no. 5 (2016): 877–78.

226. Khiara M. Bridges, "Race, Pregnancy, and the Opioid Epidemic: White Privilege and the Criminalization of Opioid Use During Pregnancy," *Harvard Law Review* 133, no. 3 (January 2020): 771. See also Nicole L. G. Villapiano et al., "Rural and Urban Differences in Neonatal Abstinence Syndrome and Maternal Opioid Use, 2004–2013," *JAMA Pediatrics* 171, no. 2 (February 2017): 1943–96.

227. Jennifer Egan, "Children of the Opioid Epidemic," *NYT*, May 9, 2018, https://www.nytimes.com/2018/05/09/magazine/children-of-the-opioid-epidemic.html; and Kennedy-Hendricks et al., "Effects of Competing Narratives," 875–76.

228. This account of the consequences of MAT for pregnant women, new parents, and their infants is drawn primarily from Shoshana Walter, "They Followed Doctors' Orders: Then Their Children Were Taken Away," *NYT*, June 29, 2023, updated July 1, 2023, https://www.nytimes.com/2023/06/29/magazine/pregnant-women-medication-suboxonbabies.html.

229. The provision specifically applied to providers in states receiving federal money to support certain child abuse programs, which is nearly every state.

230. Walter, "They Followed Doctors' Orders."

231. Walter.

232. Christopher Wildeman, Frank R. Edwards, and Sara Wakefield, "The Cumulative Prevalence of Termination of Parental Rights for U.S. Children, 2000–2016," *Child Maltreatment* 25, no. 1 (2020): 32–42.

233. Quoted in Shoshana Walter, "A Mother's Worst Nightmare," *Reveal News*, June 29, 2023, https://revealnews.org/article/a-mothers-worst-nightmare-medication-assisted-treatment/.

234. As of 2015, nearly forty states permitted the involuntary commitment of people for substance use disorder, more than double the number in 1991. Steve Horn, "Opioid Epidemic Impacts Prisons and Jails," *PLN* 30, no. 9 (2019): 11; and Leo Beletsky, Elizabeth J. Ryan, and Wendy E. Parmet, "Involuntary Treatment for Substance Use Disorder: A Misguided Response to the Opioid Crisis," *Harvard Health Blog*, January 24, 2018, https://www.health.harvard.edu/blog/involuntary-treatment-sud-misguided-response-2018012413180.

235. Kimberly Sue, *Getting Wrecked: Women, Incarceration, and the American Opioid Crisis* (Oakland: University of California Press, 2019), 55.

236. Horn, "Opioid Epidemic Impacts Prisons and Jails," 11; and Dan Werb et al., "The Effectiveness of Compulsory Drug Treatment: A Systematic Review," *International Journal of Drug Policy* 28 (2016): 1–9.

237. Marianne Møllmann and Christine Mehta, "Neither Justice nor Treatment: Drug Courts in the United States," Physicians for Human Rights, June 2017, https://phr.org/our-work/resources/niether-justice-nor-treatment/, 18.

238. Leora Smith, "West Virginia Cities Use Evictions to Combat the Opioid Epidemic," *Appeal*, June 9, 2020, https://theappeal.org/west-virginia-evictions-opioids/.

239. Mark A. R. Kleiman, Jonathan P. Caulkins, and Angela Hawken, *Drugs and Drug Policy: What Everyone Needs to Know* (New York: Oxford University Press, 2011), 55. See also Reuter, "Why Has U.S. Drug Policy Changed So Little?," 101.

240. A RAND Corporation analysis of the illicit drug market calculated that people in the United States spent $150 billion (in 2018 dollars) on cocaine, heroin, marijuana, and methamphetamine in 2016. Gregory Midgette, Steven Davenport, Jonathan P. Caulkins, and Beau Kilmer, *What America's Users Spend on Illegal Drugs, 2006–2016* (Santa Monica, CA: RAND, 2019), xi. See also Channing May, *Transnational Crime and the Developing World* (Washington, DC: Global Financial Integrity, May 2017), xi.

241. Kleiman, Caulkins, and Hawken, *Drugs and Drug Policy*, 56; and Eric Schneider, *Smack: Heroin and the American City* (Philadelphia: University of Pennsylvania Press, 2008).

242. Humphreys, testimony, Hearing on Immigration and the Opioid Crisis, 3.

243. John P. Walters and David W. Murray, "Kill All the Poppies," *Foreign Policy*, November 22, 2017, https://foreignpolicy.com/2017/11/22/kill-all-the-poppies-afghanistan-heroin-taliban/.

244. See, for example, David Farber, ed., *The War on Drugs: A History* (New York: New York University Press, 2022), chaps. 4, 8, and 9; Kleiman, Caulkins, and Hawken, *Drugs and Drug Policy*, chap. 8; and Peter Reuter, "Can the Borders Be Sealed?," *Public Interest* 92 (Summer 1988): 51–65.

245. Richard Nixon, "Remarks About an Intensified Program for Drug Abuse Prevention and Control," June 17, 1971, American Presidency Project, https://www.presidency.ucsb.edu/documents/remarks-about-intensified-program-for-drug-abuse-prevention-and-control.

246. Michael Massing, *The Fix* (Berkeley: University of California Press, 1998), 112, 119–20.

247. Barbara Andraka-Christou, *The Opioid Fix: America's Addiction Crisis and the Solution They Don't Want You to Have* (Baltimore: Johns Hopkins University Press, 2020), 44–45. For more on drug policy under Nixon's successors, see Reuter, "Why Has U.S. Drug Policy Changed So Little?," 81–85.

248. Reuter, "Why Has U.S. Drug Policy Changed So Little?," 84.

249. David Bewley-Taylor, *International Drug Control: Consensus Fractured* (Cambridge: Cambridge University Press, 2012), 115.

250. Annual spending on treatment increased from $8 billion to $15 billion between fiscal 2007 and fiscal 2016. Spending on interdiction increased from about $22 billion to $31 billion over the same period. These figures do not include the full costs associated with the US military's role in waging the wars on drugs abroad. Diana C. Maurer, director, Homeland Security and Justice, prepared testimony, US Senate Committee on Homeland Security and Governmental Affairs, May 17, 2016, https://www.gao.gov/assets/680/677235.pdf, 1.

251. Christopher Ingraham, "The Radical Way Obama Wants to Change the Drug War," *WP*, February 10, 2016, https://www.washingtonpost.com/news/wonk/wp/2016/02/10/the-radical-way-the-presidents-spending-plan-would-change-the-drug-war/.

252. Editorial Board, "America Has Lost the War on Drugs: What Needs to Happen Next?," *NYT*, February 22, 2023, https://www.nytimes.com/2023/02/22/opinion/harm-reduction-public-health.html.

253. Peter Reuter, "Eternal Hope: America's Quest for Narcotics Control," *Public Interest* 79 (Spring 1985): 79–95.

254. Sue, *Getting Wrecked*, 197.

11. Undertreated and Mistreated: The Opioid Crisis and a Nation in Pain

1. Quoted in Dan Lieberman, Sean Ryon, and Ed Ou, "Rise in Overdose Deaths During the Pandemic Has Renewed Push to Open America's First Legal Safe Injection Site," NBC News and Quibi, August 2, 2020, https://www.nbcnews.com/news/us-news/overdose-deaths-during-pandemic-philadelphia-fights-legal-safe-injection-site-n1235583. Rosalind Pichardo has administered Narcan to hundreds of people who have overdosed in Philadelphia.

2. Thomas Babor et al., *Drug Policy and the Public Good*, 2nd ed. (Oxford: Oxford University Press, 2018), 61.

3. Calculated from an overdose rate of 7 per million people for Portugal and 321 per million for the United States in 2021. Maia Svalavitz, "Portugal Has Succeeded Where We've Failed with Addiction," *NYT*, August 29, 2023, https://www.nytimes.com/2023/08/29/opinion/arrest-drug-treatment-addiction.html; and KFF, "All Drug Overdose Deaths, 2021," n.d., kff.org, https://www.kff.org/other/state-indicator/opioid-overdose-deaths/?currentTimeframe=1&selec

tedDistributions=all-drug-overdose-deaths&sortModel=%7B%22colId%22:%22Location%2
2,%22sort%22:%22asc%22%7D (accessed December 14, 2024).

4. People with opioid use disorder typically need eight years and four to five attempts at treatment to achieve remission for a single year. John Kelly, "Reasons for Optimism: Recovery Science," Association of Health Journalists Conference," Orlando, FL, April 2017, slide 14, cited in Beth Macy, *Dopesick: Dealers, Doctors, and the Drug Company That Addicted America* (New York: Little, Brown), 243, 351.

5. Estimates of the number of people with opioid use disorder in the United States range from 2.5 million to 7.6 million individuals. Only about one-quarter to one-third of them are under treatment for substance use disorder. Christopher Jones et al., "Use of Medication for Opioid Use Disorder Among Adults with Past-Year Opioid Use Disorder in the US, 2021," *JAMA Network Open* 6, no. 8 (August 7, 2023): e2327488, https://doi.org/10.1001/jamanetworkopen .2023.27488; Noa Krawczyk et al., "Has the Treatment Gap for Opioid Use Disorder Narrowed in the U.S.? A Yearly Assessment from 2010 to 2019," *International Journal of Drug Policy* 110 (December 2022), https://doi.org/10.1016/j.drugpo.2022.103786; Li-Tzy Wu, He Zhu, and Marvin S. Swartz, "Treatment Utilization Among Persons with Opioid Use Disorder in the United States," *Drug and Alcohol Dependence* 169 (2016): 117–27; and NIDA, "Only 1 in 5 U.S. Adults with Opioid Use Disorder Received Medications to Treat It in 2021," press release, August 7, 2023, https://nida.nih.gov/news-events/news-releases/2023/08/only-1-in-5-us-adults -with-opioid-use-disorder-received-medications-to-treat-it-in-2021#:~:text=Researchers%20 found%20that%20in%202021,medications%20for%20opioid%20use%20disorder.

6. G. William Hoagland et al., *Tracking Federal Funding to Combat the Opioid Crisis* (Washington, DC: Bipartisan Policy Center, 2019), 6.

7. Benjamin Bearnot et al., "Access to Treatment for Drug Use Disorders at U.S. Health Centers: A National Study," *Journal of General Internal Medicine* 34, no. 12 (2019): 2724; and Alexander C. Tsai et al., "Stigma as a Fundamental Hindrance to the United States Opioid Overdose Crisis Response," *PloS Medicine* 16, no. 11 (November 2019): e1002969, https://doi .org/10.1371/journal.pmed.1002969.

8. Emma McGinty et al., "Public Support for Safe Consumption Sites and Syringe Services Programs to Combat the Opioid Epidemic," *Preventive Medicine* 111 (2018): 73–77; and Brea L. Perry, Bernice A. Pescosolido, and Anne C. Krendl, "The Unique Nature of Public Stigma Toward Non-Medical Prescription Opioid Use and Dependence: A National Study," *Addiction* 115, no. 12 (December 2020): 2317–26.

9. HHS, *Facing Addiction in America: The Surgeon General's Report on Alcohol, Drugs, and Health* (Washington, DC: HHS, 2016), v; and Anne Schneider and Helen Ingram, "Social Construction of Target Populations: Implications for Politics and Policy," *American Political Science Review* 87, no. 2 (1993): 334–47.

10. Emma E. McGinty et al., "Criminal Activity or Treatable Health Condition? News Media Framing of Opioid Analgesic Abuse in the United States, 1998–2012," *Psychiatric Services* 67, no. 4 (April 2016): 405–11.

11. Alene Kennedy-Hendricks at al., "News Media Reporting on Medication Treatment for Opioid Use Disorder amid the Opioid Epidemic," *Health Affairs* 38, no. 4 (2019): 643–51.

12. Barbara Andraka-Christou, *The Opioid Fix: America's Addiction Crisis and the Solution They Don't Want You to Have* (Baltimore: Johns Hopkins University Press, 2020), 46–51.

13. Robert Blendon and John Benson, "The Public and the Opioid-Abuse Epidemic," *NEJM*, 378, no. 5 (2018): 411; and Lydia Aletraris et al., "Counselor Training and Attitudes Toward Pharmacotherapies for Opioid Use Disorder," *Substance Abuse* 37, no. 1 (2016): 47–53.

14. NIDA, "Is Medication to Treat Opioid Use Disorder Available in the Military?," April 13, 2021, https://nida.nih.gov/publications/research-reports/medications-to-treat-opioid-addic tion/medication-to-treat-opioid-use-disorder-available-in-military.

15. Sarah Wakeman et al., "Internal Medicine Residents' Training in Substance Use Disorders: A Survey of the Quality of Instruction and Residents' Self-Perceived Preparedness to Diagnose and Treat Addiction," *Substance Abuse* 34, no. 4 (2013): 365–66. See also Andraka-Christou, *Opioid Fix*, 147–52, 158–63.

16. Editorial Board, "America Has Lost the War on Drugs: What Needs to Happen Next?," *NYT*, February 22, 2023, https://www.nytimes.com/2023/02/22/opinion/harm-reduction-public-health.html.

17. Colleen M. Grogan et al., "Survey Highlights Differences in Medicaid Coverage for Substance Use Treatment and Opioid Use Disorder Medications," *Health Affairs* 35, no. 12 (December 2016): 2289.

18. Babor et al., *Drug Policy and the Public Good*, 145.

19. Sarah E. Wakeman et al., "Comparative Effectiveness of Different Treatment Pathways for Opioid Use Disorder," *JAMA Network Open* 3, no. 2 (2020): e1920622, https://doi.org/10.1001/jamanetworkopen.2019.20622.

20. Babor et al., *Drug Policy and the Public Good*, 145.

21. Kennedy-Hendricks et al., "News Media Reporting on Medication Treatment," 643–44 and 650n6–9; and Maia Szalavitz, "The Wrong Way to Treat Opioid Addiction," *NYT*, January 17, 2018, https://www.nytimes.com/2018/01/17/opinion/treating-opioid-addiction.html.

22. Andraka-Christou, *Opioid Fix*, 125. However, methadone for pain management is available by a prescription from a physician, nurse practitioner, or physician assistant that can be filled at the local pharmacy. Andraka-Christou, 123.

23. Eric Schneider, *Smack: Heroin and the American City* (Philadelphia: University of Pennsylvania Press, 2008), 159–70.

24. David Courtwright, *Dark Paradise: A History of Opiate Addiction* (Cambridge, MA: Harvard University Press, 2001), cited in Andraka-Christou, *Opioid Fix*, 45.

25. Richard Rettig and Adam Yarmolinsky, eds., *Federal Regulation of Methadone Treatment* (Washington, DC: National Academies Press, 1995), 3, emphasis in the original.

26. Lily Dobberteen, "Orange Handcuffs, Part of an (In)Complete Breakfast: Methadone's Failure to Address Structural Inequalities in the Civil Rights Era," BA thesis, Barnard College, April 2015, 24. In the Tuskegee syphilis study, this disease went untreated in hundreds of African American people as part of research by the US Public Health Service on the long-term effects of syphilis.

27. Dobberteen, "Orange Handcuffs," 22.

28. Schneider, *Smack*, 170.

29. Dobberteen, "Orange Handcuffs," 24, 19.

30. Andraka-Christou, *Opioid Fix*, 40.

31. Barbara Andraka-Christou, "Addressing Racial and Ethnic Disparities in the Use of Medications for Opioid Use Disorder," *Health Affairs* 40, no. 6 (June 2021): 920–27; and Schneider, *Smack*, 178.

32. Quoted in Patricia Strach, Katie Zuber, and Elizabeth Pérez-Chiqués, "Why Policies Fail: The Illusion of Services in the Opioid Epidemic," *Journal of Health Policy, Politics and Law* 45, no. 2 (2020): 354.

33. Strach et al.

34. Roger Rosenblatt et al., "Geographic and Specialty Distribution of U.S. Physicians Trained to Treat Opioid Use Disorder," *Annals of Family Medicine* 13, no. 1 (2015): 23–26; C. Holly A. Andrilla and Davis G. Patterson, "Tracking the Geographic Distribution and Growth of Clinicians with a DEA Waiver to Prescribe Buprenorphine to Treat Opioid Use Disorder," *Journal of Rural Health* 38, no. 1 (2022): 87–92; and Andraka-Christou, *Opioid Fix*, 52.

35. Andraka-Christou, "Addressing Racial and Ethnic Disparities."

36. Tsai et al., "Stigma as a Fundamental Hindrance."

37. Andraka-Christou, *Opioid Fix*, 93. As of 2016, only about one out of every three substance use treatment facilities offered MAT for opioid use disorder, and just 6 percent offered all three FDA-approved medications—methadone, buprenorphine, and naltrexone. Ramin Mojtabai et al., "Medication Treatment for Opioid Use Disorder in Substance Use Treatment Facilities," *Health Affairs* 38, no. 1 (2019): 14–23.

38. Andraka-Christou, *Opioid Fix*, 10.

39. Quoted in Cleve R. Wootson Jr., "Why This Sheriff Refuses to Let His Deputies Carry Narcan to Reverse Overdoses," *WP*, July 8, 2017, https://www.washingtonpost.com/news/to -your-health/wp/2017/07/08/an-ohio-countys-deputies-could-reverse-heroin-overdoses-the -sheriff-wont-let-them/.

40. See Wootson.

41. Christine Vestal, "Still Not Enough Treatment in the Heart of the Opioid Crisis," Pew Charitable Trusts, September 26, 2016, https://www.pewtrusts.org/en/research-and-analysis /blogs/stateline/2016/09/26/still-not-enough-treatment-in-the-heart-of-the-opioid-crisis; "Nope-ioids," *Economist*, February 4, 2023, 25; Zachary Siegel, "The Great Overdose Grief Divide," *NR*, July–August 2023, 41; and Abby Goodnough, "Helping Drug Users Survive, Not Abstain," *NYT*, June 27, 2021, updated July 14, 2021, https://www.nytimes.com/2021/06/27 /health/overdose-harm-reduction-covid.html.

42. Kennedy-Hendricks et al., "News Media Reporting on Medication Treatment," 644.

43. With abstinence-only treatment programs, people who relapse "drop out and are invisible; with medication, they often remain in treatment," which cuts the overdose risk. Szalavitz, "Wrong Way to Treat."

44. Kimberly Sue, *Getting Wrecked: Women, Incarceration, and the American Opioid Crisis* (Oakland: University of California Press, 2019), 78–79; Macy, *Dopesick*, 216–19; and Andraka-Christou, *Opioid Fix*, chap. 2.

45. NIDA, "Medications to Treat Opioid Use Disorder Research Report," December 2, 2021, https://nida.nih.gov/publications/research-reports/medications-to-treat-opioid-addiction/ overview eports/medications-to-treat-opioid-addiction/.

46. Macy, *Dopesick*, 213.

47. Macy, 213–14.

48. Alec MacGillis, "The Last Shot," *ProPublica*, June 27, 2017, https://www.propublica.org /article/vivitrol-opiate-crisis-and-criminal-justice.

49. For more on the Cures Act, see pp. 318–19.

50. Tami Mark et al., "Medicaid Coverage of Medications to Treat Alcohol and Opioid Dependence," *Journal of Substance Abuse Treatment* 55 (August 2015): 1–5.

51. Leo Beletsky, "21st Century Cures for the Opioid Crisis: Promise, Impact, and Missed Opportunities," *American Journal of Law and Medicine* 44, no. 2–3 (Summer–Fall 2018): 375.

52. Beletsky: 378, 380.

53. Andrilla and Patterson, "Tracking the Geographic Distribution," 87–92.

54. "Medicaid Provisions in Support Act," commonwealthfund.org, November 13, 2018, https://www.commonwealthfund.org/blog/2018/medicaid-provisions-support-act-important -step-forward-opioid-epidemic-road-ahead-long.

55. Ryan Hampton with Claire Rudy Foster and Hillel Aron, *Unsettled: How the Purdue Pharma Bankruptcy Failed the Victims of the American Overdose Crisis* (New York: St. Martin's, 2021), 155.

56. The Biden administration removed patient caps, slashed red tape, and even permitted online prescribing of buprenorphine. Ethan Brooks, "The Drug That Could Help End the Opioid Epidemic," *Atlantic*, n.d., https://www.theatlantic.com/podcasts/archive/2024/08/drug -could-help-end-opioid-epidemic/679397/ (accessed August 19, 2024).

57. Strach, Zuber, and Pérez-Chiqués, "Why Policies Fail," 342.

58. Aubrey Whelan, "Addiction Medications Shown to Save Lives," *PI*, January 16, 2021, A4.

59. "Nope-ioids."

60. M. Fatseas and Marc Auriacombe, "Why Buprenorphine Is So Successful in Treating Opiate Addiction in France," *Current Psychiatry Reports* 9, no. 5 (2007): 358–64; and Andraka-Christou, *Opioid Fix*, 205–10.

61. James S. Goodwin et al., "Association of Chronic Opioid Use with Presidential Voting Patterns in US Counties in 2016," *JAMA Network Open* 1, no. 2 (2018): e180450, https://doi.org/10.1001/jamanetworkopen.2018.0450; Travis Johnson, "Americans Think Opioid Addiction Is a Crisis: They're Not Sure Federal Dollars Will Solve It," *WP*, August 10, 2017, www.washingtonpost.com/news/monkey-cage/wp/2017/08/09/americans-think-opioid-addiction-is-a-crisis-theyre-not-sure-federal-dollars-will-solve-it/.

62. As of November 2024, forty states and the District of Columbia had opted to expand Medicaid under the ACA. KFF, "Status of State Action on the Medicaid Expansion Decision," n.d., https://www.kff.org/affordable-care-act/state-indicator/state-activity-around-expanding-medicaid-under-the-affordable-care-act/?currentTimeframe=0&sortModel=%7B%22colId%22:%22Location%22,%22sort%22:%22asc%22%7D (accessed February 12, 2025).

63. Colleen M. Grogan et al., "Are Policy Strategies for Addressing the Opioid Epidemic Partisan? A View from the States," *Journal of Health Politics, Policy and Law* 45, no. 2 (April 2020): 279.

64. KFF, "Status of State Action on the Medicaid Expansion Decision"; and Lisa Rab, "The Medical Crisis That Finally Convinced Republicans in North Carolina to Expand Medicaid," *Politico*, August 14, 2022, https://www.politico.com/news/magazine/2022/08/14/new-moms-convinced-republicans-to-expand-medicaid-00049534.

65. Grogan et al., "Are Policy Strategies," 303; see also 293–96.

66. Grogan et al., 299, 302, table 5c, and 296–97, table 3.

67. Lisa Clemans-Cope et al., "State Variation in Medicaid Prescriptions for Opioid Use Disorder from 2011 to 2018," Urban Institute, August 2019, https://www.urban.org/sites/default/files/publication/100817/2019.08.19_av_state_medicaid_rx_oud_final_v3_4.pdf.

68. These strategies included, for example, attempting to impose co-pays and work requirements on Medicaid recipients in the name of siphoning off "deserving" recipients from "undeserving" ones. Grogan et al., "Are Policy Strategies," 287.

69. Grogan et al., 287–88.

70. Babor et al., *Drug Policy and the Public Good*, 68.

71. Grogan et al., "Are Policy Strategies," 292–93.

72. Colton Wooten, "My Years in the Florida Shuffle of Drug Addiction," *NY*, October 14, 2019, https://www.newyorker.com/magazine/2019/10/21/my-years-in-the-florida-shuffle-of-drug-addiction.

73. Grogan et al., "Are Policy Strategies," 290.

74. Laura Katz Olson, *Ethically Challenged: Private Equity Storms US Health Care* (Baltimore: Johns Hopkins University Press, 2022), especially chap. 7; and Colleen M. Grogan, "States, Federalism, and Medicaid: Medicaid's Post-ACA Paradoxes," *Journal of Health Politics, Policy and Law* 45, no. 4 (August 2020): 625.

75. Andraka-Christou, *Opioid Fix*, 101; Erica Goode, "Centers to Treat Eating Disorders Are Growing, Raising Concerns," *NYT*, March 14, 2016, https://www.nytimes.com/2016/03/15/health/eating-disorders-anorexia-bulimia-treatment-centers.html; Brian Mann, "As Addiction Deaths Surge, Profit-Driven Rehab Industry Faces 'Severe Ethical Crisis,'" NPR, February 15, 2021, https://www.npr.org/2021/02/15/963700736/as-addiction-deaths-surge-profit-driven-rehab-industry-faces-severe-ethical-cris; and Wooten, "My Years in the Florida Shuffle."

76. Wooten, "My Years in the Florida Shuffle."

77. David W. S. Lieberman, "EKRA—a Guide to the Eliminating Kickbacks in Recovery Act," Whistleblower Law Collaborative, n.d., https://www.whistleblowerllc.com/ekra-eliminating-kickbacks-in-recovery-act/ (accessed October 6, 2020).

78. Jack Healy, "They Wanted to Get Sober: They Got a Nightmare Instead," *NYT*, November 11, 2023, https://www.nytimes.com/2023/11/11/us/arizona-native-american-addiction.html.

79. Wooten, "My Years in the Florida Shuffle."

80. Wooten.

81. Lieberman, "EKRA."

82. About four out of ten people serving a jail or prison sentence reported having a drug use disorder in the year before they were admitted. But only about one-quarter of them reported participating in any kind of drug treatment program while serving time. Fewer than one in six incarcerated people said they received professional treatment for their affliction. Jennifer Bronson et al., "Drug Use, Dependence, and Abuse Among State Prisoners and Jail Inmates, 2007–2009," DOJ BJS, June 2017, 1, https://www.bjs.gov/content/pub/pdf/dudaspji0709.pdf; and Nazgol Ghandnoosh and Casey Anderson, "Opioids: Treating an Illness, Ending a War" (Washington, DC: Sentencing Project, 2017), 12, table 6. See also Christy K. Scott et al., "The Impact of the Opioid Crisis on U.S. State Prison Systems," *Health and Justice* 9 (December 2021): 1–17.

83. WHO, *Guidelines for the Psychosocially Pharmacological Treatment of Opioid Dependence* (Geneva, Switzerland: WHO, 2009), 12.

84. NAS, *Medications for Opioid Use Disorder Save Lives* (Washington, DC: National Academies Press, 2019), 10–11, 100, 103.

85. Only about 13 percent of the country's roughly five thousand jails and prisons offer some form of MAT maintenance programs for people with opioid use disorder, according to the Jail and Prison Opioid Project. Barely 2 percent of incarcerated people have received such treatment while in prison or jail. Noah Weiland, "In Jails and Prisons, the White House Sees a Chance to Curtail Opioid Overdoses," *NYT*, April 21, 2023, https://www.nytimes.com/2023/04/21/us/politics/prisons-opioid-addiction-treatment.html; and Beth Schwartzapfel, "These Meds Prevent Overdoses: Few Federal Prisoners Are Getting Them," Marshall Project, August 10, 2021, https://www.themarshallproject.org/2021/08/10/these-meds-prevent-overdoses-few-federal-prisoners-are-getting-them.

86. Jill A. McCorkel, *Breaking Women: Gender, Race, and the New Politics of Imprisonment* (New York: New York University Press, 2013), x. See also Sue, *Getting Wrecked*, chaps. 2–4.

87. J. B. Nicholas, "Drug Treatment Is Reaching More Prisons and Jails," *Appeal*, July 31, 2019, https://theappeal.org/a-shot-over-the-bow-to-all-jails-and-prisons/.

88. In specialized detox units, medical providers use a wide range of medications, including methadone and buprenorphine, to ease the symptoms and ensure the health and safety of people who are detoxing. Many incarcerated people undergo withdrawal with no medical support or only minimal medical support, such as Tylenol, Imodium, and other over-the-counter medications to treat pain, chills, fever, and diarrhea.

89. Christine E. Grella at al., "A Scoping Review of Barriers and Facilitators to Implementation of Medications for Treatment of Opioid Use Disorder within the Criminal Justice System," *International Journal on Drug Policy* 81 (July 2020): 102768.

90. Beth Schwartzapfel, "When Going to Jail Means Giving Up the Meds That Saved You," *PLN* 30, no. 9 (September 2019): 15.

91. See Eric Westervelt, "County Jails Struggle with a New Role as America's Prime Centers for Opioid Detox," NPR, April 24, 2019, https://www.npr.org/2019/04/24/716398909/county-jails-struggle-with-a-new-role-as-americas-prime-centers-for-opioid-detox.

92. Joanne Csete, "United States Drug Courts and Opioid Agonist Therapy: Missing the Target of Overdose Reduction," *Forensic Science International: Mind and Law* 1 (2020): 1–4; and MacGillis, "Last Shot."

93. Andrew Klein, email message to author, March 12, 2022.

94. MacGillis, "Last Shot."

95. Westervelt, "County Jails Struggle."

96. NIDA, "Medications to Treat Opioid Use Disorder Research Report."

97. Bill Meagher, "Trump's Opioid Plan Gives Alkerme's [sic] Vivitrol Drug Sales a Boost," *Street*, March 26, 2018, https://www.thestreet.com/opinion/trump-opioid-plan-gives-alkermes-vivitrol-boost-14534801#:~:text=Alkermes%20has%20spent%20money%20lobbying, becomes%20part%20of%20prison%20protocol.

98. Abby Goodnough and Kate Zernike, "Seizing an Opioid Crisis, a Drug Maker Lobbies Hard for Its Product," *NYT*, June 11, 2017, https://www.nytimes.com/2017/06/11/health/vivitrol-drug-opioid-addiction.html.

99. MacGillis, "Last Shot."

100. Goodnough and Zernike, "Seizing an Opioid Crisis"; MacGillis, "Last Shot"; Center for Responsive Politics, "Alkermes, Inc.: Expenditures, 2018 and 2020 Cycles," OpenSecrets.org, n.d., https://www.opensecrets.org/pacs/expenditures.php?cmte=C00525063&cycle=2018 and https://www.opensecrets.org/pacs/expenditures.php?cmte=C00525063&cycle=2020 (accessed August 21, 2020); and Paul Gaita, "Senator Kamala Harris to Investigate Vivitrol Maker's 'Aggressive' Marketing Practices," *Fix*, November 8, 2017, https://www.thefix.com/senator-kamala-harris-investigate-vivitrol-makers-aggressive-marketing-practices.

101. Goodnough and Zernike, "Seizing an Opioid Crisis."

102. Rachel Roubein, "HHS Chief Pitches New Measures to Expand Opioid Addiction Treatment," *Hill*, February 24, 2018, https://thehill.com/policy/healthcare/375455-hhs-chief-pitches-new-measures-to-expand-opioid-addiction-treatment/.

103. For a state-by-state overview of MAT-related litigation in penal facilities, see Shelly Weizman et al., "National Snapshot: Access to Medications for Opioid Use Disorder in U.S. Jails and Prisons," O'Neill Institute for National and Global Health Law at Georgetown Law Center, July 2021, https://oneill.law.georgetown.edu/wp-content/uploads/2021/07/National-Snapshot-Access-to-Medications-for-Opioid-Use-Disorder-in-U.S.-Jails-and-Prisons.pdf.

104. Steve Horn, "Opioid Epidemic Impacts Prison and Jails," *PLN* 30, no. 9 (2019): 1–13.

105. Schwartzapfel, "When Going to Jail Means Giving Up the Meds," 14–15; and Sarah N. Lynch, "Woman with Opioid Addiction to Get Regular Methadone Treatment in Prison," Reuters, June 7, 2019, https://www.reuters.com/article/us-usa-prisons-opioid-addiction/woman-with-opioid-addiction-to-get-regular-methadone-treatment-in-prison-idUSKCN1T903F.

106. Jeffrey A. Burkett as reported in Schwartzapfel, "These Meds Prevent Overdoses."

107. Weiland, "In Jails and Prisons."

108. The rate of drug- and alcohol-related deaths increased sevenfold in state prisons from 2001 to 2018 and fourfold in county jails from 2000 to 2018. E. Ann Carson, "Mortality in State and Federal Prisons, 2001–2018," DOJ BJS, April 2021, https://bjs.ojp.gov/content/pub/pdf/msfp0118st.pdf, 8, table 4; and E. Ann Carson, "Mortality in Local Jails, 2000–2018," DOJ BJS, April 2021, https://bjs.ojp.gov/content/pub/pdf/mlj0018st.pdf, 7, table 3.

109. They must retrieve it from a storage unit or call medical personnel to administer it, even though this opioid reversal drug is relatively easy to use. A delay of even a few minutes can be fatal for someone who is overdosing. Andy Potter, "Prisons Are Overlooked in Opioid Crisis," *Detroit News*, September 5, 2010, https://www.detroitnews.com/story/opinion/2018/09/05/prison-overlooked-opioid-crisis/1192865002/.

110. Elizabeth L. C. Merrall et al., "Meta-Analysis of Drug-Related Deaths Soon After Prison," *Addiction* 105, no. 9 (September 2010): 1545–54.

111. Even a year after release, they were eleven times more at risk of a fatal opioid overdose. Shabbar I. Ranapurwala et al., "Opioid Overdose Mortality Among Former North Carolina Inmates: 2000–2015," *American Journal of Public Health* 108, no. 9 (September 2018): 1207–13.

112. A pilot program in New York State that provided people released from state prison with naloxone kits had mixed results. Some people refused to take the kits, citing, among other

reasons, distrust of the criminal legal system and fears of being charged with violating parole if they were caught carrying the opioid reversal drug. Vedan Anthony-North et al., "Corrections-Based Responses to the Opioid Epidemic: Lessons from New York State's Overdose Education and Naloxone Distribution Program," Vera Institute of Justice, March 2018, 10; and Szalavitz, "Portugal Has Succeeded Where We've Failed."

113. Weiland, "In Jails and Prisons"; and Editorial Board, "America Has Lost the War on Drugs."

114. Traci C. Green et al., "Postincarceration Fatal Overdoses After Implementing Medications for Addiction Treatment in a Statewide Correctional System," *JAMA Psychiatry* 75, no. 4 (2018): 405–7.

115. Drug Policy Alliance, "Drug Courts Are Not the Answer: Toward a Health-Centered Approach to Drug Use," March 2011, https://drugpolicy.org/wp-content/uploads/2023/09/Drug-Courts-Are-Not-the-Answer_Final2.pdf, 14, emphasis in the original. See also Sue, *Getting Wrecked*, 22.

116. MacGillis, "Last Shot."

117. David Lilley, Megan Stewart, and Kasey Tucker-Gail, "Drug Courts and Net-Widening in U.S. Cities: A Reanalysis Using Propensity Score Matching," *Criminal Justice Policy Review* 31, no. 2 (March 2020): 287–308.

118. National Association of Drug Court Professionals, *Adult Drug Court Best Practice Standards*, vol. 1 (Alexandria: National Association of Drug Court Professionals, 2013), 6.

119. Marianne Møllmann and Christine Mehta, "Neither Justice nor Treatment: Drug Courts in the United States," Physicians for Human Rights, June 2017, https://phr.org/wp-content/uploads/2017/06/phr_drugcourts_report_singlepages.pdf, 14.

120. Eric Sevigny, Brian K. Fuleihan, and Frank V. Ferdik, "Do Drug Courts Reduce the Use of Incarceration? A Meta-Analysis," *Journal of Criminal Justice* 41, no. 6 (2013): 416–25.

121. Drug Policy Alliance, "Drug Courts Are Not the Answer," 14.

122. John Roman quoted in Samantha Melamed and Dylan Purcell, "Punishing Addiction: The Probation Trap," *PI*, October 24, 2019, https://www.inquirer.com/news/inq/probation-parole-pennsylvania-philadelphia-criminal-justice-system-20191024.html.

123. Shelli B. Rossman et al., *The Multi-Site Adult Drug Court Evaluation: The Impact of Drug Courts*, vol. 4, December 2011, https://www.ncjrs.gov/pdffiles1/nij/grants/237112.pdf, 3.

124. Møllmann and Mehta, "Neither Justice nor Treatment," 15.

125. Elizabeth Drake, Steve Aos, and Marna Miller, "Evidence-Based Public Policy Options to Reduce Crime and Criminal Justice Costs: Implications in Washington State," *Victims and Offenders* 4, no. 2 (2009): 170–96. See also Susan L. Ettner et al., "Benefit-Cost in the California Treatment Outcome Project: Does Substance Abuse Treatment 'Pay for Itself'?," *Health Services Research* 41, no. 1 (2006): 206.

126. Rebecca Tiger, *Judging Addicts: Drug Courts and Coercion in the Justice System* (New York: New York University Press, 2013); and Kerwin Kaye, *Enforcing Freedom: Drug Courts, Therapeutic Communities, and the Intimacies of the State* (New York: Columbia University Press, 2020).

127. Drug Policy Alliance, "Drug Courts Are Not the Answer," 16.

128. Daniel Abrahamson, "Legal Experts Urge UN to Reject Drug Courts," Drug Policy Alliance blog post, April 6, 2016, https://www.drugpolicy.org/blog/legal-experts-urge-un-reject-drug-courts.

129. Møllmann and Mehta, "Neither Justice nor Treatment," 14 and 27n113.

130. MacGillis, "Last Shot."

131. Melamed and Purcell, "Punishing Addiction."

132. UN Human Rights Special Procedures, "Drug Courts Pose Dangers of Punitive Approaches Encroaching on Medical and Health Matters, UN Experts Say," press release, March 22,

2019, https://www.unodc.org/documents/commissions/CND/2019/Contributions/UN
_Entities/InfoNote20March2019.pdf; and Møllmann and Mehta, "Neither Justice nor Treat-
ment," 1.

133. MacGillis, "Last Shot."

134. Faith E. Lutze and Jacqueline G. van Wormer, "The Nexus Between Alcohol Treatment
Program Integrity and Drug Court Effectiveness," *Criminal Justice Policy Review* 18, no. 3 (September 2007): 234, 236.

135. See Andraka-Christou, *Opioid Fix*, 176.

136. Harlan Matusow et al., "Medication Assisted Treatment in U.S. Drug Courts: Results
from a Nationwide Survey of Availability, Barriers and Attitudes," *Journal of Substance Abuse
Treatment* 44, no. 5 (2013): 477; and Barbara Andraka-Christou and Danielle Atkins, "Beliefs
About Medications for Opioid Use Disorder Among Florida Criminal Problem-Solving Court
and Dependency Court Staff," *American Journal of Drug and Alcohol Abuse* 46, no. 6 (November 2020): 749–60.

137. For example, women with substance use disorder are much more likely than men with
the affliction to have experienced sexual abuse, to be the primary caregivers for their children,
and to have employment problems. Bernadette Pelissier and Nicole Jones, "A Review of Gender
Differences Among Substance Abusers," *Crime and Delinquency* 51, no. 3 (July 2005): 343–72.
See also Kaye, *Enforcing Freedom*.

138. Drug Policy Alliance, "Drug Courts Are Not the Answer," 12.

139. Møllmann and Mehta, "Neither Justice nor Treatment," 11.

140. Elaine Pawlowski, "Malpractice and Injustice Continues [*sic*] in Drug Treatment
Court," *HuffPost*, June 8, 2017, https://www.huffpost.com/entry/malpractice-and-injustice
-continues-in-drug-treatment_b_5939738de4b094fa859f1655.

141. Drug courts often insist that defendants waive patient-doctor confidentiality as a condition for participation. Judges and other drug court personnel openly discuss personal information about the defendant during drug court proceedings, including items that are not relevant
"to the person's drug use, addiction, or alleged criminal behavior." Møllmann and Mehta, "Neither Justice nor Treatment," 4.

142. Møllmann and Mehta, 20.

143. MacGillis, "Last Shot."

144. MacGillis.

145. Noa Krawczyk et al., "Only One in Twenty Justice-Referred Adults in Specialty Treatment for Opioid Use Receive Methadone or Buprenorphine," *Health Affairs* 36, no. 12 (2017):
2046–53.

146. Csete, "United States Drug Courts," 3.

147. Møllmann and Mehta, "Neither Justice nor Treatment," 7.

148. Møllmann and Mehta, 12.

149. Andraka-Christou, *Opioid Fix*, 191.

150. See the discussion of *Robinson v. California* in Leo Beletsky, "America's Favorite Antidote: Drug-Induced Homicide in the Age of the Overdose Crisis," *Utah Law Review* 4, no. 4
(2019): 856–57.

151. In the 1968 *Powell v. Texas* decision, the Supreme Court declined to invalidate a Texas
law criminalizing public intoxication. Beletsky: 857 and 857n177.

152. Another major example is the Police Assisted Addiction and Recovery Initiative, which
operates in hundreds of communities and dozens of states. It permits people seeking treatment
for a drug problem to turn themselves (and their drugs) in to police stations, where police officers
take the lead in getting them into treatment. Katharine Q. Seelye, "Massachusetts Chief's Tack
in Drug War: Steer Addicts to Rehab, Not Jail," *NYT*, January 24, 2016, https://www.nytimes.com
/2016/01/25/us/massachusetts-chiefs-tack-in-drug-war-steer-addicts-to-rehab-not-jail.html.

153. Melamed and Purcell, "Punishing Addiction."

154. Sheryl Gay Stolberg, "Clinton Decides Not to Finance Needle Program," *NYT*, April 21, 1998, https://www.nytimes.com/1998/04/21/us/clinton-decides-not-to-finance-needle-program.html.

155. John Stanton, "After Decades, Congress Effectively Lifts Ban on Federally Funded Needle Exchanges," *BuzzFeed News*, January 5, 2016, https://www.buzzfeednews.com/article/johnstanton/after-decades-congress-effectively-lifts-ban-on-federally-fu.

156. Sheryl Gay Stolberg, "Uproar over 'Crack Pipes' Puts Biden Drug Strategy at Risk," *NYT*, February 21, 2022, https://www.nytimes.com/2022/02/21/us/politics/biden-harm-reduction-crack-pipes.html.

157. Aris Folley, "Advocates Scorn Lawmakers over 'Crack Pipe' Uproar," *Hill*, February 23, 2022, https://thehill.com/policy/finance/595409-advocates-scorn-lawmakers-over-crack-pipe-uproar/.

158. Peter Reuter, "Why Has U.S. Drug Policy Changed So Little over 30 Years?," *Crime and Justice* 42, no. 1 (2013): 106.

159. Anna Orso and Aubrey Whelan, "Mayor Cherelle Parker Says 'Not One City Dollar' Will Fund Syringe Exchange," *PI*, March 15, 2024, https://www.inquirer.com/news/philadelphia/philadelphia-syringe-exchanges-not-one-city-dollar-20240315.html.

160. Aubrey Whelan, "Providers Say Help for Those in Addiction Is at Risk," *PI*, January 2, 2025, A1.

161. Maia Szalavitz, "A Tale of Two Cities in the Grips of the Opioid Crisis," *Nation*, February 21, 2019, https://www.thenation.com/article/archive/opioid-epidemic-sif-harm-reduction/.

162. Jeremey Roebuck and Audrey Whelan, "Justice Department Reevaluating Supervised Injection Sites After Its Yearslong Effort to Block One in Philly," *PI*, February 9, 2022, https://www.inquirer.com/news/safe-injection-sites-safehouse-philadelphia-justice-department-20220209.html. During their first year of operation, the twenty supervised consumption sites in British Columbia had about 550,000 visits and not a single fatal overdose. Safe consumption sites operate in a legal gray zone in the United States. Federal prosecutors claim they violate the so-called crack house statute of the Anti–Drug Abuse Act of 1986, which criminalizes knowingly maintaining any property where illicit drugs are consumed.

163. MyNorthwest Staff, "'Dozens and Dozens' of Underground Safe Injection Sites in Seattle," *MyNorthwest*, November 1, 2018, https://mynorthwest.com/1167554/seattle-underground-safe-injection-sites/; and Alex H. Kral et al., "Evaluation of an Unsanctioned Safe Consumption Site in the United States," letter to the editor, *NEJM*, August 6, 2020, 589–90, https://www.nejm.org/doi/full/10.1056/NEJMc2015435.

164. Noah Weiland, "Cities Face Epidemic, and Backlash over Response," *NYT*, October 21, 2023, A14; and Nancy Lavin, "Four Years After R.I. Lawmakers OK Safe Injection Site Program, They're Still Debating Its Merits," *Rhode Island Current*, April 2, 2025, https://rhodeislandcurrent.com/2025/04/02/four-years-after-r-i-lawmakers-ok-safe-injection-site-program-theyre-still-debating-its-merits/.

165. Bruce Wallace, Flora Pagan, and Bernadette (Bernie) Pauly, "The Implementation of Overdose Prevention Sites as a Novel and Nimble Response During an Illegal Drug Overdose Public Emergency," *International Journal of Drug Policy* 66 (2019): 64–72; and Sue, *Getting Wrecked*, 194.

166. Jennifer Murphy, "Here's How Philly Can Learn from the Netherlands on the Opioid Crisis," *PI*, August 5, 2019, https://www.inquirer.com/opinion/commentary/philadelphia-safe-injection-site-netherlands-heroin-addiction-20190812.html; and Transform Drug Policy Foundation, "Heroin-Assisted Treatment in Switzerland," n.d., https://transformdrugs.org/heroin-assisted-treatment-in-switzerland-successfully-regulating-the-supply-and-use-of-a-high-risk-injectable-drug/ (accessed November 20, 2020).

167. "Fentanyl v. Vancouver," *Economist*, June 29, 2024, 25–26.

168. Hannah Laqueur, "Uses and Abuses of Drug Decriminalization in Portugal," *Law and Social Inquiry* 40, no. 3 (Summer 2015): 764. Peter Reuter contends that it is impossible to forecast "even roughly how much prevalence of use or dependence would increase." Reuter, "Why Has U.S. Drug Policy Changed So Little?," 11. See also Robert MacCoun and Peter Reuter, *Drug War Heresies: Learning from Other Vices, Times, and Places* (Cambridge: Cambridge University Press, 2010).

169. Richard G. Frank, Keith N. Humphreys, and Harold A. Pollack, "Policy Responses to the Addiction Crisis," *Journal of Health Politics, Policy and Law* 46, no. 4 (August 2021): 592; MacCoun and Reuter, *Drug War Heresies*; and Mark A. R. Kleiman, Jonathan P. Caulkins, and Angela Hawken, *Drugs and Drug Policy: What Everyone Needs to Know* (New York: Oxford University Press, 2011).

170. This is thanks partly to flat US federal excise taxes on alcoholic beverages that were "set almost thirty years ago and have declined in real terms every year since." Kleiman et al., *Drugs and Drug Policy*, 38.

171. Babor et al., *Drug Policy and the Public Good*, 253–54.

172. One study based on data from the 2010s found that 20 percent of people who used marijuana accounted for 80 percent of the quantity consumed. Jonathan P. Caulkins, "The Real Dangers of Marijuana," *National Affairs* 26 (2016): 21–24, cited in Babor et al., *Drug Policy and the Public Good*, 32.

173. Katie Thomas and Sheila Kaplan, "E-Cigarettes Went Unchecked in 10 Years of Federal Inaction," *NYT*, October 14, 2009, https://www.nytimes.com/2019/10/14/health/vaping-e-cigarettes-fda.html#:~:text=A%20decade%20after%20Congress%20gave,that%20could%20have%20protected%20teenagers. See also Lauren Etter, *The Devil's Playbook: Big Tobacco, Juul, and the Addiction of a New Generation* (New York: Crown, 2021).

174. Babor et al., *Drug Policy and the Public Good*, 250.

175. Smart Approaches to Marijuana, "Revenues vs. Reality," n.d., https://learnaboutsam.org/wp-content/uploads/2022/02/Revenues-vs-Reality.pdf (accessed February 17, 2024).

176. Early initiation of use—which is a high risk factor for marijuana's harmful effects—is a major concern, with the mean age of first use in the mid-to-late teens. Robin Room et al., *Cannabis Policy: Moving Beyond Stalemate* (Oxford: Oxford University Press, 2010), 25. See also Alejandro Azofeifa et al., "National Estimates of Marijuana Use and Related Indicators—National Survey on Drug Use and Health, United States, 2002–2014," *Morbidity and Mortality Weekly Report Surveillance Summaries* 65, no. 11 (September 2, 2016): 1–25.

177. The NAS report noted the lack of high-quality randomized studies investigating the medical benefits of marijuana. Even for well-controlled trials that have substantiated certain medical claims, "very little is known about the efficacy, dose, routes of administration, or side effects of commonly used" cannabis products. For decades, cannabis was categorized as a schedule I drug (that is, a tightly controlled substance illegal under most circumstances), which impeded research on its medicinal effects. The Biden administration proposed categorizing it as a schedule III drug. NAS, *The Health Effects of Cannabis and Cannabinoids: The Current State of Evidence and Recommendations for Research* (Washington, DC: National Academies Press, 2017), 16–22, 90. See also Room et al., *Cannabis Policy*, chap. 2; Babor et al., *Drug Policy and the Public Good*, table 4.1, "Overview of Causal Impact of Cannabis According to Outcome," 45–52; and Malcolm Gladwell, "Unwatched Pot: Do We Know Enough About Marijuana?," *NY*, January 14, 2019, 18–21.

178. Megan Twohey, Danielle Ivory, and Carson Kessler, "As America's Marijuana Use Grows, So Do the Harms," *NYT*, October 4, 2024, updated October 7, 2024, https://www.nytimes.com/2024/10/04/us/cannabis-marijuana-risks-addiction.html. See also Roni Caryn Rabin, "Marijuana Dependence Linked to Higher Risk of Death," *NYT*, February 6, 2025, https://www.nytimes.com/2025/02/06/health/cannabis-marijuana-death-psychosis.html.

179. Carrie Bearden quoted in Twohey et al., "As America's Marijuana Use Grows."

180. Babor et al., *Drug Policy and the Public Good*, chap. 8.

181. Reuter, "Why Has U.S. Drug Policy Changed So Little?," 97–99; Mohammad Rifat Haider et al., "Psycho-Social Correlates of Opioid Use Disorder Among the US Adult Population: Evidence from the National Survey on Drug Use and Health, 2015–2018," *Substance Use and Misuse* 55, no. 12 (September 2020): 2002–10; and Michael William Flores et al., "Associations Between Neighborhood-Level Factors and Opioid-Related Mortality: A Multi-Level Analysis Using Death Certificate Data," *Addiction* 115, no. 10 (October 2020): 1878–89.

182. This account of decriminalization in Portugal is largely based on Laqueur, "Uses and Abuses of Drug Decriminalization in Portugal," 746–81.

183. Drug Policy Alliance, "Drug Decriminalization in Portugal: Learning from a Health and Human-Centered Approach," n.d., https://drugpolicy.org/wp-content/uploads/2023/08/dpa-drug-decriminalization-portugal-health-human-centered-approach_0.pdf (accessed December 14, 2024): 2–5; and Michael Specter, "Getting a Fix," *NY*, October 10, 2011, https://www.newyorker.com/magazine/2011/10/17/getting-a-fix.

184. Laqueur, "Uses and Abuses of Drug Decriminalization": 750.

185. Laqueur.

186. Maintaining the public health system's share of total health expenditures at its 2002 level for the years 2015 to 2023 would have required an additional $248 billion. David U. Himmelstein and Steffie Woolhandler, "Public Health's Falling Share of U.S. Health Spending," *American Journal of Public Health* 106, no. 1 (January 2016): 57; Matt McKillop and Vinu Ilakkuvan, *The Impact of Chronic Underfunding on America's Public Health System: Trends, Risks, and Recommendations, 2019* (Washington, DC: Trust for America's Health, 2019), 3; and Nason Maani and Sandro Galea, "COVID-19 and Underinvestment in the Public Health Infrastructure of the United States," *Milbank Quarterly* 98, no. 2 (June 2020): 250–59.

187. Lauren Weber et al., "Hollowed-Out Public Health System Faces More Cuts amid Virus," AP, August 24, 2020, https://apnews.com/article/e28724a125a127f650a9b6f48f7bb938.

188. Jonathon P. Leider et al., "Reconciling Supply and Demand for State and Local Public Health Staff in an Era of Retiring Baby Boomers," *American Journal of Preventive Medicine* 54, no. 3 (2018): 334.

189. McKillop and Ilakkuvan, *Impact of Chronic Underfunding*, 5, fig. 2.

190. The Obama administration had established this office in 2014 after the Ebola outbreak. Lena Sun, "Nearly 700 Vacancies at CDC Because of Trump Administration's Hiring Freeze," *WP*, May 19, 2017, https://www.washingtonpost.com/news/to-your-health/wp/2017/05/19/nearly-700-vacancies-at-cdc-because-of-trump-administration-hiring-freeze/.

191. The CDC's annual funding for opioid overdose prevention and surveillance rose to $475 million in fiscal 2018 and 2019, an increase of $350 million compared to fiscal 2017. McKillop and Ilakkuvan, *Impact of Chronic Underfunding*, 12. On the proposed cuts to the CDC under Trump 2.0, see Sheryl Gay Stolberg, "Trump's Budget Calls for Deep Cuts to Public Health Programs and Research," *NYT*, May 2, 2025, https://www.nytimes.com/2025/05/02/us/politics/trump-budget-cdc-nih-cuts.html.

192. Weber et al., "Hollowed-Out Public Health System."

193. Mike Stobbe, "CDC Ordered to Stop Working with WHO Immediately, Upending Expectations of an Extended Withdrawal," AP, January 27, 2025, https://apnews.com/article/cdc-who-trump-548cf18b1c409c7d22e17311ccdfe1f6; and Will Stone and Selena Simmon-Duffin, "Trump Administration Purges Websites Across Federal Health Agencies," NPR, January 31, 2025, https://www.npr.org/sections/shots-health-news/2025/01/31/nx-s1-5282274/trump-administration-purges-health-websites.

194. Alison Frankel, "Purdue's Sackler Family Wants Global Opioids Settlement," Reuters, April 22, 2019, https://www.reuters.com/article/world/purdues-sackler-family-wants-global-opioids-settlement-sackler-lawyer-mary-jo-idUSKCN1RZ01L/.

195. Aneri Pattani, "The Biden Administration Vowed to Be a Leading Voice on Opioid Settlements but Has Gone Quiet," *KFF Health News*, April 21, 2023, https://kffhealthnews.org /news/article/biden-administration-opioid-settlements-federal-government/.

196. Colleen Walsh, "Learning the Hard Way," *Harvard Gazette*, August 4, 2021, https://news .harvard.edu/gazette/story/2021/08/applying-lessons-learned-from-the-tobacco-settlement -to-opioid-negotiations/.

197. Pattani, "Biden Administration Vowed."

198. Pattani.

199. Aneri Pattani, "$50 Billion in Opioid Settlement Cash Is On the Way: We're Tracking How It's Spent," *KFF Health News*, March 30, 2023, https://kffhealthnews.org /news/article/opioid-drugmakers-settlement-funds-50-billion-dollars-khn-investigation -payback/.

200. Aneri Pattani, "Where Opioid Money Goes," *PI*, November 17, 2024, G2.

201. Jan Hoffman, "Opioid Settlement Money Is Being Spent on Police Cars and Overtime," *NYT*, August 14, 2023, https://www.nytimes.com/2023/08/14/health/opioids-settlement -money.html; Pattani, "$50 Billion in Opioid Settlement Cash"; and Ed Mahon and Kate Giammarise, "Expecting More Than $1 Billion in Opioid Settlement Money, Pa. Grapples with Policing Versus Treatment," *Spotlight PA*, April 18, 2023, https://www.spotlightpa.org/news/2023 /04/pa-opioid-settlement-money-cases.

202. Aneri Pattani and Rae Ellen Bichell, "In Rural America, Deadly Costs of Opioids Outweigh the Dollars Tagged to Address Them," *KFF Health News*, December 12, 2022, https:// kffhealthnews.org/news/article/rural-america-opioid-settlement-funds-inequity/.

203. Pattani and Bichell.

204. Aneri Pattani, "Meet the People Deciding How to Spend $50 Billion in Opioid Settlement Cash," *KFF Health News*, July 10, 2023, https://kffhealthnews.org/news/article/opioid -settlement-funds-state-council-members-database/.

205. Aneri Pattani, "How States Are Spending Billions in Funds from Opioid Settlements," *PI*, December 30, 2024, A1.

206. City of Philadelphia, "City Announces Spending Plan for Opioid Settlement Funds," press release, January 5, 2023, https://www.phila.gov/2023-01-05-city-announces-spending -plan-for-opioid-settlement-funds/.

207. City of Philadelphia.

208. Caitlin O'Brien, "Overdose Prevention and Community Healing Awards Fund Awards $1.9 Million in Grants to 27 Organizations," June 8, 2023, https://www.scattergoodfoundation .org/overdose-prevention-community-healing-fund-awards-1-9-million-in-grants-to-27 -organizations/.

209. Samantha Melamed and Ryan W. Briggs, "Philly Poured $222M into an Anti-Violence Grant Program: It Picked Some Groups Unable to Deliver on Their Proposals," *PI*, April 23, 2023, https://www.inquirer.com/news/philadelphia-antiviolence-expansion-grant-money -waste-20230427.html.

210. Aubrey Whelan and Anna Orso, "Parker: No Opioid Settlement to Be Used on Safer Drug Use," *PI*, March 7, 2024, A1.

211. German Lopez, "Hillary Clinton Has One of the Most Progressive Anti-Drug Plans in Decades," *Vox*, September 4, 2015, https://www.vox.com/2015/9/4/9261359/hillary-clinton -drug-abuse; and Jacqueline Alemany, "Opioid Epidemic Fades from Campaign Trail as Death Toll Rises," CBS News, November 1, 2016, https://www.cbsnews.com/news/once-the-talk-of -the-primary-opiate-epidemic-fades-from-the-trail-as-death-toll-rises/.

212. Sari Horwitz et al., "Trump Administration Struggles to Confront the Fentanyl Crisis," *WP*, May 22, 2019, https://www.washingtonpost.com/graphics/2019/national/fentanyl -epidemic-trump-administration/; and Shannon M. Monnat, "Deaths of Despair and Support for Trump in the 2016 Presidential Election," Pennsylvania State University, Department of

Agricultural Economics, Sociology, and Education, Research Brief, December 4, 2016, https://aese.psu.edu/directory/smm67/Election16.pdf.

213. Sessions, his first attorney general, had been a federal prosecutor in Alabama during the crack hysteria of the 1980s and 1990s. During his two decades in the US Senate, he was a leading opponent of even modest sentencing reforms to roll back harsh drug laws and other hard-line policies.

214. Horwitz et al., "Trump Administration Struggles."

215. Edwin Meese III, "Jeff Sessions Is the Most Underrated Member of the Trump Administration," USA Today, January 30, 2018, https://www.usatoday.com/story/opinion/2018/01/30/jeff-sessions-most-underrated-member-trump-administration-edwin-meese-column/1074410001/.

216. Julie Hirschfeld Davis, "In Declaration, No New Funds for the Drug Crisis," NYT, October 27, 2017, A1.

217. Keith Humphreys, testimony, US House Judiciary Subcommittee on Immigration and Border Security, Hearing on Immigration and the Opioid Crisis, February 18, 2020, https://republicans-judiciary.house.gov/wp-content/uploads/2018/02/Witness-Testimony-Keith-Humphreys.pdf, 3.

218. German Lopez, "Trump Declared an Emergency over Opioids: A New Report Finds It Led to Very Little," Vox, October 23, 2018, https://www.vox.com/policy-and-politics/2018/10/23/18010304/trump-opioid-epidemic-emergency-gao-report; and Davis, "In Declaration, No New Funds for Drug Crisis," A1.

219. President's Commission on Combating Drug Addiction and the Opioid Crisis, final report, November 2017, https://www.whitehouse.gov/sites/whitehouse.gov/files/images/Final_Report_Draft_11-15-2017.pdf, 22.

220. President's Commission on Combating Drug Addiction, 22.

221. President's Commission on Combating Drug Addiction, especially 6, 10, and 22. See also Horwitz et al., "Trump Administration Struggles."

222. Ali Rogin and Jordyn Phelps, "Trump Calls for Death Penalty for Drug Dealers but Says Country Might Not Be Ready," ABC News, March 19, 2018, https://abcnews.go.com/Politics/trump-calls-death-penalty-drug-dealers-country-ready/story?id=53857260.

223. The full name of the legislation was the Substance Use Disorder Prevention that Promotes Opioid Recovery and Treatment for Patients and Communities Act. This summary of the bill is based on Bill Wynne, "The 660-Page Opioids Bill Is Now the Law: Here's What's in It," California Health Foundation, November 1, 2018, https://www.chcf.org/about/; and German Lopez, "Trump Just Signed a Bipartisan Bill to Confront the Opioid Epidemic," Vox, October 24, 2018, https://www.vox.com/policy-and-politics/2018/9/28/17913938/trump-opioid-epidemic-congress-support-act-bill-law.

224. Horwitz et al., "Trump Administration Struggles."

225. Carrie Johnson, "Lawmakers Consider Tough New Penalties for Opioid Crimes, Bucking Trend," NPR, June 6, 2017, https://www.npr.org/2017/06/06/531787093/lawmakers-consider-tough-new-penalties-for-opioid-crimes-bucking-trend; and US Senate Judiciary Committee, "Feinstein, Grassley Introduce Bill to Confront Rising Threat of Methamphetamine," press release, August 7, 2020, https://www.judiciary.senate.gov/press/dem/releases/feinstein-grassley-introduce-bill-to-confront-rising-threat-of-methamphetamine/.

226. Families Against Mandatory Minimums, "Summary: First Step Act, S.756 (115th Congress, 2018)," n.d., https://famm.org/wp-content/uploads/FAMM-FIRST-STEP-Act-Summary-Senate-version.pdf (accessed August 29, 2020), 3. See also Marie Gottschalk, "Incorrigible: The First Step Act and the Carceral State," PLN 30, no. 4 (April 2019): 1–13.

227. Horwitz et al., "Trump Administration Struggles."

228. Roman Gressier, "White House Opioid Plan: Recycled 'War on Drugs'?," CR, February 5, 2019, https://thecrimereport.org/2019/02/05/white-house-opioid-plan-recycled-war-on

-drugs/; and Mike Riggs, "Trump's First National Drug Control Strategy Reads Like a High School Book Report Written 30 Minutes Before Class," *Reason*, February 1, 2019, https://reason .com/2019/02/01/trumps-first-national-drug-control-strat/.

229. See "Willie Horton 1988 Attack Ad," *YouTube*, n.d., https://www.youtube.com/watch?v =Io9KMSSEZ0Y (accessed December 13, 2023); and DOJ, Office of Policy and Communications, "The Case for More Incarceration," 1992, https://www.ojp.gov/pdffiles1/Digitization /139583NCJRS.pdf.

230. "William Barr, Confirmation Hearing," cnn.com, January 15, 2019, https://transcripts .cnn.com/show/ath/date/2019-01-15/segment/01.

231. See, for example, Jeremy Travis, Bruce Western, and Steve Redburn, eds., *The Growth of Incarceration in the United States: Exploring Causes and Consequences* (Washington, DC: National Academies Press, 2014), especially chap. 5.

232. Opioids are a group of drugs that fall under various classifications—or so-called schedules—in accordance with the 1970 Controlled Substances Act. Schedule I drugs, including heroin, are considered illegal except for tightly controlled authorized uses and are subject to harsh mandatory minimum penalties. The DEA, which is overseen by the DOJ, had temporarily designated certain fentanyl-related substances as schedule I controlled substances, but that designation was due to expire in February 2020. Michael Collins, "The Inside Story of the SISTA Win," Drug Policy Alliance, September 28, 2020, https://drugpolicy.org/blog/inside-story-sitsa-win.

233. William Barr, "Fentanyl Could Flood the Country Unless Congress Passes This Bill," *WP*, January 10, 2020, https://www.washingtonpost.com/opinions/william-barr-congress-pass -this-bill-so-we-can-attack-the-onslaught-of-illegal-fentanyl/2020/01/10/cbb8ccdc-33cb-11ea -a053-dc6d944ba776_story.html; and Nancy Gertner, "William Barr's New War on Drugs," *WP*, January 26, 2020, https://www.washingtonpost.com/opinions/2020/01/26/william-barrs -new-war-drugs/.

234. A New PATH, et al., letter to Nancy Pelosi et al., January 27, 2020, https://docs.house .gov/meetings/JU/JU08/20210311/111301/HHRG-117-JU08-20210311-SD007.pdf.

235. Sarah N. Lynch, "Trump Administration Drug Officials Clash over How to Combat Fentanyl Copycats," Reuters, July 9, 2019, https://www.reuters.com/article/us-usa-congress -fentanyl-idUSKCN1U4105.

236. Maritza Perez Medina, "Biden Administration's Fentanyl Proposal Would Create Severe Penalties for People Struggling with Addiction and Restrict Research," Drug Policy Alliance, August 1, 2024, https://drugpolicy.org/news/biden-administrations-fentanyl-proposal-would -create-severe-criminal-penalties-for-people-struggling-with-addiction-and-restrict-research/.

237. "H.R. 27—HALT Fentanyl Act," congress.gov, n.d., https://www.congress.gov/bill /119th-congress/house-bill/27 (accessed February 8, 2025).

238. Quoted in Bethany McLean, "'We Didn't Cause the Crisis': David Sackler Pleads His Case on the Opioid Epidemic," *Vanity Fair*, June 19, 2019, updated August 2019, https://www .vanityfair.com/news/2019/06/david-sackler-pleads-his-case-on-the-opioid-epidemic.

239. Beth Macy, "Failures That Fueled the Opioid Epidemic," *NYT*, February 24, 2021, A23.

240. Sheryl Gay Stolberg and Sheila Kaplan, "Biden Chooses Robert Califf to Lead F.D.A., Despite Drug Industry Ties," *NYT*, November 12, 2021, https://www.nytimes.com/2021/11/12 /us/politics/robert-califf-fda.html; and Melody Schreiber, "What the $%&! Is Going On at the FDA?," *NR*, July 14, 2021, https://newrepublic.com/article/162975/alzheimers-fda-covid -vaccines.

241. "Why America's Republicans Want to Bomb Mexico," *Economist*, September 14, 2023, https://www.economist.com/the-economist-explains/2023/09/14/why-americas-republi cans-want-to-bomb-mexico.

242. Ben Makuch, "Green Berets and Reaper Drones: Trump's Shadow War in Mexico," *New Republic*, February 21, 2025, https://newrepublic.com/article/191774/green-berets-reaper

-drones-trumps-shadow-war-mexico; and Julian E. Barnes et al., "C.I.A. Expands Secret Drone Flights Over Mexico," *NYT*, February 18, 2025, https://www.nytimes.com/2025/02/18/us /politics/cia-drone-flights-mexico.html.

243. Brian Mann, "Trump Used Fentanyl to Justify Tariffs, but the Crisis Was Already Easing," NPR, February 2, 2025, https://www.npr.org/2025/02/02/nx-s1-5283957/fentanyl -trump-tariffs-china-canada-mexico.

244. Goodnough, "Helping Drug Users Survive."

245. Reuter, "Why Has U.S. Drug Policy Changed So Little?," 109.

246. Nabarun Dasgupta, Leo Beletsky, and Daniel Ciccarone, "Opioid Crisis: No Easy Fix to Its Social and Economic Determinants," *American Journal of Public Health* 108, no. 2 (2018): 182.

247. Nick Heather, "Q: Is Addiction a Brain Disease or a 'Moral Failing'? A: Neither," *Neuroethics* 10 (2017): 115–24; Beletsky, "America's Favorite Antidote": 856; and Helena Hansen, Jules Netherland, and David Herzberg, *Whiteout: How Racial Capitalism Changed the Color of Opioids in America* (Oakland: University of California Press, 2023), 138.

248. Szalavitz, "Wrong Way to Treat."

249. Flores et al., "Associations Between Neighborhood-Level Factors"; and Haider et al., "Psycho-Social Correlates."

250. Beletsky, "America's Favorite Antidote": 844.

251. Beletsky: 844; Humphreys, testimony, Hearing on Immigration and the Opioid Crisis, 2; and Louisa Degenhardt et al., "Toward a Global View of Alcohol, Tobacco, Cannabis, and Cocaine Use: Findings from the WHO World Mental Health Surveys," *PLOS Medicine* 5, no. 7 (July 2008): 1065.

252. The more widely cited figure is 80 percent, which has been discredited by experts. See Gary Garrison, "Claire McCaskill Cites Disproven Figure on Opioid Use," PolitiFact Missouri, May 10, 2017, https://www.politifact.com/missouri/statements/2017/may/10/claire-mccaskill /mccaskill-cites-long-disproven-figure-opioid-use/.

253. Dasgupta et al., "Opioid Crisis," 182.

254. Beletsky, "21st Century Cures": 364.

255. Humphreys, testimony, Hearing on Immigration and the Opioid Crisis, 4.

256. Chris Fox, executive director, Voices for Non-Opioid Choices Coalition, letter to the editor, *NYT*, April 12, 2023, https://www.nytimes.com/2023/04/12/opinion/letters/blindness .html.

257. Maia Szalavitz, "An Encouraging Decline in Overdose Deaths," *NYT*, December 4, 2024, A23; and CDC, "12 Month-Ending Provisional Number and Percent Change of Drug Overdose Deaths," January 5, 2025, https://www.cdc.gov/nchs/nvss/vsrr/drug-overdose-data .htm, fig. 1a.

258. Friedrich Engels, *The Condition of the Working-Class in England in 1844* (London: George Allen and Unwin, 1892), trans. Florence Kelley Wischnewetzky, https://www.gutenberg .org/cache/epub/17306/pg17306-images.html, 95–96. For a further discussion of social murder in the present book, see p. 4, above.

12. Fraught: Where Do We Go from Here?

1. James Baldwin, "As Much Truth as One Can Bear," *NYT*, January 14, 1962, https://www .nytimes.com/1962/01/14/archives/as-much-truth-as-one-can-bear-to-speak-out-about-the -world-as-it-is.html.

2. Martin Luther King Jr., "Where Do We Go from Here?," August 16, 1967, Martin Luther King, Jr. Research and Education Institute, https://kinginstitute.stanford.edu/where-do-we-go -here.

3. Allegra McLeod, "An Abolitionist Critique of Violence," *University of Chicago Law Review* 89, no. 2 (2022): 538.

4. PRC, "Most Americans Point to Circumstances, Not Work Ethic, for Why People Are Rich or Poor," March 2, 2020, https://www.pewresearch.org/politics/2020/03/02/most -americans-point-to-circumstances-not-work-ethic-as-reasons-people-are-rich-or-poor/; Lydia Saad, "More in U.S. See Unions Strengthening and Want It That Way," Gallup, August 30, 2023, https://news.gallup.com/poll/510281/unions-strengthening.aspx; Amina Dunn, "Most Americans Support a $15 Federal Minimum Wage," PRC, April 22, 2021, https://www.pewresearch.org /short-reads/2021/04/22/most-americans-support-a-15-federal-minimum-wage/; Jessica D. Blankshain and Max Z. Margulies, "The Downside of High Trust in the Military," *NYT*, September 16, 2021, https://www.nytimes.com/2021/09/16/opinion/americans-trust-us-military. html; William Ruger, "Public Realism on Afghanistan," RealClear Politics, October 8, 2018, https://www.realclearpolitics.com/articles/2018/10/08/public_realism_on_afghanistan _138280.html; Data for Progress poll, May 3–4, 2024, https://www.filesforprogress.org/datasets /2024/5/dfp_climate_homicide_oil_gas_tabs.pdf; Kate Aronoff, "The Planet Is Screwed, Says Bank That Screwed the Planet," *NR*, February 25, 2020, https://newrepublic.com/article /156657/planet-screwed-says-bank-screwed-planet; and Natalie Venegas, "Luigi Mangione: Nearly 30 Percent 'Understand' Anger at UnitedHealthcare," *Newsweek*, January 18, 2025, https:// www.newsweek.com/luigi-mangione-voters-understand-anger-unitedhealthcare-poll-2017226.

5. Quoted in Tamara K. Nopper, introduction, in Mariame Kaba, *We Do This 'Til We Free Us: Abolitionist Organizing and Transforming Justice* (Chicago: Haymarket Books, 2021), xxiii.

6. Francis Bacon, "Of Revenge," in *Essays: Or Counsels, Civil and Moral* (1625; Auckland: Floating, 2014), 17.

7. Jeremy Yurow and Hannah Hudnall, "'Lock Her Up': Trump Now Claims He Never Said or Backed This. But He Did. A Lot.," *USA Today*, June 4, 2024, updated June 7, 2024, https:// www.usatoday.com/story/news/politics/elections/2024/06/04/trump-hillary-clinton-lock -her-up-fact-check/73962711007/; "Transcript: Donald Trump Announces His Presidential Candidacy," CBS News, June 16, 2015, https://www.cbsnews.com/news/transcript-donald -trump-announces-his-presidential-candidacy/; and Zachary B. Wolf, "Trump Explains His Militaristic Plan to Deport 15–20 Million People," CNN, May 1, 2024, https://www.cnn.com /2024/05/01/politics/trump-immigration-what-matters/index.html.

8. Danielle Sered, *Until We Reckon: Violence, Mass Incarceration, and a Road to Repair* (New York: New Press, 2019); and Kaba, *We Do This 'Til We Free Us.*

9. Quoted in Sered, *Until We Reckon*, 36. (Within this book, long quotes were italicized in full; I have not reproduced this all-italics style here.)

10. Brandon L. Garrett, "How Biden Should Prosecute Corporate Crime," *TAP*, January/ February 2021, 60.

11. Graham Dukes, John Braithwaite, and James Maloney, *Pharmaceuticals, Corporate Crime and Public Health* (Cheltenham, UK: Edward Elgar, 2014), 276, 303–5; and Samuel W. Buell, *Capital Offenses: Business Crime and Punishment in America's Corporate Age* (New York: W. W. Norton, 2016), 241.

12. For more on the Bernie Madoff case, see pp. 167 and 249–50.

13. Ken Sweet and Larry Neumeister, "Fallen Crypto Mogul Sam Bankman-Fried Sentenced to 25 Years in Prison," AP, March 28, 2024, https://apnews.com/article/sam-bankman-fried-ftx -cryptocurrency-sentencing-sbf-d7bb1a5e94b4c22039d74dfeab1a2ff1; and Joey Cappelletti, Ken Sweet, and Jill Colvin, "Coinbase Hires Top Political Strategist as Crypto Industry Flexes Its Newfound Political Might," WSB-TV Atlanta, June 12, 2025, https://www.wsbtv.com/news /politics/coinbase-hires-top/MOHHJ6M23JANRKHLRO4WC6BRUI/.

14. Daniel Richman, "Overcriminalization for Lack of Better Options," in *The Political Heart of Criminal Procedure: Essays on Themes of William J. Stuntz*, ed. Michael Klarman, David Skeel, and Carol Steiker (New York: Cambridge University Press, 2012), 85.

15. Richman, 86.

16. The United States has a long history of so-called leveling down, which helps explain why its penal system is so expansive and abusive compared to the carceral apparatus in other Western countries. James Q. Whitman, *Harsh Justice: Criminal Punishment and the Widening Divide Between America and Europe* (New York: Oxford University Press, 2003).

17. For more on the relationship between crime rates and incarceration rates, see pp. 6 and 408n15.

18. As Allegra M. McLeod explains, a prison abolitionist framework does not necessarily deny that some people pose a major threat to society and might need to be "forcibly contained." But "this course of action ought to be undertaken with moral conflict, circumspection, and even shame, as a choice of the lesser of two evils, rather than as an achievement of justice." Allegra M. McLeod, "Prison Abolition and Grounded Justice," *UCLA Law Review* 62, no. 5 (June 2015): 1171.

19. Quoted in Rachel Kushner, "Is Prison Necessary? Ruth Wilson Gilmore Might Change Your Mind," *NYT*, April 17, 2019, https://www.nytimes.com/2019/04/17/magazine/prison -abolition-ruth-wilson-gilmore.html, emphasis in original.

20. Dukes et al., *Pharmaceuticals, Corporate Crime and Public Health*, 303–5.

21. It is well established that certainty of punishment is a more powerful deterrent than severity of punishment with respect to so-called street crimes. The deterrent value of certainty versus severity is less certain in the case of crime in the suites, partly because there has been far less research on elite-level offending. See pp. 21–22.

22. John C. Coffee, *Corporate Crime and Punishment: The Crisis of Underenforcement* (Oakland, CA: Berrett-Koehler, 2020), 8–9.

23. Dukes et al., *Pharmaceuticals, Corporate Crime and Public Health*, 363.

24. Beginning in the 1990s, the FDA significantly relaxed restrictions on direct-to-consumer advertising of drugs. New Zealand is the only other Western country that specifically permits direct-to-consumer advertising by pharmaceutical companies. Drug companies spend twice as much money on marketing as they do on research and development. The marketing tab for US pharmaceuticals is more than $25 billion per year. Those expenditures are tax deductible, so the public is subsidizing the pharmaceutical industry, which is one of the most profitable sectors of the economy. Dukes et al., *Pharmaceuticals, Corporate Crime and Public Health*, chap. 3; Richard G. Frank, Keith N. Humphreys, and Harold A. Pollack, "Policy Responses to the Addiction Crisis," *Journal of Health Politics, Policy and Law* 46, no. 4 (August 2021): 593; Shahram Ahari, "I Was a Drug Rep.: I Know How Pharma Companies Pushed Opioids," *WP*, November 26, 2019, https://www.washingtonpost.com/outlook/i-was-a-drug-rep-i-know-how-pharma-companies -pushed-opioids/2019/11/25/82b1da88-beb9-11e9-9b73-fd3c65ef8f9c_story.html; and David E. Mitchell, "Taxpayers Fund Research and Drug Companies Make a Fortune," *NYT*, March 24, 2021, https://www.nytimes.com/2021/03/24/opinion/coronavirus-vaccine-cost -pfizer-moderna.html.

25. Dana G. Smith, "Experts Clash with Kennedy on F.D.A.," *NYT*, December 24, 2024, A11.

26. Laura Antonini and Harvey Rosenfield, *Reboot Required: The Civil Justice System Has Crashed*, #Represent, February 2022, https://www.representconsumers.org/wp-content /uploads/2022/02/2022.02.15_Reboot-Required.pdf.

27. C. Fred Alford, *Whistleblowers: Broken Lives and Organizational Power* (Ithaca, NY: Cornell University Press, 2002).

28. Jennifer Taub, *Big Dirty Money: The Shocking Injustice and Unseen Cost of White Collar Crime* (New York: Viking, 2020), 146 and chap. 7; Dukes et al., *Pharmaceuticals, Corporate Crime and Public Health*, chap. 10.

29. See, for example, Benjamin Mullin, "Obama Administration Sets Record for Unfulfilled FOIA Requests," poynter.org, March 18, 2016, http://www.poynter.org/2016/obama -administration-sets-record-for-unfulfilled-foia-requests/402326/; Trevor Timm, "Important

Lessons from Obama's Mistakes in Trump's New Crackdown on Leaks," *Columbia Journalism Review*, June 11, 2018, https://cjr.org/opinion/obama-trump-leaks.php; Amy Davidson Sorkin, "The Troubled History of the Espionage Act," *NY*, December 11, 2023, https://www.newyorker.com/magazine/2023/12/18/state-of-silence-the-espionage-act-and-the-rise-of-americas-secrecy-regime-sam-lebovic-book-review; James C. Goodale, "More Than a Data Dump: Why Julian Assange Deserves First Amendment Protection," *HM*, April 2019, 63–65; Jon Allsop, "The Trump Administration Spied on Journalists: The Biden Administration Defended It," *Columbia Journalism Review*, May 10, 2021, https://www.cjr.org/the_media_today/trump_washington_post_surveillance_biden.php; Kevin Gosztola, "Biden's Legacy: Leaving FOIA in Shambles," Freedom of the Press Foundation, November 22, 2024, https://freedom.press/issues/bidens-legacy-leaving-foia-in-shambles/; Kevin Gosztola, "Biden's Legacy: Fundamentally Changing Nothing for Whistleblowers," *Dissenter*, January 8, 2025, https://thedissenter.org/bidens-legacy-fundamentally-changing-nothing-for-whistleblowers/; David Sanger and Charlie Savage, "Trump Takes Aim at Watergate Reform: The Independent Inspector General," *NYT*, May 23, 2020, https://www.nytimes.com/2020/05/22/us/politics/trump-inspectors-general.html; Leonard Downie Jr, "The Trump Administration and the Media," Committee to Protect Journalists, April 20, 2020, https://cpj.org/reports/2020/04/trump-media-attacks-credibility-leaks/; Max Kozlov, "'Never Seen Anything Like This': Trump's Team Halts NIH Meetings and Travel," *Nature*, January 23, 2025, https://www.nature.com/articles/d41586-025-00231-y; and Harold Varmus, "Why Would We Undermine the Marvel of American Science?," *NYT*, February 14, 2025, https://www.nytimes.com/2025/02/14/opinion/trump-public-health-funding-nih.html.

30. "Squeeze Play," *Nation*, special issue on the media, December 25, 2023 / January 1, 2024; Marc Tracy, "A Paradox at the Heart of the Newspaper Crisis," *NYT*, August 1, 2019, https://www.nytimes.com/2019/08/01/business/media/news-deserts-media-newspapers.html; Margaret Sullivan, "The Constitution Doesn't Work Without Local News," *Atlantic*, July 14, 2020, https://www.theatlantic.com/ideas/archive/2020/07/constitution-doesnt-work-without-local-news/614056/; and Penelope Muse Abernathy, "The State of Local News 2023," Northwestern University, Medill School of Journalism, November 16, 2023, https://localnewsinitiative.northwestern.edu/projects/state-of-local-news/2023/report/.

31. Dominick Mastrangelo, "*Washington Post* Reels from Bezos Decision Not to Endorse," *Hill*, October 25, 2024, https://thehill.com/homenews/media/4954196-bezos-decision-post-endorsement/; and James Rainey, "L.A. Times Owner's Decision Not to Endorse in Presidential Race Sparks Resignations, Questions," *LAT*, October 25, 2024, https://www.latimes.com/business/story/2024-10-25/latimes-no-presidential-endorsement-decison-resignations.

32. Lester K. Spence, *Knocking the Hustle: Against the Neoliberal Turn in Black Politics* (New York: Punctum Books, 2015), 145.

33. Spence, 145–46.

34. Cedric Johnson, *After Black Lives Matter: Policing and Anti-Capitalist Struggles* (London: Verso 2023), 162.

35. For a lucid overview of some of these challenges, see Keeanga-Yamahtta Taylor, *From #BlackLivesMatter to Black Liberation*, rev. ed. (Chicago: Haymarket Books, 2021), chap. 8. See also Ian Haney López, *Merge Left: Fusing Race and Class, Winning Elections, and Saving America* (New York: New Press, 2019).

36. Barry Friedman, *Unwarranted: Policing Without Permission* (New York: Farrar, Straus and Giroux, 2017), xii.

37. Friedman, xii–xiii, emphasis in the original, and chap. 2.

38. David M. Kennedy, "State Violence, Legitimacy, and the Path to True Public Safety," *CLN*, September 2020, 6.

39. James Forman Jr., *Locking Up Our Own: Crime and Punishment in Black America* (New York: Farrar, Straus and Giroux, 2017), 12; Marie Gottschalk, *Caught: The Prison State and the*

Lockdown of American Politics, rev. ed. (Princeton, NJ: Princeton University Press, 2016), 154–55; Shom Mazumder, "What Black People Really Think About the Police," *NR*, December 15, 2020, https://newrepublic.com/article/160532/what-black-people-think-police; Elizabeth Hinton, Julilly Kohler-Hausmann, and Vesla M. Weaver, "Did Blacks Really Endorse the 1994 Crime Bill?," *NYT*, April 16, 2013, https://www.nytimes.com/2016/04/13/opinion/did-blacks-really-endorse-the-1994-crime-bill.html; and Anna Orso and Julia Terruso, "Most Philadelphians Think the City Needs More Cops: They're Split on More Money," *PI*, March 15, 2023, https://www.inquirer.com/news/crime-guns-police-philadelphia-voters-2023-mayor-race-poll-20230315.html.

40. Oliver Wendell Holmes, dissenting opinion, *Compania General de Tabacos v. Collector*, 275 U.S. 87 (1927), 275.

41. Bruce Western, *Homeward: Life in the Year After Prison* (New York: Russell Sage Foundation, 2018), 182.

42. Daniel Hemel, Janet Holtzblatt, and Steve Rosenthal, "The Tax Gap's Many Shades of Gray," Tax Policy Center, Urban Institute and Brookings Institution, n.d., https://www.taxpolicycenter.org/sites/default/files/publication/163544/brief-the-tax-gaps-many-shades-of-gray.pdf (accessed March 18, 2024).

43. This figure includes a loss of about $140 billion due to corporate tax avoidance and evasion and another $37 billion to tax avoidance and evasion by individuals. The International Monetary Fund estimates that the worldwide indirect costs of global corporate tax abuse are at least three times greater than direct losses because of a "race to the bottom" as countries reduce tax rates and modify tax policies in a doomed effort to lure corporations and increase tax revenues. Tax Justice Network, "State of Tax Justice 2023," July 23, 2023, https://taxjustice.net/wp-content/uploads/SOTJ/SOTJ23/English/State%20of%20Tax%20Justice%202023%20-%20Tax%20Justice%20Network%20-%20English.pdf, 25, 75.

44. Matthew Desmond, *Poverty, by America* (New York: Crown, 2023), 104–5.

45. This is according to a financial adviser to ultrawealthy individuals who is quoted in Evan Osnos, "Trust Issues," *NY*, January 23, 2023, 32.

46. Nicholas Shaxson, *Treasure Islands: Uncovering the Damage of Offshore Banking and Tax Havens* (New York: St. Martin's Griffin, 2011), quoted in Alan Rusbridger, "The Big Stash of the Big Rich: What Can We Know?," *NYRB*, November 10, 2016, 48. An estimated 8 percent of the financial wealth of households is held in tax havens around the world—or about $7.6 trillion as of a decade or so ago. Gabriel Zucman, *The Hidden Wealth of Nations: The Scourge of Tax Havens* (Chicago: University of Chicago Press, 2015), 3.

47. Jesse Drucker and Danny Hakim, "How Accounting Giants Craft Favorable Tax Rules from Inside Government," *NYT*, September 19, 2021, https://www.nytimes.com/2021/09/19/business/accounting-firms-tax-loopholes-government.html.

48. "The Land of Milk and Honey," *Jacobin*, no. 49 (Spring 2023): 97.

49. Data from UC Berkeley economists Emmanuel Saez and Gabriel Zucman cited in Osnos, "Trust Issues," 32.

50. Jesse Eisinger, Jeff Ernsthausen, and Paul Kiel, "The Secret IRS Files: Trove of Never-Before-Seen Records Reveal How the Wealthiest Avoid Income Tax," *ProPublica*, June 8, 2021, https://www.propublica.org/article/the-secret-irs-files-trove-of-never-before-seen-records-reveal-how-the-wealthiest-avoid-income-tax.

51. Eisinger et al.

52. Eisinger et al.

53. Alan Rusbridger, "Panama: The Hidden Trillions," *NYRB*, October 27, 2016, 33.

54. Many "tax avoidance schemes are considered legitimate only because they have not been challenged" or tested in court. Alex Ross, *The Raging 2020s: Companies, Countries, People—and the Fight for Our Future* (New York: Henry Holt, 2021), 150.

55. An estimated 40 percent or so of multinational profits are shifted to tax havens. American multinational corporations "appear to book a particularly large fraction of their foreign income in low-tax places." Gabriel Zucman, "International Tax Avoidance by Multinational Firms," *NBER News*, 2022, https://www.nber.org/reporter/2022number3/international-tax-avoidance-multinational-firms.

56. Richard Phillips et al., *Offshore Shell Games 2017: The Use of Offshore Tax Havens by Fortune 500 Companies*, US PIRG [Public Interest Research Group] Education Fund and Institute on Taxation and Economic Policy, October 2017, 2. See also Ross, *Raging 2020s*, 153–55.

57. Alec MacGillis, *Fulfillment: Winning and Losing in One-Click America* (New York: Farrar, Straus and Giroux, 2021) cited in Alexander Sammon, "In Bezosworld," *TAP*, March/April 2021, 57.

58. Lisa De Simone, "How the Inflation Reduction Act Imperiled the OECD's Plans for a Global Minimum Tax on Corporations," *Fortune*, September 23, 2022, https://fortune.com/2022/09/23/inflation-reduction-act-imperiledoecd-plans-global-minimum-tax-corporations-yellen-politics-lisa-de-simone/; and Mark Bou Mansour, "UN Adopts Plan for Historic Tax Reform," Tax Justice Network, November 22, 2023, https://taxjustice.net/press/un-adopts-plans-for-historic-tax-reform/.

59. Zucman, "International Tax Avoidance by Multinational Firms."

60. CBO, "The Budget and Economic Outlook: 2018 to 2028," April 9, 2018, https://www.cbo.gov/publication/536510, 106; and Jesse Drucker and Jim Tankersley, "How Big Companies Won New Tax Breaks from the Trump Administration," *NYT*, December 30, 2019, https://www.nytimes.com/2019/12/30/business/trump-tax-cuts-beat-gilti.html.

61. Taub, *Big Dirty Money*, 210. See also Jesse Drucker, "The Tax-Break Bonanza Inside the Economic Rescue Package," *NYT*, April 24, 2020, https://www.nytimes.com/2020/04/24/business/tax-breaks-wealthy-virus.html.

62. The 2010 Financial Assets Tax Compliance Act (FATCA) compels foreign financial institutions to divulge to the US government any American-owned assets. In response to the measure, other countries joined the Common Reporting Standard, a global agreement "to exchange information on the assets of each other's citizens kept in each other's banks." But the United States did not join the Common Reporting Standard. Its own system collects information from foreign countries on American assets held abroad but does not divulge information on foreign assets held in the United States. Oliver Bullough, "The Financial Black Hole at the Heart of America," *Guardian Weekly*, November 22, 2019, 38.

63. Tax Justice Network, "State of Tax Justice 2023," 11.

64. Bullough, "Financial Black Hole," 36, emphasis in the original.

65. Doubts are growing that the 2021 Corporate Transparency Act—which went into effect in early 2024 and requires more companies doing business in the United States to report who owns or controls them to the US Treasury Department—will succeed in curbing fraud, money laundering, tax evasion, and other illicit activities. Kate Kelly, "Judge's Ruling Sets Back Law Meant to Fight Money Laundering," *NYT*, March 3, 2024, https://www.nytimes.com/2024/03/03/us/politics/judge-ruling-corporate-transparenct-act.html; and Mae Anderson, "Corporate Transparency Act Still on Hold After Supreme Court Lifts Injunction," AP, January 24, 2025, https://apnews.com/article/small-business-corporate-transparency-fincen-80c4b7348a50df073d6128d42bbac716.

66. A 2021 Treasury report estimated that the top 1 percent of US taxpayers are responsible for over one-quarter of the country's unpaid taxes, which adds up to a shortfall of more than $160 billion each year. Reported in Hemel et al., "Tax Gap's Many Shades of Gray."

67. Jesse Eisinger and Paul Kiel, "The IRS Tried to Take on the Ultrawealthy: It Didn't Go Well," *Mother Jones*, April 9, 2019, https://www.motherjones.com/politics/2019/04/the-irs-tried-to-take-on-the-ultrawealthy-it-didnt-go-well/.

68. The Biden administration pushed for a major increase in IRS funding, but as of fiscal 2022, the agency's full-time workforce was still 17 percent below its 2010 peak—or about sixteen thousand fewer workers. Calculated from IRS, "IRS Budget and Workforce," various years, https://www.irs.gov/statistics/irs-budget-and-workforce (accessed March 18, 2024).

69. The IRS has ten years to pursue delinquent taxes, after which the debt expires. In 2017, over $8 billion in tax debt expired compared to only $540 million in 2010 before lawmakers began slashing the IRS budget. Taub, *Big Dirty Money*, 207–8.

70. Taub, *Big Dirty Money*, 208n12.

71. David Cay Johnston, "The IRS Finally Takes the Gloves Off," *Nation*, March 1, 2024, https://www.thenation.com/article/society/irs-wealthy-tax-cheats/.

72. Alan Rappeport, "I.R.S. Crackdown on the Wealthy Yields a Billion Dollars in Unpaid Taxes," *NYT*, July 12, 2024, B3.

73. Andrew Duehren, "How a Consulting Firm and Trump's I.R.S. Pick Pushed a Problematic Tax Credit," *NYT*, December 24, 2024, https://www.nytimes.com/2024/12/24/business/billy-long-irs-tax-credit.html.

74. Andrew Duehren, "At 'Tax Prom,' Washington Prepares for a Lobbying Frenzy Over Cuts," *NYT*, December 13, 2024, B1.

75. Tony Romm, "Poorest Americans Dealt Biggest Blow Under Senate Republican Tax Package," *NYT*, July 1, 2025, https://www.nytimes.com/2025/07/01/business/poor-americans-senate-legislation.html.

76. Ryan Mac and Stacy Cowley, "Federal Financial Watchdog Ordered to Cease Activity," *NYT*, February 8, 2025, https://www.nytimes.com/2025/02/08/us/politics/cfpb-vought-staff-finance-watchdog.html; Sarah Klieff and Noah Weiland, "Republicans Eye Medicaid Slashes and Work Rules," *NYT*, November 21, 2024, A1; "August 2024 Medicaid and CHIP Enrollment Data Highlights," Medicaid.gov, n.d., https://www.medicaid.gov/medicaid/program-information/medicaid-and-chip-enrollment-data/report-highlights/index.html (accessed December 18, 2024); David Stockman, "Trump's $30 Trillion Debt Disaster," *BG*, February 11, 2025, https://www.bostonglobe.com/2025/02/11/opinion/trump-30-trillion-added-debt/; and Katie Bergh, Dottie Rosenbaum, and Catlin Nchako, "Republican SNAP Proposals Could Take Food Away From Millions of Low-Income Individuals and Families," Center on Budget and Policy Priorities, January 13, 2025, https://www.cbpp.org/research/food-assistance/republican-snap-proposals-could-take-food-away-from-millions-of-low-income.

77. Howard Schneider and Chris Kahn, "Majority of Americans Favor Wealth Tax on Very Rich: Reuters/Ipsos Poll," Reuters, January 10, 2020, https://www.reuters.com/article/us-usa-election-inequality-poll/majority-of-americans-favor-wealth-tax-on-very-rich-reuters-ipsos-poll-idUSKBN1Z9141.

78. Benjamin I. Page, Jason Seawright, and Matthew J. LaCombe, *Billionaires and Stealth Politics* (Chicago: University of Chicago Press, 2018); Alexander Hertel-Fernandez, *State Capture: How Conservative Activists, Big Business, and Wealthy Donors Reshaped American States—and the Nation* (New York: Oxford University Press, 2019); Gordon Lafer, *The One Percent Solution: How Corporations Are Remaking America One State at a Time* (Ithaca, NY: ILR Press of Cornell University Press, 2017); and Christopher Leonard, *Kochland: The Secret History of Koch Industries and Corporate Power in America* (New York: Simon and Schuster, 2019), 478–82.

79. Nearly all of the hundred wealthiest US billionaires made a reportable federal or state campaign contribution in the dozen years between 2001 and 2012. The billionaires who contributed invested on average $509,000 each year. These figures do not include the so-called dark money by undisclosed donors that the *Citizens United* decision unleashed. Page et al., *Billionaires and Stealth Politics*, 2, 43 and 49.

80. Page et al., 59–60; and Anand Giridharadas, *Winners Take All: The Elite Charade of Changing the World* (New York: Alfred A. Knopf, 2018).

81. Zephyr Teachout, "Change Our Minds, Change the World," *TAP*, March/April 2021, 61. The United States has a long and troubling history of public-private partnerships and what historian Brent Cebul calls "supply-side liberalism," which he shows has its origins in the New Deal and Great Society. See Brent Cebul, *Illusions of Progress: Business, Poverty, and Liberalism in the American Century* (Philadelphia: University of Pennsylvania Press, 2023), chap. 1.

82. Peter Fleming and Marc T. Jones, *The End of Corporate Social Responsibility: Crisis and Critique* (Los Angeles: Sage 2013).

83. Giridharadas, *Winners Take All*, 8. See also Michael Mechanic, "Givers and Takers," *Mother Jones*, January–February 2024, 37–40.

84. Kaba, *We Do This 'Til We Free Us*, 101.

85. Dwight D. Eisenhower, "The Chance for Peace," April 16, 1953, American Presidency Project, https://www.presidency.ucsb.edu/documents/address-the-chance-for-peace-delivered -before-the-american-society-newspaper-editors.

86. In the 1890s and 1920s, active-duty US military forces constituted about 0.1 percent and 0.2 percent, respectively, of the US population, or just 10 to 20 percent of the forces that France and Britain were maintaining at the time. By the 1950s and 1960s, the figure had skyrocketed to 1.3 to 1.8 percent of the total population. American military expenditures in peacetime constituted just 0.4 to 0.9 percent of the annual GNP until well into the twentieth century. Michael S. Sherry, *In the Shadow of War: The United States Since the 1930s* (New Haven, CT: Yale University Press, 1995), 5–6.

87. Michael Kazin, *War Against War: The American Fight for Peace, 1914–1918* (New York: Simon and Schuster, 2017); and Oona A. Hathaway and Scott J. Shapiro, *The Internationalists: How a Radical Plan to Outlaw War Remade the World* (New York: Simon and Schuster, 2017).

88. Simon Callow, "The Emperor Robeson," *NYRB*, February 8, 2018, https://www.nybooks .com/articles/2018/02/08/emperor-paul-robeson/.

89. That is beginning to change. See Peniel E. Joseph, *The Sword and the Shield: The Revolutionary Lives of Malcolm X and Martin Luther King, Jr.* (New York: Basic Books, 2020).

90. Brandon M. Terry, "What Dignity Demands," *NYRB*, March 11, 2021, 13. See also Aziz Rana on how King's deep-seated anti-imperialism is either ignored or sanitized in public discussions of his work. Aziz Rana, "Against National Security Citizenship," in *Fifty Years Since MLK*, ed. Brandon M. Terry (Cambridge, MA: Boston Review, 2018), 81–91.

91. Martin Luther King, "Beyond Vietnam—a Time to Break Silence," Riverside Church, New York City, April 4, 1967, http://www.worldfuturefund.org/Reports2013/Martinluther kingspeech1967.html.

92. Heidi Peltier, "We Get What We Pay For: The Cycle of Military Spending, Industry Power, and Economic Dependence," Watson Institute, Brown University, June 8, 2023, https:// watson.brown.edu/costsofwar/files/cow/imce/papers/2023/Peltier%202023%20-%20 We%20Get%20What%20We%20Pay%20For%20-%20FINAL%20-%200608.pdf, 1–2.

93. William D. Hartung, "Conservatives Are Gearing Up for a Major Military Expansion Under Trump 2.0," *Nation*, June 5, 2024, https://www.thenation.com/article/society/project -2025-military-pentagon-spending/.

94. GAO, "F-35 Sustainment: Costs Continue to Rise While Planned Use and Availability Have Deceased," April 15, 2024, https://www.gao.gov/products/gao-24-106703; and Peltier, "We Get What We Pay For," 19.

95. Rebecca U. Thorpe, *The American Warfare State: The Domestic Politics of Military Spending* (Chicago: University of Chicago Press, 2014).

96. Peltier, "We Get What We Pay For," 18.

97. Peltier, 17, table 4.

98. Robert L. Borosage, "Roll Back Empire," *Nation*, January 2024, 8.

99. Peltier, "We Get What We Pay For," 21–22.

100. Jonathan Stevenson, "Owned by the Army: Has the President Lost Control of the Generals?," *HM*, May 2011, 34–36, 38, 40.

101. Jordan Fabian, "White House Defends Kelly as Above Reproach," *Hill*, October 20, 2017, https://thehill.com/homenews/administration/356444-white-house-defends-kelly-as-above-reproach/.

102. Phil Williams, "Isolationism or Discerning Internationalism: Robert Taft, Mike Mansfield, and US Troops in Europe," *Review of International Studies* 8, no. 1 (January 1982): 27–38.

103. Secretary of State Madeleine K. Albright, interview on *Today Show*, NBC, February 19, 1998, US Department of State Archive, n.d., https://1997-2001.state.gov/statements/1998/980219a.html (accessed February 15, 2025).

104. Neta C. Crawford, *The Pentagon, Climate Change, and War: Charting the Rise and Fall of U.S. Military Emissions* (Cambridge, MA: MIT Press, 2022).

105. Michael T. Klare, *All Hell Breaking Loose: The Pentagon's Perspective on Climate Change* (New York: Metropolitan Books, 2019).

106. Crawford, *Pentagon, Climate Change, and War*.

107. Mark Hertsgaard, "The Climate Crisis Is a Crime That Should Be Prosecuted," *Guardian*, June 30, 2021, https://www.theguardian.com/environment/2021/jun/30/climate-crisis-crime-fossil-fuels-environment.

108. Quoted in Alan Weisman, "Burning Down the House," *NYRB*, August 15, 2019, https://www.nybooks.com/articles/2019/08/15/climate-change-burning-down-house/.

109. Ronald C. Kramer, *Carbon Criminals, Climate Crimes* (New Brunswick, NJ: Rutgers University Press, 2020).

110. David Whyte, *Ecocide: Kill the Corporation Before It Kills Us* (Manchester, UK: Manchester University Press, 2020), 2. See also Michael J. Lynch, "Green Criminology and Environmental Crime: Criminology That Matters in the Age of Global Ecological Collapse," *JWCCC* 1, no. 1 (2020): 50–61.

111. Paul M. Reeping and David Hemenway, "The Association Between Weather and the Number of Daily Shootings in Chicago (2012–2016)," *Injury Epidemiology* 7, no. 31 (2020): https://doi.org/10.1186/s40621-020-00260-3; and Cynthia Golembeski et al., "The Deadly Link Between Climate Change and Incarceration," *CR*, July 5, 2022, https://thecrimereport.org/2022/07/05/the-deadly-link-between-climate-change-and-incarceration/.

112. Robert Agnew, "Dire Forecast: A Theoretical Model of the Impact of Climate Change on Crime," *Theoretical Criminology* 16, no. 1 (2011): 21.

113. Kevin Fiscella, "New Position Statement Addresses Health Risks of Extreme Temperatures," National Commission on Correctional Health Care, October 29, 2024, https://www.ncchc.org/new-ncchc-position-statement-addresses-health-risks-for-incarcerated-people-and-carceral-facility-workers/; and Matt Clarke, "In the Eye of the Storm: When Hurricanes Impact Prisons and Jails," *PLN*, May 17, 2018, https://www.prisonlegalnews.org/news/2018/may/17/eye-storm-when-hurricanes-impact-prisons-and-jails/.

114. Naomi Oreskes, "The Greatest Scam in History: How the Energy Companies Took Us All In," *Common Dreams*, November 11, 2019, https://www.commondreams.org/views/2019/11/11/greatest-scam-history-how-energy-companies-took-us-all; and James Gustave Speth, *They Knew: The US Federal Government's Fifty-Year Role in Causing the Climate Crisis* (Cambridge, MA: MIT Press, 2022).

115. Exxon internal documents quoted in Lee Wasserman, "Exxon's Climate Change Deceit," *NYT*, October 23, 2019, A27.

116. Geoffrey Supran and Naomi Oreskes, "The Forgotten Oil Ads That Told Us Climate Change Was Nothing," *Guardian*, November 18, 2021, https://www.theguardian.com/environment/2021/nov/18/the-forgotten-oil-ads-that-told-us-climate-change-was-nothing. See also Naomi Oreskes and Erik M. Conway, *Merchants of Doubt: How a Handful of Scientists Obscured the Truth on Issues from Tobacco Smoke to Global Warming* (New York: Bloomsbury, 2010).

117. Quoted in Ron Suskind, "Faith, Certainty and the Presidency of George W. Bush," *NYT*, October 17, 2004, https://www.nytimes.com/2004/10/17/magazine/faith-certainty-and-the -presidency-of-george-w-bush.html.

118. Bruce Gil, "U.S. Cities and States Are Suing Big Oil Over Climate Change. Here's Where They Stand.," *Frontline*, PBS, August 1, 2022, https://www.pbs.org/wgbh/frontline/article /us-cities-states-sue-big-oil-climate-change-lawsuits/.

119. Office of US Senator Bernie Sanders, "Sanders, Markey, Merkley, and Warren Send Letter to Attorney General Urging DOJ to Bring Lawsuits Against the Fossil Fuel Industry," press release, July 31, 2023, https://www.sanders.senate.gov/press-releases/news-sanders-markey -merkley-and-warren-send-letter-to-attorney-general-urging-doj-to-bring-lawsuits-against-the -fossil-fuel-industry/ ; and DOJ, "Justice Department Files Complaint Against Hawaii, Michigan, New York, and Vermont Over Unconstitutional State Climate Actions," press release, May 1, 2025, updated May 12, 2025, https://www.justice.gov/opa/pr/justice-department-files-complaints -against-hawaii-michigan-new-york-and-vermont-over.

120. See Aronoff, "Planet Is Screwed."

121. Bill McKibben, "A World at War," *NR*, August 15, 2016, https://newrepublic.com/article /135684/declare-war-climate-change-mobilize-wwii. See also Kate Aronoff et al., *A Planet to Win: Why We Need a Green New Deal* (London: Verso, 2019).

122. Sherry, *In the Shadow of War*, 15.

123. Sherry, 17 and 31.

124. Centers for Medicare and Medicaid Services, "National Health Expenditures 2018 High-lights," n.d., https://www.cms.gov/files/document/highlights.pdf (accessed October 31, 2020); and Roosa Tikkanen and Melinda K. Abrams, "U.S. Health Care from a Global Perspective, 2019: Higher Spending, Worse Outcomes?," Commonwealth Fund, January 30, 2020, https://www.com monwealthfund.org/publications/issue-briefs/2020/jan/us-health-care-global-perspective-2019.

125. Committee on Public Health Strategies to Improve Health, Board on Population Health and Public Health Practice, and the Institute of Medicine, *For the Public's Health: Investing in a Healthier Future* (Washington, DC: Institute of Medicine, 2012), 2.

126. Elizabeth Bradley and Lauren Taylor, *The American Health Care Paradox: Why Spending More Is Getting Us Less* (New York: PublicAffairs, 2013).

127. Alexander Sammon, "It's Time for Public Pharma," *TAP*, August 2022, 30–32; Laura Katz Olson, *Ethically Challenged: Private Equity Storms US Health Care* (Baltimore: Johns Hopkins University Press, 2022); and California Department of Health Care Access and Information, "CalRx Update: Initial Progress Under the California Affordable Drug Manufacturing Act," April 2023, https://calrx.ca.gov/uploads/2023/05/CalRx-Legislative-Report-Initial-Progress -Under-the-California-Affordable-Drug-Manufacturing-Act-April-2023.pdf.

128. People in the United States spend anywhere from 54 percent to 209 percent more per capita on medications compared to people in other wealthy countries. Nathan E. Wineinger, Yunyue Zhang, and Eric J. Topol, "Trends in Prices of Popular Brand-Name Prescription Drugs in the United States," *JAMA Network Open* 2, no. 5 (May 2019): 2.

129. Thomas Hwang et al., "Association Between FDA and EMA Expedited Approval Pro-grams and Therapeutic Value of New Medicines: Retrospective Cohort Study," *BMJ* 371 (2020), https://doi.org/10.1136/bmj.m3434.

130. Dukes et al., *Pharmaceuticals, Corporate Crime and Public Health*; and Alexander Zait-chik, *Owning the Sun: A People's History of Monopoly Medicine from Aspirin to Covid-19 Vaccines* (New York: Counterpoint, 2022).

131. Delshad Irani and Priyanka Nair, "Big Pharma and the Covid-Era Reputation Reset," ET Brand Equity.com, January 20, 2021, https://brandequity.economictimes.indiatimes.com/news /business-of-brands/big-pharma-and-the-covid-era-reputation-reset/80352919.

132. Daniel J. Kevles, "Unreasonable Terms," *NYRB*, October 5, 2023, 39–42; and David E. Mitchell, "Taxpayers Fund Research and Drug Companies Make a Fortune," *NYT*, March 24,

2021, https://www.nytimes.com/2021/03/24/opinion/coronavirus-vaccine-cost-pfizer
-moderna.html.

133. J. David McSwane, *Pandemic, Inc.: Chasing the Capitalists and Thieves Who Got Rich While
We Got Sick* (New York: Simon and Schuster, 2022); Ankush Khardori, "The DOJ Failed on
Pandemic Fraud," *Politico*, April 22, 2022, https://www.politico.com/news/magazine/2022/04
/22/justice-department-pandemic-fraud-enforcement-00027092; Zoe Richards and Sarah Fitz-
patrick, "White House Pitches $1.6 Billion Plan to Combat Covid Relief Fraud," NBC News,
March 3, 2023, https://www.nbcnews.com/politics/white-house/white-house-pitches-16
-billion-plan-targeting-covid-relief-fraud-rcna73013; Kanishka Singh, "U.S. Watchdog Identifies
$5.4 Billion in Potentially Fraudulent COVID-19 Loans," Reuters, January 30, 2023, https://www
.reuters.com/world/us/us-watchdog-identifies-54-billion-potentially-fraudulent-covid-19
-loans-2023-01-30/; and David Fahrenthold, "Prosecutors Struggle to Catch Up to a Tidal Wave
of Pandemic Fraud," *NYT*, August 16, 2022, https://www.nytimes.com/2022/08/16/business
/economy/covid-pandemic-fraud.html.

134. John Nichols, "It's Now Clearer Than Ever: The US Is Choosing to Impoverish Children,"
Nation, September 13, 2023, https://www.thenation.com/article/politics/child-poverty-rise
-census/; and Claire Cain Miller and Alicia Parlapiano, "The U.S. Built a European-Style Welfare
State: It's Largely Over," *NYT*, April 6, 2023, updated May 11, 2023, https://www.nytimes.com
/interactive/2023/04/06/upshot/pandemic-safety-net-medicaid.html.

135. Artie Vierkant and Beatrice Adler-Bolton, "Cut and Run," *In These Times*, April 2023,
14–21; and Gregg Gonsalves, "The 'You Do You' Pandemic," *Nation*, September 18, 2023, 5–6.

136. Zeynep Tufekci, "A Bird Flu Pandemic Would Be One of the Most Foreseeable Catas-
trophes in History," *NYT*, November 29, 2024, https://www.nytimes.com/2024/11/29
/opinion/bird-flu-pandemic.html; and Siddhartha Mukherjee, "Covid's Deadliest Effect Took
Five Years to Appear," *NYT*, March 10, 2025, https://www.nytimes.com/2025/03/10/opinion/
covid-public-health-privatization.html.

137. Jacob Bor et al., "Missing Americans: Early Death in the United States—1933–2021,"
PNAS Nexus 2 (2023), https://doi.org/10.1093/pnasnexus/pgad173, 8. See also Eugenio Pa-
glino et al., "Monthly Excess Mortality Across Counties in the United States During the
COVID-19 Pandemic, March 2020 to February 2022," *Science Advances* 9, no. 25 (June 23, 2023),
https://www.science.org/doi/10.1126/sciadv.adf9742, 1–14.

138. John Gramlich, "What We Know About the Increase in U.S. Murders in 2020," PRC,
October 27, 2021, https://www.pewresearch.org/short-reads/2021/10/27/what-we-know
-about-the-increase-in-u-s-murders-in-2020/; and Marin Cogan, "Why the US Had a Violent
Crime Spike During Covid—and Other Countries Didn't," *Vox*, July 8, 2023, https://www.vox
.com/politics/358831/us-violent-crime-murder-pandemic.

139. David Wallace-Wells, "Why Is America Such a Deadly Place?," *NYT*, August 9, 2023,
https://www.nytimes.com/2023/08/09/opinion/mortality-rate-pandemic.html; and Emily
Badger and Alicia Parlapiano, "The Exceptionally American Problem of Rising Roadway
Deaths," *NYT*, November 27, 2022, https://www.nytimes.com/2022/11/27/upshot/road
-deaths-pedestrians-cyclists.html.

140. For a nuanced discussion of the imperative for government-led solutions, see Mariana
Mazzacato, *Mission Economy: A Moonshot Guide to Changing Capitalism* (New York: HarperCol-
lins, 2021). For a subtle analysis of antigovernment sentiment in the United States, see Amy E.
Lerman, *Good Enough for Government Work: The Public Reputation Crisis in America (And What
We Can Do to Fix It)* (Chicago: University of Chicago Press, 2019).

141. Quoted in Editorial Board, "Rethinking Their Pledge," *NYT*, April 21, 2011, https://www
.nytimes.com/2011/04/22/opinion/22fri1.html.

142. I am indebted to Touré Reed, Cedric Johnson, Katherine Rader, and others for their help
in developing and refining this argument. See, for example, Touré Reed, *Toward Freedom: The
Case Against Race Reductionism* (London: Verso, 2020); Cedric Johnson, *After Black Lives Matter:*

Policing and Anti-Capitalist Struggles (London: Verso, 2023), 90–94; and Katherine Rader, "Delineating Agriculture and Industry: Reexamining the Exclusion of Agricultural Workers from the New Deal," *Studies in American Political Development* 37, no. 2 (October 2023): 146–63.

143. Powerful economic and agricultural interests did not want to pay for any social benefits or cede any control over their Black or white labor force. Rader, "Delineating Agriculture and Industry."

144. For more on discrimination and the CCC and WPA, see, for example, Sherry, *In the Shadow of War*, 21; Cedric Johnson, "What Black Life Actually Looks Like," *Jacobin*, April 29, 2019, https://jacobin.com/2019/04/racism-black-lives-matter-inequality; and Cybelle Fox, *Three Worlds of Relief: Race, Immigration, and the American Welfare State from the Progressive Era to the New Deal* (Princeton, NJ: Princeton University Press, 2012).

145. Joseph A. McCartin, "U.S. Labor and the Struggle for Democracy," *New Labor Forum* 32, no. 1 (2023): 26.

146. Robin D. G. Kelley, *Hammer and Hoe: Alabama Communists During the Great Depression* (Chapel Hill: University of North Carolina Press, 1990).

147. Keeanga-Yamahtta Taylor, *Race for Profit: How Banks and the Real Estate Industry Undermined Black Homeownership* (Chapel Hill: University of North Carolina Press, 2019). See also Chloe N. Thurston, *At the Boundaries of Home Ownership: Credit, Discrimination, and the American State* (Cambridge: Cambridge University Press, 2018).

148. Even Robert Kuttner, one of the shrewdest analysts of the US political economy, remarked: "FDR's New Deal was largely for whites." See Robert Kuttner, "Dividends of a Just Economy," *NYRB*, April 29, 2021, 15.

149. In his memoir *Between the World and Me*, Ta-Nehisi Coates, a prominent Black public intellectual, paints a bleak future that suggests politics is irrelevant. Coates concludes that it would take nothing short of an ecological apocalypse to dismantle white supremacy and racial inequality. Ta-Nehisi Coates, *Between the World and Me* (New York: Spiegel and Grau, 2015). I am grateful to Thomas Chatterton Williams for this point and example from Coates. See Thomas Chatterton Williams, "Easy Chair," *HM*, August 2021, 6. Brandon M. Terry makes a similar point in "MLK Now," in Terry, *Fifty Years Since MLK*, 16.

150. Rebecca Solnit, "The Habits of Highly Cynical People," *HM*, May 2016, 7.

151. See David M. Kennedy's discussion of Dewey in *Over Here: The First World War and American Society* (New York: Oxford University Press, 1980), 50.

152. For an excellent development of this point with respect to the presidency of Bill Clinton, see Nelson Lichtenstein and Judith Stein, *A Fabulous Failure: The Clinton Presidency and the Transformation of American Capitalism* (Princeton, NJ: Princeton University Press, 2023).

153. Joshua Green, *The Rebels: Elizabeth Warren, Bernie Sanders, Alexandria Ocasio-Cortez, and the Struggle for a New American Politics* (New York: Penguin, 2024), 241.

154. Ben Fountain, *Beautiful Country, Burn Again: Democracy, Rebellion, and Revolution* (New York: Ecco/HarperCollins, 2018), 250–51.

155. Green, *Rebels*, chaps. 8 and 11.

156. Green, chap. 9.

157. Theodore Roosevelt, "December 3, 1901: First Annual Message," Miller Center, University of Virginia, n.d., https://millercenter.org/the-presidency/presidential-speeches/december-3-1901-first-annual-message (accessed February 15, 2025).

158. "Remarks by President Biden at Signing of an Executive Order Promoting Competition in the American Economy," July 9, 2021, https://www.whitehouse.gov/briefing-room/speeches-remarks/2021/07/09/remarks-by-president-biden-at-signing-of-an-executive-order-promoting-competition-in-the-american-economy/.

159. That is if—and it's a big if—the measures are implemented so as to address the special needs of rural America in successfully competing for the federal windfall and developing the capacity to spend it well. Tony Pipa, "Aid for Rural America Works Only If It Gets There," *NYT*,

May 29, 2024, A23. See also Robert Leonard, "Biden Has Already Done More for Rural America Than Trump Ever Did," *NYT*, April 26, 2022, https://www.nytimes.com/2022/04/26/opinion /biden-trump-democrats-rural-america.html.

160. For more on the Biden administration and crime in the suites, see pp. 286–87.

161. Michelle Goldberg, "Billionaire Donors Have It Out for This Legal Prodigy, but President Harris Will Need Her," *NYT*, August 23, 2024, https://www.nytimes.com/2024/08/23 /opinion/lina-khan-antitrust-harris.html.

162. Nicholas Nehamas, Andrew Duehren, and Reid J. Epstein, "Harris Tells the Business Community: I'm Friendlier Than Biden," *NYT*, September 4, 2024, https://www.nytimes.com /2024/09/04/us/politics/harris-tax-break-small-business.html; and Andrew Duehren and Theodore Schleifer, "Donors Quietly Push Harris to Drop Tax on Ultrawealthy," *NYT*, August 29, 2024, https://www.nytimes.com/2024/08/29/us/politics/donors-harris-tax -ultrawealthy.html.

163. Will Bunch, "Joe Biden's Pander to Fox News Tropes Is the Worst Move of His Presidency," *PI*, March 7, 2023, A13. For more on the Biden administration's war on drugs, see pp. 358–59.

164. "The Bernie Sanders Doctrine on Foreign Policy: An Interview with Matt Duss," *Jacobin*, August 20, 2020, https://jacobin.com/2020/08/bernie-sanders-foreign-policy-matt-duss; and Alex Pareene, "Democratic Hawks Declare War on Bernie Sanders," *NR*, January 31, 2020, https://newrepublic.com/article/156374/democratic-hawks-declare-war-bernie-sanders.

165. Spencer Ackerman, *Reign of Terror: How the 9/11 Era Destabilized America and Produced Trump* (New York: Viking, 2021), 314–15.

166. John Brennan was interim director of the National Counterterrorism Center under President George W. Bush. President Obama withdrew Brennan's nomination in 2009 to be his first director of the CIA after reports surfaced that Brennan had supported the use of torture. Four years later, after the controversy cooled, Brennan became CIA director. During Brennan's controversial tenure, the CIA hacked into the computers of staffers on the US Senate Select Committee on Intelligence who were investigating the use of torture by the CIA. The agency unsuccessfully sought to have the staffers criminally charged with possession of classified documents. It also stymied release of the "torture report" and insisted that the report be heavily redacted. Senator Dianne Feinstein (D-CA), chair of the committee and a longtime champion of the intelligence community, excoriated the agency in a March 2014 speech on the Senate floor. Among other things, she denounced the extensive torture program and the CIA's efforts to spy on the congressional committee that was legally empowered to oversee the agency. Connie Bruck, "The Inside War," *NY*, June 15, 2015, https://www.newyorker.com/magazine/2015/06/22/the-inside-war.

James Clapper, who had deep ties to the defense industry and intelligence community, became Obama's director of National Intelligence in 2010. In March 2013, Clapper testified before the Senate Intelligence Committee that the NSA did "not wittingly" collect data on millions of US citizens. But two months later, classified documents leaked by whistleblower Edward Snowden revealed that Clapper had lied to Congress. The documents disclosed how the NSA ran a massive surveillance program that vacuumed up the phone records, electronic communications, computer search histories, and even the Fitbit records of millions of Americans. Ackerman, *Reign of Terror*, 201–8.

167. Jefferson Morley, "The 'Deep State' Is a Political Party," *NR*, November 8, 2019, https:// newrepublic.com/article/155629/deep-state-political-party.

168. See, for example, Garrett M. Graff's unctuous review of James Clapper's memoir, *Facts and Fears*. Clapper's staff members once made him a t-shirt, in the style of one for a heavy metal band, that proclaimed, "James Clapper and the Litany of Doom." Garrett M. Graff, "How Former US Spy Chief Became Trump's Fiercest Critic," *Wired*, May 30, 2018, https://www.wired .com/story/how-a-former-us-spy-chief-became-trumps-fiercest-critic/.

169. "Remarks by President Joseph R. Biden, Jr. Before the 76th Session of the United Nations General Assembly," US Mission to the UN, September 21, 2024, https://usun.usmission

.gov/remarks-by-president-joseph-r-biden-jr-before-the-76th-session-of-the-united-nations
-general-assembly/.

170. Eric Lipton, Michael Crowley, and John Ismay, "Bonanza for Arms Makers as Military
Budget Surges," *NYT*, December 18, 2022, A1.

171. Theodore A. Postol, "How the Obama Administration Learned to Stop Worrying and
Love the Bomb," *Nation*, December 10, 2014, https://www.thenation.com/article/archive/how
-obama-administration-learned-stop-worrying-and-love-bomb/.

172. Jim Carrier, "Playing with Fire," *Progressive*, August–September 2023, 41–43; and Alfred
Meyer, "The Bipartisan Atom," *Progressive*, August–September 2023, 44–46.

173. Noam Chomsky and Vijay Prashad, *The Withdrawal: Iraq, Libya, Afghanistan, and the
Fragility of U.S. Power* (New York: New Press, 2022).

174. Quincy Institute for Responsible Statecraft, "Overview," n.d., https://quincyinst.org
/about/# (accessed May 7, 2024). See also the apparent shift by Ben Rhodes, a close foreign
policy adviser to President Obama who recently appeared to break ranks with the Washington
rules. Rhodes questioned whether the United States should continue to strive for US primacy as
the "indispensable nation" when much of the world is antagonistic to US hegemony, and many
Americans have turned on the forever wars. See Ben Rhodes, "A Foreign Policy for the World as
It Is: Biden and the Search for a New American Strategy," *Foreign Affairs*, July–August 2024,
https://www.foreignaffairs.com/united-states/biden-foreign-policy-world-rhodes.

175. Quoted in Dan Lamothe and Alex Horton, "Vance's Marine Buddies Back His Service
Over His Politics," *PI*, August 5, 2024, A5. See also Quil Lawrence, "JD Vance and the Republican Vets Who Think America Should Do Less, Not More, Abroad," NPR, July 29, 2024, https://
www.npr.org/2024/07/29/g-s1-13741/jd-vance-republican-veterans-war.

176. "Full Transcript of Kamala Harris's Democratic Convention Speech," *NYT*, August 23,
2024, https://www.nytimes.com/2024/08/23/us/politics/kamala-harris-speech-transcript
.html. Philip H. Gordon, her top foreign policy adviser, has severely criticized aspects of US
foreign policy, especially the pursuit of regime change in Iraq and elsewhere, but did not advocate for a regime change in US foreign policy and for jettisoning the Washington rules. Michael
Brenes, "The Harris Doctrine," *BR*, August 26, 2024, https://www.bostonreview.net/articles
/the-harris-doctrine/.

177. Donald Trump quoted in Charles Homans, "Donald Trump Has Never Sounded Like
This," *NYT*, April 27, 2024, https://www.nytimes.com/2024/04/27/magazine/trump-rallies
-rhetoric.html.

178. Hartung, "Conservatives Are Gearing Up"; and Tony Romm, "Trump Seeks Drastic
Cuts to Core of U.S. Spending," *NYT*, May 3, 2025, A1.

179. Cybele Mayes-Osterman, "Hegseth Orders $50 Billion of Defense Budget Redirected
from Biden to Trump Priorities," *USA Today*, February 20, 2025, https://www.usatoday.com
/story/news/politics/2025/02/20/pete-hegseth-defense-budget-directive/79244204007/.

180. Susan B. Glasser and Peter Baker, "Inside the War Between Trump and His Generals,"
NY, August 8, 2022, https://www.newyorker.com/magazine/2022/08/15/inside-the-war
-between-trump-and-his-generals; Noah Lanard, "Republicans Are Now Parroting Trump's
Attacks on 'Woke' Generals," *Mother Jones*, August 10, 2022, https://www.motherjones.com
/politics/2022/08/donald-trump-republicans-war-woke-generals-mark-milley/; and Eric
Schmitt, Helene Cooper, and Jonathan Swan, "Trump Fires Joint Chiefs Chairman Amid Flurry
of Dismissals at Pentagon," *NYT*, February 21, 2025, https://www.nytimes.com/2025/02/21
/us/politics/trump-fires-cq-brown-pentagon.html.

181. Donald Trump quoted in Katherine Stewart, "Christian Nationalists Are Excited About
What Comes Next," *NYT*, July 5, 2022, https://www.nytimes.com/2022/07/05/opinion
/dobbs-christian-nationalism.html.

182. Donald Trump, quoted in Homans, "Donald Trump Has Never Sounded Like This."

183. Indeed, David Mayhew emphasizes the centrality of Senator Robert Wagner (D-NY) in the creation of the New Deal and suggests that the 1930s, legislatively speaking, were as much "the age of Wagner" as the "age of Roosevelt." David Mayhew, *America's Congress: Actions in the Public Sphere, James Madison Through Newt Gingrich* (New Haven, CT: Yale University Press, 2000), 212–13.

184. Heather McGhee, *The Sum of Us: What Racism Costs Everyone and How We Can Prosper Together* (New York: One World, 2021).

185. Martin Luther King Jr., "The Power of Non-Violence," June 4, 1957, https://www .barnstableacademy.com/app/uploads/2021/02/MKLjr-Power-of-Non-Violence.pdf.

186. Randall Kennedy, "Martin Luther King, Jr.: The Prophet as Healer," *TAP*, April 3, 2018, https://prospect.org/infrastructure/martin-luther-king-jr.-prophet-healer/.

187. For an excellent overview of scholarship on how economic justice and robust unionism were pillars of Martin Luther King Jr.'s agenda on par with his commitment to civil rights, see Annette Gordon-Reed, "MLK: What We Lost," *NYRB*, November 8, 2018, 48–50.

188. Quoted in Keeanga-Yamahtta Taylor, "The Pivot to Class," *BR*, September 10, 2018, https://www.bostonreview.net/forum_response/keeanga-yamahtta-taylor-pivot-class/.

189. Karen E. Fields and Barbara J. Fields, *Racecraft: The Soul of American Inequality* (New York: Verso, 2012), 261.

190. For an excellent analysis of the historical development of political polarization between rural and urban areas in the United States, see Trevor E. Brown and Suzanne Mettler, "Sequential Polarization: The Development of the Rural-Urban Political Divide, 1976–2020," *Perspectives on Politics* 22, no. 3 (September 2024): 630–58.

191. As Randall Kennedy observes, "If King were alive he would surely seek to find ways of addressing these internal disputes with candor and generosity, realism and graciousness, keeping in mind the immensity of the larger stakes." Kennedy, "Martin Luther King, Jr." See also Maurice Mitchell, "Building Resilient Organizations," *Forge*, November 22, 2022, https:// forgeorganizing.org/article/building-resilient-organizations; and Ryan Grim, "Elephant in the Zoom: Meltdowns Have Brought Progressive Advocacy Groups to a Standstill at a Critical Moment in World History," *Intercept*, June 13, 2022, https://theintercept.com/2022/06/13 /progressive-organizing-infighting-callout-culture/.

192. Manuel Funke, Moritz Schularick, and Christoph Trebesch, "Going to Extremes: Politics After Financial Crises, 1870–2014," *European Economic Review* 88 (September 2016): 227–60.

193. For two representative works that focus on identity factors to explain Trump's success in 2016, see Diana C. Mutz, "Status Threat, Not Economic Hardship, Explains 2016 Presidential Vote," *Proceedings of the National Academy of Sciences*, 115 no. 19 (2018): E4330–E4339; and John Sides, Michael Tesler, and Lynn Vavreck, *Identity Crisis: The 2016 Presidential Campaign and the Battle for the Meaning of America* (Princeton, NJ: Princeton University Press, 2018). For a critique of Mutz and overview of sociological and other research emphasizing multiple factors to explain Trump's electoral success, see Stephen L. Morgan, "Status Threat, Material Interests, and the 2016 Presidential Vote," *Socius* 4 (2018): 1–17.

194. Kathleen R. McNamara, "Explaining the New Class Cleavages: Geography, Post-Industrial Transformations and Everyday Culture," SSRN Scholarly Paper, 2017, https://papers.ssrn.com /sol3/papers.cfm?abstract_id=3059222; and Justin Gest, *The New Minority: White Working Class Politics in an Age of Immigration and Inequality* (New York: Oxford University Press, 2016).

195. Estimates of the number of Obama–Trump voters range from about seven million to nine million. Geoffrey Skelley, "Just How Many Obama 2012–Trump 2016 Voters Were There?," *Sabato's Crystal Ball*, June 1, 2017, https://centerforpolitics.org/crystalball/articles/just-how -many-obama-2012-trump-2016-voters-were-there/.

196. Karthick Ramakrishnan, "Trump Got More Votes from People of Color Than Romney Did," *WP*, Monkey Cage, November 11, 2016, https://www.washingtonpost.com/news/monkey

-cage/wp/2016/11/11/trump-got-more-votes-from-people-of-color-than-romney-did-heres
-the-data/.

197. "Illness as Indicator," *Economist*, November 19, 2016, https://www-economist-com.proxy
.library.upenn.edu/united-states/2016/11/19/illness-as-indicator.

198. "Illness as Indicator."

199. Political scientist Brian Schaffner estimated that the proportion of Sanders voters who
defected to Trump in the 2016 general election was 12 percent. Jeff Stein, "The Bernie Voters
Who Defected to Trump, Explained by a Political Scientist," *Vox*, August 24, 2017, https://www
.vox.com/policy-and-politics/2017/8/24/16194086/bernie-trump-voters-study.

200. Robert Kuttner, "Dividends of a Just Economy," *NYRB*, April 29, 2021, 17.

201. Jennifer McCoy et al., "Historical Analysis of Depolarization," Carnegie Endowment for
International Peace, May 5, 2022, https://carnegieendowment.org/research/2022/05/reducing
-pernicious-polarization-a-comparative-historical-analysis-of-depolarization?lang=en.

202. Dominic Erdozain, *One Nation Under Guns: How Gun Culture Distorts Our History and
Threatens Our Democracy* (New York: Crown, 2024), chap. 2.

203. Calculated from Aaron Karp, "Estimating Global Civilian-Held Firearms Numbers,"
Small Arms Survey Briefing Paper, June 2018, https://www.smallarmssurvey.org/sites/default
/files/resources/SAS-BP-Civilian-Firearms-Numbers.pdf, 3, table 1.

204. Nathan P. Kalmoe and Lilliana Mason, *Radical American Partisanship: Mapping Violent
Hostility, Its Causes, and the Consequences for Democracy* (Chicago: University of Chicago Press,
2022); Charles Homans, "How Americans Justify Political Violence," *NYT*, July 20, 2024, updated July 22, 2024, https://www.nytimes.com/2024/07/20/magazine/us-political-violence
.html; Jennifer Carlson, *Merchants of the Right: Gun Sellers and the Crisis of American Democracy*
(Princeton, NJ: Princeton University Press, 2023), 162–63; and Jenna Russell, Emily Rhyne, and
Noah Throop, "The Tipping Point: America's Newest Gun Owners Are Upending Preconcep-
tions About Who Buys a Gun and Why," *NYT*, February 16, 2025, https://www.nytimes.com
/interactive/2025/02/16/us/new-gun-owners.html.

205. For a prominent example of that fantasy, see "Is America Dictator-Proof?," *Economist*,
May 16, 2024, https://www.economist.com/leaders/2024/05/16/is-america-dictator-proof.
For a sharp critique of that fantasy, see Rosa Brooks, "The Liberal Fantasy Is Just That: On the
Military in a Fascist America," *NR*, May 16, 2024, https://newrepublic.com/article/181222
/liberal-fantasy-military.

206. "President Dwight D. Eisenhower's Farewell Address," January 17, 1961, National Archives, https://www.archives.gov/milestone-documents/president-dwight-d-eisenhowers
-farewell-address.

207. David Runciman, *How Democracy Ends* (New York: Basic Books, 2018), 131–32. See also
Otto Kirchheimer, "Changes in the Structure of Political Compromise," in *Politics, Law and
Social Change: Selected Essays of Otto Kirchheimer*, ed. Frederic S. Burin and Kurt L. Shell (New
York: Columbia University Press, 1969), 131–59.

208. Jane Mayer, "The Big Money Behind the Big Lie," *NY*, August 21, 2021, https://www
.newyorker.com/magazine/2021/08/09/the-big-money-behind-the-big-lie; Isaac Kamola,
"Manufacturing Backlash: Right-Wing Think Tanks and Legislative Attacks on Higher Education, 2021–23," American Association of University Professors, May 2024, https://www.aaup.org
/sites/default/files/Manufacturing_Backlash_final.pdf; and Theda Skocpol and Alexander
Hertel-Fernandez, "The Koch Network and Republican Party Extremism," *Perspectives on Politics* 14, no. 3 (September 2016); 681–99.

209. Alex Kingsbury, "Who Is Financing Trump's 'Big Lie' Caucus? Corporations You
Know," *NYT*, June 15, 2022, https://www.nytimes.com/2022/06/15/opinion/jan6-companies
-donate.html.

210. During the 2024 World Economic Forum in Davos, Switzerland, JPMorgan's Jamie
Dimon said of Trump: "He's kind of right about NATO. Kind of right about immigration. He

grew the economy quite well. Tax reform worked." "CNBC Transcript: JPMorgan Chase Chairman and CEO Jamie Dimon Speaks with CNBC's 'Squawk Box,'" CNBC, January 17, 2024, https://www.cnbc.com/2024/01/17/cnbc-transcript-jpmorgan-chase-chairman-ceo-jamie -dimon-speaks-with-cnbcs-squawk-box-from-the-world-economic-forum-in-davos -switzerland-today.html; and Will Bunch, "Is Corporate America Welcoming a Trump Dictatorship? History Says Yes," *PI*, January 23, 2024, A11. See also Erin Griffith, "Silicon Valley Notables Are Shifting to the Right," *NYT*, May 24, 2024, B1.

211. Josh Dawsey et al., "'Economic Nationalism' at the RNC Clashes with Trump's Pitch to Donors," *WP*, July 17, 2024, https://www.washingtonpost.com/business/2024/07/17/trump -vance-economy-workers/; and Lauren Hirsch and Michael J. de la Merced, "Some of the Loudest Cheers for Trump's Campaign Are Coming from Tech Titans," *NYT*, July 22, 2024, B3.

212. James Franey and Charles Gasparino, "Donald Trump Has Been Secretly Communicating with 'Man Crush' Jamie Dimon About White House Agenda for Months: Sources," *NYP*, November 29, 2024, https://nypost.com/2024/11/29/business/jamie-dimon-has-been -secretly-communicating-with-donald-trump-on-white-house-agenda-for-months-sources/.

213. Nabil Ahmed et al., "Inequality Kills: The Unparalleled Action Needed to Combat Unprecedented Inequality in the Wake of COVID-19," Oxfam, January 2022, https://www .oxfam.org.au/wp-content/uploads/2022/01/Inequality-Kills_EN_web.pdf, 10, 18.

214. Douglas Rushkoff, quoted in Eveline Chao, "How the Ultra-Wealthy Plan to Escape the Rest of Us," *Princeton Alumni Weekly*, November 2022, 38; and Douglas Rushkoff, "The Super-Rich 'Preppers' Planning to Save Themselves from the Apocalypse," *Guardian*, September 4, 2022, https://www.theguardian.com/news/2022/sep/04/super-rich-prepper-bunkers -apocalypse-survival-richest-rushkoff.

215. See, for example, Evan Osnos, "Doomsday Prep for the Super-Rich," *NY*, January 22, 2017, https://www.newyorker.com/magazine/2017/01/30/doomsday-prep-for-the-super -rich; and Douglas Rushkoff, *Survival of the Richest: Escape Fantasies of the Tech Billionaires* (New York: W. W. Norton, 2022).

Appendix: On Use of Language and Data

1. See, for example, Marshall Project, "The Language Project," n.d., https://www .themarshallproject.org/2021/04/12/the-language-project (accessed October 3, 2024); and Alexandra Cox, "The Language of Incarceration," *Incarceration* 1, no. 1 (July 2020), https://journals.sagepub.com/doi/epub/10.1177/2632666320940859.

2. Bryan Betancur, "Why I Hate the Term 'Latinx,'" *Inside Higher Education*, January 24, 2023, https://www.insidehighered.com/views/2023/01/26/why-i-hate-term-latinx-opinion; and Nancy Rodriguez and Rebecca Tublitz, "Exploring Latino/a Representation in Local Criminal Justice Systems: A Review of Data Collection Practices and Systems-Involvement," University of California Irvine, Department of Criminology, Law, and Society, March 2023, School of Ecology, https://socialecology.uci.edu/sites/default/files/users/mkcruz/sjc_latinos_in_cjs _march_2023.pdf, 4n1.

3. Sarah Eppler-Epstein, Anne Gurvis, and Ryan King, "The Alarming Lack of Data on Latinos in the Criminal Justice System," Urban Institute, December 15, 2016, https://apps.urban .org/features/latino-criminal-justice-data/.

4. See, for example, Manvir Singh, "It's Time to Rethink the Idea of 'Indigenous,'" *NY*, February 20, 2023, https://www.newyorker.com/magazine/2023/02/27/its-time-to-rethink-the -idea-of-the-indigenous.

5. For a development of this point, see Marie Gottschalk, "Incorrigible: The First Step Act and the Carceral State," *Prison Legal News* 30, no. 4 (April 2019): 1–13; and Marie Gottschalk, *Caught: The Prison State and the Lockdown of American Politics*, rev. ed. (Princeton, NJ: Princeton University Press, 2016), 252–56.

6. Ram Subramanian, Kristine Riley, and Chris Mai, *Divided Justice: Trends in Black and White Jail Incarceration, 1990–2013* (New York: Vera Institute of Justice, February 2018), 14.

7. Eppler-Epstein et al., "Alarming Lack of Data on Latinos."

8. Eppler-Epstein et al.

9. Eppler-Epstein et al.

10. Subramanian et al., "Divided Justice," 26–27; see also 2, 7, and 14.

11. Eppler-Epstein et al., "Alarming Lack of Data on Latinos."

A NOTE ON THE TYPE

This book has been composed in Arno, an Old-style serif typeface in the classic Venetian tradition, designed by Robert Slimbach at Adobe.